LOVE AND POWER

LOVE
AND
POWER

Caribbean Discourses on Gender

EDITED BY

V. Eudine Barriteau

University of the West Indies Press
Jamaica • Barbados • Trinidad and Tobago

Institute for Gender and Development Studies: Nita Barrow Unit
Cave Hill, Barbados

University of the West Indies Press
7A Gibraltar Hall Road, Mona
Kingston 7, Jamaica
www.uwipress.com

Institute for Gender and Development Studies: Nita Barrow Unit
University of the West Indies
Cave Hill, Barbados

A catalogue record of this book is available from the
National Library of Jamaica.

ISBN 978-976-640-265-5

Cover illustration: Rex Dixon, *Profile of a God*
(24 × 18 inches, acrylic on canvas, 2010)

Cover and book design by Robert Harris

Set in Adobe Garamond 11/14.5 x 27

Printed in the United States of America

DEDICATED TO THE PIONEERING WORK OF THE WOMEN
WHO FORGED INTO AN INSTITUTIONAL REALITY THE CENTRE
FOR GENDER AND DEVELOPMENT STUDIES:

ELSA LEO-RHYNIE

BARBARA BAILEY

LOURAINE EMMANUEL (who left us on 22 April 2007)

AND

MARLENE HAMILTON, THE FIRST WOMAN APPOINTED
PRO VICE CHANCELLOR AT THE UNIVERSITY OF THE WEST INDIES AND
THE FIRST PRO VICE CHANCELLOR TO HOLD GENDER STUDIES
AS PART OF HER PORTFOLIO

———————§———————

Contents

Acknowledgements

THIS CURRENT VOLUME OF ESSAYS from the Nita Barrow Unit of the Institute for Gender and Development Studies is the third publication to interrogate the intersections of relations of power in Caribbean culture, history, society and political economy. On this occasion we intersect love for (and of) power, pleasure, sexualized erotica with relations of gender. The result is a compelling volume of scholarly contributions and I want to thank all my colleagues who once more trusted me to provide an overarching, analytical framework for their insights and ideas. I am particularly pleased that comparatively newer academics such as Halimah A.F. DeShong, Gabrielle J. Hosein, Kristina Hinds Harrison, Roxanne Burton, Tonya Haynes and Tara Inniss have joined more established scholars like Patricia Mohammed, Aviston Downes, Jessica Byron and Don D. Marshall in offering their work.

Through the committed involvement of the staff of the Institute for Gender and Development Studies, Nita Barrow Unit, this project, which started as a one-day symposium, has matured into an exciting collection. I thank Deborah Deane, Rhonda Walcott, Olivia Birch, Carmen Hutchinson Miller, Sanielle Hinds and Suzanne Archer. They were later joined by Alicia Croney and Kerri-Ann Haynes-Knight at the Office of the Deputy Principal. When Joan Cuffie became acting head of the Nita Barrow Unit of the Institute for Gender and Development Studies, she maintained the institutional support and I am grateful for her commitment.

Probing new ideas on gender in feminist scholarship is always an exhilarating process. Conversations with good friends and colleagues spark ideas, fuel debates and ultimately advance the goals of critical social theorizing and analysis. I thank Rhoda Reddock, Alissa Trotz, Roberta Clarke, Linden Lewis,

Hilbourne Watson, Piya Pangsapa, Leith Dunn, Deborah Thomas, Annie Paul, Aaron Kamugisha, Kamala Kempadoo, Joan French, Rawwida Baksh and, most of all, Jane Flax. Diasporic and transatlantic locations and colleagues provided intellectual spaces and discourses to nurture the ideas presented here. The Women's Resource Centre and the Audrey Lorde Archives, both at Spelman College, and its indefatigable and generous director, Beverley Guy Sheftall, the GExcel Project at Örebro University, Sweden, and the generosity of its international scholars and students programme led by feminist philosopher Anna Jónasdóttir enabled satisfying feminist engagements. The GExcel Project welcomed Institute for Gender and Development Studies lecturer Halimah DeShong and graduate students Tonya Haynes and Andrea Baldwin to experience and participate in exciting feminist intellectual discourses. I developed enduring friendships with Kimberley Crenshaw, Kathy Jones, Stevi Jackson, Valerie Bryson and Ann Fergusson.

I am fortunate to be nurtured and supported by an inner circle of friends: Joy Workman, Camille Samuel, Pansy Hamilton, Jennifer Woodroffe, Darnley Thomas, Patricia Mohammed, Donna Banks, Maxine McClean, Patricia Brathwaite-Marshall, Marcia Martindale, Cheryl Linton, Margaret Gill, Diane Cummins, Rollins "Grandmaster" Alleyne, Bonnie Lewis, Randy Hallett, Colin Bellamy, Elizabeth Bernard, Desiree Simpson, Rodney Marshall, Mark Cadogan, Harold Codrington, and the High Priestess, Verna St Rose Greaves.

My anchor, my family, my clan, the Barriteaux – operationalizing Rosina Wiltshire's concept of the transnational family – living in London; Grenada; Atlanta; Washington, DC; and New York, and since 2006 living without my eldest sister, Shirley. I am grateful for your unconditional love. Mr Cabral Barriteau-Foster, what a journey you and I are having together, site engineer, no less, perhaps the only young Caribbean engineer who can hold his own in a conversation about Caribbean feminism and postcoloniality. I am thrilled to see the man you have become and you will always be the favourite of my sons. Thank you for always standing tall for your feminist mother.

PART 1

Destabilizing Discourses and Practices

1

Disruptions and Dangers
Destabilizing Caribbean Discourses on Gender, Love and Power

V. EUDINE BARRITEAU

> But what is in the past remains unchanged, doesn't it? I think the past does change. The present changes the past. Looking back you do not find what you left behind.
>
> – Kiran Desai, *The Inheritance of Loss*

Disruptions and Dangers of . . .

The chapters in *Love and Power* continue an ongoing project of the Institute for Gender and Development Studies to deploy feminist scholarship to confront issues of gender and power circulating in Caribbean societies. Here the contributors continue conversations, collaborations and contestations among scholars about what constitutes knowledge about feminisms, gender, masculinities and political economy in the Commonwealth Caribbean. Brian Meeks will find the contributors have taken up the challenge to correct what he describes as a failing of contemporary social science research. The authors simultaneously engage with the messy details of political economy as well as question the assumptions of contemporary theories and philosophies (Meeks 2007, 2–3). These chapters engage with the materiality of gender as well as the discursive systems and ideological architectures that constantly shape the contours of gender systems and the ways in which relations of gender are experienced by women and men, boys and girls. The systems of meanings called into question here are not viewed as unrelated to the societies in which their effects are played out. I share Michel Foucault's situating of discourse within social practice, as summarized by Paul Rabinow. He insists Foucault "never intended to isolate discourse from the social practices that surround it" (Rabinow 1984, 10). Anna Jónasdóttir and Kathleen Jones support this claim. They state, "Discursive representations of gender can persist and continue to shape social relations and structure social activities" (Jónasdóttir and Jones 2009, 6).

In the process of building a distinct system of communicating about issues of gender in Caribbean societies, readings of the past change even as understandings of the present become more fluid, more contingent. In these chapters one discerns a confidence in the authors' abilities to rediscover, reclaim and construct distinct perspectives on Caribbean relations of gender, knowledge and power. By problematizing what we think we know and how we come to know it, the works simultaneously critique and create knowledge about women's and men's lives within Caribbean societies or related Diasporas. By challenging existing knowledge claims or producing new generalizations on gender and power, my colleagues and I are continuing to disrupt and destabilize embedded and resilient patriarchal knowledge claims. Specifically we are:

- Interrogating and confronting how, in all its currencies and circulations, power works, corrupts or empowers.
- Rupturing the feminist silence around love, lust and loving in Caribbean discourses and societies. Is there love beyond sex? And, given the sharp bifurcation in popular discourses about love, is there scope for women and men to demonstrate love for each other both with and without sexual connotations? How comfortable are we within scholarship and society with same-sex and heterosexual loving? Why haven't we problematized desire and what Jane Flax calls the scandal of desire, since, as she demonstrates, desire "further undermines conventional ideas about masculinity and femininity, sexuality and rationality" (Flax 2004, 47)? What is the part played by narratives of self in the performance of constructed gender identities?

- Problematizing love and the power of the erotic. What do we mean when we talk about love? What have we avoided in not theorizing love, lust and desire in Caribbean scholarship? How can we move beyond an exploration of the character of homosexual and heterosexual relations as necessarily problematic and oppressive?
- Demonstrating the existence and intersectionality of love, lust, passion and gender in international political economy, and specifically the contours of the lust for power in state and international relations. How does the lust for power mask itself in the finance rhetoric of international economic relations?
- Maintaining and supporting meaningful dialogues with the study, issues, questions and concerns of masculinities. That is, we are nurturing an intellectual space to "converse with masculinities beyond the necessary, but generally reactive responses that have been generated so far" (Barriteau 2009, 417).

This chapter considers competing epistemological perspectives on how knowledge is created, marketed and consumed to examine the intersecting issues of power, knowledge, "love" and gender in the anglophone Caribbean. How do we come to know, especially when our knowledge is not perceived to be born solely of Platonic philosophical inquiry but is seen as dependent on experience and interpretation of events and occurrences as posited by David Hume? Are there observable patterns of exploitation and the exclusion of women and other marginalized groups? Is feminist scholarship pressured disproportionately to produce evidence before its knowledge claims can be considered valid? Are asymmetrical, punitive relations of gender a feminist invention? Are events of the past and knowledge of these finite or fixed? More precisely, how much of the accepted understanding of past events or "known" facts is an outcome of the interpretation of these phenomena? Is there a pristine, unadulterated log of occurrences, untroubled by subjectivities, relationships of power, gender or domination?

A Changeable, Ever-Present Past

In the award-winning novel *The Inheritance of Loss*, Kiran Desai offers another philosophical perspective on how knowledge is constructed, and on the destabilizing notion that multiple readings of what may appear to be an agreed-upon, settled and known past are possible. In a conversation between two of Desai's characters, one seeks assurance, reveals anxieties, craves certainties, even as he betrays a belief that the past is indeed fluid and changeable. He asks, "But what is in the past remains unchanged, doesn't it?" And the other confirms his doubts: "I think the past does change. The present changes the past. Looking back you do not find what you left behind."

These chapters attempt to revisit, re-examine and rethink what existing scholarship has left behind. For a very long time Caribbean scholarship has left women and issues of gender behind. For far too long the historiography and genealogies of Caribbean intellectual traditions have left behind feminist inquiries and gender analysis. Writing on civilization, culture and identity, Jessica Byron is aware that many aspects of the Caribbean's past refuse to be left behind, refuse to be silenced: "We will be forced to revisit and re-interpret our history over and over again as new voices and formerly invisible or over-looked aspects of what is perceived to be Caribbean identity struggle to the surface. Cultural, ethnic and political identities will forever be fields of contestation in the region" (Byron, chapter 6). Tonya Haynes implicates Caribbean feminist thought itself in the selective silencing of an indigenous epistemic opening. She argues that Caribbean feminist thought has left behind Sylvia Wynter's offering of the liminal category of the subaltern Caribbean woman as a vantage point from which to interrogate the relationship between a Caribbean feminist project and Western feminist theory towards "imagin-ing new worlds outside of our current discursive frameworks" (Haynes, chapter 3).

In her introduction, Tara Inniss returns to the past of nineteenth-century medical records to build a narrative about the contemporary. In this instance, she returns to the contested site of authoring knowledge about gendered and racialized bodies. Aviston Downes, Inniss and Carmen Hutchinson Miller look back to the past and, in the process, unsettle conventional readings of colonial masculinities, the gendering of science and medicine, and the expe-riences of gender relations among Afro-Costa Ricans. Hutchinson Miller's analysis takes seventeenth- and nineteenth-century African and Afro-Caribbean migrations to Costa Rica as the point of entry for examining contemporary gender relations among Afro-Costa Ricans. The past is present and ever changeable; looking back you do not find what you thought you left behind. Their work demonstrates the continuing dynamics of relations of power that coalesce around social relations of gender.

One of the perverse permutations of history is how the past continually ruptures the present, destabilizing linear notions of accomplishment, progress, achievement and completion. Events, occurrences and ideas thought to be confined to history suddenly reappear, forcing scholars, politicians, policy-makers, practitioners and the public to become once again occupied with what they thought they had left behind.[1] Alissa Trotz reminds us of what she probes as an overall investment in silencing the past in the specific context of Guyana's politics of 1964 and the insistent intrusion of this past into the Guyanese contemporary, an intrusion she describes as "infiltrating the inter-stices of everyday life and imprisoning our imaginations" (Trotz 2008, 6).

These analyses reveal an awareness that there are still new sites of inequal-ities to be interrogated, many unheard stories to be narrated, and a number of "facts" to be unearthed about that seemingly known past. I complicate this idea that the past is available for re-examination, that it is fluid and changeable, by advising these contributions are probing relations of gender and power left behind in earlier explorations. These authors suggest there is no stable, fixed past. Instead, their analyses imply the past is continuously constructed. Problems may remain permanent and perennial, even as their proposed solu-tions are constantly changing.

Furthering Feminist Knowledge

In *Envisioning Caribbean Futures*, Brian Meeks devotes a section entitled "Explorations in New Caribbean Thought" to "Eudine Barriteau's Caribbean Feminism: Critical Modifier or New Paradigm?" He then undertakes a thought-provoking, constructive critique of some of my earlier theoretical pieces (Meeks 2007, 11–17). I do not intend to rebut Meeks's critique; neither do I think I have to.[2] Meeks poses very relevant questions as well as offers several assertions that require revisiting and elaboration. I welcome the recog-nition and critical involvement of a leading Caribbean intellectual that there is a body of work called Caribbean feminist thought, and that this work con-stitutes a critical dimension of the Caribbean's intellectual tradition. In 2003 I noted that "the documentation and theorization of a Caribbean intellectual tradition has not yet fully discovered Caribbean feminist thought or women's subjectivity" (Barriteau 2003a, 78). With few exceptions,[3] too many intellectuals have been too comfortable in simultaneously professing their ignorance yet offering scathing dismissals of the relevance of Caribbean feminist thought to helping us make sense of our societies and economies.[4] Meeks makes amends. My colleagues' work, and my own, makes it even more challenging for future anthologies to circumvent feminist ideas, even as they acknowledge internal contradictions and crises in feminist thought and activism. Haynes's chapter simultaneously signals rupture and continuity. She returns to the works of Wynter, whom she describes as arguably the Caribbean's pre-eminent intellectual alive today, to demonstrate that Wynter's work has been "grossly misrepresented" in Caribbean feminist thought. In the process, Haynes does not just trouble what may have looked like the stable ground of Caribbean feminist theorizing, but her contribution also serves to solidify the existence of feminist epistemology in the Caribbean.

The work of feminist theorists Jónasdóttir and Jones assists in sharpening the analytical focus of this collection. Jónasdóttir and Jones contend that there is an impasse in the intellectual project of feminist political theory, and that impasse constitutes a crisis within contemporary feminist theory (Jónasdóttir and Jones 2009, 2). They locate the impasse on their identification of implicit tensions between two trends characterizing "approaches to the concept of gender in political studies" (2). One approach strategically centres gender in social and political analysis; the other explicitly deconstructs gender. One trend states gender is essential to a feminist political project; the other insists gender is essentialist, and thus reactionary and dangerous. Jónasdóttir and Jones accept that there is a crisis coming out of this impasse, but contend that this crisis exists for entirely different reasons (3). They insist that the crisis is not about *how to think about what can be known* about gender, identity or representation in the epistemological sense, but rather about *how to think about what we can do* about gender, identity or representation in the ethical political sense (2).

I support Jónasdóttir and Jones's position and incorporate Laurel Weldon's observation of Iris Young's work, that "feminist theory is not only about theorizing subjectivity, identity or experience. It is also importantly aimed at social critique and exposing relations of power and domination" (Weldon 2007, 282). All of these chapters investigate some dimension of gender and power, and they are all positioned in the interstices of these tensions, as identified by Jónasdóttir and Jones. Caribbean feminist and progressive scholars are mining the seams of historiography, culture and political economy to reveal and reconfigure deeper layers of what we thought we knew about these societies. In the process of excavation and inquiry, the authors suggest how we should think about what we can do about punitive relations of gender. The outcomes of their examinations underscore the resiliency and residual character of patriarchal and other challenges.

The ways in which knowledge about relations of gender is created, disseminated and consumed in the Caribbean illustrate the resiliency of patriarchal knowledge claims and the continuous nurturing of a public discourse hostile to women.[5] The following example illustrates some of these systemic features. John Jeremie, former attorney general of the Republic of Trinidad and Tobago, once lamented the high prison population of young men in his country, stating plainly, "The high influx of women into the teaching service may be the main reason why there are so many men in jail today" (Allaham 2009). If they did not know it before, young male criminals were now being told who in society was responsible for their life of crime. Jeremie of course went on to issue a qualifying statement which, in its utterance, licensed the speaker to blatantly ignore the very disclaimer issued and to continue to dissemble about ideologies of gender. In the second statement, Jeremie maintains that he is not an expert in the field of gender studies, and thereby clears the way for his questionable knowledge claims. He further states that his statements were spurred by the results of a study conducted by the Secretariat of the Commonwealth Heads of Government in 2008, a study which found that, "while education and schooling do not rely on the norms of patriarchy, males limit themselves in society by making it difficult for young boys to have a role model" (ibid.). Despite the findings of the study he referred to, how does Jeremie arrive at and disseminate his knowledge claim on this specific aspect of gender-identity formation within Trinidad? "I can express no expert view on this", he states, "but I can say [it] without fear of contradiction, because in two hours I will tour a prison facility in Tobago, with my friend the Honourable Chief Justice, and I know from previous visits that what I will see there will be these young, disadvantaged, poorly educated males" (ibid.).

The minister of education in Barbados refuses the male victimization model and proffers a counterview on men by admonishing them publicly to take responsibility for their roles as fathers. In an address marking Barbados's forty-third independence celebrations, the minister said to his audience, "Men must stand up and take responsibility because there are too many of our children who have mothers that have to run to the courts to get a few cents to support their children" (Lazare 2009, 7). A government minister publicly chastising men and speaking on behalf of women is welcome and rare. It runs counter to the trend of public officials and commentators blaming the ills of Caribbean society on its women (Barriteau 2003a, 2003b, 1998). I commend Minister Jones for attempting to rupture public discourses on gender governed by systematic attacks on women. By not providing support to their children, Jones said, some men were doing something "that is wrong. Do not cause that anguish to women and children. Make sure that child is taken care of and not leaving strangers and charities to do it. Make sure that the mother does not have to prostitute herself" (Lazare 2009, 7).

What can scholars working in the field of feminist, masculinity and other schools of critical theory do about gender, identity and, more importantly, representation, in the political sense? By "political sense" I mean recognizing that relations of gender are not benign and are driven by relations of power. This collection continues to expose the ongoing, relentless contestations over who will exercise power, how power is deployed, where authority resides, who concedes, who gains, and the state of negotiations. The subjects implied by "who" are nation states or political institutions as demonstrated in the chapters by Wendy Grenade, Kristina Hinds Harrison and Jessica Byron. The subjects of analysis are also institutions, organizations or discourses, as demonstrated in the works by April Bernard, Aviston Downes, Charmaine Crawford, V. Eudine Barriteau, Don Marshall, Patricia Mohammed, Tonya Haynes, Roxanne Burton, Halimah DeShong and Tara Inniss. Hutchinson Miller, Crawford, Hosein, and Annecka Marshall reveal agency and subjectivity in the actions of Afro-Costa Ricans, transnational mothers, students and feminist activists.

The chapters in this volume are informed by a willingness to continue to take on contradictions, continuities, change and transitions confounding and configuring the social, political and knowledge economy of the Commonwealth Caribbean. The contributors continue the tradition of seeking to make sense of the enduring conundrums disrupting relations of gender and power in the region. They add to an established body of scholarship as shown in the works of Heron and Nicholson (2006); Bailey and Leo-Rhynie (2004); Reddock (2004, 1994); Tang Nain and Bailey (2003); Barriteau (2003c, 2001);

Mohammed (1998, 2002a, 2002b); Lewis (2003a); Chevannes (2001); Kanhai (1999); Peake and Trotz (1999); Kempadoo (1999); Shepherd (1999, 1994); Barrow (1998); Leo-Rhynie, Bailey and Barrow (1998); Lopez Springfield (1997); Shepherd, Brereton and Bailey (1995); Safa (1995); Miller (1994); Momsen (1993); Beckles (1989); Morrisey (1989); Hart (1989); Mohammed and Shepherd (1988); Massiah (1986); and the foremother of feminist research in the anglophone Caribbean, Mair (1974). Collectively these constitute a partial sampling of the extensive research undertaken to create meaning, knowledge and change around issues of gender and power.

A Language of Caribbean Relations of Gender

Collectively the chapters in this volume apply or create new epistemological frames for enduring sociological, cultural, economic and political challenges that complicate and continuously alter the meanings and experiences of Caribbean relations of gender. The authors are actively involved in what Don Marshall has theorized as "meaning-capture" (Marshall 2009), a concept that speaks eloquently to capturing and defining new meaning and thus contributing to a multi-disciplinary language on relations of gender. Rhoda Reddock advises that "academic-based work interrogates concepts and categories and contributes to theory, challenging traditional approaches in addition to supplying new knowledge" (Reddock 2009, 218).

One of the outcomes of the process of producing knowledge is the formulation of distinctive theoretical frameworks, key conceptual tools, a critical vocabulary and a set of knowledge claims. Eventually, these evolve cumulatively into a disciplinary language. To communicate within a discipline, one has to possess the vocabulary and the ability to converse in the language of that discipline. In the same trajectory in which postcolonial and proto-independence scholars enriched Caribbean sociological, anthropological and development discourse with such critical concepts[6] as the Creole Family (R.T. Smith 1956), Creole Society (Goveia 1965; R.T. Smith 1967; Brathwaite 1971), Dual Sector Economy and Industrialization by Invitation (Lewis 1955, 1954, 1950), Sociology of Slavery (Patterson 1967), Plural Society (M.G. Smith 1965),[7] Plantation Economy and Dependency (Best 1968; Beckford 1972; Thomas 1974; Girvan 1971), "Mother-Fathering" (Lamming 1953; Clarke 1957), and Reputation and Respectability (Wilson 1969).

Caribbean feminist and other scholars have been building a lexicon of gender. Feminist and masculinity scholarship is solidifying a language of Caribbean feminist/gender/masculinity studies. These contributors enrich the existing stock of concepts, which include the reluctant matriarch, rebel woman (Mair 1977, 197), female-headed households (Massiah 1980), the paradox of matrifocality (Momsen 1993),[8] transnational family (Wiltshire-Brodber 1986), the empowered sex worker, sexual economic exchange (Kempadoo 2004, 1996), women-empowered communities (Antrobus 1993a, 1993b, 1989), gendering of transnational workers (Freeman 1998), male marginality (Wilson 1971), male marginalization thesis (Miller 1991, 1986), strategies of survival (Barrow 1986), gender negotiations, Caribbean feminist historiography, disciplinary promiscuity (Mohammed 2009, 2003, 1994), working-class women's autonomy, historicizing Caribbean women's movements (Reddock 1998, 1994), states of in-betweenness (Boyce-Davies 1994), gendered testimonies (Brereton 1998, 1994), the myth of the male breadwinner (Safa 1995), dougla poetics (Puri 2004), geographies of desire and belonging, the gift of sociality (Trotz 2008), material and ideological relations of gender, Caribbean gender systems, compensatory masculinity, politicized sexuality (Barriteau 2008, 2003a, 2003b, 1998, 1994), erotic autonomy, economies of the erotic (Alexander 1997), matri-folk, erotic feminist pedagogy (Rowley 2007, 2002), masculine gender identities, Caribbean men and fatherhood (Chevannes 1999, 1997), property rights in pleasure, historicizing black masculinity, enslaved women's sexuality (Beckles 2004, 2000, 1996a, 1996b, 1989), Caribbean masculinity in the global political economy (Lewis 2004), defining masculine construction (Lewis 2003), masculinity change (Lewis 2007, 2004), colonial education and colonial masculinities, black colonial masculinities (Downes 2005, 2004, 2003), gender somethings, Caribbean feminist ethics (Robinson 2007, 2004), Caribbean mothers and mothering ideologies (Reynolds 2005), and genderism (Soares 2006).

Claiming Power through Producing/Rethinking Knowledge and Pedagogies

In section two, Roxanne Burton argues that the goal of social epistemologies is to broaden the understandings of how we develop new fragments of knowledge. Burton states that she aims to employ a feminist, social-epistemological approach to explore how to improve the process of producing knowledge in the context of the academy in the anglophone Caribbean. Burton is interested in proving whether or not approaches rooted in social epistemologies are useful in generating shifts in teaching and research in the Caribbean context. She insists that the extent to which the range of local knowledge that researchers can develop and transmit to students and the wider society can be expanded, and that the region should benefit from this expansion. Burton shares a quote from Linda Alcoff and Elizabeth Potter, that "the history of feminist episte-mology itself is the history of the clash between the feminist commitment to the struggles of women to have their understandings of the world legitimated and the commitment of the traditional philosophy to various accounts of knowledge . . . that have consistently undermined women's claim to know" (Alcoff and Potter 1993, 2; quoted in chapter 2).

I view this history as the history of denying women's claims to power through producing knowledge. Feminists' determination to generate alternative ways of knowing, as Hosein and several other authors do, disrupts traditional claims to power, however. Burton's point that the aim of feminist epistemolo-gies is to lay bare the idea that one must take subjectivity into account is borne out and replicated throughout the collection. The authors prioritize subjective locations, whether they are dealing with gender relations of Afro-Costa Ricans, examining Caribbean diasporic communities in Canada, or probing what it means to be wo/man in the gender narratives of women and men.

Hosein seeks to answer the question posed by Burton. Her chapter is a wel-come reflection on and assessment of the politics of pedagogy. She offers a sustained, analytical discussion about politics in the classroom, the interface of feminist scholarship, the politics of producing knowledge and of the learn-ing process. What is also refreshing about Hosein's analysis is the honest assessment of what she was able to accomplish in her attempt to inspire stu-dents to be more reflective of the process by which feminist knowledge is produced and reproduced. Hosein's objective was to explore how pedagogical choices and strategies shape students' approaches to understandings of feminist politics. She engages in a critical appraisal of pedagogical practices and evalu-ation of the goals of women studies. She employs a popular-action assignment to *assess* the interface between feminist activism/politics and feminist politics. She maintains that, as a pedagogical strategy, popular actions enable students to challenge a range of received orthodoxies, including feminist versions.

Both Hosein and Annecka Marshall politicize pedagogical strategies in the classroom and insist on being reflective about how knowledge is produced. Hosein deploys her pedagogical strategies to advance feminist activism. Marshall uses her methodologies of interrogating received knowledge to encourage students to re-examine their ideas and attitudes towards sexual fantasies and desires. For both scholars the college campus is a site to problematize and produce knowledge. Hosein and Marshall are putting into practice what Elsa Leo-Rhynie advocates when she advises a critical re-examination and alteration of those methods of teaching which stress the power of the teacher as expert and knower (Leo-Rhynie 2004, 420–27).

If Marshall and Hosein force a rethinking of feminist pedagogical strategies, Haynes leads us to reconsider unproblematized adoptions of epistemic approaches and peels away another layer of the obfuscation imported in knowledge production strategies that are taken for granted. Returning to the work of Sylvia Wynter, Haynes takes exception to arguments that suggest that Wynter has rejected feminism. Instead, Haynes maintains that the relationship between Wynter's work and Caribbean feminist thought is far more complex. Rather than invalidating a feminist project, Haynes insists, "Wynter's work emerges as extremely useful for Caribbean feminisms . . . If Caribbean feminists are preoccupied with constructing and reconstructing knowledge, Wynter is preoccupied with the need to change the episteme itself" (chapter 3). In a careful and lucid interrogation of Wynter's thought, Haynes demonstrates that Wynter's work exposes the governing system of meaning which privileges and overrepresents a particular ethno-class while recreating the Caribbean woman within the liminal category of other. According to Haynes, "Wynter demonstrates that the 'governing system of meaning' is unable to 'voice' the silenced ground of subaltern Caribbean women and unable to 'make thinkable' the possibility of a new system of meaning from the vantage point of this silenced ground." Haynes uses Wynter's reference to this silenced ground as demonic as her entry point to locate the relevance of Wynter's work to Caribbean feminist epistemology. She creates the concept of an ethic of unmanageability, which she not only views as animating the theorizing of Caribbean feminist scholars such as Michelle Rowley, M. Jacqui Alexander and V. Eudine Barriteau, but also goes on to theorize as a way of living at epistemological and ontological frontiers while facing a future with unfulfilled possibilities.

Love, Lust and Sexuality

One of the contemporary problems of and disruptions of gender is the relative feminist silence on lust, loving, intimacy and sexuality. Although, paraphrasing Jackson, we suspect that even feminists fall in love (Jackson 1993), in this collection the concept of love is not seized upon and pinned down with cited references to delineate its etymology. Instead, the concept hovers, familiarly threading through the works of several contributors. In Annecka Marshall's chapter it moves from being a destination to a journey, from a place of arrival to a process. Patricia Mohammed invokes love in a profound and provocative way. She forces us to consider romantic love between two men as refracted through the cinematic gaze. I consider whether love power or the power of the erotic empowers or hinders women in their sexual relationships with men.

The turn to love, lust and theorizing sexual power continues in the work of Marshall, Mohammed, DeShong and Barriteau. Our work explores differing but complementary aspects of these themes. We are responding to Linden Lewis's concern that "not much sustained and systematic treatment of sexuality in the scholarly literature of the region exists" (Lewis 2003, 9). We are also deepening feminist knowledge of the intersectionality of love, lust, sexuality and intimacy.

In "Coming Home", I continue to focus on how knowledge is produced and the effect or outcome of that process. I examine an area that has been largely underexplored in Caribbean feminist scholarship – "love power" and the power of the erotic. I am deeply interested in revealing the sexualized power relations embedded in women's heterosexual relationships. By building on Jónasdóttir's theorization of "love power" (Jónasdóttir 2009), I tackle the question as to whether or not Caribbean feminist analysis has dismissed, downplayed or ignored heterosexual attraction and relationships as having any significance in yielding knowledge about relations of domination in women's public and private lives. I use Jónasdóttir's conceptualization of "love power" to generate a theory of women's sexualized power in the contemporary Caribbean. I then map the powerful epistemological oeuvres offered by black lesbian feminist and theorist Audre Lorde.

I argue that Lorde's epistemic openings illuminate what is simultaneously problematic and possible in apprehending the phenomenon of women's love power. Besides offering significant theoretical openings, Lorde's work exposes what I see as a limitation in Jónasdóttir's work, which is akin to the problem I have identified as bedevilling much of socialist feminist analysis (Barriteau 1995). It is the determination to make Marxist theory do what, in my analysis, it was not specifically interested in doing: answer questions about women. Jónasdóttir states that she is interested in showing the relevance of Marx's historical method. I think that this objective limits her from perceiving what Lorde does. Lorde's definition of the power of the erotic as a life force shifts the epistemological base. In Lorde's theorizing, love power or the power of the erotic is ontological; it is a condition of being, and a quality inherent in all of us if we will only embrace it and be empowered by it. I attempt to demonstrate that this nexus of political sexuality and political economy is dynamic and contested, and that not only may there be ongoing attempts to "extract" or contain women's power in sexual unions, but that women who prove powerful in other social, political and economic relationships experience continuous attempts to force them into powerless positions in their sexual relationships with men.

Annecka Marshall's work echoes the theme of socio-sexual power and powerlessness in her exploration of students' perceptions of sexual paraphilias. She examines female undergraduate students' beliefs about the regulation of sexuality in Jamaican society. In doing so, she employs a pedagogical approach that views the classroom as a space for offering new debates about sexual liberation, particularly as related to multiple sexual identities and same-sex sexual relationships.

The ruptures Marshall introduces into Caribbean feminist thought are multiple. She confronts homophobia, lust, desire and passion among young women. Usually, when scholars analyse the sexuality of young persons, they approach it in an instrumentalist manner, such as whether or not it complies with prescribed behaviours, in order to enhance programme delivery and policy refinement. Work on family planning and the prevention of HIV/AIDS are examples of this approach (Lewis 2003, 9). Alternatively, there is a discussion of women in sex work, whether it recognizes their right to view this occupation as a legitimate economic activity (Della Giusta, Di Tommaso and Strom 2008), or speaks to the abuse or victimization of women as sex workers (Kempadoo and Doezma 1998). Marshall's approach to the sexuality of young women is both ontological and existential. She frees sexuality from procreation and religion, and metaphorically liberates the womb from being in the eternal service of nationhood. Instead, Marshall seeks to generate knowledge about sexual desires and eroticism.

Love is the rubric under which discourses about desires, lusts and passions are supposed to be ordered, especially in the case of young people. There seem to be two avenues through which sexual fantasies are then entertained or spoken about. In popular discourse, sexual desire involves a facile elision – that the individuals who experience desire are in love. Even when this assumption is acknowledged to sanction the realization of those desires, the two people should then become married, at which point sexual desire should now be targeted towards procreation. Instead of following popular opinion, Marshall turns the regulatory power imbued in popular discourses about "love" on its head. The love in her analysis is a verb – love for sexual varieties, love for pleasure and love for the right to pleasure. Love shifts from being a destination, a safe harbour in which one may anchor actions and desires, to being a journey towards pleasure and all its attendant complications. Marshall concludes by raising questions for social groups and key institutions in order to move beyond opposition to, and distortion of, sexual minorities.

If love is the rubric under which popular discourses about desires, lusts and passions are supposed to be ordered and subsumed, Halimah DeShong problematizes romantic love as posing life threatening challenges for women in intimate partner relationships. She revealed this notion as part of an overall analysis that examines the construction and presentation of self in narratives of gender by women and men. DeShong uses interviews with thirty-four women and men to foreground a feminist poststructural understanding of subjectivity, power and discourse. Her account reveals the power relations of gender that operate in the narratives of self and the gender identities that are refracted through these narratives. She exposes the heterogeneity of the meanings ascribed to women and the contradictions between gender ideologies and realities of women and men. DeShong's chapter exposes physical and psychological dangers in women and men's lives even as it disrupts conventional interpretations of the system of meanings captured in self-authored narratives. DeShong observes that while "participants subscribed to traditional stereotypes of gender roles within the family . . . there were varying degrees of departure and commitment across any single account" (chapter 5).

Masculinity, Brotherhood and Loving

Patricia Mohammed, who routinely breaks new ground, delves into the destabilizing, intersecting notions of masculinity, eros and love. She defines and
demarcates love by using the classic bifurcation of eros and agape. Mohammed
states that if eros is used as erotic love and desire, then agape is used as an
unconditional, self-sacrificing, active, volitional and thoughtful love (chapter
18). As a feminist and cultural studies scholar, Mohammed looks at romantic
and platonic love through the cinematic gaze and prioritizes men's subjectivity,
masculinity and homosexual loving. Mohammed offers an evocative summary
of the film *Brokeback Mountain* as a backdrop for introducing and interrogating other archetypes of masculinity portrayed in the classic Caribbean film
The Harder They Come. Mohammed observes that although these two films
deal with vastly different versions of masculinity (one recasts the boundaries
of masculinity, while the other reinscribes a hard, heteronormative revision),
both position manhood as an unfinished project.

Mohammed informs us that the directors of both films present the raw
underbelly of a range of masculine emotions that is rarely dissected and scru-
tinized. Mohammed is drawn to these two films because, even though
superficially they seem to deal with two oppositional storylines, she surmises
that they are both linked by the "idea" of the cowboy on which generations
have relied for the prototypical definition of masculinity in the American
West. In *The Harder They Come*, Jimmy Cliff performs the role of the island-
style, urban cowboy. In *Brokeback Mountain*, the two main actors are in a
more conventional setting for cowboys. Mohammed uses these two films to
focus on the multiple masks which men wear, whether willingly or under pressure, in their desire and determination to be "masculine". Her incisive analysis
enables us to reflect on shifting charades of masculinity – compulsory homosociality as boys, compulsory heterosexuality as men. Ultimately, the cinematic
gaze she deploys enables us to see that we inhabit many different sexual worlds
in which our sexual desires are innate as well as learnt, influenced by biological
as well as psychological drives over which we have little control. She concludes
by noting that both films "destabilize some of the widely held myths about
gender and sexuality that are guilty of other kinds of imprisonment" (chapter
18). Mohammed is disrupting conventional understandings of manhood and
masculinity. Masculinity is usually portrayed in daily life with certainty. Men

know or should know who they are, appear and should be certain of where they are going. Women, however, always seem to be in a process of becoming, forever a work in progress, yet Mohammed tells us that these films position *masculinity* as an unfinished product.

Aviston Downes delivers a very sophisticated analysis of colonial masculinities in the context of fraternal societies. He focuses explicitly on interrogating gender relations in multiple masculine identities in the context of fraternal societies in the nineteenth-century Caribbean. Downes makes the observation that socio-economic dominance alone cannot guarantee hegemonic masculinity. Hence he calls into question the analysis of Linden Lewis (2005) which reads masculinity through capitalist labour relations. The self-appointed civilizing mission of Victorian England to its colonial relations meant constant tensions between the desire to impose on Barbadian men the Victorian construct of appropriate manhood, and the equally determined response of Barbadian men to reject exported prescriptions of moral and civilized masculinities (chapter 17).

Downes provides great insight into the construction of gender ideologies, identities and relations, and the maintenance of gender arrangements in his compelling study of fraternal organizations and masculinities in eighteenth-century Barbados. From their inception, working-class friendly societies admitted women, unlike their secret middle-class counterparts, albeit in separate sexual spheres. Separation by sexes reflected a preoccupation with controlling alleged "loose" sexual morality. Some of Downes's more telling contributions are his insights on men caring about the social and economic well being of other men in a sanctioned site, such as that of fraternal organizations. I argue that this demonstration of agape love occurs in such protected sites because, whether in the eighteenth or the twenty-first century, the Caribbean's social and cultural climate is overtly heteronormative, homophobic and highly sexualized, and thus requires established and protected niches for male expression of mutual caring.

Gendered Citizenship, the State and International Relations

Four scholars working differing disciplinary angles confront androcentricity in the fields of international relations and the international political economy. Jessica Byron, Wendy Grenade, Kristina Hinds Harrison and Don Marshall talk back to their respective sub-fields from the perspective of insisting on revealing gendered constructs of power and exclusionary practices. Collectively, they serve notice that these fields, in the Caribbean context, cannot now maintain academic integrity and continue to ignore how gendered relations of power alter what we know about issues of civilization, culture, identity, security, trade and international finance. These colleagues are confronting in international relations and international political economy what Spike Peterson refers to as the enduring legacy of patriarchy – "a binary construction of gender that casts women and femininity as essentially different from and inferior to men and masculinity" (Peterson 2003, 9). Their contributions substantiate Ann Tickner's theorizing of mainstream international relations as a masculine, gendered discipline (Tickner 1992, 49).

If, as Byron acknowledges, the discipline of international relations is Eurocentric, the examination of the field from a feminist perspective is embryonic in the Caribbean. Byron, Grenade and Hinds-Harrison contribute to the earlier work by Byron and Thorburn (1998) to disrupt the homogeneity and androcentric character of existing research on international relations as they relate to Caribbean states.

Byron explores the notion of civilization and the objectives of a discourse on this subject within the region. She states that contemporary discussion on culture and civilization has failed to integrate two central elements, a gendered perspective and the impact of migration and diaspora on civilization, citizenship, culture and identity. She devotes her attention to the latter concepts and, in the process, echoes the concerns of Jónasdóttir and Jones. She states that the concept of civilization is at the core of national and international power contests, and is deeply imbued with universalizing and exclusionary dimensions. One of these dimensions of exclusion relates to women. Byron goes on to discuss a gendered understanding of citizenship. She argues that cultural discourses and the notion of a Caribbean civilization can play a useful role in enabling us to look critically at societies, to acknowledge their patterns of exclusion and inequity. These concepts offer another frame of analysis for comprehending the contemporary Caribbean and unearthing some of the narratives that have been left behind.

Byron offers an extensive discussion of what an expanded definition of Caribbean citizenship would look like if it were approached from a feminist perspective. She examines mythological symbols of gender roles from cultures of origins, endemic violence in Caribbean social relations, issues of gender equity and development, and the inclusion of caring functions, along with individual rights and political participation, as dimensions of citizenship duties. She maintains that any expansion of the criteria that maps the contours of a Caribbean civilization has to include the struggle for gender equality among others. Byron's analysis suggests that even as those who craft the conventional discourse on Caribbean civilization and identity cling doggedly to historical images and traditions, attempting to preserve a pristine, nostalgic (non-existent) past, complex, contemporary realities keep erupting, refusing to be left behind and refusing to be unavailable. It is not accidental that Byron's work provides "valuable insights into the past and future constructions of Caribbean societies" (chapter 6). The past will continue to disrupt the selectively, homogenously constructed contemporary until we render more heterogeneous, inclusive narratives.

Grenade continues the focus on international relations, with a specific interest in the intersection of gender and Caribbean security. She seeks simultaneously to broaden the security discourse and to offer a synthesizing analysis of the multidimensional features of security. She deliberately seeks to fill the gap in Caribbean scholarship, which hitherto has either addressed feminist concerns or security issues. She states she seeks to unsettle the Western-centric international relations discourse and bring to the fore Caribbean realities within international relations. She zeroes in on the security concerns of Caribbean women, whom she argues are the catalysts for Caribbean economies and societies. By examining women's insecurity in relation to health, economic activity and personal safety, Grenade builds a credible case for reconceptualizing security concerns in Caribbean international relations studies. She also challenges feminist scholars to interrogate the gendered features of the Caribbean political economy as it intersects with issues of human security.

Hinds Harrison challenges the implied gender neutrality of Caribbean trade negotiations. She uses a statement from a representative of a private sector organization that trade negotiations are gender neutral as an entry point to question the assumed neutrality of international relations and political economy. Hinds Harrison discusses how the neo-liberal slant of current trade negotiations leads negotiators and academics to conduct allegedly neutral discussions about the state's economies that focus on the international trade system. Her main point is that trade arrangements have an impact on people's lives in the Caribbean in different ways, based on individuals' locations in gendered social hierarchies. Not only is she concerned about revealing those gendered hierarchies, but she is also occupied with the absence of humans from the jargon of trade negotiations, what she calls "trade-speak". In this jargon, humans are extracted and replaced by terms such as "labour markets".

Filtering Economic Analysis through a Gendered Lens

While both Kristina Hinds Harrison and Don Marshall take on the androcentric character of international political economy, Marshall is specifically interested in exposing masculinist gender tropes in the rhetoric of international finance. He interrogates the disruptions caused by creating, within finance, a discourse of danger and by painting this danger as feminine. Marshall states that his contribution is an attempt to broaden the conversation across the social and human sciences on the issue of the rise of global finance, and to reveal how the social construction of the discourse of finance has also been framed in gender terms. Marshall's piece is ambitious and imaginative. He moves back and forth between the sixteenth-century historical construction of finance as a scientific discourse governed by statistical rules, models and theories,[9] and the contemporary global meltdown of the world economy, beginning in the Wall Street-driven financial markets of 2007. His analysis traces the genealogy of financial trading and gender tropes in the construction of risk. He is particularly careful to demonstrate the creation of finance as a scientific concept, and makes clear how that scientific status bestows on its practitioners a certain authority, a sense of knowing, of authoritatively defining the rules, processes and outcomes of financial operations.

   In mapping the development of the concept of finance from being governed by behaviours of gambling and speculation to theoretical modelling, Marshall tracks how notions of gender enter the discourse on finance. This discourse deploys the loaded imagery of gender to establish that, just as previous centuries perceived nature as feminine, capable of being mastered by the male scientific mind, modern society views finance in the same way, capable of being managed, subdued and controlled by a series of techniques and strategies. He demonstrates that this artifice becomes even more problematic for Caribbean countries engaged in offshore financial operations. Accompanying the layered and well-known hierarchies and binaries in the international political economy literature of industrialized versus developing economies, imperial versus former colonial countries, metropolitan versus peripheral societies, is a more recent complication. It is the intersecting depiction of offshore financial centres as risky and dangerous temptresses operating in exotic, feminized spaces such as the Caribbean, luring good capital into destabilized, rule-evading geographical spaces which seem to exist in defiance of financial regulation and rationality.

Of Gendering Entrepreneurial Analysis

Jonathan Lashley interrogates economic theorizing and its intersections with entrepreneurship to expose how economic discourses have marginalized issues of gender. While other researchers have sought to explain entrepreneurial intentions in the Caribbean (Devonish et al. 2010), Lashley focuses particularly on how economic theory "others" gender, and the implications of this "othering" for studies of entrepreneurship in the Caribbean. He does so by demonstrating how mid-twentieth-century economic theorists sought to centralize the agency and activities of entrepreneurs in discourses on economic growth. But these theorists, while centralizing the entrepreneur, pushed any considerations of issues of gender to the margins of mainstream theorizing.

From the perspective of feminist economic analysis, these developments are neither surprising nor unexpected. Besides contributing new fields of specialization – such as the care economy (Folbre 2001), time use analysis (Floro 1995), household production (Agarwal 1997) and the gendered division of labour – to the discipline of economics, feminist economists have exposed the gendered character of economic theory and its applications (Waring 1988; Ferber and Nelson 1993; Bergeron 2004; Barker and Feiner 2004; Kuiper and Barker 2006). They have "questioned the central emphasis placed on choice as the focus of mainstream analysis, contrasting it with an emphasis on provisioning for individual and collective well being as the central alternative objective of economics" (Benería 2003, 43). Lashley provides a specific analysis relevant to the development strategies pursued by Caribbean states. He argues that if the approach of critical theories, as opposed to positivist approaches, inform economic theorizing, relations of gender are less likely to be elided from economic theory and analysis. One of the main reasons he thinks a critical theory approach should be more fruitful in centring relations of gender in economic theorizing is that critical theories recognize agency and multiple possible outcomes for any course of action. Lashley argues that this foundational assumption within critical theory creates conceptual sites for the emergence and cross-fertilization of entrepreneurship and gender.

April Bernard continues the interrogation of entrepreneurial policies and schemes and their impact on women. She does so by evaluating the potential of radical and liberal feminism to offer new perspectives on women's involvement in micro-enterprise development. She takes us into the Caribbean world of micro-entrepreneurship by exploring the programmes, policies, problems and products of eight public and private entrepreneurial development schemes in Barbados and Trinidad and Tobago. Bernard undertakes a unique synthesizing of theoretical approaches to provide a framework for comprehending non-traditional micro-enterprise initiatives for women. She blends a neo-Weberian approach, particularly the concept of *Verstehen*, with radical and liberal feminist perspectives in a study of female entrepreneurs in Barbados and Trinidad. Bernard is particularly interested in the issues affecting the success of female entrepreneurs and the structural considerations needed to address them.

Diasporic Communities, Diverse Sexualities and Gendered Genealogies

Shalini Puri reminds us that "the centrality of migration as a defining force of Caribbean societies has never been in dispute" (Puri 2004, 1). What have been generally overlooked in this context are the experiences of women as migrants. In a pioneering study, Tracey Reynolds provides analytical accounts of the historical and cultural patterns of mothering and family ideologies of Caribbean mothers, primarily in the United Kingdom (Reynolds 2005). By focusing her feminist lens on Caribbean mothers in Canada, Charmaine Crawford disrupts the discourse on mothering, migration and diasporic studies, and systematically confronts and contains the myths of mothering and migration. She examines the pre- and post-migratory experiences of African female migrants from the anglophone Caribbean who left their children with relatives while pursuing better economic opportunities in Canada. Crawford problematizes the intersectional relationship among female migrant labour, transnationality and motherhood within the rubric of globalized gender, race and class relations. She situates "African-Caribbean mother–child relations in the context of the global political economy to highlight the significance of advanced capitalism for understanding these kinds of relations" (chapter 12). Crawford's research constitutes a fascinating study that confronts advanced capitalist relations in the globalized political economy. She explores an area that scholars often examine singularly through the lens of migrant labour, sociology or gender. Through a dissection of transnational mothering, Crawford forces a re-examination of the myths of motherhood and their implications for the enduring concepts of matrifocality, matriarchy and maternalist ideology. Through this study Crawford simultaneously nuances and enriches our understanding of classic concepts of Caribbean anthropological and gender studies such as female-headed households, matrifocality, extended families and kinship networks.

Tara Inniss returns to the past to produce a narrative about the contemporary, in this case the contested site of who defines authoritative knowledge on the female body. There is good evidence for Inniss's observation that deep silences exist in historical records "between and among Caribbean women and men about several sexual and reproductive disorders that often result in social isolation and poor survival rates" (chapter 15). As she accurately points out, the experiences and voices of enslaved women and men emerge from a gleaning of plantation records and journals of the main actors and supporting cast of the plantocracy. Thomas Thistlewood's detailed recording of his sexual adventures and diseases as a plantation overseer in eighteenth-century Jamaica is but one example of these sources (Hall 1989). Inniss's investigation of early colonial medical practices exposes the androcentricity of the practice of medicine in the Caribbean at that time. By investigating then-prevailing perceptions of human physiology, she reveals the masculinist bias in Western knowledge traditions. Inniss's contribution is singular in that she provides a rare glimpse into the asymmetrical power relations involved in the production of medical knowledge about racialized and gendered subjects in the Caribbean. Inniss concludes by arguing for a need to establish a history of science, technology and medicine in the region, a history in which issues of gender are centralized.

Costa Rican researcher Carmen Hutchinson Miller provides a welcome examination of the dynamics of gender relations in a Hispanic Central American society. In an investigation that engages with the racialized subjectivity of Afro-Costa Ricans, Hutchinson Miller also makes explicit unequal

relations of gender affecting all Costa Rican women. Yet the minority status
of Afro-Costa Ricans, and the fact that official statistics have not been disaggregated to reflect the ethnic composition of the population, suggest that
unequal relations of gender affect Afro-Costa Rican women and men in ways
that are dissimilar from the larger population. Hutchinson Miller offers primary data from interviews with sixteen Afro-Costa Rican women and men.
Additionally, she supplies visual representation of this minority population of
Afro-Caribbean descent in Central America. Even though both Hutchinson
Miller and Crawford deal with themes of migration and diaspora, they
approach these issues from differing perspectives. For Hutchinson Miller,
migrants constitute a settled community; for Crawford, migrant mothers are
relatively mobile and are, in fact, very fluid with their definitions of self, home
and kinship networks. Of course, the communities are different. The Costa
Ricans represent an older wave of migration, having moved to Costa Rica
from Jamaica in the nineteenth century. The Caribbean women in Crawford's
study, by contrast, have moved to Canada more recently and they still occupy
what Boyce-Davies describes as a state of in-betweenness (Boyce-Davies 1994).

Of Caribbean Feminist Futures: Ideological Architectures and the Materiality of Gender

I conclude where I began, by calling attention to the cautionary reminders
issued by Meeks (2007, 2–3), Foucault (Rabinow 1984, 10), Jónasdóttir and
Jones (2009, 6), and Barriteau (2003b, 23–24), that discourse should not be
isolated from the social practices that surround it. Too much is at stake if we
do not insist that Caribbean realities be filtered through the lens of feminist
and other progressive frames of analysis. These analytical essays have simultaneously interrogated and contributed to the discursive systems and ideological
architectures that continuously configure the contours of gender systems. The
depth and range of the theoretical investigations provide us with new conceptual tools and methodological strategies necessary to confront the continuously
permutating materiality of relations of gender as relations of power. We would
be betraying the emancipatory potential of feminist projects if we allowed the
cumulative effects of these analyses to remain textual and discursive. The essays
point the way to engaging with the messy multiplicity of social life and political economy in the contemporary Caribbean and its diasporas. If Jane Flax is

correct that, "feminist attempts to alter gender relations stir up intense anxieties and threaten many apparently unrelated aspects of psychological and social organization" (Flax 2004, 63), then current discourses about women and sexuality in the Caribbean are an indication that the distances between feminist analyses and activism and women's lives are receding. She continues, "People may feel driven to protect existing gender arrangements by an unconscious fear of disrupting basic ways of organizing life" (ibid.).

The public discourse on women's sexuality in Barbados is symptomatic of intense anxieties being stirred up and major moves to protect existing gender arrangements in the region. There is ongoing widespread coverage in the print media of a rabid spread of lesbianism among women and schoolgirls. Headlines include, "Schoolgirls Look to Each Other for Love: Counsellor Worried about the Rising Practice of Lesbianism" (Harewood 2010c), "Girls Gone Wild" (Harewood 2010a), "Nothing Funny about Sexuality" (Goddard 2010), "Parents Must Speak to Girls" (Harewood 2010b), "God Will Not Tolerate Same-Sex Unions" (Macdonald 2010). The reporting is sensational. The coverage feature "reformed" lesbians now repackaged as born again Christians repenting for their lives of sin and debauchery and thanking God and the church for saving them (Macdonald 2010). An interesting feature of these narratives is the insistence of widespread practices in secondary schools: "It is horrible in one of the older top schools, where girls make out in front of each other – even on the corridors. Most of these are fourth and fifth formers. What is more of a concern is that they are aggressive, operate in groups, stick together, and recruit younger students" (Harewood 2010c).

Is this evidence that the unconscious fear that basic ways of organizing social life is being disrupted? Is there a fear that women and girls are internalizing a sense of sexual autonomy and reproductive freedom and that this claiming of the power of the erotic or love power is deeply disruptive of societal expectations of how women should experience their sexual lives? Traditionally an effective way to police women's lives was to accuse them of lesbianism, especially if the women were or are feminists. The charge of homosexuality was to induce silencing in a region notorious for its homophobia (Atluri 2001). What happens if women subvert this attempt at, and remove the power of, social death and silencing (the Taliban model), by claiming a lesbian sexual identity,[10] when the impression is created that there is a lesbian menace threatening and overtaking heteronormative social life? Davina Goddard starts her letter to the press, "I am a Lesbian, well, at least politically I am" (Goddard 2010).

The policing of women's gender identities has now shifted to the ultimate terrain in heterosexist discourses, women's sexuality. Fifteen years ago the public discussions were dominated by a determined blaming of women for all the ills of Caribbean society (Barriteau 1998). This even included the demise of the West Indies cricket team. Now it is the lesbian menace. The constant scrutiny and blaming of women is no longer focused exclusively on women not wanting to be mothers and wives. The ongoing preoccupation and societal need to constantly tell women who they are and how they should live their lives has shifted to a higher ground. Those invested in protecting the status quo are very much aware that gender arrangements are always in a state of flux and are always governed by overarching material and ideological relations of gender. These relations themselves are always intersecting with oppressive relations of class, race and unequal capitalist relations. Women's sexuality and the transgression of women loving women have ruptured popular discourses on relations of gender, love and patriarchal power. Looking back to an uncertain future, we do not find what we have left behind.

Notes

1. I wrote this statement in December 2009. I am rereading three days after an earthquake has devastated Haiti on 12 January 2010. Haiti's history and contemporary realities underscore why the past does change and cannot be considered closed. France has not confronted and acknowledged its role in the depletion of the Haitian state. The massive exploitation of the immediate post-revolutionary nineteenth-century Haitian state is returning time and time again to demonstrate the past is alive and fluid and forever changing, see Beckles 2010.

2. I have every confidence in the group of young scholars-in-the-making pursuing research degrees in the Institute for Gender and Development Studies postgraduate programmes. They are undertaking internal critiques of Caribbean feminist thought as well as engaging the intellectual contributions of the mainstream. The doctoral dissertation of Tonya Haynes, "Mapping the Knowledge Economy of Gender in the Caribbean: 1974–2010", is a good example.

3. George Lamming is a noticeable exception. He has a history of engaging with issues confronting the lives of Caribbean women and, since his seminal novel *In the Castle*

of My Skin (1953), documenting the struggles and contributions of Caribbean women. See Lamming 1992, 1995.

4. See, for example, Lloyd Best's bold assertion that he does not know Caribbean gender theories but still finds these theories infertile (quoted in Sylvester 2005, 261). I thank PhD student Tonya Haynes for drawing this quote to my attention.

5. In 1998 I wrote about the expressed hostility towards and blaming of women for all wrongs in Caribbean societies. This trend continues well into the twenty-first century. See Barriteau 1998.

6. The concepts presented are merely representative and I am making no attempt here to track their evolution or the various debates about their application. The references given are to theorists generally associated with the conceptualization or application of these concepts. It is a separate and exciting project to track the genealogies of these concepts.

7. According to Glenn Sankatsingh, M.G. Smith drew heavily on the work of Rudolf Van Lier's 1949 study of Surinamese society to apply what was originally Furnivall's concept of the plural society. See Sankatsingh 1989, 63, 70.

8. I have to thank my colleague Patricia Mohammed for reminding me of the considerable stock of concepts generated by feminist research in the region.

9. He shifts between the two, as if these kinds of methodological framing can wilfully remove the capriciousness, greed and speculation at the heart of this aspect of economic behaviour.

10. That is, women pursue what I call the Taliban model. They remove the power of being labelled "lesbian" and "deviant" and the almost-guaranteed "social death" by claiming the status themselves, emptying the labels of their policing and regulatory power.

References

Agarwal, B. 1997. Bargaining and gender relations: Within and beyond the household. *Feminist Economics* 3 (1): 1–51.

Alcoff, L., and E. Potter. 1993. When feminisms intersect epistemology. In *Feminist epistemologies*, ed. L. Alcoff and E. Potter, 1–14. New York: Routledge.

Alexander, M.J. 1997. Erotic autonomy as a politics of decolonization: An anatomy of feminist and state practice in the Bahamas tourist economy. In *Feminist genealogies, colonial legacies, democratic futures*, ed. M.J. Alexander and C. Mohanty, 63–100. London: Routledge.

Allaham, A. 2009. Jeremie: Nation losing young males to crime. *Trinidad and Tobago Express*, 12 November. http://www.trinidadexpress.com/index (accessed 17 January 2010).

Antrobus, P. 1989. The empowerment of women. In *The women and international development annual*, ed. R.S. Gallin, M. Aronoff and A. Ferguson, 189–208. Boulder: Westview Press.

———. 1993a. Setting the context. In *Women at the center: Development issues and practices for the 1990s*, ed. G. Young, V. Samarasinghe and K. Kusterer, 9–14. West Hartford, CT: Kumarian Press.

———. 1993b. Structural adjustment: Cure or curse? *Gender and Development* 1 (3): 13–18.

Atluri, T.L. 2001. *When the closet is a region: Homophobia, heterosexism and nationalism in the commonwealth Caribbean*. Working paper no. 5. Bridgetown: Centre for Gender and Development Studies, University of the West Indies.

Bailey, B., and E. Leo-Rhynie, eds. 2004. *Gender in the 21st century: Caribbean perspectives, visions and possibilities*. Kingston: Ian Randle.

Barker, D.K., and S. Feiner. 2004. *Liberating economics: Feminist perspectives on families, work, and globalization*. Ann Arbor: University of Michigan Press.

Barriteau, E. 1994. Gender and development planning in the postcolonial Caribbean: Female entrepreneurs and the Barbadian state. PhD diss., Howard University.

———. 1995. Postmodernist feminist theorizing and development policy and practice in the postcolonial Caribbean: The Barbados case. In *Feminism/postmodernism/development*, ed. M.H. Marchand and J.L. Parpart, 142–58. London: Routledge.

———. 1998. Liberal ideologies and contradictions in Caribbean gender systems. In *Caribbean portraits: Essays on gender ideologies and identities*, ed. C. Barrow, 436–56. Kingston: Ian Randle.

———. 2001. *The political economy of gender in the twentieth-century Caribbean*. New York: Palgrave.

———. 2003a. Confronting power and politics: A feminist theorizing of gender in Commonwealth Caribbean societies. *Meridians: Feminism, Race, Transnationalism* 3 (2): 57–92.

———. 2003b. Confronting power, theorizing gender in the Commonwealth Caribbean. In *Confronting power, theorizing gender: Interdisciplinary perspectives in the Caribbean*, ed. E. Barriteau, 3–24. Kingston: University of the West Indies Press.

———, ed. 2003c. *Confronting power, theorizing gender: Interdisciplinary perspectives in the Caribbean*. Kingston: University of the West Indies Press.

———. 2008. "Coming, coming, coming home": Applying Anna Jónasdóttir's theory of "love power" to theorizing sexuality and power in Caribbean gender relations. *GEXcel Work in Progress Report* 3: 13–25.

———. 2009. The relevance of black feminist scholarship: A Caribbean perspective. In *Still brave: The evolution of black women's studies*, ed. S.M. James, F. Smith Foster and B. Guy-Sheftall, 413–34. New York: Feminist Press.

Barrow, C. 1986. Finding the support: A study of strategies for survival. *Social and Economic Studies* 35 (2): 131–76.

———, ed. 1998 *Caribbean portraits: Essays on gender ideologies and Identities*. Kingston: Ian Randle.

Beckford, G.L. 1972. *Persistent poverty: Underdevelopment in plantation economies of the Third World*. New York: Oxford University Press.

Beckles, H. McD. 1989. *Natural rebels: A social history of enslaved black women in Barbados*. London: Zed Books.

———. 1996a. *Black masculinity in Caribbean slavery*. WAND Occasional Paper no. 2. Bridgetown: Women and Development Unit, School of Continuing Studies, University of the West Indies.

———. 1996b. Property rights in pleasure: The marketing of slave women's sexuality in the West Indies. In *West Indies accounts: Essays on the history of the British Caribbean and the Atlantic economy in honour of Richard Sheridan*, ed. R.A. McDonald, 169–87. Kingston: University of the West Indies Press.

———. 2000. Female enslavement and gender ideologies in the Caribbean. In *Identity in the shadow of slavery*, ed. P.E. Lovejoy, 163–82. London: Continuum.

———. 2004. Black masculinity in Caribbean slavery. In *Interrogating Caribbean masculinities: Theoretical and empirical analyses*, ed. R. Reddock, 225–43. Kingston: University of the West Indies Press.

———. 2010. The hate and the quake. *Sunday Sun*, 17 January.

Benería, L. 2003. *Gender, globalization and development: Economics as if people mattered*. New York: Routledge.

Bergeron, S. 2004. *Fragments of development: Nation, gender and the space of modernity*. Ann Arbor: University of Michigan Press.

Best, L. 1968. Outlines of a model of pure plantation economy. *Social and Economic Studies* 17 (September): 283–326.

Boyce-Davies, C. 1994. *Black women, writing and identity: Migrations of the subject*. London: Routledge.

Brathwaite, E. 1971. *The development of Creole society in Jamaica, 1770–1820*. London: Oxford University Press.

Brereton, B. 1994. Gendered testimony: Autobiographies, diaries and letters by women as sources for Caribbean history. Elsa Goveia Memorial Lecture. Department of History, University of the West Indies, Mona, Jamaica.

———. 1998. Gendered testimonies: Autobiographies, diaries and letters by women as sources for Caribbean history. *Feminist Review* 59:143–63.

Byron, J., and D. Thorburn. 1998. Gender and international relations: A global perspective and issues for the Caribbean. *Feminist Review* 59 (Summer): 211–32.

Chevannes, B. 1997. Helping men become better fathers: A case study of Jamaica. In *Caribbean social structures and the changing world of men*, 24–26. Port of Spain: United

Nations Economic Commission for Latin America and the Caribbean, Sub-regional Headquarters for the Caribbean.

———. 1999. *What we sow and what we reap: Problems in the cultivation of male identity in Jamaica.* Grace, Kennedy Foundation Lecture Series. Kingston: Grace, Kennedy Foundation.

———. 2001. *Learning to be a man: Culture, socialization and gender identity in five Caribbean communities.* Kingston: University of the West Indies Press.

Clarke, E. 1957. *My mother who fathered me.* London: George Allen and Unwin.

Della Giusta, M., M.L. Di Tommaso and S. Strom. 2008. *Sex markets: A denied industry.* London: Routledge.

Devonish, D., P. Alleyne, W. Charles-Soverall, A. Young Marshall and P. Pounder. 2010. Explaining entrepreneurial intentions in the Caribbean. *International Journal of Entrepreneurial Behaviour and Research* 16 (2): 149–71.

Downes, A. 2003. Gender and the elementary teaching service in Barbados, 1880–1960: A re-examination of the feminization and marginalization of the black male theses. In *Confronting power, theorizing gender: Interdisciplinary perspectives in the Caribbean,* ed. E. Barriteau, 303–23. Kingston: University of the West Indies Press.

———. 2004. Boys of the empire: Elite education and the socio-cultural construction of hegemonic masculinity in Barbados, 1875–1920. In *Interrogating Caribbean masculinities: Theoretical and empirical analyses,* ed. R. Reddock, 105–36. Kingston: University of the West Indies Press.

———. 2005. From boys to men: Colonial education, cricket and masculinity in the Caribbean, 1870–c. 1920. *International Journal of the History of Sport* 22 (January): 3–21.

Ferber, M.A., and J.A. Nelson, eds. 1993. *Beyond economic man: Feminist theory and economics.* Chicago: University of Chicago Press.

Flax, J. 2004. The scandal of desire: Psychoanalysis and disruptions of gender: A meditation on Sigmund Freud's *Three essays on sexuality. Contemporary Psychoanalysis* 40 (1): 47–68.

Floro, M. 1995. Economic restructuring, gender and the allocation of time. *World Development* 23 (November): 913–30.

Folbre, N. 2001. *The invisible heart: Economics and family values.* New York: New Press.

Freeman, C. 1998. Island-hopping body shopping in Barbados: Localising the gendering of transnational workers. In *Caribbean portraits: Essays on gender ideologies and identities,* ed. C. Barrow, 14–27. Kingston: Ian Randle.

Girvan, N. 1971. *Foreign capital and economic underdevelopment in Jamaica.* Kingston: Institute of Social and Economic Research, University of the West Indies.

Goddard, D. 2010. Nothing funny about sexuality. *Midweek Nation,* 28 April.

Goveia, E. 1965. Slave society in the British Leeward Islands at the end of the eighteenth century. In *The birth of Caribbean civilization: A century of ideas about culture and identity, nation and society*, ed. O.N. Bolland, 421–45. Kingston: Ian Randle.

Hall, D. 1989. *In miserable slavery: Thomas Thistlewood in Jamaica, 1750–86*. London: Macmillan.

Harewood, Cheryl. 2010a. Girls gone wild. *Sunday Sun*, 11 April, 5A.

———. 2010b. Parents must speak to girls. *Sunday Sun*, 11 April, 15A.

———. 2010c. Schoolgirls look to each other for love: Counsellor worried about the rising practice of lesbianism. *Sunday Sun*, 11 April, 14A.

Hart, K., ed. 1989. *Women and the sexual division of labour in the Caribbean*. Kingston: Consortium Graduate School of Social Sciences, University of the West Indies.

Haynes, T. 2012. Mapping the knowledge economy of gender in the Caribbean: 1974–2010. PhD diss., University of the West Indies, Cave Hill, Barbados.

Heron, T., and H. Nicholson. 2006. Unravelling gender, development and civil society in the Caribbean. *Caribbean Quarterly* 52 (June–September): v–ix.

Jackson, S. 1993. Even sociologists fall in love: An exploration in the sociology of emotions. *Sociology* 27 (2): 201–20.

Jónasdóttir, A.G. 2009. Feminist questions, Marx's method, and the theorisation of "love power". In *The political interests of gender revisited: Redoing theory and research with a feminist face*, ed. A.G. Jónasdóttir and K.B. Jones, 58–83. Manchester, UK: Manchester University Press.

Jónasdóttir, A.G., and K.B. Jones. 2009. The political interests of gender revisited: Reconstructing feminist theory and political research. In *The political interests of gender revisited: Redoing theory and research with a feminist face*, ed. A.G. Jónasdóttir and K.B. Jones, 1–16. Manchester, UK: Manchester University Press.

Kanhai, R., ed. 1999. *Matikor: The politics of identity for Indo-Caribbean women*. St Augustine: School of Continuing Studies, University of the West Indies.

Kempadoo, K. 1996. Prostitution, marginality and empowerment: Caribbean women in the sex trade. *Beyond Law* 5 (14): 69–84.

———, ed. 1999. *Sun, sex and gold: Tourism and sex work in the Caribbean*. Lanham, MD: Rowman and Littlefield.

———, ed. 2004. *Sexing the Caribbean: Gender, race and sexual labour*. London: Routledge.

Kempadoo, K., and J. Doezma, eds. 1998. *Global sex workers: Rights, resistance and redefinition*. London: Routledge.

Kuiper, E., and D. Barker. 2006. *Feminist economics and the world bank: History, theory and policy*. Oxford: Routledge.

Lamming, G. 1953. *In the castle of my skin*. London: Longman Group.

———. 1992. Coming, coming, coming home. Address to the Caribbean Festival of Creative Arts Symposium in Trinidad. *Daily Nation*, 15 September, 14–15.

———. 1995. Coming, coming, coming home. In *Coming, coming home: Conversations II: Western education and the Caribbean intellectual*, 29–49. St Martin: House of Nehesi.

Lazare, E. 2009. Men must man up, says Jones. *Barbados Advocate*, 3 December.

Leo-Rhynie, E. 2004. Gender studies: Interdisciplinary and pedagogical challenges. In *Gender in the 21st century: Caribbean perspectives, visions and possibilities*, ed. B. Bailey and E. Leo-Rhynie, 419–36. Kingston: Ian Randle.

Leo-Rhynie, E., B. Bailey and C. Barrow, eds. 1998. *Gender: A Caribbean multi-disciplinary perspective*. Kingston: Ian Randle.

Lewis, L., ed. 2003. *The culture of gender and sexuality in the Caribbean*. Gainesville: University Press of Florida.

———. 2004 . Masculinity, the political economy of the body and patriarchal power in the Caribbean. In *Gender in the 21st century: Caribbean perspectives, visions and possibilities*, ed. B. Bailey and E. Leo-Rhynie, 236–61. Kingston: Ian Randle.

———. 2005. *Unsettling masculinities in the Caribbean: Facing a future without guarantees*. Working paper no. 13. Bridgetown: Centre for Gender and Development Studies, University of the West Indies.

———. 2007. Man talk, masculinity, and a changing social environment. *Caribbean Review of Gender Studies* 1 (1): 1–21.

Lewis, W.A. 1950. The industrialization of the British West Indies. *Caribbean Economic Review* 2 (1): 1–51.

———. 1954. Economic development with unlimited supply of labour. *Manchester School of Economic and Social Studies* 22: 139–91.

———. 1955. *The theory of economic growth*. Homewood, IL: Richard D. Irwin.

Lopez Springfield, C. 1997. *Daughters of Caliban: Caribbean women in the twentieth century*. Bloomington: Indiana University Press.

MacDonald, C. 2010. God will not tolerate same-sex unions. *Midweek Nation*, 28 April.

Mair, L. Mathurin. 1974. A historical study of women in Jamaica 1655–1844. PhD diss., University of the West Indies, Mona, Jamaica.

———. 1977. Reluctant matriarchs. *Savacou: A Journal of the Caribbean Artists' Movement* 13:1–6.

Marshall, D.D. 2009. Gender tropes and colonial discourses in the turbulence of global finance. *Contemporary Politics* 15 (4): 413–27.

Massiah, J. 1980. Female-headed households and employment in the Caribbean. Paper presented to the International Centre for Research on Women, Workshop on Women-Headed Households and Employment in the Third World, NGO Forum, World Conference on the UN Decade for Women, Copenhagen, 14–24 July.

———. 1986. Women in the Caribbean project: An overview. *Social and Economic Studies*. 35 (2): 177–239.

Meeks, B. 2007. *Envisioning Caribbean futures: Jamaican perspectives.* Kingston: University of the West Indies Press.

Miller, E. 1986. *Marginalization of the black male: Insights from the development of the teaching profession.* Kingston: Institute of Social and Economic Research, University of the West Indies.

———. 1991. *Men at risk.* Kingston: Jamaica Publishing House.

———. 1994. *Marginalization of the black male: Insights from the development of the teaching profession.* 2nd ed. Kingston: Canoe Press.

Mohammed, P. 1994. A social history of post-migrant Indians in Trinidad from 1917 to 1947: A gender perspevtive. PhD diss., Institute of Social Studies, The Hague, The Netherlands.

———.1998. Towards indigenous feminist theorizing in the Caribbean. *Feminist Review* 59 (1): 6–23.

———.2002a. *Gender negotiations among Indians in Trinidad, 1917–1947.* Basingstoke, UK: Palgrave.

———, ed. 2002b. *Gendered realities: Essays in Caribbean feminist thought.* Kingston: Centre for Gender and Development Studies, University of the West Indies Press.

———. 2003. A symbiotic visiting relationship: Caribbean feminist historiography and Caribbean feminist theory. In *Confronting power, theorizing gender: Interdisciplinary perspectives in the Caribbean,* ed. E. Barriteau, 101–25. Kingston: University of the West Indies Press.

———. 2009. *Imaging the Caribbean: Culture and visual translation.* London: Macmillan.

Mohammed, P., and C. Shepherd, eds. 1988. *Gender in Caribbean development: Papers presented at the inaugural seminar of the University of the West Indies Women and Development Studies Project.* Kingston: University of the West Indies Press.

Momsen, J., ed. 1993. *Women and change in the Caribbean.* Kingston: Ian Randle.

Morrisey, M. 1989. *Slave women in the New World: Gender stratification in the Caribbean.* Lawrence: University Press of Kansas.

Patterson, O. 1967. *The sociology of slavery: An analysis of the origins, development and structure of Negro slave society in Jamaica.* London: McGibbon and Kee.

Peake, L., and A.D. Trotz. 1999. *Gender, ethnicity and place: Women and identities in Guyana.* London: Routledge.

Peterson, V. Spike, ed. 2003. *A critical rewriting of global political economy: Integrating reproductive, productive and virtual economies.* London: Routledge.

Puri, S. 2004. *The Caribbean post colonial: Social equality, post-nationalism and cultural hybridity.* New York: Palgrave Macmillan.

Rabinow, P., ed. 1984. *The Foucault reader.* New York: Pantheon Books.

Reddock, R.E. 1994. *Women, labour and politics in Trinidad and Tobago: A history.* London: Zed Books.

————. 1998. Contestations over national culture in Trinidad and Tobago: Considerations of ethnicity, class and gender. In *Caribbean portraits: Essays on gender ideologies and identities*, ed. Christine Barrow, 414–35. Kingston: Ian Randle.

————. 2004 *Interrogating Caribbean masculinities: Theoretical and empirical analyses*. Kingston: University of the West Indies Press.

————. 2009. Feminist research and theory: Contributions from the anglophone Caribbean. In *Global gender research: Transnational perspectives*, ed. C. Bose and M. Kim, 215–26. New York: Routledge.

Reynolds, T. 2005. *Caribbean mothers: Identity and experience in the U.K.* London: Tufnell Press.

Robinson, T. 2004. Gender, feminism and constitutional reform in the Caribbean. In *Gender in the 21st century: Caribbean perspectives, visions and possibilities*, ed. B. Bailey and E. Leo-Rhynie, 592–625. Kingston: Ian Randle.

————. 2007. A loving freedom: A Caribbean feminist ethic. *Small Axe: A Caribbean Journal of Criticism* 24 (October): 118–29.

Rowley, M. 2002. Reconceptualising voice: The role of matrifocality in shaping theories of Caribbean voices. In *Gendered realities: Essays in Caribbean feminist thought*, ed. P. Mohammed, 22–43. Kingston: University of the West Indies Press.

————. 2007. Rethinking interdisciplinarity: Meditations on the sacred possibilities of an erotic feminist pedagogy. *Small Axe: A Caribbean Journal of Criticism* 24 (October): 139–53.

Safa, H. 1995. *The myth of the male breadwinner: Women and industrialization in the Caribbean*. Boulder: Westview Press.

Sankatsingh, G. 1989. *Caribbean social science: An assessment*. Caracas, Venezuela: URSH-SLAC-UNESCO.

Shepherd, V. 1994. *Transients to settlers: The experiences of Indians in Jamaica 1845–1950*. Leeds and Warwick: Peepal Tree and the University of Warwick.

————. 1999. *Women in Caribbean history: An introductory text for secondary schools*. Kingston: Ian Randle.

Shepherd, V., B. Brereton and B. Bailey, eds. 1995. *Engendering history: Caribbean women in historical perspective*. Kingston: Ian Randle.

Smith, M.G. 1965 . *The plural society in the British West Indies*. Berkeley and Los Angeles: University of California Press.

Smith, R.T. 1956. *Negro family in British Guiana*. London: Routledge and Kegan Paul.

————. 1967. Social stratification, cultural pluralism and integration in West Indian societies. In *Caribbean integration: Papers on social, political and economic integration*, ed. S. Lewis and T.G. Matthews, 226–58. Rio Pedras: Institute of Caribbean Studies, University of Puerto Rico.

Soares, J. 2006. Addressing the tensions: Reflections on feminism in the Caribbean. *Caribbean Quarterly* 52 (June–September): 187–97.

Sylvester, M. 2005. Old concepts, new theories? Caribbean radical thought at the cross-roads. MA thesis, University of the West Indies, St Augustine.

Tang Nain, G., and B. Bailey, eds. 2003. *Gender equality in the Caribbean: Reality or illusion?* Kingston: Ian Randle.

Thomas, C.Y. 1974. *Dependence and transformation: The economics of transition to socialism.* New York: Monthly Review.

Tickner, J.A. 1992. *Gender in international relations: Feminist perspectives on achieving global security.* New York: Columbia University Press.

Trotz, A. 2008. *Gender, generation and memory: Remembering a future Caribbean.* Working paper no. 14. Bridgetown: Centre for Gender and Development Studies, University of the West Indies.

Waring, M. 1988. *If women counted: A new feminist economics.* San Francisco, CA: Harper and Row.

Weldon, S.L. 2007. Difference and social structure: Iris Young's critical social theory of gender. *Constellations* 14 (2): 280–88.

Wilson, P. 1969. Reputation and respectability: A suggestion for Caribbean ethnology. *Man* 4 (1): 70–84.

———. 1971. Caribbean crews: Peer group and male society. *Caribbean Studies* 10 (4): 18–34.

Wiltshire-Brodber, R. 1986. The Caribbean transnational family. Paper prepared for UNESCO/Institute of Social and Economic Research seminar on changing family patterns and women's role in the Caribbean. University of the West Indies, Cave Hill, Barbados, 24–27 November.

PART 2

Epistemic Excavations, Narrative Negotiations and Sexualized Power

2

Feminist Social Epistemologies and Caribbean Scholarship
Exploring a Potential Paradigm Shift

ROXANNE BURTON

Introduction

Knowledge is traditionally understood as being objective and as having atomistic knowers, but social epistemologies make the argument that much of what is labelled "knowledge" is situated, that is, it is based on social power relations and interactions between categories of power such as race, class and gender. Social epistemologies generally posit that society is a crucial aspect of the knowledge-formation process, while feminist social epistemologies further posit that the situatedness of knowers, and the resulting relations, is essential to knowledge production and understanding. This chapter explores the merit of the arguments proffered by feminist social epistemologies in rejecting the traditional, abstract, individualistic understanding of knowledge, and examines how the approach which these epistemologies offer may lead to important positive shifts in teaching and research within the Caribbean context.

The greater involvement, in more recent times, of women in the production of knowledge at the tertiary level – and, more specifically, at the University of the West Indies (UWI) – has inspired this discussion. Women have a presence on the campuses not just as researchers and teachers, but also, importantly, as administrators who are actively engaged in steering research and teaching agendas. These women are in addition to the large numbers of women who are pursuing graduate or undergraduate studies. In the Caribbean, women have generally played a significant role in teaching and research, especially the former, from the home to the classroom. One may intuit that these developments would eventually lead to a change in culture in the academic sphere, but what would such a change entail? As a possibility, could these new leadership positions for women mean a different approach to the production and dissemination of knowledge within the institutions in which women are assuming these roles? And could this new approach be seen as allowing for a greater positive, transformative process to take place within the society? I suggest that greater benefits for students and researchers can be derived by having a shift in the understanding of knowledge production, a change proposed by feminist social epistemologies. I do so by initially dis-cussing feminist criticisms of the traditional understanding of knowledge. I then present proposals from feminist social epistemologists as to the most appropriate methods of knowledge production. My discussion then turns to the importance of research and teaching in shaping a society's development, before showing how these issues may affect Caribbean scholarship.

Assumptions of Mainstream Epistemology

From the modern period in Western philosophy to the present, a particular way of thinking about the nature of knowledge and the nature of the knower has dominated epistemology. This approach takes "How can one acquire knowledge?" as the standard question to be asked. It is within this context that mainstream epistemology tries to respond to sceptical claims, by aiming to identify an adequate conceptualization of knowledge and attendant con-cerns. Discussions in the field therefore tend to focus on the appropriate definition of knowledge itself, on reliable sources of knowledge (which are generally identified as reason and perceptual experience) and issues related to justification (who or what can know). The standard position is that of a realist, the general view that objects which we perceive exist and do so independently of our perceptions or the operations of our minds.[1] Knowledge of the world therefore involves being able to develop those principles that would allow us to represent these perceptions accurately and draw inferences from them. A crucial aspect of this process of knowledge acquisition is assuming a stance of neutrality on the part of the knower. As Thomas Nagel puts it, "To acquire a more objective understanding of some aspect of life in the world, we step back from our critical view of it and form a new conception which has that view and its relation to the world as its object" (Nagel 1989, 4). This task is achieved by forming a detached view of the world, one not linked to any specific point of view – in other words, "a view from nowhere" (ibid., 70).[2]

Stressing the objectivity of knowledge, for mainstream epistemology, also implies the neutrality of the knower. This kind of neutrality is a presupposition of this conception of knowledge production, *as well as* the knower, that is epitomized in the Cartesian tradition, and which has permeated significant aspects of Western philosophy. The received view in this paradigm is a conception of humans as beings whose minds are independent of the body and can conceivably survive in a disembodied state. The hallmark of the knower is one's rationality, unencumbered by subjective concerns. The objectivity, "the view from nowhere", therefore allows this disembodied ego to see the world in its neutral state, not thinking of any particularities. It means, then, that the knower in mainstream analytic epistemology is one whom Lorraine Code calls a "surrogate", one who is interchangeable (Code 1991). As an example, while a man currently cannot give birth to a child, and so cannot experience the pain and the joy of childbirth, if technological changes facilitated a brain transplant such that the brain of a man could be transferred into the body of a woman (or vice versa), or if his brain received the same inputs, then he would be able to know what she does about the birthing experience.[3] As Louise M. Antony notes, epistemology is not concerned with the characteristics that make humans distinct (whether biological or social) because such issues do not affect *what knowledge is*. Epistemology, she argues, is not concerned with what enters our "cognitive machinery", but rather with the machinery itself, and that machinery allows for S (the subject, the knower) to know that p (a proposition) is true for any S, in spite of the internal or external conditions of that knower (Antony 2002, 463–64).

Feminist Criticisms of Mainstream Epistemology

This view of the neutral knower is the starting point for criticisms of traditional epistemology by feminists. Alcoff and Potter (1993) note that "the history of feminist epistemology itself is the history of the clash between the feminist commitment to the struggles of women to have their understandings of the world legitimated and the commitment of the traditional philosophy to various accounts of knowledge – positivist, postpositivist, and others – that have consistently undermined women's claim to know" (2). Like other disciplines, feminist presence within philosophy began at the so-called periphery, with questions being raised about issues of practical significance, and so generally falling into the realm of ethics, given feminism's "mandate" to explore practical and live issues (ibid.). But these questions were generally not deemed to be of great philosophical significance, given that male philosophers were not discussing them (issues such as rape and housework). Philosophy is often seen to be "better" practised where there is a "great degree of abstraction from concrete material reality and with pretensions to universality" (ibid., 2). The feminist foray into the area of epistemology happened because of the recognition that both within philosophy and in other disciplines there were inherent male biases that typically discounted or undermined the woman's way of knowing.

Lorraine Code's analysis of the foundational principles of traditional epistemologies, which led to her classification of these approaches to knowledge as "S-knows-that-p epistemologies", highlights the main flaws that feminists have identified in the approach taken to knowledge acquisition and production. These epistemologies, she argues, try to identify those necessary and sufficient conditions for justifying that S knows that p, with the assumption that there are indeed "universally necessary conditions" that can actually be identified. It is also crucial to place stress on "value neutrality", "pure objectivity" and the ability to transcend "particularity and contingency", and to "presuppose a universal homogenous and essential" human nature "that allows knowers to be substitutable for one another" (Code 1993, 16). Stated another way, "all knowers are believed to be alike with respect to both their cognitive capacities and to their methods of achieving knowledge" (Code 1991, 6). But the idea of the "surrogate knower" already means that the knower is an individual, an individual who is interchangeable and self-sufficient (a la Descartes' thinker, who can arrive at knowledge independently).

The problem with this model, however, is that it rules out important areas that could be deemed knowledge: given that the knower must be self-sufficient, one can only conceive of a range of knowledge that can be achieved alone, meaning that complex social phenomena cannot be known. The paradigm of this type of knowledge is therefore the simple proposition, which can be known as being all or nothing. The standard definition of knowledge as justified, true belief works very well under these conditions (Code 1993, 1991). Further, one's socio-political location is not relevant to the knowledge that can be grasped. But the problem here, for Code, is that no attention is paid to the S; all emphasis is placed on the *p*, since the S is simply a surrogate. Given that particulars are indeed attached to each person, however, "socio-political–historical locations", such as gender, race, class and ethnicity, must be given value, because the notion of the neutral S is one that hides the very specific "subject" on which that S is built, namely the dominant group in Western society (and some may say, at this point, in all societies) – rich, educated white men. So, even in the professed objective realm of mainstream epistemology, subjectivity is embedded.

The aim of revisionist epistemologies, such as the feminist, is to lay bare the idea that one must take "subjectivity into account". There are different ways in which this subjectivity can manifest itself. Firstly, with the assumption of the neutrality of the knower comes the rejection of the consideration of any relationship among power, emotions and subjective commitments and knowledge (Code 1993). When translated into practices, there may be certain groups of persons who are privileged in terms both of knowledge acquisition and of access to opportunities for knowledge production (Bergin 2002, 198). Further, when subjectivity is ignored, it can lead to problems related to homogeneity. According to Helen Longino, a major impact of the idea of a neutral knower has been the resulting homogeneity that exists in the male-dominated field of epistemology (Longino 1990, cited in Antony 2002, 470). A bias is likely to develop when the investigators are too similar to each other, and where ideas are therefore not subjected to the rigorous analysis that comes from differing points of view. Also, entrenched in mainstream epistemologies are distinct ideas of what a knower is, and these characteristics are generally in opposition to what is seen to be female (or negative characteristics which are assigned to females): "whenever a dichotomy is employed to explicate an epistemic distinction, the higher valued term will be the one more strongly associated with men and masculinity" (Antony 2002, 466).[4] Feminist epistemologists argue that unearthing the assumption of the sex of the knowers opens a space for questions to be raised about whether differences in "socio-political–historical locations" are significant. Feminist epistemologists certainly believe it is significant because the understanding that arises from thinking of epistemology solely as exploring propositional knowledge is too narrow, and is simply a "narrow range of artificially isolated and purely empirical knowledge claims, which might be paradigmatic by fiat but are unlikely to be so in 'fact'" (Code 1993, 15).

Feminist Social Epistemology: An Overview

The question can then be posed: what is the wider range of knowledge that is likely to be seen once the situatedness and embodiment of the knower is taken into account? Several answers have been posited, which form the existing variations of feminist social epistemology. The main point stressed, however, is that socially constructed understandings of gender affect knowledge production (Anderson 2007). So, feminists emphasize the experiential aspect of knowledge; no longer is there the neutral knower (after all, there never was, only a pretence at such), but rather a situated knower. The understanding of who that situated knower is varies among theorists (Grasswick 2006), but I believe that there is some merit to the two main variations of the feminist social epistemology position, each of which I will briefly outline.

The first position articulated is that of *Standpoint theory*, so called because it stresses that knowers are always situated and that the epistemic awareness that one has can be broadened or limited since "differing social positions generate variable constructions of reality and afford different perspectives on the world" (Code 1993, 39). Therefore, "experiential differences lead to differences in perspective, and these perspectival differences carry epistemic consequences" (Grasswick 2006). As a black woman, I therefore have a particular location from which I view the world, and it is from this location that I have a particular epistemic position. Standpoint theorists tend to argue, though, that because I am in a subordinated position within Western capitalist society, I actually have an important, epistemologically informative view (Anderson 2007). This view arises because persons who hold marginal social positions will know both the "knowledge" that is presented by those who are socially more powerful and maintain the dominant position, and their own experiences of the world as exploited. Theorists such as Sandra Harding and Patricia Hill Collins therefore argue that the non-dominant standpoint and the experiences of subordinated groups are useful, in fact crucial, for arriving at knowledge that is wider, including being able to identify significant moral and political truths (Collins 1990/1991; Harding 1993; Anderson 2007). The second grouping of feminist social epistemologies stresses the relational aspects of knowledge acquisition and production. The model of the *relational knower* speaks of "individuals-in-communities", recognizing that, as humans, a high level of interdependence exists (Grasswick 2006). This understanding of the knower is one that shifts the focus away from the atomistic knower of traditional epistemology and instead recognizes that the creation of knowledge (especially knowledge that will be valuable to society) is often very dependent on the interactions that we have with others (Code 1991, 83). In fact, basing her argument on Annette Baier's view that we are "second persons", guided by others to become persons ourselves, including knowers (ibid., 82–83), Code argues that we depend on others to recognize us as epistemic agents so that we can actually act as autonomous knowers.

From both of these perspectives, it is evident that what feminist social epistemologists attempt is an abandonment of the idea of a knower as being separated from the process of knowing on the basis of the need for objectivity, universality and impartiality (Collins 1990/1991; Code 1991; Harding 1993). The call is for a transformation of the structures of the epistemological enterprise, such that, while searching for knowledge, any ethical and political questions that arise receive important consideration. Different approaches must be taken to understanding the concept of objectivity; the idea of removing all concern with social values cannot be the standard for objectivity. There is a need to recognize that the knower and her community must be given consideration in order for knowledge production really to occur. Harding posits a view of objectivity that embraces the fact that knowledge and our ideas generally are socially located and that the knower is therefore "placed on the same critical, causal plane as the objects of knowledge" (Harding 1993, 69). Collins highlights social interaction, using concrete experiences, the use of dialogue, and the ethic of care and personal accountability as a model of specifically Afrocentric feminist epistemology, one which does not separate the knower from the community, and which embraces the emotional aspect of the knower, which must be present in order for reason to be fully articulated. Further, Collins argues that "values lie at the heart of the knowledge validation process such that inquiry always has an ethical aim" (1990/1991, 219).

Criticisms of Feminist Social Epistemology

Criticisms of feminist social epistemologists have unsurprisingly been harsh, especially coming from practitioners of and sympathizers with the S-knows-that-p epistemologies. As Alcoff and Potter note, there is a "philosophical myth" which states that, though the philosopher may be motivated by political concerns, "the philosopher's work is good to the extent that its substantive, technical content is free of political influence. Holding to this myth, traditional philosophers conclude . . . , a priori, [that feminist epistemology] is bad philosophy" (1993, 13).

The fact that these epistemologies clearly highlight the interrelatedness of politics and knowledge means that they cannot be deemed pure and good philosophy. Other criticisms speak of the seeming lack of rigour in outlining the standards that should be used for judging information and attaining knowledge. For example, Shelton (in criticizing Code) says that "her proposals are really of an ethical, political, and humanistic nature. If she calls these areas 'epistemology', that is her right" (2006, 85). He argues that feminist epistemology is based on an idea for which there does not appear to be any evidentiary basis, namely that there are differences between the gender groups and that these differences have "epistemological implications" (88). But I believe Shelton misses the point, because the aim of social feminist epistemology (and all feminist epistemologies) is not to say necessarily that there are different ways of knowing for women and men, but rather that the range of what is classified as knowledge, the methods of attaining knowledge, and the practice of ignoring the nature of the knower and his or her social location is problematic. In fact, the vision of feminist epistemology that he seems to be advocating is one that aims to maintain the very position that Code criticizes, without even realizing that that is what he is doing. Feminist social epistemologies, however, have as their foundation the view that "to be *adequate*, an epistemology must attend to the complete ways in which social values influence knowledge, including the discernible social and political implications of its own analysis" (Alcoff and Potter 1993, 13). Embedded in that is a clear value judgement regarding how epistemology should be understood and practised.

Caribbean Scholarship

A growth in the representation of women at the level both of students and teachers as well as researchers typifies the changing demographics of Caribbean scholarship. Women are now more concentrated in senior administrative and academic positions, ideal positions for influencing both the creation and dissemination of knowledge. I use the changes in demographic only to point to shifts that are taking place within the UWI academy, and to posit how these changes may be useful for thinking about developing new approaches to the task of the university. I focus on the gender demographic shifts, but one must remember that there are several social identities that, as human beings, we all assume. The Caribbean is a developing region of the world, made up of small, developing states, with a history of slavery and colonialism, and the citizens are, by and large, of African and mixed-race heritage. Additionally, as in all other societies, there are socio-economic class concerns that must be considered. Therefore, as alluded to earlier, when one speaks of "socio-political–geographical locations", all of these factors will play a role. I use gender, however, as a representative of these various concerns, especially given the developments in that area and the real potential that it may present.

Knowledge production and dissemination are the main roles that a university should assume, since it is able, in that way, to influence the wider society, as well as policymakers, in any of the four ways identified by Don Marshall: "the provision of alternatives, information, sensitization and criticism" (2000, 81). To that end, research and teaching should take into account value judgements as to how educational goals, considered broadly, are connected to the concerns of the society. These activities cannot, however, be seen as being there simply to serve the dictates of governments and their policy decisions. Instead, research should be transformative and interrogative of ideas to allow for development in the society, grounded in the experience of Caribbean peoples. Furthermore, if there is a growth in attendance at the university, and the presence of more women in teaching, research and policy-making positions, and there is a continuation of the practices that were there before, without giving due consideration to a change in culture which will ensure that the university continues to be relevant to the people and nations it serves, these changes will also mean nothing. What I suggest is that consideration of feminist social epistemologies can foster a paradigm shift that can lead to the university's research and teaching becoming more meaningful to the region.

Typical of feminist epistemology is the discussion of the oppression and/or domination of groups of a particular gender, ethnicity, class, etc., and, more importantly, the ways in which these characteristics or social locations affect knowledge production and acquisition. Starting from gender initially, the areas in which feminist social epistemologists examine the intersection of knowledge and power have broadened. When taken within the Caribbean context, the region, given its historical background, faces several areas of oppression/domination. Because small-island Caribbean nations are still developing as states, globalization and climate-change issues raise concerns, as do cultural changes which affect aspects of life such as diet. But we also know that much of the knowledge that we use and adapt to our region has been developed from the standpoint of theorists in developed countries (especially western Europe and North America). But, one could argue that this approach is akin to the presence of the mainstream assumption of who the S is in the "S knows that-p" formulation. Thus, by more vigorously questioning the assumptions involved in the types of questions asked and the answers given, we as Caribbean researchers can be more discriminating in utilizing these approaches, and even recognizing that some of these theories are not best suited for meeting our development targets. Doing so will open the space for developing home-grown theoretical outlooks that target our specific concerns and strengths. Situated as part of the Western capitalist structure, with its historical experiences of discrimination based on ethnicity, race, gender and class, the Caribbean should produce a unique appreciation of the world and, therefore, knowledge. To reiterate an earlier point, we have to become actively engaged in understanding our own experiences and our Caribbean situation as non-whites and citizens of developing countries while being cognisant of what is happening in the wider global community and how those events affect us. There is another aspect to this issue, however. Recognizing that the university has a privileged status within Caribbean society, persons within the university should be cognisant that, as knowers linked to the university, we are more likely to be listened to more attentively, and our ideas accepted and applied. Taking this position seriously, and in so doing, demonstrating "epistemic responsibility" (Code 1991, 72) is crucial. There is an ethical dimension to what we do, and this ethical dimension cannot be ignored in the process of knowledge production. We must be responsible in what we explore, since what we do has repercussions outside of the university.[5]

Earlier I highlighted the view that a reason for the negative impact of mainstream epistemology is the homogeneity of male voices, but this hypothesis can be expanded to include other voices as well, such as those of the elite, the European, or the neo-liberal. Inviting and allowing heterogeneity allows for a greater range of knowledge to be created because people will come in with different preoccupations and issues they want to explore. Women's history has become prominent at UWI only in the past twenty years because women scholars have become concerned with giving a voice to a group of persons who were once invisible (Brereton 2002), but this area of scholarship is still very young because of a lack of heterogeneity in the academy. We can ask: how many other areas are we not fully exploring as researchers because we enter the university and also become homogenized? Alcoff and Potter state that the role of feminist social epistemology is "the expansion of democracy in the production of knowledge" (1993, 13). We can help to ensure that feminist social epistemology fulfils this role by expanding our understanding of what is a fruitful subject for research by bringing our whole selves to the research experience. Further, by bringing the voices of students and the wider community into research activities, we enhance the democratic and interactional approach that knowledge production can take.

The last point raised is connected to another consequence of assuming the broader perspective that feminist social epistemology posits and encourages – namely, yielding more and varied approaches to the creation and dissemination of knowledge. No longer are propositional knowledge and the privileged knower the norm; nor does knowledge seemingly arise in a vacuum. Instead, one takes into account the subjectivity of both knowers and learners, and the recognition that dialogue is crucial in knowledge generation (Bergin 2002). We should be involved in more learning activities that incorporate these assumptions. Additionally, we must recognize that the community of learners and the wider society should be brought more into the process of knowledge creation (especially when the issues are about them) through the use of research tools such as ethnographic techniques and participatory learning approaches. Furthermore, interaction with others develops the relational knower. This kind of knower values collaborative creation of knowledge, which is a more realistic concept than that of the fabled atomistic knower, and generates knowledge using a different type of methodology. The methodology used would generally involve working in groups and in discussion-oriented deliberations, specifically cross-faculty collaborations and interdisciplinary approaches. Altogether, this approach would allow different knowers from differing positions within the university community, as well as organizations and groups in the society, to facilitate knowledge creation and dissemination.

There is evidence that some of these types of activities are already being undertaken. The rate at which these changes are occurring, however, is insufficient, especially for a university that is presently trying to reposition itself to meet the demands of its students better, and for a region seeking to meet the developmental goals of the twenty-first century. The challenge is to embrace quickly the different approaches that feminist social epistemologies present, to interrogate and evaluate old and new ideas, and to generate Caribbean perspectives to realize regional collaborative development goals.

Notes

1.   The realist position is traditionally seen as being in opposition to the position of idealism, which argues that reality is accessible only through the operation of the mind. The issue, then, revolves around the mind-independence, or lack thereof, of our perceptions, and hence our knowledge claims.

2.   Interestingly, when one looks closely at Nagel's examples, one sees that they are all related to scientific knowledge and perceptual knowledge (which forms the basis for scientific knowledge). This view ties in with the idea of knowledge that is often posited in mainstream epistemology and could allow Karl Popper to understand epistemology solely as the study of scientific knowledge. The critiques of the traditional view of knowledge raises the questions whether there are other types of knowledge, and, if there are, what the reason is for viewing scientific knowledge as the epitome or paradigm.

3.   With respect to this example, the question could arise as to whether, within the context of mainstream epistemology, this experience would be classified as knowledge. Epistemology typically places emphasis on scientific knowledge, and the experience of birth, in itself, cannot be classified as such. One could argue that what may be classified as knowledge would be the mechanisms involved in the process rather than the experience of the process itself, and a male as well as a female could certainly conceivably understand these mechanisms.

4. It should be noted that a similar practice can be identified for subordinated racial and ethnic groups. The result is that the white, western European male is rational, strong, intelligent and active, and has a well-directed moral compass (Antony 2002, 466).

5. I am concerned that the ethical responsibility that comes with this privileged status is one to which many colleagues only pay lip service; at other times, I think we become involved in service because it is professionally expedient to do so.

References

Alcoff, L., and E. Potter. 1993. When feminisms intersect epistemology. In *Feminist epistemologies*, ed. L. Alcoff and E. Potter, 1–14. New York: Routledge.

Anderson, E. 2007. Feminist epistemology and philosophy of science. In *Stanford encyclopaedia of philosophy*, ed. E.N. Zalta. http://plato.stanford.edu/archives/win2007/entries/feminism-epistemology.

Antony, L. 2002. Embodiment and epistemology. In *Oxford handbook of epistemology*, ed. P.K. Moser, 463–78. New York: Oxford University Press.

Bergin, L. 2002. Testimony, epistemic difference, and privilege: How feminist epistemology can improve our understanding of the communication of knowledge. *Social Epistemology* 16 (July): 197–213.

Brereton, B. 2002. Gender and the historiography of the English-speaking Caribbean. In *Gendered realities: Essays in Caribbean feminist thought*, ed. P. Mohammed, 129–44. Kingston: University of the West Indies Press.

Code, L. 1991. *What can she know?* Ithaca: Cornell University Press.

———. 1993. Taking subjectivity into account. In *Feminist epistemologies*, ed. L. Alcoff and E. Potter, 15–48. New York: Routledge.

Collins, Patricia Hill. 1990/1991. *Black feminist thought: Knowledge, consciousness, and the politics of empowerment*. New York: Routledge.

Marshall, D.D. 2000. Academic travails and a crisis-of-mission of the University of the West Indies' social sciences: From history and critique to anti-politics. In *Higher education in the Caribbean: Past, present and future directions*, ed. G.D. Howe, 59–84. Bridgetown: University of the West Indies Press.

Grasswick, H. 2006. Feminist social epistemology. In *Stanford encyclopaedia of philosophy*, ed. E.N. Zalta. http://plato.stanford.edu/archives/win2006/entries/feminist-social-epistemology.

Harding, S. 1993. Rethinking standpoint epistemology: "What is strong epistemology"? In *Feminist epistemologies*, ed. L. Alcoff and E. Potter, 49–82. New York: Routledge.

Nagel, T. 1989. *The view from nowhere*. New York: Oxford University Press.

Shelton, J.D. 2006. The failure of feminist epistemology. *Academic Questions* 19 (June): 82–92.

3

The Divine and the Demonic
Sylvia Wynter and Caribbean Feminist Thought Revisited

TONYA HAYNES

Introduction

Sylvia Wynter has been described as the "Divine one of Caribbean letters" and as the reluctant matriarch of Caribbean feminism (Barnes 1999; Henry 2000, 118). In this chapter I explore the tension between Wynter's prominence as a Caribbean intellectual and her alleged antagonism to a Caribbean feminist liberation project. Although she is arguably the Caribbean's pre-eminent intellectual alive today, and in spite of her international recognition as a scholar, her work is largely absent from courses on Caribbean feminist thought at the University of the West Indies, Cave Hill. Moreover, Caribbean feminist scholars in the social sciences cite her work infrequently.[1] While she has been accused of rejecting feminism, Caribbean feminist scholars have hardly explored her ideas sufficiently enough to make an accurate assessment of that claim.

It has been argued that Wynter "leaves theorizing about gender dynamics within the community to us and she wishes us well", and that she "leave[s] the development of alternative counterhegemonic womanist/feminist discourse to the next generation of the native women intelligentsia" (Toland-Dix 2008, 76). I want to suggest that Wynter does more than these comments suggest. Wynter challenges us to activate the epistemological demonic ground of Caribbean women. Given that this demonic ground is the Achilles heel of the episteme (to borrow Paget Henry's formulation), Caribbean feminist thought has the possibility to effect an epistemic shift. As gender is a constitutive part of Western bio-logic, however, Caribbean feminisms must confront the hegemony of gender within their own theorizing. The challenge to gender which Wynter mounts reveals the tensions between Western feminist theory and indigenous Caribbean feminist theorizing, and it is more a fruitful contribution to Caribbean feminisms than a rejection of their premises. This chapter represents a fundamental quarrel with Caribbean feminist engagements with Wynter's ideas (and the lack thereof), and attempts to resolve the purported antagonism of Wynter's ideas to Caribbean feminism.

Reading Wynter

The argument that Woman is not Man's other represents a challenge to the very foundations of feminism. For if woman is not man's other then gender functions differently from the way in which Western feminist theory has articulated it. Gender, Wynter insists, is part of genre, or different kinds of the human. Gender is always a key feature of how each genre of the human understands itself, but it is not the only feature. Part and parcel of our globalized understanding of the world is the overrepresentation of a particular genre of the human as the human itself. This localized, ethnocentric understanding of the human misrepresents itself as a universal understanding. Man's others, she insists, include all that is not simultaneously white, bourgeois, Western and male.[2]

Whereas Barnes sees Wynter as denying the salience of a Caribbean feminist project, and Wynter's alleged rejection of feminism has been understood as the inability of nationalisms to apprehend feminist concerns, I propose that, far from invalidating a feminist project, Wynter's arguments provide productive engagements with feminist theory (Barnes 1999). I wish to complicate the claim that Wynter "has consistently written from a feminist perspective, although she has not been consistently claimed by the Caribbean feminist community" (Josephs 2009, 194). And while I agree that Caribbean feminist thinkers have neither claimed her nor extensively engaged with her work, I want to suggest that Wynter's relationship to feminism is more complex. What does it mean to "consistently write from a feminist perspective", especially when your work contains a fundamental critique of Western/normative feminism? A reading of Wynter's non-fiction work provides a fuller understanding of her ideas on race and gender. That "Wynter privileges neither race nor gender" but "holds them both as equally important" (ibid., 195) is not a conclusion one could reasonably come to after reading Wynter's non-fiction work; indeeed, Wynter herself clearly underscores that "race" is epistemologically primary (Scott 2000, 183). Wynter has expanded her theorizing of race beyond a Western bio-logic to a conceptualizing of genre, within which she collapses gender.[3] Wynter rejects normative "Westocentric" deployments of gender outright, so to argue that she views race and gender as equally important is fundamentally to misunderstand her arguments.[4]

Feminist claims made in the name of gender have sought to remake Woman in the image of Man – a move which Wynter rejects as inadequate because it still excludes the nigger/native (and a long list of Others) from the human (Wynter 1990). It is this limitation of gender which Wynter rejects – a rejection which, I argue, contains fruitful possibilities for Caribbean feminisms. In addition, considering that Wynter explicitly includes those who reject compulsory heterosexuality among those excluded from the current ethnocentric conceptualization of the human (Thomas 2009, 49), which misrepresents itself as the only and universal conceptualization of what it means to be human, her theorizing opens a space from which Caribbean feminist thought can "divest itself of heterosexual precepts" (Robinson 2007, 127).

Feminism, like all other -isms, mistakes the map for the territory, to use Wynter's apt formulation (Wynter 2006, 117–19). In other words, a simultaneous revalorization of blackness/Otherness and of the "feminine" requires a revaluing of the human outside of Western biocentric terms. The revalorizing of the human cannot take place from within the current episteme because Western humanism has devalued the human itself and reduced it to a particular genre or way of being human: Man, of which both "race" and "gender" are key constitutive elements (ibid.). Wynter's work emerges as extremely useful for Caribbean feminisms as she articulates a human liberation project which must of necessity challenge the humanism of Western feminism. If Caribbean feminists are preoccupied with constructing and reconstructing knowledge, Wynter is preoccupied with the need to change the episteme itself. For Wynter, challenges to global inequalities must simultaneously be challenges to the very "order of knowledge" which presents these inequities as self-evidently normal (Wynter 1995).

Patricia Mohammed asserts that "to the casual onlooker or observer, sexual difference as a conceptual tool of social analysis might not appear to be a valuable one, but it is one which cannot be ignored" (Mohammed 2003a, 13). Wynter is by no means a casual onlooker, and her quarrel with feminism warrants further exploration. Using Shakespeare's play *The Tempest* as allegory, Wynter examines gender and race in the Caribbean. For Wynter, Miranda, the daughter of the sorcerer Prospero, possesses power and privilege, neither of which the enslaved Caliban enjoys (Wynter 1990, 363). Wynter therefore questions the salience of Western feminist deployments of gender for Caribbean women, since the universal subject Woman clearly does not exist in the Caribbean. The fact that Caliban has no female counterpart, Wynter explains, is functional to human/savage Western dualism, which replaced the male/female binary as the primary signifier of difference and relations of power (ibid., 361).

While feminists have questioned the usefulness of gender as an analytical tool, arguing that gender "is so thoroughly fragmented by race, class, historical particularity and individual difference as to self-destruct as an analytical category" (Bordo 1990, 133), or have asked whether feminism itself serves to reify gender (Butler 1990/1999, 7), Wynter's critique is different. For Wynter, then, all contemporary struggles are essentially struggles against the white Western bourgeois overrepresentation of itself as the human – as The Man – and relegating the rest of us to varying subject positions as lesser Others (Wynter 2004, 260–61). Rather than seeing her analysis as invalidating the entire premise of Caribbean feminist scholarship (Barnes 1999, 37), she insists on a wider project of social justice than that which is made possible by limited deployments of gender. After Wynter's deconstructive work comes her reconstructive project. Wynter proposes genre as a means of understanding how "race" and "gender" function:

> Although I use the term "race," and I have to use the term "race," "race" itself is a function of something else which is much closer to "gender." . . . So I coined the word "genre," or I adapted it, because "genre" and "gender" come from the same root. They mean "kind," one of the meanings is "kind." Now what I am suggesting is that "gender" has always been a function of the instituting of "kind." . . . I am trying to insist that "race" is really a code-word for "genre." Our issue is not the

issue of "race." Our issue is the issue of the genre of "Man." It is this issue of the "genre" of "Man" that causes all the "*–isms.*" (Thomas 2009, 55)

Wynter's analysis here suggests the simultaneity of "race" and "gender" in constituting different genres of the human. Hers is a rejection of a humanist feminist project which would seek to include bourgeois Woman as the counterpart of the Man, while leaving intact a long list of Others. For Wynter, there is no liberation in Woman's access to the world of bourgeois Man (the public sphere of the world of work under capitalism), as it does nothing to challenge the inequities which constitute that world. Wynter is not denying gendered power relations; she is essentially arguing that "gender" is part and parcel of the Western bio-logic which naturalized both the human/savage binary and the male/female binary. Challenges to gendered power relations must be made from a vantage point outside of the episteme, not from within it. That Wynter poses fruitful challenges to Caribbean feminism is evident, as Caribbean feminists themselves are now questioning the conceptual usefulness of gender (Rowley 2010).

Gender Trouble

Western feminist concerns with defining gender away from sex, and therefore away from biological determinism, are unnecessarily distracting (e.g., Hawkesworth 1997; Nicholson 1999, chap. 5) and miss the point that, within Western bio-logic, sex is inseparable from gender.[5] Gender may be understood as part of genre, of which race, ethnicity, class, sexuality and other relations of domination and subordination are a part, and are all grounded in a Western bio-logic. As has been argued, "it is not [an] accident . . . that 'race' and 'sex' in their primarily naturalized or biological meaning emerged in the eighteenth century, when the new political concept of the individual self and the individual bearer of rights was being articulated" (Stepan quoted in Fausto-Sterling 2004, 3). The invention of Man required a delineation of its ontological limits.

Wynter's analysis should therefore resonate with Caribbean feminists who have themselves sensed gender trouble. Andaiye's recognition that "working for gender justice, like working for gender equality, will not lead to a transformation of all the interacting power relations against which we must organise" is an acknowledgement that Caribbean feminist politics in the past may have mistaken the map for the territory (Andaiye 2002, 17). This understanding has led to the accusation that Caribbean feminisms have sold out to "genderism" (Soares 2006, 190). Gender as a feminist analytical tool has been replaced by the more palatable "gender somethings" (Robinson 2007, 121). Rowley's questioning of gender and her invocation of Wynter in order to do so points to the necessity of including Sylvia Wynter within the Caribbean feminist intellectual tradition (Rowley 2010). Moreover, it represents a timely rapprochement between Sylvia Wynter and other Caribbean feminist thinkers.

Our indigenous theoretical conceptualizations of gender have served to suggest an intransigence of patriarchal relations of domination, and in many ways have undercut a vision of radical change. Caribbean feminists have neglected to problematize the extent to which gender as a concept is rooted in Westocentric bio-logic, the very bio-logic which denies Caribbean people access to the human. In theorizing from within the West, rather than from the vantage point of their demonic ground at its margins, Caribbean feminists fail to challenge the episteme in the way in which Wynter suggests that they should.

Wynter does not provide a theory of gendered power within heterosexual relationships; nor does she provide a theory of power relations between generic men and women. What her work does, by not accepting these relationships as given or as the norm, is provide the tools, not for bargaining with patriarchy but for undoing gender altogether. By demonstrating the centrality of racial and gendered divisions to our understanding of the world, and insisting on the cultural specificity of this understanding and its link to Western, masculinized, imperial power, Wynter challenges both feminist deployments of gender and gendered asymmetries in society.

Caribbean Feminist Theorizing of Gender

Two Caribbean feminist theorists have provided extensive explorations of gender and gender systems which have enriched feminist thought. Mohammed's focus is on sexuality and culture, and Barriteau foregrounds economic questions in her analysis. Both models, however, seek to account for gendered power relations in society and have broad explanatory power.

For V. Eudine Barriteau, gender is a sophisticated feminist analytical category which brings with it methodologies and conceptual tools for social analysis (Barriteau 2003a, 59). The key methodological input is its rejection of male-centred approaches (Barriteau 2001, 29). She defines gender as "referring to complex systems of personal and social relations through which women and men are socially created and maintained and through which they gain access to, or are allocated, status, power and material resources within society" (ibid., 26).

While socialist and Marxist feminist approaches dominated earlier theorizing (ibid.; Reddock 2009, 219), Barriteau's theory-building revealed a direct attempt to move away from this trend and to use postmodernist feminism's break with dualisms to explain Caribbean women's multiple realities (Barriteau 1995b). Barriteau's model is a broad-based one which recognizes the political, economic, social and psychological elements of gender, and which emphasizes power. Drawing on a postmodernist feminist analytical frame, it views both men and women as gendered (Barriteau 2001, 26). An important contribution of hers to Caribbean feminist theory and practice is her understanding of the social relations of gender as consisting of ideological and material relations (Barriteau 2003a, 59). The material refers to women's access to the resources of the state, and the ideological refers to "belief systems" about gender. Barriteau insists, however, that a gender system is not a separate system but exists within all other subsystems: "Gender is within race, within class, within economic activity, within sexualities and sexual orientations, within language" (ibid., 67).

While this framework rejects additive models, it is not an intersectional model. It suggests that what gender does is complement and complicate existing analytical tools. Barriteau's rejection of liberal feminist and socialist feminist models which have sought to add feminist concerns to a liberal and socialist framework paves the way for her postmodernist feminist approach to gender (Barriteau 1995b, 1992): "This approach seeks to move the analysis away from an additive approach to one that simultaneously incorporates what is known about the older and more researched social antagonisms of class and race and mediate these through a commingling with the relatively more recent social relations of gender" (Barriteau 2003a, 67). Barriteau defines gendered relations separately from gender relations. While "gender relations" has been used to refer to social relations between women and men, "gendered relations" refers to "the asymmetry in the contemporary social relations of gender that generally inscribe inequalities for women materially and ideologically" (Barriteau 2001, 27).

The importance of this framework is underscored by its use in the Caribbean Community's (CARICOM) plan of action for gender mainstreaming (Massiah 2004, 12). Barriteau remains adamant that what is at issue in the proliferation of meanings assigned to "gender" is the anti-feminist/anti-woman discourse pervasive in the Caribbean during the 1990s and 2000s, and not any "internal flaw" in gender analysis itself (Barriteau 2003b, 29).

Mohammed wants to return the study of sexuality to investigations of gendered power relations (Mohammed 1994, 1995). She signals the need for feminism to explicitly include sexuality – "the idea of sex (as activity), sexual symbolism and imagery" in definitions of gender (Mohammed 1995). She argues that, even though sexuality and domesticity are among the prime sites for the production of gendered power relations, feminist theorizing of gender does not always reflect this detail (ibid.). Drawing on Joan Scott's definition of gender, she sees society as constituted by multiple gender systems. She takes from Joan Scott an understanding of gender as the social and cultural organization of sexual difference. Such organizing of society takes the form of gender systems which are "best perceived as the rules governing, social, sexual and reproductive behaviour of both sexes in any given society" (Mohammed 1995, 21). Gender systems comprise the social roles assigned to men and to women, cultural definitions of masculinity and femininity, the sexual division of labour, rules regarding marriage and kinship, and women's position relative to men in political and economic life. For Mohammed, the components of gender systems are highly variable within and among societies, and therefore gender systems and, by extension, gender itself remain "elusive concept[s]" (ibid.). She does, however, offer some definitions, taking gender relations, for example, to refer to relations between men and women (ibid.). Her theory is therefore one which seeks to account for gendered power relations within a heteronormative society.

Mohammed introduces the concept of gender negotiations to explain how Indian communities reconstituted patriarchy in Trinidad and Tobago and negotiated gender identities. She also theorizes gender as a process of negotiations which take place at the micro and macro levels (ibid., 29). The major contributions of this work are that it allows for the study of both men and women simultaneously, accounts for the change in gender systems over time, and demonstrates the importance of gender to culture. By demonstrating that "culture and gender are inextricably meshed", she accounts for both the change in gender relations over time through a process of negotiation, and the fixity of patriarchal dominance (Mohammed 2001/2002, 267). Her model is a complex one which suggests both fixity and change. If gender can be understood as a process of negotiations at the macro and micro level, then we must ask: Who initiates the negotiations? Who controls the negotiations? Who is most often asked to compromise on their demands? Are negotiations about carving out space within an unjust system? Do they suggest the impossibility of transforming the system itself? By demonstrating the importance of gendered meanings to culture, Mohammed explains why gender remains such a fixed aspect of societal organization. Her dialectical approach to negotiations of masculinity and femininity, however, takes masculinity and femininity as given. Nonetheless, her insistence that sexuality is an important dimension of gendered power relations is an important insight.

Tensions with Theory

An examination of the development of Caribbean feminist thought reveals a complex relationship between Caribbean feminisms and theory. Barriteau argues that "feminist knowledge in developing countries has never fully escaped its origins in an economistic type of *raison d'être*" (Barriteau 2004, 447). Massiah here underscores this point: "But while these academic explorations are admirable in their own right, they are of limited utility if not related to action designed to improve the situation which the theories explain. Here the idea is to ensure that those objectives of the programme which are concerned with theory building also relate to the priority development of issues as articulated by governments and regional development agencies" (Massiah 1993, 20).

Massiah's caution that theory must not be divorced from activism is relevant and has been articulated by many Caribbean feminists (see Mohammed 2003a; Providence 2005; Vassell 2003). Her suggestion that Caribbean feminist theorizing should operate within the confines of the goals of Caribbean governments and development organizations, however, is limiting in that it would deny Rowley's vision of the limitless possibilities of indigenous Caribbean feminist theorizing (Rowley 2002, 39). Furthermore, considering women's historical relegation to the margins of "development", it signals a kind of self-cooptation of Caribbean feminist thought, as well as a rejection of Caribbean women as theorists and an understanding of theorizing as foreign to Caribbean interests. The discipline of Gender and Development Studies accounts, in part, for perceptions of Caribbean feminist work as derivative and untheoretical: the Caribbean is the *field* which provides the case studies which feed into the *great house* of Western feminist theory (Barriteau, quoted in Rowley 2003, 91).

Massiah's comments highlight a tension between Caribbean feminisms and theory. Caribbean feminists have not shied away from theory, and their vision of liberation is arguably the most radical twenty-first-century vision articulated in the region. The relationships of Caribbean feminisms to Western metanarratives remain to be interrogated, however. The researchers of the Women in the Caribbean Project (WICP) sought to avoid outside theories and build theories from the lived experiences of Caribbean women. Barriteau has criticized the WICP for failing to make explicit their theoretical investments, which have been masked by their claims of avoiding theory (Barriteau 1995a, 145–46). If "habits of thought organise social relations as much as social relations organise habits of thought" (Young-Bruehl 1989, 37), then the need to "emancipate [ourselves] from mental slavery" becomes even more urgent (Marley 1980/2001). Theorizing, then, is not an ivory-tower indulgence but a necessity, in any project of human liberation.

Do Caribbean feminists produce theory or do they just use the theories produced by others? Barriteau asserts that "of all the feminist theories available to explain the day-to-day realities of Caribbean women only the postmodernist feminist frame provides an adequate fit" (Barriteau 1995a, 158). While Barriteau has been identified as the most consistently theoretical of Caribbean feminists (Meeks 2007, 11), and indeed her work is often engaged more than that of any other Caribbean feminist scholar, here she approaches theory in the pose of consumer. Of the Euro-American theories proffered to explain the subordination of Woman – radical, socialist, Marxist and liberal feminist theories – she finds postmodernist feminist theory most fruitful for understanding Caribbean women's lives. I am not contesting her conclusion here, but rather I want to use it as an example of the way in which Western feminism often figures as a kind of normative feminism within Caribbean feminist theorizing.

Mohammed identifies Western feminism as dating back to fourteenth-century Europe, and acknowledges that "Caribbean gender theory has

borrowed generously from the global expansion of feminist theory", thus linking Caribbean and Western feminism (Mohammed 2003b, 102, 108). In
describing the relative ease and comfort within which the Caribbean women's
movement operates, she compares contemporary Caribbean feminists to the
suffragettes and not to their indigenous, Afro- and Indo-Caribbean foremoth-
ers in their struggles for autonomy, humanity and liberation:

> The feminist movement in the Caribbean is a predominantly middle class move-
> ment. We have been fortunate to receive funding which has poured into the "woman
> question" over the last decade . . . In addition there is greater acceptability of the
> movement for female liberation at this time. Where the suffragettes of the early
> twentieth century suffered great ignominy, the employment of our energies in the
> feminist cause is rewarded with both recognition and recompense. (Mohammed
> 1991, 20)

Mohammed's reference to the suffragettes highlights the preponderance of
European and North American frames of reference in Caribbean feminisms
(Mehta 2004, 96). The intention here is not to foreground the "foreignness"
of Caribbean feminisms but to acknowledge the articulations of "discourses
from 'outside'" and within the region (Smith 1994, 916). Caribbean feminists
strategically select from "feminist genealogies and histories of struggle" in a
way which adds complexity to their work and cannot be read as mere outside
influence (Alexander 2005, 22). In light of Wynter's insistence on the need to
exoticize Western thought in order to disrupt the taken-for-grantedness of the
episteme, this selective genealogy, however, is not unproblematic. Historical
analysis provides the grounds for an indigenous Caribbean feminist theorizing
and a break with Western hegemony in feminism through locating feminist
thought in the historical specificities of the Caribbean.[6] Historical analysis
serves to connect Caribbean feminist theorizing to the history of struggle of
Caribbean women:

> It was important for us, as Third World women, to establish the extent to which
> there was a tradition of women's struggle in our region, and what form, if any, it
> had taken. Deep down, many of us suspected that there had to be such a history[;]
> it seemed inconceivable that there was any group of women who over time did not
> make some overt or covert effort to transform their exploited and subordinate social
> situation. But this has not been part of the collective knowledge or history which
> had been passed down to us. (Reddock 1994, 1)

Caribbean feminist scholars see their work as a part of and a contribution to Western and transnational feminist theory, while at the same time it serves as a trenchant critique of Caribbean society and politics. Caribbean feminists have sought to appropriate these Western feminist theories for their own purposes, adapting these theories to Caribbean realities and using them as the raw material from which they build indigenous understandings of gender and gendered relations (Mohammed 1994). The tensions, compromises and syntheses between indigenous and Western frames of reference, scholarship and activism, scholarship and society, and local, national, regional and international feminisms, must be explored in any attempt to engage with Caribbean feminist ideas. I want to suggest that the relationship of Caribbean feminist theory to Western feminism is one of continuity and rupture, critical engagement and departure – certainly a much more complex one than has been suggested in the past.[7] The conceptualization of feminist theory as inherently North American/European, however, contributes to the relegation of Caribbean feminist thinkers to the epistemological margins. Western feminism emerges as the normalized feminism: "After a relatively delayed start, Caribbean feminist scholarship, has, since the late 1970s, moved rapidly to become established as an exciting field of epistemological, theoretical and methodological advance" (Barrow 1998, xi).

Exactly what would have been an appropriate start for Caribbean feminism, however, remains unstated, but implicit is some standard of feminism to which the Caribbean is now playing catch-up. This subjection of Caribbean realities to a Western measuring stick results in an analysis which, even while celebratory of Caribbean feminist scholarship, results in distortions (Paravisini-Gebert 1997, 4). More importantly, however, the Westocentric framing of Caribbean feminisms silences the demonic ground from which the Caribbean subaltern woman could disrupt the episteme. What are the productive possibilities of the Caribbean's location in the West, yet at its margins?

Towards the Demonic Ground

Marlene Nourbese Philip sees the productive possibilities of living at the epistemological and ontological frontiers, facing outwards towards yet-unfulfilled possibilities. Marginality, then, does not signal inferiority but a strategic vantage point from which to imagine the future (Nourbese Philip 1990, 300). To live productively at the margins, then, is to refuse to be manageable. This commitment to being unmanageable is revealed in the epistemological positions of other Caribbean women writers and within the critical vocabulary of Caribbean feminist scholars. Barriteau's postmodernist feminist theory is a recognition of unmanageability as a defining feature of Caribbean women's lives and an attempt to do the reconstructive work necessary to make these lives readable (Barriteau 1992, 1995a). Likewise, Alexander's erotic autonomy is a politics of decolonization which refuses colonial and post-independence containment of Caribbean sexuality. Erotic autonomy therefore signals a refusal to be manageable and to be managed. Alexander links sexuality to the colonial and postcolonial Caribbean state and the international political economy, and writes her personal life into a trenchant critique of Caribbean citizenship and nationalism (Alexander 1994). If Foucault is correct that we must understand power at "the point where power reaches into the very grain of individuals, touches their bodies" (Foucault 1981, 39), then Alexander's erotic autonomy makes the intimate the highest political project.

Erna Brodber, too, refuses to be manageable. In arguing that her "fiction writing is part of [her] sociological method", she blends objectivity and subjectivity, fiction and science (Brodber 1990, 164). Of her fiction, she says, "It has to have space in which people could do their own dreaming, their own thinking, and their own planning" (ibid., 166). In dismantling epistemological hierarchies, she also produces spaces for the visioning, theorizing and creative energies of others. In writing the novel *Jane and Louisa Will Soon Come Home* as a case study for sociological training, she blends both her fiction and her work as a sociologist with her activism (Brodber 1980).

It is this politics of unmanageability which holds the potential for the activation of the epistemological demonic ground of subaltern Caribbean women.[8] In conceptualizing the demonic model, Wynter demonstrates that the "governing system of meaning" is unable to "voice" the silenced ground of subaltern Caribbean women and unable to "make thinkable" the possibility of a new system of meaning from the vantage point of this silenced ground (Wynter 1990, 363). This demonic model allows for a vantage point outside of the governing system of meaning; rooted in subaltern Caribbean realities, it is demonic because it institutes itself outside of our current discursive frameworks (ibid., 364). The demonic model contains the capacity for an epistemic shift precisely because it is not a standpoint epistemology with the vantage points of race, gender and class, which form part of the bio-logic of the governing system of meaning.[9] Rather, the demonic ground is the liminal category – that which has the potential to disrupt the episteme precisely because it is that which must be managed in order to maintain the stability of the system of meaning.

While gender as a concept has been theorized by Caribbean feminists and deployed to make demands of the state on behalf of women, as well as to expose inequities that were previously justified as natural, gender itself has revealed its limitations as being too embedded within our current techno-scientific-capitalist episteme, which relegates the Caribbean to a liminal position. Wynter argues, however, that the liminal category of the Caribbean subaltern woman is the Achilles heel of the episteme and the vantage point from which we may begin to imagine new worlds outside of our current discursive frameworks. It is the activation of this epistemological demonic ground that is the site of divine possibilities.

Notes

1. Michelle Rowley is a notable exception. See Rowley 2010.
2. Wynter articulates these ideas throughout a series of essays and interviews, including Scott 2000; Thomas 2009; Wynter 1990; Wynter 1995; Wynter 2006; Wynter 2003
3. Oyèrónké Oyewumi conceptualizes Western rationality as a bio-logic rooted in an understanding of the social, which is constructed in biological terms. See Oyewumi 1997, 11.
4. Oyewumi uses the term Westocentric to reach "beyond 'Eurocentric' to include North America" (ibid., 18).
5. Oyèrónké Oyewumi and Ann Fausto-Sterling both arrive at this insight from two completely different vantage points. See Fausto-Sterling 2003, 131; Oyewumi 1997.
6. Mohammed 2003b, 124. Shepherd, Brereton and Bailey 1995 present not just women's history but feminist approaches to history.
7. Janet Momsen argues that anglophone Caribbean feminists have been largely influenced by white Western, middle-class feminist ideas. See Momsen 1993, 4.
8. Katherine McKittrick's work must be acknowledged as a fine example of feminist application of Wynter's work. She uses Wynter's conceptualisation of demonic ground as a vantage point outside the norm – a way of viewing the West from outside the West – but also as a description of black women as a silenced, absent presence, as outside of categorization as a means of understanding black women's geography. See McKittrick 2006.

9. Implicit in this demonic model is a critique of feminist standpoint theory. The demonic model is therefore not an articulation of a black feminist standpoint. For examples of feminist standpoints see Hartsock 2003; Hartsock 2004; Collins 2003.

References

Alexander, M.J. 1994. Not just (any) body can be a citizen: The politics of law, sexuality and postcoloniality in Trinidad and Tobago and the Bahamas. *Feminist Review* 48 (Autumn): 5–23.

———. 2005. *Pedagogies of crossing: Meditations on feminism, sexual politics, memory, and the sacred*. Durham, NC: Duke University Press.

Andaiye. 2002. The angle you look from determines what you see: Towards a critique of feminist politics in the Caribbean. Lucille Mathurin Mair Lecture. Centre for Gender and Development Studies, Old Library, University of the West Indies, Mona, Jamaica, 6 March.

Barnes, N. 1999. Reluctant matriarch: Sylvia Wynter and the problematics of Caribbean feminism. *Small Axe* 5 (March): 34–47.

Barriteau, E. 1992. The construct of a postmodernist feminist theory for Caribbean social science research. *Social and Economic Studies* 41 (2): 1–43.

———. 1995a. Postmodernist feminist theorizing and development policy and practice in the anglophone Caribbean: The Barbados case. In *Feminism / Postmodernism / Development*, ed. M.H. Marchand and J.L. Parpart, 142–58. London: Routledge.

———. 1995b. Socialist feminist theory and Caribbean women: Transcending dualisms. *Social and Economic Studies* 44 (2–3): 25–63.

———. 2001. *The political economy of gender in the twentieth-century Caribbean*. New York: Palgrave.

———. 2003a. Confronting power and politics: A feminist theorizing of gender in commonwealth Caribbean societies. *Meridians: Feminism, Race, Transnationalism* 3 (2): 57–92.

———. 2003b. Theorizing the shift from "woman" to "gender" in Caribbean feminist discourse. In *Confronting power, theorizing gender: Interdisciplinary perspectives in the Caribbean*, ed. E. Barriteau, 27–45. Kingston: University of the West Indies Press.

———. 2004. Constructing feminist knowledge in the commonwealth Caribbean in the era of globalization. In *Gender in the 21st century: Caribbean perspectives, visions and possibilities*, ed. B. Bailey and E. Leo-Rhynie, 437–65. Kingston: Ian Randle.

Barrow, C. 1998. Introduction and overview: Caribbean gender ideologies. In *Caribbean portraits: Essays on gender ideologies and identities*, ed. C. Barrow, xi–xxxviii. Kingston: Ian Randle.

Bordo, S. 1990. Feminism, postmodernism, and gender scepticism. In *Feminism / postmodernism*, ed. L. Nicholson, 133–56. New York: Routledge.

Brodber, E. 1980. *Jane and Louisa will soon come home*. London: New Beacon Books.

———. 1990. Fiction in the scientific procedure. In *Caribbean women writers: Essays from the first international conference*, ed. S.R. Cudjoe, 164–68. Wellesley, MA: Calaloux.

Butler, J. 1990/1999. *Gender trouble: Feminism and the subversion of identity*. New York: Routledge.

Collins, P. Hill. 2003. The politics of black feminist thought. In *The feminist theory reader: Local and global perspectives*, ed. C.R. McCann and S. Kim, 318–33. London: Routledge.

Fausto-Sterling, A. 2003. The problem with sex/gender and nature/nurture. In *Debating biology: Sociological reflections on health, medicine and society*, ed. L. Birke, G.A. Bendelow and S.J. Williams, 123–31. New York: Routledge.

———. 2004. Refashioning race: DNA and the politics of health care. *Differences: A Journal of Feminist Cultural Studies* 15 (3): 1–31.

Foucault, M. 1981. Prison talk. In *Power/knowledge: Selected interviews and other writings, 1972–1977*, ed. C. Gordon, 37–54. New York: Harvester Press.

Hartsock, N. 2003. The feminist standpoint: Toward a specifically feminist historical materialism. In *The feminist theory reader: Local and global perspectives*, ed. C.R. McCann and S. Kim, 292–307. New York: Routledge.

———. 2004. Comment on Hekman's "Truth and method: Feminist standpoint theory revisited": Truth or justice. In *The feminist standpoint theory reader: Intellectual and political controversies*, ed. S. Harding, 243–46. London: Routledge.

Hawkesworth, M. 1997. Confounding gender. *Signs: Journal of Women in Culture and Society* 22 (3): 649–85.

Henry, P. 2000. *Caliban's reason: Introducing Afro-Caribbean philosophy*. New York: Routledge.

Josephs, K. Baker. 2009. The necessity for madness: Negotiating nation in Sylvia Wynter's *The hills of Hebron*. In *The Caribbean woman writer as scholar: Creating, imagining, theorizing*, ed. K.N. Abraham, 179–204. Florida: Caribbean Studies Press.

Marley, B., and the Wailers. 1980/2001. Redemption song (track 10). *Uprising*.

Massiah, J. 1993. Feature address. Symposium celebrating the 10th anniversary of the Women and Development Studies Programme, University of the West Indies, Cave Hill, 2 December.

———. 2004. Feminist scholarship and society. In *Gender in the 21st century: Caribbean perspectives, visions and possibilities*, ed. B. Bailey and E. Leo-Rhynie, 5–34. Kingston: Ian Randle.

McKittrick, K. 2006. *Demonic grounds: Black women and the cartographies of struggle*. Minneapolis: University of Minnesota Press.

Meeks, B. 2007. *Envisioning Caribbean futures: Jamaican perspectives*. Kingston: University of the West Indies Press.

Mehta, B. 2004. *Diasporic (dis)locations: Indo-Caribbean women writers negotiate the* kala pani. Kingston: University of the West Indies Press.

Mohammed, P. 1991. Towards a Caribbean feminist philosophy. *CAFRA News: Newsletter of the Caribbean Association for Feminist Research and Action* 5 (2–3) (March–August): 19–21.

———. 1994. Nuancing the feminist discourse in the Caribbean. *Social and Economic Studies* 43 (3): 135–67.

———. 1995. Writing gender into history: The negotiation of gender relations among Indian men and women in post-indenture Trinidad society, 1917–47. In *Engendering history: Women in historical perspective*, ed. B. Brereton, V. Shepherd and B. Bailey, 20–47. Kingston: Ian Randle.

———. 2001/2002. *Gender negotiations among Indians in Trinidad, 1917–1947.* Basingstoke, UK: Palgrave.

———. 2003a. Like sugar in coffee: Third wave feminism and the Caribbean. *Social and Economic Studies* 52 (3): 5–30.

———. 2003b. A symbiotic visiting relationship: Caribbean feminist historiography and Caribbean feminist theory. In *Confronting power, theorizing gender: Interdisciplinary perspectives in the Caribbean*, ed. E. Barriteau, 101–25. Kingston: University of the West Indies Press.

Momsen, J.H. 1993. Introduction to *Women and change in the Caribbean*, ed. J.H. Momsen, 1–11. Kingston: Ian Randle.

Nicholson, L. 1999. Feminism and Marx: Integrating kinship with the economic. In *The play of reason: From the modern to the postmodern.* Buckingham: Open University Press.

Nourbese Philip, M. 1990. Managing the unmanageable. In *Caribbean women writers: Essays from the first international conference*, ed. S.R. Cudjoe, 295–300. Wellesley, MA: Calaloux.

Oyewumi, O. 1997. *The invention of women: Making an African sense of Western gender discourses.* Minneapolis: University of Minnesota Press.

Paravisini-Gebert, Lizabeth. 1997. Decolonizing feminism: The home-grown roots of Caribbean women's movements. In *Daughters of Caliban: Caribbean women in the twentieth century*, ed. C. Lopez-Springfield, 3–17. Bloomington: Indiana University Press.

Providence, D. 2005. Caribbean feminism in transition: An interview with Professor V.E. Barriteau. *Journal of Eastern Caribbean Studies* 30 (4): 62–78.

Reddock, R.E. 1994. *Women, labour and politics in Trinidad and Tobago: A history.* London: Zed Books.

———. 2009. Feminist research and theory: Contributions from the anglophone Caribbean. In *Global gender research: Transnational perspectives*, ed. C. Bose and M. Kim, 215–26. New York: Routledge.

Robinson, T. 2007. A loving freedom: A Caribbean feminist ethic. *Small Axe: A Caribbean Journal of Criticism* 24 (October): 118–29.

Rowley, M. 2002. Reconceptualising voice: The role of matrifocality in shaping theories of Caribbean voices. In *Gendered realities: Essays in Caribbean feminist thought*, ed. P. Mohammed, 22–43. Kingston: University of the West Indies Press.

———. 2003. A feminist's oxymoron: Globally gender conscious development. In *Confronting power, theorizing gender: Interdisciplinary perspectives from the Caribbean*, ed. E. Barriteau, 75–97. Kingston: University of the West Indies Press.

———. 2010. Whose time is it? Gender and humanism in contemporary feminist advocacy. *Small Axe: A Caribbean Journal of Criticism* 14 (1): 1–15.

Scott, D. 2000. The re-enactment of humanism: Interview with Sylvia Wynter. *Small Axe: A Caribbean Journal of Criticism*, no. 8 (September): 119–207.

Shepherd, V., B. Brereton and B. Bailey, eds. 1995. *Engendering history: Caribbean women in historical perspective*. Kingston: Ian Randle.

Smith, F. 1994. Coming home to the real thing: Gender and intellectual life in the anglophone Caribbean. *South Atlantic Quarterly* 93 (4): 895–923.

Soares, J. 2006. Addressing the tensions: Reflections on feminism in the Caribbean. *Caribbean Quarterly* 52 (June–September): 187–97.

Thomas, G. 2009. Yours in the intellectual struggle. In *The Caribbean woman writer as scholar: Creating, imagining, theorizing*, ed. K.N. Abraham, 31–69. Coconut Creek, FL: Caribbean Studies Press.

Toland-Dix, S. 2008. The hills of Hebron: Sylvia Wynter's disruption of the narrative of the nation. *Small Axe* 25 (February): 57–76.

Vassell, L. 2003. Women, power and decision-making in CARICOM countries: Moving forward from a post-Beijing assessment. In *Gender equality in the Caribbean: Reality or illusion?*, ed. G. Tang Nain and B. Bailey, 1–38. Kingston: Ian Randle.

Wynter, S. 1990. Afterword. Beyond Miranda's meanings: Un/silencing the "demonic ground" of Caliban's "woman". In *Out of the kumbla: Caribbean women and literature*, ed. C. Boyce-Davies and E. Savory Fido, 355–72. Trenton, NJ: Africa World Press.

———. 1995. The pope must have been drunk, the king of Castile a madman: Culture as actuality, and the Caribbean rethinking modernity. In *The reordering of culture: Latin America, the Caribbean and Canada in the hood*, ed. A. Ruprecht and C. Taiana, 17–41. Ottawa, ON: Carleton University Press.

———. 2003. Unsettling the coloniality of being/power/truth/freedom: Towards the human, after man, its overrepresentation – An argument. *New Centennial Review* 3 (Fall): 257–337.

———. 2006. On how we mistook the map for the territory, and re-imprisoned ourselves in our unbearable wrongness of being, of Désêtre: Black studies toward the human project. In *Not only the master's tools: African-American studies in theory and practice*, ed. L.R. Gordon and J.A. Gordon, 107–69. Boulder: Paradigm.

Young-Bruehl, E. 1989. The education of women as philosophers. In *Feminist theory in practice and process*, ed. J. O'Barr, M. Malson, S. Westphal-Wihl and M. Wyer, 35–49. Chicago: University of Chicago Press.

4

Coming Home to the Erotic Power of Love and Desire in Caribbean Heterosexual Unions

V. EUDINE BARRITEAU

The core of my theory is that women and men as socio-sexual beings constitute the main parties of a particular exploitative relationship, a relationship in which men tend to exploit women's capacities for love and transform these into individual and collective models of power over which women lose control.

— Anna Jónasdóttir, "Feminist Questions, Marx's Method, and the Theorisation of 'Love Power'"

What's love got to do? Got to do with it?
What's love but a second hand emotion?
What's love got to do with it?
What's love but a sweet, old-fashioned notion?
What's love got to do with it?
Who needs a heart when a heart can be broken?
— Tina Turner, "What's Love Got to Do with It?"

By analyzing the institution of heterosexuality, feminists learned what is oppressive about it and why people cooperate with it or don't. But we didn't learn what is sexual. We don't really know for instance why men and women are still attracted to each other, even through all that oppression. There is something genuine that happens between heterosexuals, but gets perverted in a thousand different ways. There is heterosexuality outside of heterosexism.

– Amber Hollibaugh and Cherrie Moraga, "What We Are Rolling Around in Bed with: Sexual Silences in Feminism"

Introduction

Coming – To a New Epistemological Base[1]

Suspended between Anna Jónasdóttir's prescient theorization of women and men needing, seeking and practising love, and the equally powerful insight by Hollibaugh and Moraga that heterosexuality exists outside of heterosexism,[2] is Tina Turner's advice to regard love as a second-hand, overrated emotion. Where is that heterosexual, socio-sexual union in Caribbean feminist scholarship? What have we done about Hollibaugh and Moraga's suggestion that feminists "don't really know for instance why men and women are still attracted to each other, even through all that oppression" (Hollibaugh and Moraga 1983, 395)? Has Caribbean feminist analysis dismissed, downplayed or ignored heterosexual attraction as having any significance in yielding knowledge about relations of domination in women's public and private lives? What is love power and the power of the erotic?[3] What happens to women and men, but especially to women, when driven by the energies and desires which these concepts seek to analyse and explain?

I tackle these questions and apply Anna Jónasdóttir's construction of "love power" as an entry point for generating a theory of women's sexualized power in the contemporary Commonwealth Caribbean.[4] To the openings created by her theorizing, I map the powerful epistemological oeuvres offered by black feminist and lesbian theorist Audre Lorde. Even though most of my analysis focuses on Jónasdóttir's work, I maintain that it is Lorde's epistemic openings that illuminate what is simultaneously problematic and possible in apprehending the phenomenon of women's love power.

In generating my theory, I engage in a triple play on the meanings of the word "coming" and anchor these meanings to black feminist theorizing of the concept of "home" (Barriteau 2007a, 21–22; Carby 1982/1997, 47; Smith 1983, 64–72). At the first level, "coming" evokes the sense of a prodigal daughter returning to an unexplored epistemological base, a base which, I am positing, houses an explanatory framework for examining women's contradictory and, often, power-deprived experiences in our societies. Coming home to a new epistemological base on women's sexuality and power resonates with the politics of knowledge production. In as much as I view Jónasdóttir's work as extremely useful in creating new insights about women's intimate relations in Caribbean societies, I come home to Lorde's work on the erotic as pointing the way towards grasping the meaning and magnitude of love power and the operations of the erotic in women's lives (Lorde 1984).

In much of my work, I have been exploring what is wrong and goes wrong for women at different sites within the Caribbean political economy. However, I have never examined why unequal conditions continue to exist and/or persist for women from the vantage point of what Jónasdóttir has theorized as political sexuality (Jónasdóttir 1994, 227; 2009), and the socio-sexual relationship, as governed by Jónasdóttir's concept of "love power" (Jónasdóttir 1994, 223). The growing body of feminist work in the anglophone Caribbean has not done so either. Although there have been a number of studies of sexualities, none have sought to link the widespread and persistent practice of patriarchal relations of domination with an exploration of the dynamics within the basic socio-sexual union.

Elsewhere I have examined the intersections of gender and power, or gender, power and public policy (Barriteau 1992; 1994; 1995; 1996; 1998a; 1998b; 2001; 2003b; 2004). Even though I noted, in 1995, that women's approaches to their sexuality and sexual choices were largely ignored subjects in general, and in Caribbean feminist sociological analyses (Barriteau 1995, 26) in particular, I have not explored gender and sexuality, nor the power and politics of sexuality, until now. Jónasdóttir's theory of love power, especially the questions which she poses, underscores that there are both unitary/individual and societal dimensions to the things that often go consistently wrong for women.

In my current theorizing I am specifically interested in the complications that romantic loving may pose for women in sexual relationships with men. I am beginning to explore the intersections of desire and power or the relations of power embedded in desire. As Jane Flax surmises, "Desire really has a kind of energy or force of its own, and more than that, since it is within us, it operates and undermines various other processes which like to look at themselves as separate from desire" (Grant and Rubens 1997, 5).

Do Caribbean women understand the power of the erotic in their lives or even the erotic as a source of power? Audre Lorde's pioneering work on the power of the erotic is a critical, contributing strand of feminist theorizing on which I draw. Lorde declares: "When I speak of the erotic then I speak of it as an assertion of the life force of women, of that creative energy, empowered, the knowledge and use of which we are now reclaiming in our language, our history, our dancing, our loving, our work, our lives" (Lorde 1984, 55). Lorde's theorizing suggests that if women can come to appreciate the erotic as a source of power within themselves, they can come to intimate relationships, and enter the social world with a wholesome understanding of themselves as social-sexual beings. Lorde's theorizing of the erotic is much more comprehensive and encompasses more than a notion of sexual relations, however. In Lorde's analysis, the erotic includes a passion to live fully, to experience feeling (ibid.). She speaks of work having an erotic value of which women can be robbed: "The erotic – sensual – those physical, emotional and psychic expressions of what is deepest and strongest and richest within each of us, being shared. The passion of love, in its deepest meanings" (56). According to Lorde, when women accept the erotic within themselves, they negate powerlessness (58).

In spite of their pursuit of sexual relations with men, have heterosexual women (or, for that matter, homosexual women) embraced the power of the erotic in their lives? Or have they instead distanced themselves from this "life force", and contributed in this way to their own powerlessness? I am particularly interested in ongoing attempts to subordinate women, even as women continue to pursue erotic and sexual pleasure. I want to track how these complications become extrapolated into wider systemic inequalities, even as these inequalities are simultaneously reflected back onto individual relationships and their representations of gendered hierarchies of power and inequalities.

I view women and men as coming to sexual unions along a fluid and changeable continuum of sexual desires, sexual relations and sexual identities. At the two conventional extremes are heterosexuality and homosexuality. Many individuals experience their sexual relations and desires through bisexual, homosexual, heterosexual, polysexual and transgender relations.[5] Some people harbour sexual desires that remain unfulfilled for a range of reasons. In this analysis I am specifically interested in unwrapping the mystique of love power and the power of the erotic in the socio-sexual unions women have with men.

I prioritize women's intimate relations with men (that is, heterosexual sexual unions) for several reasons:

- In the Caribbean it is an unexplored dimension in the search to explain women's experience of dis-empowerment in these relations and the wider political economy.
- The contours of our dominant social, economic, cultural and political institutions are shaped by heteronormativity, yet we have not theorized this union at the centre of a normalized notion of heterosexual society. Neither have we examined how this "normalized" heterosexuality feeds homophobia and its flip side, heterosexism.
- The existence of differing forms of sexual unions does not change the heteronormativity and heterosexism of a society. I maintain that interrogating the socio-heterosexual union can provide insights into combatting heterosexism and homophobia.[6]

Coming – To a New Understanding

I agree with Jónasdóttir that there are no mono-causal explanations for what goes wrong for women (Jónasdóttir 2009, 61). I therefore believe it is necessary to integrate this unfolding investigation of political sexuality with ongoing work on Caribbean political economy while maintaining an explicit focus on women.[7] This approach points to a new understanding of the centrality of political sexuality within political economy – hence my focus on George Lamming's address on Caribbean Women Traders, whom he terms "the Miracle Managers". Lamming states:

> We can say that all women irrespective of their social origins are an example, perhaps the most extreme example, of a dominated class. Social theorists of the Left have difficulty with that formulation. But historical and personal evidence is abundant that all men, irrespective of their economic or racial status, hold a common belief about the subordinate role of women in their lives. The Black male labourer and the White male executive director share a profound bond of allegiance and solidarity on that question of the relation of woman to man, whether that union is marital, extra-marital, or ultra-marital. (Lamming 1995, 37–38)

Lamming's identification of the union as marital, extra-marital or ultra-marital in respect of the sexual relations between women and men is significant because of the central role marriage holds in Jónasdóttir's theorizing and the multiple forms of man–woman unions in the Caribbean. Because marriage still functions as a disciplinary norm for women, it is crucial to recognize how the many variants of sexual unions influence the power dynamics within those unions. This is necessary, not from a narrow perspective of insisting on cultural specificity, but because of the material and ideological implications of these socio-sexual unions, which span a range of spatial, material and emotional arrangements.

I foreground this analysis in the centrality of sexuality and sexual relations as women navigate the intersections of the public and the private, production and reproduction, caring and desiring, pursuing sexual pleasure, and (often) receiving and giving emotional pain.[8] My challenge is to work backwards and forwards from the power dynamics of that basic union (played out in private, intimate spaces such as the home, as well as in sexual relations) to contemporary manifestations of power negotiations and imbalances in the Caribbean political economy.

Coming – To Sexuality, Pleasure, Desire and Power

In everyday Caribbean culture,[9] the word "coming" has an excitement and anticipation that I hope to capture and convey in creating new theoretical insights about power and pleasure in women's lives. While "coming" is used to refer to the eve of the orgasmic climax in sexual intercourse, in my analysis I want to capture the exhilaration, tension and anticipation of "coming" in another layer of the complexities of asymmetric gender relations in the Caribbean.

I am intrigued by Lorde's and Jónasdóttir's theorization of "love power" and the power of the erotic, and the way these elements may work in women's lives. In discerning love and erotic power in women's lives, these are some of the questions my theorizing seeks to answer:

- Do dynamics within women's socio-sexual unions influence their public lives? Or, posed differently, are the ways in which women interact or experience economic or other social relations an outcome of what happens in their private, intimate spaces?

- If we accept the premise that there is a connection between public action and private experience, does Jónasdóttir's thesis that women's love power can be extracted account for women's experiences of ongoing asymmetric relations of gender in their public and private lives?
- Does this type of explanation shift blame onto women for systemic conditions of inequality?
- In what particular ways does love power or the power of the erotic manifest itself in women's sexual relations with men?
- Should women have power in intimate relations with men?
- Do women have power in love relationships with men?
- Do women enter socio-sexual unions, as Jónasdóttir has stated (1994, 224), as owners of their capacity to love, able to give of their own free will, yet without effective control over how or in what forms they can legitimately use that capacity?
- Building on Flax's observations, where does desire enter and to what extent does its energy undermine or expand women's capacity to negotiate in love relationships?
- Is the situation more like an observation made to me by a close friend who has been married three times, and has had numerous lovers, that in his experience women enter relationships with power and confidence, but give up their power within six months, thinking this is what men want?
- Is women's love power extracted, as Jónasdóttir maintains? Or do women willingly surrender or compromise more readily in their intimate relationships?
- Assuming that men do "extract" women's love power, what is the process and outcome of that extraction?
- Do women experience, understand or accept the power of the erotic as theorized by Lorde?

Unlike Jónasdóttir, I am not interested in the development of historical materialism generally, or in proving the relevance of Marx's method to feminist theorizing, or even in filling "the potential gap" in the historical materialist tradition (Jónasdóttir 2009). Jónasdóttir states that "her point is to show that a feminist use of Marx's method can both reactivate certain underdeveloped, constitutive elements of Marx's approach to the study of society and history, and also bring forward others, which are in some sense new" (ibid., 59).

Mining Jónasdóttir's work enables new theoretical offerings, not through reactivating Marx's method but because her theorizing facilitates the creation of new understandings about sexualized power in women's lives.

Through examining "love power" and "the power of the erotic", I am seeking explanations of, or at least insights into, the continuing but changing manifestations of male dominance in Caribbean societies. This kind of analysis is especially relevant because a range of material and empirical indicators seem to suggest that women are not being exploited, and academic and popular commentators have long concluded that women have taken over and have surpassed men in every arena of public life (Miller 1994 and 1991; de Albuquerque and Ruark 1998; Barriteau 1998a and 2003d). Jónasdóttir's theory provides the foundation for a powerful and compelling feminist explanatory framework that links two new dimensions of analysis: a micro-level, women and men as socio-sexual beings, with a macro-dimension, political sexuality.

As a later project, I intend to use Jónasdóttir's and Lorde's theories and their sets of assumptions to assist me in refining a model I constructed in 1998 about gender systems in Caribbean societies (Barriteau 1998b). When, in designing that model, I examined late-twentieth-century Caribbean societies, I concluded that while women had made significant gains in material relations of gender, ideological relations of gender continued to construct women as inferior and subordinate, and to rank their gender identities and roles as subordinate to those of men (Barriteau 1998b and 2001). My level of analysis remained at the macro-level and I paid no attention to sexuality or women and men as socio-sexual beings. Jónasdóttir's and Lorde's theories of "love power" and "the power of the erotic" link the material and the ideological as well as move between the micro (socio-sexual beings in relation) and the macro – political sexuality and political economy, respectively. Lorde, in particular, introduces a psychological and ontological dimension to assessing the ideologies of intimacy.

Jónasdóttir's redefinition of sexuality away from being perceived only as an identity category to being understood "as a set of relations, activities, needs and desires, productive/reproductive powers and capacities, identities, values, institutions, and organizational and structural contexts" (Jónasdóttir 2007, 19), offers great possibilities for producing new knowledge about the centrality of sexual relations in women's and men's lives. This definition shifts the terrain of studies of sexuality to "a broad and complex dimension of historically changing socio-cultural and human-material reality" (ibid.). This redefinition provides a broad conceptual framework for investigating the power and politics inherent in the discourse and experiences of sexuality in the twenty-first-century Caribbean.

In focusing on the point at which politicized sexuality and political economy converge – that is, the point at which state policies, societal norms and views interact with privatized and politicized sexual relations in women's lives – I employ Jónasdóttir's and Lorde's conceptual tools to generate feminist insights on sexuality in anglophone Caribbean societies. This emergent theorizing not only recognizes historically fluid and contested features of Caribbean women's sexuality, but also seeks to explore desire, sensuality, pleasure and power in formulating a woman-centred discourse on sexuality in the region. Specifically, I am attempting to extend Jónasdóttir's and Lorde's theorization of "love power" and the power of the erotic to women's realities.

Who Needs a Heart?

It is somewhat ironic that notions of love, sex and romance are everywhere embedded in the Caribbean imaginary, yet these same notions remain unexamined in the day-to-day lives of women in their sexual relations with men,[10] and in the implications of these relations for ongoing conditions of inequality in women's lives. It is not just in the marketing campaigns of tourist destinations that the Caribbean seems filled with desire, lust and the promise of more love, more sex and more romance. In a plethora of popular expressions, musical forms and folk tales, love and sex are critical to, and fully articulated in, the rhythms of everyday life. Evidence abounds in social commentaries sung by calypsonians, in dance hall lyrical chants by reggae and dub artists, in folk songs about love affairs gone awry, in letters to the press seeking advice on relationships, in popular concoctions for building sexual stamina, in "putting it back in the back", and in obeah remedies for recapturing straying lovers or claiming new ones.[11] These examples all underscore the foundational location of "making love" as opposed to just "making tools" (Jónasdóttir 1994), in arriving at new insights about both "political sexuality" (ibid.) and political economy in Caribbean societies.

Feminist research in the region has explored almost every dimension of women's lives, yet we have not turned the lens "on women and men – needing, seeking and practising love" (Jónasdóttir 1994, 63). Increasingly, sex and romance tourism is being used to market Caribbean destinations.[12] The majority of Caribbean countries, including Cuba, are now heavily dependent on tourism as the major earner of foreign exchange and an extremely valuable, even if vulnerable, economic activity (McDavid and Ramajeesingh 2003). Given the region's heavy reliance on tourism, sex tourism has become an important but unofficially acknowledged product (or prop) of that sector.

There is a substantive and growing body of literature on sex tourism in the anglophone, francophone and Hispanic Caribbean (Chanel 1994; de Albuquerque 1998; Kempadoo 1999, 2001, 2003; Cabezas 1999, 2004; Sanchez-Taylor 2001; Sharpe and Pinto 2006). Differing feminist and other ideological prisms and perspectives have also examined homosexual and heterosexual sex tourism and/or trade between gay tourists and Caribbean women and men, and to Caribbean destinations (Alexander 2005 and 1997; Kempadoo 2003; Puar 2001). There is research on Caribbean women working as prostitutes/sex workers, and, increasingly, UN bodies in collaboration with US agencies have been examining trafficking in women and girls for sex work in the region (Thomas Hope 2007). There is exciting, newer work which explores many dimensions of sexual and reproductive health and rights (DAWN 2006), as well as "risk, sexuality, rights, power, culture, and vulnerability in the context of HIV in the Caribbean" (Barrow, de Bruin and Carr 2009, xvii).

Yet there are almost no feminist investigations of love, sexuality and sexual relations with men, or the complications these relationships pose for women in their everyday lives.[13] Even more intriguing, there have been no attempts to interrogate these relationships as possible contributing factors to the unequal relations of domination that women experience in wider society as well as in intimate spaces. Jónasdóttir's theorization of "love power" and its attendant assumptions provide a compelling frame of analysis for investigating Caribbean women's socio-sexual relationships and their impact or influence on ongoing unequal relations of gender.

It's Only the Thrill of Boy Meeting Girl: Opposites Attract

In theorizing about love power, Jónasdóttir presents a theory as to why or how men's positions of power with respect to women persist even in contemporary Western societies (2009, 60). She builds her process of inquiry around a series of questions, and moves from this groundwork to her primary analytical tool: love power. She developed her theory of love power after making her assumption "that a crucial part of the theoretical analysis of women's exploitation must be done within the field of sexuality, and not limited to economy or work, and also that the analysis has to be extended 'beyond oppression'" (ibid., 61). Jónasdóttir refines her discussion of the basic assumptions of this concept further. She emphasizes that the appropriative practice of exploiting women's love power produces and reproduces contemporary patriarchal relations or male-dominated society. She also states that she has never intended this analytical framework to serve as a mono-causal explanation for women's exploitation or experiences of relations of domination (ibid.). I present the contours of Jónasdóttir's theory in Table 4.1.

Table 4.1. Building Blocks of Jónasdóttir's Theory

A priori conditions	Feminist questions; why or how men's power vis-à-vis women is reproduced and augmented
Core of theory	Women and men as socio-sexual beings constitute the main parties of a particular exploitative relationship in which men tend to exploit women's capacity for love and transform these capacities into individual and collective modes of power over women who lose control
Foundation of socio-sexual existence	Production and reproduction of life and living people
Vantage point of analysis	Political sexuality
Link between the private and the public	Significance and status of marriage, men's "right" to appropriate women's sexual resources
Basis of exploitation	Love as a practical, human, sensuous activity; the organization of love

Source: Jónasdóttir 2009, 58–65.

The fact that Jónasdóttir has politicized sexuality by problematizing it and treating it as systemic to the basic marital (read: sexual) union, provides a crucial entry point for examining the interconnections between what happens between men and women in sexual relations and what happens between women and men in the economy and state. Her emphasis that this union has a wider meaning that pertains to people other than those who are legally married or cohabiting is especially relevant in Caribbean societies, where the majority of sexual unions and relationships exist outside of legal marriages and even cohabitation. I agree with Jónasdóttir's statement that "social interactions between women and men in direct person to person relations are consistently overlooked" (1994, 213).

Jónasdóttir insists on exposing and centralizing the power dynamics of a politicized sexuality. She offers epistemological and methodological signposts that deal with the complications of socio-sexual relations and move beyond the public/private divide which haunted and limited much of earlier feminist theorizing. This impasse has often made the prescriptions of the early feminist scholars irrelevant in Caribbean societies. By advising that we approach the study of political sexuality through existing empirical data about the impact of increased needs and new social relations within the family and economy, Jónasdóttir expands the range of epistemological and methodological tools that can be used or created for understanding what goes wrong in women's lives. "The aim", she writes, "is to understand the significance of sexuality and love in social life today" (Jónasdóttir 2007, 20).

We Don't Really Know Why Men and Women Are Still Attracted to Each Other . . .

Jónasdóttir's other major theoretical breakthrough is the articulation of the concept of love power. She positions a transformative, creative power at the centre of the love relationship which echoes the power of the erotic as articulated since the 1970s by Audre Lorde. Jónasdóttir poses the question of what is being done to us as women in free and equal, yet still patriarchal, Western society, and points out that "men exploit a certain power resource in women, namely the power of love" (1994, 214). Continuing, she states that this kind of exploitation is at the centre of the contemporary, Western sex-struggle (ibid.). In searching for "a term that could denote precisely this 'practical, human sensuous activity', a term that could distinguish it both from the power of labor or work", she notes that she "came to believe that love is the best term available if care and erotic ecstasy are incorporated as its two main elements" (221). Here she does two things: she differentiates the power of love, a practical, human sensuous activity, from the power of labour, and she identifies the two main components of love – care and erotic ecstasy. I am particularly drawn to Jónasdóttir's conceptualization of love power as care and erotic ecstasy, and to applying this framework to the analysis of Caribbean women's heterosexual unions.

As separate categories of analysis, some aspects of the two dimensions of Jónasdóttir's concept of love power have been covered extensively in investigations of Caribbean women's lives, but they have never been disaggregated or recombined to create any type of explanation of power imbalances in women's lives. Perhaps because of the influence (or bias) of the Women in Development discourse, and its early impact on feminist scholarship in regions such as the Caribbean, a great deal of intellectual energy has been expended on women's work and women's work as caring work,[14] whether within families and households or the state and the economy.[15] There is an extensive literature on the work that Caribbean women do (Gill and Massiah 1984; Massiah 1986b; Massiah 1991; Scott 1992; Denis 2003; Elliot 2006), not only in households and in pursuing strategies for survival (Barrow 1986; French 1994; Bolles 1983), but also in informal and formal economic activities (Seguino 2003; Bolles 1983; Jayasinghe 2001; Barriteau 2002; Lagro and Plotkin 1990; Freeman 2000, 1998, 1997).

Although it has come later than research on women's work, the type of research in the Caribbean that comes closest to approximating an investigation into the realm of the erotic (the other component of love power) is investigation into sex work. I maintain that this kind of work is another dimension of women's care work, fulfilling the sexual needs of others.[16] A gap remains. We need research that treats the sexual relationship as constitutive in what women experience as relationships of domination or oppression. It is my thesis that women's pursuit of what they define as erotic ecstasy is what propels and maintains heterosexual women in intimate relations with men, and what becomes, for many women, the eventual source of their powerlessness.

This condition directly contradicts the sense of the erotic as developed by Lorde. In Lorde's theorizing, pursuit of, or rather the embrace of, the erotic within ourselves is a source of empowerment; it is an internal life force. I argue that many women conceptualize and grasp the erotic as an external condition gained within intimate relations not as an organic source of energy embedded within their own psyches. I also posit that, in their pursuit of the conventional understanding of the erotic, women end up with the care and continue with the caring. Many either continue hoping that the erotic will materialize, or eventually replace their desires to be cared for and fulfil other dimensions of their sexual pleasure with caring for others. Jónasdóttir's theorization of love power and its twin components of care and ecstasy are compelling. In one sense, I hypothesize that women pursue erotic ecstasy and end up with the care work.[17] Women are generally responsible for, or accept that they are responsible for taking care of relationships, men,[18] children and elders of the family, and the organizations in which they are members,[19] in addition to providing most of the care work in the economy (Folbre 2003).[20] Women expend a lot of "emotional labour" in providing care (Hochschild 2002, 194). In another sense, in the pursuit of erotic ecstasy, there is that man–woman dynamic which Jónasdóttir calls "women and men – needing, seeking and practicing love" (1994, 63). Accordingly, women may experience satisfying heterosexual encounters, and we may have deeply fulfilling sexual relations characterized by multiple orgasms, but often what many women want is a desire to be cared for by men beyond sexual encounters.[21]

In terms of Lorde's theorizing, the erotic is a condition of being rather than a state of relating. Most women do not grasp this distinction. Lorde's work shows the erotic to be first existential and ontological rather than relational. Often women look to men to supply them with erotic power when, according to Lorde, women already have that power within them and need only embrace it. Jónasdóttir's work does suggest that women can possess this power of the erotic as Lorde theorizes it, but she also states that men exploit and "extract" women's power. Elsewhere I have hypothesized that women's powerlessness in love exists at the point at which their love power becomes "extracted" – a concept that falls within the erotic dimension of Jónasdóttir's love power (Barriteau 2011). Jónasdóttir perceives that most women interpret the erotic as an outcome of their socio-sexual unions. Lorde states that the power of the erotic is an internal condition that is expressed or repressed in socio-sexual and other unions. According to Lorde's theorizing, women's love power cannot be "extracted"; however, she suggests, women can ignore or surrender it.

Because of the foregoing arguments, I disagree with Valerie Bryson when she states she is "inclined to prioritise the caring rather than the erotic element of love power as a central political issue, along with more general reproductive rights" (2008, 34), even as I agree with her statement that old forms of oppression and exclusion remain in place for many women. It is precisely because these forms persist that we should shift the frames of analysis, as Jónasdóttir's and Lorde's theories suggest. I want to prioritize the erotic, the erotic ecstasy of love power.[22] When I think of Jónasdóttir's two components of love power, I think of the dimension in which (according to her theories) women experience powerlessness in their sexual relations with men. Lorde and Jónasdóttir differ as to how that powerlessness arises, however. As challenging as it is to unravel, I think we have to explore what happens to women and between women and men in the realm of erotic ecstasy. Unlike Bryson (2008, 29), I agree with Jónasdóttir that making love is as foundational and necessary as making tools, and that a lot of what women do as socio-sexual beings in their intimate relations is making love. Lorde states that the erotic is sensual, that it is the passion of love in deepest meanings: "the erotic is the nurturer or nursemaid of all our deepest knowledge" (1984, 56). When I use the term "making love", I mean that women engage in a range of activities that are inclusive of, but beyond, sexual intercourse, and that in those activities they are pursuing the erotic dimension of love power. I maintain, however, that, in the process, many are often forced into conditions of powerlessness or make accommodations. They either surrender their love power or have it extracted from them. Following Lorde, women would be surrendering their love power since it is an internal condition of being. She suggests that when women accept the erotic within themselves they negate powerlessness (Lorde 1984, 56).

There Is Something Genuine Between Heterosexuals

Four of Jónasdóttir's core assumptions stand out in applying her model to women's sexual relations: understanding and conceptualizing power as part of sexuality; marriage/socio-sexual unions as linking the domains of the private and the public; women's love as a practical, human, sensuous activity; and the organization (and expression) of that love as the basis of women's "exploitation". Lorde's work would certainly support Jónasdóttir's first three assumptions. She identifies sexuality as powerful, and power as intrinsic to sexuality. Lorde would also agree not only that sexual unions link the private and the public, but also that issues of sexuality affect every dimension of women's lives (Lorde 1984). An aspect of my larger project is to determine whether Lorde would conclude that the organization and expression of women's love is the basis of their exploitation.

I have noted in earlier publications that gendered relations are characterized "as the ways in which *social realities* between women and men are socially constructed to perpetuate male dominance" (Barriteau 1992, 15; Barriteau 2003c, 4). Drawing on Jónasdóttir's and Lorde's theories, I shall now re-examine this statement to determine how or whether *sexual realities* between women and men are socially constructed to perpetuate male dominance.

In reviewing the Caribbean evidence, it becomes clear that Jónasdóttir's sense that women's experiences of relations of domination arise from something other than the conditions and terms on which labour is organized and exploited is valid. What her analysis suggests is that, by the time we recognize that women are being exploited in their work, there are a set of a priori conditions in which unequal relations are already a factor. More women than men are enrolled in tertiary educational institutions and graduate in larger ratios,[23] are relatively highly skilled, and possess fair to high levels of social capital (Bailey 2003; Elliot 2006). Simultaneously, women experience higher levels of unemployment, and are the first to be retrenched or the last to receive training when factories begin to need more highly skilled workers. Daphne Jayasinghe's research (2003) demonstrates that, as manufacturing becomes more technologically driven, an inverse relationship quickly develops between technological expertise and women's training, with women becoming increasingly de-skilled. Caribbean women receive lower wages than men for comparable levels of work, except in the state or governmental sector, and more women than men head households in households below the poverty line (Seguino 2003; Jayasinghe 2001; Andaiye 2003). In 2008, the Economic Commission for Latin America and the Caribbean expressed concern that the current economic crisis would increase unemployment among women in Latin America and the Caribbean in productive sectors such as commerce, the manufacturing industry, financial services, tourism and domestic help services (*Barbados Advocate*, 15 Dec 2008).

In the political sphere, political parties and electoral contests have met all conditions of formal equality of access since the 1950s, but in the area of political leadership and the occupation of cabinet positions and senior governmental appointments, the ratio of women to men is still uneven and in no way parallels men's dominance of political positions and power (Vassell 2003). As Joan French has concluded, "women's political participation in the Caribbean is still generally well below parity and even the 30% target" (2008, 33).

Since the early 1970s, Caribbean governments have established state machineries on women and/or gender in almost all government administrations. They have removed or modified several pieces of punitive legislation and introduced more egalitarian laws. These governmental bodies have produced numerous reports and recommendations on how to improve the conditions of women and have undertaken more or less consistent reporting to United Nations bodies on governments' attempts to work towards gender equality in Caribbean societies (Tang Nain and Bailey 2003). Yet relations of domination remain. Six in-depth regional studies of efforts to promote gender equality in the Commonwealth Caribbean concluded:

- Increases in the number of women in leadership positions do not necessarily lead to greater influence on policy.
- New issues, such as HIV/AIDS, have a greater impact on women than men, but the general public seems reluctant to support an agenda for the empowerment of women.
- Although women display higher levels of participation and performance in education at the secondary and tertiary levels, this participation does not translate into significant gains in their economic, political or personal empowerment.
- While some women have benefited from new opportunities opened by globalization, many others have experienced new or deepening inequalities in access to opportunities and resources.
- Despite the apparent contradictory situation of women and the concern with the so-called marginalization of men, the elimination of gender inequities is not yet a part of core values, policy developments, programme action or administrative systems.
- Although states have signed on to various international instruments, there is no regionally agreed-upon system for measuring progress towards the achievement of gender justice (Massiah 2003, xii–xiv).

Missing from all these studies is a focus on women as socio-sexual beings in their sexual relations with men, and how these relations interface with economic and political developments – in other words, how politicized sexuality affects political economy. These studies have investigated macro-level conditions in material relations of gender in Caribbean gender systems.

Women and Men Needing, Seeking and Practising Love[24]

Given that both Jónasdóttir and I view socio-sexual unions as a link between the private and the public, we need to examine these relations. Research seems to indicate that motherhood and, to a lesser extent, marriage are the primary sources of identity for Caribbean women (Powell 1986, 83; Anderson 1986; Mohammed and Perkins 1999, 121; Robinson 2003, 246). The Women in the Caribbean Project (WICP) also found that working-class women who were in long-term unions with men postponed decisions about marriage if the change in the legal status of their relationships would not entail a change in their material level of comfort (Anderson 1986; Senior 1991).

According to the WICP survey conducted in the late 1970s, for many women of the working class, marriage should mean an observable change in their standard of living. These findings need to be contextualized, however. Rates of marriages and/or legal unions have been historically low in the Caribbean and continue to be so. For example, data from a period similar to that of the WICP survey provides a historical snapshot. In Barbados, the illegitimacy ratio (the total number of births out of wedlock, calculated as a percentage of total live births) climbed steadily from 62.0 per cent in 1961 to 74.2 per cent in 1974,[25] meaning that, in 1974, nearly 75 per cent of all children were born to unmarried parents (Barriteau 1994, 151). The marriage ratio (as the number of marriages per 1,000 people, calculated as a percentage of total population) declined from 4.2 per cent to 3.8 per cent for the same period (ibid.).

Caribbean family structures come in multiple variations, running from the small nuclear family to extended families of several generations occupying one dwelling space, and encompassing what Rosina Wiltshire-Brodber (1986) has classified as the transnational family. The latter has key members located in several different countries and diasporic communities with several, especially female, members who are very mobile and living in what Carol Boyce-Davies terms a state of "in-betweenness" (Boyce-Davies 2007; Trotz 2008). The sexual relations Caribbean women have and their attendant complications are threaded through these family structures. Without further probing, it is difficult to determine whether Caribbean women truly do not desire formal marriages over motherhood,[26] or the ranking given by the WICP is a form of adaptation, an adjustment to the realities of the instability of marital and other forms of sexual unions within the fluid family arrangements that many women experience.

Marriage is still a dominant ideological force and regulatory norm in Caribbean women's lives. As Tracy Robinson observes, "Caribbean women generally begin their reproductive life without marriage, but that reality cannot deny the considerable force that marriage still has as an ideal for women. Being able to define one-self socially and legally by reference to a man through marriage provides a distinct form of legitimacy and acceptance for women in the eyes of the community that should not be underestimated" (2003, 248).

An interesting observation that I have made from frequent conversations with some undergraduate and postgraduate female students at the Cave Hill campus of the University of the West Indies is that the majority do state that they want to be mothers; however, none of them has expressed a willingness to enter motherhood outside of marriage, citing the need for a stable relationship first. Is that the exercise of power in sexual unions or the pursuit of a romanticized ideal?[27] Do these women assume that, once they are married, they will have no need to negotiate power arrangements in their intimate relations? The majority of women in Barbados who are single parents have been in committed relationships with the fathers of their children, and many are currently in relationships with men who may also have children with other women. Common Caribbean expressions are "the baby father" or "my child mother". The use of these kinds of expressions indicates the relationship status of the other parent – that there is usually no longer a viable emotional or sexual relation, and often very contentious interpersonal relations, between a child's parents.[28]

Anthropologists Connie Sutton and Susan Makiesky-Barrow have said of sexual relations in Barbados in the 1950s, 1960s and 1970s, that "both men and women regard sex as pleasurable, desirable, and necessary for health and general well-being, and they discuss, separately and together, how to improve sexual performance and pleasure. Stylized sexual banter between women and men occurs in public and private settings and is enjoyed by both sexes" (Sutton and Makiesky-Barrow 1981, 492). According to them, West Indian men's preoccupation with sexual activities is very pro-female, the opposite of machismo. They maintain that a man's reputation as a lover is not based on the conquest of the inaccessible woman but on his success in sexual performance, in knowing techniques that give a woman pleasure.[29]

Evidence suggests that many Caribbean men are relatively open about having multiple sexual partners, even though there are contrasting anthropological perspectives on this aspect of Caribbean life. About men in Trinidad, for example, Michael Lieber states that "wives and lovers [tend] to be mere 'chicks' – women to be exploited for their sexual availability, their services, and sometimes for their money . . . Men are unwilling to make sacrifices and to work out problems with women; it is too easy to walk away from problems and go searching for new women. Women know this and fortify themselves with a resiliency and resignation attuned to the unreliability of men" (1981, 108). Similarly, Barry Chevannes informs us that "in Jamaica multiple partnerships are a feature of male sexual behaviour" (Chevannes 1999, 5; Barriteau 2003d, 343). He also found, in a 1985 survey, that "only 50% of the males he interviewed acknowledged that they had more than one partner. However, many more indicated that they would have liked to have more, implying that the lack of finance was the limiting factor" (Chevannes 1999, 5–6; Barriteau 2003d, 343). In another survey Chevannes found that women also had multiple partners and that these partnerships were motivated by women's need for money and feelings of sexual independence (Chevannes 1999, 5–6; Barriteau 2003d, 343). Clearly there are situations within women's sexual unions that are in need of further exploration.

A Particularly Exploitative Relationship

Danielle Toppin's work with young women in Jamaica underscores the intersection of economic vulnerability and sexual relations, as well as working-class women's early start to reproduction in Jamaica. She presents information on the sexual relations of three teenage girls, one of whom is fourteen years old, five months pregnant and living with a man ten years older than herself (Toppin 2007a). Another is fifteen and also lives with an older man. She moved out of her mother's home to avoid sexual molestation by her stepfather.

The third is still at home, has a teenaged boyfriend, a good relationship with her mother, and has discussed with her mother her decision to be sexually active.

Toppin submits that these young women are grappling with the feelings and consequences of their early entry into sexual relationships. She reports that the pregnant young woman attends an organization that allows teenaged mothers to complete their education and to receive developmental counselling, with one of the core areas of concern being delaying unwanted pregnancies. Even so, the young woman states that she doubts she would use condoms with her partner. She states that he will not use them, and she will not push him to, because he might think she has another man, even though she suspects he is sexually active with other people (Toppin 2007a).

Toppin also notes that, according to a report by the Statistical Institute of Jamaica, one in every ten Jamaican women is married or in a common-law union before her eighteenth birthday, with approximately one per cent doing so before the age of fifteen (Toppin 2008). Toppin continues: "Although ideas regarding men's right to ownership over 'their' women in intimate relationships can be found across communities, the practice of cohabitation between under-aged females and older men is predominantly found in communities marked by poverty. In many instances, young girls become bargaining tools for economic improvement, placing them in relationships in which the power imbalances affect them negatively" (ibid., 1).

Two of the young women in Toppin's analysis are living with older men because of issues of economic deprivation, and for one the additional grief of sexual harassment at her mother's home.[30] The information on cohabitation between older men and girls in poor communities underscores the troubling dynamics of developments in political economy that affect women's sexual lives. Here girls' opportunities are being shaped in a context that breeds powerlessness, despair, and a lack of sexual and social autonomy.

It Scares Me to Feel that Way

Another way to examine the intersection of politicized sexuality and political economy is to link the economic violence done to women and men in the workplace with the sexualized violence which occurs in privatized spaces such as the home and in intimate relations. There is ample evidence that when men

suffer economic hardship, job loss or reduced income, the incidence of violence against women rises. What has not been adequately tracked is how
women's experience of that same form of economic violence in their working
lives increases their vulnerability in their relationships in the absence of any
state-sponsored protective mechanisms. Economic hardship reduces women's
economic autonomy and leaves them more susceptible to abuses in their sexual
unions because of their dependence (real or perceived) on men for financial
support (Pargass and Clarke 2003, 43).

In a 2003 study, Gaitery Pargass and Roberta Clarke reviewed studies on
violence against women in the Caribbean and examined some of the beliefs
about what causes this kind of violence, as well as established some continuities
between domestic violence and sexualized violence (Pargass and Clarke 2003,
39–72; Barriteau 2003a, 213). They found that a key factor in a study of violence in Suriname was that, when many women made their first report about
domestic violence, their partners had been violent for many years before
(Pargass and Clarke 2003, 43).[31]

Continuing the link between sexualized violence and political economy,
Toppin holds the media accountable for the prevalence of sexual violence in
Caribbean society. She cites a case in which a popular reggae artist was jailed
for the rape of a young girl, and many artists, radio personalities and popular
local figures came out in support of him, ignoring the plight of the young victim and elevating the convicted rapist to the false status of "a wrongfully
imprisoned political prisoner" (Toppin 2007b). Toppin concludes: "Sexual
violence is a weapon. Our sexuality becomes a tool to be used against us. How
can we even begin to talk about sexual and reproductive health in a culture in
which sexually violent art is acceptable?" (ibid.).

Taking on a New Direction

Lorde and Jónasdóttir's theories begin from vastly different positions, yet they
seem to make a similar journey to the common destination of wanting to
improve the lives of women. It is this common thread with which I seek to
work in my commitment to theorize how desire, passion and the power of
the erotic operate in the lives of women. Kathleen Jones advises that "the test
of Jónasdóttir's theory should not be the degree of generality, but whether its
account of the construction of women as loving caretakers 'for' men, instead

of as desiring subjects in reciprocally erotic relations, is persuasive" (Jones 1994, xii–xiii). I accept that in order to test the applicability of Jónasdóttir's theory I need to know more about the organization of sexual unions and how love power operates in women's lives. Feminist research needs to determine whether women enter socio-sexual unions as desiring subjects in reciprocally erotic relationships.

The information gleaned from the evidence I have examined indicates intense negotiations and accommodations of power, and, for some women, their love power seems to have been extracted. The situation with young girls is starker; they are indeed economically and socially powerless in their sexual unions. But what of the situation of women who have considerable economic resources and social capital, but whose sexual unions seem to be just as problematic?

Applying Jónasdóttir's assumptions, I have tried to demonstrate that the nexus of political sexuality and political economy is dynamic and sometimes contested but largely underexamined. I maintain that not only are there ongoing attempts to "extract" or contain women's power in sexual unions, but that for women who prove powerful in other social, political and economic relations, there are continuous attempts to use their sexual relations with men to force them into powerless positions. Flax offers insights into another profoundly unsettling dimension of whether women's love power is extracted or they willingly surrender it. Drawing on her experience as a licensed, practising psychotherapist, Flax reveals:

> In my clinical practice, I see all too often how women deny their own desire; how they over idealize its object because acknowledging their longings for pleasure produces too much anxiety. The over idealized object is bound to disappoint, but they remain reluctant to recognise the unconscious dynamics at work. My patients inhibit their own aggression; self-generated activity unsettles the stability they seek through a (passive) gender identity. They enact the norm that their best chance for success is to get others, usually more powerful men, to like/idealize them and then wait patiently until such relationships pay off. When success can no longer be attained this way, they panic or become depressed. (Flax 2004, 61)

Equally troubling from the perspective of investigating what happens to women's love power, Flax continues: "Often female patients prefer to see themselves as selflessly serving others rather than pursuing their own desire.

This denial frequently results in self-undermining behavior, hurting others and unconsciously seeking control through induced guilt and shame. Some women collude with conventional ideas of femininity by relentlessly disciplining their body and monitoring and judging those of other women (including their own daughters)" (ibid.). Flax complicates the situation further by noting that, with these types of behaviours, women's willing repression of their desires does produce secondary gains of social approval, avoidance of responsibility, and probably less loneliness and anxiety. And, of course, this kind of behaviour is happening in societal contexts in which it is traditionally expected that women will sacrifice for spouses, families and society.

I conclude with an identification of three areas in which further research is needed. (1) Have women's experiences of accommodations and compromises in their socio-sexual unions predisposed and conditioned them to accept powerlessness in their intimate spaces, in the state, the economy and civil society?[32] (2) Where women hold institutional power or power of office, has their conditioning to compromise continuously in the pursuit of the erotic dimension of love power left them unwilling to use their institutional power to challenge relations of domination in the state, in the economy and civil society, and in political economy? (3) Will the use of Audre Lorde's theorization of the erotic as women's life force – a creative, empowering energy, "physical, emotional and psychic expressions of what is deepest and strongest and richest within each of us" (Lorde 1984, 56) – shift the terrain of analysis of love power, albeit to an analysis that requires more rigorous development and application? This constitutes my ongoing project.

Influenced by her desire to redeem Marx's method, on the one hand, Jónasdóttir theorizes love power as arising from material relations of production within intimate relations. Her theory also reflects how the majority of women conduct their lives in socio-sexual unions with men. Their relationships are often a pursuit of the unobtainable holy grail of erotic fulfilment – unobtainable because most women believe that their love power, their erotic power, exists outside of themselves, and is an outcome of their experiences in their socio-sexual unions. On the other hand, Lorde's construct of the "power of the erotic" takes the analysis of love power in a completely new direction. Her theorizing forces feminist scholarship that investigates love power in women's lives to come home to a radical reconceptualization of the erotic. Rather than apprehend love power as something that is extracted or surrendered, Lorde offers the erotic (i.e., love power) as an internal life force, a source of power and passion that drives every dimension of women's and men's lives. We need to know more about how care and erotic ecstasy shape women's private and public lives. Jónasdóttir's theory of love power indicates the need for an in-depth study of women's sexual relations with men. Lorde's contribution suggests that women need to accept or embrace that erotic power that already exists within themselves.

Notes

1. This chapter advances a theoretical analysis of the presence or absence of love power in the lives of Caribbean women, and draws on the theoretical work of Anna Jónasdóttir and Audre Lorde. It expands on earlier arguments I presented in Barriteau 2011. I gave an outline of the earlier essay in a seminar at the University of Örebro, Sweden, in 2008 (Barriteau 2008). In the current work, I advance my earlier analyses and provide significant points of departure by critically examining the relevance of Audre Lorde's much earlier work on the power of the erotic.
2. Perhaps "in spite of" would be more appropriate.
3. As I will show, I do not mean to suggest that these two concepts can be used interchangeably. Instead, they are two similar yet differing conceptual tools that seek to analyse the same phenomenon.
4. By "Commonwealth Caribbean" I refer to the independent anglophone island states and British dependencies within the Caribbean Sea, the Central American country of Belize, and the South American country of Guyana. These countries share similar historical, political, social and cultural legacies. They are either former colonies of Britain or, in a few cases, British Protectorates. I view neighbouring countries as equally Caribbean but recognize and respect their differing historical, political, economic, social and cultural legacies, as well as my limited knowledge of these.
5. In response to Sigmund Freud's point that bisexuality is the decisive factor in human sexuality, Jane Flax states she prefers the term "polysexual": "Polysexual conveys the sense of a complex, usable range of possibilities, of sites with varying attributes in multiple mixtures and forms" (Flax 2004, 58).
6. I am aware of the symbiotic relationship between heterosexism and homophobia, and believe that patriarchal relations of power reproduce these exclusions and inequalities. In this project I focus on heterosexuality and heterosexism.
7. I cannot help but think that in the present-day Caribbean it seems almost reactionary, backward and dated to say that one is interested in maintaining a research focus on women. Within both the academy and popular culture there is a sense that

cutting-edge work is on men and masculinity, or alternative sexualities, which are, of course, of incredible importance. I remain intrigued that research on heterosexual women seems to be out of style, when heteronormativity and patriarchal relations continue to be dominant. I am also mindful of Hollibaugh and Moraga's observation (1983, 395) that there is heterosexuality outside of heterosexism.

8.   Either with or without sexual pleasure. We need empirical studies in this area.

9.   And elsewhere too: "So, like, you feel like you have to be this fabulous lover and they have *to come* at least three times" (Kimmel 2008, 62; emphasis added).

10. As my friend and colleague Pat Mohammed reminded me, sex and love are "reflected all around us in the music, which, out of fear of emotional entanglements, the capacity/incapacity for Caribbean men and women to profess to, admit to, [or] speak of love equates and embeds love and desire in material things – "mi love mi car, mi love mi bike, mi love mi money and ting, but most of all mi love mi browning" (e-mail correspondence, Mohammed to Barriteau, 16 April 2008). I must thank Pat for this wonderful insight.

11. The Mighty Sparrow sings, "You can't make love without money." Reggae artist Buju Banton declares, "mi love mi car, mi love mi bike, mi love mi money and ting, but most of all mi love mi browning [brown-skin black woman]." In another calypso by Sparrow, a woman named Melda visits an obeah man to try to get her man to marry her (an attempt to gain guaranteed status and respectability, even if emotional stability is not assured). Drinks for sexual stamina include bois bandé and sea moss. Similarly "putting it back in the back" means undertaking activities for sexual prowess, building sexual stamina which is often referred to as having a strong back.

12. Michelle Belgrave, a graduate student at the Institute for Gender and Development Studies, Nita Barrow Unit, University of the West Indies, Cave Hill, who was researching sex tourism in the Caribbean states: "The advertisements for these countries [Barbados, Jamaica and Dominica] were remarkably similar. Sex tourism is coded into the ads, with varying degrees of subtlety, as part of the services or attractions which a visitor can expect to consume whilst on holiday. As a consequence, sex tourism plays a distinctive role in the branding of Caribbean countries as tourist destinations" (e-mail correspondence, Belgrave to Barriteau, 20 April 2008). She goes on to link Caribbean governments to these ads through their membership in the Caribbean Tourism Organization and the fact that the CTO's promotional activities are linked to national tourism organizations.

13. Caribbean women writers such as Edwidge Danticat, Oona Kempadoo and Shani Mootoo have addressed women's sexuality. Dorian Powell, a researcher on the Women in the Caribbean Project, has looked at women's sexuality through family planning and fertility, and in fact the closest one can come to getting information about women's sexual lives is through studies of population, reproductive health

and fertility. Patricia Mohammed has also examined women's sexuality in Dominica and St Lucia through family planning (Mohammed and Perkins 1999). In her doctoral dissertation, Mohammed theorized the way early Indo-Trinidadian women negotiated sexual relations, expanding their personal and sexual power in the context of migration, indentureship and the comparatively smaller number of Indian women in Trinidad during the early period of indentureship. Roseanne Kahnai, in *Matikor*, also looks at the sexuality of Indo-Trinidadian women. None of the existing works, however, has made women's sexual relations the central focus of analysis in the way that scholars have examined the role of work in Caribbean women's lives. I am indebted to my colleague Patricia Mohammed for the foregoing information (e-mail correspondence, Mohammed to Barriteau, 21 April 2008).

14. Please note that I do see this research as vital.

15. At the level of informing policy there is a great deal of convergence between Liberal and Socialist feminist theories. Both emphasize women in the public sphere, but from differing theoretical positions. Liberal feminists want to increase women's participation in the state and the economy. Socialist feminists have done valuable work on showing how women have been exploited as workers and as housewives, while also emphasizing how women's household work goes unremunerated even as it underwrites capitalist production. On Socialist Feminist theory and Caribbean women, see Barriteau 1994 and 1995.

16. I do not deny that there are women engaged in sex work who get sexual satisfaction from it.

17. Perhaps without even recognizing that, in the pursuit of the erotic, they also want to be cared for by their men.

18. Even for nurturing the scholarly discourse on men and masculinity, see Hamilton 1999.

19. In many political and social organizations women serve as the fundraisers, the secretaries, the organizers of social activities, key organizers of constituencies, or rank-and-file members (but not presidents) of parent–teachers associations. For some of these dynamics in political organizations, see Clarke 1986; Barriteau 1992.

20. According to Folbre, "historically women have done a very large proportion of our care work, and that is still true today" (2003, 1).

21. I would like to prove this assumption in a study of women's sexual relations and unions.

22. I recognize a caring dimension within the erotic, however. That is to say, within the erotic, caring for and being cared for also have multiple modes of expression.

23. On average there is about a 70:30 ratio of women to men for the three main campuses of the University of the West Indies, although at the Mona campus in Jamaica the enrolment ratio is now 80:20 women to men.

24. I agree with Jónasdóttir that marriage, relationships or unions are the link between

the private and the public, so I draw attention to women's experiences of sexual unions. In subsequent work I would like to examine how the institutionalization of sexual unions within the state and civil society may reinforce the gradual weakening of women's love power so it ends up being something that is more or less absent from women's lives.

25. Legislation in the 1980s removed the legal discrimination and social stigma between legitimate and illegitimate children.

26. I can almost hear the strong condemnation of this point by some feminists in the region, given our heavy investment in mythologizing Caribbean women as mothers above all else. This is not to suggest that Caribbean women do not make incredible sacrifices for their children and even their men. The point I am questioning is the suggestion that they actively choose motherhood over marriage rather than coming to this position as a result of the tenuous character of many sexual relations.

27. Or is it the exercise of power in pursuit of a romanticized ideal?

28. This is not to suggest that neither party is interested in reviving the sexual/emotional relation.

29. Their view seems somewhat idealized, even though they are correct about the sexual banter. Compare with Michael Lieber's view on Trinidadian men (Lieber 1981).

30. I have learned from social workers attending CGDS's gender training programmes that many mothers deny their daughters' claims of being sexually assaulted by their stepfathers, many out of fear of losing their partners and/or the economic support those partners provide. Evidence from court cases shows that stepfathers are sometimes charged for rape, and that girls do run away from home because of sexual aggression from their relatives.

31. This fact suggests that the women waited for some time before taking action to end their experiences of abuse and violence.

32. This statement leads me to wonder whether one of the reasons why so many lesbian feminists are so vocal about exposing conditions of inequality for women is that they do not deal with patriarchal relations of domination in their own intimate spaces.

References

Alexander, M.J. 1997. Erotic autonomy as a politics of decolonization: An anatomy of feminist and state practice in the Bahamas tourist economy. In *Feminist genealogies, colonial legacies, democratic futures*, ed. M.J. Alexander and C. Mohanty, 63–100. London: Routledge.

———. 2005. Imperial desires / sexual utopias: White gay capital and transnational tourism. In *Pedagogies of crossing: Meditations on feminism, sexual politics, memory and the sacred*, by M.J. Alexander, 66–90. Durham, NC: Duke University Press.

Andaiye. 2003. Smoke and mirrors: The illusion of CARICOM women's growing economic empowerment, post-Beijing. In *Gender equality in the Caribbean: Reality or illusion?*, ed. G. Tang-Nain and B. Bailey, 73–107. Kingston: Ian Randle.

Anderson, P. 1986. Conclusion: Women in the Caribbean. *Social and Economic Studies* 35 (2): 291–324.

Bailey, B. 2003. The search for gender equity and empowerment of Caribbean women: The role of education. In *Gender equality in the Caribbean: Reality or illusion?*, ed. G. Tang-Nain and B. Bailey, 108–45. Kingston: Ian Randle.

Barriteau, E. 1992. The construct of a postmodernist feminist theory for Caribbean social science research. *Social and Economic Studies* 41 (2): 1–43.

———. 1994. Gender and development planning in the postcolonial Caribbean: Female entrepreneurs and the Barbadian state. PhD diss., Howard University.

———. 1995. Socialist feminist theory and Caribbean women: Transcending dualisms. *Social and Economic Studies* 44 (2–3): 25–63.

———. 1996. Structural adjustment policies in the Caribbean: A feminist perspective. *National Women's Studies Association Journal* 8 (1): 142–56.

———. 1998a. Theorizing gender systems and the project of modernity in the twentieth-century Caribbean. *Feminist Review* 59 (June): 186–210.

———. 1998b. Liberal ideology and contradictions in Caribbean gender systems. In *Caribbean portraits: Essays on gender ideologies and identities*, ed. C. Barrow, 436–56. Kingston: Ian Randle.

———. 2001. *The political economy of gender in the twentieth-century Caribbean*. New York: Palgrave.

———. 2002. Women entrepreneurs and economic marginality: Rethinking Caribbean women's economic relations. In *Gendered realities: Essays in Caribbean feminist thought*, ed. P. Mohammed, 221–48. Kingston: University of the West Indies Press, Centre for Gender and Development Studies.

———. 2003a. Conclusion: Beyond a backlash – The frontal assault on containing Caribbean women in the decade of the 1990s. In *Gender equality in the Caribbean: Reality or illusion?*, ed. G. Tang-Nain and B. Bailey, 201–32. Kingston: Ian Randle.

———. 2003b. Confronting power and politics: A feminist theorizing of gender in commonwealth Caribbean societies. *Meridians: Feminism, Race, Transnationalism* 3 (2): 57–92.

———. 2003c. Confronting power, theorizing gender in the commonwealth Caribbean. In *Confronting power, theorizing gender: Interdisciplinary perspectives in the Caribbean*, ed. E. Barriteau, 3–24. Kingston: University of the West Indies Press.

———. 2003d. Requiem for the male marginalization thesis in the Caribbean: Death of a non-theory. In *Confronting power, theorizing gender: Interdisciplinary perspectives in the Caribbean*, ed. E. Barriteau, 324–55. Kingston: University of the West Indies Press.

———. 2004. Constructing feminist knowledge in the commonwealth Caribbean in the era of globalization. In *Gender in the 21st century: Caribbean perspectives, visions and possibilities*, ed. B. Bailey and E. Leo-Rhynie, 437–65. Kingston: Ian Randle.

———. 2007a. The theoretical strengths and relevance of black feminist scholarship: A Caribbean perspective. *Feminist Africa* 7 (1): 9–31.

———. 2007b. Thirty years towards gender equality: How many more? *Journal of Gender Studies* 1 (1): 1–17.

———. 2008 . "Coming, coming, coming home": Applying Anna Jónasdóttir's theory of "love power" to theorizing sexuality and power in Caribbean gender relations. *GEXcel Work in Progress Report* 3: 13–25.

———. 2011. Theorising sexuality and power in Caribbean gender relations. In *Sexuality, gender and power: Intersectional and transnational perspectives*, ed. A. Jónasdóttir, V. Bryson and K. Jones. London: Routledge.

Barrow, C. 1986. Finding the support: A study of strategies for survival. *Social and Economic Studies* 35 (2): 131–76.

Barrow, C., M. de Bruin and R. Carr, eds. 2009. *Sexuality, social exclusion and human rights: Vulnerability in the Caribbean context of HIV*. Kingston: Ian Randle.

Bolles, L. 1983. Kitchen hit by priorities: Employed working-class Jamaican women confront the IMF. In *Women, men and the international division of labor*, ed. J. Nash and M.P. Fernandez Kelly, 138–60. Albany: SUNY Press.

Boyce-Davies, C. 2007. "Con-di-fi-cation": Black women, leadership and political power. *Feminist Africa* 7:67–88.

Bryson, V. 2008. *From making tools to making love: Marx, materialism and feminist thought.* GEXcel Work in Progress Report, vol. II. Proceedings from GEXcel Theme 1. Gender, Sexuality and Global Change, 23–34.

Cabezas, A.L. 1999. Women's work is never done: Sex tourism in Sosua, the Dominican Republic. In *Sun, sex and gold: Tourism and sex work in the Caribbean*, ed. K. Kempadoo, 93–123. Lanham, MD: Rowman and Littlefield.

———. 2004. Between love and money: Sex, tourism and citizenship in Cuba and the Dominican Republic. *Signs: Journal of Women in Culture and Society* 29 (4): 987–1016.

Carby, H.V. 1982/1997. White woman listen: Black feminism and the boundaries of sisterhood. In *Black British feminism: A reader*, ed. H. Safia Mirza, 45–53. London: Routledge. [Originally published 1982 in *The empire strikes back: Race and racism in seventies Britain*, by the Centre for Contemporary Cultural Studies, 212–35 (London: Hutchinson).]

Chanel, I.M. 1994. Haitian and Dominican women in the sex trade. *CAFRA News: Newsletter of the Caribbean Association for Feminist Research and Action* 8:13–14.

Chevannes, B. 1999. *What we sow and what we reap: Problems in the cultivation of male identity in Jamaica.* Grace, Kennedy Foundation lecture series. Kingston: Grace, Kennedy Foundation.

Clarke, R. 1986. Women's organisations, women's interests. *Social and Economic Studies* 35 (3): 107–55.

Development Alternatives with Women for a New Era (DAWN). 2006. *Sexual and reproductive health and rights in the English-speaking Caribbean: A study of maternal mortality, abortion and health sector reform in Barbados, Jamaica, Suriname, and Trinidad and Tobago.* Calabar, Nigeria: DAWN Secretariat.

De Albuquerque, K. 1998. Sex, beach boys, and female tourists in the Caribbean. *Sexuality and Culture* 2 (1): 87–112.

De Albuquerque, K., and S. Ruark. 1998. "Men day done": Are women really ascendant in the Caribbean? In *Caribbean portraits: Essays on gender ideologies and identities*, ed. C. Barrow, 1–13. Kingston: Ian Randle.

Denis, A. 2003. Theorizing the gendered analysis of work in the commonwealth Caribbean. In *Confronting power, theorizing gender: Interdisciplinary perspectives in the Caribbean*, ed. E. Barriteau, 262–82. Kingston: University of the West Indies Press.

Elliot, D. Richards. 2006. The Jamaican female skills surplus and earnings deficit: A holistic explanation. *Journal of International Women's Studies* 8 (1): 70–87.

Flax, J. 2004. The scandal of desire: Psychoanalysis and disruptions of gender: A meditation on Sigmund Freud's *Three essays on sexuality. Contemporary Psychoanalysis* 40 (1): 47–68.

Folbre, N. 2003. Caring labor. Transcription of a video by O. Ressler, recorded in Amherst, MA. 20 minutes. http://www.republicart.net/disc/aeas/folbre01_en.htm (accessed 26 December 2008).

Freeman, C. 1997. Reinventing higglering across transnational zones: Barbadian women juggle the triple shift. In *Daughters of Caliban: Caribbean women in the twentieth century*, ed. C. Lopez Springfield, 68–95. Bloomington: Indiana University Press.

———. 1998. Island-hopping body shopping in Barbados: Localising the gendering of transnational workers. In *Caribbean portraits: Essays on gender ideologies and identities*, ed. C. Barrow, 14–27. Kingston: Ian Randle.

———. 2000. *High tech and high heels in the global economy: Women, work, and pink-collar identities in the Caribbean.* Durham, NC: Duke University Press.

French, J. 1994. Hitting where it hurts most: Jamaican women's livelihoods in crisis. In *Mortgaging women's lives: Feminist critiques of structural adjustment*, ed. P. Sparr, 165–82. London: Zed Books.

———. 2008. Women's leadership in the Caribbean: Evolution and challenges in IADB member countries post-Beijing. Paper produced for the tenth anniversary of PRO-LEAD.

Gill, M., and J. Massiah, eds. 1984. *Women, work and development.* Women in the Caribbean Project no. 6, ed. J. Massiah. Bridgetown: Institute of Social and Economic Research (Eastern Caribbean), University of the West Indies.

Grant, M., and A. Rubens. 1997. Feminism, psychoanalysis and identity politics: An interview with Jane Flax. *Melbourne Journal of Politics* 1: 1–16.

Hamilton, M. 1999. *Women and higher education in the commonwealth Caribbean: UWI — A progressive university for women?* Working paper no. 2. Bridgetown: Centre for Gender and Development Studies, University of the West Indies, Cave Hill.

Hochschild, A. 2002. Emotional labour. In *Gender: A sociological reader*, ed. S. Jackson and S. Scott, 192–96. London: Routledge.

Hollibaugh, A., and C. Moraga. 1983. What we are rolling around in bed with: Sexual silences in feminism. In *Powers of desire: The politics of sexuality*, ed. A. Snitow, C. Stansell and S. Thompson, 394–405. New York: Monthly Review.

Jayasinghe, D. 2001. "More and more technology, women have to go home": Changing skill demands in manufacturing and Caribbean women's access to training. *Gender and Development* 9 (1): 70–81.

———. 2003. *Changing skills demands in manufacturing and the impact on Caribbean female workers.* Working paper no. 9. Cave Hill, Barbados: Centre for Gender and Development Studies, University of the West Indies.

Jónasdóttir, A.G. 1994. *Why women are oppressed.* Philadelphia: Temple University Press.

———. 2007. Theme 1: Gender, sexuality and global change. GEXcel Work in Progress, vol. 1: *Proceedings from GEXcel kick-off conference*, 19–21. Örebro , Sweden: Center of Gender Excellence, Örebro University.

———. 2009. Feminist questions, Marx's method, and the theorisation of "love power". In *The political interests of gender revisited: Redoing theory and research with a feminist face*, ed. A.G. Jónasdóttir and K.B. Jones, 58–83. Manchester, UK: Manchester University Press.

Jones, K.B. 1994. Foreword. In *Why women are oppressed*, by A.G. Jónasdóttir, xi–xiv. Philadelphia: Temple University Press.

Kempadoo, K., ed. 1999. *Sun, sex and gold: Tourism and sex work in the Caribbean.* Lanham, MD: Rowman and Littlefield.

———. 2001. Women of color and the global sex trade: Transnational feminist perspectives. *Meridians: Feminism, Race, Transnationalism* 1 (2): 28–51.

———. 2003. Theorizing sexual relations in the Caribbean: Prostitution and the problem of the "exotic". In *Confronting power, theorizing gender: Interdisciplinary perspectives in the Caribbean*, ed. E. Barriteau, 159–85. Kingston: University of the West Indies Press.

Kimmel, M. 2008. *Hooking up, party rape and predatory sex: The sexual culture of the American college campus.* GEXcel Work in Progress Report, vol. 1, 49–64. Örebro , Sweden: Center of Gender Excellence, Örebro and Linkoping Universities .

Lagro, M., and D. Plotkin. 1990. *The suitcase traders in the free zone of Curaçao.* Port of Spain: Economic Commission for Latin America and the Caribbean, Sub-regional Headquarters for the Caribbean.

Lamming, G. 1995. Coming, coming, coming home. In *Coming, coming home: Conversations II: Western education and the Caribbean intellectual*, 29–49. St Martin: House of Nehesi.

Lieber, M. 1981. *Street scenes: Afro-American culture in urban Trinidad*. Cambridge: Schenkman.

Lorde, A. 1984. Uses of the erotic: The erotic as power. In *Sister outsider: Essays and speeches*, by A. Lorde, 53–59. Freedom, CA: Crossing.

Massiah, J. 1986b. Work in the lives of Caribbean women. *Social and Economic Studies* 35 (2): 177–239.

———. 1991. Defining women's work in the commonwealth Caribbean. In *Persistent inequalities: Women and world development*, ed. I. Tinker, xx. Oxford: Oxford University Press.

———. 2003. Preface. In *Gender equality in the Caribbean: Reality or illusion?*, ed. G. Tang-Nain and B. Bailey, xi–xxiv. Kingston: Ian Randle.

———. 2004. Feminist scholarship and society. In *Gender in the 21st century: Caribbean perspectives, visions and possibilities*, ed. B. Bailey and E. Leo-Rhynie, 5–34. Kingston: Ian Randle.

McDavid, H., and D. Ramajeesingh. 2003. The state and tourism: A Caribbean perspective. *International Journal of Contemporary Hospitality Management* 15 (3): 180–83.

Miller, E. 1991. *Men at risk*. Kingston: Jamaica Publishing House.

———. 1994. *Marginalization of the black male: Insights from the development of the teaching profession*. 2nd ed. Kingston: Canoe.

Mohammed, P., and A. Perkins. 1999. *Caribbean women at the crossroads: The paradox of motherhood among women of Barbados, St Lucia and Dominica*. Kingston: Canoe.

Pargass, G., and R. Clarke. 2003. Violence against women: A human rights issue post-Beijing five-year review. In *Gender equality in the Caribbean: Reality or illusion?*, ed. G. Tang-Nain and B. Bailey, 39–72. Kingston: Ian Randle.

Powell, D. 1986. Caribbean women and their response to familial experiences. *Social and Economic Studies* 35 (2): 83–130.

Puar, J. Kuar. 2001. Global circuits: Transnational sexualities and Trinidad. *Signs: Journal of Women in Culture and Society* 26 (4): 1039–65.

Robinson, T. 2003. Beyond the bill of rights: Sexing the citizen. In *Confronting power, theorizing gender: Interdisciplinary perspectives in the Caribbean*, ed. E Barriteau, 231–61. Kingston: University of the West Indies Press.

Sanchez-Taylor, J. 2001. Dollars are a girl's best friend: Female tourists' sexual behaviour in the Caribbean. *Sociology* 35 (3): 749–64.

Scott, K. Mackinnon. 1992. Female labour force participation and earnings: The case of Jamaica. In *Case studies on women's employment and pay in Latin America*, ed. G. Psacharopoulos and Z. Tzannatos, 323–38. Washington DC: World Bank.

Seguino, S. 2003. Why are women in the Caribbean so much more likely than men to be unemployed? *Social and Economic Studies* 52 (4): 83–120.

Senior, O. 1991. *Working miracles: Women's lives in the English-speaking Caribbean.* London: Currey.

Sharpe, J., and S. Pinto. 2006. The sweetest taboo: Studies of Caribbean sexualities: A review essay. *Signs: Journal of Women in Culture and Society* 32 (1): 247–77.

Smith, B. 1983. *Home girls: A black feminist anthology.* New York: Kitchen Table.

Sutton, C., and S. Makiesky-Barrow. 1981. Social inequality and sexual status in Barbados. In *The black woman cross-culturally,* ed. F. Chioma Steady, 469–98. Cambridge, MA: Schenkman.

Tang Nain, G., and B. Bailey, eds. 2003. *Gender equality in the Caribbean: Reality or illusion?* Kingston: Ian Randle.

Thomas Hope, E. 2007. Human trafficking in the Caribbean and the human rights of migrants. http://www.eclac.org/celade/noticias/paginas/2/11302/Thomas-Hope.pdf (accessed 20 April 2008).

Toppin, D. 2007a. Centralizing Stories. *Reproductive Health / RH Reality Check,* 31 October. http://www.rhrealitycheck.org (accessed 21 April 2008).

———. 2007b. Sexual violence more than just rape. *Reproductive Health / RH Reality Check,* 28 September. http://www.rhrealitycheck.org (accessed 21 April 2008).

———. 2008. Child brides in Jamaica, too. *Reproductive Health / RH Reality Check,* 4 March. http://www.rhrealitycheck.org (accessed 21 April 2008).

Trotz, A. 2008. *Gender, generation and memory: Remembering a future Caribbean.* Working paper no. 14. Bridgetown: Centre for Gender and Development Studies, University of the West Indies.

Vassell, L. 2003. Women, power and decision-making in CARICOM countries: Moving forward from a post-Beijing assessment. In *Gender equality in the Caribbean: Reality or illusion?,* ed. G. Tang-Nain and B. Bailey, 1–38. Kingston: Ian Randle.

Wiltshire-Brodber, R. 1986. The Caribbean transnational family. Paper prepared for UNESCO/ Institute of Social and Economic Research seminar on changing family patterns and women's role in the Caribbean. University of the West Indies, Cave Hill, Barbados, 24–27 November.

5

What Does It "Really" Mean to Be a Wo/Man?

Narratives of Gender by Women and Men

HALIMAH A.F. DeSHONG

Sometimes I don't even know who is the man from the woman.[1]

—Lionel, interview participant

Introduction

People invariably convey impressions about themselves in their everyday verbal interactions. Individuals may manage these portrayals more carefully in the context of official interviews, and the promise of anonymity does not guarantee full disclosure from participants about their experiences and thoughts. This chapter explores the narratives of gender that emerged from a series of interviews with women and men. The work forms part of a larger study which addresses the interstices of intimate partner violence, other acts of coercive control and gender in women's and men's interview talk. This study does not purport to mirror the precise realities of participants' lives. My concern is to analyse those presentations of self that people often quite carefully manage during interviews, as these self-portrayals provide a useful site for a discursive analysis of gender in speech. The contribution represents a feminist poststructuralist discourse analysis of narratives of gender produced during these interviews. Feminist poststructuralism is concerned with the ways in which hegemonic discourses function to subjugate women (Gavey 1992), and the points at which individuals complicate these discursive practices.

The meanings which participants (men in particular) attached to violence can often be tied to a number of conventional stereotypes about what it means to be a man or what it means to be a woman. In the opening quotation, Lionel suggests that there ought to be clearly demarcated roles for women and men in intimate relationships, and that women sometimes usurp men's power. He engages in a binary depiction of gender as he laments the confusion which arises when the so-called boundaries of womanhood and manhood are crossed. This kind of response provides a backdrop for the chapter, which seeks to address the following questions:

1. How do men and women define themselves in these interviews and in relation to their intimate partners?
2. What are the culturally available explanatory frameworks that inform participants' narratives of gender?
3. How do these narratives implicate particular relations of power?
4. What are the meanings of these relations for individual women and men?
5. In what ways do individuals commit to or subvert dominant discourses on gender?
6. How are egalitarian values expressed in these narratives?

Setting the Agenda of "Gender" as a Feminist Resource

Gender in the context of this study is not to be confused with its reductionist usage; it is not simply a matter of counting male and female bodies. I use gender as an analytical tool; however, its use has become so commonplace that it is worth spending some time exploring its utility as a feminist resource. Barriteau (2001, 25) speaks to the confusion which arises when the term "gender" is used in both popular and academic discourses: "At one level gender has come to stand erroneously as a trendier synonym for the biological differences and signifiers implied by the word 'sex'. Now, on almost all questionnaires there is the mandatory category 'gender' in which one is supposed to reply male or female." She is careful to note that the term "gender" has been used historically in the grammatical sense (masculine gender, feminine gender and neuter gender), deriving its identity in the disciplines of biology, linguistics and psychology. Feminist scholarship, however, appropriated the term to signify complex social relations between women and men that are historically characterized by a disproportionate distribution of power and material resources (Barriteau 2001).

Notwithstanding its feminist etymology, gender has been deployed in a variety of ways within the social sciences. The study of sex roles in sociology and psychology provides one of the most popular examples of the application of the term "gender" outside of feminist frameworks. Talcott Parsons and Robert Bales (1964) applied sex-role theory to explain how a series of normative attributes become attached to various members of the nuclear family through the process of socialization. Their schema allocates to men the instrumental roles of courage, roughness, self-reliance and aggression, whereas it designates for women the expressive roles which embody timidity, tenderness and dependence. In other words, monolithic notions of masculinity and femininity are attributed to male and female bodies, respectively, in the process of becoming men and women. The main critique of sex-role theory is that it reinforces asymmetrical relations of power based on biological determinism, with its implied commitment to fixed-gender essences. There is no discussion of how policing the boundaries of gender actualizes power. The inadequacy of sex-role theory to a study of Caribbean gender relations becomes quite apparent when we consider the privileging of the nuclear family.

Caribbean feminist scholars and other social scientists have critiqued early anthropological and sociological works on gender roles within the family for their emphasis on the Parsonian and other structural–functionalist models (Barriteau 2003; Barrow 1996; Hodge 2002; Reddock 1994; Rowley 2002). These early scripts portray Caribbean men as absent and marginal in relation to the normative nuclear family, while they often construct Caribbean women as matriarchs in families characterized by matrifocality (Rowley 2002). By implying that roles within Caribbean households are reversed, these studies construct families in the region as disorganized and dysfunctional (Reddock 1994), and read women's putative power in relation to families as a form of emasculation which results in men's paralysis and disenfranchisement. A discourse which positions women as usurpers in the context of the family is based on the following assumptions:

1. That women occupy positions of power which are manifested in material and other benefits;
2. That men's "rightful" place as heads of households have somehow been hijacked in so-called atypical arrangements of power.

For Barriteau (2003) and Lindsay (2002), headship status should not be confused with economic or social empowerment, since there is greater likelihood for households headed by women to experience financial deprivation. It is also important to analyse whether the absence or transitory nature of some men as partners signifies a break with traditional ideologies of gender. This study addresses the meanings of these arrangements for individual women and men.

Apart from the study of gender in the context of the family, feminist theorists have also presented gender as social construct, as discourse (Weedon 1997, 2000), as performative (Butler 1993, 1990/1999, 2000, 2004), and as institutional practice (Barriteau 2001). Contemporary scholars also point to the need to take account of various other social indices of difference even as we seek to accent gender. These perspectives converge in their rejection of biological determinism, and they are by no means mutually exclusive. Barriteau, in her definition (2001), speaks to the notion of gender as socially constructed in her reference to those complex personal and social relations that feature in the process of becoming a man or woman. She also alludes to the institutionalization of gender in particular societal practices. Judith Butler's (1993, 1999, 2000, 2004) performativity theory offers a way of viewing gender as something performed. The idea that gender is performative repudiates the view that there exists an internal essence of gender. Instead, "a sustained set of acts, posited through the gendered stylization of the body" produces gender (Butler 1990/1999, xv). Butler's constant reference to the significance of bodies in perpetuating (and sometimes resisting) commonsensical ideas of gender rests primarily on the notion that particular texts are metaphorically written onto male and female bodies in a dichotomous and thus constraining fashion. Specific practices are expected and sometimes demanded of individuals, depending on whether they are biologically female or male. This explains why we imagine men's power as natural and why we reject non-normative enactments of sexuality. Though there is a tendency to assume that we create our "own" gender or that it comes from within, Butler (2004, 1) argues that it is contingent on "a sociality that has no single author". In other words, one does not "do" one's gender alone; instead, gender is actualized as social practice. It is here that performativity intersects with the idea of gender as social construct. Finally, the idea of gender as discourse speaks to the ways in which language produces, reproduces and even subverts notions of gender. This idea most often finds articulation within feminist poststructuralist frameworks, and will be discussed in greater detail later in this chapter. These approaches point to the need to study the power dynamics which facilitate the policing of gender. This kind of surveillance also begs the question: what accounts for both the privileging and the marginalization of particular gendered practices? Moreover, how might ideas of gender bear meaning to participants' understandings of what it "really" means to be a woman or a man?

Feminist Poststructuralist Discourse Analysis

This work is informed by two distinct yet intersecting theoretical traditions: feminism/s[2] and poststructuralism. Both traditions challenge existing power relations that have the effect of marginalizing individuals as well as groups. Not all versions of feminism, however, celebrate the utility of poststructuralist insights, and those that do, do so with varying degrees of commitment. In this chapter, I examine the language produced about meanings of womanhood and manhood. In so doing I apply a feminist poststructuralist approach to discourse analysis to the study of these accounts. While I privilege the use of feminist poststructuralism because of the centrality it accords to language in the construction of subjective meanings, I am also committed to understanding the significance of these meanings in contemporary Caribbean societies. I argue that these insights can be mobilized in a contribution to Caribbean feminist epistemologies.

Feminist poststructuralism is a mode of knowledge production which applies poststructuralist notions of language, subjectivity, social processes and institutions to analyses of existing power relations, while also suggesting possibilities for change (Weedon 1997). My point of departure from this method of analysis is the examination of the power relations implicated by women's and men's accounts, and the ways in which culturally specific narratives inform these relations. This framework endorses the poststructuralist view of language (and other non-linguistic practices) as structuring social reality, and ratifies its rejection of universals as well as its embrace of the notion of multivocality or the multiple meanings present in texts. In addition to its approach to language, this schema also employs poststructuralist understandings of subjectivity, power and discourse.

Poststructuralism emerged as both an extension and a critique of structuralism, and expanded mainly on the structuralist linguistics of Ferdinand de Saussure (2001). Saussure refers to language as a system of signs, and the sign as a "double-entity" which unites a concept or *signified* and a sound-image or *signifier*. He posits that the sign is both *arbitrary* and *differential*. In his reference to the sign as differentially derived, Saussure explains that it is determined by reference to what it is not rather than what it is. This theory can be applied to an understanding of how individuals come to terms with their gendered identities. In many instances femininity is defined as what masculinity is not, and vice versa. Negatively derived meanings limit possibilities for both women and men. Historically, through a process of "Othering", ontologies of difference have been applied to justify unequal relations of power which position some groups (including women, blacks, East Indians and indigenous people) at the margins of society, while at the same privileging an Anglo-American male "Self". Of course, this process has never occurred without various modes of contestation. For Saussure, arbitrary does not mean that the choice of signifier is entirely up to the speaker. In fact, the individual does not have the power to change the sign once the linguistic community has established it. By "arbitrary", Saussure implies that the connection is "unmotivated"; that is, there is no natural connection between signified and signifier, or between the sign and the referent: "The community is necessary if values that owe their existence solely to usage and general acceptance are to be set up; by himself the individual is incapable of fixing a single value" (Saussure 2001, 967). In other words, the relationship between the sign and the reality it purports to represent is based on convention. The value of Saussure's claims to a poststructuralist epistemology is that they unsettle what we have come to know as the "natural" or "real". Saussure, however, views meaning as determined by a unitary sign system. According to Brooker (1999), meanings for Saussure are ordered or centred within closed linguistic or cultural systems. Poststructuralist thought decentres the idea of language as a system of signs and opens up the possibilities for meaning in language as contextually derived.

In trying to outline a clear definition for the broad field of works which have come to be identified as poststructuralist, what is most striking is "the purposeful elusiveness of work that can be variously classified as poststructural and/or postmodern" (Agger 1991, 112).[3] Poststructuralism problematizes linguistic referentiality, emphasizes heteroglossia (multivocality), decentres the subject, rejects the idea that "reason" is universal or foundational, criticizes humanism and stresses difference (Leitch 2001). It emphasises plurality as opposed to homogeneity, and rejects the universalizing of human experience.

Poststructuralist thought emphasizes the importance of language and discourse in understanding human relations. Towns and Adams (2000) posit that discourses govern people's actions, thoughts and feelings, and are in turn produced (and reproduced) as individuals use language in talk and action. As we confront and navigate across these discourses, we create different subject positions or subjectivities. It is not, however, simply a matter of choosing or rejecting this or that discourse. These discourses have varying appeal and institutional legitimacy, and although dominant discourses tend to be normalized in everyday practices and speech, on occasion, they are contested. In the context of gender ideologies, they are (re)produced as natural and immutable, with the emerging power dynamics tending to favour men in heterosexual relationships. It is for this reason that an analysis of power is central to poststructuralist-oriented scholarship. In the case of gender discourses, Weedon (1997) refers to the appeal of the natural in sustaining unequal relations of power between men and women.

The works of Michel Foucault find appeal among feminists who employ poststructuralist insights. His focus on historically specific discursive relations and social practices (see Weedon 1997) provides a platform from which feminists can problematize the appeal of the natural. In this regard, Foucault's formulation offers a useful approach to the analysis of gender power. Rather than conceptualizing power as some transcendental element of society, Foucault refers to power relations that are actualized in day-to-day practices (Foucault 1982). They are made manifest in various ways and are "brought to bear on permanent structures" (ibid., 789).

For Foucault (1998), power is always local. The exercise of power takes place from countless points, "in the interplay of nonegalitarian and mobile relations" (ibid., 1,472). His approach facilitates a focus on how individuals construct power from moment to moment within speech. There is no singular way in which power is exercised, as Mohammed (2004) reminds us, and what makes gendered power relations in the form of patriarchal power so resilient is their amoebic quality. This idiosyncrasy renders asymmetrical relations of gender all the more difficult to contest.

So, what are the implications of these insights for feminist research? In some circles poststructuralism is regarded as inimical to the emancipatory goals of feminist politics. It is often censured as an exercise in relativism, in which a feminist politics (with the aim of ending women's marginalization) is obscured. In Weedon's view, "not all forms of poststructuralism are necessarily productive for feminism" (1997, 20). In fact, some strands of poststructuralism, particularly deconstruction, focus exclusively on the texts and tend to disregard the social power relations within which texts are located. These power relations manifest themselves in various forms. In her formulation of feminist poststructuralism, Weedon explains that it must take full account of "the social and institutional context of textuality in order to address the power relations of everyday life" (ibid., 24). She explains that, in order for "a theoretical perspective to be politically useful for feminists, it should be able to recognise the importance of the *subjective* in constituting the meaning of women's lived reality. It should not deny subjective experience, since the ways in which people make sense of their lives is a necessary starting point for understanding how power relations structure society" (ibid., 8). A theory is useful for feminism if it problematizes the exercise of social power. This idea dovetails well with the intent of this chapter. Feminist poststructuralism guides the analysis of how women and men negotiate different gendered identities in talk. I analyse the points at which they position themselves in discourses on gender by identifying the cultural reproduction of meanings inherent in these accounts.

I have based my analysis of the interviews on the assumption that language is a central component in the way that we structure and (re)produce our realities. Language acts as a mediator between the personal and the social; it mediates reality. These assumptions necessitate the application of an analytical technique that is attentive to this kind of a view of language and one that is congruous with a feminist poststructuralist framework. As an analytical tool, discourse analysis is compatible with a feminist poststructuralist framework (Baxter 2007; Gavey 1997), as is evidenced by the use of language as the main unit of analysis. Discourse analysis involves a particular reading of texts by focusing on how "speakers draw from culturally available explanatory frameworks to construct the objects about which they speak and an array of subject positions" (Avdi 2005, 498). It is concerned with what language is used for (Brown and Yule 1983). In fact, discourse analysis examines the ways in which talk and texts are used to perform actions (Potter 2003). It is an umbrella term that captures a range of approaches to the study of talk and texts. These approaches have developed from different theoretical traditions and from diverse disciplinary locations (Gill 2000). Gill, however, explains that "what these perspectives share in common is a rejection of the realist notion that language is simply a neutral means of reflecting or describing the world, and a conviction to the central importance of discourse in constructing social life" (ibid., 172). Discourse analysis facilitates an analysis of the social languages at work as individuals' attempts to attach meanings to their experiences. In the following analysis, I examine the discourses at work as participants position themselves and others as gendered subjects.

A Note on Data Collection

I collected the data for this analysis between 2007 and 2008 in St Vincent and the Grenadines as part of my doctoral research on the interstices of gender and intimate partner violence. I conducted in-depth interviews with a total of thirty-four persons (including eight couples), of whom nineteen were women and fifteen were men. All participants were involved in heterosexual relationships in which men were the main perpetrators of violence. I contacted them through counsellors at the family court, family case workers at the Family Affairs Division in the Ministry of National Mobilization, members of staff at Her Majesty's Prison, and with the aid of a few police officers at one community police station.[4]

Here I focus on those portions of the interviews in which participants discussed meanings of womanhood and manhood, and in which I posed direct as well as more subtle questions about gender. In fact, large portions of the accounts were imbued with various ideas on what it means to be a wo/man. The emerging texts form the basis of the following analysis.

On Being a Woman

Participants' ideas generally endorsed, but sometimes subverted, binary discourses on gender by ascribing conventional scripts of femininity and masculinity to female and male bodies, respectively. A further dichotomization occurred as individuals distinguished between "good" and "bad" femininity – the archetype of the Madonna being the measure of a good woman, while ideas about women as whores or jezebels signified the bad woman. Women often distanced themselves from the latter images, with some aspiring to the ideals of the former. Participants often defined femininity in relation to and in opposition to masculinity. They usually defined these terms negatively – with femininity being what masculinity is not, and vice versa – and sometimes presented states of gender as idealized. The practices in which participants claimed to be engaged, however, sometimes complicated binary discourses on gender. Binary notions of gender appear with varying levels of approval and rejection in the accounts.

In this first example, Rose outlines her ideas on what she thinks it means to be a woman:

> Interviewer: OK, and for you, what do you think it means to be a woman?
>
> Rose: Well it's many things. Most of all it's education, and you have to live up to your expectations, not other people['s] expectations, and your mind . . . I have two girl children. I have to show respect for myself, show respect for my children, make sure I am a good role model for my children, so sometimes the things that you do, the children does look at that. You know, you understand and copy from that.

She explains that being a woman is "many things". Attaching significant value to education, Rose believes that she has a responsibility to be a good role model. While the idea of being a good role model points to a broader discourse on adult responsibility, for her this responsibility is enacted in specific ways. In her description of a good role model Rose speaks to the importance of having self-respect and respect for her children. Notions of femininity as the embodiment of good morals, particularly when her role as mother is considered, become the focus of her response. Embedded in what, from the outset, appears to be a gender-neutral articulation of women's identity, are latent meanings about the importance of women's respectability in the construction of femininity.

Janet's account of femininity draws more specifically on traditional discourses of gender, but it also exemplifies the heterogeneity of the ideas informing her understanding of self:

OK, with me, there are basically two or three kinds of women out there. There are those who are just the family type, who take care of everything. They make sure that the world goes good. There are some who just think about themselves and what they could get out of you and some who don't know what they're doing. So, on that point I put myself as the kind that, as the family kind who wants to see the world a better place.

Janet creates a typology of womanhood, identifying "two or three kinds of women". First, "the family type, who take care of everything" and who "make sure that the world goes good". This definition is akin to a femininity which draws on the nurturer–homemaker motif, in which women are considered carers. Second, she disapprovingly presents a construction of femininity in which women are described as self-centred and self-interested. This description resonates with the derogatory images of women as opportunistic and manipulative, evoking colloquial monikers such as "whore" and "gold digger", which are only used in relation to women. There is a sense in which these women enter relationships for material gain, rather than the more culturally esteemed motive of love. Third is a woman who is unsure of her role ("some who don't know what they're doing"), oblivious to her responsibilities or her place in the familial and societal contexts. While describing these three types of women, Janet positions herself as the family-oriented type.

As in other societies, traditional views about a good wife feed the expectations of both women and men as they negotiate power in relationships. The idea of a good wife draws on the essentialist discourse on sex roles. In this sense, an accomplished gender performance is based on women's mastery of domestic duties. Ricky, for example, referring to his partner, says, "you come off work five o'clock, so after five, after six, all six o'clock you could leave from your mother and come home and cook something for me to eat because we live in a house" . There is the expectation that, although Ricky and his partner both work outside of the home, she must continue to fulfil the traditional duties assigned to a housewife. In Ricky's view, this is the "true" measure of her identity. He laments how much time she spends at her parents' home at the expense of performing these duties. Feminist scholars have conceptualized this arrangement as the "double burden" or "double day" of paid employment and housework that is disproportionately borne by women (Freedman 2001). Similarly, Gary endorses a discourse on femininity based on women's role as housewives. Describing his expectations of a partner, he says, "I would need somebody loving, somebody caring who is always there. You know, make sure, well, you have your lunch, your breakfast, always keep the place clean, you know them sort o' things. Make sure you comfortable at home." In describing his ideal partner, Gary engages a feminine subjectivity which draws on traditional symbols of women as housekeepers, carers and homemakers – the woman who looks after her home and provides all of her partner's physical and emotional needs. His account has the effect of limiting the possibilities available to women in their pursuit of various aspirations.

Bruce describes the differences between a good woman and a bad woman, drawing on the archetype of the housewife. In reference to his partner he says, "I always, since I growing up, I always say I would like to meet a nice woman. She could cook. She could clean. She could, like good in everything, although she's so young. She started when she was young coming up. So those are the kind o' quality ladies, so that is why when she left I could've leave and just let her go, but I know the kind o' quality she is." Bruce's ideas are indicative of the pressure placed on many young girls and women in Vincentian society to master the traditional art of home management, which remains a major marker of femininity. Of course, the same is not expected of men. In spite of increased educational opportunities for women there remains the belief that the transition from childhood and adolescence to fully mature woman is actualized when a woman can prove her domestic capabilities. The problem does not lie in women's work within the home or in their positions as homemakers or housewives, but the ways in which these practices have always been ascribed an inferior status to paid employment and have been almost exclusively assigned to women. In many instances there is a lack of opportunity for women to choose to do otherwise, whether or not they are engaged in paid work. The naturalization of these kinds of roles serves to preserve power relations which place women at a disadvantage in relationships, limiting the options open to them.

Implicit in these accounts is the idea that the responsibility of the breadwinner is of far greater importance than that of the housewife. Whereas paid employment is presented as an option open to women, it is considered an absolute requirement for men. These historical discourses on women's and men's duties and responsibilities continue to support asymmetrical relations of power in which men's position as breadwinners accord them headship status within the context of the family.

Among female participants, Yvette also assigns housework to women, but her account of women's identity is more extensive, although it draws from an essentialist scripting of gender:

> Interviewer: For you, what does it mean to be a woman?
>
> Yvette: Well, I enjoy being a woman, but [I] end up ain't getting the right, ain't satisfying myself by doing what I want . . . I never feel bad being a woman because that is how God make me and I never refuse from doing a woman's work.
>
> Interviewer: What do you think a woman's work is?
>
> Yvette: Well, being around her children, when she has children. Well, at first have a boyfriend {mm hmm} so that you could have kids or have a husband, and you raise the children and you have a house and you take care of the house and so. Well, if you have an education and you have a career – well, at least I didn't have an education, but I have a career {mm hmm}. I had something in mind because I usually do craft work; make fans and purses and things and so. I could do a lot of craft.
>
> Interviewer: And you do them and you sell them?
>
> Yvette: I don't do them anymore because I don't have the time. I have things home doing, but I can't get the time to sit down [at] home and sew them. By the time I leave here it's already dark. On Sundays, I have to do my Sunday chores, clean-up, and sometimes I don't even get to finish cleaning up by the time night comes in. When I finish cooking, I feel [too] tired to sit down and eat.

At the beginning of her response, Yvette declares that she embraces those conventional role expectations that have been scripted as part of a dominant narrative on what it means to be a woman. She presents these expectations as part of a broader set of directions that comes from a higher power – God. She draws on a socio-religious discourse in which individuals are called to fulfil their duties according to the laws of a Christian God, legitimized by the Bible and supported by various denominations of Christianity. Being a woman is essentially good in Yvette's view, as it is what God intended for her. This belief suggests a transcendental femininity with its attachment to bodies that have historically been designated female. In this corporeal scripting of femininity, Yvette privileges discourses on motherhood, marriage, home management and self-sacrifice. She presents heteronormative practices of courtship, marriage, and child bearing and rearing as necessary in the pursuit of feminine completeness. The privileging of a conventional femininity based on the archetypes of woman as nurturer, mother and homemaker contextualizes the need for self-sacrifice. Yvette adds that educated women are expected to pursue their careers, but admits that she does not have a formal education. Although she describes her craftwork as a career, there is a sense in which she sacrifices her craft to satisfy the responsibilities of a housewife. It is evident that having a career does not necessarily mean an abandonment of traditional relations of gender. By the end of the extract there is a shift in the tone of her talk about these role expectations. Although she speaks of embracing her traditional responsibilities at the beginning of the excerpt, by the end she depicts her life as dominated by a range of household chores with little relief or time to follow her own interests. She ties these practices to the notion of self-sacrifice, which places certain restrictions on women who might otherwise pursue different experiences.

The idea of a transcendental femininity also features in Stacey's narrative. She regards her identity as an inherited script that she ought to embrace:

> Interviewer: OK, now, ahm, for you, what you think it means to be a woman?
>
> Stacey: What it means to be a woman?
>
> Interviewer: Mm hmm.
>
> Stacey: Well growing up from small, as you come up, well, God bring you a woman so it's just left to yourself and your thinking to bring yourself how you want it.

Religion is a central authority informing Stacey's discourse as she echoes the idea of a transcendental essence of womanhood, which hints at her reliance on Christianity as an authoritative force. It appears as though Christian ideals about womanhood govern her self-regulation, and she positions herself within a broader religious discourse on gender. She suggests that the potential for successful femininity is present, as God instils this capacity, but that the individual also has to embrace the scripted ideals of femininity in order to satisfy the requirements of womanhood. Another participant, Eve, also engages the sentiment of an essence of womanhood when she states, "I want to be as a woman because I am a woman." Being a woman is presented as a given, something innate, a biological fact.

In their accounts, participants supported essentialist readings of gender in which they used traditional values to define the self. There were moments in which these values were subverted, however. Counter-hegemonic discourses on women's identity tended to be espoused mainly by women. There were moments in the interviews when these women countered traditional readings of gender, with some shifting between articulating dominant and subversive ideas about identity. In the example provided by Rose earlier in this chapter, I suggested that embedded in her talk were latent meanings on the traditional idea about the need for women to be respectable. In the following example, Rose articulates ideas about the importance of women's autonomy:

> Interviewer: When would you say you're most comfortable as a woman?
>
> Rose: Well, you see, I am a person like this, eh, sometimes I'd rather be alone, me and my kids. I feel much better because nobody there to come and harass me. Nobody there to come and tell me do this and do that, go there, you know what I mean {mm hmm}. I just relax. I get up when I want to get up. I move when I want to, you know what I mean {mm hmm}. That is one of the happiest moments of my life.

Rose engages a counter-hegemonic discourse on femininity, in favour of a position which values women's autonomy. When asked about when she is most comfortable as a woman, Rose refers to a state of spatial freedom – having no boundaries in her everyday practices – as offering a sense of empowerment. In this sense she engages in a discourse on self-determination that departs from the notions of male support and interdependence between partners in a relationship. Moreover, she privileges the value of freedom in the construction of her gender identity, and it is almost as if this is an ideal, utopian even, alternative to a more restrictive, regimented everyday existence.

Dawn's account is an example of how both hegemonic and counter-hegemonic discourses informed participants' narratives. She declares her independence while at the same time endorsing a heteronormative narrative which privileges the heterosexual union as a marker of identity: "Well, I usually tell people I'm an independent woman. I don't sit down. I go and work for my money . . . I usually say that I don't just want a man for things. I want somebody to keep me comfort and talk to me at night and we could discuss how we want the things to turn out." Dawn subverts dominant narratives on gender by resisting the historically subordinated positions of homemaker and what is culturally known as the "kept woman", that is, a woman whose financial needs are met by a male partner, usually in the context of a transaction in which, in exchange for financial provision, the woman is expected to remain fully committed to her partner. The term resonates with particular negative and reductionist stereotypes of women as the property of men. Dawn, however, places far greater value on independence. The ability to provide for her own financial needs is the means by which she secures personal autonomy. Participants often stated that they invest great importance in the intimate heterosexual union. For Dawn, a male partner should provide companionship and comfort. Her final statement appears to indicate strong societal support for the heterosexual union and its defining role in the pursuit of the social completeness of the individual.

Angie's account also exemplifies the push and pull of dominant discourses on gender. Parallels can be drawn between the accounts of Dawn and Angie, for, while they celebrate women's independence as a kind of epiphany, they place great value on the heterosexual union:

> Interviewer: What do you think it means to be a woman?
>
> Angie: Hmm [pause]. Well, you have to be independent. You have to be independent in one's self. That is the important thing right now for me. If you had asked me this a couple years ago I might have said being in a relationship – being independent because if you independent you could have any relationship.

Angie registers two distinct stages in her development, which she uses to define herself as a woman. The first subject position she creates is that of the independent woman, which encompasses ideas of liberation or freedom to pursue her ambitions. There is a sense in which the experience of her current relationship has shaped her views. She indicates that, had she been asked the same questions a few years prior, she would have defined her gendered identity as a product of being a part of an intimate union. Ideas of independence form part of the language of women's autonomy to pursue their own desires. There are tensions between ideas on women's liberation and the centralizing tendency of the heteronormative discourse, however. Angie describes the ultimate goal of women's independence as a means of allowing women the choice of having the kinds of intimate relationships they wish to pursue. There is an overall sense that becoming a woman or successfully performing femininity centres on a person's ability to maintain a heterosexual union.

The women interviewed sometimes shifted between hegemonic and counter-hegemonic ideas about femininity as they defined themselves. Endorsing personal autonomy, in some cases, appears to be the result of past experiences of violent victimization and control by their partners. Participants often positioned women within traditional narratives which privileged an essentialist scripting of gender – the transcendental woman as a creation of God. An emergent trend in the negotiation of gender in these interviews was the occasional destabilization of conventional ideas about gender in general, and women's identity in particular, by the presence of counter-hegemonic discourses which support the idea of personal autonomy as a value which women should pursue.

The "Villainous" Woman

Constructions of femininity represented in participants' accounts sometimes resonated with the image of women as whores or jezebels. Some participants distinguished between archetypes of the "good" (the Madonna) and the "bad" (the jezebel) woman. Women admitted that their partners often attempted to attach the latter image to them, which they rejected in their talk on identity. They also support the notion of the "bad" woman with loose sexual morals as a form of contrast to their articulations of personal identity. In the examples that follow, both men and women privilege an idea of a virtuous femininity as the ideal to which all women should aspire. Participants sometimes used women's attire as a marker of particular kinds of gender performances, with some pointing to women's dress sense as a signifier of loose sexual morals. Consequently, they advocated modesty in dress for women as an appropriate gender performance. In addition to sexual practices, the idea of the villainous woman is exemplified as an effect of women's participation in taboo socio-religious practices in their attempt to control men. Participants viewed such practices as a means through which women usurped power in intimate relationships.

In the first example, Lionel describes the views about women that emerged from conversation with his male friends:

Interviewer: When you'll talk about women, what exactly would you say?

Lionel: Well, sometimes it could be a good story about woman. {mm hmm} I mean sometimes we don't really want [to] call woman bad because we love them, but sometimes definitely there are some girls you have to talk about and say you don't like how she's dealing with a man because it's not easy sometimes to see a man going out to work in the hot sun and she's there home and when he gone, you see, you call in another man to give you a work out [i.e., to have sex with you], and the man that['s] home now you playing you ain't want me touch you and them kind o' stuff, and it's not right. It's not right. You think it's easy you working in the hot sun, you come home back, you cussing the man and all them kind o' things, behind the man['s] back and the man still have to turn around and give you money. You must talk about them things. Some people don't like when we talk about it, but if she's wrong, she's wrong.

As he describes his conversations with his friends, Lionel draws on notions of the bad woman, that is, the whore or jezebel. He attempts to tap into a sense of morality as he presents a hypothetical scenario in which a man goes out to work, only to have another man visit his partner to engage in sexual intercourse. The terminology he uses to refer to sexual activity, "give you a work out", creates a subordinate subject position for women in relation to men because of its objectifying effect. Sexual intercourse is treated as something "done" to women; when "done" with a man other than one's partner, it represents a form of bodily defilement. What is more, the woman in Lionel's scenario refuses to acquiesce to her partner's sexual requests, in spite of his hard work as breadwinner. In this story Lionel constructs the female partner as the villain, and her industrious, long-suffering partner as the victim. There is an overall sense that this situation is a common occurrence in intimate relationships, making men a target for this sort of victimization and, by extension, emasculation. Although Lionel says that he and his friends sometimes discuss "a good story about woman", he opts to centre his talk on an anecdote about a "bad" woman. It is important to mention that, in reference to women, the word "bad" in Vincentian parlance is synonymous with whore, bitch or jezebel. It suggests that a woman has loose sexual morals, or that she is promiscuous. Lionel deploys the man-as-provider discourse as he depicts a hard-working man engaging in manual labour in order to provide for his family. The level of the man's commitment is emphasized in his reference to the man labouring in "the hot sun". The way he tells the story seems to convey the impression that he identifies with those men who have been "wronged" by their female partners.

Other participants' interviews focused, in greater detail, on how rationalizations of violence are often linked to the discourse on a villainous femininity. Men described being provoked into violence because of women's (presumed) infidelity. And women, in fact, outlined various forms of violence and controlling practices meted out to them because their partners believed they were having intercourse outside of their relationships. By their actions, the men point to a need to suppress women's perceived proclivity for sex, and they sometimes use women's style of dress as a measure of these supposed desires. In his discussion of his partner's view of herself as a woman, Lance talks about changes in Linda's sense of dress: "Before, the kind o' clothes she used to wear, like of late now she start wearing some pieces o' pants going down the road now. She was even leaving home without underwear." The act of leaving home without underwear signifies, in Lance's view, a change in his partner's moral purview. He alludes to a loss of respectability and her subsequent (suspected) infidelity. The regulation of women's dress thus becomes one of the many practices used to police femininity in an effort to maintain respectability among women while at the same time affirming hegemonic masculine performances.

In the interviews, the idea of the "bad" or villainous woman sometimes revealed other socio-cultural and socio-religious discourses. Participants alluded to women's involvement with proscribed rituals in order to control men in intimate relationships. In the following excerpt, Bruce describes the traits of a bad woman:

> I have a friend. He would have to stay home with the baby and she gone party, party, and he can't say anything. You would tell him that you see her such and such and what he would do now is to go and he would tell her what you say. He's already addicted. He would go and tell her, "Boy, Bruce, Bruce tell me blah, blah, blah", so not even if I see my brother['s] girlfriend or my good friend['s] girlfriend anywhere messing around I would say anything. I would just leave them. I don't have nothing to say again.

Bruce distances himself from the image of the bad woman, who can embarrass a man by acting outside of the boundaries that dictate culturally acceptable gender norms. These kinds of unconventional practices have an emasculating effect. The idea of his friend staying at home with the baby departs completely from the conventional symbol of a good woman as nurturer/carer. Also, the public sphere is often defined as reserved for men's recreation. Bruce's account draws on a popular discourse that speaks of the wiles of women as they engage mystical or magical powers to trap men. It is a popular belief in Vincentian society that men can be trapped by women's use of obeah – hence Bruce's statement that his friend was "already addicted". Interestingly, the reverse (a man's use of obeah) does not obtain, since trickery is usually associated with the image of the jezebel, the manipulative woman. This idea appears to be an assumed extension of women's inherent deceit, which men ought to curb. Collins describes obeah as "an Afro-Caribbean practice that utilizes herbal remedies, possession by ancestral spirits or African-based deities, and diagnosis or divination through trancework . This practice is used not only to cure physical illnesses or wounds but also to work out (or intensify) social problems" (1995, 147). It exists as a form of magical spiritualism and is believed to possess the ability to alter biological, economic or socio-cultural relations (ibid.). I grew up hearing about people who had visited the village obeah man or woman for sinister reasons. Although works have emerged which try to shore up the socio-cultural value of these practices, the dominant idea about obeah is that it exists in the realm of witchcraft and sorcery and that only those with malicious intent engage in such practices. When Bruce says "he's already addicted", it means that his friend has fallen prey to trickery, he has been emasculated, he is at the whim of his partner, and he cannot be trusted to deal with his partner in a way that would redeem his manhood.

Like Bruce, Yvette distances herself from these practices. She labels actions deemed to be attempts by women to control their partners as having sinister origins. She says, "I never hit him because I don't want anybody to say I'm controlling him and I give him things to eat and all those things, 'cause you done know once a woman doing all them things to man, they usually say that, well, that the man stupidy [i.e., foolish] and all those sorts o' things." She suggests that her reason for not using violence against her partner is that she does not want to be identified as a woman who controls a man. Yvette implicates a vile femininity in much the same way Bruce does in his talk. She suggests that the kind of woman who hits her partner with no fear of reprisal possesses a power derived from some sinister force. Yvette subscribes to a particular socio-religious worldview that is partly responsible for shaping her views on women's and men's places in the context of the family and relationships. Next, she describes men as heads of households, based on the laws of God. She uses this notion, along with a socio-religious and cultural discourse on Obeah as witchcraft and trickery, to explain how some women use evil forces to derive power over men in relationships. She implicitly presents this kind of "evil" as the cause of changes in a putative natural order between men and women. Her statement "I don't want anybody to say I'm controlling him and I give him things to eat" refers to a popular belief in Vincentian society that the so-called obeah man or woman can perform rituals and prepare potions which women can give to men in their food. This action, in turn, gives women the power to control their partners, keeping them committed forever to these relationships. These kinds of practices are felt to rob men of their "naturally" dominant identities, while at the same time emphasizing women's putative capacity for evil.

On Being a Man

Ideas about men's identity in participants' accounts tend to endorse traditional discourses on gender. The most common theme emerging from these accounts is that of men as providers. This theme features in the accounts of both women and men, with varying levels of support and rejection. The section which follows, on power in relationships, will explore the extent to which the provider motif is used to justify asymmetrical relations of power. The current section, however, begins the discussion of the meanings of these narratives for understanding particular gendered practices. Other, albeit conventional, scripts on gender also define masculinities. These scripts include ideas about men's entitlement to freedom to navigate between domestic and social spaces, the naturalization of men's presumably higher sex drive relative to women's, and the image of men as the protectors of their partners.

In the following dialogue, Ricky points to a man's decision to take responsibility in the context of the family as a defining moment in becoming a man:

Interviewer: What does it, for you, what does it mean to be a man?

Ricky: What it means for me to be a man?

Interviewer: Mm hmm.

Ricky: Let me see now. Let me see how to put it. [He laughs.] Responsibility. {mm hmm} That is one. Most of all, you have to take in life. I used to move a kind o' lackadaisical towards that. Sometimes when you and your friends having a nice time, sometimes you does go overboard, and forget that you have family values to take care of. I would admit that I'm wrong on them things. Yeah, I used to move lackadaisical towards my responsibility.

Ricky mentions the importance of taking responsibility as the defining principle of his manhood. He contrasts the responsibility of looking after one's family with the nonchalant existence of having a good time with friends. Portrayals of gender are by no means monolithic. There are two competing archetypes of masculinity here. Ricky advocates a masculinity based on the notions of responsibility and good family values, while at the same time lamenting an indifferent or "lackadaisical" masculinity based on the principles of freedom, personal autonomy and few restrictions. There is a sense in which he has the choice to determine which of these scripts of gender he should assume. His decision to set aside the latter implies a process of self-realization, of maturing and of becoming a man by relinquishing boyish things.

Floyd's beliefs about men's identity resonate with popular cultural narratives on the possible fallout when men fail to fulfil their obligations as providers. His response to the question about the meaning of manhood is below:

> Interviewer: What do you think it means to be a man?
>
> Floyd: Well, you have to take responsibility. You can't expect somebody else to do it for you. If you have children, you have to take care of them. If you not working, you find yourself in a lot o' trouble because if you sit down and don't go look for work and ain't go do anything, you girlfriend would get tired o' that and – Let me put it this way: You would find she would butt you [i.e., she would cheat on you]. Any woman would butt you because you would find that she ain't got anything to go by, no money and so on, so she would butt you. Your children, you need to look up to your children as they look up to you because it's like you can't sit down and watch your children hungry and you yourself hungry and everybody just watching one another in their faces.

Floyd cites the significance of the provider motif in the construction of his gendered self. Not fulfilling this role could lead to, in his view, his partner's infidelity. He explains that the role of provider is a societal expectation. For him, women's infidelity is justified when men fail to satisfy this obligation. These principles are often reproduced in calypso music – an important musical tradition emerging within Caribbean societies whose roots can be traced back to plantation society and the enslaved peoples. One song that became popular in the early 2000s is "You Looking fuh Horn", rendered by Trinidadian calypsonian the Mighty Shadow. The word "horn" is used in the Caribbean to refer to a person's experience when his or her partner has been unfaithful. In St Vincent and the Grenadines, the terms "horn" and "butt" are used interchangeably. Below are excerpts from the song:

> You working? No.
> You joking? No.
> You stealing? No.
> You dealing? No.
>
> You looking for horn.
> Plenty, plenty horn, boy.
> You looking for horn.
> You want to get horn, boy.
>
> Why you want to marry?
> You don't have no money.
> You ain't working no way [i.e., nowhere].
> You don't have a payday.
>
> . . . . . .
>
> Without money to buy honey
> You heading for misery.
> She want hairdo and callaloo [a green, leafy vegetable used in Caribbean cuisine]
> And you ain't have nutten [i.e., nothing].
>
> Somebody will horn you,
> You better believe it.
> Somebody will horn you.
> I hope you could take it, partner [i.e., friend]

There are obvious parallels between the sentiment of this song and Floyd's response. The boy in the song is cautioned about his decision to marry because he is unemployed. Besides the noticeable reference to men as providers, the song portrays women as expecting men's support. The writer alludes to the emasculation that results from being "horned": "I hope you could take it, partner." In the late 1990s the Vincentian soca/calypso band Touch released a song entitled "Man Can't Tek [Take] Butt" in which they poked fun at men's feelings of emasculation when they believe their partners are unfaithful. They cite a range of men's responses to being "horned", including suicide and mental illness. Both of these calypso songs encompass Floyd's ideas on manhood.

Calypsonians try to capture an array of social and political views, as well as popular beliefs within the contexts of Caribbean societies (Rohlehr 2004). Both the songs and Floyd's account exemplify the pull of the discourse of men as providers in the construction of masculinities. Women's infidelity is considered to have a destabilizing effect on men's identities.

Women sometimes support the traditional scripting of gender in which men's identity and power are based on the idea of men as providers; for example, Yvette's views on what it means to be a man. She says:

> Well, seeing that he's around a woman, he does a lot o' things, a lot o' things. He would buy Kentucky. He would buy clothes, you know. He would do different things, but sometimes he would, like, nail up things in the home when he in a good mood, otherwise he would mostly want to pay somebody. I does tell him you don't pay, you don't pay people to do things because there are times men would pay people to do things in their house and the men end up with their wife, you understand. You have to learn to do things in you[r] home as a man, so that your children could see you doing things and they could in turn join with you, and be able to come up to be along with you.

Yvette identifies two markers of masculinity. First, she positions her partner as the family's provider, and she defines this position as a man's obligation to his partner. The second marker has to do with a man's duty to perform masculinity in a particular way that could project an image of him as an exemplar for his children, particularly of the man who does repairs on his home. Yvette attaches great value to this function, arguing that men who avoid performing what she presents as male-oriented duties are in fact inviting other men to replace them as patriarchs. Importantly, she makes certain demands of her partner in the domestic sphere. She presents these demands as a sort of masculine performance that reminds women of their partners' self-worth, value and success at being men. They also serve to reinforce the gendered division of labour in which men and boys are usually assigned outdoor chores, as well as home repair work. Later in the interview, Yvette says:

> I find they [men] should be able to have certain respect for their children so people could see that and at least you would usually work and bring home a dollar and so, but with the women . . . they looking for them to be in the home all the time, if you go out it's a problem and all them kind o' things. I find that a woman should have the same rights as a man, as long as she's not doing anything that is wrong, like to

disrespect or like to break the relationship, like to butt him or anything, I find she should have the right to go when she want to go because if I can't tell you not to go, how you want to tell me not to go?

There are competing voices in this particular example from Yvette. In the first instance she deploys a traditional discourse on masculinity in which she positions men as role models for their children and as breadwinners within families. There is also an expectation that women allow their partners freedom of movement between domestic and social spaces. She then engages an egalitarian discourse and declares that men and women should have equal rights, but these rights come with particular conditions. She advocates that freedom of movement be granted to women who are faithful in their relationships. The same condition is not mentioned for men in relationships. In Mohammed's explication of "the essentialist contouring of gender", she remarks that "the gender system has recurrently relegated the activities and lives of men and women into two ideologically separate spheres: that of the male to a public realm and that of the female to the private and domestic domain" (2002, xiv–xv). This might explain why men's freedom to pursue public/social activities is normalized in Yvette's account as a right bequeathed to all men. Yvette, however, rejects the constant tying of women to the home in her call for women's freedom to pursue their own public recreational activities. Her account touches on the idea that public spaces provide opportunities for women to be unfaithful, thus compromising their respectability and damaging their partners' reputations. This notion helps to contextualize her inclusion of a caveat to women's pursuit of autonomy as they attempt to navigate the supple boundaries of public and private spaces.

"Who *Is* the Man"? Arrangements of Power in Intimate Relationships

It is important to consider participants' interpretations of the question "Would you say that one of you was in charge or head of the relationship/household?" Some persons interpreted the idea of headship as holding onto or conceding power, the overall power dynamics within relationships. The original intent of the question was to elicit these meanings. Some participants, however, focused on the management of the household in terms of planning the family's activities, preparing meals and doing other general household chores. The latter interpretation meant that women were sometimes identified as leaders, whereas the former interpretation positioned men as heads of the household. Most participants identified one partner as the head of the family or relationship. Men were generally positioned as heads of relationships. Discourses on their responsibilities as the main breadwinners mainly supported this idea. Counter-hegemonic discourses in which egalitarian values were articulated sometimes complicated this schema.

Women deployed the archetype of provider or breadwinner, although it is traditionally associated with men, as a measure of their entitlement to greater power in their relationships. The dominance of the discourse of men as providers and women as homemakers is incompatible with the realities of a wide cross section of Caribbean people. Barriteau (2001) reminds us that, historically, Caribbean women have utilized a number of strategies to survive economic and other hardships, and the extent to which women are involved in various sectors of Caribbean economies is often missed. This point is echoed by Hodge (2002, 474), who explains that the tradition of the male-as-breadwinner, often presented as a universal historical legacy of nations, does not readily apply to the Caribbean, where "breadwinners are both male and female".[5] That so many participants engaged this narrative is, in part, a reflection of the resilience of colonialist discourse, which places great value on Victorian ideals of the family. Both women and men position women as the heads of their families, identifying women's superior organizational skills as the rationale for women's leadership. In some cases they engaged narratives which normalize men's authority by implicating religious discourses that have the effect of naturalizing men's power in relation to women.

The archetype of breadwinner is the most significant attribute that is used to assign power to individuals in intimate relationships. In this binary scripting of gender, the idea of the family's breadwinner has been historically linked to male bodies, with paid work accorded greater value than domestic duties. In some situations, however, in which women are the only partners involved in paid work, these women position themselves as heads of households. Some respondents described women as leaders in the home based on organizational skills, but they hardly ever spoke of women in positions of authority or influence outside of these limited spheres. In some instances men lamented what, in their view, is their partners' attempt to usurp men's putative authority, a position exemplified by the quotation from Lionel cited at the beginning of this chapter.

In situations in which women were positioned as the persons in charge of their relationships, this idea was sometimes linked to women's earning power. This is the case in Giselle's explanation of why she considers herself the person in charge of her relationship:

> Interviewer: Would you say that one of you was in charge of the relationship?
>
> Giselle: I was in charge of everything.
>
> Interviewer: Why you say that?
>
> Giselle: Because I spending the money. If he was spending the money he would've been like, you know what I mean, head, but he doesn't care whether he's spending money or not. He just wants to be a bully, but he can't be a bully.

Giselle positions herself as the person in charge of the relationship because she provides the financial needs of the family. She criticizes what, in her view, is her partner's refusal to engage in paid work. Authority in the relationship is centred on one's ability to provide the family's financial sustenance. Her account creates a paradox because, while she engages in a conventional discourse that centres on the notion of power residing with the breadwinner, her response seems to be counter-hegemonic at first glance, as there appears to be no implication that the provider archetype is aligned with anatomically male bodies. She suggests, however, that, had her partner been earning money for the family, she would have conceded headship. The statement has the effect of normalizing asymmetrical relations of power in which men are privileged as leaders so long as they assume the responsibility of being providers.

Participants sometimes positioned women as the ones in charge of the home, based on their involvement in housework. This is not to be confused with articulations of power based on the couples' decision-making practices. Betty's comments exemplify these arrangements. There is, however, a sense in which she positions her partner as the overall authority figure because of his responsibility as provider of the family's financial needs:

> Interviewer: And would you say that one of you is in charge, or head of the relationship or head of the family?
>
> Betty: Like?

Interviewer: Head of the family?

Betty: The home?

Interviewer: Yeah.

Betty: Me.

Interviewer: Why would you say that?

Betty: Because I am the woman. I'm supposed to be responsible for everything in the home.

Interviewer: But in terms of the relationship and the family, who you think is head of the house?

Betty: The man is to be the head of the house.

Interviewer: Why do you say that?

Betty: Because they are the ones who are working and bringing in things in the home so they're supposed to be the head of the house.

In terms of power in the relationship, she separates responsibility for domestic duties from providing the family's financial needs. In this division of labour and/or power, she positions her partner as head of the household and assigns greater significance to paid work. She uses conventional discourses on gender to explain what it means to be a man and what it means to be a woman. In explaining why she names herself as head of the household she endorses a masculinist discourse which naturalizes men's power as a by-product of their traditional responsibility as providers. Implicitly, she attributes housework a secondary status to paid work. The former is also normalized as women's work. Betty's narrative reinscribes those binary arrangements of gender in which men's dominance in relationships is both naturalized and normalized.

In the next example Chantal describes a paradoxical situation in which she presents herself as the person in charge of the relationship, but explains that she was limited in her capacity to exercise autonomy because of her partner's extreme methods of control:

Interviewer: OK. At the time when you'll were living together, would you say one of you was in charge of the relationship?

Chantal: Well, me. He wasn't in charge of it because he didn't care. All he wanted a woman to do was when he wanted sex, and when he wanted his clothes washed and something to eat.

> Interviewer: Did you feel like he was bossing you around?
>
> Chantal: Yes. He didn't even want me to go by my mom['s], and my mom lived in Deacons and I lived in Atkins. He didn't want me to go cross to where my mother was living. My mother never even used to come to visit me. It's now that my mother comes to visit me.

Chantal situates herself as the one in charge because her partner was unconcerned about issues related to the relationship. In her view, he considered women objects for his own sexual gratification, and as necessary caretakers. Even though she identifies herself as head of the relationship, the implication of her response is that power resides with him to dictate the roles that she ought to fulfil. Thus her position as head does not convey ideas about personal autonomy. Later in the interview, she goes on to describe her partner's extreme forms of control over her movement between the home and public spaces. His restrictions on her freedom of movement indicate the extent to which he exercised authority in the relationship.

Conventional gender norms dominate men's accounts about identities and power. There is a tendency to engage in essentialist discourses in order to describe the arrangements of power within intimate relationships. In the following excerpt, Lenny draws on two discourses of gender and power:

> Interviewer: I just want go back to something because you were saying that you're the head of the household. Could you just explain that to me? What does this mean?
>
> Lenny: Well, actually, I'm responsible. I'm responsible for her. She's away from her mother, so anything she has to look to, anytime she's in trouble, if she's in trouble with the police it's me. I'm the one who['s] working. I'm the one who's bringing in the finances. I'm the one who's providing for the kids, for them to go school, preschool and stuff like that, making sure they ain't go hungry, making sure to leave money home, food home so they ain't have to go to beg any neighbour or anything like that, so I have a very hard responsibility to fulfil, but I intend to do it, eh.

Lenny is assertive about his function in this relationship. His masculine performance draws on two different, yet equally conventional, archetypes of manhood. First, there is the idea of men as protectors or guardians of their partners and families. He presents himself as assuming the role of his partner's parent now that she is in a relationship with him. Girls shift from being subordinate to their parents to being subordinate to their partners. The second archetype is one which features in the accounts of both men and women –

the idea of men as breadwinners. He emphasizes his importance as provider by cataloguing his obligations. There is an overall sense of the enormity associated with the myriad financial responsibilities he undertakes. The emphasis on his role as provider would appear to suggest that this is the more significant of the two roles in support of his position as head of the household.

Participants often stated men's power as a biological fact. Dominant discourses on masculinities focused on men's right to rule as a consequence of history, religion and culture. These beliefs reinforce the difficulties associated with challenging patriarchal norms. The following examples demonstrate the normalization of men's power in speech:

> Interviewer: Who would you say is the head of the household or the relationship?
>
> Eve: The head?
>
> Interviewer: Yeah.
>
> Eve: Well, I have to say him because he is the man. [She laughs.]
>
> Interviewer: Could you explain that to me?
>
> Eve: I say so because you have to say he is the head. I can't head over him.
>
> Interviewer: And why you say so?
>
> Eve: Because I always say that the house belongs to him and I can't rule over him in his own house.

Eve draws on a conventional discourse on gender which has the effect of supporting patriarchal relations. She identifies her partner as head of the household "because he is the man". There is a tacit understanding of men's power to rule households based on an assumed natural order of things. To rule over him is read as an attempt to usurp power. Power also comes as an effect of his ownership of the house they occupy. The implication here is that she has to know her place in his house or risk displacement.

Similarly, Cheryl positions her partner as head of the household by offering religious support for his status:

> Interviewer: Would you say that one of you is the head of the family or household?
>
> Cheryl: Well, I always say the man is to be the head of the family. I can't discredit him or demote him from that.
>
> Interviewer: Why, why?

> Cheryl: Because biblically that is it, so I leave that to him. You supposed to be the head of the family. If you instruct I would follow your instruction.

Cheryl deploys a patriarchal discourse based on religious ideas in which she proclaims that the man is head of the household. She implies that she never seeks to unsettle this arrangement. Her talk is performative of the notion of the obedient wife who follows the laws of God by deferring to her husband. The discourses which support men's authority are myriad. From the traditional narratives of men as breadwinners to locating men's power within the context of a biological script on gender, both men's and women's accounts support asymmetrical relations of power.

Some men in the study also share the view of men's natural place as heads of their families. Colin declares that all men are head of households. He implies that being a man is a privileged existence because of the wisdom and power associated with it:

> Interviewer: For you, what do think it means to be a man?
>
> Colin: It's good because if you check it out a man is a leader in every household, and as a man, the same way you want the other individual to give you respect you have to give them respect and take care around the house so things could work. See, that is living happy. Make sure they eat and drink and every thing is well, you know. Sometimes you take the garbage outside and throw it away and things like that. Keep around the yard clean and things like that. But it's good, good when you are a man.

Colin's answer has the effect of normalizing men's power. He engages in a discourse of men's roles in the context of the household by endorsing a division of labour in which men are responsible for performing the chores outside of the physical structure of the house – keeping those areas tidy. Men are expected to do the gardening and keep the yard clean, that is, the more labour intensive tasks. This statement is comparable to Yvette's ideas that a man should complete jobs around the house to ensure that he protects his home and partner from other men. Colin suggests that women are incapable of doing some of the things that men do, and that men have knowledge that only they possess. For him, it is important that men impart wisdom and display leadership to ensure the successful functioning of the family unit. This leadership is defined as a quality possessed only by men as rational beings.

These direct articulations of power were a feature of several men's accounts. Sometimes participants stated them as if to correct the researcher's apparent ignorance regarding interpersonal relations. This was the case when I interviewed Andrew:

> Interviewer: Who would you say is the head of the relationship? Who's in charge?
>
> Andrew: The head. I am the head. Come on. [He chuckles.] I am the man. No other man can't come in my place, that is all I know. Since I name man, nobody can't run things other than me.

Andrew's expectation is that I should have known the answer to this obvious question. The statement "Come on" and his subsequent chuckle signals his disappointment in my lack of understanding of human relations. It is almost as if he is surprised both by the question and my lack of knowledge. This response also indicates that, for Andrew, men's power is something natural, a privilege bequeathed to all men as a consequence of their biology: "The head. I am the head. I am the man." This articulation of a masculinist/macho discourse normalizes the idea of power as residing with men. Andrew expresses readiness to defend his authority in the event of any challenges from another man. Inadvertently, he suggests that although another man might attempt to challenge his authority, it is inconceivable that a woman might attempt to do the same. Andrew's talk is performative of a dominant masculinity in which he reproduces ideas about men's natural right to have dominion over their households. The naturalization of men's power is exemplified by the overall sentiment of his response that such power "goes without saying". No explanation is required; it just *is*.

Ideas about the distribution of power were often anchored in different discourses in which participants shifted between patriarchal and egalitarian values. Lenny's example, featured below, shows how separate and sometimes contradictory positions inform people's ideas about identity:

> We know that men are the head of the home, but really and truly, if, if you have a balance, if you and – I wouldn't really want be above my girlfriend. I wouldn't want to be above my wife. I would want to be equal, but if a decision is to be made we would use the best one out of the both of us. If her ideas are better than mine I would use her idea instead of my idea. It would be easier. It would be cheaper and we don't have to get any hassle at all. {OK} It wouldn't be any hassle at all.

Lenny's account has the effect of normalizing the notion of men as heads of their households, which he presents as a transcendental truth. Cloaked in an egalitarian discourse on gender is an understanding that, ultimately, decision-making power rests with men. He talks about wanting equality or balance with his partner but, paradoxically, his position of authority is reinforced by the statement "If her ideas are better than mine, I would use her ideas instead of mine." The decision about whose ideas are best within a given situation ultimately resides with him.

Gendered Constructions of Love

In the main, respondents presented dominant portrayals of romantic love to describe either their feelings towards their partners or the scenario of an ideal relationship. For some, love acts as a cohesive force which sustains relationships. Participants often discussed decisions to remain within or to end a relationship in the context of love between partners. Some participants problematized the traditional stereotypes of romantic love and rejected the prototypical forms of heterosexual relationships. The suggestion here is that discourses on romantic love coexist with traditional beliefs about gender and, in this sense, have implications for the experiences of individuals in the context of intimate relationships.

Regina discusses love by describing what women need in a relationship. In her explanation she draws on cultural constructions of love as an emotion. She says:

> Sometimes we as woman need a companion in love, someone to give you hugs and kisses, you know, someone to make you feel like a woman, make you feel appreciated. The other thing is, when you live with someone and you see their ways, you do try to cope. I never butt [i.e., cheat on] him or anything, you know, but it was too much. I feel so free, like a weight is off my shoulder. Sometimes I come home, I used to have to be cooking, bathe my children, cleaning. If you see the amount o' work I used to have to do in the little time I come from work. By 8:00, I'm tired. No appreciation. Some men don't show any appreciation for woman, none whatsoever, and the kind o' words he used to use to me, oh my God, how my "this yah" [she does not want to repeat the word her partner was supposed to have used to refer to her vagina, so instead she uses the phrase "this yah"] stink, and when the night comes he used to want to tell me how he's sorry. He was angry. It's not an easy, it

wasn't easy . . . You see, he is a guy like this, he don't know how to show love. He's not compassionate. He's not passionate. It's just sex and go to sleep. If you show him love he takes advantage of you.

Regina ties notions of romantic love, companionship, the heterosexual union and their associated practices – hugs and kisses – to ideas about gender. In her view, femininity is affirmed when a man engages in these kinds of practices. She uses her fidelity to explain why her partner's maltreatment of her was unconscionable. She explains that her hard work in satisfying the role of housewife – cooking, cleaning and taking care of the children – was not rewarded by any outward show of his affection. In fact, the ideals of love she describes are not realized in her relationship with her partner. His actions are presented as antithetical to her views on love. She presents him as unreasonable, uncompassionate and unable to show love – "it's just sex and go to sleep". Regarding her feelings, there are overtones of a kind of bodily defilement. "Just sex" has a reductive resonance. It is not part of the vocabulary of romantic love. "Just sex" implicates the other half of a binary, that is, "making love or love-making". Her depiction of how love ought to be performed draws from the archetype of the chivalrous lover that appears in many popular romantic fictional novels and films.

Cheryl distinguishes between women's and men's approaches to each other within intimate relationships. She argues that women tend to be more aware of their partners' emotional needs than men:

> A woman needs to be loved, not to be taken advantage of, not to be underestimated. Like I was telling Mrs Smith [the counsellor] yesterday, when a woman would take the time to learn about her partner, to pinpoint every little aspect about him, a man will not take the time to know his. He will just see her there to cook, wash, iron, supply his bedroom needs, and that's it. {Mm hmm.} As long as he gets what he wants, that's it, but to think about what she wants, they don't take time to do that.

Cheryl believes that there is a significant difference between men's and women's actions in relationships. She contends that women are more attuned to the emotional needs of their partners, observing and noting all of their idiosyncrasies. She rejects a functionalist discourse in which men consider women necessary in a utilitarian sense. Instead, she alludes to an ideal love as a human need that all women share, reinforcing a heteronormative discourse that values the intimate heterosexual union as a necessary part of women's lives. A binary view of gender is articulated in this account, which presents women as sensitive and compassionate, and men as domineering and brutish.

The idea of unrequited love featured in some men's accounts. They talked about the loss of love, while others referred to experiencing the pretensions of love. Randy explains his perpetration of violence as a consequence of the latter:

> OK, if I meet a, I just met a girl, right, and she is a woman that, OK, you just meet a guy and you want to have sex and that is it. If they do that to me I will feel bad because I had a girl who did that to me already and I actually end up hitting her. Her boyfriend was sailing and she met me and told me that she liked me, and stuff like that. She used me to have sex. She used to always come by my place, you know, always want it, you know, and when her boyfriend coming back now she had the nerve to tell me her boyfriend was sailing and he's coming back. So I felt hurt. If somebody just come and tell you that and you love that person and you doing anything for them, what would be your reaction? First things first, my reaction was like "yeah right" because I didn't believe she would do that to me, and then she told me that she was serious, and then afterwards I saw her crying so, you know, so I know it was the truth, so I snap right there, so I end up, I hit her and she ran out.

Randy describes a situation of nonreciprocal love. He justifies his use of violence as a consequence of his feelings of being used and deceived: "She used me to have sex." His discussion is atypical insofar as he presents a situation in which the body objectified is a male body. There is an overall impression of his emasculation implied by the realization that his declaration of love was in vain. He engages in the traditional language on love as he asks rhetorically, "If somebody just come and tell you that and you love that person and you doing anything for them, what would be your reaction?" The question functions as a persuasive device intended to convince the listener about the power of love, and it serves as a rationalization of his so-called loss of control and subsequent violent reaction. Love means doing "anything for a person", or, according to Angie, "giving your all". These statements exist as part of the vocabulary of love in which the notion of self-sacrifice is presented as a prerequisite of love.

In the next example, Lance conflates ideas about men as providers with the notion of being in love: "The first time we were together everything was fine, you know. I was there. I was supplying everything she needed and I don't know if she was expecting more of me or what, but, you know, in relationships people get fed up o' people and I think that was it. She wasn't in love after a while." Constructions of love intersect with ideas about gender in this example. Lance talks about taking care of his partner's needs before the relationship had ended, but he suggests that what he provided may not have been sufficient to satisfy her. This response is contrary to his partner's claim that she was the family's sole provider. His version suggests that she expected him to perform the role of breadwinner, and he presents himself as complying with this role, particularly when he says, "I was supplying everything she needed." Implicitly he suggests that providing for his partner is a way of demonstrating love – the materiality of love. He suggests, however, that there was a loss of love in the relationship. He juxtaposes the idea of being in love, which points to a state of happiness and contentment, with his partner's loss of love. Lance rationalizes her loss of love as a result of her displeasure with his ability to function as breadwinner.

In the context of violent relationships, some female participants depicted love as a barrier that prevented them from leaving their partners. Chantal describes how she remained in her relationship with her partner because she loved him. She explains, however, that once she had ended the relationship her partner continued to harass and threaten her. Her description of these experiences is indicative of broader narratives on the nexus between romantic love and violence:

> Chantal: He was calling my phone, he was calling my fiancé's phone and telling my fiancé how he would come up here and chop him up and he would go on his workplace and do him all sorts of things.
>
> Interviewer: He would do what?
>
> Chantal: He would go on his work and do him what he has to do him if he's not giving me up.
>
> Interviewer: What does that mean, if he not –
>
> Chantal: Kill him, lash him and tell him if he can't have me, if he, Larry, can't have me, ahm, Richard can't have me, Juliet and Romeo. He would kill me, kill himself and kill Richard . . . When his mother found out he does abuse me she came down and told me to leave him and tell him to leave her home. {Mm hmm.} But I couldn't send him away. When you love somebody it doesn't matter what they do. You like you blind to the love. You can't see it and that was [how it was] with me. It didn't

matter what Larry did to me, and people told me to leave him, even my mother. It was just like I, it was going through this ear and coming through the next [i.e., she was not heeding the advice].

Chantal deploys the tragedy of Shakespeare's *Romeo and Juliet* in her declaration of fatal love. She presents her ex-partner as engaging narratives of romantic love in which unrequited love precipitated the threat of a murder-suicide. This narrative also positions Chantal as an object he possessed: "If he, Larry, can't have me, ahm, Richard can't have me . . . Juliet and Romeo." Later in the interview she presents love as having a powerful, hypnotic influence that prevents her from heeding the advice of family and friends. She uses the idealized narrative of romantic love, particularly the notions that love is blind, that love endures or that love has the effect of veiling its victims, to explain why she remained for so long in this violent relationship. It is love that impaired her judgement. Jackson contends that "the classical romantic love narrative reinforces the fusion of love and violence" (2001, 307). In other words, narratives of romantic love can have debilitating effects for women, who often rationalize their decision to remain in violent relationships as a consequence of being in love.

Conclusion

Women and men deployed a range of narratives that drew on culturally available explanatory frameworks as they constructed gendered selves in these accounts. Although participants' talk often reinscribed binary understandings of gender, there were a few instances of subversive speech. Discourses of femininity – almost always tied to female bodies – often resonated with traditional narratives which valued some forms over others. There was a privileging of depictions of women as mothers, carers and workers (for paid work); housework was usually defined as women's work. Although some men tended to liken their partners to images of the "bad woman" – read: whore/jezebel – women always resisted these characterizations. Participants' often presented respectability as a 'virtue' idiosyncratic of a celebrated femininity, with men pointing to a loss of respectability as resulting from women's presumed infidelity.

There were moments when participants countered these kinds of hegemonic discourses on women's identities. Women often articulated notions of self-determination, and sometimes rejected the centrality of the heterosexual union in the construction of self. This was not a case of the subversive versus the traditional woman, however. Individuals usually engaged a combination of conventional, egalitarian and resistant discourses. Participants, particularly men, were more likely to subscribe to conventional views of women's identity, as these views function to justify men's power in relationships. The idea of a transcendental femininity based on socio-religious and biological narratives was quite pervasive in these accounts. Participants often used these ideas to position women as men's subordinates.

The naturalization of men's power in relation to women guaranteed men freedom to navigate across various social spaces. In addition to ideas about men's "true" nature, some respondents used a socio-religious discourse to position men as protectors and providers, notwithstanding Caribbean women's historical involvement in various areas of the labour force and in the general upkeep of their families. Shifts between egalitarian and asymmetrical discourses on gender also featured in discussions of manhood, albeit to a lesser extent than existed in the construction of women's identities. The resilience of the breadwinner motif (a locus of men's power) is, in part, a residual effect of a colonial discourse that values Victorian ideals of the nuclear family. These ideals continue to shape relations of gender in the Caribbean. For some women, men's power resides in their ability to exert forms of coercive, aggressive and violent intimidation and control, which creates boundaries for women and severely curtails their movement between the home and other social spaces.

In addition, participants sometimes used ideas of romantic love, "being in love" and love as a cohesive force to situate men and women in intimate relationships. These notions shaped participants' expectations of their partners. Women felt that they were more attuned to men's needs than men were to women's needs. They often characterized men as domineering and brutish, juxtaposed against descriptions of women as sensitive and compassionate. In this sense love was often defined as a constraining force for women in these intimate unions. Not only is this fact evidenced in instances in which participants presented love as a barrier which prevented women from leaving their abusive partners, but it also explains why some women positioned themselves outside of heteronormative discourses on love.

Throughout this analysis, I have focused on the (re)production of various discourses, archetypes and ideologies of gender in women's and men's talk. Participants' accounts of gender were multiple, with varying degrees of devotion to the traditional dichotomous representations of manhood and womanhood. For the most part, participants subscribed to traditional stereotypes of gender roles within the family, but there were different levels of departure and commitment across any single account. Some participants were more resistant to prototypical accounts of gender than others, and women tended to be more subversive in speech than men. That women were more inclined to resist dominant narratives and practices of gender can be read as an effect of the boundaries of space created for women in the context of relationships characterized by men's violence and other forms of control. Moreover, this resistance is probably emblematic of an overall response to the constraints experienced by women as a consequence of a variety of patriarchal practices. There is need to interrogate the extent to which individuals subscribe to or reject traditional narratives of gender, and embrace egalitarian values in a variety of contexts within and outside of heterosexual unions.

Notes

1. This statement was made by a participant during an interview.
2. It is impossible to capture the diversity of the sign "feminism" and the feminist movement in any brief discussion. Some explanation is required, however, in order to anchor the argument that follows. In a broad sense, feminism signifies, in the words of Weedon, "a politics directed at changing existing power relations between men and women in society", the catalyst for feminist theorizing (1997, 1). Early feminist theories have met with criticism for privileging an all-encompassing, monolithic subject as the face of feminism – Woman – from feminists who argue that "She" is incapable of representing the concerns of women from various social locations (Barriteau 2007; Collins 1991; Lorde 2007; Mama 1989; Mohammed 1998; Mohanty 1988). They argue that the generic "Woman" usually signifies a white, middle-class, Anglo-American female subject. These criticisms have changed the face of contemporary feminist theorizing, as scholars recognize that gender is often, if not always, complicated by other social markers of difference, such as race, class and sexuality. Moreover, contemporary scholars prefer to speak of "feminisms" in order to capture the variation in approaches to feminist theorizing. These variations include radical,

Marxist, liberal, psychoanalytic, standpoint theory, postcolonial and postmodern and/or poststructuralist (the latter two are often conflated) (Elliot and Mandell 1995; Mohanty 1988; Spivak 1998; Tong 1997; Weedon 1997 and 2000), and these are by no means hermetically sealed off from each other.

3.   Agger (1991) differentiates between poststructuralism and postmodernism by arguing that the former is a theory of knowledge and language, while the latter is a theory of society, culture and history.

4.   I wish to convey my sincerest gratitude to the counsellors, police officers, family case workers and senior prison officers who so kindly assisted with this research. I also want to say a very special thanks to all of the women and men who so generously shared their stories, and without whom this research would have been impossible.

5.   According to Hodge (2002), the only women in the Caribbean who might now be entering the workforce are women of the upper echelons of society. She continues to explain that, since the bulk of Caribbean women were brought here from Africa during the slave trade, and later from India during the indentureship period, women first worked as enslaved labourers, then indentured labourers, and later as small farmers, cane cutters, domestic workers, seamstresses, market vendors, inter-island traders, washers, ironers, roadside sellers of food, and child-minders, *inter alia*.

References

Agger, B. 1991. Critical theory, poststructuralism, postmodernism: Their sociological relevance. *Annual Review of Sociology* 17:105–131.

Avdi, E. 2005. Negotiating a pathological identity in the clinical dialogue: Discourse analysis of a family therapy. *Psychology and Psychotherapy: Theory, Research and Practice* 78:493–511.

Barriteau, E. 2001. *The political economy of gender in the twentieth-century Caribbean*. New York: Palgrave.

———. 2003. Requiem for the male marginalization thesis in the Caribbean: Death of a non-theory. In *Confronting power, theorizing gender: Interdisciplinary perspectives in the Caribbean*, ed. E. Barriteau, 322–53. Kingston: University of the West Indies Press.

———. 2007. The relevance of black feminist scholarship: A Caribbean perspective. *Feminist Africa* 7:9–31.

Barrow, C., ed. 1996. *Family in the Caribbean: Themes and perspectives*. Kingston: Ian Randle.

Baxter, J. 2007. *Positioning gender in discourse: A feminist methodology*. Houndmills: Palgrave Macmillan.

Brooker, P. 1999. *A concise glossary of cultural theory*. London: Arnold.

Brown, G., and G. Yule. 1983. *Discourse analysis*. Cambridge: Cambridge University Press.

Butler, J. 1993. *Bodies that matter: On the discursive limits of "sex"*. New York: Routledge.

———. 1990/1999. *Gender trouble: Feminism and the subversion of identity*. New York: Routledge.

———. 2000. Changing the subject: Judith Butler's politics of radical resignification. In *The Judith Butler reader*, ed. S. Salih and J. Butler, 325–56. Oxford: Blackwell.

———. 2004. *Undoing gender*. New York: Routledge.

Collins, P.H. 1991. *Black feminist thought: Knowledge, consciousness, and the politics of empowerment*. New York: Routledge.

Collins, L. 1995. "We shall all heal": Ma Kilmah, the Obeah woman, as mother-healer in Derek Walcott's *Omeros*. *Literature and Medicine* 14 (1): 146–62.

de Saussure, F. 2001. Course in general linguistics. In *The Norton anthology of theory and criticism*, ed. V.B. Leitch et al., 960–77. New York: Norton.

Elliot, P., and N. Mandell. 1995. Feminist theories. In *Feminist issues: Race, class and sexuality*, ed. N. Mandell, 3–31. Scarborough, Ontario: Prentice Hall.

Foucault, M. 1982. The subject and power. *Critical Inquiry* 8 (4): 777–95.

———. 1998. The history of sexuality. In *The critical tradition: Classical texts and contemporary trends*, ed. D.H. Richter, 1472–81. Boston: Bedford Books.

Freedman, J. 2001. *Feminism*. Buckingham: Open University Press.

Gavey, N. 1992. Technologies and effects of heterosexual coercion. *Feminism and Psychology* 2 (3): 325–51.

———. 1997. Feminist poststructuralism and discourse analysis. In *Toward a new psychology of gender: A reader*, ed. M.A. Gergen and S.N. Davis, 49–64. New York: Routledge.

Gill, R. 2000. Discourse analysis. In *Qualitative researching with text, image and sound*, ed. M.W. Bauer and G. Gaskell, 172–90. London: Sage.

Hodge, M. 2002. We kind of family. In *Gendered realities: Essays in Caribbean feminist thought*, ed. P. Mohammed, 474–85. Kingston: University of the West Indies Press.

Jackson, S. 2001. Happily never after: Young women's stories of abuse in heterosexual love relationships. *Feminism and Psychology* 11 (3): 305–21.

Leitch, V.B. 2001. Introduction to theory and criticism. In *The Norton anthology of theory and criticism*, ed. V.B. Leitch et al., 1–28. New York: Norton.

Lindsay, K. 2002. Is the Caribbean male an endangered species? In *Gendered realities: Essays in Caribbean feminist thought*, ed. P. Mohammed, 56–82. Kingston: University of the West Indies Press.

Lorde, A. 2007. *Sister outsider: Essays and speeches*. Berkeley, CA: Crossing.

Mama, A. 1989. *The hidden struggle: Statutory and voluntary sector responses to violence against black women in the home*. London: London Race and Housing Research Unit.

Mohammed, P. 1998. Towards indigenous feminist theorizing in the Caribbean. *Feminist Review* 59 (Summer): 6–33.

———. 2002. Introduction: The material of gender. In *Gendered realities: Essays in*

Caribbean feminist thought, ed. P. Mohammed, xiv–xxi. Kingston: University of the West Indies Press.

———. 2004. Unmasking masculinity and deconstructing patriarchy: problems and possibilities within feminist epistemology. In *Interrogating Caribbean masculinities: Theoretical and empirical analyses*, ed. R. Reddock, 38–67. Kingston: University of the West Indies Press.

Mohanty, C. Talpade. 1988. Under Western eyes: Feminist scholarship and colonial discourses. *Feminist Review* 30 (Autumn): 61–88.

Parsons, T., and R.F. Bales. 1964. *Family: Socialization and interaction process.* London: Routledge and Kegan Paul.

Potter, J. 2003. Discourse analysis and discursive psychology. In *Qualitative research in psychology: Expanding perspectives in methodology and design*, ed. P.M. Camic, J.E. Rhodes and L. Yardley, 1–30. Washington, DC: American Psychology Association.

Reddock, R. 1994. *Women, labour and politics in Trinidad and Tobago: A history.* London: Zed Books.

Rohlehr, G. 2004. I Lawa: The construction of masculinity in Trinidad and Tobago Calypso. In *Interrogating Caribbean masculinities: Theoretical and empirical analyses*, ed. R. Reddock, 326–403. Kingston: University of the West Indies Press.

Rowley, M. 2002. Reconceptualising voice: The role of matrifocality in shaping theories of Caribbean voices. In *Gendered realities: Essays in Caribbean feminist thought*, ed. P. Mohammed, 22–43. Kingston: University of the West Indies Press.

Spivak, G. Chakravorty. 1998. Can the subaltern speak? In *Marxism and the interpretation of culture*, ed. C. Nelson and L. Grossberg, 271–315. Urbana: University of Illinois Press.

Tong, R. 1997. *Feminist thought: A comprehensive introduction.* London: Routledge.

Towns, A., and P. Adams. 2000. "If I really loved him enough, he would be okay": Women's accounts of male partner violence. *Violence against Women* 6 (6): 558–85.

Weedon, C. 1997. *Feminist practice and poststructuralist theory.* 2nd ed. Oxford: Blackwell.

———. 2000. *Feminism, theory and the politics of difference.* Oxford: Blackwell.

PART 3

Gendering Caribbean Civilization, Security and Trade

6

Regional Integration and Caribbean Civilization
Continuing the Debate

JESSICA BYRON

Introduction

A few years ago, the prime minister of St Vincent and the Grenadines reflected at length on the existence of a Caribbean civilization, its function as the underpinning for enhanced regional integration, and the potential for the process of regional integration to advance that civilization further (Gonsalves 2001, 2003, 2006). In his own contribution on the subject, Kirk Meighoo points out the wider societal interest in Caribbean civilization that has been manifested in other statements and publications, as well as the development of an academic curriculum on the subject (Meighoo 2006). This chapter adds to the discussion, a logical one to have arisen in a globalized era in which identities and lifestyles are less stable and are subject to multiple transnational influences and challenges which at times threaten to overwhelm them completely.

I begin by exploring the notion of civilization and the objectives of a discourse on this subject both within the Caribbean itself and more generally. I discuss the term "civilization" together with the terms "culture" and "identity" because the three concepts are closely linked, particularly in the current age. My analysis points out the contradictions inherent in these concepts and the challenges they pose for national and regional communities in the Caribbean. It also identifies some gaps in the contemporary discussion, as it has developed, on Caribbean culture and civilization. In particular, current viewpoints have failed to integrate two central elements, namely, gender perspectives and the impact of migration and diaspora on civilization, citizenship, culture and identity.

Ultimately, I concur with those who feel that the hybrid cultures of the Caribbean are part of a broader Western civilization, despite their unique character derived from diversity and hybridity (Meighoo 2006; James 1962/1992). Nonetheless, Caribbean societies are constantly evolving, propelled by the dynamics of the contestations among their domestic populations and the tensions generated by their interaction with the global community. Although there is not yet an autonomous "Caribbean civilization", there may eventually be one. The debate over Caribbean civilization invites us to examine critically our societies from normative and developmental perspectives in order to consider how we might best influence this evolution. Regional integration may indeed serve as a tool for constructing, directing and strengthening Caribbean societies, and the latter part of this chapter considers past regional integration initiatives. I advocate processes of regional integration that incorporate more flexible interpretations of Caribbean identities and more feminist perspectives on citizenship, and conclude with proposals for some new regional goals and projects.

Civilization, Culture and Identity

Civilization may be defined as "a human society with a complex cultural, political and legal organization", or as "the total culture and way of life of a particular people, nation, region or period" (*Collins Dictionary* 1993). Culture, by contrast, is defined as "the ideas, customs and art produced or shared by a particular society", or as "a particular civilization at a particular time" (ibid.). Emphasizing the overlapping elements of meaning in the two terms, the *Chambers Pocket Thesaurus* (1993) lists culture as "civilization, customs, education, enlightenment, lifestyle, mores", and civilization as "advancement, enlightenment, cultivation, culture, development". I interpret culture as the lifestyle, customs and values of a particular group, while I argue that civilization has a broader connotation. Several distinct cultures which share certain common features may be encompassed within one civilization. In that sense, I concur with the second definition put forward by the *Collins Dictionary*. Meighoo speaks in the same vein but goes further in his claim that "a civilization is often composed of many societies, nations and peoples. But there is usually an identifiable cultural, and often geographic centre . . . A civilization provides for its peoples a primary point of reference and orientation" (Meighoo 2006, 3). Meighoo, in fact, proceeds to argue that the Caribbean is an offshoot of Western civilization rather than an autonomous civilization in its own right. He feels that Caribbean societies are deeply influenced by external centres of authority and are still not fully developed in their national or regional identities, despite their potential to have much greater autonomy (ibid., 3–4). Lloyd Best has followed a similar line of reasoning in his references to "Afro-Saxon" elites in the region (Best 2003).

It is important to explore the terms used above, and to clarify our own understanding of them. Contending civilizations, cultures and identities, both historical and present, are among the main driving forces of international and domestic politics – witness Huntington's controversial paradigm of the "Clash of Civilizations" (Huntington 1993). As Stuart Hall reminds us, "the question of cultural identity [is] at the very centre of the contemporary political agenda" (Hall 2001, 25).

In international relations, a discipline with heavy Eurocentric overtones (Jones 2006), the term "civilization" has traditionally carried much imperial resonance. It has been used to justify colonialism, to establish and maintain hierarchies of peoples and ethnicities, and to determine which ones are entitled to nationhood or citizenship, or to be *bona fide* members of the international community, and which ones should be excluded on the grounds of barbarism.[1] "Civilization" has served to justify all kinds of violations, dispossession, oppression and elimination of other peoples. William Walker (quoted in Salter 2002, 12) writes that "culture, like civilization, becomes something we have, distinguishing us from the barbarians outside . . . the possession of civilization justifies the conquest of barbarism. The possession of civilization is marked by artifacts of culture."

Both Walker and Salter argue that the binary concepts of civilization and barbarism have performed the important function of differentiating between the Self and the Other for European states, thus facilitating the coalescing of a European state system. The term "civilization" therefore often has both a universalizing and an imperialist dimension. It can be used to gloss over many national and cultural differences by enveloping them in a broader identity. Likewise, it is often used as an excluding device, both within societies and internationally. It is a concept at the core of national and international power contests.

One of these dimensions of exclusion relates to women. The Western concept of civilization is imbued with deep patriarchal overtones, a fact that calls for reflection as we situate the Caribbean within the Occident and debate the possibilities for the emergence of a Caribbean-specific civilization. Western philosophical thought has often viewed women as a group that should be subordinated within its civilizational arrangements.[2] Feminist readings of Western political thought point out that, whereas men have traditionally been expected to act as rational beings, women are often held to be incapable of transcending their biological nature, and therefore incapable of making a positive contribution to the institutions and citizenship routines of the public sphere (Pateman 1989; Shanley and Pateman 1991). By this logic, women are best suited to confinement in the private sphere of social existence, where they engage only in reproductive and domestic tasks (Rousseau 1911 and 1968, both quoted in Pateman 1989, 17, 19, 21; Hegel 1949 and 1952, both quoted in Pateman 1989, 17, 20, 21). Ultimately, women are subversive elements at the heart of an ordered, rational, liberal civil society; if given the reins, they can destabilize the entire enterprise. As Freud once expressed it, women are "malcontents . . . in opposition to civilization" (Freud 1961, quoted in Pateman 1989, 17, 22).

Carole Pateman argues that two types of contracts underlie modern Western civilization. The first is the social contract from which are derived understandings of human rights, equality, civil liberties and the rule of law, which are deemed to govern the public sphere of society. The second is the sexual contract which operates in the private sphere and establishes the man's conjugal rights and authority over the woman. These spheres are interconnected, and the subordination of women in the domestic sphere is replicated in unequal relations in a wide range of commercial arrangements in the public sphere. Thus, "the original contract is a sexual-social pact . . . the new civil society created through the original contract is a patriarchal social order . . . the social contract is a story of freedom; the sexual contract is a story of subjection" (Pateman 1989, 1–2). This perception of the gendered and unequal nature of rights and obligations in modern civil society has led many feminist thinkers to interrogate liberal concepts of gender-neutral citizenship and equality, and to elaborate feminist visions and discourses of citizenship (e.g., Lister 1995 and 1997). I will explore these concepts later in the chapter.

To return to Salter's reflections on civilization: the term "culture", in his usage, is more particularistic than the term "civilization". It highlights what is unique to a particular community or people and is closely linked with the construction of national identities. The cultural expressions of elite groups have generally dominated and driven the development of nationalisms. Salter, however, reminds us that culture can also be seen as "a field of representations in which power and identities are constructed, reified, negotiated and resisted" (Salter 2002, 13). Therefore, cultural discourses, rituals and icons may perform many different functions. They may be used to dominate and subjugate, but they may also be liberating, and they can certainly be divisive, possibly leading to conflict and fragmentation more than they promote unification. Both concepts – civilization and culture – have traditionally been invoked as instruments of power and as attributes which confer legitimacy on a group. In engaging in a Caribbean discourse on civilization, one must bear in mind these traditional functions. Would the concepts have the same utility value for the Caribbean, or, given the legacies of oppression and exploitation and the cultural diversity of our societies, would they end up having a divisive boomerang effect? It is my contention that, in the Caribbean, cultural discourses are of the greatest importance in helping us to understand our own societies, while the notion of a Caribbean civilization is somewhat less important. This notion can, however, play a useful role in enabling us to look critically at Caribbean societies, to acknowledge their patterns of exclusion and inequity, and to debate on the normative themes and values which we might wish them to reflect and to evolve towards.

Civilization, Culture and Community in the Caribbean

In the Caribbean context, most observers, including Ralph Gonsalves, highlight the diversity of cultures found in the region. Gonsalves does it in lyrical, somewhat romanticized fashion: "We are a unique civilization: we are the songs of the Caribs, Arawaks and the Amerindians, we are the rhythm of Africa, the melody of Europe, the chords of Asia, and we are the home-grown lyrics of the Caribbean . . . we occupy an especial seascape and landscape" (Gonsalves 2003). His words are reminiscent of a similar theme uttered by three French Caribbean writers, Jean Bernabe, Patrick Chamoiseau and Raphael Confiant, who published their *Manifesto of Creolite* in 1989: "We cannot reach Caribbeanness without interior vision. And interior vision is nothing without the unconditional acceptance of our Creoleness. We declare ourselves Creoles . . . Creoleness is the cement of our culture and it ought to rule the foundations of our Caribbeanness . . . [It] is the interactional or transactional aggregate of Caribbean, European, African, Asian and Levantine cultural elements, united on the same soil by the same yoke of history . . . Creoleness is the world diffracted but recomposed" (Bernabe, Chamoiseau and Confiant 2004, 254–55).

Both reflections emphasize the region's diversity and the interaction among its various cultural and ethnic groups. They define the Caribbean as a composite of all its cultures. They also illustrate the complexities and discontinuities of defining the Caribbean that its diversity imposes. Gonsalves proposes his "Caribbean civilization" primarily in response to British colonial influences and the contemporary reality of North American hegemony. Bernabe, Chamoiseau and Confiant propose Creoleness as a necessary post-colonial alternative to both French colonialism and the earlier *Negritude* movement proclaimed by Senghor and Cesaire during the anti-colonial struggles of the 1930s to 1960s.[3] Both run the risk of selectively delineating "their" Caribbean analytical and operational spaces and avoiding the territorial, cultural and ideological spaces in the Greater Caribbean that would render its contours less manageable.[4] This intellectual tendency is a potential pitfall for the region as a whole, and has already perpetuated the colonial legacy of fragmented political, economic and linguistic groupings within the broader geographical zone.

Other commentators, notably Stuart Hall, have problematized the diversity of the region to a greater extent, and, in so doing, they shed light on the conceptual challenges that confront those who attempt to define Caribbean culture or a Caribbean civilization. Hall reminds us that one of the principal commonalities across the Caribbean is that almost everyone originated from somewhere else. As a result, most societies have been composed of several diasporic and polarized cultures which have had to embark on a long, painful process of assimilation and integration or accommodation of one another. He also reminds us that diasporic cultures have to reinvent themselves: "they are always exercises in selective memory and they almost always involve the silencing of something in order to allow something else to speak" (Hall 2001, 26). Caribbean cultural diversity is thus simultaneously an invaluable resource and an incredible challenge to the peoples and the institutions of the region. Undoubtedly, we will be forced to revisit and reinterpret our history over and over again as new voices and formerly invisible or overlooked aspects of what is perceived to be Caribbean identity struggle to the surface. Cultural, ethnic and political identities will forever be fields of contestation in the region.

Rhoda Reddock, in a study of Trinidad, makes the point that the rejection of colonial hegemony is only the beginning of a much more arduous struggle to construct appropriate replacements, marked by "a continuous struggle and negotiation over representation" (Reddock 1998, 414). To a greater or lesser extent, the same could be said about many other parts of the region, including Guyana, Suriname, Jamaica, Belize, the French Caribbean, Puerto Rico, Cuba and the Dominican Republic. In fact, the truth of this remark is evidenced in the vibrant, often acrimonious debates over identity, citizenship and entitlements that are still very much in process and focus on achieving greater acknowledgement, visibility and power for communities and minorities that have long been part of the ethnic kaleidoscope of our societies.

Numerous other thinkers have considered the burden of history for Caribbean societies, political cultures and national identities. I mention a couple whose reflections seem particularly relevant to this discussion. Elsa Goveia, in her 1965 study of slave societies in the Leeward Islands, made the point that "the foundations of the free society were built upon a social structure which had been shaped by the necessities of the slave system, with its basic principles of racial inequality and subordination . . . [E]ver since the time of emancipation, we have been trying to combine quite opposite principles in our social system . . . [and] a most profound incompatibility necessarily results from the uneasy union which joins democracy with the accumulated remains of enslavement" (Goveia 2004, 439, 444). Goveia was prescient in her observations on the challenges that would be encountered in the search for democracy, social justice and citizenship in a region with a legacy of multiple forms of oppression and exploitation. More recently, Baronov and Yelvington (2003, 212, 223–29), in their reflections on the themes of ethnicity and identity, race, class and nationalism in the Caribbean, highlight the challenges of nation-building amidst diversity compounded by the history of domination, exploitation and resistance that exists among the ethnic groups. They argue that national elites have adopted varying national and societal responses, including the *Creolite* of the French Caribbean, the somewhat contested notion of "racial democracy" in Cuba,[5] the equation of race with the nation-state in the Dominican Republic and the increasingly stretched multiculturalism of the English-speaking territories. In their view, there are challenges and contradictions inherent in each of these formulae, and they conclude, like Reddock, that nation-building projects remain fluid sites of struggle and contestation in the Caribbean.

Gender and Caribbean Civilization

Among the most prominent voices in the current conversation on Caribbean civilization, there are few references to the theme of gender; yet, gender is extremely pertinent to any discussion of civilization, community, culture and identity, especially in the Caribbean. In most civilizations, gender-specific spheres of activity are evident. Men may tend to dominate the major political, economic and religious institutions, while women are often the custodians of cultural norms and values, the ones who socialize successive generations into observing and preserving them. In most societies, sexual unions involving individuals from different ethnicities have historically been a sensitive issue, a challenge to dominant cultural identities and at times a flashpoint for communal conflict. In wars, the appropriation and sexual exploitation of the women of the defeated group by the conquerors have been key symbols of subordination. Even when these unions have been based on violence and extreme oppression, women have tended to be the "gatekeepers" in encounters between different ethnic and cultural groups, and have played a crucial role in merging communities, transmitting traditional practices and memories, and eventually modifying cultural norms.[6]

All these points are relevant in a discussion about Caribbean civilization and culture. Caribbean gender relations have emerged from the unique history of the region, which involves colonial exploitation, slavery and indentureship, forced and voluntary migration, poverty, and inequalities of class, gender and ethnicity. Gender relations have been a vital dynamic underlying the construction of our hybrid societies. Caribbean societies are often described as matrifocal, since kinship structures and family welfare revolve overwhelmingly around female figures (Clarke 1972/1999; Senior 1991). Another significant aspect of Caribbean culture concerns the diversity of family structures and the strength of family networks that operate both in the region and in far-flung diasporas.[7] Gender relations provide a lens through which feminist theorists give us additional critical insights into important aspects of Caribbean culture and identity. They challenge us to reflect on the sources and the norms of the Caribbean civilization that we are constructing. The following discussion, although not exhaustive, attempts to identify some of the main themes relating to gender and civilization that Caribbean gender theorists have touched on.

One of the issues explored concerns how gender roles evinced by mythological symbols from cultures of origin may have an enduring and powerful influence on various ethnicities in the Caribbean who are seeking to re-create their communities far from their places of origin. Patricia Mohammed (1998) reflects on the significance of this process for East Indians in Trinidad. While acknowledging the weight of tradition, Mohammed (1994 and 1995) also emphasizes the ongoing process in Caribbean societies of negotiating new gender systems and of constructing new gender identities. In contrast, Rhoda Reddock, exploring the impact of globalization on Caribbean societies, argues that fundamentalism and conservative, traditional gender ideologies have experienced a resurgence during the last fifteen years, in response to globalized, homogenized modernity and to Neoliberalism (Reddock 2004). Both authors remind us of the complex ways in which cultural legacies from the past feed into the present-day Caribbean and continue to influence the evolution of gender relations.

Gender analysts have also highlighted the issue of endemic violence in Caribbean social relations. Merle Hodge (2004) argues that, in societies in which many people have historically been subordinated and stripped of their dignity and rights, the quest for power and recognition manifests itself in high levels of domestic and sexual violence, largely but not exclusively male violence against female partners. In Caribbean culture, physical aggression and the possession of weapons often more easily expresses masculinity than access to material resources and high social status. Reddock (2004), Clarke and Pargass (2003), Barriteau (2003) and Ffolkes (1997) have underlined the high rates of domestic violence in the Caribbean and its possible causes, including pathological factors, structural socio-economic factors, and culture and gender ideologies. Hodge (2004) observes that while male violence is often evident in male–female relations, women are also perpetrators of verbal and physical violence, often against children. Gender-based violence is a disturbing pattern in Caribbean communities which spills over into increasing levels of criminality and violence in the wider regional society. In general, these authors portray institutional responses to domestic violence as inadequate and ineffective. Domestic violence data and violent crime statistics underscore the fact that the sanctity of human life and the integrity of the person may not be deeply rooted norms in Caribbean civilization; moreover, contemporary violent trends increasingly threaten the value of these norms.

Gender equity and human development, themes which have major implications for the future of a Caribbean civilization, feature prominently in Caribbean feminist discourse. Various writers point to the perennial paradox facing Caribbean women, who are generally strong, resilient and economically active, occupy an increasing share of the labour market and participate in education up to the tertiary level. Yet, several categories of Caribbean women continue to earn less than their male counterparts in equivalent jobs, and women account for a disproportionate share of the unemployed and the poor, despite the fact that they bear a heavier share of the responsibility for household upkeep and the care of dependents (Andaiye 2003; Barriteau 2003). Gender researchers across the board have also engaged with the theme of masculinity crises in Caribbean societies, whether to confirm or deny that they are taking place, to explore their causes and to suggest institutional and individual responses. They have also worked to keep the many unresolved issues related to women firmly on the policy agenda as part of the quest to achieve more equitable and sustainable Caribbean development (Barriteau 2003, 2004; Andaiye 2003; Lewis 2002, among many others).

Many feminist writings beyond the Caribbean have considered citizenship to be a crucial area for engendering political community. In this light, Dietz (1987, 14) defines citizenship as a "collective and participatory engagement in the determination of the affairs of the community". Lister (1997, 2008), while noting women's progression from exclusion from the political sphere to acquiring citizen status, critiques the failure of twentieth-century ideas of citizenship to incorporate gender differences fully into their conceptual frameworks. Liberal citizenship aspires to be gender-neutral and fails to take sufficient account of the sexual division of labour, which results both in individuals' gendered performance of duties and in unequal access to political, economic and social entitlements. Lister advocates a re-gendering of citizenship which would consider both individual rights and political participation, and would emphasize the function of care-giver as an important dimension of citizenship duties. Finally, this re-gendering would widen the concept of the political space to include informal spaces such as non-governmental organizations or community associations (e.g., churches, consumer associations, nurses and teachers' associations, soup kitchens) where women tend to play active roles.

This kind of approach resonates with the realities of Caribbean societies and would contribute greatly towards our construction of a gendered understanding of citizenship. To date, our Caribbean discourse has not explored all these angles. Gendered considerations of citizenship in the region initially focused on questions of women's and children's rights in family law and in the wave of legislative reforms derived from international and regional initiatives during the International Decade for the Advancement of Women (1975–1985) (see Boxill 1997). Researchers have also noted some significant legislative reforms of the labour market in this era, most notably the creation of paid maternity leave, but they underline that Caribbean societies have eradicated neither average earning differentials nor differential rates of employment between Caribbean men and women. Gender-based violence became an issue of rising concern in the 1980s and 1990s (Clarke and Pargass 2003; Ffolkes 1997) and, while there have been some advances in legislation, police training and response, and the availability of protective facilities, there is general agreement that Caribbean societies still have a long way to go in protecting their citizens from gender-based violence, or even violence in general.

Tracy Robinson (2004, 593) agrees that "the question of citizenship offers a critical lens to theorize the 'woman question' and to continue political work around it", and she focuses her analysis on constitutional reform initiatives across the Caribbean region. Robinson gives a nuanced interpretation of Commonwealth Caribbean constitutional provisions, pointing not only to some recent advances but also to many contradictions. She argues that comprehensive reading of an entire constitution, rather than just the sections on fundamental rights and freedoms, may bring to light discriminatory or contradictory provisions in other areas of the text. Likewise, there are various aspects of gender equality that the text upholds but that are, in reality, not justiciable. Robinson feels that Caribbean women have been moderately successful in their involvement in constitutional reform processes and in increasing the awareness of political citizenship issues for and among women. Their representation on constitutional reform commissions, however, has remained minimal, and some of the most controversial constitutional reform debates and impasses have erupted over gender-related issues, such as constitutional provisions to strengthen women's participation in public life and provisions about freedom from discrimination on the grounds of sexual orientation. These sorts of controversies give insight into the continuity of power relations and of conservative gender ideologies, even while there is evidence of some progress towards greater equity.

Civilization, Culture, Regional Autonomy

What fully inclusive possibilities exist for constructing a sense of community and identity at the regional level? Nigel Bolland (2004), while agreeing that there are cultural and political schisms in the Caribbean, argues that there are nonetheless striking aspects of unity which are rooted in state and non-state regional organizations; in a common history of European colonialism, plantation society and economy; in an all-pervasive Afro-creole culture; and in common intellectual traditions. He optimistically describes the latter as "an emerging pan-Caribbean civilization" (ibid., xxii). A dominant feature of this civilization lies in the complicated multiple identities manifested by its people as a result of migration and transculturation. Bolland lists three important themes which engage many Caribbean intellectuals, who are both the products and the spokespersons of this "civilization": (1) responses to the oppression of slavery, colonialism, racism; (2) the development of a creole, multicultural society; (3) relationships between the Caribbean Self and the external Others. In a contemporary update to the list, one might argue for the addition of three further themes, namely: (4) the struggle for gender equality in the Caribbean, (5) the connection of the Caribbean diaspora with the evolution of Caribbean societies, and (6) a consciousness that is born of existence in a small-scale community and polity.

Themes two, three and six seem to be uppermost in the writings of anglophone Caribbean political thinkers and actors like Ralph Gonsalves and, before him, Errol Barrow in 1986 (see Barrow 2000). Their assertion of the existence of a Caribbean civilization is an assertion that Caribbean territories have their own distinct and valid political and cultural traditions, that they are viable societies and valuable members of the international community, and that this community owes them respect. These kinds of assertions are aimed at the spectre of increasing global and hemispheric political and economic marginalization for small Caribbean states. They are voiced in the context of a problematic and uneven process of globalization and a Western neoliberal ideology which claims that its principles of political and economic organization have universal applicability. Gonsalves (2006) argues that the preservation of an autonomous Caribbean cultural identity and civilization requires deepening and strengthening regional integration via the construction of confederal institutions among the countries of the Caribbean community. He fears that the alternative to political union might be cultural domination and political absorption into either the United States or the European Union.

This scenario points us to the fifth theme mentioned above. Migration and transnational networks are a quintessential part of Caribbean culture, and pervade every aspect of contemporary Caribbean development (Nurse 2004). As expressed by Trotz (2008, 23), "it is movement and not borders which is naturally Caribbean . . . a continuously defining moment of our collective historical experience and memory". The multi-faceted support provided by migratory networks is vital to the well-being and stability of Caribbean societies. Migration and large Caribbean diasporas have, over time, created a "Caribbean America" (Payne and Sutton 2001, 240) and have forged strong ties of interdependence between North American and Caribbean societies, which have both experienced the positive and negative interchanges that such interdependence implies. The anti-hegemonic civilizational discourse in the region has to confront the contradictions of this interdependence. Diasporic communities draw on Caribbean culture as part of their self-definition and are widely acknowledged to make crucial contributions to the development of the region. They are also conduits, however, for introducing or reinforcing, in the Caribbean, values and cultural elements drawn from their host societies. Caribbean societies which have high rates of migration cannot be hermetically sealed off from metropolitan societies. Regional integration or even political union cannot prevent the inexorable process of cultural symbiosis that will take place between Caribbean communities in the region and in the diaspora.

The merging of cultures is bound to have unanticipated, perhaps undesirable (for some) yet inevitable, civilizational effects.

The subjects of migration and diaspora also raise unequivocal questions of citizenship rights in Caribbean societies. As the globalized labour market has obliged growing numbers of Caribbean people to commute between their countries of origin and the countries where they live and work, the question of voting rights for nationals overseas has arisen in constitutional reform discussions across the region. Likewise, we witness the steady growth of a regional labour market that is only partially covered by agreements about freedom of movement and social protection for migrants and their families. On the one hand, regional migration can function as a catalyst for deepening economic and social integration. During periods of economic recession, however, like the present period, migration becomes a source of conflict. Intraregional migration became the principal issue in the rising societal and intergovernmental tensions that surrounded Caribbean integration in 2008–2009, and unilateral moves by various countries to limit freedom of movement have plunged the Caribbean Single Market and Economy (CSME) into crisis (Girvan 2009; Ramphal 2009). President Jagdeo of Guyana makes a critical point here: "The maltreatment of CARICOM [Caribbean Community] citizens is repugnant . . . If we treat our own people badly, how can we expect third countries to receive them with respect?" (Jagdeo 2009, 6).

Alissa Trotz makes some incisive observations in her analysis of Caribbean migration issues. First, she argues that Caribbean migration is cyclical, based on historical phases and economic developments. Many contemporary migrants are merely returning to the lands which their ancestors left for greener pastures one or two generations earlier. This is true of many Haitians in the Dominican Republic, of many Dominicanos in the Eastern Caribbean, of many Cubans in Jamaica, and of many Guyanese in Barbados. As Ramphal puts it, "the roots of family trees are now spread out in the sub-soil of the Caribbean" (Ramphal 2009). Second, Trotz emphasizes the place that migration now occupies in the survival strategies of both men and women, its tremendous support to household welfare, and the seminal contributions of migrants to vital service industries across the Caribbean. In the case of female migrant workers, these contributions are usually in the tourism sector, the care sector or in small commercial enterprises. Finally, Trotz points to the underlying inequalities and injustices within Caribbean societies which not only contribute to the exodus of migrants from their home societies but also fuel anti-migrant hostilities in the receiving societies. Migration is often the symptom of this deeper societal malaise and not the root cause of the problems (Trotz 2008).

I conclude, therefore, that Caribbean societies have evoked the concept of civilization to reaffirm a distinct, unique identity vis-à-vis the outside world. They have drawn on it as a nation-building tool to promote national and regional unity and, in this context, the concept has been part of the rationale underlying projects of regional integration. Given the region's diversity and fragmentation, however, assertions of Caribbean identity and civilization are rife with contradictions. Interpretations of these concepts may be static, clinging doggedly to historical images and traditions, refusing to confront either the present or the future. They may emphasize the identity of some ethnic, linguistic, economic, political or geographical groups in the region to the exclusion of others, and so exacerbate internal divisions. Concepts of "civilization" often thrive on the notion of external "Others". In a region like the Caribbean, where there are also many internal Others, the civilization and cultural identity debate remains an area of fierce contestation.

Rather than promoting dialogue and an understanding of the differences in political culture around the Caribbean, the civilization discourse and the policy responses influenced by this discourse have tended to gloss over these formidable barriers to regional integration. Regional groupings are often constructed on and perpetuate partial representations of the Caribbean. One example of this kind of grouping is the Caribbean Community (CARICOM), an intergovernmental integration initiative founded in 1973 that rests on the shared colonial history, institutional heritage and cultural commonalities of the English-speaking Caribbean territories. Expansion of the grouping has been halting and cautious, and membership has only been extended to two other countries that have a different colonial and post-colonial heritage (Suriname in 1995, Haiti in 2002). Meaningful incorporation of Haiti, in particular, is taking much longer than the formal process of accession. The member governments may well view the Dominican Republic's recent application for membership in CARICOM as a dilemma and not as a welcome opportunity to widen the community.

Current discourse has likewise failed to incorporate gender perspectives sufficiently into reflections on Caribbean civilization and culture. My discussion, therefore, has sought to demonstrate that these perspectives provide valuable insights into the past and future construction of Caribbean societies. Finally, given the fundamental significance of migration to Caribbean societies, discussions of Caribbean civilization and culture are obliged to take into account the wider Caribbean socio-cultural, economic and political spheres generated by the large and vibrant diasporas of Caribbean migrants in Europe, North America and elsewhere, as well as the dynamics of intraregional migration.

Regional Integration

My discussion now shifts gear to focus on regional integration. In recent years, regional integration theory and praxis have gone through a rapid evolution. On the one hand, the World Trade Organization–compatible "Open Regionalism" of the 1990s was characterized by a heavily economistic approach that emphasized trade liberalization and neoliberal macroeconomic reforms.[8] There are some regional groups, most notably the European Union, which have also emphasized the political and cultural dimensions of integration. For many regions, however, trade liberalization has dominated the agenda, with the GATT/ World Trade Organization having received 273 notifications of regional trade agreements by 2003 (WTO 2003). Since the dawn of the twenty-first century, this trend has been more contested in the Western Hemisphere and there has been a discernible shift in focus. The North American Free Trade Area provides one example of the new trends. At the inception of the North American Free Trade Area, the United States showed a clear preference to maintain the area's exclusive emphasis on the free movement of goods, services and investments. Partly because of US national security preoccupations since 2001, however, and the inevitable spillover effect of integration initiatives, the North American Free Trade Area has engendered growing debates in North America on cultural identity, political values, security and hegemony in the trade zone.[9] In Latin America, regional integration debates have reintroduced political issues such as the rejection of US hegemony and the assertion of alternative priorities in integration policy – energy security and social policy, to name two prominent themes. The culmination of this process was the Venezuelan–Cuban initiative in 2004 to form the Bolivian Alternative for the Americas (ALBA), an organization which seeks to build an explicitly non-neoliberal model of South–South trade and development cooperation among countries in Latin America and the Caribbean (Harris and Azzi 2006; Arreaza 2004). A number of Caribbean states are either full members or observers of the ALBA integration process.

It is not surprising, therefore, that, on the theoretical front, discussions and investigations of the driving forces behind regionalism have turned more and more towards the cultural and the political. International Relations theory posits that this shift of focus is evident in the rise of Constructivism in the 1990s and in critical responses to globalization (Reus-Smit 2005). Constructivist approaches draw heavily on historical and sociological analyses to explain integrationist tendencies, and they emphasize the importance of cognitive forces – culture, identities, shared experiences, common interests and shared value systems, for example – in the development of communities, whether at the subnational, national or regional levels.

An important aspect of the Constructivist perspective is that it does not focus primarily on external factors, but rather on the internal, societal dynamics of building a community. It also stresses that identities, values and interests are not static but subject to change over time, and that these changes will lead to the emergence of new forms of communities (Hurrell 1995; Hveem 1999). These kinds of perspectives feature, for example, in contemporary studies of the European Union, where issues of identity and culture are as significant as the economic questions and the evolution of political institutions.

The Caribbean contains diverse interstate cooperation projects, each of which is based on a distinct expression of regionalism. The Organization of Eastern Caribbean States draws its membership from the micro-states of the Leeward and Windward Islands. It operates on the premise that their development needs are very specific and cannot always be met exclusively within the wider ambit of CARICOM, and it seeks to pool their limited resources to provide a number of common services. CARICOM began life as the institutional expression of the English-speaking Caribbean. The group based its subregional unity on shared historical experiences and colonial heritage and on a sense of having an identity distinct from the wider region and the rest of the world. Both CARICOM and the Organization of Eastern Caribbean States are, to some extent, examples of defensive regionalism, small-state initiatives to survive in the international environment, to build closer relationships among themselves and to promote economic development through cooperation. Both have been relatively successful in their functional cooperation but have an unimpressive record of integrating markets and productive processes. Both have found it difficult to demonstrate greater relevance since the early 1990s. While CARICOM embarked on the bureaucratically and technically complex "nuts and bolts" process of constructing the CARICOM CSME, the Organization of Eastern Caribbean States found itself obliged to reduce the scale of its regional cooperation activities in the 1990s in order to remain on a sustainable footing, but it has since regained some equilibrium with the adoption of an agreement towards closer economic union in 2006 (Ishmael 2006). CARICOM's CSME project has suffered from interminable delays in implementation by member states, from institutional shortcomings and a lack of adequate resources to meet the high costs of regional agencies, and from the tough challenges posed by the free movement of people and the ongoing question of widening the community's membership.[10]

The Central American community has had a similar ethos but a longer history than CARICOM and has experienced much higher levels of internal strife (Solis and Solano 2001). Since the late 1990s, its membership has focused increasingly on economic integration into the North American market, and these efforts culminated in the adoption of the Central American/Dominican Republic Free Trade Agreement with the United States in 2004. Some other countries with a geographic presence in the Caribbean basin, namely Mexico, Colombia and Venezuela, have membership in other regional groupings, North American Free Trade Area, the Andean Community and MERCOSUR, respectively. Finally, since December 2004, the South American Community of Nations has emerged, in which Guyana and Suriname, Venezuela and Colombia are members. The rules and hegemonic and counter-hegemonic projects of these groupings vis-à-vis the now suspended project for a Free Trade Area of the Americas have shifted the centre of gravity for Caribbean regionalism, exposing it much more to hemispheric dynamics and to the multilateral trading system.

At the beginning of this renewed focus on continental and hemispheric economic integration and expanded docket of regional cooperation projects came the attempt to reconceptualize the various post-colonial fragments of the Caribbean as the Greater Caribbean. Questions of identity, culture and community-building became more insistent, both in the Association of Caribbean States, formed in 1995 to encompass various subregional groupings, and in CARICOM, which was grappling with a more diversified membership and the launch of new institutions. Subregional integration projects have experienced a type of crisis of relevance during the past decade. Vaughan Lewis (1999), Havelock Brewster (2000, 2003, 2005) and Patsy Lewis (2003) have all argued that economic integration alone cannot serve as the basis for unity in the Caribbean. They have called for a greater focus on questions of cultural identity and joint political institutions, if subregional integration is to survive in the current age. While Brewster made reference to "political expressions of cultural identity and kinship" (2000, 39), Vaughan Lewis posed the following question: "Is there any longer something that can be defined as a 'West Indian' interest as we pursue our widening towards the Association of Caribbean States or our integration into the Free Trade Area of the Americas? . . . Have time and the tide of international relations processes now brought an end to the Montego Bay dream that there is a West Indies for which practical, political integration is the instrument prerequisite to economic well-being and the maintenance of cultural identity?" (1999, 91).

The only regional body which has sought to incorporate most of the disparate geographical and political elements is the Association of Caribbean States, which includes all the countries, territories and subregions bordering on the Caribbean Sea. Norman Girvan, former secretary-general of the association, in underlining the heterogeneity and historical fragmentation among the member territories, describes it as a "Zone of Cooperation based on shared geographic space" (Girvan 2003, 537). He identifies the tremendous obstacles posed both by competing allegiances and by contradictory economic interests, which have bedevilled the economic integration project among countries in the Association of Caribbean States. He argues, however, that in such a culturally diverse region as the Caribbean, cooperation can still take place on the modest, pragmatic basis of shared interests – conservation of the marine environment, development of sustainable tourism, disaster management, implementation of more effective regional transport networks, for instance. These functional activities may eventually spread to other areas and cause them to build up a stock of mutual trust and greater cultural awareness of one another.

But the Association of Caribbean States has also encountered major constraints in its integration activities which have resulted in a very low profile for the group. There has been a lack of strong political support from its member states. And, in addition to having a very small operational budget, the organization has had to contend with low rates of ratification of important legal instruments that are seminal to its main activities. Another former secretary-general, Ruben Sillie, in a January 2007 speech to the ministerial council of the association, acknowledged that, "even though we have begun to create new links, we are still far from our goal. We need to go beyond simply having put government leaders in contact with each other" (http://www.acs-aec.org; accessed April 2007).

In a sense, time has provided an answer to the question Vaughan Lewis posed. The experience of the Association of Caribbean States suggests that a sense of greater Caribbean identity will evolve only very gradually. That ambitious hemispheric integration project, the Free Trade Area of the Americas ran aground in 2003–2004 and was shipwrecked on the conflicting interests and rivalries of the two largest economic powers and blocs in the Americas. Subregional integration groupings like the Caribbean Community will therefore continue to have the opportunity to play a meaningful role in building community and promoting development among their member territories, and in providing them with a platform from which to define, coordinate and voice their interests vis-à-vis the wider international community. The group's success in doing these things will, however, depend on its capacity to adapt its institutions, to change its programmes in response to new needs and changing regional and international conditions, and, above all, to respond to the concerns of ordinary Caribbean people. The latter represents the most profound challenge.

The Advancement of Caribbean Civilization through Regional Integration

In conclusion, I pose the following question: Have regional integration efforts preserved and improved Caribbean peoples' ways of life, cultures or human security? The response is twofold. The first part affirms that regional integration initiatives and institutions have preserved and improved these areas in a number of ways.

All regional organizations in the Caribbean promote democratic institutions and democratic governance as fundamental to the construction of wholesome societies and to the maintenance of national and regional peace, stability and order. Still, much remains to be done to strengthen the protection of human rights in Caribbean societies and to build just, humane societies that place the highest value on human life and safeguard people's political, social, cultural and economic rights – in short, that have a holistic understanding of national and regional citizenship. The foregoing discussion has identified major shortfalls in engendering citizenship so that it meets the needs and life experiences of Caribbean men and women. Likewise, there are glaring deficiencies in the project to construct a regional citizenship that respects the rights and provides for the civic participation of migrant workers and their families across the Caribbean. CARICOM appears to be the regional grouping that has concerned itself more than any other with issues of gender equality and regional citizenship. It has created structures such as the Women's Desk in the 1970s and 1980s, later to become the Gender and Development Unit within the Secretariat, which drafted and promulgated model legislation on women's rights to member states, coordinated regional responses to global gender initiatives, and in 1996 prepared a Regional Policy on Gender Equality and Social Justice. Likewise, freedom of movement and related policies on social security and other entitlements have formed part of the CSME agenda, and CARICOM has a mechanism for routine consultations with non-state representatives, its "Social Partners" on regional issues. Even so, current tensions and expressions of disillusionment with CARICOM illustrate the shortcomings in realizing these regional policy goals.

To a greater or lesser degree, all regional organizations also promote conflict management and peaceful settlement of disputes, although at times with limited success. Central America in the 1980s demonstrated the terribly destructive consequences of the absence of these kinds of mechanisms and the absolute necessity of regional bodies' complementing the roles of national conflict management bodies and promoting the peaceful settlement of disputes. Haiti, in particular, now poses a similar challenge to CARICOM, to which the organization has only partially responded (Granderson 2004). The Association of Caribbean States embarked upon a novel area of conflict management in 2005, working in collaboration with UNESCO and the Human Rights Internet to explore the mitigation of societal tensions caused by transnational migration. Despite its relevance to Caribbean and global realities, however, the project does not appear to have become a mainstream activity of the organization.[11]

Regional organizations have the promotion of economic well-being through cooperation in trade, investment, sustainable development and other areas, as a fundamental objective. All societies and civilizations must have a material base. Without material resources, they either wither away or subsist at a very basic level. Although there is sometimes an excessive concern with the economic aspects of regional integration, it is an indispensable area for cooperation which will contribute to the advancement of Caribbean societies. The current crop of regional groupings has contributed in varying degrees to economic growth, but it has continued to be the Achilles' heel for CARICOM and other organizations because of the slow pace and deficiencies of the various groups' economic integration activities (IDB-INTAL 2005; Bernal 2005; Girvan 2005).

Disaster preparedness and response are other essential activities that have been carried out with some success at the regional level. They have provided a basis for cooperation and consensus because of the nature of the environment and the high frequency of natural disasters within the region. The promotion of resilience in the face of disasters is crucial for small societies such as those in the Caribbean and has increasingly become a reference point in analyzing the security and strength of societies more generally (Flynn 2008).

Finally, through activities such as the Caribbean Festival of Creative Arts (CARIFESTA) and through providing some support for cultural industries, regional organizations have contributed to increasing cultural interchange and understanding in the wider Caribbean. There is still much more that can be done, however, to preserve and strengthen cultural traditions, build cultural industries and expand the appreciation of Caribbean people for the wealth and diversity of Caribbean culture.

A second question devolving from the above would be: What are the areas of weakness in which regional organizations can do more to preserve and enhance Caribbean ways of life? Several authors have already addressed this theme. Brewster (2000), writing in the CARICOM context, suggests that states and societies should agree on a given number of regional public goods, and should then organize regional functional cooperation around these goods, so as to maximize returns from scarce resources. Gonsalves (2006) lists three crucial areas for integration: public policy which develops the marine resources of the Caribbean; confederal institutions for the Organization of Eastern Caribbean States and CARICOM; and promoting freedom of movement to the greatest extent possible in the Caribbean. The latter point has received the endorsement of Trotz (2008), who writes in a somewhat different context but nonetheless emphasizes the value of free movement in the construction of regional integration and citizenship. Freedom of movement is essential for the integration process and for building any type of Caribbean civilization. The present cautious liberalizing steps in the Organization of Eastern Caribbean States and CARICOM should continue to include other categories of workers. Greater efforts should also be made on a reciprocal basis to facilitate the movement of people among the countries of the Greater Caribbean. But it should also be borne in mind that increased regional mobility carries the potential for greater inter- and intra-societal conflict, and must therefore be accompanied by improved conflict management institutions and tighter security cooperation. It is essential for regional organizations to spearhead the promotion of freedom of movement, to set standards for the treatment of migrants across the Caribbean, to monitor their implementation and to serve as active fora for intergovernmental and societal consultations on the management of freedom of movement.

Related to the issue of freedom of movement, and also to the question of "regional public goods", is the need to prioritize the improvement and safety regulation of regional transport networks. These networks are essential for the movement of goods, services and people across the Caribbean, where, for the most part, large tracts of water separate economies and societies. Maritime transport seems to have received little sustained policy attention, save in the French Antilles. Yet it is vital to the agricultural marketing trade in the Eastern Caribbean, to the safety and security of the regional fishing industry, and to links among a number of smaller island societies in the Eastern Caribbean.

In their projects, regional organizations must place more emphasis on the goals of poverty eradication and social justice, and should prioritize activities oriented towards these objectives. Otherwise, regional integration will have little relevance for the majority of Caribbean people. In this context, there should be much greater emphasis on supporting the agricultural sector, and on the production of and trade in Caribbean food crops in the interest of food security and income-generation for rural populations. Belatedly, we witness the issue of food production and security rising higher on the regional policy agenda, in response to global food shortages and rising prices. Linked to the issue of agriculture is the need to place even greater emphasis on the conservation of Caribbean ecological systems, the basis of all life in the region. Included in this kind of policy area should be the exploration and exploitation of sustainable energy systems that draw from the wind, solar, wave and geothermal energy sources in abundance throughout much of the region.

Although there has been important progress in this direction, a greater proportion of regional resources should be devoted to exploring and expressing the diverse cultural identities that exist in the Greater Caribbean. At present, the English-speaking Caribbean pays little attention to the indigenous heritage that remains in a number of territories. Likewise, greater priority must also be given to populations who attain proficiency in the different official languages of the zone, as well as the languages spoken by a majority of people in the area. One example concerns Haitian membership in CARICOM and the question of incorporating French and, perhaps more importantly, Kweyol. Radio, television and online media can be harnessed to greater effect to promote wider access to Caribbean films, documentaries, music and news items, to build a stronger regional consciousness.

Interstate regional bodies have to increase their collaboration with civil society groups at national and regional levels, and work to facilitate these groups' projects. Quite often, people perceive the collaboration between state and civil society as the civil society providing support for what the state does, rather than the state giving greater support to the priorities and agendas set by the civil society. In addition to strengthening connections with civil societies in the region, organizations must explore ways of fully incorporating Caribbean diasporas into regional structures and programmes. The diasporas are a significant sector of the region's human and economic resources and they exhibit vibrant cultural and political activity. They are also the Caribbean region's strongest, and perhaps most viable, attachment to the global political economy and to the metropolitan societies in which they are based.

Education is a vital element in building any society or civilization. Caribbean states and societies need to reflect deeply on the essential components of their educational curricula that draw on and further develop cultural identities and produce Caribbean consciousness. Many states have engaged in educational liberalization and reform processes driven by globalization. In the midst of these undoubtedly necessary activities, there is still the need to define and protect core elements of the national and regional curricula and determine which institutions will deliver them. Education can never be completely reduced to a commercial commodity; it is a valuable tool for cultural interventions. Among the many other priorities, educational curricula should give prominence to questions of gender justice and to promoting more equitable gender ideologies in the Caribbean. Likewise, formal and public education processes must focus much more on the central and historical role of migration in the social and economic development of the region, as well as in constructing kinship bonds across Caribbean societies. Both issues are crucial to the task of building national and regional citizenship.

Regional agendas need to focus, even more than at present, on providing services and opportunities for Caribbean youth (the majority of our population) and on strengthening support for family structures and the maintenance of kinship ties, both within the Caribbean itself and between the Caribbean and its various external diasporas. This kind of focus requires engendering every aspect of regional social and economic policy far more than is the case today. Despite the 1995 Regional Policy on Gender Equality and Social Justice (Hall 2000), many observers contend that these kinds of policies have lost ground since the 1990s, and that further improvements for the status of women have lagged (Tang and Bailey Nain 2003). Yet, working towards gender equality is a core element in the development and well-being of Caribbean societies.

Acknowledgements

This paper was first prepared for the Ninth Annual Research Conference of the Eastern Caribbean Central Bank, Basseterre, St Kitts, 1–3 December 2005.

Notes

1.   The very word "barbarian" has been linked with the geographical concept of the "Barbary Coast" of North Africa, which stretches from Egypt to Tunisia, Libya, Algeria and Morocco. Some say that the word is of Greek origin, while others derive it from the name of the Berber inhabitants of the region. The Barbary Coast, which lies just outside Europe and was for a long time a part of the Ottoman Empire, represents a civilization and religion different from those of Europe. In the long series

of conflicts between the Muslim world and Europe, moreover, it has exemplified "the Other" in the European mind, even more so because the Barbary Coast has been extensively associated with piracy and the exaction of tribute as a protection against pirate attacks. See *Lexicon Universal Encyclopedia* 1989, 3:76.

2. For example, Aristotle and Plato in their conceptions of the family unit, its place in society, and woman's place in relation to man, the head of the household. See the excerpts from Plato's *Republic* and Aristotle's *Politics* 1 in Foster 1977, 86–89, 123–29; and Jean Bodin, excerpts from *Les Six Livres de la Republique*, in Jones 1980, 55–57.

3. In fact, they speak of the French Caribbean's sharing cultural affinities with other French creole societies, such as the Seychelles or Reunion, and of its having "geopolitical solidarity" with Caribbean neighbours. They do, however, point out that these other Caribbean societies are themselves creole in nature (Bernabe, Chamoiseau and Confiant 2004, 255–57).

4. For example, Gonsalves speaks of the central influence of the Caribbean Sea in his Caribbean civilization. Undoubtedly this is correct, yet it is insufficient. What of those designated parts of "Caribbean civilization" – such as the Guyanas – that have no Caribbean seaboard at all and whose consciousness is shaped by other dominant environmental and ethno-historical influences? See E. Kamau Brathwaite's "Timehri" (2004) or McWatt 2006. Likewise, the discourse on Caribbean civilization and culture is yet to explore such crucial topics as the syncretism of Latin, Anglo-Saxon, Afro-Caribbean and (sometimes) Amerindian cultures which has occurred in places such as the Garifuna communities of Central America or San Andres y Providencia, south-western Caribbean island territories of Colombia. See alternative understandings, for example, in Vives 2006.

5. See Helg 2005, 183–206; Martinez 2007.

6. One Caribbean example of this phenomenon is the indigenous Kalinago people who inhabited the Lesser Antilles in large numbers in pre-Columbian times. The Kalinago women spoke an Arawak-based language, while the men spoke a language called Kariban. One historical theory is that the Kalinago or Carib men often captured Arawak (Taino) women, whom they took back to Kalinago villages. The women retained their own language and taught it to their children. See Shepherd 1999, 3; Trillos Amaya 2006, 70–71.

7. For more recent discussions about the paradoxes and questions surrounding portrayals of the family in the Caribbean, see Barrow 1999 and Mohammed 1999.

8. WTO 1995; Bulmer-Thomas 2001.

9. The most recent initiative of the North American Free Trade Area has been the Security and Prosperity Partnership of North America, launched in 2007. See *Building a North American Community* 2005; *SPP* 2009; *Joint Statement by Ministers* 2009.

10.   CARICOM faces operational crises at present. Member states are reeling from the effects of the global economic recession, and there has been a widespread political and social backlash against migrant labour and the CSME encouragement of free movement for many categories of CARICOM citizens, in addition to several recent trade disputes and the failure of member states to use the dispute settlement mechanisms provided for either in the Revised Treaty of Chaguaramas or in the Caribbean Court of Justice. The Dominican Republic has also reapplied for membership of the organization, forcing the existing member states to confront again issues of cultural diversity, competitiveness and the challenges of absorbing a much larger population grouping. For recent commentary, see Girvan 2009, Ramphal 2009, and Jagdeo 2009.

11.   See ACS Secretariat 2005.

Reference List

Andaiye. 2003. Smoke and mirrors: The illusion of CARICOM women's growing economic empowerment, post-Beijing. In *Gender equality in the Caribbean: Reality or illusion?*, ed. G. Tang Nain and B. Bailey, 73–107. Kingston: Ian Randle.

Arreaza, T. 2004. ALBA: Bolivarian alternative for Latin America. 30 January. http://www.venezuelanalysis.com/analysis (accessed 2 July 2009).

Association of Caribbean States (ACS) Secretariat. 2005. *ACS building a culture of peace and preventing conflict in the greater Caribbean: Workshop summary.* 28 January.

Baronov, D., and K. Yelvington. 2003. Ethnicity, race, class and nationality. In *Understanding the contemporary Caribbean*, ed. R.S. Hillman and T.J. D'Agostino, 209–38. Boulder: Lynne Rienner.

Barriteau V.E. 2003. Beyond a backlash: The frontal assault on containing Caribbean women in the decade of the 1990s. In *Gender equality in the Caribbean: Reality or illusion?*, ed. G. Tang Nain and B. Bailey, 201–32. Kingston: Ian Randle.

———. 2004. Constructing feminist knowledge in the Commonwealth Caribbean in the era of globalisation. In *Gender in the 21st century: Caribbean perspectives, visions and possibilities*, ed. B. Bailey and E. Leo-Rhynie, 437–65. Kingston: Ian Randle.

Barrow, C. 1999. Men, women and family in the Caribbean: A review. In *Gender in Caribbean development*, ed. P. Mohammed and C. Shepherd, 149–63. Kingston: Canoe.

Barrow, E. 2000. Address to the seventh meeting of CARICOM Heads of Government. Georgetown, Guyana, July 2, 1986. In *Integrate or perish! Perspectives of leaders of the integration movement 1963–1999*, ed. K. Hall, 331–37. Kingston: Office of the Principal, University of the West Indies.

Bernabe, J., P. Chamoiseau, and R. Confiant. 2004. Manifesto of Creolite. In *The birth of Caribbean civilization: A century of ideas about culture and identity, nation and society*, ed. O.N. Bolland, 250–66. Kingston: Ian Randle.

Bernal, R. 2005. The CSME and CARICOM's external trade negotiations. *Journal of Caribbean International Relations* 1 (April): 35–50.

Best, L. 2003. Afro-Saxon heritage. *Trinidad Express*. 14 June.

Bolland, O.N., ed. 2004. *The birth of Caribbean civilization: A century of ideas about culture and identity, nation and society*. Kingston: Ian Randle.

Boxill, E. 1997. The reform of family law as it affects women. In *Gender: A Caribbean multi-disciplinary perspective*, ed. E. Leo-Rhynie, B. Bailey and C. Barrow, 91–105. Kingston: Ian Randle.

Brathwaite, E.K. 2004. Timehri. In *The birth of Caribbean civilization: A century of ideas about culture and identity, nation and society*, ed. O.N. Bolland, 504–15. Kingston: Ian Randle.

Brewster, H. 2000. Identity, space and the West Indian Union. In *Contending with destiny: The Caribbean in the twenty-first century*, ed. K. Hall and D. Benn, 37–44. Kingston: Ian Randle.

———. 2003. CARICOM: From community to single market and economy. In *Governance in the age of globalisation: Caribbean perspectives*, ed. K. Hall and D. Benn, 499–508. Kingston: Ian Randle.

———. 2005. Mature regionalism and the Rose Hall declaration on regional governance. In *Caribbean imperatives: Regional governance and integrated development*, ed. K. Hall and D. Benn, 88–93. Kingston: Ian Randle.

Building a North American Community. 2005. Report of an independent task force, no. 53. New York: Council on Foreign Relations.

Bulmer-Thomas, V. 2001. *Regional integration in Latin America and the Caribbean: The political economy of "open regionalism"*. London: ILAS, University of London.

Chambers pocket thesaurus. 1993. Ed. C. Schwarz. Edinburgh: W. and R. Chambers.

Clarke, E.C. 1972/1999. *My mother who fathered me: A study of the families in three selected communities of Jamaica*. Kingston: University of the West Indies Press.

Clarke, R., and G. Pargass. 2003. Violence against women: A human rights issue. In *Gender equality in the Caribbean: Reality or illusion?*, ed. G. Tang Nain and B. Bailey, 39–72. Kingston: Ian Randle.

Collins Paperback English Dictionary. 1993. Glasgow: HarperCollins.

Dietz, M.G. 1987. Context is all: Feminism and theories of citizenship. *Daedalus* 116 (4): 1–24.

Flynn, S. 2008. America the resilient: Defying terrorism and mitigating natural disasters. *Foreign Affairs* 87 (2): 1–6, http://www.nyu.edu/intercep/lapietra/Flynn_Americathe Resilient.pdf (accessed 6 February 2012).

Ffolkes, S. 1997. Violence against women: Some legal responses. In *Gender: A Caribbean multi-disciplinary reader*, ed. E. Leo-Rhynie, B. Bailey and C. Barrow, 118–29. Kingston: Ian Randle.

Foster, M. 1977. *Masters of political thought: From Plato to Aristotle*. London: Harrap.

Girvan, N. 2003. Regional cooperation and economic governance: The case of the Association of Caribbean States. In *Governance in the age of globalisation: Caribbean perspectives*, ed. D. Benn and K. Hall, 535–54. Kingston: Ian Randle.

———. 2005. Whither CSME? *Journal of Caribbean International Relations* 1 (1): 13–32.

———. 2009. Is CARICOM at risk? 11 June. http://www.nomangirvan.info/wp-content/uploads/is-caricom-at-risk.pdf (accessed 4 July 2009).

Gonsalves, R.E. 2001. The OECS in our Caribbean civilization. Speech delivered on the occasion of the twentieth anniversary of the Organization of Eastern Caribbean States, Kingston, St Vincent, 18 June. http://www.caricom.org/jsp/speeches/oecs_gonsalves .jsp (accessed 6 February 2012).

———. 2003. Our Caribbean civilization and its prospects. Paper presented at the CARICOM distinguished lecture series, Port of Spain, Trinidad, 12 March.

———. 2006. Our Caribbean civilization and its political prospects. In *Integration: CARICOM's key to prosperity*, ed. K. Hall and M. Chuck-A-Sang, 1–18. Kingston: Ian Randle.

Goveia, E. 2004. Slave society in the British Leeward Islands at the end of the eighteenth century. In *The birth of Caribbean civilization: A century of ideas about culture and identity, nation and society*, ed. O.N. Bolland, 421–45. Kingston: Ian Randle.

Granderson C. 2004. The CARICOM initiative towards Haiti: A case of small states diplomacy. *Focal Point* 3 (6): 1–4.

Hall, K., ed. 2000. *Reinventing CARICOM: The road to a new integration*. Kingston: Ian Randle.

Hall S. 2001. Negotiating Caribbean identities. In *New Caribbean thought: A reader*, ed. B. Meeks and F. Lindhal, 24–39. Kingston: University of the West Indies Press.

Harris, D., and D. Azzi. 2006. Venezuela's answer to free trade: The Bolivarian alternative for the Americas. Occasional paper no. 3. October – Focus on the Global South, Sao Paulo and Bangkok. http://www.focusontheglobalsouth.org (accessed 2 July 2009).

Helg, A. 2005. Race and politics in Cuba. In *Contemporary Caribbean cultures and societies in a global context*, ed. F. Knight and T. Martinez-Vergne, 183–206. Kingston: University of the West Indies Press.

Hodge, M. 2004. The shadow of the whip: A comment on male–female relations in the Caribbean. In *The birth of Caribbean civilization: A century of ideas about culture and identity, nation and society*, ed. O.N. Bolland, 524–30. Kingston: Ian Randle.

Huntington, S. 1993. The clash of civilizations? *Foreign Affairs* 72 (3): 23–49.

Hurrell, A. 1995. Regionalism in theoretical perspective. In *Regionalism in world politics: Regional organization and international order*, ed. L. Fawcett and A. Hurrell, 37–73. Oxford: Oxford University Press.

Hveem, H. 1999. Political regionalism: Master or slave of economic internationalization? In *Globalism and the new regionalism*, ed. B. Hettne, A. Inotai and O. Sunkel, 85–115. Basingstoke, UK: Macmillan.

IDB–INTAL. 2005. CARICOM report, no. 2. Washington DC: IDB. http://www.iadb .org.

Ishmael, L. 2006. The OECS model of integration in the context of Caribbean regionalism. *Pensamiento Propio* 23:37–70.

Jagdeo, B. 2009. CARICOM at a crossroads: Finding the way forward. Address delivered at the opening of thirtieth CARICOM Heads of Government Conference, Georgetown, Guyana. CARICOM press release, no. 264/2009. 3 July. http://www .caricom.org.

James, C.L.R. 1962/1992. From Toussaint L'Ouverture to Fidel Castro. Reprinted in *The C.L.R. James reader*, ed. A. Grimshaw, 296–314. Oxford: Blackwell.

Joint statement by ministers responsible for the security and prosperity partnership of North America, 28 February 2009, Los Bayos, Baja California Sur, Mexico. http://www .spp.gov (accessed 2 July 2009).

Jones, B.G., ed. 2006. *Decolonizing international relations*. Lanham, MD: Rowman and Littlefield.

Jones, W.T. 1980. *Masters of political thought: From Macchiavelli to Bentham*. London: Harrap.

Lewis, L. 2002. Envisioning a politics of change within Caribbean gender relations. In *Gendered realities: Essays in Caribbean feminist thought*, ed. P. Mohammed, 512–30. Kingston: University of the West Indies Press, Centre for Gender and Development Studies.

Lewis, P. 2003. Is the goal of regional integration still relevant among small states? The case of the OECS and CARICOM. In *Living at the border lines*, ed. C. Barrow-Giles and D. Marshall, 325–52. Kingston: Ian Randle.

Lewis, V. 1999. Time and tide: Changing orientations towards Caribbean integration. *Social and Economic Studies* 48 (4): 83–95.

Lexicon universal encyclopedia. 1989. Vol. 3. New York: Lexicon Publications.

Lister, R. 1995. Dilemmas in engendering citizenship. *Economy and Society* 24 (1): 1–40.

———. 1997. Citizenship: Towards a feminist synthesis. *Feminist Review* 57 (1): 28–48.

———. 2008. Citizenship and gender. http://www.socsci.aau.dk/cost/gender/working papers/lister.pdf (accessed 28 June 2009).

Martinez, I. 2007. *The open wound: The scourge of racism in Cuba from colonialism to communism*. Kingston: Arawak.

McWatt, M. 2006. *Suspended sentences: Fictions of atonement*. Leeds: Peepal Tree Press.

Meighoo, K. 2006. Caribbean civilization? *Integrationist* 3 (2): 1–7.

Mohammed, P. 1994. A social history of post-migrant Indians in Trinidad from 1917 to 1947: A gender perspective. PhD diss., Institute of Social Studies, The Hague, Netherlands.

————. 1995. Writing gender into history: The negotiation of gender relations among Indian men and women in post-indenture Trinidad society, 1917–47. In *Engendering history: Women in historical perspective*, ed. B. Brereton, V. Shepherd and B. Bailey, 20–47. Kingston: Ian Randle.

————. 1998. Ram and Sita: The reconstitution of gender identities among Indians in Trinidad through mythology. In *Caribbean portraits: Essays on gender ideologies and identities*, ed. C. Barrow, 391–413. Kingston: Ian Randle.

————. 1999. The Caribbean family revisited. In *Gender in Caribbean development*, ed. P. Mohammed and C. Shepherd, 164–75. Kingston: Canoe.

Nurse, K. 2004. Diaspora, migration and development in America. *Internationale Politik und Gesellschaft* 2:107–27.

Pateman, C. 1989. *The disorder of women*. Stanford, CA: Stanford University Press.

Payne, A., and P. Sutton. 2001. *Charting Caribbean development*. London: Macmillan.

Ramphal, S. 2009. Address at inauguration of Caribbean Association of Judicial Officers, Port of Spain, Trinidad, 25 June. http://www.normangirvan.info/caribbean-judicia ries-in-an-era-of-globalisation-sir-shridath-ramphal (accessed 4 July 2009).

Reddock, R. 1998. Contestations over national culture in Trinidad and Tobago: Considerations of ethnicity, class and gender. In *Caribbean portraits: Essays on gender ideologies and identities*, ed. C. Barrow, 414–35. Kingston: Ian Randle.

————. 2004. Caribbean masculinity at the fin de siècle. In *Interrogating Caribbean masculinities: Theoretical and empirical analyses*, ed. R. Reddock, 244–66. Kingston: University of the West Indies Press.

Reus-Smit, C. 2005. Constructivism. In *Theories of international relations*, ed. S. Burchill, A. Linklater et al., 194–201. Basingstoke, UK: Palgrave.

Robinson, T. 2004. Gender, feminism and constitutional reform in the Caribbean. In *Gender in the 21st century: Caribbean perspectives, visions and possibilities*, ed. B. Bailey and E. Leo-Rhynie, 592–625. Kingston: Ian Randle.

Salter, M. 2002. *Barbarians and civilization in international relations*. London: Pluto.

Senior, O. 1991. *Working miracles: Women's lives in the English-speaking Caribbean*. London: Currey.

Shanley, M.L., and C. Pateman, eds. 1991. *Feminist interpretations and political theory*. University Park: Pennsylvania State University Press.

Shepherd, V. 1999. *Women in Caribbean history: An introductory text for secondary schools*. Kingston: Ian Randle.

Sillie R. 2007. Speech of the secretary-general of the Association of Caribbean States to the twelfth Ordinary Meeting of the Ministerial Council, Guatemala City, Guatemala, 26 January. http://www.acs_aec.org (accessed April 2007).

Solis, L., and P. Solano. 2001. *Central America: The difficult road towards integration and the role of Canada*. FOCAL policy paper FPP-01-07. Ottawa: Canadian Foundation for the Americas (FOCAL).

The SPP: Myths vs. facts. http://www.spp.gov (accessed 2 July 2009).

Tang Nain, G., and B. Bailey, eds. 2003. *Gender equality in the Caribbean: Reality or illusion?* Kingston: Ian Randle.

Trillos Amaya, M. 2006. Fronteras y limites linguisticos en el Caribe Colombiano. In *El Caribe en la nacion Colombiana*, ed. A.A. Vives, 67–85. Bogota: Museo Nacional de Colombia/Observatorio del Caribe Colombiano.

Trotz, A. 2008. *Gender, generation and memory: Remembering a future Caribbean.* Working paper, no. 14. Bridgetown: Centre for Gender and Development Studies, The University of the West Indies.

Vives, A.A. 2006. *El Caribe en la nacion Colombiana.* Bogota: Museo Nacional de Colombia/Observatorio del Caribe Colombiano.

World Trade Organization (WTO). 1995. *Regionalism and the world trading system.* Geneva: WTO.

———. 2003. *Report 2003 of the committee on RTAs to general council WT/REG/13.* http://docsonline.wto.org (accessed 5 December 2009).

7

Engendering Security
HIV/AIDS and Human (In)Security in the Caribbean

WENDY C. GRENADE

Introduction

In this chapter I combine the concept of human security and a Caribbean feminist perspective to explore the intersection between security and gender in the Caribbean. My central question is: How can gender analysis advance the discourse on Caribbean security? My main contention is that gender analysis is intrinsic to security, and any conceptualization of Caribbean security cannot ignore the important category of gender. Why illuminate the intersection between Caribbean security and gender? I argue that Caribbean international relations scholars and feminists are seeking to understand the Caribbean problematic but that they are doing so from separate vantage points. While this approach may be useful for interrogating certain dimensions of the Caribbean's condition, an interdisciplinary approach is required to understand the complexity of Caribbean security.

Caribbean security goes beyond the Western state-centric, military paradigm. For the Caribbean, security is intricately linked to development. It is simultaneously a precondition for development and a desired outcome of the development process. Therefore, the quest to achieve security is compounded in the context of post-coloniality and underdevelopment. Poverty breeds insecurities, which in turn perpetuate further poverty. Given the historical evolution of the Caribbean and its location in the global political economy (Beckford 1972, 1999; Best 1966), Caribbean security must by necessity be concerned with the well-being and survival of Caribbean people and the viability of Caribbean economies.

I agree with Griffith, who argues that "the nature of the security challenges facing the Caribbean makes it imperative that scholars go beyond single disciplinary boundaries and adopt an interdisciplinary approach because meaningful examination of the region's security situation requires drawing on several fields of study, including economics, political science, history, psychology, sociology, geography, and environmental science" (1995, 13). While Griffith acknowledges the need for interdisciplinarity, his work does not go far enough to include the security concerns of Caribbean women (Griffith 1991, 1995, 2003, 2004, 2008).

Similarly, despite the richness of Caribbean feminist scholarship (Reddock 1994, 2004; Barrow 1998; Parpart, Connelly and Barriteau 2000; Mohammed 2002; Barriteau 1994, 2003; Slocum and Shields 2008), Caribbean feminists have not sufficiently interrogated the gendered nature of Caribbean security. As Byron and Thornburn observe, "little work has so far been done on the gender dimensions of conflict and security in the Caribbean" (1998, 217). There is therefore a gap in Caribbean scholarship, on the critical question of security and gender.

In this chapter, I seek to do two things. First, I aim to unsettle Westocentric international relations discourses and bring the Caribbean's reality to the fore. Mainstream international relations is concerned with "high politics" among great powers and ignores the plight of weaker states, such as those in the Caribbean. Given the Caribbean's postcolonial condition, Caribbean international relations must by necessity focus on the region's search to break from a history of poverty and underdevelopment, and to gain respect in the international community. Some of the central issues which preoccupy Caribbean international relations scholars and practitioners include poverty, unfair trade, high debt, HIV/AIDS, the illicit drug trade and environmental disasters. These forces threaten the capacity of Caribbean states to navigate effectively the global system, and undermine the security of Caribbean people. I focus specifically on the security concerns of Caribbean women, who I argue are the catalysts of Caribbean economies and societies.

Second, I will use security as a platform to marry the conversations between Caribbean international relations scholars and Caribbean feminists. Why is it necessary to do so? Caribbean women face a number of (in)securities in their everyday lives which are insufficiently captured in the security discourse. As heads of households and burden bearers in society, Caribbean women are particularly vulnerable to security threats. A large number of Caribbean women struggle consistently with poverty and other dimensions of economic insecurity. Many Caribbean women experience the negative impacts of natural disasters, human trafficking, the illicit drug trade, violence and criminality. Women and girls are most vulnerable to HIV/AIDS, which breeds human insecurity. Yet, despite the insecurities which surround women's lives, Caribbean scholarship does not sufficiently bring together in one place the gendered nature of Caribbean security.

The chapter is divided into four sections. Following the introduction, section two provides a broad overview of the security discourse. It includes the traditional paradigm, arguments to broaden the security debate, and a feminist and Caribbean perspective on security. In the third section I analyse the gendered nature of HIV/AIDS and the implications for human (in)security in the Caribbean. I use a framework which combines aspects of human security and gender analysis. Finally, I conclude with a discussion of the implications for Caribbean international relations theory and praxis.

An Overview of the Security Discourse

The Traditional Paradigm

> In anarchy, security is the highest end. Only if survival is assured can states safely seek such other goals as tranquillity, profit, and power. (Waltz 1979, 126)

Traditionally, realist thought has dominated the security discourse (Waltz 1959, 1979; Mearsheimer 1994/95, 1995, 2000; Glaser 2000; Van Evera 2000). The above observation by Kenneth Waltz epitomizes the realist perspective on security. This hegemonic theorizing of security confines the concept of security to the military sphere, making it part of the grand strategy of great powers preoccupied with state survival in an anarchical world characterized by a Hobbesian "war of all against all". Security is viewed merely as "the study of the threat, use and control of military force, especially of specific policies that states adopt in order to prepare for, prevent or engage in war" (Walt 1991). This conception of security was useful to explain the dynamics of the Cold War.

Realism still has great explanatory powers, particularly following the attacks on the United States on 11 September 2001, and the subsequent wars in Afghanistan and Iraq. Yet, it is limited for several reasons. It focuses on great powers and ignores the security concerns of weaker, less powerful states. It overemphasizes nuclear deterrence, privileges the military sphere and fails to grapple sufficiently with non-military threats (Balwin 1996). Realist conceptualizations of security are also state-centric and disregard the security concerns of people and communities. Therefore, realism is insufficient to analyse the convergence of old and new security challenges in the twenty-first century.

Broadening the Security Discourse

> The lives of billions of people are not merely "nasty, brutish and short", they are also full of uncertain horrors. An epidemic can wipe out a community, a famine can decimate a nation, unemployment can plunge masses into extreme deprivation, and insecurity in general plagues a large part of mankind with savage persistence. (Dreze and Sen, cited in Ahmad et al. 1991, 3)

The above observation aptly captures several key aspects of global (in)security. The end of the Cold War coincided with the intensification of the new wave of globalization. This process created a complex world order, with several overlapping security threats, such as "global crime; human trafficking; financial market instability and contagion (the spread of capital market collapse and sudden threats that can have extensive impact on the economy and people's lives); threats to job security (through global economic restructuring); the spread of diseases and conflict within national borders" (Fukuda-Parr 2004, 35–36). No longer could the concept of security be confined solely to the military sphere.

In the post–Cold War environment a body of work emerged which sought to broaden and deepen the security discourse to include military, economic, societal and environmental threats (Ullmann 1983; Rubenstein 1988; Matthews 1989; Eberstadt 1991; Moran 1991; Roberts 1990; Buzan 1991; Grant and

Newland 1991; Buzan, Weaver and de Wilde 1998; Buzan and Weaver 2004). This re-conceptualization of security seeks to incorporate the complex and multiple dimensions of security in the twenty-first century.

Attempts to broaden and deepen the concept of security have met with criticism. Critics argue that this makes the field intellectually incoherent and practically irrelevant (Dorff 1994; Mearsheimer 1994/95; Gray 1995). Mearsheimer (1995, 92) maintains that alternative approaches have neither provided a clear explanatory framework for analysing security nor demonstrated their value in concrete research. Walt (1991, 213) cautions that the adoption of alternative conceptions is not only analytically mistaken but also politically irresponsible (cited in Krause and Williams 1996, 230). Despite criticisms, new security paradigms continue to challenge realism.

Human Security

> [T]he concept of security has for too long been interpreted narrowly: as security of territory from external aggression, or as protection of national interests in foreign policy or as global security from the threat of nuclear holocaust . . . Forgotten were the legitimate concerns of ordinary people who sought security in their daily lives. (UNDP 1994, 22)

The concept of human security is a central pillar of the new security paradigm. It is generally concerned with protecting the vital core of human life and the welfare of ordinary people. It challenges state centrism and argues that threats to people's safety often come from states themselves. Human security covers insecurities related to the failure to meet basic economic and social needs as well as those related to conflicts between groups of nations and the failures of communities, nations and the global community to provide protection against threats (see Fukuda-Parr 2003). Human security proponents argue that people should be the primary referent of security. In this way, emphasis shifts from "a security dilemma of states to a survival dilemma of people" (Hudson 2005, 163).

The first major reference to human security occurred in the 1994 United Nations Development Programme Human Development Report. The report identified seven elements of human security: (1) economic security (freedom from poverty); (2) food security; (3) health security (access to health care and protection from diseases); (4) environmental security; (5) personal security (for example, physical safety from such things as torture, war, criminal attacks, domestic violence, drug use, suicide and traffic accidents); (6) community security (survival of traditional cultures and ethnic groups as well as the physical security of these groups); and (7) political security (enjoyment of civil and political rights and freedom from political oppression) (UNDP 1994, 24–25). I will draw on aspects of this framework to explore the intersection of gender, HIV/AIDS and human (in)security in the Caribbean.

There is now an emerging literature which examines the concept of human security in the context of globalization (Nef 1999; Stoett 1999; Thomas and Wilkin 1999; Khong 2001; Fukuda-Parr 2003 and 2004). The general contention is that globalization has exacerbated old insecurities and created new ones. "Human security goes beyond concepts of poverty, inequality and human rights, and emphasizes the downside risks or changes in the level of human well-being due to sudden changes that threaten the vital core of human lives", Fukuda-Parr states (2004, 35).

Critics warn that human security lacks a precise definition and it is expansive and vague, As Paris states, it appears to be "slippery by design, rendering it an effective campaign slogan but diminishing the concept's usefulness as a guide for academic research or policymaking" (2001, 88). Paris further argues that the United Nations Development Programme's list is so broad that it is difficult to determine what, if anything, might be excluded from the definition of human security (ibid., 90). Feminists also warn that there is a real danger that collapsing femininity or masculinity into the term "human" could conceal the gendered underpinnings of security practices. Indeed, the term "human" is typically presented as though it were gender-neutral, but very often it is an expression of the masculine (Hudson 2005, 157). And although we must be mindful of the criticisms, human security is still a useful concept to analyse gender and security.

Security: A Feminist Perspective

> A feminist perspective extends the general arguments about the nature of society to the realm of security and reminds us that comprehensive security can only be achieved if the relations of domination and submission in all walks of life are eliminated and gender justice is achieved. (Hudson 2005, 162)

In the above observation, Hudson summarizes the core of the feminist perspective on security. Since the mid-1980s, feminist challenges to the study of international relations have explored the role that gender plays in areas such as war, conflict and global security (Elshtain 1987; Enloe 1990; Tickner 1992, 1997; Peterson 1992; Baud and Smyth 1996; Youngs 2004; Singh 2006). Feminist perspectives on security take women's security as their main concern. Their definitions begin with the individual or community rather than the state or international system. Feminists view the military not as an assurance against outside threats, but as a source of women's insecurity.

Feminists focus on both the causes and consequences of war. They advocate a bottom-up approach to security in order to understand how social relations affect world politics. As Youngs observes, traditional approaches to security "fail to take account of the specific ways in which women and children are affected by war, military occupation, militarization, (forced) migration, human trafficking, sexual and other forms of slavery and (forced) prostitution" (2004, 83).

There is empirical evidence which suggests that war severely afflicts and affects women and children. For instance, rape has traditionally been viewed as a side-effect of war. In Darfur, for example, rape is used as a tool for subjugation of the black population in the region. Rape victims include children and women as old as seventy years (Singh 2006, 9). Another major consequence of war is human displacement. Again, women and children are the most vulnerable. For example, in Darfur over 90 per cent of people forced to leave villages have been women and children (UN Office for the Coordination of Humanitarian Affairs 2004). Singh (2006) points out that, since the end of the Cold War, women have been the primary victims in ethnic conflicts, and constitute the bulk of civilian deaths and displaced refugees.

Women and children constitute 80 per cent of the world's refugees (Tickner 1997, 625). Migration and human trafficking are also posing serious challenges: "Each year, between 700,000 and two million women and children are trafficked across international borders, falling victim to a growing and particularly exploitative category of global crime" (Fukuda-Parr 2004, 38). In essence, security threats have an impact on the everyday lives of women. Even so, traditional notions of security do not adequately capture these realities.

Security: A Caribbean Perspective

The contemporary Caribbean Community (CARICOM)[1] faces myriad security challenges. The structure of the current global political and economic order has exacerbated old insecurities and created new ones in every sphere of Caribbean life. Geopolitical rivalries contribute to energy and food insecurity, particularly for the most vulnerable persons, such as women and children. The intensification of globalization and trade liberalization has exacerbated poverty for many countries in CARICOM:

> The net effect of globalisation, trade liberalisation, privatisation, and market-driven policies on the small, open economies of CARICOM has been to create new tension and insecurity in the society. The promise of increased jobs, improved market access, new technologies, and financial and other resources to alleviate poverty has not materialized. In spite of modest macro-economic growth in most of the region, there is a new class of poor people in many countries . . . WTO rules that have threatened preferential market access for the main . . . have led to new, increased insecurities in the job market and the society as a whole, and raise the question of the long-term viability of some of the smaller states . . . Across the region, there is hidden poverty even in those countries whose per capita incomes rank them highest among developing countries. (Andaiye 2003, 75–76)

Andaiye (2003) points to the structural conditions which continue to plague the Caribbean in its search for economic security. In addition, money laundering, human trafficking, and the illicit drug trade and its attendant violence and criminality threaten societal safety, order and national security. The frequency and intensity of natural disasters increase environmental insecurity. The relatively high prevalence of HIV/AIDS undermines human security and overall development.

What is emerging in the Caribbean is a multidimensional, multilevel, interwoven maze of (in)securities. While this situation is not entirely new, it is problematic for CARICOM states, individually and collectively, and threatens the present and future well-being of Caribbean people. Within this context, in 2007 CARICOM Heads of Government recognized security as the fourth pillar of the Community, "given its ever-increasing importance and its cross-cutting and fundamental nature" (Caribbean Community 2007).

How then is Caribbean security conceptualized? The Caribbean security discourse has never focused solely on the traditional, state-centric, military notions of security. Caribbean security is multidimensional and has never been viewed merely as protection from military threats. It is, instead, "protection and preservation of a people's freedom from external military attack and co-ercion, from internal subversion and from the erosion of cherished political, economic and social values. These values include democratic choice and polit-ical stability in the political arena, sustainable development and free enterprise in the economic domain, and social equality and respect for human rights in the social arena" (Griffith 2004, 10). In essence, for the Caribbean, security is fundamentally about developmental security. That is, there is a direct interplay between security and development. Both concepts are intricately linked and one cannot be achieved without the other. For example, insecurities perpetuate underdevelopment and conditions of underdevelopment breed insecurities.

Griffith's work (1991, 1993, 1995, 2003, 2004, 2008) contributes immensely to the security discourse, especially in his advancement of a "new conceptual approach to Caribbean security" (2008, 221). His central question is: "What is an appropriate conceptual framework to examine contemporary security challenges?" In answering this question, Griffith recommends a "back to basics" mode whose ambit extends beyond US–Caribbean security relation-ships and aims to construct a holistic schema, not a segmented one, in the context of twenty-first-century realities (2008, 222).

Griffith reviews the Caribbean security discourse and points out that Robert Pastor's "whirlpool" approach is valuable and has relevance to the secu-rity area, but that it is an approach for interpreting US–Latin American/ Caribbean dynamics and is not designed purely with security in mind (Pastor 1982, cited in Griffith 2008, 222). He also notes that Anthony Maingot's appli-cation of interdependence theory pays considerable attention to security matters, but that his approach is intended essentially to explain and interpret US–Caribbean realities writ large (Maingot 1994, cited in Griffith 2008, 222). Similarly, James Rosenau (1998), Edward J. Greene (1990), Leslie Manigat (1988), Andrés Serbin (1990), Andy W. Knight and Kenneth B. Persaud (2001) and Tyrone Ferguson (2002) focus on the Caribbean in the context of inter-national politics, geopolitics and ideology, regional–international architecture for security governance, and management modalities and coping strategies (all cited in Griffith 2008, 222).

Griffith seeks to go beyond a limited conceptualization of security and emphasizes that security is multidimensional, with military, political, economic and other dimensions. He quotes Owen Arthur, who asserts that "it would be a fundamental error on our part to limit security concerns to any one area while the scourge of HIV/AIDS, illegal arms and drug trafficking, transnational crime, ecological disasters and poverty continue to stare us in the face" (Arthur 2002, cited in Griffith 2008, 222).

Griffith's article on "discrete multidimensional security framework" outlines traditional and non-traditional issues, core and peripheral threats which play out in both internal and external arenas and in which threat intensity can range from low to medium and high. He identifies poverty, political instability, drugs, crime, HIV/AIDS, terrorism, border and territorial disputes, and hurricanes as threats. Griffith highlights responses such as diplomatic, economic, emergency management, law enforcement, military and political instruments. He identifies actors within the national and international spheres and national and international security engagement zones (2008, 235). I accept the broad tenets of Griffith's framework. As mentioned above, however, he does not go far enough to address the specific security concerns of Caribbean women.

Gender, HIV/AIDS and Human (In)Security

> Cultural, social and economic pressures make women more likely to contract HIV infection than men, since they are unable to negotiate for safe sex because of their lower social and economic status and fear of violence. Men are vectors for transmission because of socialized sexual behavior patterns which allow them to have multiple sex partners. Young women and girls are increasingly being targeted for sex by older men seeking safe partners with virgins. Women and girls tend to bear the main burden for caring when they themselves are infected. (Noel-DeBique 2003, 167–68)

As Noel-DeBique (2003) points out in the above observation, gender dynamics in Caribbean societies exacerbate the spread of HIV/AIDS. Gender refers to "a system of social relations through which women and men are constituted and through which they gain differential access and are unequally allocated status, power and material resources within a society" (Barriteau 1994, cited in Barriteau 2002, 222). Several factors shape the gender–HIV/AIDS–human (in)security problematic in the Caribbean.

Social and cultural definitions of gender shape female and male behaviour, particularly in the realm of sexuality: "From the earliest age boys and girls are socialized to adopt specific ideals of femininity and masculinity. The social construction of gender portrays the ideal woman as being modest, pure, dependent, weak, acquiescent, vulnerable and abstinent until marriage, at which point the woman becomes subordinate to and obedient of her spouse. Masculinity defines male sexuality as heterosexual, virile and even promiscuous, knowledgeable, aggressive and in control of his environment, including the women around him" (Stevens 1973, cited in Anderson, Marcovici and Taylor 2002, 7). Research shows that multiple partnership is a demonstration of masculinity for men in the Caribbean (Anderson, Marcovici and Taylor 2002, 11–12). These gender dynamics have serious implications for the spread of HIV/AIDS. As one Jamaican study demonstrates, many women will tolerate a husband with multiple sexual partners, or they themselves will have multiple sexual partners in order to guarantee financial stability for themselves and their children (Weiss and Rao Gupta 1998; Blanc 2001; both cited in Anderson, Marcovici and Taylor 2002, 11–12).

Unequal power relations between women and men place women at a higher risk for contracting HIV. Empirical evidence supports the fact that Caribbean societies, apart from displaying cleavage between class and race divisions, are organized around hierarchical gender power relations with male domination reducing women to economic and emotional dependency (Clarke 1998, cited in Pargass and Clarke 2003, 40). Results of a household-based general population survey in six countries in the Organization of Eastern Caribbean States revealed that "it was striking that although 8 out of 10 respondents knew that condom use during sex was preventative against HIV infection, less than half of the sexually active male respondents reported consistent condom use with casual partners . . . [and] less than 1 in 5 women reported consistent condom use with casual partners" (Caribbean Epidemiology Centre 2007, 9). This data suggests that the susceptibility and vulnerability of women to HIV/AIDS surround unequal power relations in the "negotiation" of sex. Why is this so? Several factors, including women's subordinate social status and their need for emotional and economic security, usually influence women's (in)ability to insist on condom use and safely negotiate sex.

The unequal social status of women places them at a higher risk of contracting HIV/AIDS. Women are at a disadvantage with respect to access to information about HIV/AIDS prevention, the ability to negotiate safe sexual encounters and access to treatment for HIV/AIDS once infected (Anderson, Marcovici and Taylor 2002). In fact, "women often cannot control with whom or under what circumstances they have sex, whereas men often feel pressured to have sex with many different partners. Both are victims of the social construction of gender, but men's risk of HIV infection is primarily determined by their own proactive behaviour, whereas women's vulnerability to HIV infection is largely beyond their control" (ibid., 5). This problem is a gendered security dilemma which has negative consequences for both women and men in the Caribbean.

The need for emotional security – for instance, fear of losing a male partner and the perceived loneliness or emotional dependency which may ensue – is yet another reason why some women do not insist on condom use. Generally, if a woman insists that her male partner use a condom, she may undermine trust in the relationship. She may even be accused of cheating. This need for emotional security is often linked to the need for economic security.

Economic dependence is another factor which prevents women from insisting on condom use. In the Caribbean some women are still economically dependent on men and are often trapped in violent and abusive relationships which make them powerless to negotiate safe sex.

Gender dynamics are therefore compounded in the context of poverty and underdevelopment. The dilemma is: In the context of poverty, as women seek to satisfy short-term security needs, they can jeopardize their long-term security and survival. This endangerment, in turn, has negative implications for human security. In the rest of this chapter, I will specifically examine three dimensions of human (in)security in the Caribbean: economic (in)security, health (in)security and personal (in)security.

Economic (In)Security

At its core, economic security is freedom from poverty. In the Caribbean, however, there is "hidden poverty even in those countries whose per capita incomes rank them highest among developing countries" (Andaiye 2003, 75–76). Poverty is a serious factor that undermines security and development. HIV/AIDS has implications for an individual's ability to consume, produce and contribute meaningfully to the economy. In many cases, when an indi-

vidual is infected with or affected by HIV/AIDS, he or she is less able to purchase goods and services, pay taxes, contribute to health and welfare services
and influence the market. HIV/AIDS also affects production through loss of
labour and reduced savings. It also has a negative impact on family members
who are income earners, care givers and educators. The impact of the epidemic
erodes communities. Community members are often unable to provide services, leadership and support to their communities (Allen, McLean and Nurse
2004, 232).

In the Caribbean, heavy dependency on tourism and power differentials
between locals and tourists exacerbate the problem (Pritchard and Morgan
2000; Boxill et al. 2005). For example, among female sex workers, HIV prevalence has been found to be 3.5 per cent in the Dominican Republic, 9 per cent
in Jamaica and 31 per cent in Guyana (Allen, McLean and Nurse, 2004).
Across the region, sex tourism or tourism-oriented prostitution has become
an important topic of research and discussion because of the growing reliance
of national governments on income generated by tourism and tourism-related
activities. Karch and Dann's research (1981) on "beach boys" in Barbados
draws attention to the negotiations that take place between black Barbadian
men and white women around their sexual, gendered and racialized identities,
as well as the way in which the relationships are shaped by the location of
Barbados as a developing country locked into dependency on the global economy. The Dominican Republic, Cuba and Jamaica have also been sites for
research on tourism-related prostitution (O'Connell 1996; Brennan 1998). It
is not surprising that tourism-dependent economies have some of the highest
HIV prevalence rates and reported AIDS incidences in the region (Allen,
McLean and Nurse 2004). For example, HIV prevalence rates are relatively
high in the Bahamas, Barbados, the Dominican Republic and Jamaica, which
are key tourist destinations (see Kempadoo 1999, 2003, 2004). In a previous
work I referred to HIV/AIDS as an "unwelcome guest" in the tourism sector
and pointed to the policy dilemma which surrounds tourism dependency and
the threat of HIV/AIDS (Grenade 2008). There is, therefore, a negative relationship between the spread of HIV/AIDS and the quest for economic security
in the Caribbean.

Health (In)Security

In addition to economic security, another key aspect of human security is health security, which includes access to health care and protection from diseases (UNDP 1994, 27–28). Women's health involves their emotional, social and physical well-being, and is determined by the social, political and economic contexts of their lives, as well as by biology (United Nations 1996, 56, cited in Noel-DeBique 2003, 146). Severe threats to health can undermine human well-being, productivity and development. The HIV/AIDS pandemic is a grave source of health insecurity which transcends the health sector. The Caribbean's case must be understood within the larger global context. In 2000 the United Nations Security Council passed resolution 1308, which indicated that HIV poses a security threat to the nations of the world (United Nations Security Council 2000). Similarly, in that same year, the United States declared HIV a threat to national security (Allen, McLean and Nurse 2004, 221–22). In 2007 approximately 33 million persons were living with HIV worldwide. Of that number, 30.8 million were adults, 15.4 million were women, and 2.5 per cent were children under fifteen years of age (see table 7.1). AIDS remains one of the leading causes of death among persons aged twenty-five to forty-four (UNAIDS 2007, 29).

Women are disproportionately infected and affected by the disease. In sub-Saharan Africa, almost 61 per cent of adults living with HIV in 2007 were women. In the Caribbean, that percentage was 43 per cent, compared with 37 per cent in 2001. In eastern Europe and Central Asia, it is estimated that women accounted for 26 per cent of adults with HIV in 2007, compared with 23 per cent in 2001, while in Asia that proportion reached 29 per cent in 2007, compared with 26 per cent in 2001. UNAIDS reports that the proportion of women versus men has been increasing. For example, the proportion of women living with HIV in Latin America, Asia and eastern Europe is slowly growing, as HIV is transmitted to the female partners of men who are likely to have been infected through drug use or during unprotected paid sex or sex with other men (UNAIDS 2007).

The Caribbean has the second highest HIV/AIDS adult prevalence rate (1.1 per cent) in the world, after sub-Saharan Africa (5.0 per cent). During 1982 to 2005, a cumulative total of approximately thirty-one thousand AIDS cases were reported to the Caribbean Epidemiological Centre (CAREC) from

Table 7.1. Regional Statistics for HIV and AIDS (End of 2007)

Region	Adults and Children Living with HIV/AIDS	Adults and Children Newly Infected	Adult Prevalence* (percentage)	Deaths of Adults and Children
Sub-Saharan Africa	22,000,000	1,900,00	5.0	1,500,00
North Africa & Middle East	380,000	40,000	0.3	27,000
Asia	5,000,000	380,000	0.3	380,000
Oceania	74,000	13,000	0.4	1,000
Latin America	1,700,000	140,000	0.5	63,000
Caribbean	230,000	20,000	1.1	14,000
Eastern Europe & Central Asia	1,500,000	110,000	0.8	58,000
North America, Western & Central Europe	2,000,000	81,000	0.4	31,000
Global total	33, 000,000	2,700,000	0.8	2,000,000

*Proportion of adults aged fifteen to forty-nine who were living with HIV/AIDS.
Note: "The ranges around the estimates in this table define the boundaries within which the actual numbers lie,based on the best available information" (UNAIDS 2007, 1).
Source: UNAIDS 2007.

its member countries (CAREC 2007). In 2007 approximately seventeen thousand people in the Caribbean became infected with HIV, and more than eleven thousand died of AIDS. Haiti has the highest HIV prevalence in the entire Western Hemisphere (3.8 per cent), while Cuba has one of the lowest (0.1 per cent). The Bahamas (3.3 per cent), Trinidad and Tobago (2.6 per cent), and Guyana (2.4 per cent) are all heavily affected, while Puerto Rico is the only Caribbean country apart from Cuba where it is thought that less than 1 per cent of the population is living with HIV. Despite differences between countries, the spread of HIV in the Caribbean has taken place against a common background of poverty, gender inequalities and a high degree of HIV-related stigma (see Pan Caribbean Partnership Against HIV/AIDS 2008).

Biological factors place women and girls at a higher risk of contracting HIV/AIDS. The "soft tissue in the female reproductive tract tears easily, producing a transmission route for the virus. Additionally, vaginal tissue absorbs fluids more easily, including sperm, which has a higher concentration of the HIV virus than female vaginal secretions and may remain in the vagina for hours following intercourse" (Anderson, Marcovici and Taylor 2002, 8). This biological vulnerability is a dangerous threat to women's health security. When biological factors are combined with gender inequalities and poverty, the threat to health security in the region is all the more significant. There is then a multiplier effect. Women are often the caregivers of their families, and work within the home as well as pursuing paid employment. In most Caribbean countries nurses and teachers are predominantly women. The severe illness or death of women has a negative ripple effect throughout the society and the economy. The absence of a mother's care and strong influence in the home and society can encourage delinquency and social disorder. The decline in women's work, in and out of the home, can undermine productivity and further perpetuate economic (in)security.

Young women are particularly vulnerable to HIV/AIDS. HIV prevalence is two to four times higher in women fifteen to twenty-four years old than in their male counterparts. This pattern is consistent with findings from several surveys conducted in the Caribbean which indicate that females usually have their first sexual experience with an older male. Qualitative research has shown that females choose older men partly because they can gain access to goods that offer status, such as brand-name clothes, fast food and rides in cars (Allen, McLean and Nurse 2004, 224–25). Gender dynamics in Caribbean societies influence the interrelationship between health (in)security and economic (in)security. This problem is exacerbated in the context of personal (in)security in the Caribbean.

Personal (In) Security

> The fear of violence permeates women's daily lives, curtailing their freedom of movement and limiting what they do. (Pargass and Clarke 2003, 39)

Personal security includes physical safety from such things as torture, war, criminal attacks, domestic violence, drug use, suicide and traffic accidents (UNDP 1994, 30–31). I focus here on gender-based violence, which leads to women's increased susceptibility to HIV infection by limiting their physical and mental freedom:

> Men are the main perpetrators of violence against each other and against women. Socialized into a generally accepted warriorhood in defence of honour, nation, country and God, we find it difficult to seek other ways to negotiate autonomy, difference and change. It is in such a broad context that one must place the question of violence in society. Caribbean colonial society was forged in the crucible of violence. European occupation, the destruction of the indigenous peoples of the region and the enslavement of millions of African men and women are all fundamentally acts of violence, perpetrated on the minds and bodies of people . . . In this sense, therefore, violence is endemic to the system we have inherited and seek to reproduce. (Lewis 2002, 520)

When domestic violence is coupled with economic dependency, the resulting combination has direct implications for the spread of HIV/AIDS and human (in)security in the Caribbean. A study on urban poverty and violence in Jamaica suggests that there is a relationship between economic dependence and violence. Female participants from five communities perceived that high rates of unemployment led to greater dependency on men for income, which in turn led to an increase in domestic violence (Moser and Holland 1997, cited in Pargass and Clarke 2003, 44). This search for economic security can lead to unsafe sexual practices, which in turn can jeopardize health and personal security.

The trafficking of girls and women into prostitution is another form of violence against women which places them at risk for HIV infection. Because many of these women enter countries illegally and commercial sex is usually illegal, they receive no protection in law, experience social stigma and have almost no access to social and medical services (Anderson, Marcovici and Taylor 2002). In a documentary which highlights the plight of illegal Guyanese migrants in Barbados, one woman explained her predicament: "She [i.e., the woman who recruited her] would be telling the people that you would be coming to Barbados to work and when you come in Barbados here, . . . she just want you go work on the street. Some people does and some people don't. Some girls don't even know what they come here for. For example, like me. I never know I was coming to work on a street as a prostitute" (Davis 2007). This speaks to a larger question. In the context of the Caribbean Single Market (CSM), intra-CARICOM migration is necessary but problematic. The free movement of skills of both women and men is critical to advance human resource capacity and promote economic security in the region. Yet, as people move, state borders cannot be easily protected against the spread of diseases such as HIV/AIDS. In addition, given the gendered nature of the Caribbean's political economy, many women work in hotels, brothels, nightclubs and other high-risk jobs, which increases their chances of being exposed to HIV. Again, the search for economic security can undermine other dimensions of human security. The undocumented migrant mentioned above referred to the fact that it was a woman who recruited her from Guyana to work on the streets in Barbados. This admission throws light on the contradictions which surround gender dynamics in the Caribbean.

The question of intra-Caribbean migration is not new. In the contemporary era, however, new challenges emerge which can complicate existing realities. Unmanaged intra-Caribbean migration can generate social dislocations in the receiving country, encourage xenophobia and breed migrant insecurities. According to another Guyanese woman who explains her predicament as an illegal migrant in Barbados: "It's very scary. In a sense, you're always wondering if something is going to happen. You're not free, in the sense that you feel as though you're in a mental prison. But on the other hand it's a risk that I'm willing to take in the sense that I have a job, I'm working, I'm saving and I'm making a sacrifice that I'm willing to make right now because I'm young. But it is very difficult to be in this position" (Davis 2007). This is a dilemma which confronts Caribbean women as they search for security. In the case of Guyanese women, they are forced out of their country as a consequence of several factors, including racial politics, crime and poor governance. As they capitalize on the opportunities which the CSM may present, they are further exposed to exploitation and various forms of violence and insecurity.

Conclusion

In the context of post-coloniality, the search for Caribbean security and development is both necessary and problematic. As Caribbean states, individually and collectively, continue to grapple with old and new security threats, and as people in general and women in particular search for security in their everyday lives, understanding the social relations of gender must be central to the security discourse.

As I set out to establish throughout this chapter, the intersection of gender and HIV/AIDS complicates the security development nexus in the Caribbean. There is a gendered dynamic which undermines human security. I have used the case of HIV/AIDS to argue that, as women search for economic security they can often jeopardize their health security and their personal security. This endangerment, in turn, further undermines their economic security. There is, then, a gendered multiplier effect. Women are economic agents, caregivers and burden bearers within society. Their insecurity has a negative impact on a country's productive capacity; it threatens societal stability and national order.

What are the implications for theorizing Caribbean security? The case of gender, HIV/AIDS and human security in the Caribbean suggests the need for a more comprehensive dialogue between Caribbean international relations scholars and Caribbean feminists to probe the gaps which exist and to offer alternative frameworks for understanding the complexity of security and gender in the Caribbean. There is, therefore, scope for an interdisciplinary research agenda which continues to unpack traditional international relations paradigms. In particular there is a need to find the intersection between security and gender to explore how gender analysis can advance a more informed conceptualization of security. Developing a research agenda is critical since security threats pose a clear and present danger not only to global order and stability but also to the very lives of women, men and societies.

Notes

1. The Caribbean Community (CARICOM) is a regional arrangement which comprises fifteen states in the Caribbean Basin, which includes the anglophone, francophone and Dutch Caribbean. The states are: Antigua and Barbuda, Barbados, Belize, the Commonwealth of the Bahamas, the Commonwealth of Dominica, the Federation of St Christopher and Nevis, Grenada, Guyana, Jamaica, Haiti, Montserrat, St Lucia, St Vincent and the Grenadines, Suriname, and the Republic

of Trinidad and Tobago. In this paper I use "the Caribbean" and "CARICOM" interchangeably.

References

Ahmad, E., J. Dreze, J. Hills, and A. Sen, eds. 1991. *Social security in developing countries.* Oxford: Clarendon Press.

Allen, C., R. McLean, and K. Nurse. 2004. The Caribbean, HIV/AIDS and security. In *Caribbean security in the age of terror*, ed. I.L. Griffith, 219–51. Kingston: Ian Randle.

Andaiye. 2003. Smoke and mirrors: The illusion of CARICOM women's growing economic empowerment, post-Beijing. In *Gender equality in the Caribbean: Reality or illusion?*, ed. G. Tang Nain and B. Bailey, 73–107. Kingston: Ian Randle.

Anderson, H., K. Marcovici, and K. Taylor. 2002. *The UNGASS, gender and women's vulnerability to HIV/AIDS in Latin America and the Caribbean.* Washington DC: Pan American Health Organization.

Balwin, D. 1996. Security studies and the end of the Cold War. *World Politics* 48 (1): 117–41.

Barriteau, E. 1994. Gender and development planning in the postcolonial Caribbean: Female entrepreneurs and the Barbadian state. PhD diss., Howard University.

———. 2002. Women entrepreneurs and economic marginality: Rethinking Caribbean women's economic relations. In *Gendered realities: Essays in Caribbean feminist thought*, ed. P. Mohammed, 221–48. Kingston: Centre for Gender and Development Studies, University of the West Indies Press.

———, ed. 2003. *Confronting power, theorizing gender: Interdisciplinary perspectives in the Caribbean.* Kingston: University of the West Indies Press.

Barrow, C., ed. 1998. *Caribbean portraits: Essays on gender ideologies and identities.* Kingston: Ian Randle.

Baud, I., and I. Smyth, eds. 1996. *Searching for security: Women's responses to economic transformations.* London: Routledge.

Beckford, G.L. 1972. *Persistent poverty: Underdevelopment in plantation economies of the Third World.* New York: Oxford University Press.

———. 1999. *Persistent poverty: Underdevelopment in plantation economies of the Third World.* 2nd ed. Kingston: University of the West Indies Press.

Best, L. 1966. Size and survival. *New World Quarterly* 2 (3): 58–63.

Boxill, I., K.-A. Lewis, R. Frey, P. Martin, D. Treasure, W. Bowen, and T. Joseph. 2005. *Tourism and HIV/AIDS in Jamaica and the Bahamas.* Kingston: Arawak.

Brennan, D.E. 1998. Everything is for sale here: Sex tourism in the Soscia, the Dominican Republic. PhD diss., Yale University.

Byron, J., and D. Thorburn. 1998. Gender and international relations: A global perspective and issues for the Caribbean. *Feminist Review* 59 (Summer): 211–32.

Buzan, B. 1991. *People, states and fear.* 2nd ed. New York: Harvester Wheatsheaf.

Buzan, B., and O. Weaver, eds. 2004. *Regions and powers: The structure of international security.* Cambridge: Cambridge University Press.

Buzan, B., O. Weaver and J. de Wilde, eds. 1998. *Security: A new framework for analysis.* Boulder: Lynne Rienner.

Caribbean Community. 2007. Communiqué issued at the conclusion of the eighteenth inter-sessional meeting of the Conference of Heads of Government of the Caribbean Community (CARICOM), 12–14 February 2007, Kingstown, St Vincent and the Grenadines.

Caribbean Epidemiology Centre (CAREC). 2007. *The Caribbean HIV/AIDS epidemic and the situation in member countries of the Caribbean Epidemiology Centre.* Port of Spain: Caribbean Epidemiology Centre.

Davis, A. 2007. *On the map.* Film. St George, Barbados: [Annalee Davis].

Dorff, R.H. 1994. A commentary on security studies for the 1990s as a model core curriculum. *International Studies Notes* 19:23–31.

Eberstadt, N. 1991. Population change and national security. *Foreign Affairs* 70 (3): 115–31.

Elshtain, J.B. 1987. *Women and war.* New York: Basic Books.

Enloe, C.H. 1990. *Bananas, beaches and bases: Making feminist sense of international politics.* Berkeley and Los Angeles: University of California Press.

Fukuda-Parr, S. 2003. New threats to human security in the era of globalisation. *Journal of Human Development* 4 (2): 167–79.

———. 2004. Gender, globalization and new threats to human security. *Peace Review* 16 (1): 35–42.

Glaser, C. 2000. Realist as optimist: Cooperation as self-help. In *Theories of war and peace,* ed. M. Brown, O.R. Coté Jr., S.M. Lynn-Jones and S.E. Miller, 94–134. Cambridge, MA: MIT Press.

Grant, R., and K. Newland. 1991. *Gender and international relations.* Bloomington: Indiana University Press.

Gray, C. 1995. *Villains, victims and sheriffs: Security studies and security for an inter-war period.* Hull, UK: University of Hull Press.

Grenade, W.C. 2008. An unwelcome guest: Unpacking the tourism HIV/AIDS dilemma in the Caribbean (Grenada). In *New perspectives in Caribbean tourism,* ed. M. Daye, D. Chambers and S. Roberts, 188–218. New York: Routledge.

Griffith, I.L., ed. 1991. *Strategy and security in the Caribbean.* Westport, CT: Praeger.

———. 1993. *The quest for security in the Caribbean: Problems and promises in subordinate states.* Armonk, NY: Sharpe.

———. 1995. Caribbean security: Retrospect and prospect. *Latin American Research Review* 30 (2): 3–32.

———. 2003. Security and sovereignty in the contemporary Caribbean: Probing elements of the local–global nexus. In *Living at the borderlines: Issues in Caribbean sovereignty and development*, ed. C. Barrow-Giles and D.D. Marshall, 209–25. Kingston: Ian Randle.

———, ed. 2001/2004. *Caribbean security in the age of terror*. Kingston: Ian Randle.

———. 2008. A new conceptual approach to Caribbean security. In *The Caribbean community in transition: Functional cooperation as a catalyst for change*, ed. K. Hall and M. Chuck-A-Sang, 221–40. Kingston: Ian Randle.

Hudson, H. 2005. Doing security as though humans mattered: A feminist perspective on gender and the politics of human security. *Security Dialogue* 36 (2): 155–74.

Karch, C.A., and G.H.S. Dann. 1981. Close encounters of the third kind. *Human Relations* 34:249–68.

Kempadoo, K., ed. 1999. *Sun, sex and gold: Tourism and sex work in the Caribbean*. Lanham, MD: Rowman and Littlefield.

———. 2003. Theorizing sexual relations in the Caribbean: Prostitution and the problem of the "exotic". In *Confronting power, theorizing gender: Interdisciplinary perspectives from the Caribbean*, ed. E. Barriteau, 159–85. Kingston: University of the West Indies Press.

———. 2004. *Sexing the Caribbean: Gender, race and sexual labour*. London: Routledge.

Khong, Y.F. 2001. Human security: A shotgun approach to alleviating human misery? *Global Governance* 7 (3): 231–36.

Krause, K., and M.C. Williams. 1996. Broadening the agenda of security studies: Politics and methods. *Mershon International Studies Review* 40 (2): 229–54.

Lewis, L. 2002. Envisioning a politics of change within Caribbean gender relations. In *Gendered realities: Essays in Caribbean feminist thought*, ed. P. Mohammed, 512–30. Kingston: Centre for Gender and Development Studies, University of the West Indies Press.

Matthews, J. 1989. Redefining security. *Foreign Affairs* 68 (2): 162–77.

Mearsheimer, J.J. 1994/95. The false promise of international institutions. *International Studies* 19:5–49.

———. 1995. A realist reply. *International Studies* 20:82–93.

———. 2000. Back to the future: Instability in Europe after the Cold War. In *Theories of war and peace*, ed. M. Brown, O.R. Coté Jr., S.M. Lynn-Jones and S.E. Miller, 3–54. Cambridge, MA: MIT Press.

Mohammed, P., ed. 2002. *Gendered realities: Essays in Caribbean feminist thought*. Kingston: Centre for Gender and Development Studies, University of the West Indies Press.

Moran, T. 1990. International economics and national security. *Foreign Affairs* 69:5.

Nef, J. 1999. *Human security and mutual vulnerability: The global political economy of development and underdevelopment*. 2nd ed. Ottawa: International Development Research Centre.

Noel-DeBique, D. 2003. Gender equality and women's health. In *Gender equality in the Caribbean: Reality or illusion?*, ed. G. Tang Nain and B. Bailey, 146–77. Kingston: Ian Randle.

O'Connell, D.J. 1996. Sex tourism in Cuba. *Race and Class* 38:39–48.

Pan Caribbean Partnership against HIV/AIDS. 2008 *Overview of HIV/AIDS in the Caribbean*. http://pancap.org/index.php?option=com_content&task=view&id=52&It emid=1 (accessed 12 December 2008).

Pargass, G., and R. Clarke. 2003. Violence against women: A human rights issue post-Beijing five-year review. In *Gender equality in the Caribbean: Reality or illusion?*, ed. G. Tang Nain and B. Bailey, 39–72. Kingston: Ian Randle.

Paris, R. 2001. Human security: Paradigm shift or hot air? *International Security* 26 (2): 87–102.

Parpart, J.L., P. Connelly and E. Barriteau, eds. 2000. *Theoretical perspectives on gender and Development*. Ottawa: International Development Research Centre.

Peterson, V.S. 1992. Transgressing boundaries: Theories of knowledge, gender and international relations. *Millennium: Journal of International Studies* 21 (2): 183–206.

Pritchard, A., and N.J. Morgan. 2000. Privileging the male gaze: Gendered tourism landscape. *Annals of Tourism Research* 27 (4): 884–905.

Reddock, R.E. 1994. *Women, labour and politics in Trinidad and Tobago: A history*. London: Zed Books.

———, ed. 2004. *Interrogating Caribbean masculinities: Theoretical and empirical analyses*. Kingston: University of the West Indies Press.

Roberts, B. 1990. Human rights and international security. *Washington Quarterly* 13:65–75.

Rubenstein, R.A. 1988. Cultural analysis and international security. *Alternatives* 13:529–42.

Singh, A. 2006. Women and security: Addressing ethnic conflict through a gendered lens. Paper presented at the first annual graduate symposium, Centre for Foreign Policy Studies, Dalhousie University, Halifax, Canada, 24–26 March.

Slocum, K., and T.L. Shields. 2008. Critical explorations of gender and the Caribbean: Taking it into the twenty-first century. *Identities: Global Studies in Culture and Power* 15 (6): 687–702.

Stoett, P. 1999. *Human and global security: An exploration of terms*. Toronto: University of Toronto Press.

Thomas, C., and P. Wilkin, eds. 1999. *Globalization, human security and the African experience*. Boulder: Lynne Rienner.

Tickner, J.A. 1992. *Gender in international relations: Feminist perspectives on achieving global security*. New York: Columbia University Press.

———. 1997. You just don't understand: Troubled engagements between feminists and IR theorists. *International Studies Quarterly* 4:611–32.

Ullmann, R. 1983. Redefining security. *International Security* 8 (1): 129–53.

United Nations Development Programme (UNDP). 1994. *Human development report.* New York: Oxford University Press.

United Nations Office for the Coordination of Humanitarian Affairs. 2004. SUDAN: Militias ravage Darfur in gangs of hundreds. http://www.irinnews.org (accessed 5 June 2008).

United Nations Programme on HIV/AIDS (UNAIDS). 2007. United Nations AIDS, 2007 AIDS epidemic update. http://www.unaids.org/en/KnowledgeCentre/HIVData /EpiUpdate/EpiUpd Archive/2007/default.asp (accessed 6 June 2008).

United Nations Security Council. 2000. *Resolution 1308.* New York: United Nations Security Council.

Van Evera, S. 2000. Offense, defense, and the causes of war. In *Theories of war and peace,* ed. M. Brown, O.R. Coté Jr., S.M. Lynn-Jones and S.E. Miller, 55–93. Cambridge, MA: MIT Press.

Walt, S.M. 1991. The renaissance of security studies. *International Studies Quarterly* 35 (1): 211–39.

Waltz, K.N. 1959. *Man, the state and war.* New York: Columbia University Press.

———. 1979. *Theories of international politics.* New York: McGraw Hill.

Youngs, G. 2004. Feminist international relations: A contradiction in terms? Or: Why women and gender are essential to understanding the world "we" live in. *International Affairs* 80 (1): 75–87.

8

"These Issues Are Gender Neutral"

Caribbean Gender-Free Trade Relations

KRISTINA HINDS HARRISON

> Gender-neutral terms . . . frequently obscure the fact that so much of the real expe-
> riences of "persons", so long as they live in gender-structured societies, does in fact
> depend on what sex they are.
>
> – Susan Moller Okin, "Gender, the Public and the Private"

IN JUNE 2005 I CONDUCTED an interview with a representative of a private-
sector association in Trinidad and Tobago. The interview aimed to find out
the extent to which government and regional officials on international trade
matters consulted this organization, among others in Trinidad and Tobago.
The interview was pleasant and informative but became uncomfortable
towards the end when I asked the interviewee whether women's groups were
included in the trade consultations that he attended. The interviewee looked
at me in puzzlement and after a brief pause told me that women's groups were
not included because "these issues are gender neutral".

The interviewee is certainly not alone in his view that international trade
and other political and economic issues of international scope are gender
neutral. Views of this sort signal an assumed divorce between gender
and politico-economic affairs that can be linked to what Julie Nelson terms
"the Cartesian model of objectivity" (Nelson 1993, 25). Objectivity is often

conflated with masculinity, particularly white European masculinity. Thereafter, economic and political concerns can be treated as neutral. Although it can be beneficial to assume neutrality, particularly for economic modelling, doing so leads to the erasure of the lived experiences and concerns of women in general, and also of many men. Viewing international trade matters that have an impact on the Caribbean as gender neutral follows this gender-erasing pattern of Cartesian objectivity to the detriment of Caribbean people. Consequently, in this chapter I will contest this kind of neutrality by challenging conventional "gender-forgetting" ways of viewing Caribbean[1] international relations and international political economy in order to assert that more useful policy positions can emerge from recognizing and correcting the fallacy of gender neutrality. In order to situate my work as a challenge to conventional approaches to international relations and international political economy in general, and to Caribbean international political economy in particular, I provide a brief presentation of the basic assumptions and gender biases of these academic co-disciplines in the following section.

Gender, International Relations and International Political Economy: The Caribbean Context

Following the First World War, international relations emerged as a field of inquiry into matters of war and peace in world affairs. International relations was born as a Westocentric field which focused on the activities of Westphalian states (mostly on world powers), and has been dominated by debates between realists and liberals. Many of the divergences between realist and liberal international relations stem from the realist focus on the primacy of power and self-interest in interstate relations in contrast to liberals' concentration on the potentials and dynamics of cooperation.[2] Although international relations has changed over time, realist and liberal approaches continue to comprise the mainstream and, in so doing, perpetuate analyses which privilege the state in analyses of international affairs.

International political economy sits alongside international relations as the field that examines economic aspects of world affairs, in recognition that states can derive power from economic wealth and in light of the significance of economic interdependence and globalization to world politics.[3] Susan Strange defines international political economy as "the social, political and economic arrangements affecting the global systems of production, exchange and distribution, and the mix of values reflected therein" (Strange 1994, 18). International political economy emerged as a parallel discipline to international relations in the 1970s and draws on wide philosophical backgrounds, including classical economic liberalism, mercantilism, and the works of Marx and Gramsci, which have inspired neo-liberal, economic nationalist and critical-theory approaches to international political economy. Yet, like broader international relations, international political economy tends to be a white, male-dominated field of inquiry that focuses on the concerns and issues of significance to powerful or influential states in world politics.

Critical theorists have attacked the statist, elitist and capitalist nature of international relations and international political economy. Work focused on the economic South has also challenged the mainstream by taking critical perspectives and by casting a bright light on "Third World" issues that have an impact on, or are affected by, international affairs. Scholarship in the Caribbean forms part of this Third World challenge to mainstream international relations and international political economy. Caribbean works elevate concerns and issues of microstates that are heavily influenced by international politics but are often forgotten in international relations/international political economy analyses, which tend to focus on influential states in world affairs. For example, Ivelaw Griffith's *Caribbean Security in the Age of Terror* (2001) presents Caribbean perspectives on (in)security. Similarly, Ramesh Ramsaran's *Caribbean Survival and the Global Challenge* (2002) provides useful insights into international relations and international political economy.

Constructivists have also called into question the supposedly objective nature of statist, self-interested and power-absorbed neo-realist analyses. For instance, Alexander Wendt asserts that relations among states and other actors are socially constructed, as opposed to following some neo-realist logic of self-help based on state power and interests (Wendt 1992). Moreover, constructivists such as Blyth (2002, 2003), Woods (1995) and Wendt (1999) note that ideas are important in constituting interests. Therefore, international affairs are inter-subjective. Many of these critiques of the mainstream in international relations and international political economy omit gender, however.

Postmodern approaches have gone further, though, by exposing the power relations which plague claims to truth and objectivity in international relations. For instance, Smith notes that "all power requires knowledge and all knowledge relies on and reinforces existing power relations" (Smith 1997, 181). Consequently, neither realist perspectives which elevate powerful states and their interests, nor liberal ones which elevate cooperation between states are objective. To post-modernists, much of mainstream international relations/ international political economy is subjective.

Feminist perspectives in international relations and international political economy tend to pick up on post-modernist critiques by highlighting the exclusion of gender in these disciplines. In her discussion of feminist method-ologies in international relations, for instance, Ann Tickner has noticed "the often unseen androcentric or masculine biases in the way that knowledge has traditionally been constructed in all the disciplines" (Tickner 2005, 3). In addi-tion to Tickner, Cynthia Enloe, Spike Peterson, and Anne Sisson Runyan provide a wealth of feminist readings of international occurrences in response to the masculine bias of the traditional approaches of international relations (Tickner 1997, 2002; Enloe 1990, 1993; Peterson 1992; Peterson and Sisson Runyan 1993). In international political economy, feminist scholars such as Carla Freeman (2001) and Lourdes Benería (1999) have examined the often-omitted intersections between globalization and gender. Meanwhile, Diana Thorburn and Jessica Byron have advised Caribbean scholars of the necessity of using the lens of gender to view international relations/international polit-ical economy issues such as (in)security brought by crime, domestic violence, economic privation or narco-trafficking; human rights; and international trade and finance (Thorburn and Byron 1998; Thorburn 2000).

My analysis continues along the lines of these feminist challenges to international relations/international political economy by problematizing gender-"neutral" approaches to the study and negotiation of Caribbean inter-national trade relations. Focusing on trade within the realm of international political economy also signals a challenge to gender biases in the field of eco-nomics, as international political economy discusses the intersections between international political and economic occurrences. Gender is not simply a mat-ter of sex; it also involves socially created, accepted and recreated power relations. V. Eudine Barriteau aptly notes that gender refers to "complex sys-tems of personal and social relations of power through which women and men are socially created and maintained and through which they gain access to, or are allocated, status, power and material resources within society" (Barriteau 1994, cited in Barriteau 2003, 31). Thus, taking a gender-sensitive approach to international trade relations entails bringing to the fore power dynamics of negotiating processes and the differential impacts of issues under negotiation on men and women. Serious consideration needs to be given to gendered power relations as treatments of Caribbean international trade politics that disregard the power relations that govern the abilities of women and men to access resources are complicit in reinforcing injustices within Caribbean societies. Consequently, my analysis takes a feminist perspective that urges correcting the biases complicit in ignoring and oppressing women, through the emancipatory act of putting women at the centre. This approach draws on sentiments expressed by bell hooks (1989) which see placing women at the centre as a necessary part of the struggle to end inequalities caused by the domination of women, and by domination in general.

Within the Caribbean, appeals for Special and Differential Treatment, or for acknowledgment of the particular needs of small island developing states in trade and economic affairs (e.g., Bernal 2001), do speak to the need for equity in international trade affairs. All the same, these kinds of calls for equity remain incomplete, so long as they continue to use "neutral" approaches that are complicit in marginalizing women in both theory and practice. We can only truly strive toward Caribbean approaches to international trade politics based on equity if we halt and reverse injustices committed under the veil of gender neutrality. In brief, this work joins feminist Caribbean international relations/international political economy, which seeks to incorporate women's lives into scholarship and practice, in asserting that the social relations of gender should be systematically incorporated in the study and negotiation of Caribbean trade affairs.

People-Free, Gender-Free Trade and Economic Man

The World Trade Organization (WTO) came into being in 1995 following the Uruguay Round of the General Agreement on Tariffs and Trade (GATT). Along with the WTO came the requirement that trade agreements between WTO members be WTO compatible. As a result, current trade agreements have become ever more "free trading", "market oriented" or "neo-liberal". These terms suggest that free markets should facilitate international trade. States should decrease tariffs on imported goods in order to make products more affordable for consumers. Decreasing barriers to trade in this way should provide all countries with opportunities they can exploit, based on the neo-classical economic notion of comparative advantage. In the end, a more efficient allocation of resources brought about by negotiating freer trade agreements and by specializing on the basis of comparative advantage will benefit the states involved and should contribute to enhancing world welfare. From this perspective, all that Caribbean states need to do to benefit from the neo-liberal bounty in the pursuit of economic growth is to develop the capacity to allow producers and traders to make use of these opportunities (Ramesar 2002, 349) and be ready to face some adjustments.

This market-oriented world is one of abstractions, however. It appears to be void of people. There are states, issues, statistics, tariff rates, schedules and all sorts of "factors" that relate to trade, but there are hardly any people. Markets and economies are viewed as objects to be manipulated. Further, international negotiations related to these objects are treated as gender neutral and technical in nature. The neo-liberal slant of current trade negotiations leads negotiators and academics to conduct allegedly neutral discussions about states' economies or the international trade system. This neutrality is not altogether surprising, since neo-classical economics, on which these concepts are based, begins with abstractions to homo-economicus, or economic *man*, which are then generalized to all individuals.

Economic man is self-interested; he is the egoist whose aim is to maximize utility. He can make rational choices and undertakes economic activities in the competitive market. Based on these assumptions about human behaviour one can predict economic behaviours by using mathematical modelling without necessarily having to return to people, especially when it comes to macroeconomic activities. Again, Julie Nelson's discussion of Cartesian objectivity proves useful in highlighting that masculine models and perspectives have crafted actors within economics (Nelson 1993). Similarly, Paula England discusses the androcentric bias in neo-classical economics which begins with masculine assumptions about human nature and tends to focus on men's interests by concentrating on markets (England 1993). The economy is theorized as public and male, even though the term "economy" can be connected in European thought to the Greek *oikonomikos*, which equates to household or estate management (Backhouse 2002, 16–17; Rousseau 1775/1923). Instead of focusing on the household, though, studies of economics make a jump to the public sphere. For instance, in *Discourse in Political Economy* (1775),

Rousseau states that *"public* economy . . . has been rightly distinguished from *private* economy" (Rousseau 1775/1923; emphasis added). Additionally, Adam Smith's *Wealth of Nations* (1776) places the man, the husband specifically, as the economic actor in society since his wages function to support the family (see Bodkin 1999; Ferber and Nelson 1993). According to classical political economy, men's actions drive the economy, while women conduct invisible and unpaid reproductive work in the home. Economic life is male and, since the economy is created through economic life, it too becomes a male object. This kind of objectification and abstracting of human activity is further facilitated by the professionalization of economics as a discipline that coincided with an increasing focus on mathematics and modelling towards the end of the nineteenth century (Backhouse 2002, chaps. 8 and 9; Nelson 1993).

In European political and economic thought the nation-state is also somehow a male entity. Once more, Rousseau's *Discourse in Political Economy* is informative in asserting that a state has "nothing in common with the family except the obligations which their heads [fathers/husbands] lie under of making both of them happy" (Rousseau 1775/1923). Canonical international relations texts which speak to the nature of the state and to sovereignty also subjugate and then banish women from the masculine state (Sylvester 1998). It is no surprise, then, that gender rarely enters the discussion when macro-economic issues are studied in connection with states' activities in international political economy. Gender-neutrality is achieved through generalizing to masculinity and then, as if by magic, making the maleness of it disappear.

Although the macro-economy and the state are often central in international political economy analyses, there is scope for other actors. For example, the work of authors such as Peter Gourevitch (1978, 1986), Ronald Rogowski (1987, 1990) and Jeffrey Frieden (1988, 1991), highlight that the interests of economic sectors are important in international political economy because sector-based concerns inform the interests of states. A look at the impact on people's lives, particularly differentiated by gender, is markedly absent from such discussions, however. But should gender feature into these types of discussions?

A look at the various impacts of the banana disputes within the WTO demonstrates both that gender needs to be considered in the study and in negotiation of commercial pacts, and that neo-liberal trade agreements may not be as beneficial as predicted. Focusing on the banana disputes forces one to see the problems associated with using gender-neutral abstractions to make decisions about various aspects of people's lives. The following discussion signals that complying with economic agreements can bring insecurity and instability, not only to economies, states and sectors, but also to people's – to women's – lives. As a consequence, gender should, and indeed must, be considered in appraising and negotiating trade arrangements.

Bananas!

In 1997 a WTO dispute settlement body found the European Union to be acting at odds with GATT rules in the famed banana dispute in which Ecuador, Guatemala, Honduras, Mexico and the United States challenged the European Union's preferential regime for the importation of bananas from the African, Caribbean and Pacific (ACP) group of countries. Following this WTO ruling, the European Union reduced the quotas it had offered to ACP banana producers under the Lomé agreements, and replaced these quotas with tariffs (also called "tariffication") in 2005.

Latin American banana producers gained their desired outcome through this WTO dispute. These countries' more competitively priced bananas gained improved access to European markets through a challenge to the WTO's inconsistent policies on the Lomé agreements. Much of the gains of this WTO victory accrued to multinational corporations such as Chiquita Brands, Dole Food Company and Del Monte Fresh Produce, however. Such corporations wield a great deal of power over production, finance and technology in the Latin American banana industries. Multinational corporations act as owners of many of the plantations, as employers of labourers at rather low wages, and as implementers of production systems that make wide use of technology and agrochemicals in order to increase yields and profits (Sutton 1997; Thompson 1987, 22–24). Wage suppression has been an important element in maintaining the competitiveness of Latin American bananas. Consequently, plantation labourers have had to battle, with the help of often-struggling unions, to have their demands for higher wages heard by the management of agricultural multinational corporations (Frundt 2002, 11–13). Latin American banana farmers want higher wages, but an increase in wages would contribute to higher banana prices – exactly the opposite of what the corporations and consumers want.

Unlike banana production in Latin America, banana production in the Caribbean's Windward Islands relies heavily on peasant farming. In the Windward Islands, banana farming has typically been conducted on relatively infertile, steep land that was often the only land to which the ex-slave population had access (Barrow 1992, 24–28). Furthermore, in 1983 the British-owned firm Geest gave up ownership of its banana plantations in the Windward Islands to focus on the more lucrative shipping business. Geest's withdrawal from the plantations allowed local farmers to buy the land and, consequently, to see more of the profits from banana farming (Thompson 1987, 30–31). Therefore, banana farmers in the Windward Islands have gained significant control over their livelihoods. These farmers have been able to earn better livings than Latin American banana growers, who usually work on foreign-owned plantations. This independence has, however, meant that individual farmers have often borne the brunt of the risks and costs of growing and producing bananas. Small-scale independent production has also contributed to the Windward Islands' banana farmers' seeing smaller returns on their produce than are seen on Latin American bananas (Ransom 1999). The loss of preferential access to European markets that followed the WTO dispute has led farmers in the Windward Islands to work ardently at becoming more efficient in order to stay in the production of bananas in the face of competition from large-scale Latin American competitors. Farmers have also made use of the Fair Trade label to market Windward Island bananas in Europe, in the hope that consumers will be empathetic to the cause of small farmers (Oxfam 2007; Godfrey 1998).

More broadly, changes to the European Union's banana regime that followed the WTO ruling have had negative impacts on household incomes in banana exporting islands. To be specific, the proportions of banana growers and those directly employed in banana farming declined substantially by 1998 (Pantin, Sandiford and Henry 2005, 155), and it has been predicted that Windward Island bananas will suffer from tariffication to the tune of US$100 million annually (Gillson, Hewitt and Page 2004, 3), even though in April 2008 the WTO still found the European Union's amendments to its regime for ACP bananas to be GATT inconsistent (WTO 2008, 224–25).

Declines in employment and shifts away from banana farming have had different impacts on women and men. These differentiated impacts can be understood in light of gender roles. According to Michaeline Crichlow, in the transition to small-farmer banana production for export in the region (and away from estate-based production), "many women . . . placed themselves under their male partners' leadership in order to sustain family farms and relinquished their independent earning potential" (2003, 43). Although women undertook little of the actual farming of bananas, they were involved in marketing activities, in trading bananas informally across borders and in subsistence production of vegetables and livestock (ibid., 44; Garcia 2005, 19). Women tended to perform functions which were supportive of the banana industry or to perform household work, while "they relied on their spouses to engage in the public domain" (ibid., 44). These shifts denote not only the movement from dual to single incomes within some banana-producing households but also the placement of women, to some extent, at the mercy of those formally employed in the banana industry. As a consequence, declines in household income which have resulted from the WTO trade ruling have adversely affected women in the Windward Islands in ways directly linked to their gender roles. For example, Zoraida Garcia notes that increases in levels of female unemployment and poverty have stemmed from the declining fortunes of bananas in the Windward Islands (Garcia 2005, 20).

Another alleged outcome of the decline of bananas in the region has been the upsurge in marijuana cultivation for export (Godfrey 1998; Crichlow 2003, 38). The farming of this illicit crop has raised security concerns of an international scope and should not be disconnected from the declining fortunes of Caribbean bananas. Although it does not connect a 2008 drug raid in St Vincent to the decline of bananas, a report by Barry Alleyne in Barbados's *Nation* newspaper (3 May 2008) speaks to the fact that growing marijuana has provided a lucrative though risky economic option in the region. This illegal trade not only contributes to the international drug trade and to crime rates in the region; it also has specific, gendered impacts including the use of women as "mules" in the transportation of these "valuable" commodities across territorial borders. This manner of drug trafficking has negative social consequences for the Caribbean as a result of the incarceration of some of these women in prisons across the region and around the world. Further, securitization and criminalization of both the luggage and bodies of female Caribbean travellers at international borders follows. Trade agreements negotiated under the pretext of gender neutrality have an impact on lives, not simply on abstract economies, sectors or markets.

Even when one sets aside the banana issue, the impacts of trade relations on people's lives, and specifically on women's lives, should not be forgotten in Caribbean international political economy, and the potentials opened by negotiating free trade agreements should not be taken for granted either. Some key questions should be asked about the opportunities created by trade pacts. First, for whom will enlarging market access generate opportunities? Indeed, scholars and officials have often asked this question but they tend to focus on sectors or industries within the region rather than on people. In addition, there is an equally significant question needed to qualify this query: Will women – particularly poor women with limited access to resources (including credit) and burdened with much of society's reproductive work – be able to reap benefits from improved market access? The point here is that trade arrangements affect people's lives in the Caribbean in different ways, depending on each person's location within gendered social hierarchies. This is so despite the fact that trade and economic issues tend to be treated as technical matters up for negotiation between states. Treatments of trade relations need to be altered to consider people's lives, and taking a gender-based approach is a useful way of doing so. Considering gender in discussions about trade is significant for limiting the forgetful harm that gender neutrality can inflict on people's lives.

Here, a useful parallel may be drawn between liberalizing commercial pacts and structural adjustment programmes, which have been implemented in the Caribbean under the guidance of the International Monetary Fund and the World Bank from the late 1970s.[4] In order to gain International Monetary Fund/World Bank assistance in times of financial crisis, governments were advised, particularly in the 1980s and 1990s, to reduce their spending by privatizing state-owned enterprises, decreasing or stabilizing public-sector wage bills, cutting back on social services spending and ending subsidization schemes wherever possible. Countries were also advised to devalue their currencies and to introduce new taxes to generate supplementary government revenue (McAfee 1991, 68–69). These policies were thought to allow struggling countries to recover and were based on generalizations and abstractions about developing countries' governments, economies and economic actors. People only entered this policy advice as secondary concerns, and women appear not to have been considered at all. All the same, structural adjustment programmes had a direct impact on people's lives. Instead of making life better, structural adjustment programmes tended to hurt both the middle and lower echelons in Caribbean societies (Whitehead 1994, 12, 20, 22). To underscore this point, V. Eudine Barriteau states that structural adjustment programmes in the region had detrimental effects on women in light of "the gender biases inherent in these policies and in the neo-classical economic paradigm on which they are based" (1996, 142). She notes some of the deleterious effects of these supposedly gender-neutral policies on lives in the Caribbean, and places particular emphasis on the burdens carried by women who have had to craft coping strategies to deal with cuts in public-sector spending, increased taxation, increased unemployment, privatization and liberalization. Important too, especially when drawing the parallel with liberalizing trade agreements, is the tendency of these policies to "accentuate unequal relations of power" unwittingly by making use of macro-economic abstractions that disregard the economic significance of households and the "asymmetrical impact on the women and men forced to bear the burden of adjustment" (ibid., 148). Peggy Antrobus goes further in stating that, "far from not taking women into account, the structural adjustment policies are actually grounded in a gender ideology which is deeply exploitative of women's time and labour. Contrary to what we are taught in our economics courses there are no value-free theories" (1993, 13).[5] Like structural adjustment programmes, liberalizing trade arrangements tend to follow neo-liberal macro-economic logics while they forget to focus on people's lives. The potential negative outcomes for Caribbean societies of not focusing on people or gender when it comes to trade relations is parallel to the ill effects of omitting gender under structural adjustment programmes. This potential drives home the need to concentrate on gender in international political economy treatments relating to Caribbean trade relations and in processes of preparing for and negotiating commercial agreements.

My analysis insinuates that Caribbean discussions and negotiations surrounding international trade agreements are *entirely* disconnected from people's lives. To begin with, people enter trade relations as consumers. Trade liberalizing agreements should be beneficial to the region's consumers, as these pacts should enable Caribbean consumers to access lower-cost, imported commodities. Access to more affordable goods should, in turn, reduce the cost of living, thereby allowing Caribbean people to reap gains from trade liberalization. Market opening to reduce costs to consumers comes with warnings, however. For instance, there are concerns about low-cost imported foods displacing food items produced domestically or regionally. In this connection, discussions about food security in an already import-dependent region, and about declining health and nutrition standards that may accompany substituting local or regional produce with cheap imports have come to the fore (see CARDI 2005; Deep Ford and Rawlins 2007). Some analyses of Caribbean trade relations examine these consumer issues, but these analyses need to be infused with gender analysis in order to gauge the true impacts of liberalizing policies on the region's populations.

The issue of employment also introduces humans to "trade speak", but a focus on people can be easily avoided by instead speaking of labour markets. Negotiated agreements should have positive, employment-generating effects or should have a positive impact on the region's labour markets. A focus on human resources and the need to develop them so that the labour market may benefit from changes in the economic landscape also extends the discussion of people. Once more, though, people are treated as abstract entities, this time to be developed along with infrastructure and institutions. Unsurprisingly, consideration of gender rarely enters. Yet gender is significant: Which women and/or men will gain or lose employment opportunities in connection with a negotiated trade agreement? Which men and/or women will comprise the human resources to be developed in order to exploit new opportunities? Questions such as these must be posed and answered from a gender-based perspective.

Taking further the argument about the exclusion of people in discussions about trade, one can assert that the concentration of trade talks on the private sector, industry, agriculture, the economy and various technical matters drives home the insignificance of actual living, breathing people. Lucy Eugene's discussion of labour standards in international trade makes a similar point by noting that the individual in the WTO context "is subject to a rather narrow interpretation, namely, the individual economic operator – that is, the producer" (2002, 283). This type of reification allows one to treat negotiating agendas as technical issues. By discussing markets, commodities, tariff levels and the like, we may forget about the many people who trade and are affected by trade. And we may forget that negotiated trade agreements cover social relations and that several discourses, not only on Caribbean trade relations but also on the prospects of the Caribbean in a time of neo-liberal trade agreements, perpetuate this forgetfulness by concentrating on states, economies, sectors and industries.

Gender-Free Trade Discussions and Texts

Studies on the region tend to consider the power relations in international affairs that have created the neo-liberal approach to trade as the only viable option in the early twenty-first century (e.g., Samuel 1999; Pantin, Sandiford and Henry 2005; Thomas 2005). Economies and the economic sectors contained in them must seek to cope. Therefore, we see sector-based discussions on trade matters.

In agriculture, scholars have looked at the sugar industry, the banana industry and non-traditional agricultural exports. In the service sector we encounter discussions about tourism, cultural industries and information service industries. When it comes to manufactured goods there are discussions about apparel and other light industries (e.g., Ramesar 2002; Singh 2002; Nurse 2002; Barclay, Henry and James 2005; Thomas 2005).[6] These discussions are often devoid of people. Some authors, however, have spoken of the need to take a people-centred approach to trade in the region (Girvan 2006, 99–102). Additionally, some scholarship has emerged on gender and trade in the region (see the texts cited in Stuart 2003). Yet, the norm is to focus on discussions about competitiveness and the impacts of liberalizing agreements on industries, sectors and, ultimately, on state economies, while hardly taking people into account and hardly ever taking gender relations into consideration. If equity for the region is a significant concern, though, gender must be incorporated into analyses of Caribbean trade relations.

Caribbean discussions of trade relations are not alone in their tendency towards gender exclusion. When one considers trade agreements to which Caribbean Community members are parties and around which international political economy discussions on trade revolve, it is clear once again that gender has little or nothing to do with these arrangements. For instance, consider the WTO. Thirteen of the fifteen Caribbean Community member states are WTO members.[7] The WTO lays down rules for continual trade liberalization via three main legal agreements that accompany the Agreement Establishing the WTO: the General Agreement on Tariffs and Trade (GATT), the General Agreement on Trade in Services (GATS), and Trade-Related Aspects of

Intellectual Property Rights (TRIPS).[8] On browsing these texts it becomes clear that gender is not a concern and obviously did not enter into the minds of the persons who negotiated the terms of the WTO during the Uruguay round of the GATT. Nowhere in the Agreement Establishing the WTO, the GATT, the GATS or the TRIPS will one encounter the terms "women" or "gender". These omissions contribute to reinforcing unequal power relations, since trade affairs are not uniform in the ways in which they affect people's lives. People, however, are considered.

To begin with, the Agreement Establishing the WTO makes reference to improving standards of living and attaining full employment within member states (WTO 1994a). Also, in the GATT there are several references to improving the living standards of a country and/or its people, particularly in article 18 (Governmental Assistance to Economic Development), article 36 (relating to trade and development) and in the preamble to the agreement. The GATT again refers to people in the general exceptions listed in article 20.a–b, which authorizes states to take measures to preserve "public morals" and "human, animal or plant life and health" (GATT 1947). The GATS and TRIPS also include similar exceptions to protect people and morals under article 14 and article 27, respectively (WTO 1994b, 1994c). Compared to the GATT, the texts of the GATS and the TRIPS are much more focused on people. Within the GATS there is an emphasis on "natural persons" and their ability to cross territorial borders to supply services. Similarly, under the TRIPS, individuals (natural or legal persons) are significant, as they are some of the important bearers of the intellectual property rights to which the agreement speaks (WTO 1994b, 1994c).

Despite the fact that WTO texts speak of people, the people who are included in the texts tend to be generic, sexless entities. When the documents mention people, "people" are assumed to be undifferentiated commercial operators whom the agreements will affect or who will be able to make use of the agreements. When it comes to states, though, WTO texts and individual countries' schedules for trade liberalization take into consideration differences between industrialized and developing countries. Even if inadequate, there is recognition of the differences among countries. By extension, then, there is some recognition that people located within developing states require differentiated treatment. There is, however, no such acknowledgement of differing power relations based on class, race, ethnicity and sex that affect the quality of life of people residing within states. No doubt neo-classical economics and mainstream international relations/international political economy have shaped this neutral approach employed by the institution created to govern the neo-liberal trade order. This kind of neutrality in the WTO, then, contributes to the normalcy of gender exclusion in WTO-compatible commercial treaties. Nonetheless, there are some WTO-compatible trade agreements that attempt to include gender. One of these pacts is the European Partnership Agreement (EPA) between CARIFORUM and the European Community,[9] which was initialled on 30 December 2007.

The EPAs are intended to replace the previous Lomé agreements, which provided non-reciprocal market access for a range of ACP exports into European Union markets. Replacing the Lomé with the EPAs was important, since much of the preferential treatment accorded to the ACP states was allowed under a WTO waiver which expired on 30 December 2007. Negotiations began in 2002 to replace the Lomé with WTO-compatible agreements for trade and development in the form of EPAs to be negotiated between the European Union and the six ACP regions (West Africa, Central Africa, Eastern and Southern Africa, the Southern African Development Community, the Caribbean, and the Pacific). The framework for these agreements emerged from the Cotonou agreement, signed in June 2000, which committed the European Union and the ACP to create trade and development relationships that would lead towards fulfilment of the United Nations' Millennium Development Goals (European Commission 2007). Therefore, it is not altogether surprising that the EPA between CARIFORUM and the European Union seems somewhat socially concerned and speaks about women.

For instance, article 5 of the agreement on monitoring explicitly mentions women: "The Parties undertake to continuously monitor the operation of the Agreement through their respective participative processes and institutions, as well as those set up under this Agreement, in order to ensure that the objectives of the Agreement are realized, the Agreement is properly implemented and the benefits for *men, women, young people and children* deriving from their Partnership are maximised. The Parties also undertake to consult each other promptly over any problem arising" (CARIFORUM–EC 2007; emphasis added). Further, chapter 5 of the EPA agreement not only includes people by speaking to social aspects of the agreement but also speaks about women in article 191.2: "The Parties reaffirm their commitment to the 2006 Ministerial declaration by the UN Economic and Social Council on Full Employment and Decent Work, promoting the development of international trade in a way that is conducive to full and productive employment and decent work for all, including *men, women and young people*" (ibid.; emphasis added).

Article 192 of chapter 5 continues to speak of "the right of the Parties and the Signatory CARIFORUM States to regulate [trade and investment] in order to establish their own social regulations and labour standards in line with their own social development priorities" (ibid.). It appears, then, that there is some scope for considerations based on gender. Yet, it seems that it is up to governments to decide whether, on the basis of articles 192 and 193 (Upholding Levels of Protection), gender considerations will colour decision-making related to the restriction of certain types of trade, or the slowing of liberalization in some areas. In order for governments and negotiators to make trade decisions in light of the potential gender implications of this EPA, they would need to move away from conventional ways of handling trade by conducting gender impact assessments. In any case, the liberalizing nature of the CARIFORUM–EC EPA leaves one wondering as to the extent to which "men, women and young people" factor in, since the majority of the agreement ignores people to speak of industries, sectors, barriers to trade, customs issues and a host of other technical matters.

Caribbean thinkers such as Norman Girvan, Havelock Brewster, Vaughn Lewis and Clive Thomas have called on the region's leaders to review and overhaul drastically the initialled CARIFORUM–EC EPA (Brewster, Girvan and Lewis 2008; Brewster 2008). As with most economic and political economy approaches, though, their rationales for re-evaluating the EPAs do not include gender considerations. Without a doubt, the EPAs must be seriously evaluated to ensure that they are of benefit to the Caribbean. Consequently, the potentials opened or closed for sectors and industries in the region need to be considered. Nevertheless, if attaining some level of social and economic justice for the region is important, gender should be infused throughout these evaluations, which should not examine the implications this EPA has merely for allegedly neutral sectors and industries.

In assessing the gender blindness of trade agreements, one can go a step further by asserting that these agreements may not even address some important forms of trade for the region. By omitting certain trades, particularly informal trade, the agreements fail to address the lives of women and men; they ignore social relations of power that are indeed gendered. Addressing informal trade in the Caribbean's economic relations may make things messy, but doing so is needed in order to unearth the potentials or limits of commercial pacts.

A useful example is the forgotten informal trade conducted by higglers in their traditional and modern incarnations:

> Today, a new form of higglering has expanded in the region, in which women travel on commercial airlines, rather than on trucks, buses, or banana boats, buying clothing and other consumer goods, rather than mangoes or provision crops, and reselling these in an active (and illegal) informal market at home . . . Otherwise called "suitcase traders" or "informal commercial importers" (ICIs), Caribbean higglers are a well-known and much-discussed, but little-studied, group . . . The suitcase trade (named for the large bags carried abroad empty and returned full upon the higgler's return home) is an international phenomenon witnessed in many of today's major metropolitan areas as well as in third-world cities within Africa, Latin America, and the Caribbean. (Freeman 2001, 1020–21)

These informal trade activities may be viewed as problematic for state officials who are eager to collect customs duties and other taxes and are aware of the challenge these trades pose to commercial entities that ply similar wares in the formal economy. These informal trade activities, however, are "an expression of innovative enterprise concentrated in the hands of women who represent the highest proportion of the nation's unemployed and underemployed" (ibid., 1022). In other words, social hierarchies which keep women poor in the Caribbean tend to force them to conduct informal commercial transactions both domestically and internationally. Gender blindness allows one to forget that socio-economic relations of power make these informal options important for some women. One is then left to wonder how multilateral trade rules and other trade agreements will address these informal trades while perpetuating pretensions to gender neutrality.

Bridging the Gaps

Gender should be systematically incorporated into the study and negotiation of Caribbean international trade agreements, but how? I have already alluded to gender impact assessments as a means of countering a false sense of gender neutrality. These assessments are significant, as they can provide mechanisms for accounting for the impact of trade agreements on formal and informal economies, as well as on women employed in often invisible, unpaid work conducted within homes and communities. Accounting for this invisible and unpaid work (e.g., cleaning, cooking, childcare, elder care) is significant, since, as Susan Himmelweit states, "the impact of economic policy depends not only on its effects on the paid economy, the recognized target of such policy, but also on its effects on an unpaid economy" (2002, 51). Himmelweit notes the significance of mainstreaming gender in economic affairs for the purpose of equity. She states: "One argument for analyzing the gender impact of policy is an equity one: in order to make outcomes fairer between men and women, it is important to understand and make visible the different effects of policies on them. This argument focuses on redressing inequality, by ensuring that policies do not exacerbate, and if possible ameliorate, existing inequalities" (ibid., 50).

Ideally, the gender impacts of negotiated trade agreements should enter the discussion during negotiating phases to ensure a holistic focus on societal impacts. Incorporating gender assessment at the negotiating phase would, however, require drastic changes to norms that govern the practice of international economic relations and would require a shift in the thinking of scholars, researchers and others who focus on trade affairs. Creating this kind of cultural shift will be challenging. In the interim, the second best option – of studying gender impacts of proposed or negotiated agreements – should be considered. It is important to state here, too, that the inclusion of gender, whether by scholars, researchers or practitioners who deal with trade, must avoid being piecemeal. Appropriate tools and analytical frameworks need to be learned and then used. This appropriate use of techniques helps one to differentiate among analyses that tack on "gender speak" in order to appear equitable. Added to the need to alter perceptions about the significance of gender considerations is also a need to incorporate new skills and methods into the study and conduct of Caribbean trade affairs. This change, too, may face resistance.

Even if a gender-neutral approach in much of international relations, international political economy and economics can be seen in Caribbean approaches to the study of international trade agreements, work has to be done on gender and trade in the region in efforts to effect a shift in thinking on international trade and economic relations. Non-governmental organizations such as the Caribbean Gender and Trade Network – a regional branch of the International Gender and Trade Network coordinated by the Caribbean Association for Feminist Research and Action – have been particularly important in taking the lead in work on gender and international trade. For example, the Caribbean Gender and Trade Network has conducted studies that speak to the intersections between trade and gender in holistic ways. Rather than simply inserting gender considerations as afterthoughts, the work done by this organization places women at the centre and employs gender-based perspectives to raise awareness and to influence policy and negotiations. Work by researchers such as Denny Lewis, Judith Wedderburn, Judy Whitehead and others has also contributed to expanding the still-limited pool of research on gender and trade in the region (Stuart 2003, 21–35). Additionally, the region's trade negotiators appear to be beginning to pay some attention to gender. In February 2006 the Caribbean Regional Negotiating Machinery (now called the Office for Trade Negotiations) held a workshop in conjunction with the United Nations Development Fund for Women entitled "Gender and Labour Issues in Trade". Nonetheless, conventional ways of doing international relations, international political economy and economics seem, predominantly, to be those that inform the negotiation of agreements and the study of Caribbean trade affairs, while gender-based approaches remain on the margins.

Students of Caribbean trade relations and those involved in negotiations and policy processes may assume that there are so many things to negotiate that considering gender impacts is superfluous, especially for small states with little influence on international affairs. As a result, the mainstreaming of gender analysis may be snubbed as little more than a feminist political agenda that diverts attention from the technical issues which negotiating for economic survival in a neo-liberal trade environment requires. Some may further assert that advocating for a gender focus illustrates feminist naiveté to the realities of participating in inter-state negotiations. Yet, my analysis holds that there are serious negative implications for excluding gender perspectives. A brief glance into recent Caribbean history reveals that social problems have already arisen in connection with generic, gender-insensitive structural adjustment programmes. Difficulties similar to those that resulted from "gender-neutral" structural adjustment programmes may be avoided in Caribbean trade matters by systematically incorporating gender into trade analyses. Moreover, if nego-tiators, governments and students of international economic relations are truly interested in equity, they will recognize gender issues as significant to the study and conduct of trade negotiations in which Caribbean states are involved. Continuing to exclude gender by treating international economic affairs as "gender neutral" makes those involved in the study and conduct of Caribbean economic relations complicit in perpetuating inequity in the region and, more generally, in international relations.

Notes

1. Although this chapter uses the term "Caribbean" in discussing "normal" approaches to international relations/international political economy, the discussion here is lim-ited to the English-speaking Caribbean subregion, as I am most conversant with scholarship relating to this segment of the region.
2. Among notable realist contributions that assert that states act in their self-interests and on the basis of power are E.H. Carr's *The Twenty Years' Crisis* (1939); Hans Morgenthau's *Politics Among Nations: The Struggle for Power and Peace* (1948); and Kenneth Waltz's *Theory of International Politics* (1979). Notable liberal approaches that speak to cooperation are Woodrow Wilson's *Fourteen Points Speech* of 1918; Karl Deutsch's 1957 *Political Community and the North Atlantic Area*; and Robert Keohane and Joseph Nye's 1977 *Power and Interdependence: World Politics in Transition*.
3. For an account of international political economy in international relations, see Brown (2001, chapters 8 and 9); Strange (1970).
4. Structural adjustment programmes have been implemented in the following Caribbean states: Barbados, Belize, Grenada, Jamaica, the Commonwealth of Dominica, the Co-operative Republic of Guyana, and the Republic of Trinidad and Tobago.
5. The works of Antrobus and Barriteau are but samples of writings on gender and structural adjustment in the Caribbean. Joan French's 1994 work on the impacts of structural adjustment programmes in Jamaica is also a notable piece with Caribbean focus. Examples of further work on the effects of structural adjustment programmes on women in developing countries can be found in Thomas-Emeagwali (1995); Afshar and Dennis (1992); and Benería and Feldman (1992).
6. The works of the authors referred to here are emblematic of the approach to trade relations usually found in much of Caribbean scholarship.
7. The Bahamas and Montserrat are not WTO members but, at the time of writing, the Bahamas was under accession talks in an attempt to attain WTO membership.

8. The WTO, however, is governed by further legal texts. Information on the structure of the WTO and the substance of these texts can easily be obtained from http://www.wto.org.

9. The European Community exists within the first of three pillars of the European Union. The European Community encompasses areas in which decisions are made supra-nationally. The second and third pillars, however, entail inter-governmental decision-making and cooperative efforts. The second pillar of the European Union encompasses cooperation on Common Foreign and Security Policy, and pillar number three covers Justice and Home Affairs (Bomberg and Stubb 2003, 4–5; Van Oudenaren 2000, 55).

References

Afshar, H., and C. Dennis, eds. 1992. *Women and adjustment policies in the Third World.* London: Macmillan.

Alleyne, B. 2008. Jackpot. *Nation*, 3 May 2008. http://www.nationnews.com (accessed 3 May 2008).

Antrobus, P. 1993. Structural adjustment: Cure or curse? *Gender and Development* 1 (3): 13–18.

Backhouse, R.E. 2002. *The Penguin history of economics.* London: Penguin.

Barclay, L., R.M. Henry and V.N. James. 2005. Caribbean economies in the new international trading environment. In *The Caribbean economy: A reader*, ed. D. Pantin, 617–36. Kingston: Ian Randle.

Barriteau, E. 1994. Gender and development planning in the post colonial Caribbean: Female entrepreneurs and the Barbadian state. PhD diss., Howard University.

———. 1996. Structural adjustment policies in the Caribbean: A feminist perspective. *National Women's Studies Association Journal* 8 (1): 142–56.

———. 2003. Theorizing the shift from "woman" to "gender" in Caribbean feminist discourse. In *Confronting power, theorizing gender: Interdisciplinary perspectives in the Caribbean*, ed. E. Barriteau, 27–45. Kingston: University of the West Indies Press.

Barrow, C. 1992. *Family land and development in St Lucia.* Bridgetown: Institute of Social and Economic Research, University of the West Indies.

Benería, L. 1999. Globalization, gender and the Davos man. *Feminist Economics* 5 (3): 61–83.

Benería, L., and S. Feldman, eds. 1992. *Unequal burden: Economic crises, persistent poverty, and women's work.* Boulder: Westview.

Bernal, R.L. 2001. Small developing economies in the World Trade Organization. Paper presented at the World Bank Conference Leveraging Trade, Global Market Integration and the New WTO Negotiations for Development, Washington DC, 23–24 July. http://www.crnm.org (accessed 12 May 2008).

Blyth, M. 2002. *Great transformations: Economic ideas and institutional change in the twentieth century.* Cambridge: Cambridge University Press.

———. 2003. From comparative capitalism to economic constructivism: The Cornell series on political economy. *New Political Economy* 8 (2): 263–74.

Bodkin, R.G. 1999. Women's agency in classical economic thought: Adam Smith, Harriet Taylor Mill and J.S. Mill. *Feminist Economics* 5 (1): 45–60.

Bomberg, E., and A. Stubb. 2003. *The European Union: How does it work?* Oxford: Oxford University Press.

Brewster, H. 2008. The anti-development dimension of the European Community's economic partnership agreement for the Caribbean. Paper presented at the Cape Town Meeting on Evaluating the Interim EPAs. Revised 6 May 2008. http://www.norman-girvan.info (accessed 30 May 2008).

Brewster, H., N. Girvan, and V. Lewis. 2008. Renegotiate the EPA. *Trade Negotiations Insights* 7 (3): 8–10. http://www.ictsd.org/tni/tni_english/TNI_EN_7-3.pdf (accessed 30 May 2008).

Brown, C. 2001. *Understanding international relations.* 2nd ed. London: Palgrave Macmillan.

CARDI. 2005. Securing food and nutrition security in the Caribbean region. Press Release, 4 March 2005. St Augustine, Trinidad and Tobago: The Caribbean Agricultural Research and Development Institute. http://www.cardi.org/newsroom/03-07-2005-01.php (accessed 12 May 2008).

CARIFORUM–EC. 2007. *Economic partnership agreement between the CARIFORUM states, of the one part, and the European Community and its member states of the other part.* http://www.crnm.org/documents/ACP_EU_EPA/epa_agreement/EPA_Text_14April08.pdf (accessed 12 May 2008).

Carr, E.H. 1964. *The twenty years' crisis, 1919–1939: An introduction to the study of international relations.* New York: Harper and Row.

Crichlow, M.A. 2003. Neoliberalism, states, and bananas in the Windward Islands. *Latin American Perspectives* 30 (3): 37–57.

Deep Ford, J.R., and G. Rawlins. 2007. Trade policy, trade and food security in the Caribbean. In *Agricultural trade policy and food security in the Caribbean: Structural issues, multilateral negotiations and competitiveness*, ed. J.R. Deep Ford, C. dell'Aquila and P. Conforti, 7–40. Rome: Food and Agriculture Organization of the United Nations.

Deutsch, K.W. 1968. *Political community and the North Atlantic area: International organization in the light of historical experience.* Princeton: Princeton University Press.

England, P. 1993. The separative self: Androcentric bias in neoclassical assumptions. In

Beyond economic man: Feminist theory and economics, ed. M.A. Ferber and J.A. Nelson, 37–53. Chicago: University of Chicago Press.

Enloe, C.H. 1990. *Bananas, beaches and bases: Making feminist sense of international politics.* Berkeley and Los Angeles: University of California Press.

———. 1993. *The morning after: Sexual politics at the end of the Cold War.* Berkley and Los Angeles: University of California Press.

Eugene, L. 2002. International trade and labour standards: Prospects and problems. In *Caribbean survival and the global challenge*, ed. Ramesh Ramsaran, 280–98. Kingston: Ian Randle.

European Commission. 2007. *Partnership agreement ACP-EC: Signed in Cotonou on 23 June 2000, revised in Luxembourg 25 June 2005.* Luxembourg, Belgium: European Commission Directorate-General for Development and Relations with African, Caribbean and Pacific States.

Ferber, M.A., and J.A. Nelson, eds. 1993. *Beyond economic man: Feminist theory and economics.* Chicago: University of Chicago Press.

Freeman, C. 2001. Is local:global as feminine:masculine? Rethinking the gender of globalization. *Signs: Journal of Women in Culture and Society* 26 (4): 1007–37.

French, J. 1994. Hitting where it hurts most: Jamaican women's livelihoods in crisis. In *Mortgaging women's lives: Feminist critiques of structural adjustment*, ed. P. Sparr, 165–82. London: Zed Books.

Frieden, J.A. 1988. Sectoral conflict and foreign economic policy, 1914–1940. *International Organization* 42 (1): 59–90.

———. 1991. Invested interests: The politics of national economic policies in a world of global finance. *International Organization* 45 (4): 425–51.

Frundt, H.J. 2002. Central American unions in the era of globalization. *Latin American Research Review* 3 (3): 7–53.

Garcia, Z. 2005. *Impact of agricultural trade on gender equity and the position of rural women in developing countries.* Frederico Caffe Centre Research Report m9/2005. Denmark: Frederico Caffe Centre. http://www.ruc.dk/upload/application/pdf/f51d6748/Research%20Report%209_2005%20Zoraida%20Garcia.pdf (accessed 1 September 2008).

General Agreement on Tariffs and Trade (GATT). 1947. *General agreement on tariffs and trade.* Geneva: WTO. http://www.wto.org/english/docs_e/legal_e/legal_e.htm (accessed 6 March 2008).

Gillson, I., A. Hewitt and S. Page. 2004. *Forthcoming changes in the EU banana/sugar markets: A menu of options for an effective EU transitional package.* Policy brief. London: Overseas Development Institute. http://www.europarl.europa.eu/meetdocs/2004_2009/documents/dv/bananasugarpolbri/bananasugarpolbrief.pdf (accessed 24 October 2006).

Girvan, N. 2006. *Cooperation in the greater Caribbean.* Kingston, Jamaica: Ian Randle.

Godfrey, C. 1998. *A future for Caribbean bananas: The importance of Europe's banana mar-*

ket to the Caribbean. Oxfam GB Policy Paper. March. http://www.oxfam.org.uk/what_we_do/issues/trade/wto_bananas.htm#impact (accessed 24 October 2006).

Gourevitch, P. 1978. The second image reversed: The international sources of domestic politics. *International Organization* 32 (4): 881–912.

———. 1986. *Politics in hard times: Comparative responses to international economic crises.* New York: Cornell University Press.

Griffith, I.L., ed. 2001/2004. *Caribbean security in the age of terror.* Kingston: Ian Randle.

Himmelweit, S. 2002. Making visible the hidden economy: The case for gender-impact analysis of economic policy. *Feminist Economics* 8 (1): 49–70.

hooks, b. 1989. Talking back: Thinking feminist, thinking black. Boston: South End Press.

Keohane, R.O., and Joseph S. Nye. 1977. *Power and interdependence: World politics in transition.* Boston: Little, Brown.

McAfee, K. 1991. *Storm signals: Structural adjustment and development alternatives in the Caribbean.* Boston: South End Press.

Moller Okin, S. 1991/1998. Gender the public and the private. Reprint. In *Feminism and politics,* ed. A. Phillips, 116–41. Oxford: Oxford University Press.

Morgenthau, H.J. 1948. *Politics among nations: The struggle for power and peace.* New York: A.A. Knopf.

Nelson, J. 1993. The study of choice or the study of provisioning? Gender and the definition of economics. In *Beyond economic man: Feminist theory and economics,* ed. M.A. Ferber and J.A. Nelson, 23–36. Chicago: University of Chicago Press.

Nurse, K. 2002. Preparing for the digital age: A strategy for the cultural industries in the Caribbean. In *Caribbean survival and the global challenge,* ed. by R. Ramsaran, 416–28. Kingston: Ian Randle.

Oxfam. 2007. Fair trade banana farmers will need a year to recover from Hurricane Dean. Oxfam GB. Posted 28 September, 5:02 p.m. http://www.oxfam.org.uk/applications/blogs/pressoffice/2007/09/windward_island_fair_trade_ban.html (accessed 20 April 2008).

Pantin, D., W. Sandiford and M. Henry. 2005. Cake, mama coca or? Alternatives facing the Caribbean banana industry. In *The Caribbean economy: A reader,* ed. D. Pantin, 131–64. Kingston: Ian Randle.

Peterson, V.S. 1992. Transgressing boundaries: Theories of knowledge, gender and international relations. *Millennium: Journal of International Studies* 21 (2): 183–206.

Peterson, V.S., and A. Sisson Runyan. 1993. *Global gender issues in world politics.* Boulder: Westview.

Ramesar, M. 2002. The Caribbean after preferences. In *Caribbean survival and the global challenge,* ed. R. Ramsaran, 337–65. Kingston: Ian Randle.

Ramsaran, R., ed. 2002. *Caribbean survival and the global challenge.* Kingston: Ian Randle.

Ransom, D. 1999. Banana split. *New Internationalist,* no. 317. http://www.newint.org/issue317/keynote.htm (accessed 1 September 2008).

Rogowski, R. 1987. Political cleavages and changing exposure to trade. *American Political Science Review* 81 (4): 1121–37.

———. 1990. *Commerce and coalitions: How trade affects domestic political alignments.* Princeton, NJ: Princeton University Press.

Rousseau, J.-J. 1775/1923. *A discourse on political economy.* Reprint. In *The social contract and discourses, by J.-J. Rousseau,* ed. G.D.H. Cole. London: Dent. http://oll.liberty-fund.org/title/638 (accessed 29 May 2008).

Samuel, W.A. 1999. Small island economies in the new international environment. *Social and Economic Studies* 48 (4): 155–89.

Singh, R. 2002. Implications of liberalisation for Caribbean agriculture: Prospects for the non-traditional subsector. In *Caribbean survival and the global challenge,* ed. R. Ramsaran, 384–415. Kingston: Ian Randle.

Smith, A. 1776. *An inquiry into the nature and causes of the wealth of nations.* Dublin: Printed for Messrs. Whitestone.

Smith, S. 1997. New approaches to international relations theory. In *The globalization of world politics,* ed. J. Baylis and S. Smith, 165–90. Oxford: Oxford University Press.

Strange, S. 1970. International economic and international relations: A case of mutual neglect. *International Affairs* 46:304–15.

———. 1994. *States and markets.* 2nd ed. London: Pinter.

Stuart, S.V. 2003. *Gender, trade and investment issues in the Caribbean: A literature review.* International Gender and Trade Network. http://www.igtn.org/page/478/1 (accessed 12 April 2008).

Sutton, P. 1997. The banana regime of the European Union, the Caribbean and Latin America. *Journal of Interamerican Studies and World Affairs* 39 (2): 5–36. http://find-articles.com/p/articles/mi_qa3688/is_199707/ai_n8775638 (accessed 1 September 2008).

Sylvester, C. 1998. Homeless in international relations? "Women's" place in canonical texts and feminist reimaginings. In *Feminism and politics,* ed. A. Phillips, 44–66. Oxford: Oxford University Press.

Thomas, C. 2005. The inversion of meaning: Trade policy and the Caribbean sugar indus-try. In *The Caribbean economy: A reader,* ed. D. Pantin, 165–87. Kingston: Ian Randle.

Thomas-Emeagwali, G. 1995. *Women pay the price: Structural adjustment in Africa and the Caribbean.* Trenton, NJ: Africa World Press.

Thompson, R. 1987. *Green gold: Bananas and dependency in the Eastern Caribbean.* London: Latin American Bureau.

Thorburn, D. 2000. Feminism meets international relations. *SAIA Review* 20 (2): 1–10.

Thorburn, D., and J. Byron. 1998. Gender and international relations: A global perspective and issues for the Caribbean. *Feminist Review* 59 (Summer): 211–32.

Tickner, J.A. 1997. You just don't understand: Troubled engagements between feminists and IR theorists. *International Studies Quarterly* 4:611–32.

————. 2002. Feminist perspectives on 9/11. *International Studies Perspectives* 3 (4): 333–50.

————. 2005. What is your research program? Some feminist answers to international relations methodological questions. *International Studies Quarterly* 49 (1): 1–21.

Van Oudenaren, J. 2000. *Uniting Europe: European integration and the post-Cold War world*. Oxford: Rowan and Littlefield.

Waltz, K.N. 1979. *Theory of international politics*. New York: McGraw Hill.

Wendt, A. 1992. Anarchy is what states make of it: The social construction of power politics. *International Organization* 46 (2): 391–425.

————. 1999. *Social theory of international politics*. Cambridge: Cambridge University Press.

Whitehead, J.A. 1994. The IMF and World Bank: Policies for growth or decline? Paper prepared for the Kairos Europa Caribbean Exposure Programme, Barbados, February.

Woods, N. 1995. Economic ideas and international relations: Beyond rational neglect. *International Studies Quarterly* 39 (2): 161–80.

World Trade Organization (WTO). 1994a. *Agreement establishing the World Trade Organization*. Geneva: WTO. http://www.wto.org/english/docs_e/legal_e/legal_e.htm (accessed 16 March 2008).

————. 1994b. *General agreement on trade in services* (GATS). Geneva: WTO. http://www.wto.org/english/docs_e/legal_e/legal_e.htm (accessed 16 March 2008).

————. 1994c. *Trade-related aspects of intellectual property rights* (TRIPS). Geneva: WTO. http://www.wto.org/english/docs_e/legal_e/legal_e.htm (accessed 16 March 2008).

————. 2008. *European communities: Regime for the importation, sale and distribution of bananas — Second recourse to article 21.5 of the DSU by Ecuador: Report of the panel*, WT/DS27/RW2/ECU, 7 April. http://www.wto.org/english/tratop_e/dispu_e/27rw2_a_e.pdf (accessed 10 May 2008).

PART 4

Into the Margins
Filtering Economic Analysis
through a Gendered Lens

9

Finance Rhetoric and Gender Tropes into the Twenty-first Century

DON D. MARSHALL

IT IS WORTH ASKING WHETHER the mainstream international political economy scholars embrace awareness that its stories are stories like any other, propelled by their own modes of selection, metaphor and illustration. While the subject addresses the perennial tension and reciprocal influence of states and markets, gender has not been able to achieve more than a marginal status therein (Waylen 2006). To be sure, international political economy is marked by a diversity of approaches derivative of a wide variety of backgrounds from which international political economy scholars hail – political and social scientists, development scholars, economists – and, later, gender analysts (e.g. Mies 1986; Enloe 1989; Marchand and Runyan 2000; Barriteau 2001). To the extent that the emphasis lies with "politics", it is odd that gender analysis has rarely joined the community of international political economy. This chapter seeks to discuss the social constitution of finance largely in terms of gender, and reflects on the genealogy of financial trading and gender tropes in cultural constructions of risk before turning finally to the ongoing discussion of the global economic downturn. We learn of the battles for legitimacy and respectability among creditors and speculators in early modern finance, when the financial sphere, like the economic system, had to be presented as one of smooth and neutral functioning. Through the assumptions of science as objective, rational and secure, accounting, auditing, financial trading and credit rating came to be accorded as articulations of financial truth – co-equal in terms to notions of "economic truth". Financial authority has since posed as masculine, its identity forged out of traditional, stereotypical/hegemonic forms of masculinity, that is, the stabilized, self-disciplined, disinterested gentleman capable of mitigating risk.

To be sure, the feminist literature stresses that there are stereotypes attributed to male and female gender that deny women co-equal status with men as fully human and fully equal beings. These stereotypes derive from patriarchal understandings of statehood and social systems in which the preserve of men is bearing intellect and power, while, for women, child rearing and nurturance are treated as their domestic preserve, in keeping with an assumed weaker nature. This dichotomization of gender produces sexist biases which, in utterance, imagery and deed, render invisible the injustices women experience as a devalued feminine being. The reproduction and deployment of this kind of gender discourse unwittingly reinforce patriarchal values. And so is the case within the field of finance, where the canon of work experiences no self-doubt, given its faith in a neutral reason that goes to work on the pursuit of the liberal freedom to exchange, invest and accumulate. In a chapter entitled "Gender and the Globalisation of Finance", Tony Porter (2005) focuses on gendered occupations in finance, gendered aspects of the relationship of the international financial system with the global South, and the impact of gendered attitudes and images on global finance. He observes that traditional gendered inequality exists in the field of finance, and discusses the ways global finance is fissured with images that affirm these inequalities, a matter that de Goede (2000 and 2005) extends, of which more is discussed later in this chapter.

The emphasis on discourse is intended to highlight struggles for meaning-capture. Following Barnett and Duvall (2005, 55), discourse refers to the "social processes and systems of knowledge through which meaning is produced, fixed, lived, experienced, and transformed". Examples of discourse include both written and verbal discussion, technical manuals and reports, press releases, and the symbolic use of institutions and policies. Discourse is not a material action but it constitutes power in a much more indirect sense, endowing some actors (insiders with specialist knowledge and information) with privileges and prerogatives not enjoyed by others. This is clear in the divide between financial specialists and consumers; investors and shareholders; and between transnational networks of regulators and country officials. Here meanings and definitions of legitimate transaction, financial value, instruments and products are secured and contested. Hegemony in the Gramscian sense is achieved when there is intra-elite consensus on the universe of norms, definitions and deviations. This is the power to establish the "common sense", that is, to express the advantaged position of dominant social groups with respect to discourse. To be sure, I make references to discourses of entitlement, of science and objectivity, of risk and danger, of Nature and of gender. These are all historically grounded discourses to which financial science appeals for its legitimacy, authority and respectability. These discourses do not exist transcendentally or without contests, as there have been moments of destabilization and reaffirmation in the history of the finance industry, moments that allow for a profound questioning of financial rationalities.

In the power-relations between authority structures in Western global governance, traditional constructions of passive femininity punctuate financial stability discourse, even as the situations under scrutiny are ones in which women seldom figure physically. Offshore financial centres (OFCs) in geographies of the South often give bulk expression to the term "tax haven", and are often coded feminine, meaning a devalued version of femininity. The stock market as perfect market exists as an ideal. But the materiality of the stock market rests with the command of information, the influence of arbitrage operations, and mastery of economic tools to determine the value of financial instruments, contracts and definitions. Until very recently this was the site of late modern, masculinized financial identities featuring toughness, hubris, and a capacity to steer questions on how money, profit and value are grafted onto discussions about proper stock valuation, eliding, of course, the contestability of such modern financial practices.

Reflections on the Financial Globalization Debate

In recent decades we have come to learn of Ulrich Beck's (1992) account of high modernity through his discussion of risk, but it might be useful to draw attention to Douglas and Wildavsky's (1982) earlier argument that discussions on risk, danger and pollution are culturally embedded. There is always a moral judgement involved in the identification, selection and classification of risks. Douglas and Wildavsky conclude: "We moderns do a lot of politicising merely by our selection of dangers" (ibid., 30). Of the range of dangers in late modern capitalism, management of financial risk is held to be crucial – even as there is no clear resolution to the broader capital mobility/volatility debate or redress of the exclusionary character of international financial governance bodies (Marshall 2007). The context is of a "financial globalization" underway, marked by a dramatic expansion of liquidity. Beck (1992) would observe that the scientific and objective appearance of modern risk assessment has obscured the fact that, at the heart of these technical procedures, lies the question: How do we wish to live? Until the post-2008 financial crisis, the cultural consensus endemic among bankers and policy professionals was for capitalist growth based on creating and promising to fulfil new desires. This growth dovetailed with the discourse of finance theory and financial engineering, relayed through many different points: neoliberal development practice and personal banking and risk management. The disciplinary matrix rested on the foundational assumption of the growing power of finance. It is important therefore to consider conceptualizations and representations of finance, the manner of its knowledge apparatus, and the kinds of truths mobilized within its discursive networks if we are to make sense of financial globalization.

Generally, mainstream discourses on globalization fixate on the flows of capital and finance, as well as of people, across borders. The increasing growth of cross-border financial flows in some markets during the last thirty years has brought the debate on globalization of finance into a prominent place in current academic literature. Indeed, the rise of innovative developments in global financial markets, along with their grip on individuals, households, firms and governments, has stimulated work on *financialization*. The research probes the increasing disarticulation among the symbol economy of hedge funds, derivatives and asset reallocations between firms – and the real economy of product markets, labour markets and research and development capacities. At centre is the new universal competition of financial results, regardless of products and sectors, of pressure from shareholders in the capital market through buy, sell and hold decisions, of management's preoccupation with current and projected returns on investment, and of how, inter alia, such pressure for financial results overturns the capitalist competition of process and product of the late 1970s and 1980s (Froud et al. 2000; Langley 2004).

This chapter, however, has two core objectives: one, to highlight some key aspects of financial globalization since the 1870s, the predominant historical starting point according to various scholars; and two, to link this discussion with parallel literature that seeks to explain the rise of finance as a common-sense force. Convergence of the two narratives is required if we are to understand how consensus on the idea of free capital mobility remains steadfast, and why the stock market remains a valorized site of exchange and accumulation. Of course the consensus relied very much upon a grammar of scientific claims-making and a rhetoric featuring the mobilization of gender stereotypes and tropes.

As with globalization, financial globalization is a multidimensional topic that has no consensual description. It is generally defined as a process whereby the domestic financial markets meld into a single market of global scope. While plants and facilities are located at home, advances in technology allow for trading globally in a large variety of public and private assets and liabilities, currencies, commodities, a variety of financial services, instruments of risk management and the like. Often raised in this context is the distinction between financial internationalization and financial globalization, as some argue that we are still a long way from an interlinked network of markets that are able to negotiate products and services quickly in larger areas of the world (Bayoumi 1999; Arestis and Basu 2003).

The historically connected factors propelling financial globalization are:

1. The emergence of a world financial order during the Gold Standard (circa 1870) among a small number of leading western European countries. This development encouraged a philosophy of "playing by the rules" that led to interconnectedness and high financial integration. By the beginning of the twentieth century, the growth of cross-border financial flows among these players was higher than the growth in international trade.

2. The spread of financial deregulation and liberalization policies among the core economies in the 1970s, and among countries of the global South from the 1980s.

3. Stringent competition among offshore financial centres and core onshore financial centres and banking cities throughout the 1970s, 1980s and 1990s. Some argue that the emergence of the Eurodollar market (1957) created the stimulus. From the 1980s, competition also intensified among financial agents, both banks and non-banks. Altogether, increased competition led to the development of new products, services and markets.

4. Technological interconnection of financial systems worldwide that later led to a reduction in transaction costs of financial services.

The above developments did not unfold along a linear progression, as Rajan and Zingales (2003) explain. The 1980s and 1990s witnessed growth in international interest rates and debt financing that marked a dramatic increase in world financial instability. The waves of deregulation spawned developments such as securitization, over-the-counter (OTC) derivatives markets, institutional investors and investment banks, and allowed for a financial integration that was not only deeper but also pervasive. The advent of high-speed communications increased the risk of crisis contagion.

While the terms "financial globalization" and "internationalization of capital" are sometimes used interchangeably, two overlapping developments remain crucial in mainstream scholarship on financial globalization (Watson 2007; Cohen 1996; Helleiner 1994). One is the US-led campaign for capital mobility from the 1980s and the subsequent coercive pressure applied to governments in the global South by international financial institutions (IFIs) to deregulate their capital markets. Second, capital mobility quests merged well with parallel advances in communications technology, marked by the proliferation of Internet and high-tech stock. Where there is some recognition of the importance of historical processes, the recognition starts with the proliferation of bank-industry networks in leading nineteenth-century economies, the emergence of the Eurodollar market (1957) and, of particular emphasis, the United States' decision in 1971 to abandon a fixed exchange-rate policy by removing the peg tying the dollar to the gold standard. Altogether, these developments facilitated the quest to "go global" in search of efficiency, markets and increased returns on the part of core firms and corporations. Stock exchanges expanded to form intricate networks and offered ever more financially innovative products and opportunities for speculation. This was the stimulus for the furtherance and creation of newer "juridical enclaves" *pace* Palan (2006), which offer an equally complex basket of low regulatory attractions and financial services. Invariably, most scholars who attempt to explain financial globalization take the forging of the global financial system as largely mired in the twentieth-century incidence of transfer and diffusion of deregulatory policies across many countries. They do address these developments, noting the historical specificities of the moment, how national economies have adjusted their fiscal and monetary policies in order to become part of a "global discipline", and why panics and bubbles occur. I wish to examine the idea that financial globalization is also an expression of the epistemological confidence of the modern risk order. There are relevant, longer-run historical processes that require revisable recall.

Most accounts of the rise of finance unwittingly miss the saliency of battles for legitimacy and respectability among creditors and speculators in early modern finance. Indeed, the politics of financial identity was, for a long time, a messy, conflict-filled and dissonant affair until those same creditors and speculators re-articulated their positions by claiming that their vocations and practices were scientific. Today, discursive lines are shifting, peeling away the layers of financial authority – epistemic, gendered and imperial. How did finance rise to acquire its status as a legitimate arena for the accumulation of capital? Or, put in more explicit terms, how was legitimacy won for finance to the extent that financial "experts" could build their own sets of rules, determine their worth and, by the dawn of the twenty-first century, exercise significant authority? The work of Neal (1990), Nicholson (1994), de Goede (2005) and others refers to social tensions around financial practices and arrangements of the day, and identifies practices that encountered public opprobrium.

Historical Sketch of the Growth of Financial Trading as a Profession

In the aftermath of the recent global financial downturn, it can be recognized how much consumer and civilian publics gave ground to specialists who were (or are) "fluent in finance": they trusted their judgement on credit, their criteria of value and their calculability of future uncertainties. Of course, the application of specialist and technical knowledge to the financial sphere depoliticized issues such as financial risk management, securitization, financial modelling and financial accounting. This depoliticization arose out of the modern faith in financial science or scientific finance, as well as the new environment of accumulation, which encouraged easy loans to citizens and more jobs in the area of financial services. While the demise of the billion-dollar US hedge fund Long Term Capital Management in 1998 and the collapse of the US energy corporation Enron in 2002 would have dented modern faith in accountants, the United States' subprime mortgage crisis of August 2007, which eventually led to a run on big Wall Street financial firms in September 2008 (Goldman Sachs, American International Group Inc., Fannie Mae and Freddie Mac, Lehman Brothers, Morgan Stanley and Merrill Lynch), has opened space for debate on assessments made by financial professionals. An unravelling financial services sector, rising loan defaults and a deepening recession have meant the end of the bankers' counter-revolution, one that extends back to the 1980s. But for quite some time, bankers and others in the field of scientific finance argued that risks could be calculated, that there was no reason to fear rising levels of leverage and risk: "It [was] simply just a question of the right mathematics and enough information" (Green 2000, 86).

The genealogy, or the "moment of arising" of scientific finance, extends back to the overlapping histories of gambling and financial trading in seventeenth-century Europe and the emergence of professional speculators and their struggle for political legitimacy and respectability by the end of the nineteenth century. Gambling on a wide variety of uncertainties was part and parcel of early modern finance. For over three centuries, no conceptual distinction existed between gambling and financial practices (de Goede, 2005). The second half of the seventeenth century saw the development of institutionalized finance and public credit in England as English society was transforming from a feudal, aristocratic one to a commercial and trade-oriented one. This period saw the emergence of London as one of the principal financial centres in the world. Indeed, London, Antwerp and Amsterdam were centres of commercial capitalism, more anonymous and more coherently regulated than the frontier or the countryside. It is true that sophisticated financial networks existed earlier in Florence, Italy, in the fifteenth century, and other European cities in the sixteenth century, but the sheer volume of the English government's borrowing and investment fostered financial innovations such as new partnership banks, new insurance offices and sophisticated trade in stocks and debt certificates (Germain 1997). While the invention of state credit and national debt can be regarded as monetary transformations which inaugurated modern finance, this does not mean, however, that the conceptual apparatus of modern finance sprang up naturally and consistently in the wake of the Financial Revolution (spurred by the English need to finance the war against France). Even more than the invention of financial instruments, the Financial Revolution must be thought of as the articulation of moral and political spaces in which these instruments became possible and condoned. Here, metaphors based on stereotypes of Nature as weak and feminine, subject to mastery by males, were deployed to shape financial understanding.

Trade in derivatives has been controversial since its first appearance in early modern Europe. Financial instruments such as options and forward contracts emerged in conjunction with the longer time horizons brought about by voyages of discovery and colonial conquest. For instance, the Amsterdame Beurs (Amsterdam stock market) emerged early in the seventeenth century as a secondary market for shares of the imperial shipping company, the Dutch East-India Company (Neal 1990; Germain 2000). In this historical context, the Amsterdam money market developed sophisticated techniques of trading, including forwards, short sales and options to sell or buy stocks for a stipulated price.[1]

Indeed, intense controversies surrounded financial gambling on the exchanges. Particularly controversial was short-selling, which entailed the selling of shares or commodities without actually possessing them. Short-selling commodities emerged as a way for farmers and shippers to sell their produce for a fixed price prior to harvesting or docking. Controversies over short-selling matched parallel social objections to the invention of credit, which was regarded as morally dubious instead of naturally beneficial. The concepts of promise and pledge underlying credit were seen to deliver England to the whims and fancies of its emerging financial class. Indeed, credit became a focal point of political struggle and satirical debate in the seventeenth century. De Goede (2000) explains that these debates expressed the political confusions around the transition from feudal society, in which wealth was visibly embodied in land, to a commercial and trading society in which wealth became more intangibly located in the mechanisms of credit creation. Daniel Defoe, an early English satirist, imagined credit as a "female inconstant" (Nicholson 1994, 10). Proponents and opponents of the new credit structures also shared with Defoe his depiction of credit as an "inconstant, often self-willed but persuadable woman" (ibid., xi.). This idea merged well with parallel debates on Nature, physics and probabilistic developments in science. Today, de Goede (2000) has drawn connections between credit and truth at the birth of modern science. Scientific truth, she argues, was generated in a social network which recognized the seventeenth-century gentleman as a truth-teller *par excellence*, in contrast to women, enslaved peoples and servants. Science in this context became "gentlemanly science", for objective truth was linked to social credibility.

The use of prevailing gender imagery to explain and gain an understanding of credit was intended to present finance as a phenomenon capable of being perfectly understood, much like what those seeking to explain Nature promised. Frances Bacon, for instance, constructed "Nature" as a female whom the male scientific mind had to subdue and master. As Evelyn Fox Keller (1985) would later argue, Bacon's projection of Nature as a female to be mastered and controlled underlies modern conceptions of science and scientific facts.

By the dawn of the twentieth century, the claim to providing scientific information, along with the concept of risk, provided the possibility of a line of demarcation between gambling and finance. The argument was that speculators proceeded with careful examination and information, in contrast to gamblers, who were reckless and ill informed. While New York banker John Moody would outline the "art of Wall Street investing", the founder of the *Wall Street Journal*, Charles Dow, drew from the work of English economist William Stanley Jevons to fashion a scientific defence of investment (Bernstein 1992; de Goede 2005). He described risks as natural but humanly calculable, and thus provided the political and moral legitimacy for the creation of a range of financial instruments, including futures contracts and other speculative contracts. It was during the late nineteenth century that concepts from probability were pervasive in scientific work and were reflected in studies of stock prices. Statistical experts located the cause of price fluctuations as external to the financial system, in contrast to arguments which held that price movements depended on speculators' hopes and fears. With an upsurge in speculation underway in the 1970s, the path was clear for the practical application of mathematical science. By then, the academic theory of financial markets had begun with the random walk model, portfolio selection and the capital asset pricing model adopted by a variety of practitioners (Bernstein 1992, 233–306).

But it was the 1973 theory of option pricing developed by Robert Merton and his colleagues, following Fisher Black and Myron Scholes, professors at the Massachusetts Institute of Technology, which proved decisive. Black, Scholes and Merton argued that, with the help of options, financial practitioners could create risk-free positions. As long as one purchased a set of options comprising the opposite positions to one's bets, large financial losses would be impossible. Their work quickly became an essential resource for traders on the floor of the Options Exchange (Chicago Board Options). The legal demarcation between trading and gambling would be redrawn, and barriers to cash settlements removed, in the 1970s and 1980s. New developments, such as financial derivatives exchanges, occurred (Mackenzie 2009). Indeed, the hitherto dubious legitimacy attached to financial trading and the stock market as a research topic gave way to the growth of Chicago and the Massachusetts Institute of Technology as key sites for the development of modern finance theory. The use of a theoretically based valuation formula rather than simple intuition made it possible to speak of scientific finance. Certainly, "option dealers had newfound respect" (Mackenzie 2004, 105). The same was true for statistics experts tied to the financial industry, whom some critics considered "knights errant of the empire of chance" (Gigerenzer et al. 1989, 274). But by 1997, the *Economist* would laud Scholes and Merton with the accomplishment of having "turned risk management from a guessing game into a science".[2]

Questions over the science of money, value and the calculability of risk lessened as the idea and ideal of free capital mobility grew popular and led to a wave of deregulation occurring in leading financial markets. Major investment banks were allowed the freedom to establish hedge funds, lend to speculators, trade in financial derivatives and package and securitize credits, which were sold to third parties. These actions would transform US credit markets into the world's largest unregulated money-creation machine (Engdahl 2008). By 2005, globalized investment banking, derivatives trading, and speculation involving highly abstract financial products took on the appearance of economic necessity and scientific respectability. From the autumn of 2007, questions of legitimation and societal impact re-emerged as credit markets collapsed under the weight of defaulting loans and the complicity of "light-touch regulatory systems" governing the financial sector. The following section tracks the latest episode of historical challenge to the realm of money and finance.

Back to the Future: The Fall of Capital Markets

> The era of cowboy capitalism has died, largely of self-inflicted wounds. Who knows what's coming now? I do: A new era of tight business regulation and government intervention in the markets. For now, and perhaps for many years, there will be no going back. The Rubicon was crossed when the deal was struck for a US$700 billion federal takeover of the carcass of Wall Street. At that moment, the conservative era in America, which began with Ronald Reagan's election in 1980, ended. It did so not with a bang, but with a whimper – a cry of help from erstwhile masters of the universe who suddenly feared for their platinum-level lives. (Fineman 2008)

This passage is drawn from Howard Fineman's "Bailout Ushers in the Era of Obama" (2008). It relates to the September 2008 decision by the outgoing George W. Bush administration to bail out indebted investment banks and mortgage finance companies following the collapse of the subprime mortgage market in the United States. By then it was clear among mainstream analysts that experts in the financial sphere had underestimated the risk exposure of the US housing boom. This discourse is rife with traditional stereotypes of masculinities and femininities, and is prescient, as solutions to the financial turbulence are located in ideas about conquering and taming. The causes identified for this disturbance range from the allegedly fraudulent actions of stock traders and others in the boardrooms and CEO offices of Wall Street and London, to activities of OFCs. The range of blame queries the competencies of government regulators, politicians, bankers, ratings agencies and global financial governance institutions.

As stated earlier, a growing number of commentators, policymakers and scholars have been busily seeking to cast blame for, and find solutions to, the recent Wall Street tumult that has paralysed broader credit markets in Asia and Europe. As the dominant narrative goes, the average American had, by the 1990s, became seduced by the myth of stock ownership as a sure path to a better life now and a safe retirement later. This outlook corresponded with an emergent Westernized culture of entitlement in which elites and workers express no moral qualms over excess, whether in the form of salary bonuses, benefit levels or lifestyle-related carbon emissions, so long as capitalist economies continue to grow (Giddens 2009). This cultural sentiment is a version of L'Oreal's advertising slogan "Because you're worth it", a sort of dysfunctional meritocracy that has been implicit in how inequality is tolerated, and explicit in how hyper-consumption has taken hold over the past two decades. Banks, brokers and insurance companies besieged citizens with marketing claims that the regular purchase of shares in public companies would effortlessly grow in value forever – never mind there were long periods in the twentieth century when this was proven not to be true: 1929–1932, 1937–1949 and 1965–1982, roughly.[3] All were encouraged to fix their gaze on movements in share prices. By then, European and US investment banks had undertaken a wave of deregulatory measures whereby most of these entities changed from private, owner-responsible banks to public, limited companies which transfer risk to shareholders. The laxity in the financial environment increased in 2004, when the largest US investment banks successfully petitioned the Securities Exchange Commission (SEC) to lift further restrictions on their debt-to-equity ratios. The net result was a surge in the creation and distribution of unsecured debt as big banks and private equity firms used leverage to engage in risky ventures.

A risk-free investing culture had already set in as rating agencies bestowed market acceptability to mutual funds, bonds, stocks, auction rate securities and an increasing supply of commercial paper. The US housing market – deemed a no-risk, as opposed to a low-risk, investment option – attracted the spectacular growth of such financial products. As a result, by the time of the bailout of Fanny Mae and Freddie Mac in the subprime mortgage crisis in summer 2007, the financial sector in most leading economies was encouraging expansion in securities; dangerous levels of leverage; speculative adventures in capital markets around the world; a massive speculative asset price and debt bubble; and the regulation of this melee of activity by the banks themselves (Labaton 2008). The subprime mortgage quagmire would lead, in September 2008, to the collapse of Lehman Brothers, a 158-year-old investment bank which declared insolvency, with nearly US$650 billion in liabilities. Wall Street would remain in free-fall mode as every financial institution and production firm across different markets sought to determine their exposure to the mortgage crisis; to investment firms, including Lehman Brothers, Merrill Lynch, Goldman Sachs and Citigroup; and troubled insurance groups, including American Insurance Group (AIG) and Washington Mutual. The web of contagion soon extended to companies in the real economy, leading to job cuts, state bailouts and foreclosures that unsettled livelihoods and households.

This stock explanation has produced concerns about "the irrational exuberance of the market" (*Crash*, 2009) and has raised the question: What regulation will oversee international finance? Since financial engineering is often portrayed as a heroic masculine enterprise, it is not surprising to learn that, within the discourse of blame, men and masculinities take centre stage, with special focus on the exuberance of youthful men as stock traders and mortgage brokers, or the hubris of hegemonic men as managers and bondholders in major banks, as CEOs in Wall Street and London offices, and as specialists in risk management. Stated differently, the crisis is located in the idea of the failure of different kinds of masculinities, rather than in the need to re-examine the pillars of technical financial knowledge. In the United

Kingdom, a Channel 4 documentary chronicling the financial crisis, a senior banker remarked, "A tsunami of cash was available through the money markets. They sat in New York and London bragging that they could turn bad risks to good; that they could make dodgy loans work. It was just a bunch of young men full of testosterone" (*Crash*, 2009).

William K. Black, a bank regulation expert, argues instead that the Wall Street collapse resulted from massive fraud which originated in boardrooms and CEO offices, and extended to ratings agencies. In an interview with Bill Moyers in April 2009, he stated:

> Fraud is deceit. And the essence of fraud is, "I create trust in you, and then I betray that trust, and get you to give me something of value." And as a result, there's no more effective acid against trust than fraud, especially fraud by top elites, and that's what we have . . . Well, the way that you do it is to make really bad loans, because they pay better. Then you grow extremely rapidly; in other words, you're a Ponzi-like scheme. And the third thing you do is, we call it, leverage. That just means borrowing a lot of money, and the combination creates a situation where you have guaranteed record profits in the early years. That makes you rich, through the bonuses that modern executive compensation has produced. It also makes it inevitable that there's going to be a disaster down the road. The Bush administration essentially got rid of regulation, so if nobody was looking, you were able to do this with impunity and that's exactly what happened. Where would you look? You'd look at the specialty lenders. The lenders that did almost all of their work in the sub-prime, and what's called Alt-A, liars' loans . . . Even Ronald Reagan, you know, said, "Trust, but verify." They just gutted the verification process. We know that will produce enormous fraud, under economic theory, criminology theory, and two thousand years of life experience. This stuff, the exotic stuff that you're talking about, was created out of things like liars' loans, that were known to be extraordinarily bad. And now it was getting triple-A ratings. Now, a triple-A rating is supposed to mean there is zero credit risk. So you take something that not only has significant [risk], it has crushing risk. That's why it's toxic. And you create this fiction that it has zero risk. That itself, of course, is a fraudulent exercise. And again, there was nobody looking, during the Bush years. So finally, only a year ago, we started to have a congressional investigation of some of these rating agencies, and it's scandalous what came out. What we know now is that the rating agencies never looked at a single loan file. When they finally did look, after the markets had completely collapsed, they found, and I'm quoting Fitch [Ratings], the smallest of the rating agencies, "the results were disconcerting, in that there was the appearance of fraud in nearly

every file we examined". [Our financial system] became a Ponzi scheme. Everybody was buying a pig in the poke. But they were buying a pig in the poke with a pretty pink ribbon, and the pink ribbon said "triple-A". (Black 2009)

The idea that the American financial economy fell victim to a group of confidence men is echoed in part by John K. Galbraith, a professor of government, in an interview with Matt Renner in May 2009:

> There was a whole class of lenders out there, many of whom were completely unregulated, the Countrywide Financials of the world, others of whom should have been regulated but were effectively de-supervised, the Indymacs and the Washington Mutuals, where the business model was "Push those bonuses out the door, get as many of them signed up as possible because, if they pay for the first thirty days, we can sell them and pocket the fees. After that, it isn't our responsibility."
>
> Systematically, in this industry, the people who previously specialized in risk management used to say, "Show me the documents proving that this will be a safe mortgage", [and] were given instructions by top management, "Get out of the way, and get these mortgages issued." There are plenty of records showing that these lenders were told to drop the standards. That was the revenue model for the institution. You have a model which is fraud in origination, fraud in the conveyance and fraud in the rates.

Dominic Savage, the British television director of the drama *Freefall*, portrayed the financial collapse as the result of the moral fall-out of financial men and their clients. When asked if he spoke to any of the men involved in the mortgage market about moral issues, Savage stated:

> Yes. Of course, some couldn't think in those terms at all, as if to do so would be to show weakness. But others had a philosophy about what they did. There was greed in them, but in their hearts they believed they were doing good, creating wealth. Their identities, you see, were tied up with their jobs. I spoke to someone at UBS [a leading financial firm] who told me you could feel people's deep sense of loss once jobs began disappearing. It wasn't only losing the salary; it was a loss of self. To an extent I believe that they didn't believe things could fail. They were making money but so were their clients, so long as house prices were rising. They were deliberately vague about how much repayments could go up, but then again the people they were selling to didn't want to hear the negative. They just wanted [the dream home]. Even if they were full of doubt, their own greed would get the better of them. So the brokers were playing on other people's greed as well as their own. (Cooke 2009)

In these excerpts, there is a dual critique of the self-assuredness of male exemplars of high finance and the automatic respectability of the financial sphere. The unravelling is as rapid for the hierarchical financial masculinities as it is unsettling in the field of financial science. Recall the appeals for outgoing treasury secretary Henry Paulson to be "contained" if he was to exercise discretionary authority over the first bailout package, as he was considered "soft" and untrustworthy in relation to monitoring Wall Street activities (Malkin 2008). John McCain, a US presidential candidate at the time, condemned the risks and compensation schemes of CEOs of failing banks and firms, and then declared that, if he had been president, he would have dismissed the SEC chairman, Christopher Cox, for his lack of vigilance. This statement resonated with the opinions of other commentators, who accused Cox of being "asleep at the switch" (Westbrook and Schmidt 2008). The retreat/emasculation has been so extensive that, following the British government's intervention in the UK banking system (which ended the "love affair" with London), Sir Fred Goodwin, former CEO of the troubled Royal Bank of Scotland, was moved to observe that "the negotiations were more like a drive-by shooting" (*Crash*, 2009).

Financial authority continues to be questioned as the economic recession deepens. In the process, constructions of masculinity shaped around mastery in financial trading are destabilizing. Some commentators question the faith that re-regulation can check investment greed and restore stability and soundness to the banking system. The then Brown administration in the United Kingdom and the Obama administration in the United States, for example, had outlined programmes based on the assumption that the different classes of assets which their governments acquired in the bailout packages, and those which the banks retain, will recover values. But the underlying quality of a large part of that asset base is dubious, insofar as these assets are, in the case of subprime mortgage securities, backed by inadequate documentation, and are thus unsafe and likely to default at high rates (Dunbar and Donald 2009). Galbraith (in Renner 2009) argues that this kind of plan, in effect, rescues incumbent management and bondholders of major banks, and transfers the losses from the books of the banks to the taxpayers. It is a way of avoiding the necessity of devaluing those assets now and requiring their present owners – the banks – to take appropriate losses.

Rather than a critique of the intrinsic practice of recycling private capital through stock markets, or a critique levelled at the centres of calculation – that is, those knowledge centres where logs, diagrams, value metrics and models are accumulated and used by accountants, economists and statisticians to escalate the proof race – a discourse of delusion persists. This discourse preserves the naturalization of financial markets as essentially irrational and bedazzling and in need of regulation and mastery. The logic reinforces male–female stereotypes and tethers institutions to modes of action that tap into popular consciousness. In sum, we are to believe that the Wall Street tumult will usher in new reforms, which tougher, more vigilant men (read: experienced regulators) will execute.

At the global level, the debate turns to wider reforms when blame is extended to the role of OFCs in the international financial system. The concern with Caribbean financial jurisdictions is one that has a longer history than the current offensive. It extends to the competing conceptions of the operational activity of OFCs. The fundamental imaginative act at work is the motif of the rational, Western form at variance with the exotic and sexualized "Other". The toughness, decisiveness and hardness of financial experts clustered around the OFCs of the global South are portrayed as embracing competition in regulatory laxity in order to win more international business. Not unlike encounters in the colonial past, Caribbean and Pacific OFCs have been cast simultaneously as geographies to be conquered and temptations to be resisted. As the dominant discourse goes, limitations in financial regulation in emerging economies and offshore financial markets undermine financial rationality. The comments below reveal the official French position following the fall of capital markets in late 2008:[4]

> Is it normal that a bank to which we guarantee loans or allocate our own funds continues operating in tax havens? The answer is no. (French President Nicolas Sarkozy)
>
> Black holes like offshore centres should no longer exist. Their disappearance must be a prelude to a reform of the international financial system. (French prime minister Francois Fillon)
>
> By mid-2009, we should have established a more realistic [black]list of tax havens, and this would [have been] an indispensable step to go further. (French budget minister Eric Woerth)

The then British prime minister Gordon Brown, in an address to US congressmen in Washington, DC, on 4 March 2009, similarly opined, "How much safer would everybody's savings be if the whole world finally came together to outlaw shadow banking systems and offshore tax havens?" (Brown 2009).[5] These pronouncements, together with articles appearing in *Euromoney* and *Offshore Alert*, and in the online legal research network *Thomson Legal Record*, confine OFCs to the apocryphal field of "a shelter" for tax evaders, perpetually in need of regulatory guidelines and rules from a supranational authority whether it be from the Organization for Economic Co-operation and Development, the Financial Action Task Force, the Financial Stability Forum or the Bank for International Settlements. In today's outrage over huge pay and bonuses among the richest elites, tax evasion equals male dishonour but it touches on the idea of the OFC as a temptress and locates blame in the nature of the Caribbean as feminized space in the masculinized/patriarchal sense.

Summary

A longer historical view teaches that rationales for financial speculation have often been politically contested and are beset with their own weaknesses and internal contradictions. The gender binary system, together with its associated stereotypes, seems to be at the centre in conceptualizing banking and financial practices and in accomplishing a "buy-in" in terms of corrective measures. After all, Lady Credit has long been fabled as irrational but desirous, and capable of being mastered by those who can discover latent knowledge technologies to tame her "Nature". Tackling the discursive underpinnings of the world financial order enables one to make sense of the current crisis in global credit markets. We are learning that, contrary to the opinions of financial specialists, monetary values do not exist objectively or transcendentally but are created in human acts of valuation. We therefore have to question these discourses of valuation fundamentally in order to enable effective criticism of financial speculation and to challenge the legitimacy of current policies that relate to liberalizing financial sectors. This idea also extends to analysis of what constitutes safe and unsafe investment in stock markets and what it means to confine OFCs in the Caribbean and the Pacific to the status of the curious.

Notes

1. Short-selling is the practice of "selling a borrowed security". Short-sellers sell a security or commodity which they do not own for delivery at a later date, and thus profit from price declines. See Karpoff 1994, 445.
2. See editorial, "The Nobel Prize for economics: The right option", *Economist*, 16 October 1997.
3. For a discussion of the 1929 stock market crash, see Wheelock 1994.
4. These quotations are drawn from speeches made earlier in the week beginning 19 October 2008. See the Caribbean Net News editorial of 22 October 2008, "Caribbean tax havens: An endangered species?" (http://www.caribbeannetnews .com; accessed 12 January 2009).
5. Full text of Gordon Brown's speech available at http://www.guardian.co.uk/poli tics/2009/mar/04/gordon-brown-congress-speech-obama (accessed 11 March 2009).

References

Arestis, P., and S. Basu. 2003. *Is financial globalization truly global? New institutions for an inclusive capital market*. Public Policy Brief no. 75. New York: Levy Institute, Bard College.

Barnett, M., and R. Duvall. 2005. Power in international politics. *International Organization* 59 (1): 39–75.

Barriteau, E. 2001. *The political economy of gender in the twentieth-century Caribbean*. New York: Palgrave.

Bayoumi, T. 1999. Is there a world capital market? In *Globalisation and labour*, ed. H. Siebert, 65–86. Tubingen: Mohr Siebeck/Institut für Weltwirtschaft.

Beck, U. 1992. *Risk society: Towards a new modernity*. New Delhi: Sage.

Bernstein, P.L. 1992. *Capital ideas: The improbable origins of modern Wall Street*. New York: Free Press.

Black, W.K. 2009. Interview by B. Moyers. *Bill Moyers Journal*, 3 April. http://www .pbs.org/moyers/journal/04032009/watch.html (accessed 1 June 2009).

Brown, G. 2009. Speech before US Congress. 4 March. http://www.guardian.co.uk/pol itics/2009/mar/04/gordon-brown-congress-speech-obama (accessed 11 March 2009).

Cohen, B. 1996. Phoenix risen: The resurrection of global finance. *World Politics* 48:268–96.

Cooke, R. 2009. Making great drama out of a credit crisis. *Observer*, 10 May. http://www .guardian.co.uk/culture/2009/may/10/freefall-drama-tv-economic-collapse (accessed 1 June 2009).

Crash: How the banks went bust. A two-part investigation. 2009. UK Channel 4 feature. Produced, narrated and reported by W. Hutton. 20 April and 27 April.

de Goede, M. 2000. Mastering lady credit: Discourses of financial crisis in historical perspective. *International Feminist Journal of Politics* 2:58–81.

———. 2005. *Virtue, fortune and faith: A genealogy of finance.* Minneapolis: University of Minneapolis Press.

Douglas, M., and A. Wildavsky. 1982. *Risk and culture.* Berkeley and Los Angeles: University of California Press.

Dunbar, J., and D. Donald. 2009. Billion dollar bailout banks financed the subprime industry and America's economic meltdown. *Cutting Edge*, 18 May. http://www.the-cuttingedgenews.com/index (accessed 1 June 2009).

Engdahl, W. 2008. The financial tsunami, part IV: Asset securitisation – The last tango. http://www.engdahl.oilgeopolitics.net/AssetsecuritisationIV (accessed 11 March 2009).

Enloe, C.H. 1989. *Bananas, beaches and bases: Making feminist sense of international politics.* London: Pandora.

Fineman, H. 2008. Bailout ushers in the era of Obama. *MSNBC.COM Business.* http://www.msnbc.msn.com/id/26933982 (accessed 29 September 2008).

Fox Keller, E. 1985. *Reflections on gender and science.* New Haven, CT: Yale University Press.

Froud, J., C. Haslam, K. Sukhdev, and K. Williams. 2000. Shareholder value and financialisation: Consultancy promises, management moves. *Economy and Society* 29 (1): 80–110.

Germain, R.D. 1997. *The international organisation of credit.* Cambridge: Cambridge University Press.

———. 2000. Globalisation in historical perspective. In *Globalisation and its critics: Perspectives from political economy*, ed. R.D. Germain, 67–90. London: Macmillan.

Giddens, A. 2009. *The politics of climate change.* Boston: Polity.

Gigerenzer, G., Z. Swijtink, T. Porter, L. Daston, J. Beatty and L. Kruger. 1989. *The empire of chance: How probability changed science and everyday life.* Cambridge: Cambridge University Press.

Green, S. 2000. Negotiating with the future: The culture of modern risk in global financial markets. *Environment and Planning: Society and Space* 18 (1): 77–89.

Helleiner, E. 1994. *States and the reemergence of global finance.* Ithaca: Cornell University Press.

Karpoff, J.M. 1994 Short-selling. In *New Palgrave dictionary of money and finance*, vol. 3, ed. P. Newman, N. Milgate and J. Eatwell. New York: Macmillan.

Labaton, J. 2008. Agency's 04 rules let banks pile up new debt. *New York Times*, 2 October.

Langley, P. 2004. In the eye of the "perfect storm": The final salary pensions crisis and financialisation of Anglo-American capitalism. *New Political Economy* 9 (4): 539–58.

Mackenzie, D. 2004. Physics and finance. In *Cultural economy reader,* ed. A. Amin and N. Thrift, 101–20. Oxford: Blackwell.

———. 2009. *Material markets: How economic agents are constructed.* Oxford: Oxford University Press.

Malkin, M. 2008. Why Henry Paulson must be contained. 22 September. http://michelle-malkin.com/2008/09/22 (accessed 7 October 2008).

Marchand, M.H., and A.S. Runyan, eds. 2000. *Gender and global restructuring.* London: Routledge.

Marshall, Don D. 2007. The new international financial architecture and Caribbean OFCs: Confronting financial stability discourse. *Third World Quarterly* 28 (5): 917–38.

Mies, M. 1986. *Patriarchy and accumulation on a world scale: Women in the international division of labour.* London: Zed Books.

Neal, L. 1990. *The rise of financial capitalism: International capital markets in the age of reason.* Cambridge: Cambridge University Press.

Nicholson, C. 1994. *Writing and the rise of finance: Capital satires of the early eighteenth century.* Cambridge: Cambridge University Press.

Palan, R. 2006. *The offshore world: Sovereign markets, virtual places and nomad millionaires.* Ithaca: Cornell University Press.

Porter, T. 2005. *Globalisation and finance.* Cambridge: Polity.

Rajan, R., and L. Zingales. 2003. The great reversals: The politics of financial development in the twentieth century. *Journal of Financial Economics* 69 (1): 5–50.

Renner, M. 2009. My interview with economist John K. Galbraith. *Truthout Original.* 6 May. http://www.truthout.org/050609J (accessed 1 June 2009).

Watson, M. 2007. *The political economy of international capital mobility.* Cambridge: Palgrave Macmillan.

Waylen, G. 2006. You still don't understand: Why troubled engagements continue between feminists and (critical) IPE. *Review of International Studies* 32 (1): 145–64.

Westbrook, J., and R. Schmidt. 2008. Cox "asleep" at switch as Paulson, Bernanke encroach. 22 September. http://www.bloomberg.com/apps/news (accessed 7 October 2008).

Wheelock, D.C. 1994. "The slack banker dances": Deposit insurance and risk-taking in the banking collapse of the 1920s. *Explorations in Economic History* 31:357–75.

10

Economics, Entrepreneurship and Gender
Integrating "the Others" into Enterprise Development Strategies

JONATHAN LASHLEY

Introduction

Mainstream economics seeks to analyse the social world as a closed system, with human action relegated to rebounding "in atom-like fashion to external influences" (Lawson 1995, 11). In this conceptual framework, where equilibrium is the golden chalice, the entrepreneur has historically been ensconced in economic theory and considered only as a "mechanism" for restoring balance to an economy. Although the entrepreneur has typically had a place, albeit hidden, in economic theory, gender and its role in providing and constraining opportunities have been altogether ignored. Recent times have restored the place of the entrepreneur as the driver of economic growth, stimulating greater investigation of this once shadowy figure. Advocates for the inclusion of the entrepreneur into mainstream economic theory have noted the fallacy of removing this agent from economic analysis, and indeed the concept of entrepreneurship is now widespread. In addressing the *othering* of the entrepreneur in economic theory, however, theoreticians in the area are introducing their own *othering* by disregarding the discourse of gender in their characterization of the entrepreneur and the process of entrepreneurship.

This chapter seeks to address some of the issues involved in disregarding gender discourse by charting the development of entrepreneurship theory as it has addressed the *othering* of the entrepreneur in economic theory, followed by recent contributions that have sought to address the *othering* of gender in entrepreneurship theory. This analysis is followed by the presentation of some policy prescriptions for enhancing the inclusion of gender in enterprise development strategies, drawn from recent research in Barbados and the Eastern Caribbean.

Traditional Economics and the Lonely Hero

The discipline of economics has traditionally been noted for its simplification of reality and its desire to discover the general "laws" of economic behaviour in a search for equilibrium (Lawson 1997). In this kind of approach, individual human action has often been rejected in a search for generality. In a rejection of this approach, economic theorizing in the latter half of the twentieth century has explicitly sought to include the entrepreneur as an agent and entrepreneurship as a process in discourse on economic growth. The recent critical literature in this area has rejected the *othering* of the entrepreneur and individual human actions, and has placed the entrepreneur as an individual at the centre of this discourse.

The classic literature on the subject has represented the entrepreneur as "conqueror of unexplored territories, the lonely hero, the patriarch" (Bruni, Gherardi and Poggio 2004, 407). In this sense, scholars have been entrepreneurial in their theorizing, with their pioneering insights and inclusion of the entrepreneur in the economic literature. In these endeavours, however, scholars have been guilty of introducing another type of *othering* by disregarding the role of gender in entrepreneurship. Scholars were accepting several of the principles of mainstream economics that they had rejected. In their fight to re-establish the entrepreneur's role, they accepted a model of economic rationality that was purported to be universal and gender neutral (Bruni, Gherardi, and Poggio 2004, 406). In another pioneering effort, scholars have sought to address this other *othering* by including the issue of gender in their analyses. This inclusion is not simply modelling gender as a variable in the mainstream economic tradition, however, but also the adoption of methods thought more suitable to provide an understanding of the issue of gender. These new methods seek to understand the role that social relationships play in our analysis of the entrepreneur as an agent of change and/or economic growth, and entrepreneurship as a process.

The import of these issues is the link they have with the formulation of policy in the area of enterprise development, and its probability of success. This area is considered important for development and growth in the current era of globalization and its attendant neo-liberal underpinnings. And it relates especially to policy for the resources required for enterprise development: training, technical assistance, finance, legislation and advocacy. It is now accepted that entrepreneurs have a role to play in economic development and growth, evidenced by their inclusion in theory and policy. Despite this acceptance, however, the issue of gender has largely been ignored in both applied and theoretical research. This exclusion is even more paradoxical, given the fact that *female empowerment* is touted as a goal for policy enacted in the area of enterprise development and supported by international development agencies such as the United Nations, the Inter-American Development Bank, and the International Labour Organization. In this context, gender is often not fully researched in the context of the developing world, and where it is researched or appreciated, it is often based on a masculine conception of entrepreneurship. Some of these points form the rationale for Browne's (2001) study of female entrepreneurship in a Caribbean context. On the issue of female empowerment, Browne suggests that research in this area can ask powerful questions and challenge "patriarchal institutions and ideologies in shaping women's opportunities to achieve economic autonomy (production and control of resources) and economic mobility" (ibid. 2001, 329). She goes on to note that the literature on entrepreneurship is gender neutral, and that the gender-based analysis that does exist is mostly drawn from the United States and based on male entrepreneurs. This chapter proposes that this sequential *othering* of the entrepreneur, followed by the *othering* of gender, has resulted in an enterprise development paradigm that pays scant attention to women in economic development policy.

An A-Gendered, Entrepreneurless Economics

The general characterization of mainstream economics is positivist, one that accepts closed, universalistic, non-cultural and abstract social analyses (Jennings and Waller 1995). This approach is concerned mainly with facts and is opposed to questions about values and intentions; it is concerned with the "positive" elements of experience, and prefers to identify regularity, order and pattern. Observation and the external world are paramount; history is largely ignored. Positivists consider reality as the world that can be directly observed or sensed, rejecting any concept of metaphysics[1] and unobservable structures. In this scheme, the "oddity", the "abnormal", and the "obscure" are all ignored in favour of the normal and the observable. The motivations of the maverick computer programmer or the reasons for the sexual division of labour are of peripheral concern in this kind of conception of society. The inherent limitation of positivism is that human "choice" is externally determined, exogenous, and there is in fact no choice (Lawson 1997).

In contrast, critical theories accept that we do not live in a closed system, and we do not passively follow predetermined courses of action. We all make choices, and because we all make choices, the result of any action can have multiple outcomes. These choices are governed both by individual character, the prevailing internal and external environment, and the constraints of societal rules and structures (Lashley 2002). In taking this perspective in contrast to mainstream economics, it starts to become clear that these kinds of critical theories afford more considerations of entrepreneurship and gender. This is especially relevant, as such structures are spatially and temporally unique and governed by such factors as beliefs, interpersonal relationships, locale, history, culture and position in society. North stresses the importance of history, stating that "history matters, that the choices we make today and tomorrow are constrained by the past evolution of the belief system and institutions of the society" (1995, 11). These factors all reflect the roles we play in society, including that of entrepreneurial character, and gender as a social relation. None of these factors are ubiquitous. The premise here is that we make an active choice to do or not to do, and indeed how to do.

Critical theories have afforded a place for the entrepreneur and gender by recognizing that we are not passive recipients of information that leads us to follow passively a certain path. Within a framework of positivism, the underlying philosophy of mainstream economics, this is the course and "cause" of action. From it, we can implicitly see that gender is a casualty of generalization. Bhaskar (1978) believes that positivists oversimplify reality as they collapse the three domains of reality (the real, the actual and the empirical) into one. This is one of the reasons why economic analysis finds it difficult to get past simple sex-disaggregated analysis and progress into gender analysis. In this kind of analysis, what women do determines what they are, not what they are caused to be. Bhaskar's objection to positivism is clear. He states that causality (which critical realists believe to be grounded at the level of mechanisms, such as gender relations, that are not observable) does not necessarily follow pattern (the actual) or experience (the empirical) (ibid.).

The wholesale acceptance of the principles of positivist economics led to the lack of explicit recognition of the entrepreneur in economic theory on growth and development. This lack of explicit recognition is despite debates and discussions on the definition, role and character of the entrepreneur that have their roots as far back as the eighteenth century, with the work of economic theorist Richard Cantillon. Although Cantillon allocated a place for the entrepreneur and characterized the entrepreneur as an arbiter (Thornton n.d.), the entrepreneur has for the most part been ensconced in economics, present in some form but hidden from theory or analysis. The entrepreneur was an anomaly, and because this phenomenon could not be explained, it was relegated to being part of the ubiquitous "error term" in empirical models.

More recent discussions of the entrepreneur have their roots in the work of Baumol (1968). Baumol recognized the importance of the entrepreneur in economic growth by attributing to this agent the responsibility for the "vitality" of the free enterprise society (ibid.). When Baumol was writing, there were global divisions in economic theorizing over the merits of this free enterprise society. In the society of the twenty-first century, however, whether one agrees with it or not, the free enterprise society *is* the dominant model. If, in the late 1960s, Baumol placed the entrepreneur at "the apex of the hierarchy that determines the behaviour of the firm" (ibid., 64), today this position is of even greater importance. In the current era of "globalization", neo-liberal ideologies prevail and "the market" is seen as the panacea for all economic ills (Browne 2001). In seeking to locate what drives economic development, Baumol recognized the implicit inclusion of the entrepreneur in economic theory, citing that "he [*sic*] remained a shadowy entity without clearly defined form or function"(1968, 64). In recent times, greater study of this once shadowy figure has addressed, to a degree, the implicit role of the entrepreneur; however, the issue of a clearly defined form or function is still elusive. The lack of a clear definition may, however, be owed to a greater, rather than lesser, explicit study of the entrepreneur, as academics and practitioners from myriad disciplines have undertaken the task of revealing the very nature of this agent of economic growth that we call an entrepreneur.

In recognizing the importance of this figure, Baumol (1968) eloquently attempts to provide a rudimentary definition: "The entrepreneur (whether or not he in fact doubles as a manager) has a different function. It is his job to locate new ideas and to put them into effect. He must lead, perhaps even inspire; he cannot allow things to get into a rut and for him today's practice is never good enough for tomorrow. In short, he is the Schumpeterian inno-vator and some more. He is the individual who exercises what in the business literature is called 'leadership'" (ibid., 65). This consistent, and assumed inten-tional, masculine representation of the entrepreneur by Baumol is pervasive in much of the literature (Bruni, Gherardi and Poggio, 2004). This kind of image reinforces the entrepreneur as male. With such seminal works as Baumol's influencing consequent theorizing in the area, the entrepreneur as male has become thoroughly embedded in both pure and applied research, evident to the present day.

In speaking to the issue of the absence of the entrepreneur from economic models on economic growth at the time, Baumol notes that the references are scanty or often absent. He notes that the "firm" as a theoretical construct was "entrepreneurless", leading to the famous quote that "the Prince of Denmark has been expunged from the discussion of Hamlet" (1968, 66). It is now clear that the issue of the *othering* of the entrepreneur in economic theorizing has been addressed, as is evident from the volume of literature and debate that has emerged in the field in the last few decades, with there being over forty-four peer-reviewed English-language academic journals in entrepreneurship (Katz and Boal 2002). In addition to this increased interest in entrepreneurship in general, from the mid-1980s to the present there has been a marked increase in the attention specifically paid to the link between entrepreneurship and economic growth.

The discourse in the field emerges from a number of perspectives and approaches. In seeking to explain the various perspectives, Hebert and Link (1989) discuss the contributions of Schumpeter, Schultz and Kirzner, whom they consider to be the core scholars from whose work more recent debates have emerged. Hebert and Link cite Schumpeter as viewing development as a dynamic process *"a disturbing of the status quo"* (ibid., 43), and state that he attributes to the entrepreneur the title *persona causa* of the dynamic process of economic development. According to Hebert and Link, Schumpeter provides a role for the entrepreneur in his observation that economic processes are organic, and that change comes from within the economic system, not just from without. Schumpeter views the entrepreneur as the agent who causes economic disturbances. This view is unlike that of other schools of thought, particularly Schultz's Chicago School, which characterizes the entrepreneur as reactive to economic imbalance, a reconciling rather than a disruptive influence on the economic system.

From a Schultzian view of the entrepreneur as a reactor to imbalance, it appears that, without some exogenous shock to the economy, the entrepreneur does not exist, as "economic life proceeds routinely on the basis of past experience; there are no forces evident for any change of the status quo" (Hebert and Link 1989, 44). This kind of observation lends support to Baumol's claim (1968) that, when this view prevailed in mainstream economics, the entrepreneur was expunged from economic theory. In other words, the entrepreneur was *othered*. Schumpeter challenges the view that development only occurs following external shocks. He considers endogenous disturbance of the status quo as being the instigator of development. This process is what Schumpeter termed "creative destruction", defined as "the carrying out of new combinations on production. It is accomplished by the entrepreneur" (Hebert and Link 1989, 44).

Overall, Schumpeter identifies three main conflicts in theory development. First, there are conflicts between the tendency towards equilibrium and the tendency towards imbalance; secondly, conflicts exist between statics and dynamics; and finally, the manager is in conflict with the entrepreneur. In Schumpeter's theory the entrepreneur is more than just a manager following set procedures. The entrepreneur is the instigator of imbalance in a dynamic economic environment. In his discourse, Schumpeter further alludes to some of the characteristics of entrepreneurs as he speaks of their "pioneering and innovative spirit".

Unlike with Schultz, an examination of the works of Kirzner reveals more of an affinity with Schumpeter, although there are inherent philosophical differences relating to whether the entrepreneur is the *persona causa* of economic imbalance or of equilibrium. In this instance Kirzner assigns the entrepreneur the task of creating the adjustments necessary to move the market towards equilibrium. Kirzner identifies alertness to profit opportunities, or predation, as the essence of the entrepreneur, and identifies three main influences on his theories about the entrepreneur. He views the market process as essentially an entrepreneurial learning process, and cites as his influences the work of Mises and Hayek. He remains adamant, however, that entrepreneurial acts are acts of discovery. Kirzner states that these acts are *creative* acts, in obvious alignment with Schumpeter.

Although Kirzner attributes to the entrepreneur the role of adjuster to equilibrium, he makes clear that this state is unachievable, as in a dynamic economy: "knowledge is neither complete nor perfect, therefore markets are constantly in states of disequilibrium, and it is disequilibrium that gives scope to the entrepreneurial function" (Hebert and Link 1989, 46). In this manner, the Kirzner entrepreneur is neither Schumpeterian nor Schultzian. In summing up the main debates in the field, Hebert and Link (ibid.) dismiss as unimportant, at the elemental level, the emergent discourse on whether the entrepreneur reacts to or causes economic imbalance. The authors claim that what should be important if one seeks to promote entrepreneurship is attention to its basic elements, which they cite as perception, courage and action, all terms with distinctly masculine connotations.

In examining these basic elements of entrepreneurship, Wennekers and Thurik (1999) view the link between entrepreneurship and economic growth as indirect. Utilizing this assumption, they stress the need for, firstly, the identification of *intermediate linkages*, as well as *conditions* for entrepreneurship. In providing a rationale for their approach, Wennekers and Thurik hypothesize that personal traits lie at the root of entrepreneurship, and that entrepreneurship and intermediate linkages both depend on the underlying cultural and institutional conditions in a country. It is obvious from these more recent works that theorizing has advanced from understanding the role of the entrepreneur in economic growth, to clarifying the conditions under which entrepreneurship occurs and flourishes, as well as its determinants.

Following their analysis of data from several countries on the link between cultural conditions and entrepreneurship, Wennekers and Thurik note that the link, while significant, is not straightforward. They stress that the efficacy of the process is based on a range of determinants at various levels. Of particular relevance to the present discourse are the cultural and institutional conditions for the emergence of entrepreneurship, and the type of entrepre-

neurial character exhibited. Wennekers and Thurik outline these determinants
as follows:

- Cultural conditions: open-mindedness to other cultures, acceptance of
  risk and failure, long-term orientations, valuation of wealth and savings
- Institutional conditions: high level of incentives, clear competition rules,
  clear property rights, low entry barriers
- Character of entrepreneurship: personal traits (alertness, curiosity, creativity, experimentation, ambition, perseverance); smallness (autonomous
  role of owners of small firms); manifestations of behaviour (being innovative, entering new markets, starting a new enterprise)

The authors' observations are instructive for policymaking, conditional on an
understanding of the pre-existing conditions in the economy of concern, as
advocated by Kirzner. Indeed, in Barbados, there is some understanding of
the local environment for the promotion of entrepreneurship. Although there
are institutions and some intermediate linkages along the supply chain of support entrepreneurship, it appears that cultural inhibitions (a moderate social
valuation of entrepreneurship and a preference for employment) are constraining entrepreneurship's contribution to economic growth in Barbados (Lashley
2007).

The *Othering* of Gender

The foregoing discussion has revealed that, in breaking from a mainstream
positivist conceptualization of economics, economic theorists have included
the entrepreneur in their theories as a dynamic figure. Indeed, scholars have
identified several roles, characteristics and determinants in the sub-discipline
of entrepreneurship studies, including the concept of the entrepreneur as dis-
rupter of the status quo, and a positive correlation between social valuation
of entrepreneurship and the entrepreneur's contribution to economic growth.
What is clear, however, is that the issue of gender has been bypassed. This cir-
cumvention of gender is owed to the accepted conceptualization of the
entrepreneur as explicitly asexual but implicitly masculine. This perception
of the entrepreneur has led to theorizing and policy development that proclaim
to be gender neutral, based on the belief that entrepreneurship is gender neutral. As highlighted by Bruni, Gherardi, and Poggio, however, "when

masculinity is made invisible, the male entrepreneurial model is universalized and stripped of gender. Thus made universal, it is proposed or prescribed independently of a person's gender: women who wish to become entrepreneurs are required to comply with an apparently neutral set of values, while men are required to comply with those of 'entrepreneurial' masculinity" (2004, 410).

This type of approach suggests that there is a level playing field, that males and females have the same level of access to resources, and that society as a whole is equally accepting of both the male and female entrepreneur. Although theorizing has progressed from the traditional mainstream economic approach which precluded any place for individual human action, entrepreneurship research, while allowing for individual human action, has until recently been characterized by a universal and agendered model of economic rationality, as typified in the quote above (Bruni, Gherardi, and Poggio 2004). However, much of the recent research which has included the issue of gender in its analysis, while it has economic implications, has approached the subject from a variety of perspectives, including anthropology, sociology and management studies. Despite stating that entrepreneurship research has been overtly agendered, Bruni, Gherardi, and Poggio (2004) note that much of the literature implicitly equates entrepreneurship with the masculine, observing that the classic literature defined the entrepreneur as the "conqueror of unexplored territories, the lonely hero, the patriarch" (ibid., 406). Even more overt in this characterization is Collins and Moore's assertion that, "however we may personally feel about the entrepreneur, he emerges as essentially more masculine than feminine, more heroic than cowardly" (1964, 5).

Despite these overt references to the masculine, there have been some useful contributions to the advancement of gendered entrepreneurship research. Although they do not explicitly address the issue of gender in their proposed determinants of entrepreneurship, Wennekers and Thurik (1999) provide some useful starting points for the inclusion of gender, especially on the levels of conditions and character of entrepreneurship. The authors recognize that, at the level of conditions, culture and institutions have an important role to play; at the level of character, personal traits and manifestations of behaviour also have a role. By not explicitly recognizing the issue of gender, however, they accept the masculine orientation alluded to above. If we consider culture, institutions, personal traits and manifestations of behaviour as important in the discovery and exploitation of entrepreneurial opportunities, then this framework will give context to our examination of gender and the role it plays in defining the character of the entrepreneur, as well as the overall process of entrepreneurship.

The critical literature has given us an understanding of what entrepreneurship is in its dynamic sense. It is confronting economic disequilibrium to actualize economic growth, whether at the community, national, regional or international level. In defining the entrepreneur as the agent of entrepreneurship, however, theory has only managed to provide us with indicators that are representative of the manner in which males practice entrepreneurship.

If we pull together the insights of scholars such as Wennekers and Thurik, we can begin to construct a framework in which all aspects of the entrepreneur can be facilitated to promote economic growth. Wennekers and Thurik (1999) identify several issues related to the entrepreneur that have yet to be investigated extensively with reference to gender, including culture, institutions, personal traits and manifestations of behaviour. These issues have been interrogated with the masculine base of entrepreneurship as a foundation for analysis. From this base, policy has been developed in the areas of training, technical assistance, finance and legislative reform. The role of gender, however, has been subsumed surreptitiously within the implicit understanding of the entrepreneur.

To redress this imbalance, and in making reference to gender, the approach of Barriteau is useful. Barriteau uses gender to "refer to a system of social relations through which women and men are constituted and through which they gain differential access and are unequally allocated status, power and material resources within a society" (2002, 222). From this perspective, a new approach to enterprise development policy can be nurtured. If we can begin to understand that the exhibited characteristics of women entrepreneurs are owed to imbedded social relations because of women's assigned gender roles, then we can adopt measures to address these inequities in status, power and access to resources. In this instance, we must understand what these exhibited characteristics are, and how they differ from those of men. We then need to examine the causes of these occurrences – that is, whether men and women entrepreneurs do indeed "do business differently".

Do Men and Women Practise Entrepreneurship Differently?

Evidence from a number of studies reveals that men and women do demonstrate different entrepreneurial characteristics, and indeed do practice entrepreneurship differently (Mirchandani 1999). Specifically of relevance to the Caribbean are the findings of Barriteau, who finds that officials who provide services to entrepreneurs in Barbados have the overarching view that women "did not inculcate the values of an entrepreneurial culture" (2002, 227). This statement serves to highlight the hostile environment within which women must operate in the public sphere, and insinuates that men fully embrace and represent the entrepreneurial ideal. This conception of women as non-entrepreneurs is fuelled by views that women's work is characterized by non-entrepreneurial components, such as a focus on female-oriented businesses (hairdressing, day care, sewing and catering), small business size (fear of expansion and partnerships), employment of family members, aversion to taking risks, and basing business in the home (ibid.). All of these areas identified by officials suggest that female business owners demonstrate an element of non-professional behaviour because of inherent linkages between their businesses and the home. From this sort of commentary we can glean that if women are to be considered entrepreneurial, they must discard all vestiges of the home and exhibit professional, and hence entrepreneurial, behaviour. With these kinds of views in the public supply of enterprise development support, it is not surprising that women continue to have difficulty in accessing the support services necessary to grow and develop their businesses. It must be noted, however, that Barriteau's findings, from interviews with women entrepreneurs, did not support officials' views on the characteristics of women's businesses.

These issues identified in Barbados are not unique to that island, however. Mirchandani (1999) provides a review of research in the area of gender and entrepreneurship that includes relevant insights in this regard, as summarized below:

- Motivation for business formation: Females are less motivated by economic gain, and more by child-rearing demands and career dissatisfaction (Cromie 1987).
- Size: Female-owned businesses are typically smaller than those of males (Loscocco et al. 1991).

- Networking: Females spend more time and effort than males on building relationships with clients (Aldrich 1989).
- Work/Home Separation: Females' businesses show a greater integration with home life than those of males (Brush 1992).

Mirchandani's (1999) review of the differences between males' and females' practice of entrepreneurship is informative. The explanatory factors for these observed differences, as identified by Mirchandani, are: the roles of different socializations, and hence different orientations; the structural barriers women face; and the fact that women "do" business differently from men. In order to grasp fully the causal factors underlying the observations made, we need to unpack these issues, and we need to ask what the different socializations and structural barriers are, and why women "do" business differently. Answering these questions will require an analysis at the level of culture, institutions, personal traits and manifestations of behaviour, as suggested above in reference to the work of Wennekers and Thurik (1999). These issues are addressed in the sections to follow.

In returning to Mirchandani's (1999) review, one of the most alarming elements is the identification that recommendations for the enhancement of female entrepreneurship consistently suggest that females need to rid themselves of the characterizations listed above, and adopt an approach more in line with the masculine conceptualization of entrepreneurship. This masculine conception of entrepreneurship implicitly suggests that women must demonstrate leadership and independence, embrace risk, be hungry for profit and growth, and discard the household as a source of finance or labour. Even studies in the Caribbean have adopted this kind of approach. A study by the International Labour Organization (ILO) on gender and small enterprises in Barbados, Suriname, and Trinidad and Tobago provides recommendations for enhancing female entrepreneurship based on the goal of women's achieving the masculine version of entrepreneurship (ILO 2001). The study, for example, encourages females to undertake technical training in male-dominated areas in order to facilitate their participation, and recommends that women engage in leadership training in order to evoke the pioneering spirit that is so much the ethos of current conceptualizations of entrepreneurship. Mirchandani (1999) treats these approaches as misleading, but indeed, we need to question whether they are even feasible, given the antecedent social relations of gender that lie at the root of these kinds of occurrences.

The recommendations of the ILO study are further evidence that the current approach to enterprise development is geared towards the masculine, and provides scant attention to the role played by gender relations. These types of recommendations are opposed to understanding the underlying causes of females' alternate approaches to entrepreneurship. If women practice entrepreneurship differently from men, and define success in different ways, can a policy approach that is geared towards the masculine version of entrepreneurship then really be effective in promoting enterprise development? This is the main issue that needs attention if public policies that seek to enhance the discovery and exploitation of entrepreneurial opportunities are going to serve adequately a large percentage of the pool of potential entrepreneurs. Indeed, although women have a strong presence in the labour market in the Caribbean, it appears that they are not realizing their entrepreneurial potential. In general, women are over-represented at the lower end of the labour market and underrepresented at the high end, where the greatest potential for contributing to economic growth is located (Browne 2001).

In seeking to address this issue it is important, first, to understand the needs and approaches to entrepreneurship employed by men and women in the economies of concern, specifically Barbados and the Eastern Caribbean. The following section provides some results derived from studies on enterprise development in these societies. Although data were not primarily collected to analyse the issue of gender, they are considered useful as they provide a profile of the issues of interest. In this case, the inferences made can only be made with reference to other studies, as no gender analysis was done at the time of data collection and analysis.

Enterprise Development and Gender Differences in the Caribbean

The results outlined in table 10.1 are based on research conducted between 2002 and 2003 in Grenada, St Vincent and the Grenadines, and Barbados. The research was not concerned with the issue of gender; hence, results were only disaggregated by sex. Given this constraint, the results presented are not intended to provide any overarching conclusions about the differences observed between males and females in business, but simply to identify significant trends that may be analysed within the framework of current studies related to gender and entrepreneurship. This kind of research can provide for more effective, efficient and equitable policy formation in the area of enterprise development.

For Grenada and St Vincent and the Grenadines, the data presented below is based on a survey of 212 micro-entrepreneurs, conducted in March 2003, which sought to collect information on demographics, business character and finance. Approximately 64 per cent of respondents were female, and respondents' ages ranged from twenty years to eighty-nine years, with a median of thirty-nine years. The 212 respondents were evenly distributed among urban, suburban and rural communities, with household sizes ranging from one to fifteen, with a mean of four. Over 80 per cent of respondents were heads of household. The basis of the results for the survey of Barbadian micro-entrepreneurs is information collected in 2002 about 195 clients of two micro-finance institutions. The research sought to investigate employment history, credit history and business character. For both studies, the main significant differences between men and women are outlined in table 10.1.

The results emerging from the research in Grenada and St Vincent and the Grenadines demonstrate some clear differences between the sexes, and show that male and female micro-entrepreneurs have different demographics, operate in different sectors and have different preferences for the form and use of finance. For Barbados, the results appear to indicate that males have larger, more successful businesses than females, if assets, growth and employment are used as measures.

Analysing these results from a mainstream economics perspective would undoubtedly end in recommendations of the type outlined above, where cause and effect are expected to map neatly onto each other. From this perspective, recommendations emerge to encourage women to seek to address the observed differentials, with men's behaviour held up as the ideal. With the masculine conception of entrepreneurship as a base, women are encouraged to demonstrate leadership and independence, embrace risk, be hungry for profit and growth, and discard the household as a source of finance or labour. What this kind of approach does not consider, however, is how these characteristics and/or observations have emerged, and how to address them through public policy. Indeed, as long as men's actions are upheld as the ideal, the goal for entrepreneurship is given: do what men do and you will have successful entrepreneurship. This philosophy is essentially based on the characteristics of the entrepreneur rather than entrepreneurship as process. This kind of strategic

Table 10.1. Significant Differences between Men and Women

Issue	Grenada and St Vincent and the Grenadines	Barbados
Household Size	Female micro-entrepreneurs had larger households (4.8 persons) than males (3.7 persons).	
Size/Growth	Male-operated enterprises employed more persons (1.4) than female-operated enterprises (0.5).	Female-operated businesses were more likely to experience no change in employees since inception. Males borrowed in excess of two times that of females to start their businesses (US$7,613 versus US$3,286.65), and females were more likely not to have additional loans. Males experienced significant growth in assets (US$20,430), while females experienced significant losses in assets (US$20,505)** since the inception of their businesses.
Business Type	Males were involved in skilled/technical occupations (20.6 per cent) and sales/services (22.2 per cent), while females were mainly involved in sales/services, including retail (62.7 per cent). Females experience seasonality to a greater degree (49.7 per cent) than males (35.8 per cent).	

Table continues

Table 10.1. Significant Differences between Men and Women (*cont'd*)

Issue	Grenada and St Vincent and the Grenadines	Barbados
Finance	Males mainly sought finance for cash flow (32.6 per cent) and purchase of machinery (30.2 per cent), while females mainly sought finance for business start-up costs (46.2 per cent) and cash flow (23.1 per cent). In drawing contrasts, only 12.8 per cent of females borrowed funds to purchase machinery, and only 25.6 per cent of males borrowed for business start-up.	Males' current assets were approximately five times those of females (US$40,280 versus US$7,546). Males borrowed in excess of two times that of females to start their businesses (US$7,613 versus US$3,286.65), and females were more likely not to have additional loans.
Savings	Females (56.7 per cent) had a greater preference than males (46.6 per cent) for participating in a sou-sou* to save and provide future finance for their businesses.	

Notes:

Sou-sou is a traditional group savings system utilized in many Caribbean countries whereby participants deposit a specified amount with the group at a specific interval (weekly, monthly) and each member of the group takes turns in drawing out contributions. This form of saving is also called a "meeting turn" in Barbados, a "box hand" in Guyana, and "partner" in Jamaica.

**This result may be indicative of females' utilizing their own resources in place of additional loans.

direction fails to recognize that entrepreneurship is about dealing with dise-quilibrium to facilitate economic growth, and is more concerned with emulating the characteristics of successful (male) entrepreneurs.

If economic growth is the main concern when speaking to the issue of enterprise development, then entrepreneurship as process must be the main focus rather than policy development concerned with emulating a masculine conception of the entrepreneur. It is more important, in this regard, to accept what entrepreneurship is, and develop policy that seeks to remove the con-straints that both male and female entrepreneurs encounter in operating their businesses.

In seeking to address the *othering* of gender, we need to question what the social relations are that are causing differential access to the resources for entre-preneurial success, specifically training, technical assistance, finance and an appropriate legislative environment. This questioning of causal relations will need to be within the context of the determinants of entrepreneurship (culture, institutions, personal traits and manifestations of behaviour). The specific issues that need to be addressed are:

- What is it about culture, institutions, personal traits and manifestations of behaviour (how entrepreneurship is practised) that cause differential access to entrepreneurial resources (training, technical assistance, finance, legislation) for men and women?
- How does this differential access affect the manner in which entrepre-neurship is practised?
- What policy measures can be put in place to address the manner in which entrepreneurship is practised in order to actualize economic growth?

The results presented in table 10.1, as well as the work of Mirchandani (1999), demonstrate how differential access has affected the manner in which entrepreneurship is practised by both men and women. These results suggest that women's motivation is different, and that their businesses are generally small, have low growth and are located in sectors which have a close affinity with the home. In addition, women have a different approach to savings and finance, indicating a different approach to risk. What needs to be understood is the cause of these differential approaches, and Wennekers and Thurik pro-vide a useful starting point in this regard. If Wennekers and Thurik's (1999) determinants of entrepreneurship are considered from the gender perspective advocated by Barriteau (2002), then we can propose that these determinants perhaps have an effect on access to entrepreneurial resources (training, technical assistance, finance and legislation), which are differentially allocated among men and women because of the status allocated to their varying gender roles.

In analysing these determinants in turn, we can propose that *culture* causes differential access as a result of assigned gender roles, which determine what is acceptable for women and men. Browne speaks directly to this concept when she states that the profiles of women entrepreneurs may vary in a society, depending on the "form and strength of gendered ideologies" (2001, 333). For entrepreneurship to contribute successfully to economic growth, it needs to be accepted culturally as a viable career choice (Lashley 2007). Women's gender roles reduce this acceptance, however, because they diverge from the traditional view of the entrepreneur, who has distinctly male characteristics. This kind of point of view in the household and wider community constrains women's choices in participating in the economy, both personally and societally. This cultural influence not only affects the acceptance an individual receives, but it also has wider implications for the way in which access to entrepreneurial resources is structured and shared. The link between acceptance and access to resources further marginalises women as their entrepreneurial status is ranked lower than that of men and, as indicated by Barriteau (2002), their activities are not even considered entrepreneurial by some officials.

In terms of institutions, which can be considered the result of history and the formalization of a country's culture, the discussions have revealed that the male conceptualization of entrepreneurship, albeit not explicitly stated, has been uncritically accepted (Bruni, Gherardi and Poggio 2004). With this conceptualization, women entrepreneurs who have the potential to contribute to economic growth are considered non-entrepreneurial if they do not exhibit certain male characteristics. This perception leads institutions to provide support that does not speak directly to women's needs, and requires them to emulate a masculine conception of entrepreneurship in order to access entrepreneurial support. This need to emulate the masculine conception is specious, however, and speaks directly to the unequal status and power allocated to women in the realm of business, and hence entrepreneurship. If a country's institutions (incentives, competition rules, property rights, low barriers to entry) are determinant of entrepreneurship, then it is clear that women are at

a disadvantage, especially because of the prevailing conception of the entrepreneur as distinctly male. As discussed above, the entrepreneur is expected
to demonstrate leadership and independence, embrace risk, be hungry for
profit and growth, and discard the household as a source of finance and labour.
This definition, in essence, berates the status of the household and serves to
reinforce women's differential access to entrepreneurial resources.

Personal traits are a determinant of entrepreneurship as they affect the manner in which one approaches the tasks of entrepreneurial discovery and
exploitation. Literature on the topic has represented these traits as leadership,
independence, ambition, perseverance, risk tolerance, growth and profit orientation, and professionalism. In addition, scholarship also includes issues
related to innovation, such as alertness, curiosity, creativity and experimentation. These traits, however, describe an individual whom an innate personal
desire pulls into entrepreneurship; they do not apply to those individuals who
are pushed. From previous research on female entrepreneurs, it appears that
women are pushed into entrepreneurship more than men, as women's motivations lie with career dissatisfaction and child-rearing demands (Cromie
1987). Browne (2001) notes that career dissatisfaction rests with the imposition
of barriers by employers (the glass ceiling), as well as occupational segregation.
In addition, while women use work satisfaction, peace of mind and autonomy
as ratings of performance (Barriteau 2002), these factors suggest to resource
providers that women lack ambition and drive. These traits, when exhibited
by women, suggest to officials and practitioners in the field of enterprise development that women are not only un-entrepreneurial, but may also be
anti-entrepreneurial. The demonstration of these traits subsequently causes a
reduction in access to resources, as the gatekeepers of these resources, and
those who develop policy, do not believe that addressing these traits is in keeping with their mission of enterprise development. Instead, they leave the issue
of policies for developing female entrepreneurship to governmental and non-
governmental institutions with a distinctive social rather than economic focus.
Relegating female enterprise development to this level not only leads to foregone economic growth, but it further exacerbates the status and power
differentials between men and women, since these kinds of programmes
concentrate more on the micro-entrepreneur and survival, rather than entrepreneurship and economic growth. While there are elements of these
programmes that are laudable because they seek to address the needs of women

and the family, they are indeed perpetuating a myth of inferiority. Women are still restricted from participation in the wider economy and lack access to entrepreneurial resources to help them succeed, whatever their personal definition of success may be.

In further indicating the complexity of the issues, manifestations of behaviour, as a determinant of entrepreneurship, are not only affected by culture and institutions, but also by personal traits. In addition, and in the wider context, the social relations of gender that form some of the basis for the current discourse drive how males and females behave. At the root of this differential behaviour are assigned gender roles, whose status and assigned power have a marked influence on what is deemed acceptable. The entrepreneur is expected to be innovative, searching and willing to enter new markets and businesses as opportunities arise. Again, this description suggests a pull towards entrepreneurship and does not consider the way in which the situation of women may cause them to be pushed, because of the situation either in the labour market or in the home. In this regard, it is the image of the entrepreneur that leads to differential access and, as with the discussion of personal traits, if women do not exhibit these behaviours, they are considered to be non-entrepreneurial. Indeed, in some instances, for women to behave in this manner is deemed unacceptable. This kind of environment further alienates women and constrains their access to resources by assigning to the entrepreneur certain behaviours which do not necessarily represent the manner in which women practise "business". It also leads women not to view themselves as entrepreneurs and, in some cases, actually to seek to emulate the behaviours attributed to the entrepreneur, although these actions may not come naturally. Bruni, Gherardi and Poggio illustrate this phenomenon in their analysis of an interview with a female entrepreneur named Franca who owns and operates a manufacturing company with her sister, Enrica:

> Franca states that there exists a shared image of the "entrepreneur". Besides relating more to a man than a woman (as illustrated by Enrica's explanation of why they have decided to register the company in the Engineer's [a male] name), this image conveys an ability to be ruthless in dealing with others. Franca Somma is indeed able to behave in this way (as when she protested "vigourously" to a defaulting customer), but she does not see this as something that comes naturally to her. It is this that prevents her from seeing herself (and being seen) as a "real" entrepreneur. (Bruni, Gherardi and Poggio 2004, 417)

All of these issues are related to culture, institutions, personal traits and man-ifestations of behaviour, and all have an effect on the differential access to entrepreneurial resources experienced by men and women. In considering these issues, we can start to hypothesize about the underlying causes of the significant differences seen in table 10.1. The differences observed indicate issues related to the household, to the character of the enterprise and to finan-cial behaviour. The issue of the female household relates to its size relative to that of males. Although the specific causal relations here were not directly investigated with respondents, inferences can be made in relation to the literature. Cromie (1987) identifies child-rearing demands as one of the moti-vations for business formation by females. Owing to the larger household size identified, it can be proposed that the gender roles of caregivers and child-minders are causing these women to be pushed into entrepreneurship. It appears, in this instance, that culture has a distinct effect as a determinant in this case, with women's assigned gender roles causing them to enter entrepre-neurship in order to ensure that their households are catered for.

The greatest areas of divergence between men and women, however, were in the character of their businesses and their financial behaviours – the areas in which the determinants of entrepreneurship have the greatest effect on access to entrepreneurial resources. In this case, women's businesses were small, experienced low growth, and were mainly involved in the services sector. Women sought capital for start-up and cash-flow, and had a preference for informal savings plans. In looking at these results in light of the discussion above, it appears that culturally assigned gender roles and their related low status, as well as personal traits and behaviours that have emerged from these roles, have caused a lack of access to resources. This lack of access is owed to the role of institutions in determining entrepreneurship, and the perception that women display un-entrepreneurial tendencies and hence should be barred from access to entrepreneurial resources. In this sense, incentives and property rights as components of these institutions do not directly address the situation of women. Women's businesses are small and experience low growth because they lack access to the type of financial and technical assistance their businesses require. The incentives in this area are not geared towards women's businesses, as they do not provide for the differing financial needs of women, whose prop-erty rights are limited in some cases. With this kind of institutional framework, entrepreneurial resources are not geared towards coping with the training required by women, providing technical assistance in areas that are not considered entrepreneurial, or providing credit and savings products that cater to females' attitudes towards risk and uncertainty. This problem is further exacerbated by the fact that links between business and household are considered unprofessional, and hence too risky or unproductive for consideration by financing institutions.

The link between business and household has also influenced the types of businesses women undertake. These businesses are mainly in the service sector and draw on the everyday work of women allocated by their gender roles – cooking, cleaning, sewing and other home-based labour. Because these tasks are considered to be outside of the public sphere, they are not accommodated in the institutional structure that provides for training, technical assistance and finance. These issues have subsequently led to women's preferring informal measures of finance such as *sou-sou* in order to fund their businesses. In addition, owing to the service-oriented nature of their work, women also seek financing for start-up costs and cash flow, as these expenses are generally small and can be accommodated within the current framework. This tendency is unlike that of men, who require funds for more capital-intensive machinery because of the nature of the sectors in which they are involved.

The preceding discussion has revealed the complexity of the issues under consideration, and has shown that culture, institutions, personal traits and manifestations of behaviour have all contributed to women's lack of access to entrepreneurial resources. This is a concerning situation, as these determinants of entrepreneurship are mutually reinforcing and serve to exacerbate the problems faced by women. Women's assigned jobs or roles are considered low-status, and hence cause them to lack power. These assigned roles are then formalized in institutional frameworks which serve to stigmatize women's traits and behaviours as un-entrepreneurial. This stigmatization has the further effect of portraying women's work as low in status, contributing to a vicious cycle of further alienation from entrepreneurial endeavours. This process, coupled with the masculine conception of entrepreneurship and the entrepreneur, have served to debar women from productive enterprise development, and from contributing to economic growth.

In order to address these issues, policy will need to be developed that is not only cognizant of the reasons for the revealed characteristics of women's businesses, but also addresses the current inequities of the system. This is not to say that men's path to entrepreneurship is to be dismissed, but suggests that the current system is geared towards men's natures and characteristics. The prevailing cultural and institutional structure is geared towards an acceptance of male traits and behavioural manifestations. This is not to say that men's path to entrepreneurship is easy; indeed, many do not proceed along this kind of path. What the research does suggest is that we need to develop policies that appreciate the time and resource constraints women face because of their gender roles and the societally allocated status of their work. It is only from such endeavours that power will emerge. Although the issue of gender receives attention in policy, the current approach to addressing the revealed needs of women has been based on a framework that seeks to address the effects, rather than the cause, of the social relations of gender. Women's businesses are smaller, experience lower growth and are often based in the service sector. Current policy approaches seek to encourage women to grow their businesses by emulating entrepreneurial characteristics that are distinctly masculine, as well as participating in non-traditional professions (ILO 2001; Mirchandani 1999). These approaches do not seek to address the causes of low growth and service orientation. The issues surrounding these occurrences are difficult to address through policy because of their socially and culturally embedded nature, and the fact that policy can only have a direct effect on institutions in the short term. In order to effect change in culture, personal traits and behaviour, a more long-term approach is required, one that speaks to the base causes of the results seen.

In the short term, policy needs to address the implicit masculine conception of entrepreneurship and realize that entrepreneurship is a dynamic process for addressing economic imbalance. All persons who undertake to address this kind of imbalance should be considered entrepreneurs, whether their activities take place in the private or public sphere. In addition, any policy development must be appreciative of the dual roles played by women in the home and in the world of business.

In terms of enhancing access to entrepreneurial resources, policy will need to be cognizant that any training, technical assistance or finance that is provided to women must be structured in such a manner that it serves not only to address women's specific needs, but also to address the inequities of status and power between men and women. Although the results of recent research, as presented earlier, indicate that women's businesses are small, experience low growth and are service-oriented, and that women's financial behaviour is different from men's, the needs of women cannot be inferred, because the current research cannot specifically identify whether women in these businesses have a desire to grow and operate outside of the service sector, or whether they want the same financing options as men. This uncertainty suggests that in-depth research is required to identify the needs of women in business, rather than basing policy on the current approach to policy development, which seeks growth and formalization within the masculine conception of entrepreneurship.

Conclusion

This analysis does not seek to provide a treatise on the overall social relations of gender that cause differential access to resources, status and power. It does, however, seek to contribute to this discussion by providing an example of this process as it relates to entrepreneurship and enterprise development policy. The chronological examination of the development of theorizing on entrepreneurship has revealed that mainstream economic theory has *othered* the entrepreneur as an agent, and entrepreneurship as a process, because of inherent philosophical constraints related to positivism. Although the literature on entrepreneurship has developed to reveal determinants of entrepreneurship and the character of the entrepreneur, theoreticians in the past have *othered* gender by accepting an implicit masculine conception of the entrepreneur. This othering has, however, been addressed in recent times, with gender theorists providing insights as to the role of gender in constraining access to resources, status and power.

In relating these concepts to the growth of enterprise development policy, research has revealed that the determinants of entrepreneurship (culture, institutions, personal traits and manifestations of behaviour) cause differential access to entrepreneurial resources for men and women. In addition, it has shown that this differential access affects the manner in which entrepreneurship is practised, where significant differences in men's and women's business were seen. Policy, however, can have little short-term effect on other issues that affect how gender is performed, including ingrained cultural expectations and practices. It is these issues which will need to be addressed if both male and female entrepreneurs are to realize their full potentials. This suggests that policy measures need to be implemented to address women's needs, as well as to ensure that, in the long term, status and power are allocated in an equitable manner. A greater understanding of the causes of the observed occurrences is required – something that implicit philosophical barriers bar mainstream economics or traditional approaches to entrepreneurship research from investigating.

It is widely touted that effective enterprise development strategies can contribute to development through alleviating poverty, generating employment, enhancing competitiveness and earning essential foreign exchange. Unless the role of gender is understood in terms of the implications it has for the practice of entrepreneurship, however, a significant portion of economic development may be foregone because of policy that only caters to a masculine conception of entrepreneurship. Based on a mainstream economic philosophy that accepts a flat version of reality, policy ignores the influence of underlying structures and mechanisms which influence how society as structure interacts with society as agency.[2] Policy development needs to begin with a goal for enterprise development, and must then ascertain how best to exploit different gendered approaches to self-employment by constructing policy to serve the differential motivations and antecedent conditions experienced by men and women. This kind of approach may then be able to tailor programmes for training, technical assistance and finance for enterprise development more efficiently, and may perhaps allow for the creation of "new, alternative models of enterprise and entrepreneurship" (Lewis 2006, 456), inspired by a greater understanding of the role gender plays in the practice of entrepreneurship.

Notes

1. Metaphysics is considered to be "that which lies outside our sense perceptions or is independent of them" (Holt-Jensen 1988, 88).
2. "Society as structure" speaks to the structural component of society that empowers or constrains human actions, while "society as agency" speaks to the manner in which members of society react and interact with societal structure.

References

Aldrich, H. 1989. Networking among women entrepreneurs. In *Women-owned businesses*, ed. O. Hagan, C. Rivchun and D. Sexton, 103–32. New York: Praeger.

Barriteau, E. 2002. Women entrepreneurs and economic marginality: Rethinking Caribbean women's economic relations. In *Gendered realities: Essays in Caribbean feminist thought*, ed. P. Mohammed, 221–48. Kingston: Centre for Gender and Development Studies, University of the West Indies Press.

Baumol, W.J. 1968. Entrepreneurship in economic theory. *American Economic Review* 58 (2): 64–71.

Bhaskar, R. 1978. On the possibility of social scientific knowledge and the limits of naturalism. *Journal for the Theory of Social Behaviour* 8 (1): 1–28.

Browne, K. 2001. Female entrepreneurship in the Caribbean: A multisite, pilot investigation of gender and work. *Human Organisation* 60 (4): 326–42.

Bruni, A., S. Gherardi and B. Poggio. 2004. Doing gender, doing entrepreneurship: An ethnographic account of intertwined practices. *Gender, Work and Organisation* 11 (4): 406–29.

Brush, C. 1992. Research on women business owners: Past trends, a new perspective, and future directions. *Entrepreneurship Theory and Practice* 16 (4): 5–30.

Collins, O., and D. Moore. 1964. *The enterprising man*. East Lansing: Michigan State University Press.

Cromie, S. 1987. Motivations of aspiring male and female entrepreneurs. *Journal of Occupational Behaviour* 8 (3): 251–61.

Hebert, R., and A. Link. 1989. Search of the meaning of entrepreneurship. *Small Business Economics* 1 (1): 39–49.

Holt-Jensen, A. 1988. *Geography: History and concepts*. 2nd ed. London: Chapman.

ILO. 2001. *Jobs, gender and small enterprises in the Caribbean: Lessons from Barbados, Suriname, and Trinidad and Tobago*. SEED working paper no. 19. Port of Spain: ILO.

Jennings, A., and W. Waller. 1995. Culture: Core concept reaffirmed. *Journal of Economic Issues* 29 (2): 407–18.

Katz, J., and K. Boal. 2002. Entrepreneurship journal rankings. *Marketing Techie*. http://www.marketingtechie.com/articles/mtart20020307.pdf.

Lashley, J. 2002. The internationalisation of the small- to medium-sized enterprise (SME): A critical realist approach. PhD diss., University of Leicester.

———. 2007. The entrepreneurship challenge in a time of change. Paper presented at the Sir Arthur Lewis Institute of Social and Economic Studies eighth annual conference, Trinidad and Tobago, 28 March. http://sta.uwi.edu/conferences/salises/documents/Lashley%20J.pdf.

Lawson, T. 1995. A realist perspective on contemporary economic theory. *Journal of Economic Issues* 29 (1): 1–32.

————. 1997. *Economics and reality*. London: Routledge.

Lewis, P. 2006. The quest for invisibility: Female entrepreneurs and the masculine norm of entrepreneurship. *Gender, Work and Organisation* 13 (5): 453–69.

Loscocco, K., J. Robinson, R. Hall, and J. Allen. 1991. Gender and small business success: An inquiry into women's relative disadvantage. *Social Forces* 70 (1): 65–85.

Mirchandani, K. 1999. Feminist insight on gendered work: New directions in research on women and entrepreneurship. *Gender, Work and Organisation* 6 (4): 224–35.

North, D. 1995. The Adam Smith address: Economic theory in a dynamic economic world. *Business Economics* 30 (1): 7–12.

Thornton, M. N.d. *The origin of economic theory: A portrait of Richard Cantillon (1680–1734)*. Auburn, AL: Ludwig von Mises Institute. http://mises.org/content/cantillon.asp (accessed 8 December 2006).

Wennekers, S., and R. Thurik. 1999. Linking entrepreneurship and economic growth. *Small Business Economics* 13 (1): 27–55.

11

Fostering Freedom

A Feminist Analysis of Micro-Enterprise Development for Women in the Caribbean

APRIL BERNARD

Introduction

In the Caribbean, the gains made by women relative to men over the past five decades have spurred a widespread debate on gender. One side claims that the third millennium belongs to women and suggests that declines in male participation and performance in the educational system, the proportion of men in the highest paying and most prestigious occupations, and the earning power of men relative to women are evidence of male marginalization in the Caribbean (Miller 1991). This argument implies that the ascension of women in the public domain is displacing men, particularly those who are acutely politically, economically and socially vulnerable.

Another side of the debate points to the persistent feminization of poverty as an indication of women's continued oppression in the new millennium. Proponents of this side of the argument raise evidence that reveals women's advances in educational attainment at the primary, secondary and tertiary levels have yet to translate into equitable outcomes, relative to men's success (Barriteau 2003; Tang Nain and Bailey 2003; De Albuquerque and Ruark 1998). In the Caribbean, the marginalization of women from the political centres of power, the unequal distribution of household responsibilities, and the rise of households headed by single females are also significant indicators of women's oppression, as well as contributors to the feminization of poverty (Bailey 2003; Andaiye 2003; Wiltshire-Brodber 1999; Vassell 2003). The implications of this side of the argument are that, despite women's social and economic ascension relative to men in the last half of the previous century, women's oppression has not been eradicated, and equity has yet to be attained. The notion of fostering non-traditional micro-enterprise development opportunities for women may further ignite passions on either side of the gender debate.

Micro-enterprise development and micro-credit initiatives across the globe have helped women to set up their own businesses and obtain meaningful employment. In the Caribbean, research has shown that, through entrepreneurship, women have made significant contributions to their economic development and that of their communities (Barriteau 2002). Through mentoring relationships with established business professionals, enterprise development training and access to credit from government or private commercial lenders, micro-enterprise development initiatives function to propel some women out of poverty.

The analysis presented in this chapter emphasizes the importance of engaging women in non-traditional vocations (those that have traditionally been male dominated, such as construction, landscaping, information technology and transportation). My research provides a gendered sociological analysis of micro-enterprise development initiatives in Trinidad and Barbados. On one level, this research investigates the capacity of micro-enterprise development initiatives in Barbados and Trinidad to target women and enable their success as entrepreneurs in non-traditional fields. To this end, I will discuss findings from interviews with administrators of micro-enterprise development initiatives in both countries, highlighting their successes as well as challenges in targeting women as entrepreneurs in non-traditional areas. On another level, this analysis aims to engage in a theoretical discourse on the perspectives used to understand the nature of women's work, particularly work which is non-traditional. In this regard, my research asks which perspective or combination of theoretical perspectives may provide an effective lens for analysing the nature of women's work, and specifically their involvement in non-traditional micro-enterprise development in the Caribbean.

I begin with a discussion of the emergence of entrepreneurial schemes as economic development strategies to alleviate the problems of poverty and inequality for women. I then apply theoretical perspectives from feminist and sociological traditions to the issue of women, work and inequality, and discuss the challenges inherent within any single approach. I suggest a combined theoretical approach and apply it to an analysis of the capacity of micro-enterprise development initiatives to target women for entrepreneurial opportunities in traditionally male-dominated professions. In conclusion, I argue that efforts to build the capacity of entrepreneurial initiatives to target women for opportunities in male-dominated fields are needed and could benefit from a combined feminist–sociological approach to programme and policy design and evaluation.

Gender Inequality and the Emergence of Micro-Enterprise Development as a Poverty Alleviation Strategy for Women

Micro-enterprise development as a poverty alleviation strategy emerged in the mid-1970s in response to growing global economic disparities. The emphasis on poverty alleviation coincided with the start of the United Nations Decade for Women (1976–1985), which led to a focus on women and the potential for micro-enterprise development as a strategy for generating income, eradicating poverty and achieving greater gender equity (Tinker 2000).

The UN Decade for Women stimulated international interest in ensuring the integration of women into mainstream (or "malestream") development programmes which tended to target men as decision makers and programme participants. This Women in Development (WID) approach to integrating women into development initiatives helped to establish national infrastructure in developing countries in the form of women's departments and internationally supported non-governmental organizations that provided training and support for the development of women's income generation projects. These projects tended to be geared towards providing women with training and support that would not compromise their domestic activities, but would enable them to obtain "supplemental income" through part-time work consisting of making crafts (Tinker 2000).

Since the 1970s, changes in the global economy and corresponding shifts in the labour market occurred as the Caribbean also experienced an increase in the number of female-headed families. By the 1980s, one-third of households in the Caribbean were headed by women (Wiltshire-Brodber 1999). The combined result of globalization and the increase in female heads of household has placed the significant burden of the dual responsibilities of being both caregiver and breadwinner onto women. In the Caribbean, micro-enterprise development programmes are challenged with the need to go beyond providing the basics (access to credit, training and skilled mentors/technical support) to meet the complex needs of Caribbean women who function as both breadwinners and caregivers.

The difficulty of assisting women in meeting these dual responsibilities and the limitations of micro-enterprise development programmes to enable women to achieve economic empowerment are evident internationally (Ehlers and Main 1998; Mayoux 1995). Critics of the micro-enterprise movement in the United States, where over three hundred micro-enterprise development initiatives exist, suggest that, in order to help alleviate the threat of poverty for low-income women, support programmes which address both their economic and social welfare needs are required. At the same time, these critics caution that, for the majority of these women, self-employment does not tend to lead to self-sufficiency (Servon 2005; Sanders 2004).

Feminist theory suggests a number of reasons why micro-enterprise development programmes may not achieve the goal of poverty alleviation for women. At the crux of the problem is the persistence of historical gender ideologies which support the sexual division of labour and gender inequality. Ann Oakley, a prominent theorist in feminist sociology, has challenged the argument postulated by Murdock (1949) and Parsons (1955) that biological differences between men and women justify the sexual division of labour. Oakley (1974) describes how variance in socialization processes, rather than biological differences between the sexes, shape the behaviour and outcomes of males and females. Individuals tend to be socialized into traditional sex roles defined by a particular society. Historically, in Westernized societies, the traditional or ascribed gender roles are nurturing and non-monetized domestic functions for women, and public, monetized roles outside of the home for men.

While the "housewife" may have been a dominant role for women in some Westernized societies, women in the Caribbean, according to Massiah, "have always engaged in money making activities" (1999, 207). In the Caribbean context, women have often been able to gain nominal income from active involvement in the informal economic sector (Wiltshire-Brodber 1999), yet the sexual division of labour continues to exist. The informal sector can be characterized by small-scale, intermittent and low-paying activities that fulfil specific functions and are carried out in the home or on the street without government support or sanctions (Massiah 1999). For women, their involvement in the informal sector tends to be as providers of goods and services over which they have direct control. These goods and services typically conform to women's ascribed gender roles, are undervalued and tend to be those needed by other women or children. Women's work in the informal sector frequently includes such activities as clothing and food production, childcare and selling handicrafts.

The agricultural sector has also been a source of income for indigenous or rural workers in the Caribbean, many of whom are women. Globalization and neoliberal policies have supported a particular model of development that replaced an emphasis on agriculture and exports with increased imports and targeted growth in the services and tourism industries. In the 1970s, researchers warned that the process of globalization could displace low-income women from indigenous paid work and increasingly relegate them to the service sector and informal or unpaid work in the home (Boserup 1970). Both men and women in rural areas found their economic bases eroded, and those in urban areas faced increased competition for low-skilled jobs (Tinker 2000).

Since the 1970s, growth in the service sector and tourism industry in the Caribbean has provided opportunities for women to enter the labour force in increasing numbers, yet this increase is not an indication of a reduction in gender inequality. By 1992, unemployment among females in the Caribbean was higher than that among men in all countries except for Grenada (Andaiye 2003). Women are also more likely to enrol in and graduate from tertiary-level educational institutions, yet they experience lower financial returns for their education than men (Olsen and Coppin 2001). Although women's labour force participation and education rates have increased, they remain more likely to earn less and to be unemployed more often and for longer durations than men (Seguino 2003).

The types of work women perform in the formal labour market also tend to blend with their inherited gender roles. By the 1980s, Caribbean women in the labour force tended to be clustered in the teaching and nursing professions, and often as domestic workers in the service sector (Wiltshire-Brodber 1999; Gordon 1986). Women were also more likely than men to represent occupations in wholesale, retail, hotels and restaurant services, and were least represented in mining, refining and construction and installation fields (Andaiye 2003).

The sexual division of labour is a constraint to the achievement of gender equity and equality in the Caribbean, and it has implications for understanding the capacity of micro-enterprise development initiatives to meet the complex needs of low-income women while alleviating the threat of poverty. Micro-enterprise development programmes need to be established with supports in place to address these historical, structural and cultural issues that constrain the ability of women to experience economically viable livelihoods.

The Challenge of a Gendered Analysis of Women and Work: An Alternative

Feminist critics of these micro-enterprise development programmes point to their failure to achieve significant outcomes in regard to women's economic self-sufficiency and gender equity within the public or private sphere (Carr 1984; Rogers 1980; Mayoux 1995; Buvinic, Gwin and Bates 1996). Feminist research on women's involvement in micro-enterprise development programmes indicates that women's earned income has been insufficient, owing to the concentration of employment opportunities in a narrow range of low-paid, small-scale, home-based businesses consistent with gender roles; in addition, women entrepreneurs have remained economically vulnerable and marginalized, and programmes have failed to challenge the power relations and gender divisions within the labour market and household (Tinker 2000; Sanders 2004; Ehlers and Main 1998; Loscocco and Robinson 1991). Feminist analysis of micro-enterprise development programmes suggests that, rather than eradicating poverty and empowering women, these initiatives may serve to trap women further in the cycle of poverty while perpetuating existing power disparities and gender ideologies (Servon 2005; Sanders 2004).

The Grameen Bank in Bangladesh has become an international model for empowerment and economic development through micro-enterprise and micro-credit programmes, particularly for low-income women (Tinker 2000).

In addition to providing small loans to entrepreneurs, this empowerment-based model, created by Dr Mohammed Yunus, involves peer groups as providers of support and guidance for financial, health and family planning. Evaluations of the Grameen Bank model show mixed results. Favourable results report improvements in social and psychological indicators such as family violence and levels of self-confidence for female entrepreneurs (Hashemi, Schuler and Riley 1996; Todd 1996), yet critics suggest that these outcomes are insufficient indicators of the capacity of micro-enterprise initiatives to meet their overall goal of poverty alleviation. Critical evaluations indicate that, rather than moving poor women towards empowerment and away from poverty, the loans tend to be used to facilitate the needs of male family members (Goetz and Sen Gupta 1996), and the limited amount of credit provided does little to alleviate the drudgery of poverty in women's daily lives (Kabeer 1998).

The challenge with designing and evaluating micro-enterprise development programmes for women is that fundamental assumptions about the role and function of women's work in society underlie the framework for analysis. In the Caribbean, if these assumptions are based on inherited Enlightenment idealist principles which justify a patriarchal–capitalist sexual division of labour, then women's work is in the home (private sphere) or related to caregiving or nurturing functions, whereas the appropriate function for men is production in the public sphere, which results in their social, psychological, economic and political gain (theoretically based upon meritocracy). Women's interest in business ventures or occupations which do not support this established ideology may be viewed as problematic if one believes that adherence to these traditional gender roles provides a balanced, natural, functional or efficient way of organizing the public and private domains of society. The notion of women's involvement in opportunities to generate income in non-traditional fields may also face opposition from feminist theorizing which seeks to promote the re-valuation of women's contributions to society through their work in the private sphere, so that the work of women in the private sphere is valued, in ideological and economic terms, equally with that of men in the public sphere.

The two feminist theoretical approaches I will review in regard to their potential for developing a perspective to explore women's involvement in micro-enterprise development initiatives are radical feminism and liberal feminism. Radical feminism views the sexual division of labour as a function of patriarchy which enables men to benefit from the subordination of women (Bryson 1999). While multiple perspectives exist, Tong (1998) classifies two categories of radical feminist thought: radical-libertarian feminism and radical-cultural feminism. Radical-libertarian feminists believe the differences between men and women should be minimized, and that a state of androgyny, where men and women are free to express both masculine and feminine characteristics, is the ideal. The concept of androgyny can either be perceived as an attempt to separate or eradicate men from dominant positions in society and create conditions for female supremacy, or can be understood as an opportunity for men and women to move beyond the confines of ascribed gender roles to establish the preconditions for gender equality.

Radical-cultural feminists believe that the female/feminine characteristics (manifested at micro, mezzo and macro levels of society) are superior to the male/masculine. They deem characteristics and approaches such as value interconnectedness, interdependence and emotion as feminine, in opposition to the linear, individualist, and rational qualities attributed to a masculinist worldview. Liberation for women, according to radical feminism, is achieved not only when the differences between men and women are minimized, but when the suppressed capacity of the female or feminine nature of women is fully realized and revalued (Abbot, Wallace and Tyler 2005).

Liberal feminist theory attributes women's subjugation to discrimination within the political, economic and social systems in Western societies. Women's inferior position in these systems results in their exclusion from decision-making processes and prevents them from equally accessing opportunities in the labour market. Unlike radical feminism, liberal feminism emphasizes the primacy of rational thought over emotion as a means for both men and women to achieve autonomy and self-fulfilment, and encourages the attainment of equal rights for both sexes. Liberation, from the liberal feminist perspective, is achieved by collective action between women and men to change institutions, legislation and rigid, socialized attitudes which lead to gender inequality and discrimination against women. Explicit in liberal feminist theory is higher value accorded to opportunities to participate in the "monetarized public sphere" (Denis 2003, 267). Harriet Taylor Mill, in her seminal text *The Enfranchisement of Women* (1851/1994), insists that, to be fully liberated, both men and women should work outside the home, and women should obtain a coequal share of education and employment opportunities while actively participating in the formation and administration of laws.

The liberal feminist response to the issue of gender inequality is generally compatible with moderate ideologies about social change and the role of women in society. Change, for the liberal feminist, occurs incrementally and within the current political, social and economic context through collective action (involving men and women), legislative change, advocacy and training to reduce systemic barriers to women's economic empowerment. The conundrum is that this process of change, which is intended to liberate women, is predicated on assumptions and norms that value individualism, competition, rationality and paid work in the formal public sphere. Liberal feminism, consequently, may be perceived to create and reinforce biases in favour of males, and to perpetuate a masculinist worldview which contributes to the devaluation of contributions to society that are traditionally associated with women.

Sociologist Ann Denis (2003) describes liberal feminism as "idealist" and challenges the validity of liberal feminist approaches that fail to question the greater value placed on both the monetarized public sphere and the opportunities within it that are traditionally perceived as male dominated. Denis states that, although "the public–private divide and the male-breadwinner family may have been a part of the dominant ideologies in the Caribbean, these features, together with the overall assumptions of liberal feminism, are at odds with the experience of the majority of women there, and as a result are inadequate as a basis on which to theorize gender and work in the Caribbean" (2003, 267). The advances made towards gender equality in the public and private domains internationally and in the Caribbean over the last half of the twentieth century can primarily be attributed to movement emerging from liberal feminism. Legislation to increase equal opportunities for education, work, advocacy for health and reproductive rights, and protection from domestic violence and sexual discrimination can be directly attributed to liberal feminist thought. Despite these advances, the conundrum inherent in liberal feminism is problematic, and has led to legislative and programmatic responses to women's oppression that may sanction increased access to opportunities and the exercise of choice, yet, owing to the underlying values, these initiatives may function to reinforce existing gender ideologies that devalue the contributions of women to society. The implications of a liberal feminist approach must be considered when designing or evaluating economic development initiatives for women, yet it must be acknowledged as an effective method, but not the only method, for effecting change.

Denis suggests that gender analysis of work for women could benefit from incorporating a neo-Weberian approach: "It eschews a grand, universalizing theory of society and social change, being instead firmly rooted in the historical and socio-cultural context. It stresses the interaction of material conditions with the ideological or belief systems rather than the automatic primacy of one or the other. A crucial methodological tool is *verstehen*, the interpretive understanding of a phenomenon. It rejects the necessary use of conceptual dichotomies, focusing instead on continua or on the existence of multiple competing groups" (2003, 272). The appeal of a neo-Weberian approach to assessing micro-enterprise development programmes for women lies in the opportunity to resist the temptation to develop a conceptualization of social problems and issues from a single theoretical framework. Rather than adopting an existing theory to form the basis of a conceptual framework, the neo-Weberian approach allows for understanding to emerge from the historical, social and cultural context. In an attempt to broaden the types of information gathered through gender analysis, rather than a quantitative or positivist approach, the following analysis utilizes an interpretive approach, or *verstehen*, to understanding non-traditional micro-enterprise initiatives for women. Attempts to categorize, classify or develop a universal theory about the women involved in the programmes, or the programmes themselves, are forfeited in favour of an opportunity to gather an in-depth understanding of the contextual, structural and systemic elements that should be considered when designing micro-enterprise programmes that engage women in non-traditional fields.

The following analysis combines aspects of the neo-Weberian approach with both radical and liberal feminist perspectives. The radical feminist aspects of the study emphasize the possibilities for women's liberation through opportunities for women to build and express the capacity of their female or feminine natures. This perspective of liberation goes beyond the limitations of perceiving feminine nature as being confined to traditionally ascribed gender roles. The bounds of freedom and liberty for women in this analysis include opportunities to generate income in fields that are either traditionally male dominated or have yet to be discovered (and therefore may not be classified as either male or female in nature). In alignment with radical feminism, this alternative approach to gender analysis of women and work also includes an emphasis on group/community- (mezzo) and systemic-level (macro) structures that promote interdependence and acknowledge the efficacy of institutionalized and responsive economic, social and emotional support.

Recognizing both the conundrums and potential advances that can be realized by utilizing aspects of a liberal feminist theoretical approach, this alternative gender analysis framework is conscientiously working within the current historical, social and cultural context, which attributes higher value to opportunities to participate in the "monetarized public sphere". Based on a liberal feminist approach, this analysis underscores the ways in which micro-enterprise development initiatives include provisions that target women for: (1) liveable wage-paying (ideally high-income) employment outside the home; (2) the introduction of new skills training or preparation for women to enter previously male-dominated occupations; (3) the integration of gender issues and the needs of low-income women into malestream projects; and (4) the incorporation of social support and services to meet the complex needs of female entrepreneurs. The intention is not to devalue the contributions of women who provide traditional goods and services in the home or informal labour market, but to explore the structures needed to enable women to access opportunities for generating income in non-traditional fields while building their capacity to express other, possibly dormant dimensions of their female or feminine natures.

Methodology

This research was preliminary and exploratory and occurred from May through July 2007. The study began with a review of local, regional and international programme documents and reports related to the status of female entrepreneurs, with particular interest in those involved in non-traditional businesses. I conducted interviews with staff persons responsible for programme oversight and implementation of eight micro-enterprise development programmes, as well as programme participants and stakeholders, in Barbados and Trinidad to discuss the type of infrastructure needed to involve women effectively in non-traditional business ventures. Representatives from the Mayaro Initiative, Helping Our People Prosper Economically (HOPE),

Jubilange Cooperative Society, the Ministry of Social Development, Caribbean Microfinance Limited (Microfin), and the Youth Business Trust were interviewed in Trinidad and Tobago. In Barbados, interviews were conducted with representatives from Pinelands Creative Workshop, the Youth Entrepreneurship Scheme and the Barbados Youth Business Trust.

The interviews were unstructured and lasted for approximately one and a half to two hours each. Audiotape recordings and notes taken during interview sessions facilitated analysis of the data. This analysis was guided by themes that emerged from the interviews in relation to issues affecting the success of female entrepreneurs and the structural considerations needed to address them.

I selected the participating organizations based on their classification as micro-enterprise development programmes which provide opportunities for non-traditional business ventures for women – those ventures generally defined as entrepreneurial opportunities in which women are underrepresented as employers and employees, based on the distribution of persons in the workforce by sex. Women are said to be engaged in a non-traditional business venture if the level of their representation in the given occupation is below the percentage of their participation in the total labour market.[1]

The features of the micro-enterprise development schemes reviewed were fairly consistent across the eight organizations. The eligibility criteria tended to target both males and females, generally between the ages of eighteen and thirty-five. Another feature which the initiatives tended to hold in common was the provision of business training and support provided by programme staff, peers, mentors, and public and private sector consultants. Access to financing or credit to start or expand a business through commercial and non-commercial lenders was another shared aspect of the programmes.

Findings

Analysis of the data gathered revealed that participants' answers typically centred upon the structures needed to support female entrepreneurship in non-traditional fields, and revolved around three themes. The first theme emphasizes that targeting and training women in non-traditional entrepreneurship is an underexplored phenomenon with immediate implications for women's advancement. The second theme suggests that programmes which target women as entrepreneurs require the establishment of an infrastructure which integrates natural and effective sources of social support with constructive business-development training and aggressive financing as a means of empowering women to manage personal, family and professional demands. The final theme emerging from the findings underscores the need to identify and capitalize on efficacious roles for public, private and civil sector collaborators interested in boosting the involvement of female entrepreneurs in non-traditional business ventures.

Targeting and Training Women for Entrepreneurship in Non-Traditional Fields

Although women are engaged as entrepreneurs in each of the eight organizations included in this study, only two programmes specifically targeted women interested in non-traditional business ventures. The private and internationally funded Barbados Youth Business Trust has experienced moderate success in attracting women to training and entrepreneurial opportunities in tiling and landscaping. This ground-breaking initiative has experienced high attrition rates among participants. Just over half of the thirteen women who started the trust's tiling and landscaping programme completed the training, and only one has started a business in tiling.

The Barbados Youth Business Trust held classes on Saturdays for three months. The inopportune scheduling of these classes may have contributed to female participants' concerns about managing the multiple responsibilities entailed in their roles as mothers, wives (for some), providers and students in the training programme. The one participant who planned to start a tiling business after graduating from the programme is a single mother of five children. This participant has subsequently put her entrepreneurial ambitions on hold, and used transferable skills gained from the programme to obtain a lucrative, permanent employment opportunity in the short term, citing concerns for her family's immediate economic needs as the reason for her decision.

Although the initial results of this non-traditional business training programme for women has yet to produce its intended outcomes, the Barbados Youth Business Trust has successfully enabled several female participants to become entrepreneurs in non-traditional areas, including poultry rearing, building maintenance and publishing services. Out of the fifty-seven female-owned businesses listed in the trust's 2005–2006 business directory, eighteen can be classified as non-traditional. According to the general manager of the Barbados Youth Business Trust, female entrepreneurs who experience success in the programme tend to come to the programme with some practical skills, professional ethics and values, and an "inner motivation" to succeed in the area in which they would like to start a business.

The Pinelands Creative Workshop (Pinelands) also provides a programme that targets female entrepreneurs interested in non-traditional businesses. Pinelands currently manages a UNESCO-sponsored programme that provides on-the-job training to women interested in acquiring skills in airbrushing and business management. This programme has also experienced moderate success with engaging female entrepreneurs. In the past two years, forty-five participants have completed the programme. Once trained, women in this programme are encouraged to choose between seeking employment or starting their own businesses. Rather than becoming entrepreneurs, programme graduates have tended to pursue opportunities to gain further on-the-job training and technical skills, at auto body shops for example, before requesting financing to start their own businesses.

Pinelands and the Barbados Youth Business Trust were the only programmes that specifically targeted women for non-traditional business opportunities, yet all eight of the micro-enterprise development initiatives have successfully enabled female participants to become entrepreneurs in non-traditional areas. The most common types of non-traditional businesses for women include poultry rearing, building maintenance, transportation, and marketing and publishing services. The most promising results were experienced by the Barbados Youth Business Trust; almost half of all businesses listed in its 2005–2006 business directory were female owned.

Unlike the Barbados Youth Business Trust and Pinelands, the Youth Entrepreneurship Scheme in Barbados does not offer a specific programme that provides training to women in non-traditional business sectors, yet this programme has been successful in enabling female entrepreneurs to start businesses in non-traditional areas. Of the eighty-nine female-owned businesses listed in their 2006–2007 business directory, seventeen can be classified as non-traditional. These include graphic design, landscaping and construction businesses.

Female participants tend to enter the Youth Entrepreneurship Scheme with prerequisite skills in their areas of interest; as a result, their primary need is to obtain the training necessary to start a business. In addition to training in business and technical skills, the Youth Entrepreneurship Scheme is unique in providing opportunities for its entrepreneurs to obtain skills training to enhance their life skills and professional development.[2] All participants undergo initial training modules in self-development which emphasizes goal setting and planning skills. After this preparatory phase of the programme, participants are given the opportunity to decide formally whether they would like to continue training to become entrepreneurs, or whether they would like to seek further technical skills training to prepare them for direct employment. Those who choose the former continue in the programme, are assigned a business mentor and begin receiving training related to beginning their entrepreneurial endeavours.

The option of employment placement should not be underemphasized as an effective alternative for women interested in non-traditional fields. The findings indicate that innovative, non-traditional economic development schemes for women exist. Some programmes specifically target women, while others provide creative training options, but further exploration of ways to address the challenges of engaging women is needed.

Creating a Culture of Entrepreneurship For Women: Sustaining Integrity through Collaboration

Collaboration among public and private stakeholders at the community, national and international levels can provide opportunities and support for female entrepreneurs, yet whether funding streams are public or private has implications for the autonomy and sustainability of micro-enterprise development initiatives. The public and private sectors vary in their approaches to micro-enterprise development, and each approach has inherent benefits and challenges. The political interests of stakeholders, when aligned with the need to address persistent social issues such as poverty and unemployment, may motivate approaches to fostering entrepreneurship that are public or government driven. Micro-enterprise development driven by private sector interests is distinguished by the tendency to function with an emphasis on the bottom line, that is, on making a profit.

The primary benefit of government-driven initiatives is that a wider target population can be served with public resources so that those most in need have equal access to available services, including low-interest or no-interest loans or grants. The challenge faced by public-driven approaches is determining whether this greater breadth of service provision achieves the desired outcome of creating entrepreneurs, or fosters a culture of dependency. The dedication of resources by private lenders provides an alternative approach to micro-enterprise development, which carries higher interest rates but is of low to no cost to the general public. Private approaches to micro-enterprise development mimic a realistic economic environment for those seeking to start their businesses and tend to target those entrepreneurs who are most able, because of access to collateral or personal contacts, to secure financial and social support.

The organizations included in this study range on a continuum from public- to private-driven approaches to enterprise development. All but three of the initiatives included in this study were run by non-profit organizations. Of the three remaining initiatives, two were government based. The eighth organization is a private, for-profit microfinance entity named Caribbean Microfinance Limited (Microfin).

Microfin is based in Trinidad and has been in existence for seven years. Their mission is to fund any viable and existing micro-enterprises or small business. Unlike government-driven initiatives, such as poverty eradication or increasing the ability of individuals to become self-sufficient, Microfin's primary objective is to make a profit and maintain its own financial sustainability. Unlike non-profit initiatives, Microfin also does not provide business training or fund start-up ventures. Existing micro-enterprises are deemed viable once they pass a site inspection, undergo a review of a written or verbal business plan, along with banking records indicating that the entrepreneur has been able to accumulate assets and savings, and the entrepreneur completes an interview with a loan officer. Given the competition for limited resources, Microfin does not fund existing businesses that indicate a history of heavy depreciation of assets, buildings or equipment, and high indebtedness.

Over the past seven years, Microfin has financed over five thousand clients. Half of those clients are women. As experienced by not-for-profit micro-enterprise development initiatives, the kinds of businesses financed tend to be divided according to sex, with women in garment manufacturing, food processing, poultry raising and retail. Men tend to operate businesses in transportation services, auto repair, agricultural production and construction. The executive director of Microfin acknowledges that while garment manufacturing, food processing and poultry raising are viable businesses, the most profitable micro-enterprises tend to be transportation services and construction: "The perception is that this is a man's world; women, consciously or not, shy away from those types of businesses. Of a hundred construction or transportation businesses, only about 5 per cent of those would be owned by women. For women in the Caribbean, it is out of tradition. The mind-set is that women wouldn't go into those businesses because they may think 'it is not my place', or it goes against their culture" (Henry 2007).

According to Microfin's executive director, women who risk going into transportation and construction tend to realize profits comparable to their male counterparts, and he claims that government and for-profit entities could play pivotal roles in enabling women's entrepreneurship in non-traditional sectors. Through public and private sector collaboration, government and for-profit organizations could work together to: (1) provide training and case management to women to prepare them to start businesses in non-traditional fields, and (2) provide linkages to commercial lenders. He suggests that financing micro-enterprises should be left to for-profit organizations as a means to foster a realistic vision and culture of entrepreneurship:

> Government and non-profit micro-enterprise development programmes undermine the legitimacy of for-profit lenders and foster a culture of dependency. They are hurting the micro-finance sector by providing a service that is viewed as *help*, so customers are not inclined to pay [back their loans]. The customer must know we run a business and their company must be taken seriously. By setting an opposite trend customers lose their commitment to pay and they set up a culture of dependency and distort the market by providing interest rates that are as low as possible and encouraging customers to think it is the norm. In a small country you hurt the entrepreneurial environment. (Henry 2007)

Creating a culture of entrepreneurship may be one of the primary underlying tenets of micro-enterprise development, whether for-profit or not-for-profit driven, yet the methods government and non-profit organizations utilize to foster entrepreneurship are suspect in their ability to achieve this end. NEDCO, the National Entrepreneurship Development Company Limited, is an initiative of the Government of Trinidad and Tobago established to provide low-interest loans to small businesses and micro-businesses. In 2007 NEDCO reported TT$10 million in losses, which indicates that approximately 80 per cent of the loans financed through the organization are in arrears, leading to speculation about the genesis and rationale of the organization's lending practices.[3]

NEDCO may be an isolated case representing government's incompetence in managing the finance components of micro-enterprise development programmes, yet the argument that the non-profit impetus towards soft lending practices leads to a culture of dependency rather than entrepreneurship remains compelling. According to the executive director of Microfin, "The government and non-profit organizations involved in microfinancing encourage customers to think it is the norm [to obtain loans with low interest rates and highly flexible terms for repayment]. Then when they get to us and learn we have to operate in a fair market, they experience culture shock. If you want to help people to become true entrepreneurs and change the social and economic environment, then you have to give them a realistic picture of what to expect" (Henry 2007). The ability to eradicate a culture of dependency is linked to a commitment to create opportunities for income generation, which also include job placement. The Ministry of Social Development in Trinidad oversees and implements two micro-enterprise development initiatives, the Micro-Enterprise Training and Development Grant and the Micro-Enterprise Loan Programme. The grant is a poverty reduction programme open to clients of the ministry. Ministry social workers identify clients who may be eligible to receive grants to start or expand a micro-business, or clients who may opt to obtain employment. Social workers present their cases to a screening committee that recommends approval or rejects applications. Instead of receiving cash, approved applicants receive vouchers of up to TT$5,000 to buy requested items or receive training related to their businesses, or to enhance their chances of finding employment. Since the money received is a grant, there is no expectation of repayment. Typically grants are provided for cooking, landscaping and the purchase of construction equipment, with women receiving support primarily for traditional business ventures.

The Micro-Enterprise Loan Programme is a community-based micro-credit initiative of the Ministry of Social Development in Trinidad and Tobago in collaboration with the United Nations Development Programme designed for the purpose of poverty reduction. With an interest in reaching entrepreneurs within their communities, the Micro-Enterprise Loan Programme commissioned and trained five community-based organizations located in various districts of the country to manage the investment and lending of TT$140,000 each. The community-based organizations were to provide business loans up to a maximum of TT$10,000 to entrepreneurs at a 6 per cent rate of interest.

This pilot programme, while innovative, is not without challenges. According to a senior research officer at the Ministry of Social Development, competition, crime and capacity issues limit the effectiveness of the programme. Although each community-based organization receives training and is assigned a micro-credit expert for eighteen months, capacity issues still exist. The community-based organizations typically have limited staff and they must continue to manage the responsibilities of their existing programmes while implementing the micro-loan programme, which may require them to meet with entrepreneurs after hours.

The need to establish the level of poverty is a deterrent among applicants to the Micro-Enterprise Loan Programme. As an alternative, some potential participants are electing to seek out competitive opportunities with commercial lenders and other government-funded programmes which may require less bureaucratic red tape to obtain financing. According to the senior research officer, "Even employment relief programmes present competition. The instant gratification of obtaining employment through the government employment and training programmes meets the need of persons seeking quick money even if, in the long run, through MEL [micro-enterprise loan] they could make more money. Our own employment programme hampers the creation of an entrepreneurial culture" (Reed 2007).

The General Manager of Jubilange Cooperative Society, a community-based organization in Lavantille, East Port of Spain, Trinidad, also highlighted the issues of crime and capacity. Since 2002, Jubilange has only granted loans to twenty-two persons through the Micro-Enterprise Loan Programme. According to the general manager of Jubilange, the limited number of loans disbursed is the result of a "meticulous screening" process and the competition of larger businesses and the drug and crime industry in his community. He states that, for both males and females, "the income you can earn from micro-enterprise is no comparison to what you can earn in the drug and crime industry. In 2005, 53% of all murders were committed here. To compete with the social conditions in East Port of Spain requires increased investment. The market is saturated with these [women-owned] subsistence businesses, sewing, restaurants and retail shops, and these small businesses have to compete with the larger ones. The playing field is not level" (Kernahan 2007). Levelling the playing field requires a concerted effort on the part of public and private entities with an interest in fostering entrepreneurship. While the government should play a critical role in creating, supporting and monitoring innovative policies and approaches to micro-enterprise development, these initiatives should do so without creating a culture of dependence or worsening the situation facing persons living in impoverished conditions. Programmes like the Micro-Enterprise Training and Development Grant can work against efforts to foster entrepreneurship through microfinancing and can be perceived as an opportunity for participants to receive a hand-out rather than a hand-up.

The Mayaro Initiative and HOPE are poverty reduction and micro-enterprise development programmes in Trinidad. In addition to providing access to standard services such as personal and business development training and access to credit, both initiatives have incorporated the aspects of social support that enable them to promote fiscal sustainability. Both programmes have maintained low rates of repayment arrears and have helped to improve the quality of life for persons seeking a way out of poverty.

In 2000, Sister Rosario Hackshaw founded HOPE to provide small loans for micro-enterprises as a means of alleviating poverty. The programme replicates the Grameen Bank model created by 2006 Nobel Prize winner Dr Muhammad Yunus. Annually the organization provides over five hundred loans of up to TT$2,000 to the poorest residents in eastern Trinidad, and boasts a default rate of less than 1 per cent. A component of this model is the use of small community groups that meet weekly to collect loan payments (TT$25 per week) and review bankbooks. The group functions to model practical entrepreneurial skills and act as a source of social support.

According to Sister Rosario, a new type of social service agency is required for fostering entrepreneurship:

> He [Muhammad Yunus, founder of Grameen Bank] says, "I don't give anyone a penny"; he loans it. This practice falls under the principle of, if they don't have to reap it, they become beggars. Giving someone a hand-out takes away their dignity. It is better to make them pay or repay. When people try to thank me for a loan I tell them, "Don't", and say, "When you go and buy a piece of material in a store, do

you say thank you in that way? No, because you paid for it. This is a loan; you are
paying us for it, with interest. The interest is how I pay my staff, buy computers,
your bankbook, and everything we need to do business. You allowed me to get what
I need to run a business by paying your loan." This isn't a case of someone coming
to me with a problem, and I try to fix [it]; it's business. (Hackshaw 2007)

This new type of agency alluded to by Rosario would blend for-profit motives
and accountability with non-profit, community-based organizing and responsiveness. The Mayaro Initiative is an example of this new type of agency.

In 2002, the Mayaro Initiative received seed funds in the amount of
TT$140,000 from the Ministry of Social Development's Micro-Enterprise
Loan Programme. Although Mayaro functions as a non-profit organization,
the programmatic and fiscal sustainability of its Micro-Enterprise Loan initiative is tied to two critical decisions made by programme planners. The first
is their early investment of a portion of the seed funding they received from
the Ministry of Social Development into profitable stocks. The second critical
component of Mayaro's success is the institution of a regulation that requires
a guarantor for all loans. Since 2002, the Mayaro Initiative has loaned over
TT$600,000 to entrepreneurs. According to the Mayaro executive director,

We have a few [clients] we have to fight to get payments [from]. The people we
work with are the ones we want to see. One man we supported went to jail. We had
just gave him money to do a Christmas project. All of our loans are guaranteed by
a guarantor. His guarantor is a respectable, well-established person in the community, and although he [the guarantor] didn't want to pay, he has paid. I saw that
young man on the street the other day, so I know he is out of jail now. So the guarantor will soon know, if he doesn't already, and will look to get his money back. To
protect ourselves, we also have both spouses or partners sign the loan, and the guarantor pays if the situation arises. (Noel 2007)

The emphasis on investing a portion of funding received and the use of guar-
antors to insure the loan are two innovative aspects of the Mayaro Initiative
that could improve the viability of micro-enterprise and micro-credit programmes over time.

Private lenders are an ideal partner with government in micro-enterprise
development, as the former can continue to use their expertise and resources
to focus on the fiscal bottom line without exploiting entrepreneurs, and the
latter can create the political will, policies and environment to support sus-

tainable micro-enterprise development. This public and private partnership toward sustainable micro-enterprise development could benefit from the engagement of local or community representatives. Programmes that simply provide training or financing without a community of support are not enough to lift participants out of poverty and foster a culture of entrepreneurship. According to Sister Rosario, this is particularly the case for female entrepreneurs:

> A female in the neighbourhood came to me and said a field worker told her, "You need to get a HOPE loan." She said, "I told her to get out of my face; I have to feed my children." The field worker told her, "That is why you need to get a HOPE loan." She got the loan to raise poultry. She started off with a few chicks, and she grew the thing. She made a business out of it after four or five loans. Instead of just raising them to sell, she slaughtered them and froze them. As a result, over time she had to get water, then electricity, then a freezer and so on. Her life has changed. (Hackshaw 2007)

Sister Rosario and the HOPE staff are particularly sensitive to the needs of women and the multiple layers of social and economic challenges and demands affecting their lives. They realize that a loan to a female entrepreneur can make the difference between earning enough to feed her children and earning enough to change her quality of life. For many low-income women, the division between the public and private sphere, and the notion of being "housewife", is non-existent. They are blending the roles of caregiver and provider out of necessity, and are seeking to become entrepreneurs as a means of survival. Sister Rosario understands that creating a culture of entrepreneurship for low-income women cannot be accomplished through financing alone; the process requires a commitment and mechanisms to connect to the psyche and emotions of women who are struggling to survive:

> People who are really destitute are motivated because they have to fight for their families, especially women. We [women] have a greater responsibility for our children – well, both have it – but it weighs on men and they run or drink, [while] the women will just do without underwear. They will do without anything to help their children. I think that is the reason women repay, because they want another loan to do better and better for their children. That man [Muhammad Yunus] developed something that has come out of our psyche, the psyche of human beings. This is about helping ourselves prosper economically. (Hackshaw 2007)

The use of small community groups in the HOPE model, according to Sister Rosario, provides an effective means for building fiscal integrity and ensuring progress towards entrepreneurship through the provision of social support:

> Every week groups of people meet in a centre—under a house, classroom, church, anywhere. They come together in groups of five. A field worker looks after them, and there are eight groups of five [forty people] that are visited by each field worker. Each group elects a supervisor from one of its members. Each group comes from the same village. No group can have members of the same family. Two people in the group get a loan first. When they have repaid for a few months, the next two get a loan. The chairperson gets a loan last. The chairperson is to take up all payments and write the amount paid into each person's book, and when the field worker comes, they show the money and bankbook. Field worker signs for it in front of everyone. They only have a small amount to pay each week. Through the groups they see how each other pays. They encourage each other to pay. (Hackshaw 2007)

These local collectives are examples of community-level structures that support the radical feminist ideal of interdependence, and function to sustain mutually, and contribute to the economic development of, group members and the community at large. Interdependence, partnership and collaboration at the community, national and international levels among public and private sector stakeholders and civil society are needed to begin to foster an enabling environment and to nurture a culture of entrepreneurship for female entrepreneurs.

Challenging Traditional Gender Ideologies: Support for Female Entrepreneurs

The importance of incorporating gender issues into "malestream" economic development programmes is glaringly apparent when assessing the support mechanisms for female entrepreneurs in non-traditional fields. Legislative advances that afford women increased access to opportunities in the public sphere have ignored the need to develop the infrastructure required to assist women with managing both their domestic and professional demands. A part of that infrastructure should be systemic reforms and collective actions that challenge embedded gender ideologies. The need to sensitize entrepreneurial schemes to the complex needs of women is particularly relevant to those who have low incomes and may be struggling to balance domestic responsibilities with the *necessity* of starting a business.

Micro-enterprise development initiatives with staff and mentors who can provide personal and professional support are critical to enabling the success of female entrepreneurs. One Youth Entrepreneurship Scheme entrepreneur stated that the support she has received from her marketing coach has augmented her progress towards being a successful business owner. According to this entrepreneur, her marketing coach has been particularly effective with helping her to strengthen her accounting and marketing acumen. She states:

> My mentor helped me with identifying how much to charge clients, how much profit I need to make to sustain my business. A lot of things I was learning through trial and error. I was in business for two years before joining YES [the Youth Entrepreneurship Scheme], and now after working with my mentor, I finally got a standard price list this month. My mentor had to work hard to get me to do this; I really resisted their advice for a while. Now I try not to think about all the people I never charged or undercharged for my services because they "didn't have the money". I was naïve in not running [the business] as a profitable institution. (YS03, 2007)

The business coaches or mentors who work on a voluntary basis provide valuable support to entrepreneurship programmes. I observed all eight of the programmes involved in my study functioning with limited staff-to-participant ratios. Every eight months, the Youth Entrepreneurship Scheme involves a new cohort of seventy to eighty participants who are assigned to one of five staff persons. At any given time, the scheme works with approximately three hundred new or existing entrepreneurs, which would equate to a 1:60 staff-to-client ratio. To provide effective services, social work professionals recommend that case managers carry a reasonable caseload that allows them to plan, provide, and evaluate services effectively through meaningful face-to-face contact with clients.[4] Poverty reduction programmes that target female entrepreneurs with limited work experience, skills, and education and/or demanding family considerations may need to seek innovative ways to provide intensive support services to women to facilitate their transition into employment or business ownership.

According to Sister Rosario, the small community groups that meet weekly in the HOPE model provide an effective means of addressing personal challenges such as substance abuse or domestic violence that can limit progress toward successful business ownership. She states that the group process is successful because existing members lead the selection of group participants: "[This process] also protects against substance abuse since they have to choose who can become a member of their group. They try to deal with these issues, even if it is substance abuse by someone in the home, before it becomes a problem" (Hackshaw 2007). This element of social support could reduce the dependency on and need for programme staff or mentors as the sole providers of support to entrepreneurs, and may offer an effective means for building and sustaining a culture of entrepreneurship within communities. The use of support groups could contribute valuable human capital to understaffed programmes.

With the general manager as the sole full-time staff member of the Trinidad and Tobago Youth Business Trust, the organization has provided loans to one hundred and five entrepreneurs, of whom 48 per cent are women, in the past seven years. Only three of the female entrepreneurs are engaged in non-traditional businesses, which consist of landscaping and video/DVD rentals. Similar to the Barbados Youth Business Trust, women involved in this programme in Trinidad were reported to require interventions beyond the programme's capacity. According to the general manager of the Trinidad and Tobago Youth Business Trust, "Some of our female entrepreneurs attempt to run their businesses from home. In life they may find themselves pregnant, and as a result the child now needs care and the business takes a backseat. We also find that [business] mentors are not as effective with our female entrepreneurs and often fail to communicate with me when an intervention is needed. Case management becomes important with some entrepreneurs, both male but especially female, to help with planning and management of their family life and a business" (Samuel 2007).

Prior to joining the Trinidad and Tobago Youth Business Trust, the general manager was a loan officer at a bank. He felt that his experience with making critical decisions about the feasibility and ability of entrepreneurs to pay their debts has helped him in his current position. He states that micro-enterprise development programmes must be staffed appropriately to assist new entrepreneurs effectively: "Entrepreneurs with limited experience come with projections that tend to be above what really exists in the market. They want to impress the lender. We try to help clients get a realistic sense of their projections. We need more professionals in micro-enterprise organizations, and we need to be staffed appropriately" (ibid.). The qualities of effective programme staff include an ability to mix case management with a heightened business acumen that seeks to accentuate the entrepreneur's current and potential personal, professional and fiscal assets. According to the general manger of the Trinidad and Tobago Youth Business Trust, the traits of successful female entrepreneurs involve a combination of confidence, family stability and a commitment to progress beyond their current situations. He adds that successful male and female entrepreneurs share many traits, yet men may not have stable family lives and are distinguished by their lack of reliance on their micro-enterprises as their sole source of income: "[The] most important trait that helps women remain successful and sustain their businesses is having a stable family life. This sets women apart from the men, because some of the successful males do not have stable family lives. The men also tend to have other jobs or businesses that they can fall back on if needed. Most women are taking care of their families and trying to run a business, so the micro-business tends to be their only source of income" (ibid.). Unlike for their male counterparts, the weight of caregiving demands within the home is a disadvantage for female entrepreneurs. Women's dual responsibilities of earning an income while managing their domestic affairs has a direct impact on the ability of some women to hold a job and/or pursue a business venture. As observed by Sister Rosario, "We have many women who convert their front porches into parlours and sell staples and other items to their neighbours. Many of them have children or elderly persons living with them and they can't leave home. These businesses don't earn much money, but it provides a little subsistence, and for some of these women every bit is needed" (Hackshaw 2007). Although they may generate income through non-traditional occupations, these female entrepreneurs continue to function in a caregiving capacity by meeting the critical needs of their communities. The necessity or choice by female entrepreneurs to blend caregiving functions with income-generating opportunities in traditionally male-dominated areas, and the qualitative as well as quantifiable impact on their communities, should be further explored. While she admits that some home-based businesses are unable to generate substantial income for women, Sister Rosario acknowledges the contributions women in non-traditional businesses are making to serve the needs of the poor: "It is for this reason that I fund women who run private taxis. I get criticized, but these women are the only ones helping the poor who live in rural areas and have difficulty leaving their homes. If it wasn't for these women, others wouldn't get to work, they couldn't get their children to school, and they couldn't get the things they need to maintain their households. They are providing a service to the poor that no one else would" (ibid.).

The executive director of the Pinelands Creative Workshop calls for a concerted effort to support the entrepreneurial capacity of women and balance the unequal distribution of labour within the home by challenging traditional gender ideologies. He states: "Women are the heads of the majority of households. They are the ones caring for the household. Entrepreneurship programmes that focus on women in Barbados must have a broader base to help them support their household needs while becoming business owners. We've got to be biased in favour of women in our outreach to them and do more to help them start their businesses and go into productive sectors" (Grant 2007). Public and private sector programmes that target female entrepreneurs require a female-centred approach that acknowledges and responds to their complex needs. Innovative ways to replace socially ascribed norms which sanction the expectation that women are primarily responsible for managing the demands of the home are also needed. Policies which encourage and support the ability of women and men to share both domestic and economic responsibilities provide a step in that direction.

Discussion of the Findings

This analysis of micro-enterprise development initiatives for women in non-traditional fields uses a combined approach that incorporates components of radical and liberal feminist and neo-Weberian perspectives. Stemming from the radical feminist perspective, I explored opportunities for women to generate income in traditionally male-dominated fields and sought evidence of group-, community- and systemic-level structures that promote interdependence and acknowledge the function of social support. I assessed women's access to skills training, the integration of gender issues and the incorporation of social services based on the liberal feminist approach. In addition, I also considered an understanding of the contextual, structural and systemic elements as an aspect of the neo-Weberian approach.

In summary, opportunities for women to build their capacity for developing micro-enterprise initiatives in non-traditional sectors in Barbados and Trinidad are limited. Of the eight micro-enterprise development programmes included in this analysis, only two specifically targeted women for opportunities in non-traditional fields. The programmes generally experienced difficulties engaging women because of the reality of competing demands facing participants, particularly those who held the responsibilities of meeting domestic as well as economic demands.

The models for group-, community- and systemic-level structures emerged from programmes such as the Mayaro Initiative, HOPE and Microfin. Mayaro, with its early fiscal ingenuity, invests public dollars and uses the resulting private profits to support the entrepreneurial aspirations of low-income persons. HOPE blends a for-profit emphasis on the bottom line and innovative, community-based social support with a keen understanding of, and responsiveness to, the issues and challenges facing low-income women. Microfin suggests the need to capitalize on the shared interests and collective resources of the public and private sectors to create a comprehensive system for financing and supporting female entrepreneurs.

Targeting women for non-traditional business opportunities requires access to new skills training, which, the findings indicate, encompass three primary areas: technical skills, self-development and business management (which includes financing, marketing and accounting). Training in these areas not only helps women prepare for the demands of starting their own businesses, but also provides transferable skills that can augment women's ability to obtain permanent and gainful employment.

An essential element of entrepreneurship programmes is providing the opportunity for women to choose other viable options for generating legitimate income by linking these options to employment. Consideration must be given to persons entering an entrepreneurship programme who may be more suited for direct employment opportunities. Programmes similar to those administered by the Pinelands Creative Workshop in Barbados and the Ministry of Social Development in Trinidad and Tobago that facilitate opportunities for women to benefit from a combination of skills training, job placement and entrepreneurial opportunities in non-traditional sectors are ideal. Providing options for paid on-the-job training should be incorporated into entrepreneurial schemes to enable women to gain valuable technical skills while meeting their economic responsibilities.

As extensions of malestream development programmes, the micro-enterprise initiatives included in this analysis (with the exception of HOPE) noted challenges in their incorporation of social services and sensitivity to gender issues. The traditional financing, training and technical assistance which some programmes provided may have met the needs of some female entrepreneurs, but were admittedly unresponsive to the needs of those women managing multiple and complex responsibilities as well as businesses that were their sole source of income.

The need to identify efficacious roles for public and private entities with an interest in fostering entrepreneurship requires further assessment. Each sector tends to approach the issue of microfinancing from opposing positions. While the state's approach tends to focus on ensuring broad access to those most in need, commercial lenders have an eye on the profits. Each approach has implications for engaging women in non-traditional business ventures. The private sector approach is likely to omit training and support services essential to ensuring women's progress toward entrepreneurship, and the government-driven approach has the potential to create dependency and place women at a further disadvantage in the *real* economic market.

The role of civil society is a significant contributor to the success of public and privately funded programmes that seek to transition women from poverty to entrepreneurship and independence. In their quest to create a culture of entrepreneurship, the HOPE Initiative and the Mayaro project utilize community stakeholders as sources of fiscal integrity and social support. Both programmes have significantly high rates of repayment.

The findings of my research highlight the need to develop initiatives that specifically target women for entrepreneurship in non-traditional business sectors. Given the projected areas for economic growth in the region – such as construction, communications, and transportation – opportunities for developing female entrepreneurs in these sectors should be encouraged, yet entrepreneurs should have the option of creating enterprises based on their own interests. Subsequent analysis that includes in-depth interviews with and participant observation among female entrepreneurs involved in micro-enterprise development schemes is needed to assess further the contextual, structural and systemic elements that help or hinder their success in non-traditional fields.

Conclusion

Making traditional businesses for women more profitable is a necessary challenge which involves the complex task of modifying gender ideologies and changing social mores. These changes are necessary in order to achieve a more equitable society, yet this task is not the only means of achieving this goal. In addition to valorizing women's contributions to society, I argue that also needed is an approach that challenges social constructs and norms that fail to recognize that women's contributions can and should include those that have been traditionally ascribed to men. Underlying this argument is not an implicit assumption that male-dominated professions are the only areas in which female entrepreneurship should be developed, but rather the call is for systematic, widespread and concerted exploration of these areas, along with more traditional entrepreneurial options for women.

The intent of my argument is not to emphasize aspects of liberal and radical feminist approaches in which achieving gender equality is comparable to gender homogeneity or androgyny. Instead, my emphasis is on broadening opportunities for women to avoid or lift themselves out of poverty and to increase their options for generating income. I suggest these goals can be achieved through the creation of non-traditional entrepreneurship schemes and supportive services that address the specificities and peculiarities particular to the lives of female entrepreneurs.

In light of this argument, women's choices in regard to entrepreneurship should be prefaced with information, training and resources that expose women to the opportunities and potential for income generation in non-traditional areas, and allow them to weigh their options critically. These tools should be reviewed and assessed on an ongoing basis to ensure that women receive consideration as persons who possess capabilities comparable to those of men, and should have equal access to opportunities for becoming successful entrepreneurs in non-traditional areas.

Perhaps because of the limited integration of gender issues and lack of sensitivity to the needs of low-income women in malestream development programmes, there is a mismatch between the amount of funding available and the resources needed to obtain and sustain the engagement of low-income women in micro-enterprise development initiatives. Women with limited work experience, skills, and education and/or family considerations may require a higher allocation of resources and funding to help them to manage the multiple demands of home and work while they transition from unemployment or underemployment to entrepreneurship. This emphasis on the higher allocation needs of programmes for women is not an indication of their personal inadequacies, but rather of the limitations of systems that support the responsibilities of managing home and work demands beyond the woman. Of the various traits that enable women to become successful entrepreneurs, of primary significance is their ability to acquire and maintain stable family lives. Effective programmes must have the resources and capacity to enable female entrepreneurs to strengthen their abilities to excel at home and in their businesses.

At the macro-level, public and private sector policies which seek to foster a culture of entrepreneurship and sustainable development must begin to redress socially ascribed norms that sanction the expectation that women bear the sole responsibility for managing the demands of the home. Systemic interventions can involve the media and the government working in partnership with the private sector and civil society to promote images of women and men sharing responsibilities, recognition and status within the home and the workplace. Employers and the government should develop policies that equally encourage and support the ability of women and men to work within and outside of the home.

Women constitute a significant portion of persons engaged in microenterprises, yet variations in circumstances that enable or constrain their ability to become viable business owners and employees in non-traditional areas have tended to be underinvestigated. Perhaps as a result, women's underinvolvement in male-dominated sectors has yet to receive concerted policy or programmatic emphasis in the region. Male marginalization has somehow been coined as fallout from women's academic ascension. This perspective ignores the disparity in outcomes even for educated women when compared to men in the labour market.

The approach to women's empowerment and poverty reduction must be multifaceted, and non-traditional micro-enterprise development for women is but one of many means to be pursued. Through the use of a feminist sociological approach to gender analysis, this chapter highlights the aspects of the systemic and programmatic infrastructure that we should consider in the development of gender-responsive policies on entrepreneurship and poverty reduction for women. The time has come to revolutionize the way in which we view the means of enhancing the economic viability of unemployed or underemployed women in the Caribbean. This revolution requires the dismantling of the sexual division of labour and the inherited ("Westernized") ideology that reinforces traditionally ascribed gender roles. Micro-enterprise development for women in non-traditional fields, or opportunities in occupations historically dominated by men, is but one tool that we can use in the dismantling process.

Acknowledgements

I would like to thank Professor Ann Denis whose thoughtful comments on an earlier draft of this chapter helped to enhance the theoretical content and analysis.

Notes

1. This definition is based upon methods employed by Hughes (1990, 1995).
2. The Virtues Programme, a recently added component to the Youth Entrepreneurship Scheme training programme, is intended to prepare participants for the personal and professional ethical responsibilities of owning a business.
3. See "Conflict over $10M in NEDCO losses", *Trinidad Express*, 24 May 2007, http://www.trinidadexpress.com/index.pl/article_business?id=16115 1543.
4. See Standard 9 of the NASW Standards for Social Work Case Management, http://www.socialworkers.org/practice/standards/sw_case_mgmt.asp.

References

Abbott, P., C. Wallace and M. Tyler. 2005. *An introduction to sociology: Feminist perspectives.* 3rd ed. Abingdon, UK: Routledge.

Andaiye. 2003. Smoke and mirrors: The illusion of CARICOM women's growing economic empowerment, post-Beijing. In *Gender equality in the Caribbean: Reality or illusion?*, ed. G. Tang Nain and B. Bailey, 73–107. Kingston: Ian Randle.

Bailey, B. 2003. The search for gender equity and empowerment of Caribbean women: The role of education. In *Gender equality in the Caribbean: Reality or illusion?*, ed. G. Tang Nain and B. Bailey, 108–45. Kingston: Ian Randle.

Barriteau, E. 2002. Women entrepreneurs and economic marginality: Rethinking Caribbean women's economic relations. In *Gendered realities: Essays in Caribbean feminist thought,* ed. Patricia Mohammed, 221–48. Kingston: University of the West Indies Press.

———. 2003. Requiem for the male marginalization thesis in the Caribbean: Death of a non-theory. In *Confronting power, theorizing gender: Interdisciplinary perspectives in the Caribbean,* ed. E. Barriteau, 324–55. Kingston: University of the West Indies Press.

Boserup, E. 1970. *Women's role in economic development.* New York: St Martin's.

Bryson, V. 1999. *Feminist debates: Issues of theory and political practice.* Basingstoke, UK: Palgrave.

Buvinic, M., C. Gwin and L. Bates. 1996. *Investing in women: Progress and prospects for the world bank.* Washington DC: Overseas Development Council.

Carr, M. 1984. *Blacksmith, baker, roofingsheet maker: Employment for rural women in developing countries.* London: IT Publications.

De Albuquerque, K., and S. Ruark. 1998. "Men day done": Are women really ascendant in the Caribbean? In *Caribbean portraits: Essays on gender ideologies and identities,* ed. C. Barrow, 1–13. Kingston: Ian Randle.

Denis, A. 2003. Theorizing the gendered analysis of work in the commonwealth Caribbean. In *Confronting power, theorizing gender: Interdisciplinary perspectives in the Caribbean,* ed. E. Barriteau, 262–82. Kingston: University of the West Indies Press.

Ehlers, T., and K. Main. 1998. Women and the false promise of microenterprise. *Gender and Society* 12 (4): 424–40.

Goetz, A., and R. Sen Gupta. 1996. Who takes the credit? Gender, power and control over loan use in rural credit programmes in Bangladesh. *World Development* 23 (1): 45–63.

Gordon, D. 1986. *The sexual division of labour and inter-generational mobility in Jamaica.* Kingston: Institute of Social and Economic Research, University of the West Indies, Mona.

Grant, R. 2007. Interview by A. Bernard. Audiotape. Pinelands, Barbados, 5 May.

Hackshaw, Sister R. 2007. Interview by A. Bernard. Field notes. HOPE, Trinidad, 18 July.

Hashemi, S., S. Schuler and A. Riley. 1996. Rural credit programmes and women's empowerment in Bangladesh. *World Development* 24 (4): 635–53.

Henry, J. 2007. Interview by A. Bernard. Field notes. Microfin, Trinidad, 28 June.

Hughes, K.D. 1990. Trading places: Men and women in non-traditional occupations, 1971–1986. *Perspectives on Labour and Income* 2 (Summer): 58–68.

———. 1995. Women in non-traditional occupations. *Perspectives on Labour and Income* 7 (4): 14–19.

Kabeer, N. 1998. *Money can't buy me love: Reevaluating gender, credit and empowerment in rural Bangladesh.* Discussion paper no. 363. Sussex: Institute for Development Studies, University of Sussex.

Kernahan, M. 2007. Interview by A. Bernard. Field notes. Trinidad, 11 July.

Loscocco, K., and J. Robinson. 1991. Barriers to women's small-business success in the United States. *Gender and Society* 5:511–32.

Massiah, J. 1999. Researching women's work: 1985 and beyond. In *Gender in Caribbean development*, ed. P. Mohammed and C. Shepherd, 197–222. Kingston: Canoe.

Mayoux, L. 1995. *From vicious to virtuous circles? Gender and micro-enterprise development.* Geneva: United Nations Research Institute for Social Development.

Mill, H. Taylor. 1851/1994. Enfranchisement of women. *Westminster Review* (July): 289–311. Reprinted in *Sexual equality: Writings by John Stuart Mill, Harriet Taylor Mill and Helen Taylor*, ed. A.P. Robson and J.M. Robson, 178–203. Toronto: University of Toronto Press.

Miller, E. 1991. *Men at risk.* Kingston: Jamaica Publishing House.

Murdock, G.P. 1949. *Social structure.* New York: Macmillan.

Noel, E. 2007. Interview by A Bernard. Field notes. Mayaro, Trinidad, 18 July.

Oakley, A. 1974. *Housewife.* London: Allen Lane.

Olsen, R.N., and A. Coppin. 2001. The determinants of gender differentials in income in Trinidad and Tobago. *Journal of Development Studies* 37 (5): 31–56.

Parsons, T. 1955. The American family: Its relations to personality and social structure. In *Family, socialization and interaction process*, ed. T. Parsons and R. Bales, 3–26. New York: Free Press.

Reed, M. 2007. Interview by A. Bernard. Field notes. Ministry of Social Development, Trinidad, 27 June.

Rogers, B. 1980. *The domestication of women.* London: Kogan Page.

Samuel, G. 2007. Interview by A. Bernard. Field notes. Youth Business Trust, Trinidad, 26 June.

Sanders, C. 2004. Employment options for low-income women: Microenterprise versus the labour market. *Social Work Research* 28 (2): 83–92.

Seguino, S. 2003. Why are women in the Caribbean so much more likely than men to be unemployed? *Social and Economic Studies* 52 (4): 83–120.

Servon, L. 2005. Microenterprise programmes and women: Entrepreneurship as individual empowerment. In *Gender and planning: A reader*, ed. S.S. Fainstein and L.J. Servon, 191–212. New Brunswick, NJ: Rutgers University Press.

Tang Nain, G., and B. Bailey, eds. 2003. *Gender equality in the Caribbean: Reality or illusion?* Kingston: Ian Randle.

Tinker, I. 2000. Alleviating poverty: Investing in women's work. *Journal of the American Planning Association* 66 (3): 229–42.

Todd, H. 1996. *Women at the center: Grameen Bank borrowers after one decade.* Boulder: Westview.

Tong, R. 1998. *Feminist thought: A more comprehensive introduction.* Boulder: Westview.

Vassell, L. 2003. Women, power and decision-making in CARICOM countries: Moving forward from a post-Beijing assessment. In *Gender equality in the Caribbean: Reality or illusion?*, ed. G. Tang Nain and B. Bailey, 1–38. Kingston: Ian Randle.

Wiltshire-Brodber, R. 1999. Gender, race, and class in the Caribbean. In *Gender in Caribbean development*, ed. P. Mohammed and C. Shepherd, 136–48. Kingston: Canoe.

YS03. 2007. Entrepreneur interview by A. Bernard. Audiotape. Barbados, 22 May.

PART 5

Feminist Travels through Diasporic Communities, Diverse Sexualities and Politicized Pedagogies

12

Who Is Your Mama?

Transnational Motherhood and
African-Caribbean Women in the Diaspora

CHARMAINE CRAWFORD

Introduction

Migrancy and transnationality are integral components of global capitalism. Social relations, formations and processes influence, as well as are influenced by, changing macroeconomic conditions. During the 1970s and 1980s, Caribbean women were on the move as independent migrants, settling and establishing ties elsewhere in order to provide for their families. The heightened movement of women from the English-speaking Caribbean to Canada and other post-industrialized nations during this time was precipitated by increased unemployment, poverty and limited social mobility in the region as a result of the negative effects of debt restructuring and structural adjustment policies on local economies (Williams and Henry 1995). Asymmetrical development continues to take place between richer and poorer nations within a globalized economy, and mirrors hierarchical gender, race and class relations within the international division of labour (Basch, Schiller and Blanc 1994; Sparr 1994). Migration and gender are major factors within present-day globalization as a result of more "Third World" women seeking economic opportunities in foreign countries in order to support their weakened households through remittances (Ehrenreich and Hochschild 2002; Parrenas 2001).

While this trend of the feminization of labour migration is noteworthy, migratory economic strategies are not new for working-class African-Caribbean women, who, historically, have been viable income earners (Aymer 1997; Safa 1995; Harrison 1991).

Working-class African-Caribbean women play a central role in their families as both providers and caretakers of children and of others, marking the interconnectedness of their productive and reproductive roles. Black feminist scholar Patricia Hill Collins appropriately uses the term "motherwork" (a contraction of "motherhood" and "work") to describe the multiplicity of ways in which black women in the African diaspora have simultaneously provided for and cared for others. These ways cannot be reduced to rigid distinctions and divisions. Mothering practices among working-class African-Caribbean women comprise contradictory elements which, on the one hand, give women status and power as mothers (particularly through matrifocality), while they reinforce gender-specific norms, on the other hand, as a result of women's shouldering a disproportionate share of the social reproduction of care, childcare and socialization (Mohammed 1999; Barrow 1996; Senior 1991). African-Caribbean women's role as worker-mothers, characterized by the high visibility of female-headed households in the region, is a salient feature of their gendered identity and labour that transcends and transgresses the divisibility of private and public spheres on both a national and international level. The development of this role is owed to the fact that working-class African-Caribbean women have always had to work in order to support themselves and their families as a result of racial-economic marginalization under colonialism and thereafter (Massiah 1986; Reddock 1995; Shepherd, Brereton and Bailey 1995). This dimension of social inequality did not consolidate a European middle-class, gendered division of labour with women's isolation in the private sphere as stay-at-home mother-wives supported by male breadwinners within nuclear family units. Extended familial cultural patterns and flexible socio-sexual relations that mitigate the male breadwinner role have also influenced female economic independence and resourcefulness (including migratory strategies) (Smith 1996). Given the centrality of the worker-mother role to Caribbean societies, further exploration of this role within globalization is important in order to facilitate recognition of its significant racialized and gendered impact on migration and on Caribbean transnational relations and families.

In this chapter, I examine the pre- and post-migratory experiences of African-Caribbean female migrants from the English-speaking Caribbean who left their children with relatives in their home countries while they themselves pursued better economic opportunities in Canada during the 1970s to early 1990s. I problematize the intersectional relationship among female migrant labour, transnationality and motherhood within the rubric of globalized gender, race and class relations. I do so by examining the migrant work experiences of working-class African-Caribbean women while they adjust to new socio-cultural environments and also support their children from abroad under varying material conditions and social circumstances. Moreover, I situate African-Caribbean mother–child relations in the context of the global political economy to highlight the significance of advanced capitalism for understanding these kinds of relations.

I draw on the research that I conducted for my PhD dissertation, during 2004–2005 in Toronto. I interviewed ten female migrants about their experiences of migration, work and motherhood. The women in my study initially entered Canada on a temporary basis to work, and later decided on permanent settlement. Of the ten female migrants in the study, five were from Jamaica, four from Trinidad and Tobago, and one from St Kitts and Nevis. Five women came to Canada during the 1970s, three during the 1980s and two during the 1990s. Six women were single and/or in visiting unions, two were married and another two were in common-law relationships prior to migrating. Female migrants had similar experiences of working in domestic services while securing their residency status and supporting their children from abroad. Seven women left three to four children behind. Ten children were left at five years old and under. Of those, six were under two years of age, with the youngest being one year old. At the opposite end of the spectrum, five children were left between the ages of ten and twelve years old.

The majority of these women were undocumented migrants, so their tenuous immigration status, along with periodic changes to immigration policies, left them with few employment opportunities, other than working in private, low-paying domestic jobs in a labour market segregated along lines of race and gender. This lack of opportunities ultimately complicated or delayed women's reunification plans with their children. In exploring female migrant labour, transnationality and motherhood, I examine four central areas: (1) how female migrants are exploited in paid reproductive work within an international division of labour stratified according to gender, race and class; (2) how the African-Caribbean women in the study were viewed as migrant workers and mothers while they forged new racialized, gendered identities within Canada; (3) how African-Caribbean women, as transnational mothers, utilize their kinship networks to support their families across borders; (4) how African-Caribbean women view themselves as mothers while they reconcile old and new ways of parenting their children during the reunification process.

While some Canadian studies have critically examined the gender, race and class dynamics of female migrant labour under foreign domestic-work schemes and the systemic barriers experienced by Caribbean domestics (Bakan and Stasiulis 1997; Calliste 1996; Daenzer 1993; Jakubowski 1997; Arat-Koc 1990; Silvera 1992), few have critically examined the socio-cultural and psychological impacts of migration on African-Caribbean women's gender roles and racial and cultural identities, or how they renegotiate these factors within new environments. Additionally, although there has been significant research on Caribbean migration and diasporas, with an emphasis on cultural transplanting, social networks and kinship in host countries (Ho 1993; Chamberlain 1999; Olwig Fog 1999, 2007; Goulbourne 2002), there is a paucity of material (with the exception of Aymer 1997) on gendered dynamics of migration, specifically in relation to *theorizing female migrant work and motherhood* in Caribbean migratory processes from a transnational feminist perspective. Transnational feminism, through a postmodern lens informed by an "anti-colonial and antiracist interrogation" (Sholat 2002, 72), aims to deconstruct the hegemonic notions of gender, sexuality, race, culture and nation promoted by patriarchal and racialized discourses of nationalism, fundamentalism and militarism that produce hierarchical relations between, and among, different groups of women and men within and across geographical locations. This feminist perspective is also essential in challenging androcentric discourses on migration that overlook the different ways in which "the social relation of gender organizes, shapes and distinguishes the immigration patterns and experiences of men and women" (Parrenas 2001, 29).

Utilizing an interdisciplinary transnational feminist standpoint, I situate African-Caribbean mother–child relations in the context of the global political economy to highlight the significance of advanced capitalism in understanding these relations. Furthermore, research on transnational motherhood and the migrant experiences of Latina and Filipina domestic workers (Hondagneu-

Sotelo and Avila 1997; Parrenas 2001) is invaluable, both theoretically and cross-culturally, to my study in centring and validating the multiplicity of working-class African-Caribbean women's worker-mother roles within macro-economic processes. Since women worldwide disproportionately shoulder the burdens of social reproduction, with ostensible recognition and limited remu-neration, centring women's worker-mother activities within migration is not only meaningful in validating their experiences but it also allows for a more nuanced understanding of motherhood as a complex, gendered role that is dynamic rather than deterministic. Therefore, I critique dominant Euro-American ideologies on motherhood that privilege the exclusivity of mother–child relations and position women *primarily* as nurturers, to the exclusion of other ways of parenting, or simply *being*. I also problematize the impact of the good mother/bad mother construct on the identity and selfhood of working-class African-Caribbean women.

Under patriarchal capitalism, motherhood has been characterized as a bio-logically fixed role for women, based on exclusive mother–child relations primarily within the nuclear family unit. In reducing women to their biology (sex), this kind of gender essentialism is also apparent in maternalist ideology, which valorizes motherhood as a *natural* rite of passage for females in *being* women and proving womanhood (Rich 1995). Whether it is through maternal valorization or patriarchal dominance, sexual biological determinism promotes gender inequality and objectifies women as non-autonomous, life-reproducing vessels, or simply *things* (Oakley 1980). Varying feminist perspectives have challenged gender essentialist discourse on motherhood by highlighting the social aspects of this gendered role. The social construction of motherhood relates to how varying economic and socio-cultural factors that are neither deterministic nor universal shape motherhood, family and gender relations, and also to how women experience motherhood differently across races, classes, cultures and sexualities (Hill Collins 2000; Nakano Glenn 1994; Oakley 1980; Rich 1995; Barrow 1996; Mohammed 1999). Transnationality, as a process of social relations across borders and nations, ultimately compli-cates normative meanings and practices of motherhood.

Transnational motherhood refers to how women, as primary migrants, sup-port their children from abroad through "circuits of affection, caring and financial support that transcend national borders" (Hondagneu-Sotelo and Avila 1997, 550). Mother–child separation can be short, from a few months to a year, or over the long term for an indefinite period of time. Women usually leave children in the care of trusted female relatives, grandmothers, aunts and sisters. While this practice seems practical, and even sensible, for female migrants who have dependent children, the dominant Euro-American perception is that women who migrate without their children or "leave their children behind" *indefinitely* are somehow "bad" or "neglectful" mothers because they deny their children direct or, more so, continuous care and supervision from them. This moralistic stance, which I will debunk, contributes to "maternal blaming". This outlook positions women as lacking agency to act independently of their children and also reinforces a simplistic, causal understanding of mother–child relations, whether for better or worse. Conversely, transnational motherhood reinforces the social, rather than the biological, aspects of motherhood as a dynamic, gendered role. Motherhood is seen as complex and negotiable, with women being active agents, both in making choices for themselves and their children under changing material conditions and social circumstances, and in allowing for the transferability of the social reproduction of care among individuals. I argue that it is the *quality* of care that children receive from their caregivers, who may not necessarily be their birth mothers, which is a major factor in childhood socialization, and that the continuity of African-Caribbean extended familial formations and child-shifting practices facilitate, and are indicative of, this type of socialization on local and transnational levels.

African-Caribbean Women, Work and Migration

Migration has been a strategy for Caribbean people in countering the unemployment, poverty and limited opportunities that result from the structural inefficiencies of their dependent capitalist economies (Benería and Feldman 1992). From the nineteenth to the mid-twentieth century, men led migratory outflows to neighbouring islands, Central America, the United States and Britain (Bolles 1996; Senior 1991; Chamberlain 1998; Foner 1979), with women following in small numbers (Aymer 1997). But the late 1960s saw a reversal in this trend (Benería and Feldman 1992). Increased female out-migration from the Caribbean to Canada and the United States during the 1970s and 1980s was necessitated not only by pull factors from post-industrialized countries seeking skilled and semi-skilled labour and domestic workers (Anderson 1993;

Richmond 1989; Simmons 1990), but also by the push factors of unemployment, impoverishment and limited social advancement that resulted from Caribbean economies' being weakened by debt and structural adjustment policies. For example, in Jamaica "between 1978 and 1985, 95 percent of nurses trained in that period emigrated" (Sparr 1994, 23). With heightened globalization, the implementation of structural adjustment policies by so-called Third World countries signalled increased privatization, currency devaluation, trade liberalization and cuts to social spending (e.g., education, health and social welfare). This neo-liberal economic agenda had little to do with social and human development, and contributed to increased poverty, inflation, unemployment and general social malaise (Benería and Feldman 1992; Sparr 1994; Elu 2000).

The economic downturn was particularly hard on poor and working-class Caribbean people, especially women, many of whom were breadwinners and heads of households (Williams and Henry 1995; Harrison 1991; Freeman 1997). Peggy Antrobus argues that, "because of their primary role in the care of people, women have the most at stake when the imperatives of economic growth and trade liberalization clash with those of human development as they do today" (2004, 56). Although more working-class African-Caribbean women were engaged in wage work in order to keep their households afloat, they were highly concentrated in low-paying, informal-sector economic activities and/or in non-unionized, formal-sector multinational enterprises (Freeman 1997; Harrison 1991). Therefore, going abroad or *foreign* became even more pressing for women, who sought economic opportunities elsewhere for professional development, in order to send back remittances to support their struggling households. Migration was complicated for working mothers who had to leave their dependent children with grandmothers or other female relatives. For these women, it was not feasible to migrate with their children, either on account of immigration restrictions or because living a life of uncertainty would have been too risky for the children (Anderson 1993; Richmond 1989; Crawford 2003; Henry 1994).

The importance of Caribbean women as independent migrants has characterized their status as lead migrants, when compared to other immigrant women. Throughout the 1970s and 1980s, Caribbean women outnumbered men in migratory flows to Canada (Richmond 1989; Anderson 1993). Richmond states that "a significant feature of Caribbean immigration, in comparison with that from other regions of the world, has been the above-average proportion of women who immigrate alone" (1989, 15). In addition, Caribbean women entering other countries reported themselves as single more frequently than women in other immigrant groups. Those women who did not enter as permanent residents came under the foreign domestic work scheme. The racialization of paid reproductive work is particularly noteworthy because of the predominance of black women and women of colour in domestic service, which encompasses myriad jobs that often overlap, from household mainte-nance (cooking, cleaning, washing, etc.) to childcare and tending to the elderly and sick. Arat-Koc states that "while domestic labour under capitalism assumes several universal characteristics such as invisibility, isolation and low status, the way these are experienced by individuals performing such labour may vary significantly by class, race and citizenship" (Arat-Koc 1990, 86). Colen goes on to refer to this phenomenon as "stratified reproduction":

> By stratified reproduction I mean that physical and social reproductive tasks are accomplished differentially according to inequalities that are based on class, race, ethnicity, gender, place in the global economy, and migration status, and that are structured by social, economic and political forces. The reproductive labor – phys-ical, mental, and emotional – of bearing, raising and socializing children and of creating and maintaining households and people (infancy to old age) is differently experienced, valued, and rewarded according to inequalities of access to material and social resources in particular historical and cultural contexts. (1995, 78)

The irony about stratified reproduction is that migrant women take care of other families in order to take care of their own. Under this racialized, gen-dered division of labour, from July 1975 to June 1976, "44.8 percent of all entrants to Canada's foreign domestic program were from the Caribbean, and only 0.3 percent were from all countries in Asia" (Bakan and Stasiulis 1995, 316). Throughout the 1980s, the migratory flow of female migrants was less structured, with more women coming to Canada as visitors, after which they worked (as domestics) and stayed in the country undocumented.

Family, Motherhood and Transnationality: Contesting Dominant Constructions

Extended family and kin networks, especially among Caribbean immigrants, have adapted to the internationalization of social relations in advanced capitalism because of increased economic expansion and integration, alongside asymmetrical development through the forging of transnational social networks and families in order to support of individuals across nations (Parrenas 2001; Ho 1993; Chamberlain 1999). Transnational motherhood is an important gender-specific component of this wider social system that is particularized through Third World women's experiences across races, cultures, classes, sexualities and nationalities. Hondagneu-Sotelo and Avila (1997) point out that there are many different ways in which the social reproduction of children or childcare takes place without the immediate involvement of biological mothers, but it appears that the temporariness of these arrangements is tolerated, if not accepted, compared to the long-term and/or indefinite periods of separation characterized by transnational motherhood:

> There are, in fact, many transgressions of the mother–child symbiosis in practice – large families where older daughters care for younger siblings, child-servants who at [an] early age leave their mothers, children raised by paid nannies and other caregivers, and mothers who leave young children to seek employment – but these are fluid enough to sustain ideological adherence to the prescription that children should be raised exclusively by biological mothers. Long-term physical and temporal separation disrupts this notion. Transnational mothering radically rearranges mother–child interactions and requires a concomitant radical reshaping of the meanings and definitions of appropriate mothering. (Hondagneu-Sotelo and Avila 1997, 557)

Transnational motherhood counters dominant notions of motherhood linked to the institution of motherhood under patriarchal capitalist relations. Dominant notions of motherhood are premised on three major assumptions, which Oakley (1980) refers to as the myths of motherhood, and which serve to make motherhood appear universal, natural and unchanging for women. The myths of motherhood are: (1) children *need* their mothers; (2) mothers *need* their children; (3) women *need* to be mothers. The first assertion that *children need their mothers* relies on three assumptions: "the first is that children need their biological mothers. The second is that children need mothers rather than any other kind of caretaker. The third is that children need to be reared in the context of a one-to-one relationship" (Oakley 1980, 204).

This perspective ultimately privileges the nuclear family as the norm, based on a middle-class, gendered division of labour whereby men, as husbands, are seen as breadwinners, and women, as wives/mothers, are seen as economic dependents (Luxton, Rosenberg and Arat-Koc 1990). Motherhood, in turn, is constructed as a solitary experience within the domestic sphere, where mothers are expected to care for and raise their children exclusively, avoiding separation, voluntary or otherwise (Oakley 1980). Nancy Chodorow reinforces this perspective by stating that neglect or the wrong kind of care can affect an infant's personality and self-identity and that, "for [a] mother, the relationship has a quality of exclusivity and mutuality, in that it does not include other people and because it is different from relationships to adults" (1978, 86). Conversely, Hondagneu-Sotelo and Avila rightfully argue that "the ideal of biological mothers raising their own children is widely held but is also widely broken at both ends of the class spectrum. Wealthy elites have always relied on others – nannies, governesses, and boarding schools – to raise their children, while poor families often rely on kin and 'other mothers'" (1997, 557).

The reinforcement of the maternalist ideology that *all* children need their biological mothers and that *all* biological mothers need their children (Oakley 1980) does not hold true for working-class African-Caribbean women who participate in collective maternal practices. I argue that it is the function of African-Caribbean families through matrifocality and child-shifting practices that facilitates the occurrence and practice of transnational motherhood. These practices ultimately contest dominant notions of motherhood that privilege nuclear family norms and the exclusivity of mother–child relations.

Caribbean Women, Motherhood and Family

While western European traditions have universalized the nuclear family as the ideal family type, and have ascribed particular gender-specific roles to both men and women based on the male breadwinner/dependent housewife construct, scholars (Herskovits and Herskovits 1947; Clarke 1999; Smith 1956 and 1996; Blake 1961; Rodman 1971; Senior 1991; Barrow 1996; Sutton and Makiesky-Barrow 2001) have examined the family and household patterns of working-class African-Caribbean people based on culturally class-based standards, accounting for some of the notable, non-nuclear family formations such as female-headed households, matrifocality and the primacy of the extended family and kinship networks.

Motherhood appears to be an important rite of passage for many Caribbean women as a marker of womanhood, regardless of class and marital status (Senior 1991; Mohammed 1999). Childbearing and childrearing "may be perceived as 'natural' roles" (Mohammed 1999, 11) that women should take on. This fact supports maternalist ideology whereby mothers valorize their role as nurturers of their children as a *natural* extension of their self-identity and sense of self (Villani and Ryan 1997; Eyer 1996). While this perception may give African-Caribbean women power and status as mothers, it does little to overturn a restrictive sexual division of labour. Gender socialization in the Caribbean promotes sex differentiation between males and females and rigidly structures gender roles according to "appropriate" roles, duties and behaviours for women and men within the home and wider society (Clarke 1999; Senior 1991). Women are mainly responsible for childcare and also shoulder the bulk of household responsibilities since these activities tend to be considered "women's work" (Leo-Rhynie 1998), and therefore out of the sphere of men, who are defined primarily as providers, whether this role is achievable or not. Despite the fact that the social reproduction of care is organized along gender lines, working-class African-Caribbean women's activities are structured and experienced differently in comparison to a middle-class Euro-American familial reality. In the African-Caribbean experience, women have more personal autonomy: motherhood and wifehood are not inextricably linked because marriage is not a prerequisite for women to have children. Also, conjugal relationships within nuclear units are less important than extended family units in organizing women's reproductive responsibilities and personal relationships because of the unreliability of male economic contributions (Senior 1991; Mohammed 1999; Safa and Antrobus 1992; Barrow 1996).

The interdependence between work and motherhood for working-class African-Caribbean women, and the negotiation between the two, is supported by the extended family unit. African-Caribbean women, particularly young, single, undereducated mothers, are highly represented in extended-family households. These extended units may include biological members such as parent(s), adult children (i.e., the mother's siblings), grandchildren, grandparents, cousins and also non-biological members, or fictive kin, such as foster children who rely on one another for economic, social and emotional support (Clarke 1999; Blake 1961; Olwig Fog 1996; Smith 1996). In addition, as Sutton and Makiesky-Barrow state, "the strong sense of family based on these connections counter-balances the relative instability of conjugal unions" (2001, 379). Extended family units are usually matrifocal, a feature managed by respected elder or mature women. Adult males, whether fathers, brothers or uncles, may or may not be present, but if they are they have limited direct authority over household matters (Smith 1996; Clarke 1999). Women's economic independence, resourcefulness and decision-making power are important. Household members pool their resources together and share domestic and parental responsibilities to ensure that children, elders and the sick are not abandoned and that unemployed adults are not left homeless (Senior 1991). Women are ultimately incorporated into a wider family and kinship network that offsets economic hardship and the lack of state services (Benería and Feldman 1992).

The utilization of female kinship networks is an integral part of the migratory process for women who may leave their children behind in the care of their mothers, sisters and aunts (Olwig Fog 1996; Gordon 1995). Compared to a middle-class Euro-American stance on motherhood in relation to the exclusivity of mother–child relations, working-class African-Caribbean women's childcare and childrearing arrangements are more open and expansive, and displace notions of motherhood as an individualistic experience and practice. Birthmothers are willing to outsource care of their children for economic and personal reasons through child-shifting practices for indefinite periods of time (Senior 1991; Mohammed 1999; Barrow 1996). Child-shifting may occur for many reasons, not just because of maternal absence as a result of migration or the inability of parent(s) to care for children properly because of economic reasons (Leo-Rhynie 1997). Matthei argues that, "expanded transnationally, women's networks play [a vital] role in international migration, linking women who remain in sending communities to remittances and women who seek to migrate to employment opportunities and childcare, and, in some cases, paving the way for a potential return to their communities of origin" (1996, 39).

The Study: African-Caribbean Women in Canada

Settlement, Employment and Undocumented Status

The ten female migrants who participated in the study initially stayed with family or friends who helped them migrate as visitors to Toronto, Canada, during the 1970s to early 1990s. While most women arrived with the intention of staying, a few women just came to work and make some money and return home to repeat the cycle at another time through a revolving migratory pattern. But eager Caribbean immigrant hosts encouraged women to stay on indefinitely or permanently. Faist notes the relationship between social networking and chain migration, stating that "chain migration is a social mechanism in which numerous persons leave one well-defined area or origin serially for another well-defined location. They rely on people from the same origin and brokers for information, informal aid, and various resources" (2000, 53). Hosts admonished their visitors for wanting to go back home, since those who had settled felt that there was nothing there for them. Although these Caribbean immigrants were fighting to make ends meet, they felt that their situations abroad were better than what they had in their home countries.

Women were assured by their hosts that things would work out, and that somebody would find a "little end" or job for them to do. Extended family support was an essential part of the settlement process for newcomer females. Carol, who migrated in 1984, relied on the support of her mother and sisters to help with the settlement process.

Given their status as worker-mothers, African-Caribbean women made finding work their priority. They had their children to support back home, and needed money for remittances and savings. Eight out of the ten women in the study overstayed their time in Canada during the 1970s and 1980s, and resolved to deal with immigration issues at a later date. Economic objectives drove the actions women took to circumvent immigration policy (Henry 1994; Silvera 1992). While women received reassurance from informants that things would work out, and were given support and information about work and legal counsel at different stages of their visitations or settlements, nothing prepared them for the trials of finding employment, working and adjusting to their new environment as undocumented migrants.

Live-in domestic work was readily available, and was the main source of employment for unskilled black women and women of colour without landed status. Seven women in the study engaged in domestic live-in work as newcomers. The length of time that these women stayed with this type of employment depended on their wages, work conditions and personal circumstances. Parrenas states that "the international transfer of caretaking refers to a social, political and economic relationship between women in the global labor market. This division of labor is a structural relationship of inequality based on class, race, gender and (nation based) citizenship" (Parrenas 2001, 71). Most women did live-in domestic work for a year or less. Scholars in both Canada and the United States support the point that this type of work may not be the most desirable for female migrants, facilitating a high turnover in this sector (Hondagneu-Sotelo 2001; Romero 2002; Bakan and Stasiulis 1997; Arat-Koc 1990; Silvera 1992; Calliste 1991). Pierette Hondagneu-Sotelo points out that, "once they experience it, most women are repelled by live-in jobs. The lack of privacy, the mandated separation from family and friends, the round the clock hours, the food issues, the low pay and especially the constant loneliness prompt most [immigrant women] to seek other job arrangements" (2001, 36). Hazel was the only woman in the study who did live-in domestic work for three years. Most of the women in the study referred to this type of work as "babysitting" although they lived with their employers and engaged in a wide range of domestic duties, from taking care of children, cleaning and cooking, to doing laundry within households. For some women, this was hard, unrewarding and exploitative work, but they felt compelled to do live-in work despite the poor working conditions because they had families to support back home.

Thus, the economic imperative becomes a motivating factor in female migrant workers' decision to settle for substandard wages. Bakan and Stasiulis note that "the perception that even the lowest wages in the most undesirable type of work in Canada are still preferable to those available in the home country is a powerful incentive compelling foreign domestic workers to accept such employment" (1997, 42). Security concerns were also a reason why some women opted to do live-in domestic work. For women who had no place to stay or could no longer reside with family or friends because of conflicts, this kind of work was an alternative to homelessness. Cossette, who arrived in Canada in 1994 with limited familial and social support, shared her experience of homelessness. Other women settled for domestic live-in work because it takes place in the private sphere, away from the roving eyes of immigration officials, who made intermittent raids at factories in search of undocumented workers, especially during the 1970s. Women in the study tried their best not to be sent back home prematurely.

The issue of paid domestic work not only raises several questions about an unequal gender division of labour vis-à-vis so-called women's work and men's work, and the devaluation and underremuneration of the latter, but also exposes the stratified class and race dynamics in paid and unpaid reproductive work among different groups of women (Arat-Koc 1997). Since the racialization of black women's labour from slavery, paid domestic work has been deemed "suitable" employment for non-white women, especially those with precarious immigration statuses. This perception has often placed white female employers in a position of power to exploit domestics of colour as a "cheap", expendable labour source (Daenzer 1993). Owing to race and class privileges, white female employers are, on the one hand, benefactors of the low-cost labourers who assist them in the reproduction of their families, while, on the other hand, they contribute to economic instability among working-class African-Caribbean women by paying them substandard wages that barely keep their families afloat (Silvera 1992). This arrangement does little to transform the gendered division of labour in relation to how domestic work is organized and remunerated, or to redress female economic marginality resulting from the pervasiveness of the male breadwinner myth. In addition to the race and class dynamics of stratified reproduction among women, the racial construction of motherhood also differentially categorizes women and positions them in opposition to each other (Hill Collins 2000). Through a colonial legacy of the cult of true womanhood, white women are recognized as mothers of the nation with citizenship benefits for themselves and their children, while Caribbean migrant women/mothers are rendered invisible as mothers by being seen, first and foremost, as workers by their white employers (Crawford 2003). Nakano Glenn rightfully states that the "two fundamental elements in the construction of racial-ethnic womanhood [have been] the notion of inherent traits that suited the women for service and the denial of the women's identities as wives and mothers in their own right" (1992, 32).

Transnational Families and Motherhood

The continuity of African-Caribbean women's worker-mother role across borders is indicative of the practice of transnational motherhood. Christine Ho
states that "women are the protagonists in the drama of globalizing Caribbean
kinship, which requires the active maintenance of circuits of exchange of
goods, services, communication, travel and personnel. This is not a new challenge for Caribbean women, who for centuries have been embedded in large
kin-based support networks. Today's transnational structures are merely the
postmodern versions of this tradition on a global scale" (1999, 45). Given
women's non-reliance on male breadwinners for support, women's responsibilities to their children often drive their economic aspirations, thus linking
their productive and reproductive roles. This perspective challenges assumptions about "housewification", which Mies (1986) universally applies to all
women. Barriteau, however, argues that "Mies reduces all women's experiences, all exploitations, all their realities to economic determinism. Her
analysis reinforces the Eurocentric bias of socialist feminism and either an
inability or refusal to desegregate women in 'over-developed', industrialized
societies. Not all women in the North [or the South] are white and/or
middle-class" (1995, 53). Caribbean women's worker-mother role on the
transnational level also challenges assumptions about the inability of mothers
to act independently of their children, as proscribed by the myths of motherhood (Oakley 1980).

Rosina Wiltshire-Brodber states that "the transnational family thus represents a mutually interdependent support network which is neither bounded
by the household nor national boundaries. It enables its members to adapt
and partially transcend the realities of unemployment, very small size, limited
opportunity and mobility which characterize life for large sectors of Caribbean
people" (1986, 5). But Rhacel Parrenas (2001) contends that, since transnational families do not conform to dominant nuclear family standards,
particularly in "traditional" societies, they are labelled as "broken" for several
reasons: "First, the maintenance of this household diverges from traditional
expectations of cohabitation among spouses and children. Second, they do
not meet the traditional division of labor in the family, as transnational mothers do not maintain social expectations for women who perform domestic
chores . . . Third, they move away from traditional practices of socialization

in the family. While socialization is expected to come from direct supervision and interaction with parents as well as other adults, the geographic distance in transnational households mars the ability of mothers to provide direct supervision" (Parrenas 2001, 109).

The assumption that transnational households are "broken" reinforces dominant nuclear family bias and overlooks the diversity of family structures and mothering practices that exist, which are not necessarily a by-product of migration. Legacies of matrifocality, child-minding and female economic independence are culturally class-based characteristics of working-class African-Caribbean families (Barrow 1996; Clarke 1999; Senior 1991) that challenge the universality of the nuclear family and the exclusivity of mother–child relations, and ultimately complement transnational familial practices. In addition, the assumption that transnational families are "broken" reinforces gender bias about the primary reproduction for women as mothers, which is not expected of men as fathers. A sexual double standard plays out in border crossings, informing the perception of transnational mothers. It appears that migrant men/fathers are not criticized for leaving their children behind because of gender norms which assign women as the primary caregivers and key socializers of children (Crawford 2004). Unlike the migrant fathers, who have the privilege of passing on the social reproduction of labour onto their female counterparts while focusing on fulfilling their perceived role as providers without condemnation, female migrants who do the same are judged negatively for doing so because of the myths of motherhood and separate-sphere ideology based on the male breadwinner/housewife construct. This tendency reflects what V. Eudine Barriteau calls unequal gender relations. She states that "an unequal gender relation is a relation of domination. Its inequality is rooted in an asymmetry of power that has differential material and ideological outcomes" for women and men (1998, 188).

Maintenance and Remittances

Women in the study were conscientious about sending some form of support back home. It was both shameful and unacceptable not to do so. Like other migrants before them, they had to translate the adage of going abroad for betterment into material gains or some evidence of economic advancement (Olwig Fog 2007). Transnational families based in kinship relations facilitate the migratory objectives of migrants and also cater to needs related to social reproduction. Ho notes: "First, it [i.e., the transnational relationship] satisfies the needs of migrants who find it necessary to move in order to work and assures them the wellbeing of their children who have to remain behind until such time as they are again able to care for them. Second, it allows them to get the most out of both the sending and receiving society, and provides them with insurance against migration failure if things do not work out in their destinations" (1993, 37). Women were conscious of the sacrifices that they, and their families, had made and did not want their efforts to be in vain. Olwig Fog states that, "though the wide networks of relations help individuals migrate and sustain those individuals in the early phases of settling in a foreign place, it is the desire to increase the status of the smaller family group that motivates the migratory move" (2007, 219). With their meagre incomes, the migrant women in my study had to be both thrifty and resourceful in "stretching their money". After accounting for transportation, personal items and rent for those who lived in a rooming house or shared accommodations with someone, they set aside money as remittances to be sent back home or to buy goods that would be stacked and then shipped in a barrel or box.

Women periodically sent money to caregivers to pay for food, clothes and school supplies for their children. Hazel was proud that she was able to send money to Jamaica to pay for her children's tuition fees for private school: "They went to private school down the road, so I had to send money for that." Carol explained that most of the money she and her husband worked for went toward supporting her children back in Trinidad. Not only did she find it necessary to take care of them, but also her sister, their caregiver, in order to avoid any conflict. This point is supported by Hondagneu-Sotelo and Avila's note that "transnational mothers know that they may increase the likelihood of their children receiving adequate care if they appropriately remunerate the caregivers and treat them with the consideration their work requires" (1997, 561). Although ill advised, women usually sent remittances to caregivers in good faith and rarely questioned what portion of money or goods was actually used on their children. Tensions sometimes rose between foster children and other children in the household when the former received additional items from their migrant mothers that the latter were not privileged to. Although the reciprocity pattern between the caregiver and migrants may be initially established, there are risks involved in such an informal arrangement because either party can default on their responsibility to the other without warning or being fully accountable for their actions.

Women bought non-perishable items in discount stores and a few boasted about saving to buy the best clothes and items (e.g., tailored or name brand items) for their children. Parrenas (2001) suggests that transnational mothers may compensate for their absence by showering their children with gifts. She states that "they equate love with monthly remittances. Parents weigh the pros and cons of transnational parenting and systematically conclude that material benefits of their earnings compensate for the emotional costs inflicted in separation" (Parrenas 2001, 124). While this action may be seen as impractical or as mothers trying to buy their children's love through "gifts of guilt" to make up for their not being present (Crawford-Brown 2000), there may also have been a class and cultural motivation behind this practice. Two women reported that their children deserved the best and made attempts to achieve this goal. Sending second-hand or bargain clothes to their children was classless and unacceptable behaviour if they could do better. This idea is particularly important in a Caribbean cultural sense, in which the appearance or condition of children is often judged to be a measure of a parent's ethic of care. Unkempt children may be seen as a sign of parental neglect; in colloquial terms, "they look like they don't have an owner". In this case, a few women may have projected their ethic of care as well as their promise of betterment onto their children through outfitting or adorning them well even when they did not really have the means to do so.

Through their community networks a few women joined or later organized a "susu" or "partner", a rotating credit and savings system in which individuals take turns drawing a designated lump sum to help with saving or in generating immediate capital (Herskovits and Herskovits 1947). Susu, or partner money, is purposeful for many reasons. It can be set aside for provisions back home, for lawyer fees, airfare or settlement costs for children, and can even help with a down payment on a new home at a later date. Hazel shares her experience: "It was very hard when we were thinking about buying a house. We had to put $10,000 down, so we throw a partner and we get out [a] little money and we borrowed the rest." The practices that women engaged in, as transnational mothers, were important not only in providing support to their families but also in creating gendered Caribbean diasporic experiences. They mixed their Caribbean values and customs with new practices and ideas of acculturation, which they transmitted to their home countries via communication and support. They did not do so smoothly or without contradictions but through continuous negotiation. While holding onto memories of home, mothers projected the possibilities available abroad onto their children through the support and goods they sent from Canada. Thus, transnational mothering practices not only reflected the materiality of survival within globalization but also revealed a lot about extended familial social values and cooperation.

Separation and Maintaining Contact

Transnational motherhood not only challenges and obscures normative, day-to-day practices of mothering in relation to time, space and contact, but it also complicates maternal expectations related to role achievement and social bonding. Four women were separated from their children for three to four years; three women for five to eight years; two women for nine to twelve years; and one woman has never been reunited with her children. The average number of years of separation, for the entire sample, was 6.4 years. The age of reunification among children ranged from five to nineteen. Therefore, deterministic notions of motherhood are faulty and also unrealistic because they overlook the complexity of this gendered role that requires constant negotiation between parents and children under different circumstances.

In the study, Caribbean transnational mothers shared how they felt about being separated from their children. Some women recalled feelings of sadness and emptiness in being separated from their children. Lorna, for instance, said, "I was very sad being away from my children." And Patsy reported, "There was this emptiness inside. I can't explain that . . . I was so empty . . . anytime I would see kids I would just wish they were with me." As Parrenas notes, "emotional strains of transnational parenting include feelings of anxiety, helplessness, loss, guilt and loneliness" (2001, 120). Delores worried about whether her children were being properly cared for, especially in times of illness. Hondagneu-Sotelo and Avila state that "transnational mothers worry about some of the negative effects on their children, but they also experience the absence of domestic life as a deeply personal loss" (1997, 562). Lorna found being away from her children emotionally taxing. Birthdays and the holidays were especially difficult when she was taking care of other people's children: "It's hard. It was very hard. You tend to grow apart. You weren't there for their birthdays. You weren't there for Christmas . . . And you see it happening around with other kids' birthdays. You are here on other kids' birthdays and other families. You know. It's very hard."

Women's inability to see and/or speak to their children regularly heightened their concern about the children's wellbeing and their development. Common questions, such as how their children were doing, coping and growing, were often on their minds. Some women could not escape feelings of guilt and helplessness (Villani and Ryan 1997; Gustafson 2005) when they found out that their children were ill or needed medical attention and they could not be there to comfort or care for them. Delores remembers how helpless she felt when she found out one of her sons was ill: "I remember getting a phone call saying he is in the hospital and he isn't going to make it. They put him on . . . I spent the whole time wondering if he is okay and I wonder if this is going to happen to him. But apparently he was okay; he get over the asthma." The psychosocial dimensions of stratified reproduction were also evident (Colen 1995). Some women coped by embracing and establishing bonds with their employer's children to pass time, while others kept their distance and dissociated from emotional trappings by focusing on their work. Women experienced feelings of loneliness, especially at birthdays and during the holidays. In the absence of children and family, some women recalled "skin-grinning", or pretending, through special occasions and then crying themselves to sleep because of noteworthy reminders of the past.

Women attempted to keep in touch with their children as best they could. Letters and phone calls were the main sources of communication. Carol recalls how much she spent in phone payments: "We had to pay the telephone bills, $300–$400 because we had to talk to the children every minute." But ultimately effective communication was dependent on a variety of factors such as access, continuous follow-up and willingness to disclose information on the part of parent, child and caregiver. In a few cases, women took for granted that their children were in good hands and were not proactive enough in maintaining continuous contact and communication with their children. Parrenas points out that communication between parent and child in transnational relations is skewed: "In transnational families, power clearly lies with the parent, in particular the migrant parent. The process of 'time-space compression' is unidirectional, with children at the receiving end. Migrant parents initiate calls and children receive them . . . They are trapped as 'time space-compression' convinces parents that they have maintained close-knit ties through separation and allows parents to leave children waiting longer" (2001, 26). Mothers wrote letters to their older children, explaining their situations and inquiring about how they were doing. They also got the chance to let their children know that they missed and cared for them. Those children who were able to articulate their feelings responded in kind, often requesting that their mothers come back home or come and get them. Other women wrote directly to caregivers, giving updates and sending their regards, because they felt that their children were too young to understand the situation. It is unclear whether children got any messages or regards through these correspondences. Some caregivers sent correspondence in reply but saw fit to withhold unfortunate or upsetting news from women to prevent them from worrying. Lorna recalls her situation: "They kept things away from me. They didn't want me to worry and I guess I couldn't help anyway." Women in this situation found out about deaths and major conflicts after the fact, showing their disconnection to life back home. Nevertheless, mothers found ways to keep the lines of communication open. They sent birthday cards to their children and often enclosed a few dollar bills so that they could buy treats on their special days. This was the case for Delores: "If they want money I send money, and when it is their birthday I put $5 in the card so they know that they get it from their mom." Some mothers made an effort to send photos so that their children would have visible tokens to remind them who their mothers were. Mothers rarely received photos of their children and were often shocked by the children's growth and development once they saw them in person after many years.

Reunification

The expediency of the reunification process depended on the status of the mothers, sponsorship issues, and establishing households and provisions for the children before they migrated. While women in the early 1970s had fewer problems with the immigration process, they still took a few years to establish themselves before sending for their children. Those women who came to Canada in the late 1980s and later faced greater immigration challenges and experienced longer periods of separation, sometimes spanning more than ten years, from their children.

Caribbean transnational mothers were active agents in getting their children to Canada. In some cases, matrimonial aspirations were either postponed or advanced in the best interest of the children in order to expedite sponsorship. Both married and single women placed importance on their economic independence and the need to work in order to take care of their families, continuing their worker-mother roles abroad. Although migration offered women new opportunities and helped in personal development, the gendered division of labour within the home for married women remained unequally shared in relation to household and childcare responsibilities between themselves and their spouses. A few women took a stand and challenged their partners but were met with indifference.

Transnational motherhood also obscures parental authority through the paradoxical roles which the migrant mothers play in their children's lives upon reunification. Since children saw their migrant mothers during the separation process first as providers, and second as caregivers, both mothers and children experienced some conflict between the past way of relating and what was desired and expected upon reunification. Cossette has a difficult time reuniting with her daughter: "It is hard dealing with her now because she grew up without discipline. She grew up just doing her own thing and people just beat up on her. She comes with the same mentality and I can't even deal with her now. Now it's like a gap between me and her." Those women with limited parenting experience found the demands of childrearing overwhelming and felt that they had underestimated the magnitude of their responsibilities. This experience debunks the notion that birthmothers *naturally* possess maternal instinct instead of developing it as a product of particularized *social* bonding with their children (Oakley 1980). Because of the demands of work, mothers found it difficult to spend quality time with their children, contributing to further alienation. An extended system of family support would have been helpful in the sharing of domestic responsibilities and buffering household conflicts, but this type of support was unfortunately weakened in the post-migratory period. Carol felt the pressure of balancing both work and her familial responsibilities: "I had to work because we had our own apartment. Then I had to go to work and come [home] in the evening. They [her children] stayed with my mother. Then I had to cook and clean. It was more challenging. This was the first time I was ever on my own. Family and work. And guess what? I had no help. Back home I had help but now I was on my own."

The adjustment process for children, whether positive or negative, depended on multiple factors, such as age, length of separation, socialization, parental experience and influence. It could not be reduced to just one factor. Teenagers, compared to younger children, had greater difficulty adjusting to their new environments and re-establishing ties with their mothers. At a transitory stage of life, teenagers were not only vying for independence but also seemed to be more cognizant of losing their caregivers, friends and family because of migration. Their grief was exacerbated by the uncertainty of a new life in a foreign cultural milieu. They exhibited unresolved feelings in defiance of parental authority and resentment towards their parent(s) for past unilateral decisions about migrating without their input. At times, mothers seemed unable to handle their children's anger, criticisms and delinquency. Delores shares her experience: "[T]he oldest one and the second one, anytime we are fighting, they let me know that they did not grow with me, they grow with my mother. They show in a different sense I wasn't there for them; their grandmother was there for them." Younger children were more impressionable and were thus easily influenced by their parent(s) and less resistant to change. Childhood socialization trumped the shared biology between mother and child, with children remaining loyal to their caregivers. Oakley states that "maternal deprivation is hence a syndrome which can only occur in a culture oriented around an exclusive mother–child bond. In different cultural settings, the close and exclusive attachment of mother and child never develop. The child cannot be deprived through a lack of 'mother' love" (1980, 214). Mothers expected more from their teenage children, especially females, in terms of household tasks, but at the same time teenage children had high expectations of their mothers. Hazel had difficulties with her teenage daughter, who was also her eldest child: "My older daughter keep saying that she felt more like a maid than like my daughter when she came here. She didn't know how close we were even when we were writing. She don't care, she felt more like the maid. And then she would say, 'Oh mama', [and] would tell us that this would happen." Some teenagers were disappointed that their standards of living had not improved dramatically and that they had to care for or share resources and their mother's affection with their foreign-born siblings.

Child-shifting, as a practical strategy, had not only an economic impact on families but also a social one. Children raised by their caregivers over a long period of time were more loyal to these individuals and resented their mothers' telling them what to do because their mothers had not "raised them". This was the case for two mothers, Cossette and Hazel. Cossette stated, "My daughter loves her grandmother. She grew up with grandma; that is all she knows. She didn't grow up with her mommy." Likewise, Hazel said, "My eldest daughter loved my grandmother, her great grandmother. She could do no wrong." In these cases, socialization, not biological parenting, was the prime determinant in parent–child bonding. These children may have coped with parental loss with limited emotional support, which in turn fuelled insecurities about abandonment. Children's malevolent feelings were exacerbated, depending on their relationships with their caregivers, their experience of abuse, their childhood environments and the kind of relationships they maintained with their mothers during separation. Once again, the good mother/bad mother trope was recognizable and played out during reunification. African-Caribbean women were judged for "leaving their children behind" not only by dominant white society but also by their own children, who internalized the mothering role as one of nurturer/caregiver. Not surprisingly, children projected the "good mother" trope onto grandmothers. Diana Gustafson states that "the good mother is selfless and puts the needs of her child before her own needs in all things . . . A child's needs are advanced as the good mother's raison d'etre because biological ties are presumed to bind together mother and child emotionally, socially and morally" (2005, 26). The "bad mother", however, violates the exclusive mother–child connection, becoming everything that the "good mother" is not: "The bad mother is imagined to ignore, trivialize, or reject her child's need for love, caring and nurturance both as an intellectual understanding and as a lived practice" (ibid., 28).

Older women fit normative notions of motherhood because "they were there" to take care of their grandchildren and establish familiar bonds, while migrant mothers were deemed neglectful if not "bad" mothers because of their absence, which was seen as the cause of unfamiliarity. Some children, on the one hand, called into question their mothers' parenting styles, which they felt were too disciplinary and lacking in demonstrative love. Mothers, on the other hand, held onto the notion that their children were their blood, and expected respect, if not love, from them because of it. They saw motherhood as an extension of their identities as per maternalist ideology, and expected things to fall into place *naturally* and felt unappreciated or were disappointed when they did not. Maternal guilt surfaced for some women who felt responsible for contributing to their children's unresolved feelings and/or unmet needs (Caplan 2000).

Since the caring work of parenting is highly gendered, maternal guilt and blame are indictments of women who supposedly have not lived up to the idealized mothering role and are made to feel solely responsible for their children's failures and shortcomings because of it (Caplan 2000; Nice 1992). There is a sexual double standard when it comes to social reproduction because there is no paternal equivalent to describe the lack of care or connection that fathers have with their children. Nonetheless, mothers wanted the best for their children, especially in the area of education. Women expressed pride in the educational rewards that their children obtained because of migration and the better standards of living they provided abroad. Moreover, based on the experiences of Caribbean transnational mothers, migration in and of itself should not be considered the sole cause of precarious relations between mothers and their children. Instead, the myriad socio-economic, personal and cultural factors that affect and shape transnational relationships and the effectiveness of familial re-integration upon reunification also contribute to unstable parent–child relationships.

Conclusion

Working-class African-Caribbean women, through their experiences as transnational mothers, demonstrate how class, culture, socialization and other factors inform and shape motherhood, debunking universal assumptions about this gendered role. Centring female migrant work and mothering experiences within migratory discourse allows for a more nuanced examination of the different dimensions of racialized, gendered identities and relations within the context of globalization and on a transnational level. The multiple roles that women took on with the support of their extended kin network challenged dominant assumptions about the universality of the nuclear family and housewification based on separate-sphere ideology. Through African-Caribbean women's roles as worker-mothers, they were able to remit money and goods in order to maintain households and support their children in their home countries. The ongoing communication and exchange between female migrants and caregivers is reflective of reciprocal kin relations within globalization. Women attempted to foster positive relationships with their children but they found it difficult at times because of feelings of loneliness and loss and because of spatial and temporal distance.

The multiple feelings and emotions that women had about motherhood reflect the complexity of the gendered roles of mothers, especially on a transnational level. While African-Caribbean women viewed and practised motherhood in a collectivized way based on cultural, class-based norms, they also had personal expectations of themselves based on obligation and love for their children. Their personal expectations were complicated by their capability in fulfilling their role, their children's expectations and responses to them, and white mainstream perceptions of them. It is interesting to note that, while the exclusivity of mother–child relations may have been undermined for Caribbean transnational mothers, maternalist ideology associated with women being birth mothers, in a Caribbean context, remained ideologically strong for women in validating womanhood. Moreover, transnational motherhood exposes the paradoxical aspects of the social construction of motherhood in view of dominant notions of motherhood as examined through themes of separation, support and reunification in Caribbean transformational families.

References

Anderson, W.W. 1993. *Caribbean immigrants: A socio-demographic profile*. Toronto: Canadian Scholars' Press.

Antrobus, P. 2004. Feminist activism: The CARICOM experience. In *Gender in the 21st century*, ed. B. Bailey and E. Leo-Rhynie, 38–58. Kingston: Ian Randle.

Arat-Koc, S. 1990. Importing housewives: Non-citizen domestic workers and the crisis of the domestic sphere in Canada. In *Through the kitchen window: The politics of home and family*, ed. M. Luxton, H. Rosenberg and S. Arat-Koc, 81–103. Toronto: Garamond.

———. 1997. From mothers of the nation to migrant workers. In *Not one of the family: Foreign domestic workers in Canada*, ed. A. Bakan and D. Stasiulis, 53–80. Toronto: University of Toronto Press.

Aymer, P.L. 1997. *Uprooted women: Migrant domestics in the Caribbean*. London: Praeger.

Bakan, A., and D. Stasiulis. 1995. Making the match: Domestic placement agencies and the racialization of women's household work. *Signs: Journal of Women in Culture and Society* 20 (2): 303–35.

———, eds. 1997. *Not one of the family: Foreign domestic workers in Canada.* Toronto: University of Toronto Press.

Barriteau, V.E. 1995. Socialist feminist theory and Caribbean women: Transcending dualisms. *Social and Economic Studies* 44 (2 and 3): 25–63.

———. 1998. Theorizing gender systems and the project of modernity in the twentieth-century Caribbean. *Feminist Review* 59 (June): 186–210.

Barrow, C., ed. 1996. *Family in the Caribbean: Themes and perspectives.* Kingston: Ian Randle.

Basch, L.G., N.G. Schiller and C.S. Blanc. 1994. *Nations unbound: Transnational projects, postcolonial predicaments, and deterritorialized nation-states.* London: Routledge.

Benería, L., and S. Feldman, eds. 1992. *Unequal burden: Economic crises, persistent poverty, and women's work.* Boulder: Westview.

Blake, J. 1961. *Family structure in Jamaica.* New York: Free Press of Glencoe.

Bolles, A.L. 1996. *Sister Jamaica: A study of women, work and households in Kingston.* New York: University Press of America.

Calliste, A. 1991. Canada's immigration policy and domestics from the Caribbean: The second domestic scheme. In *Race, class, gender: Bonds and barriers*, ed. J. Vorst et al., 136–48. Toronto: Garamond.

———.1996. Anti-racism organizing and resistance in nursing: African Canadian women. *Canadian Review of Sociology and Anthropology* 33 (3): 361–90.

Caplan, P.J. 2000. *The new don't blame mother: Mending the mother-daughter relationship.* New York: Routledge.

Chamberlain, M., ed. 1998. *Caribbean migration: Globalised identities.* London: Routledge.

———. 1999. The family as model and metaphor in Caribbean migration to Britain. *Journal of Ethnic and Migration Studies* 25 (2): 251–66.

Chodorow, N. 1978. *The reproduction of mothering: Psychoanalysis and the sociology of gender.* Berkeley and Los Angeles: University of California Press.

Clarke, E.C. 1972/1999. *My mother who fathered me: A study of the families in three selected communities of Jamaica.* Kingston: University of the West Indies Press.

Colen, S. 1995. "Like a mother to them": Stratified reproduction and West Indian childcare workers and employers in New York. In *Conceiving the new world order*, ed. F.D. Ginsburg and R. Rapp, 78–102. Berkeley and Los Angeles: University of California Press.

Crawford, C. 2003. Sending love in a barrel: The making of transnational families in Canada. *Canadian Woman Studies Journal* 22 (3–4): 104–9.

———. 2004. African-Caribbean women, diaspora and transnationality. *Canadian Woman Studies Journal* 23 (2): 97–103.

Crawford-Brown, C. 2000. Separation and reunification: The effects of migration on children. *Kinesis* 3 (4): 10–11.

Daenzer, P. 1993. *Regulating class privilege: Immigrant servants in Canada, 1940s–1990s.* Toronto: Canadian Scholars' Press.

Ehrenreich, B., and A. Russell Hochschild, eds. 2002. *Global woman: Nannies, maids, and sex workers in the new economy*. New York: Holt.

Elu, J. 2000. The journey so far: The effect of structural adjustment programme (SAP), sustainable growth, and development in the Caribbean region. *Western Journal of Black Studies* 24 (4): 202–15.

Eyer, D. 1996. *Motherguilt: How our culture blames mothers for what's wrong with society*. New York: Random House.

Faist, T. 2000. *The volume and dynamics of international migration and transnational social spaces*. Oxford: Clarendon Press.

Foner, N. 1979. West Indians in New York and London: A comparative analysis. *International Migration Review* 13 (2): 284–97.

Freeman, C. 1997. Reinventing higglering across transnational zones: Barbadian women juggle the triple shift. In *Daughters of Caliban: Caribbean women in the twentieth century*, ed. C. Lopez Springfield, 68–95. Bloomington: Indiana University Press.

Gordon, S.W. 1996. "I go to 'tanties'": The economic significance of child-shifting in Antigua. In *Family in the Caribbean: Themes and perspectives*, ed. C. Barrow, 106–18. Kingston: Ian Randle.

Goulbourne, H. 2002. *Caribbean transnational experience*. London: Pluto.

Gustafson, D.L. 2005. *Unbecoming mothers: The social production of maternal absence*. New York: Haworth Clinical Practice Press.

Harrison, F. 1991. Women in Jamaica's urban informal economy: Insights from a Kingston slum. In *Third World women and the politics of feminism*, ed. C.T. Mohanty, A. Russo and L. Torres, 171–96. Bloomington: Indiana University Press.

Henry, F. 1994. *The Caribbean diaspora in Toronto: Learning to live with racism*. Toronto: University of Toronto Press.

Herskovits, M.J., and F.S. Herskovits. 1947. *Trinidad village*. New York: Knopf.

Hill Collins, P. 2000. *Black feminist thought: Knowledge, consciousness, and the politics of empowerment*. 2nd ed. New York: Routledge.

Ho, C. 1993. The internationalization of kinship and the feminization of Caribbean migration: The case of Afro-Trinidadian immigrants in Los Angeles. *Journal of the Society for Applied Anthropology* 52 (1): 32–40.

———. 1999. Caribbean transnationalism as a gendered process. *Latin American Perspectives* 26 (5): 34–54.

Hondagneu-Sotelo, P. 2001. *Domestica: Immigrant workers cleaning and caring in the shadows of affluence*. Berkeley and Los Angeles: University of California Press.

Hondagneu-Sotelo, P., and E. Avila. 1997. "I'm here but I'm there": The meaning of Latina transnational motherhood. *Gender and Society* 11 (5): 548–71.

Jakubowski, L. 1997. *Immigration and the legalization of racism*. Halifax: Fernwoood Publishing.

Leo-Rhynie, E. 1997. Class, race, and gender issues in child rearing in the Caribbean. In

Caribbean families: Diversity among ethnic groups, ed. J.L. Roopnarine and J. Brown, 25–55. Greenwich, CT: Ablex.

———. 1998. Socialisation and the development of gender identity: Theoretical formulations and Caribbean research. In *Caribbean portraits: Essays on gender ideologies and identities*, ed. C. Barrow, 234–52. Kingston: Ian Randle.

Luxton, M., H. Rosenberg and S. Arat-Koc, eds. 1990. *Through the kitchen window: The politics of home and family.* Toronto: Garamond.

Massiah, J. 1986. Work in the lives of Caribbean women. *Social and Economic Studies* 35(2): 177–239.

Matthei, L. 1996. Gender and international labor migration: A networks approach. *Social Justice* 23 (3): 38–53.

Mies, M. 1986. *Patriarchy and accumulation on a world scale: Women in the international division of labour.* London: Zed Books.

Mohammed, P. 1999. *Caribbean women at the crossroads: The paradox of motherhood among women of Barbados, St Lucia and Dominica.* Kingston: Canoe.

Nakano Glenn, E. 1992. From servitude to service work: Historical continuities in the racial division of paid reproductive labor. *Signs: Journal of Women in Culture and Society* 18 (1): 1–42.

———. 1994. Social constructions of mothering: A thematic overview. In *Mothering: Ideology, experience and agency*, ed. E. Nakano Glenn, G. Chang and L.R. Forcey, 1–32. New York: Routledge.

Nice, V.E. 1992. *Mothers and daughters.* New York: St Martin's Press.

Oakley, A. 1980. *Housewife.* Middlesex, UK: Penguin.

Olwig Fog, K. 1996. The migration experience: Nevisian women at home and abroad. In *Family in the Caribbean: Themes and perspectives*, ed. C. Barrow, 135–49. Kingston: Ian Randle.

———. 1999. Narratives of the children left behind: Home and identity in globalized Caribbean families. *Journal of Ethnic and Migration Studies* 25 (2): 267–84.

———. 2007. *Caribbean journeys: An ethnography of migration and home in three family networks.* Durham, NC: Duke University Press.

Parrenas, R.S. 2001. *Servants of globalization.* Stanford, CA: Stanford University Press.

Reddock, R. 1995. Women and slavery in the Caribbean: A feminist perspective. *We specialize in the wholly impossible: A reader in black women's history*, ed. D. Clark Hine, W. King and L. Reed, 127–41. New York: Carlson.

Rich, A. 1995. *Of woman born: Motherhood as experience and institution.* New York: Norton.

Richmond, A.H. 1989. *Caribbean immigrants.* Ottawa: Ministry of Supply and Services.

Rodman, H. 1971. *Lower-class families: The culture of poverty in Negro Trinidad.* London: Oxford University Press.

Romero, M. 2002. *Maid in the U.S.A.* New York: Routledge.

Safa, H. 1995. *The myth of the male breadwinner: Women and industrialization in the Caribbean.* Boulder: Westview.

Safa, H., and P. Antrobus. 1992. Women and economic crisis in the Caribbean. In *Unequal burden: Economic crises, persistent poverty, and women's work,* ed. L. Benería and S. Feldman, 49–82. Boulder: Westview.

Senior, O. 1991. *Working miracles: Women's lives in the English-speaking Caribbean.* London: Currey.

Shepherd V., B. Brereton, and B. Bailey, eds. 1995. *Engendering history: Caribbean women in historical perspective.* Kingston: Ian Randle.

Shohat, E. 2002. Area studies, gender studies, and cartographies of knowledge. *Social Text* 72 (3): 67–78.

Silvera, M. 1992. *Silenced.* Toronto: Black Women and Women of Colour Press.

Simmons, A.B. 1990. New wave immigrants: Origins and characteristics. In *Ethnic demography: Canadian immigrant, racial and cultural variations,* ed. S.S. Halli, F. Trovato, and L. Driedger, 141–59. Ottawa: Carleton University Press.

Smith, R.T. 1956. *The Negro family in British Guiana.* London: Routledge and Kegan Paul.

———. 1996. *The matrifocal family: Power, pluralism and politics.* New York: Routledge.

Sparr, P., ed. 1994. *Mortgaging women's lives.* London: Zed Books.

Sutton, C., and S. Makiesky-Barrow. 2001. Social inequality and sexual status in Barbados. In *Caribbean sociology: Introductory reading,* ed. C. Barrow and R. Reddock, 371–88. Princeton, NJ: Markus Wiener.

Villani, S.L., and J. Ryan 1997. *Motherhood at the crossroads: Meeting the challenge of a changing role.* New York: Plenum.

Williams, G., and R. Henry. 1995. Engendering the adjustment process in Trinidad and Tobago: Perspectives and policy issues. In *Women pay the price: Structural adjustment in Africa and the Caribbean,* ed. G.T. Emeagwali, 87–104. Trenton, NJ: Africa World Press.

Wiltshire-Brodber, R. 1986. The Caribbean transnational family. Paper prepared for UNESCO/Institute of Social and Economic Research seminar on changing family patterns and women's role in the Caribbean. University of the West Indies, Cave Hill, Barbados, 24–27 November.

13

Activism in Academia

Twenty-first-Century Caribbean Feminist Dilemmas

GABRIELLE J. HOSEIN

Introduction

Walking past classrooms and through halls on campus, I passed posters making statements about sexual harassment, domestic violence, song lyrics, body image, pornography, rape and contraception. It was late November in the first semester of 2006 and these posters were everywhere – some disturbing, some advertising events, some handmade, some downloaded from the Internet, some with graffiti, some torn down and drifting across the asphalt.

They were the outcome of a "popular action" assignment in an Introduction to Women's Studies course offered by the Centre for Gender and Development Studies,[1] at the University of the West Indies in Trinidad and Tobago. I was the course lecturer and this was the first year I had introduced the assignment. In addition to poster campaigns, the ninety-two students who were registered in the course also organized a public workshop on female condoms, created popular theatre on reproductive rights, facilitated a session on consciousness-raising,[2] and staged participatory activities on issues ranging from female genital cutting to natural hair.

In this chapter, I use these "popular actions" and the ensuing debates that emerged as a lens for reflecting on the politics of Women's Studies, the changing meaning of "gender", issues raised when engaging men, and the role of academic feminism in identifying and addressing continuing issues of gender justice. I focus on the relationship among academic feminism, activism and liberal teaching values in the twenty-first-century Caribbean.

I argue that Women's Studies and (even) Gender Studies in the anglophone Caribbean are and remain tools for feminist consciousness-raising and movement-building. This chapter discusses challenges to these kinds of positions and the valid warnings made about openly politicized education. It therefore addresses a key question drawn from a debate in feminist literature about pedagogy; yet, it also addresses my own questions about totalitarianism and propagandizing in my teaching.

In this sense, I think critically about the political goals I have taken for granted in teaching and take seriously feminists' reflections on practices of domination in classrooms (Rinehart 2002). Does bringing activism into the classroom promote or suppress learning and critical thinking? What are the possibilities for intersecting Women's Studies and women's movements? Using the popular action assignment as a case study, I argue that activist pedagogies can expand possibilities for the liberal education that, critics argue, Women's Studies often lose sight of.

I also aim to further "a critical feminist pedagogy that is open to self-reflexivity about the processes by which we produce knowledge for and with our students" (Bojar and Naples 2002, 7). Drawing on these reflections, I therefore show how peer and cooperative learning strategies, as well as public, political engagement – cornerstones of Women's Studies – can empower students to challenge masculinism,[3] interrupt "banking" approaches to knowledge, question political assumptions, bridge differences and apply a nuanced gender analysis to the lives of both women and men. To this end, I provide a detailed description of aspects of the popular actions and their impact.

Activism in Academia

The objectives of the first-year course reflect aspects of the original goals of Women's Studies programmes when they began to be introduced in the 1960s and 1970s.[4] As Charlotte Bunch has outlined, the task at hand "was to use the academic arena to deepen our understanding of the problems women face and to encourage women to be activists" (Rose 2002, 120). Since its introduction in the mid-1990s, the discipline has sought to challenge patriarchal conceptions of women, provide information about women's lives and perspectives, change women's senses of themselves, interrogate and confront illegitimate power and hierarchy, and promote knowledge and understanding of feminism. I aimed to empower students further to participate consciously in women's movements and feminist activism. In this sense, the course continued to present "a field of inquiry, a critical perspective, a center for social action" and an "academic arm of the women's movement" to students (Ruth 1990, 2, 12).

When I began to teach the course to a class of ninety women and two men, I introduced the "popular action" assignment in order to use experiential strategies to meet these goals. Through activism, students could engage in consciousness-raising, feel empowered to express their own perspectives and the perspectives of women on a range of issues, challenge male bias in various forms, and reflect on ways that Women's Studies could remain connected to women's movements. Students could also gain a more personal and nuanced appreciation of what feminist struggles entail and how much effort was needed to secure the rights and freedoms from which many women benefit today.

The assignment itself was a consciousness-raising one in the sense that it emphasized student learning through dialogue, praxis and reflecting on lived experience, as well as development of a sense of power to transform reality. It further aimed to engage and educate students outside the course on a range of women's issues and aspects of feminist politics, and, in so doing, to build a more gender-conscious community. Specifically, I asked students to take action on campus to raise awareness about an issue of their choice, the university campus being one of the few spaces that young people can fully appropriate as their own. The action had to be public, relatively short (under two hours) and interactive. The overall goal was to bring together "fundamental aspects of a feminist pedagogical praxis: making connections between feminist theory and feminist practice, and personal transformation" (Rexroat 2002, 102).

Students had to present an analysis of their actions that highlighted the reasons why they chose their issues and identified key readings and sources they used to deepen their understandings. They also had to state why they chose the actions they did as well as how they were received and whether or not they "worked", what lessons and skills they learned, and their observations and feelings about the process. As Nancy Naples points out, these kinds of projects can "teach lessons in politics, collective action, and feminist analyses" and "help students develop investigatory and political skills that can complement a developing critical consciousness" (2002b, 71).

Fears and Feelings

At first, many students were reluctant to do an assignment that required public, collective activity on campus. They were also afraid of having to "represent" feminism in the campus space (Moulds 2004). This fear of feminism could be a result of its demonization, fear of politics, of being considered lesbian or rejected by men, and fear of reprisal (Mohammed 2003). Perhaps it was also linked to perceptions that social movements are things of the past, or a sense of powerlessness to change the rules of the game (Rinehart 2002, 27). Students also thought the assignment required too much effort, did not like to work in groups and wanted something simpler, individualistic and private. Some were also worried about their grades.

Nonetheless, some students who considered themselves feminists soon began to suggest ideas that they had and still others were simply excited by the assignment. Rather than blaming students for not being part of the "women's movement", Patricia Mohammed suggests that we also recognize the generational context within which students encounter feminism as "an amorphous set of ideas and practices" rather than the "more defined and public feminism" of the 1960s (2003, 27). The success of (liberal) feminism over the past decades has also meant that many young women simply do not feel oppressed, do not identify feelings or experiences of oppression with patriarchal capitalism, and increasingly understand empowerment in terms of "difference", personal choice and individual freedom. All these aspects are also part of a "post-feminist" trend which relies on ideas regarding women's rights and power, even as it rejects too close a link with its feminist mother (Barriteau 2002).

Issues

In the middle of the semester we began to talk more about the assignment, having by this time completed course sections on the goals of Women's

Studies, women's movements and feminisms, the politics of consciousness-raising and conscientization, the significance of telling women's stories, conceptualizing masculinism, forms of violence within patriarchies and issues emerging from women's bodily experiences. Later sections would deal with activism within academia, "Third World" or decolonizing feminisms, and aspects of the "Third Wave". These themes shaped students' approaches to the assignment, their choices of foci and the analyses that they brought to their issues.

By the time real planning began for the actions, the majority of students began to get excited about the possibility of their own activities. Their aim was to create greater consciousness of what it means to be female in a society that privileges males, and some females over others. It was also to enable greater analysis of the individual and structural factors that create this situation and these relationships of power (Antrobus 2004, 41). In the end, they chose topics ranging from violence, pornography and abortion, to Afro-Trinidadian women's hair, female drug abuse, body image and the naming of women's body parts.

While some of these topics dovetailed with course readings and themes, they were prominent issues in popular discourse and in students' minds in late 2006. Reproductive rights were being hotly contested in the lead-up to the formation of a Draft National Gender Policy and close to two-thirds of the class knew someone who had had an illegal abortion; students were keenly observing the campaigns for and reactions to "gay marriage" in the United States; newspapers were highlighting stories about pornography being made and watched on cell phones in secondary schools across the country; and there was a series of rapes around campus that was drawing the attention of the Guild of Students. Portrayals of women's bodies in Jamaican dancehall music and US rap were also issues that students felt great ambivalence about, given their ubiquity in Trinidadian popular culture. Thus, overall, as Naples (2002b) points out with regard to her students' choices of action, the most prevalent area of concern was violence against women.[5]

Students' foci also showed how they "understand what counts as politics" (Naples 2002b, 82). These kinds of choices reflected a very personal level of concern rather than cognizance of issues and analyses regarding, for example, class inequity, ethnic difference and tensions, religion, globalization, trans-portation difficulties for women, food prices, minimum wage levels, patient rights, women's political participation, environmental conservation and war. Students didn't bring a sense of global, institutional or structural analysis to class discussions, and in many ways I failed to explore adequately how food security, human rights, state health care, international trade rules or simply economic inequality were areas for feminist analysis and action.

Because of this omission, the students' consciousness-raising strategies did not adequately "provide the context through which we can recognize how social structural dynamics such as capitalism, colonialism, or racism shape our experiences" (Naples 2002a, 10). As a brief moment for engaging in public deliberation, and one largely given meaning through students' own experiences or interests, the assignment can be critiqued for failing to transcend the local or create sustainable change. As Nancy Naples observes, "issue-based community activism often contributes to a narrow focus that renders invisible the larger political and economic factors in which the particular concern is embedded. Therefore, group members often have difficulty extending their political and economic analysis beyond the immediate context" (2002b, 92). Nonetheless, students' choices for actions also signalled the potential offered by a politics that emerges from personal concerns, and the possibilities for solutions that depend on the power of individual choices.

Sexuality

In terms of the actions themselves, many students (especially younger ones) liked the idea of being provocative, explicit and rebellious, and in many ways focusing on aspects of sexual politics allowed them to do so. I understood their sentiment. Yet, their actions also opened them to the risk of representing problematic perspectives.

For example, it was important that students engaged in the anti-pornography campaign consider all sides of the debates among feminists about pornography as well as some of the perspectives presented by sex-positive feminists and sex worker unions. Similarly, I did not want the students looking at song lyrics to fall easily into a censorial and simplistic approach that demanded moralistic and narrow, middle-class notions of respectability and asexuality for women and men.

At the same time, the students who focused on music designed posters that

Gabrielle J. Hosein

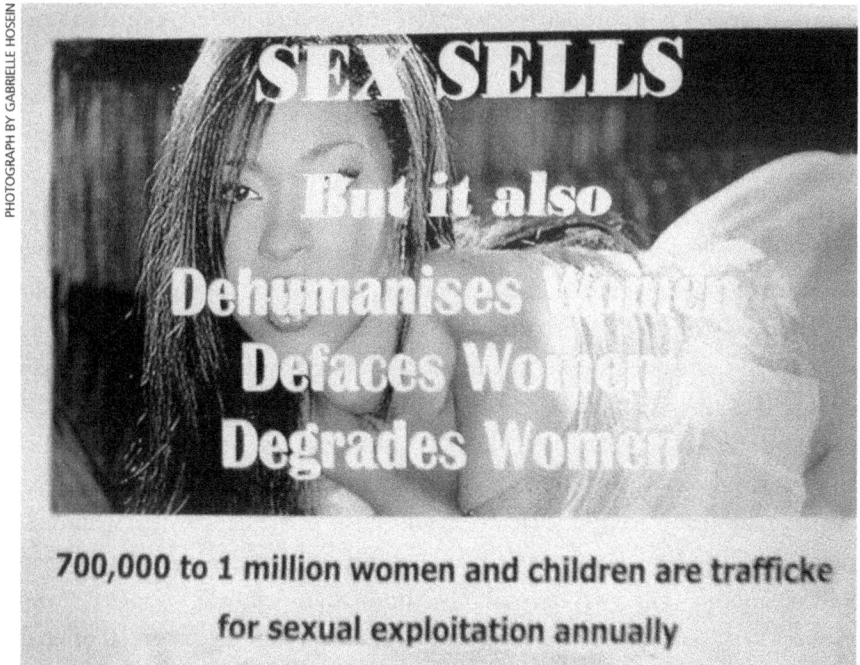

Figure 13.1: Image from an anti-pornography poster campaign.

sometimes had explicit photos of women from dancehall competitions or from rap music videos, and we discussed the ways their advertising problematically relied on women's bodies to generate interest in their workshops. I had long discussions with the students whose action was titled "Cuntspeak" (Caputi 1996) about the dilemmas regarding re-appropriating terms and the difficulties of changing the ways they are popularly used. I also pointed out to the students who made a vagina (out of brown corduroy and pink cloth) in which they put information about women's bodies and sexual health, how problematic it was that women and men had to put their hands inside to get the information. In general, students showed both a naiveté and an implicit sense of power about wielding sexuality within the more conservative campus space.

Reactions

Campus students' reactions to the popular actions varied. The anti-pornography campaign posters were graffitied and some torn down. The students paid close attention to the comments and participated in many conversations among students about the posters. The workshop on song lyrics and depictions of women was lively, with at least a dozen men and women vociferously debating different perspectives at any one time. The pillow-sized vagina with information inside attracted a huge amount of attention, causing men and women to try to figure out how informed they really were about women's sex organs. Similarly, the open-air workshop on female and male condoms drew a crowd of at least fifty participating students.

One group who had chosen to do an action on the naming of women's genitalia had debated endlessly whether to put the word "cunt" on their posters or, if it was too "offensive", to instead put a flower where the "u" should be. Within hours, someone had graffitied the "u" back onto the posters and, when the students saw it, they tried to reflect on their initial fears and explore what the change signified. I followed around a similar action, titled "Cuntspeak", as the students handed out the material they had prepared and started discussions with men and women about the shame often associated with women's bodies.

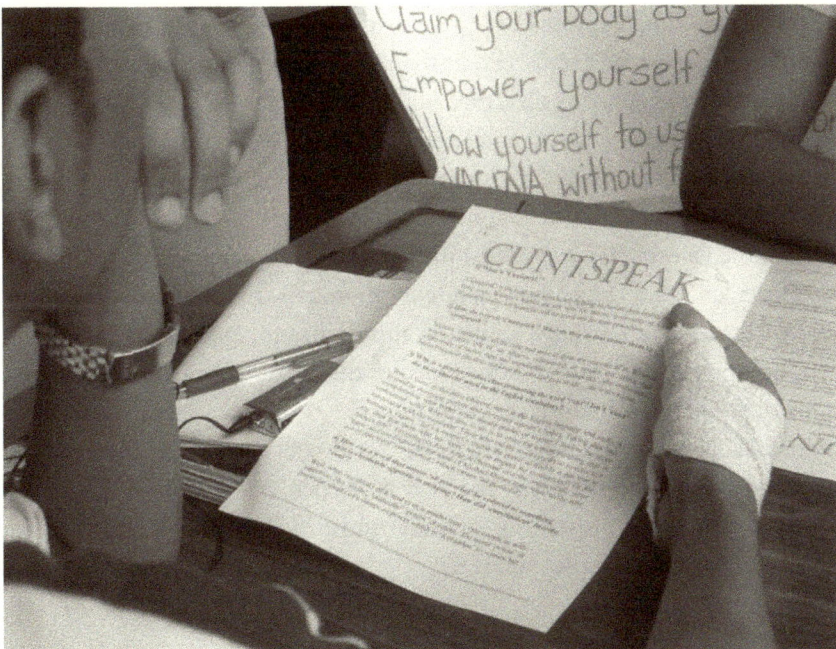

Figure 13.2: Presenting clear arguments for a political position.

The majority of *both* male and female campus students whom I observed or spoke to, or who saw or participated, said that they welcomed the popular actions because they provided interesting and relevant topics for students to debate and learn more about. Both women and men often commented that "this is what university life should be about".

Students who chose topics such as sexual harassment, domestic violence and rape were surprised that they shared the experience of having men respond to them that women sexually harass, beat and rape men too, and that the students should be *equally* dealing with men's experiences as much as they were trying to raise awareness about women's. Those responses also highlighted popular, and particularly male, notions that gender is about "doing for men what you would do for women", achieving "balance" and showing how men are victims (of women) as much as women are "victims" of men. Thus, although many men whom I observed and spoke to found the actions interesting and participated in lively debates and discussions, there were also those who sought to undermine discussions or label the young women as sexists who were "discriminating against men" because their actions focused on women.

Some men simply refused to believe that women experience violence at the hands of men to a far greater extent than men do at women's hands, refused to discuss that violence against men and boys is largely at the hands of other males,[6] or insisted on giving anecdotal stories the same validity as statistics which the students presented. Both male and female students were confused, angered, saddened, frustrated and, often, totally surprised at these reactions, despite the fact that we had talked in class about preparing for them.

These aspects of the popular action assignment highlight how pedagogical choices and strategies shape students' approaches to and understandings of feminist politics. I want to acknowledge the biases that defined my own approach, ones that I continue to try to make explicit as well as critique and contextualize in my teaching. As I discuss further below, it is important to be aware of the tension between "the goal of deepening students' awareness of feminist issues and promoting activities most likely to advance a feminist agenda" (Bojar and Naples 2002, ix).

Liberal Warnings

In *Professing Feminism* (2003), Daphne Patai and Noretta Koertge argue that any classroom driven by politics will eventually degenerate from education to indoctrination. For them, Women's Studies, because it is defined by feminist teaching, "is in the strict sense of the word totalitarian; refusing boundaries, entering the private lives of students and aiming to bring all concerns into a 'coherent and unified' pattern" (278). Their position is that Women's Studies' emphasis on the study of women and gender *and* the correction of social justice essentially leads to hostility among women and people of differing identities and views, rejection of knowledge produced by men, subordination of educational aims to political goals, silencing of dissenting views, brainwashing, academic separatism, rigidity and policing of thought, "politics-plus-therapy" (ibid.), belligerent and separatist militancy, anti-intellectualism and use of staff with inadequate academic credentials and capacity in the classroom. They describe an angry kind of Women's Studies that is hostile to "logic, the analysis of arguments, quantitative reasoning, objective evaluation of evidence, [and] fair-minded consideration of opposing views – modes of thinking central to intellectual life" (xiv).

From this perspective, Women's Studies is bound to implode. If it is too committed to the teaching of a liberal education, activists in and especially outside of the academy malign it as elitist, apolitical and even masculinist. If it gives in to these political charges of reinforcing hegemonic masculinity, it becomes a space for ideology, not education (ibid., 168–71, 178–82). For this reason, Patai and Koertge would fundamentally critique Charlotte Bunch's view that Women's Studies is the academic arm of feminism. They argue that Women's Studies uses dangerous "proselytizing" tactics such as providing comfort and support for neophytes, denouncing the enemy, and engaging in rituals of confession and celebration to keep the faithful pure and committed (81). Reliance on bias and ostracism to challenge androcentrism in actuality becomes mimicry of its power, creating "a closed worldview" (183). Furthermore, emphasis on discussion of students' feelings reproduces the traditionally gendered split between intellect and emotion (3).

Patai and Koertge argue that the feminism that defines Women's Studies is "not merely about equal rights for women or the empirical and theoretical study of gender roles and their pervasive effects in society". Rather, it "bids to be a totalizing scheme resting on a grand theory, one that is as all inclusive as Marxism, as assured of its ability to unmask hidden meanings as Freudian psychology, and as fervent in its condemnation of apostates as evangelical fundamentalism" (183). These authors contend that feminist scholars "lock students into one stage of emotional and intellectual development . . . inculcate attitudes of hostility and condescension to all prefeminist knowledge and nonfeminist individuals", and misread the purpose of academia in terms of transforming students' identities (196).

Professing Feminism was compelling reading, making me question my teaching and facilitation of the popular action assignment. One definition of Women's Studies which closely describes the goals of the introductory course was critiqued by Patai and Koertge (2003, 168–69). The authors comment that nothing in this conception "suggests that it might be the business of Women's Studies to foster research in, or at least, make students aware of, women's history, women's literature, or recent social science work on women and gender. Instead, all stated goals seek to promote processes and attitudes, and to stake out psychological and pedagogical 'space'" (169). Quoting an interviewee, Patai and Koertge conclude that "there *is* bound to be a relationship between feminism as a political enterprise and Women's Studies, but that you *can't* collapse the two, because then everything Women's Studies people do is judged by some political result, and then it's not scholarship anymore, it's something else" (29).

Challenging Perspectives

I have included so much of Patai and Koertge's critique because their warnings, though not new, should be taken seriously. In the anglophone Caribbean, academic feminism, which is the context for my teaching, needs to acknowledge when and why departments may be experienced as combat zones (Castello 2006; Soares 2006). We need to step back continually and look at how and what we teach, and why. We need to be cognizant about what female and male students' feedback suggests is their experience in our classrooms, and the utility of our course material. Nonetheless, after exploring their arguments, I conclude that activism can contribute to teaching in the spirit of liberal education in a way that Patai and Koertge deem impossible.

The popular action assignment highlights this idea because it shows how, through activism, students can be exposed to a wide range of debates, men's views, perspectives on masculinity and tough critiques of their positions on issues. At the same time, the assignment meets what a liberal view considers legitimate academic objectives: "to find and publicize information about the lives and works of women who had been forgotten and overlooked, and to make women's lives a primary focus of inquiry" (Patai and Koertge 2003, 115). I argue that, as a pedagogical strategy, the popular actions enable and encourage male and female students to "challenge received orthodoxy" (120), including feminist kinds.

The assignment required students to use the Internet and scholarship from both within and outside of the course to develop greater knowledge of the issues on which they acted. None of this information was necessarily used uncritically. One group, for example, wanted to explore the issue of abortion in Trinidad and Tobago. The group included members who held both pro- and anti-choice positions. When the young man in the group came to

Figure 13.3: Using popular theatre to create discussion on abortion.

me for more information, he said that they were going to present a pro-choice position because that is what the majority of members advocated, and the other group members were women. Instead, I suggested that they pay attention to the fact that, within the group, there was a debate and that this could be the basis for their action. The group then organized a discussion in which they presented differing arguments about abortion to participants and created a space where they could be debated. The young man later reported that, through the discussion, group members came to realize that there were criticisms of their views that they had not considered, that there were questions they needed to do more research on, and that they had agreed on some points that surprised them.

If not before, certainly after the popular actions were complete, students who advocated specific positions on issues such as pornography and abortion took more seriously the advice that they should prepare thoroughly by having a clear idea of their argument and its critiques before starting their actions. They realized how much clarity is involved in defending a position. They also emerged with a greater understanding of the debates, nuances and dilemmas surrounding their issues and, particularly, through discussions with the wider student population, came to appreciate how few easy answers exist.

The students whose action focused on music lyrics, for example, had to contend with the fact that audiences give lyrics very different meanings, or even no meanings at all. Thus, even if their peers agreed with their critiques, the songs students focused on retained wider meanings as well, and pointed to multivalence in everyday life and culture. All students learned a great deal from having to engage in public debate with others who held a wide variety of perspectives, including stereotypes about women and feminism.

We discussed the different theoretical approaches underpinning varying actions, and how students' ideas and goals fell within or crossed over different feminist frameworks. The assignment enabled a majority of the students to understand the significance of course readings to their own analyses and the debates they encountered. Finally, it made students evaluate both mainstream and feminist perspectives insofar as they reflected and explained their experiences (Lubelska 1991, 43).

In discussions with students about their actions, I emphasised that they did not have to do everything right to learn from the assignment. In fact, they often pointed out what they could have done differently. Their task was to write an almost ethnographic account of their action, noting statements made by them and others, their reactions and feelings, and the lessons they learned. In this way, they learned about gathering and assessing information, applying concepts, presenting their perspectives, working in groups, and observing, documenting and thinking critically about their experiences. At another level, they also often had ideas about how they could have expressed their own and listened to others' opinions, and managed meetings and established achievable goals during the planning process. As Naples points out, "after a short period of frustration and resistance at the very beginning of the course" students start to participate in and understand more about "their own learning process and political development" (Naples 2002b, 85, 88–89).

Overall, students also came to appreciate the difficult and sustained work that is needed to achieve the thorough and long-term changes from which they benefit and often continue to seek. In this sense, the assignment did create greater cognizance of some of the challenges to feminist struggles on a range of issues. Many students said that they gained an insider's view on the hostilities directed at feminists and feminisms or just against women and men speaking out on behalf of women and gender justice. Given the fact that, at the beginning of term, some of the female students said that they feared the class would make them "too feminist", much of the feedback was about both female and male students' greater confidence in identifying as or with feminists.

One thing that I think this kind of assignment attempts and, to some extent, accomplishes is to provide another basis for observation, questioning, debate and analysis. More than liberal critiques allow, it enables the classroom to be a "place for debate and the free expression and exchange of varied ideas and opinions, especially when the topics under discussion are open-ended and controversial" (Patai and Koertge 2003, 82). It also alerts students to the fact that sources of knowledge both inside and outside the classroom contribute to learning, and that it is possible to include different perspectives in a syllabus in this way.

These are useful considerations as I continue to refine how the popular actions fit within and provide another perspective on the goals defining the relationship of Women's Studies to academia. As I examine "both instruction and social vision" (Naples 2002a, 15), I am also encouraged to look at the extent to which my classroom practices break down my own authority, promote collaboration with students, and facilitate practice rather than receipt of a critical consciousness (Rinehart 2002, 26). As Karen Bojar points out, I need to continue to examine more critically my own assumptions about what constitutes activism and how these underlying assumptions shape my curriculum choices, and share this interrogation of my own values with my students (2002, 54). To this end, the analysis exposes areas for improvement so it can contribute to an academic feminism that "truly engages in political discussion of gender injustice" (Naples 2002a, 15).[7]

Gender and the Man Question

The popular actions raised more than pedagogical dilemmas and considerations. They also enabled me to observe conceptions of gender in practice, and the challenges of engaging men. In the Caribbean, feminist literature has wrestled with the implications of the concept of gender (Tang Nain and Bailey 2003; Barriteau 2003b; Bailey and Leo-Rhynie 2004). Pointing to at least ten different meanings and the fact that "in everyday usage gender can mean almost anything" (Barriteau 2003c, 33), Caribbean feminist V. Eudine Barriteau observes that "many scholars and practitioners are deploying the notion that a shift to gender means a change from analysing relations of domination in women's lives to a simultaneous focus on women and men in all aspects of social investigations" (43). Gender is becoming a "barren" concept, she argues, and is being used to delegitimize a focus on women as subjects of knowledge (34).

My students' popular actions showed this technology of power at work (de Lauretis 1987). In the campus space, some male students insisted that women justify their perspectives in terms of men's experiences and androcentric (male-centred) views on what constituted valid knowledge. Students also encountered how popular conceptions of gender re-centred hegemonic masculinities on the one hand, and promoted a discourse that positions men as victims (of women) on the other. Such responses "centred on the idea that Caribbean men are in crisis and that they are being marginalized by the activities of Caribbean states, the women's movement, and the decisions and lifestyle choices of individual women who may or may not be part of any organized women's networks" (Barriteau 2003a, 204).

Conceptions of gender also opened a space for critique based on numbers.

If there were more women in the class then men, the argument followed that this imbalance must result from women's discrimination against men or men's feelings of discrimination, or from women's not taking enough effort to make Women's Studies and feminism relevant to men and their preoccupations. Finally, narrowly defining the concept of gender as concerned with "balance" enabled both male and female campus students to argue that Women's Studies should be equally as concerned with men as it is with women, and made feminists "responsible" (as women traditionally are) for equally looking after women's and men's needs and problems.

Gender refers to "complex systems of personal and social relations of power through which women and men are socially created and maintained and through which they gain access to, or are allocated status, power and material resources within society" (Barriteau 2003c, 30). Yet, as Barriteau accurately notes, "the recognition that men are equally gendered does not alter the reality that social relations predominantly benefit men" (36). It is this very point that was often lost in the popular actions while students struggled to recognize and

Figure 13.4: Engaging men.

understand the legitimizing power men and masculinity (still) asserted over what women and men do.

The assignment gave them a chance both to see androcentrism and masculinism, which naturalize male domination and masculine supremacy, and to confront feminist approaches. It prompted them to wrestle with questions about focusing on women, engaging men and the space created by popular notions of "gender". On this basis, they could engage in debates about how to include men and theorizations of masculinity in a course on women's experiences and perspectives, and feminist politics. They could also identify the impact of male marginalization discourses (Miller 1989 and 1991; Lindsay 2002) on feminist and women's activism. Rather than deploying a separatist stance or fundamentally excluding men, the popular actions put feminist approaches to Women's Studies in the hot seat. They also compelled class discussion about the relationship among men, gender and feminism in a Women's Studies course in Trinidad and Tobago.

Male students have always been welcome to enrol and participate in anglophone Caribbean women's and gender studies courses, and female students frequently express a wish that there were more men in the class so that they could hear their perspectives and reactions to course material. Philips and Westland (1992, 40) suggest that female students wish to have more male lecturers and students in classes so that men can be "educated" about women and feminism, and because they assume that men bring more "balance" to classroom discussion and can represent the "other" side. In contrast to long-standing research about the impact of men on female students' learning (Philips and Westland 1992), my students did not seem to think that the presence of male students inhibited their discussion.

In class, I highlight that gender is relational as well as institutional and ideological, exemplify how hegemonic gender ideals negatively affect different kinds of women and men, investigate how women's subordination negatively affects men, and explore men's responses. This doesn't mean studying women in relation to men. Yet, it does foster "a classroom space that moves beyond 'women's space' toward a *feminist* space characterized by constant (re)negotiation and an attentiveness to the voices and experiences that continue to be attacked and marginalized in society in general" (Hughes 1999, 75). Following from this, I do not have different goals for female and male students. I expect all of them to learn more about women's experiences and perspectives, to take

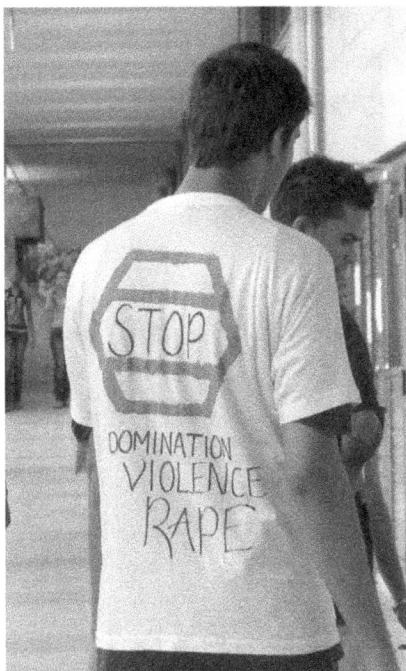

Figure 13.5: The issues also enable exploration of diverse masculinities.

action on women's issues, and to engage with feminist insights in their reading, assignments and reflections. I don't privilege male students' perspectives in class or expect men to take an oppositional "male" stance.[8]

Although boyfriends and male friends of female students sometimes attend classes (and participate), men and masculinity have generally not been an issue because of low numbers of male enrolment, as well as an historical and contemporary openness to male allies in Caribbean feminism (Mohammed 1998). Nonetheless, the popular actions made female and male students recognize dilemmas and debates raised by the "man question" in feminism. They encountered both ideological and intellectual critiques of Women's Studies' politics and focus on women, and engaged them as part of their process of learning. In this regard, the assignment enabled students to realize that the confrontation between masculinism and feminism is lived in more nuanced, contradictory and problematic ways than they imagined and hoped (Prendergast and Grace 2006). Through this process, students also came to appreciate how some conceptions of gender assume a false equality between the sexes and "may mean that women disappear (again) within the generality of humanity" (Kennedy and Piette 1991, 39).

In this sense, the popular actions stimulated both an interest and an investment in thinking about the significance of conceptions of gender and feminist engagement with both women and men. From this, we could discuss the split between women and gender, and differences among Women's Studies, Gender Studies and Masculinity Studies. Together, we could also reflect on how men and issues of masculinity were incorporated into the course. Could the actions have been on issues of masculinity? Should Women's Studies equally centre on men's experiences?

The assignment also highlighted the dilemmas involved in men's reckoning with gender. As Patricia Mohammed observes, feminism and women's everyday awareness and defence of their rights have stimulated a "gender consciousness"[9] among men and renegotiation of gender roles. For this reason, the burgeoning third feminist "wave" is also defined by "the adjustments or retaliations being made by masculinity and men" (Mohammed 2003, 14). Finally, recognizing the significance of these questions beyond intellectual debate, students could return to the readings to see how Caribbean feminist and women's writings spoke to their own positions and dilemmas.

Experiential Knowledge and Feminist Engagements

In this analysis, I have explored the relationship between feminism and education, and have argued that activism has a place in academia. Women's Studies courses should remain committed to expanding both feminist theorizing and activism, and I argue that popular actions do this effectively. Feminist activism, through its reliance on peer, cooperative and independent learning strategies, can expose students to wide sources of knowledge for interrogating ideas, writings and actions, as well as politics, subjectivity and social change.

While I agree with critiques and warnings of feminists teaching Women's Studies, I also find that Patai and Koertge's (2003) depiction of feminist academia does not fit my own experience – the reason why it stimulated me to make my own assessment. I first became active in feminism when I began to participate in activities at the Women's Centre at the University of Toronto. I also began to be involved with environmental, immigrant, LGBT (lesbian, gay, lesbian, bisexual and transgendered), media, artist and other groups, and non-governmental organizations. As I took only one Women's Studies class on women and international development during my undergraduate final year, it was through this participation that I learned about women's experiences and perspectives, and feminist politics. It was as an activist that I applied to the Centre for Gender and Development Studies (CGDS) at the University of the West Indies to do graduate research.

It was when I enrolled in the Master of Philosophy programme in Gender and Development Studies in 1997 that I took my first feminist theory classes. As I experienced it, there was never an insistence on radical feminist positions among CGDS staff, nor on conscious participation in a "lesbian continuum" (Patai and Koertge 2003, 57). Despite Indo-Trinidadian writings about exclusion (Baksh-Soodeen 1998), and generational, ideological, ethnic, national and class tensions in Caribbean feminist movements, I did not experience divisionary identity politics in my courses. It is possible that others had different perceptions or experiences, and certainly personal and "office" politics remain bases for contention among feminists in Caribbean gender studies departments.

In the centre's courses, I never experienced hostility to quantitative analysis, mathematics, science (though there is an emphasis on the social sciences and humanities), rationality, academic standards or men. In fact, to the contrary, the CGDS was soon involved in masculinity studies and in offering a course, co-taught with a man, on men and masculinities in the Caribbean. Moreover, I never experienced pressure to be loyal "to an ideological agenda rather than empirical adequacy and logical consistency" (Patai and Koertge 2003, 366), and I was encouraged to appeal to and recognize expert learning and to practise methodological rigour (173). There was never an overly emotional tenor to classroom discussion. Additionally, although I could "become personally and emotionally invested in the intellectual positions" (75) we explored, there was also an emphasis on questioning, observation and intellectual pursuit of answers.

In this way, Women's Studies courses in the anglophone Caribbean appear to serve a very different set of academic, feminist and identity politics from the North American ones surveyed by Patai and Koertge. Recognizing this departure is a key starting point for engaging literature on feminist teaching and movement-building.

In fact, the teaching, research and activism of the centre inspired me to produce sound research, to think critically about my politics, to be involved in changing unequal relations, and to teach students to think analytically, write persuasively and reflect consciously on the knowledge that they gain. As one of Patai and Koertge's informants suggest, the questions that students ask "*can* be informed by their politics – and inevitably they will be – and the more conscious they are of that, the better. But when they're devising ways to find answers, they have to adhere to the methods of our discipline, because it *checks* them against their assumptions and their biases, and in some ways their politics" (2003, 39).

The popular action assignment thus aimed to provide, even if only briefly, personal, emotional, rational, public, collective and organizational sources of knowledge to complement academic ones. As Sue Lees (1991, 91) identifies, "Women's Studies has always had the aim of bridging the gap between the subjective and experiential knowledge on the one hand, and academic knowledge on the other." The debate is whether using activism as a pedagogical strategy makes the classroom like a movement or a non-governmental organization or a campaign, instead of a place for interrogating ideas.

To this end, Patai and Koertge suggest that "what needs to be investigated is whether students are at all receptive to reasoned arguments against the basic tenets of their own framework or, to the contrary, have learned to deploy various criticism-deflecting strategies in an effort to keep their acquired ideas inviolate" (2003, 176). They argue that, ultimately, introductory courses should "perform what should be one of their vital functions: to act as independent critics of an important political movement that is going on around us" (211) and to promote "critical examination of feminist discourse itself" (181). I agree.

Informed analysis and reflective action for change is the basis of feminism, whether or not in the academy. We need to teach students to think critically about feminism and women's movements rather than enforce them and to produce, more than anything else, intellectual autonomy by using full and balanced information. After all, as Baumgardner and Richards (2000, 303) point out, "activism requires thinking outside of the box". We also need, therefore, to teach about the history of women's advocacy so that students can be aware of both past struggles and strategies to confront such problems, and of how women and men were personally involved and affected in different ways. In other words, we need to encourage students to pursue questions of gender justice both in and outside of the classroom.

If, as the course outline states, feminism is "a conscious opposition to gender hierarchies that structurally oppress some groups in society, particularly women, while privileging others", it requires intellectual and political engagement. It also requires making connections among Women's Studies, feminist organizations, women's struggles for autonomy and empowerment, progress achieved regarding the status of women (and girls) in society, and a range of social issues. At the very least, it involves a pursuit of knowledge, methods for assessment and ways of contributing to ideas, debate and change.

Added to these things, activism and reflection on feminism, even when imperfect, highlight and often further the possibilities for radically questioning all positions. Perhaps I cannot escape my bias and my training (indoctrination?). Nonetheless, debate about pedagogy, the purpose of universities, and their relationship to politics is useful for showing the contradictions that intersect with feminism, which anyone who teaches Women's Studies constantly works through. Therefore, this chapter participates in "probing the underlying assumptions that lead us to encourage some types of projects rather than others and to engage our students in the process of analyzing our choices and in developing a long-term strategy for building a powerful feminist movement" of both women and men (Bojar and Naples 2002, 8).

Conclusion

Women's Studies courses in the twenty-first-century Caribbean have to make sense in a historical moment characterized by the mainstreaming and de-politicization of gender, men's gender consciousness and the masculinist backlash against feminism, and the success of liberal feminism as well as a wave of "post-feminism". These courses have to define their differences from, as well as ways of co-existing with, Gender Studies and Masculinity Studies. Together, these subjects are specific to this phase of feminisms and the current status of girls and women. They point to the challenges of and possibilities for questioning and redefining the university, disciplinarity, and the construction of knowledge. They are also a basis for thinking about how academic feminism situates itself within the university and wider society, and enable us to use the anglophone Caribbean as a case study.

The relationship among feminist politics, the concept of gender and women's realities will be key to the future of feminism. Men's solidarities, resistances and redefinitions will also add nuances and new forms and meanings. Caribbean feminist literature has long engaged the intellectual and political problems associated with institutionalizing and professionalizing feminist thought and action, and what these problems mean for the relationship between academia and activism (Vassell 2004; McKenzie 2004).

Still, far more can be said about pedagogical strategies, classroom experiences, and the nitty gritty of feminist, counter-hegemonic teaching. How are Caribbean feminisms continuing to work through the connections between

Women's Studies and women's movements? What are the intellectual, pedagogical and institutional implications? I use experiential approaches to
knowledge to exemplify how feminist activism can promote research, analysis,
reasoning and communication skills. Far from inevitable totalitarianism in
teaching, such methods additionally enable students to evaluate the utility of
feminist concepts and critiques while wrestling with explanations for gender
relations and strategies for addressing women's realities. For this reason, as a
space for both academic and political learning, Women's Studies in the
Caribbean is here to stay.

Notes

1. The Centre for Gender and Development Studies was established in 1993 as a
    regional institute for feminist teaching, research and outreach. It has units on each
    of the three University of the West Indies campuses in Mona, Jamaica; Cave Hill,
    Barbados; and St Augustine, Trinidad and Tobago (Leo-Rhynie 2003).

2. Catherine MacKinnon (1990, 143–44) defines consciousness-raising as "a method of
    analysis, mode of organising, form of practice and technique of political interven-
    tion" to "unpack the concrete moment-to-moment meaning of being a woman in a
    society that men dominate, by looking at how women see their everyday experience
    in it".

3. Like patriarchy, masculinism is an ideology of male supremacy and domination that
    shapes ideological and material relations of gender. Its increasing use over the last
    decade signals a critique of the universalizing way that the concept of patriarchy was
    used and a challenge to the analysis of patriarchy as being centred in male bodies or
    the static category of "men" (Parpart and Zalewski 2008).

4. Renate Klein points out that there are many different "brands" of Women's Studies.
    She writes: "Women who define themselves as reformist or liberal feminist tend to
    see Women's Studies primarily as remedial: as the 'study of women', as 'adding
    women on' to the curriculum. A second group, women who identify as socialist fem-
    inists, tend to favour the integration of feminist courses into the traditional
    disciplines and many of them are taken with the development of gender studies. Yet
    another group, radical feminists, are the main promoters of women-centred,
    'autonomous' Women's Studies, preferably organized in independent programmes
    . . . They perceive Women's Studies as an entity in its own right and see knowledge
    generated in Women's Studies as valid in relation to women" (Klein 1991, 77). She
    further observes that liberal feminist students concomitantly see Women's Studies
    as helping them to acquire skills to manoeuvre around remaining sexism and to suc-
    ceed in the world. For socialist-oriented students, Women's Studies can contribute

to social change, including challenges to racism and classism. Somewhat differently, radical feminist students expect to encounter "a woman-centred power base where they can acquire intellectual and political skills" (78).

5. Primarily, her students' choice of topic for their action projects included preventing "sexual harassment and acquaintance rape as well as increasing safety on campus", eating disorders, women's reproductive health, contraception, sexually transmitted infections, child care and gender socialization, negative images of women in the media and sexist advertising, promoting Women's Studies and issues of discrimination against various groups of women (Naples 2002b, 82–85).

6. Patai and Koertge devote an entire page to an episode in which a Women's Studies lecturer made a student feel that the lecturer completely denied the importance of men's experiences of rape by other men, and humiliated her by suggesting she wanted to excuse male victims for their wrongs to women (2003, 84). In contrast, I encourage my students to affirm that men are raped, and to point out that the rape of boys and men, as with all physical and sexual violence, occurs largely at the hands of men. In affirming that this is the case, and something that men and boys fear, the students can then point out the ways that patriarchy negatively affects men and boys, and make connections among violence, masculinity and men's lives. They also affirm that many men do not exercise patriarchal hegemony or dominance in their personal relationships and practices.

7. This paper is also the basis for continuing research that seeks to provide evidence of pedagogical impact and student learning, and measures the congruence between teaching philosophy, intent and outcomes among the 2010 cohort of students.

8. In this regard, Glyn Hughes observes that introductory courses that appeal to men "can be a point of resistance to the mass-mediated, hegemonic masculinity, which imagines (and thereby conjures) the solidarity of other men clustering around kindred discourses of their own victimization . . . This particular victimization is a face of privilege, one self-righteously oblivious to its effects on Others, even viciously constructing them as the enemy. We need to . . . replace it with a set of skills: how to recognize one's own privilege at work; how privilege affects space . . . how to listen intently from a position of self-doubt. We might also not *deny* their sense of victimization so much as we name the real sources of that powerlessness while also refusing to let them settle on the notion that they *alone* (or to some *greater* degree) are the victims . . . the trick to getting men to engage feminism productively is to make . . . something that everyone can participate in: the critique and dismantling of privilege" (1999, 84).

9. Patricia Mohammed defines gender consciousness as "the self-awareness and confidence of one's rights and privileges as 'female' or 'male' in society, as well as the limits or oppressiveness [that] being male or female still imposes on the individual to realize their potential" (2003, 6).

References

Aaron, J., and S. Walby, eds. *Out of the margins: Women's Studies in the nineties.* London: Falmer.

Antrobus, P. 2004. Feminist activism: The CARICOM experience. In *Gender in the 21st century: Caribbean perspectives, visions and possibilities,* ed. B. Bailey and E. Leo-Rhynie, 34–57. Kingston: Ian Randle.

Bailey, B., and E. Leo-Rhynie, eds. 2004. *Gender in the 21st century: Caribbean perspectives, visions and possibilities.* Kingston: Ian Randle.

Baksh-Soodeen, R. 1998. Issues of difference in Caribbean feminist theory. *Feminist Review* 59 (Summer): 74–85.

Barriteau, E. 2002. Issues and challenges of Caribbean feminisms. Keynote address, Caribbean Feminisms workshop on recentring Caribbean feminisms. Centre for Gender and Development Studies and the Faculty of Law, University of the West Indies, Cave Hill, Barbados, 17 June.

———. 2003a. Conclusion: Beyond a backlash – The frontal assault on containing Caribbean women in the decade of the 1990s. In *Gender equality in the Caribbean: Reality or illusion?,* ed. G. Tang Nain and B. Bailey, 201–32. Kingston: Ian Randle.

———, ed. 2003b. *Confronting power, theorizing gender: Interdisciplinary perspectives in the Caribbean.* Kingston: University of the West Indies Press.

———. 2003c. Theorizing the shift from "woman" to "gender" in Caribbean feminist discourse. In *Confronting power, theorizing gender: Interdisciplinary perspectives in the Caribbean,* ed. E. Barriteau, 27–45. Kingston: University of the West Indies Press.

Baumgardner, J., and A. Richards. 2000. *Manifesta: Young women, feminism and the future.* New York: Farrar, Straus and Giroux.

Bojar, K. 2002. Teaching feminist activism: Probing our assumptions, analyzing our choices. In *Teaching feminist activism: Strategies from the field,* ed. K. Bojar and N. Naples, 54–70. New York: Routledge.

Bojar, K., and N. Naples, eds. 2002. *Teaching feminist activism: Strategies from the field.* New York: Routledge.

Caputi, J. 1996. Cuntspeak: Words from the heart of darkness. In *Radically speaking: Feminism reclaimed,* ed. D. Bell and R. Klein. London: Zed Books.

Castello, J. 2006. "Where have all the feminists gone": Learning lessons of a long time passed in the women's movement in the Caribbean. *Caribbean Quarterly* 52 (2–3): 1–13.

De Lauretis, T. 1987. *Technologies of gender: Essays on theory, film, and fiction.* Theories of Representation and Difference. Indianapolis: Indiana University Press.

Hughes, G. 1999. Revisiting the "men problem" in introductory Women's Studies classes. In *Teaching introduction to Women's Studies: Expectations and strategies,* ed. B. Winkler and C. DiPalma, 73–86. Westport, CT: Bergin and Garvey.

Kennedy, M., and B. Piette. 1991. Women's Studies on adult education and access courses. In *Out of the margins: Women's Studies in the nineties*, ed. J. Aaron and S. Walby, 30–40. London: Falmer.

Klein, R. 1991. Passion and politics in Women's Studies in the 1990s. In *Out of the margins: Women's Studies in the nineties*, ed. J. Aaron and S. Walby, 75–89. London: Falmer.

Lees, S. 1991. Feminist politics and Women's Studies: Struggle, not incorporation. In *Out of the margins: Women's Studies in the nineties*, ed. J. Aaron and S. Walby, 90–104. London: Falmer.

Leo-Rhynie, E. 2003. Gender Studies: Crossing boundaries, charting new direction. Paper presented at the tenth anniversary lecture of the Centre for Gender and Development Studies, University of the West Indies, St Augustine, Trinidad, 3 December.

Lindsay, K. 2002. Is the Caribbean male an endangered species? In *Gendered realities: Essays in Caribbean feminist thought*, ed. P. Mohammed, 56–82. Kingston: University of the West Indies Press.

Lubelska, C. 1991. Teaching methods in Women's Studies: Challenging the mainstream. In *Out of the margins: Women's Studies in the nineties*, ed. J. Aaron and S. Walby, 41–48. London: Falmer.

MacKinnon, C. 1990. Consciousness-raising. In *Issues in feminism: An introduction to Women's Studies,* ed. S. Ruth, 143–50. Mountain View, CA: Mayfield.

McKenzie, H. 2004. Shifting centres and moving margins: The UWI experience. In *Gender in the 21st century: Caribbean perspectives, visions and possibilities*, ed. B. Bailey and E. Leo-Rhynie, 397–416. Kingston: Ian Randle.

Miller, E. 1989. *The marginalization of the black male: Insights from the development of the teaching profession.* Rev. ed. Kingston: University of the West Indies Press.

———. 1991. *Men at risk*. Kingston: Jamaica Publishing House.

Mohammed, P. 1998. *Stories in Caribbean feminism: Reflections on the twentieth century.* St Augustine: Centre for Gender and Development Studies, University of the West Indies.

———. 2003. Like sugar in coffee: Third wave feminism and the Caribbean. *Social and Economic Studies* 52 (3): 5 –30.

Moulds, C. 2004. Feminist approaches to social justice: Activism and resistance in the Women's Studies classroom. In *Voices of a new generation: A feminist anthology*, ed. S. Weir and C. Faulkner, 108–20. Boston: Pearson.

Naples, N. 2002a. The dynamics of critical pedagogy, experiential learning, and feminist praxis in Women's Studies. In *Teaching feminist activism: Strategies from the field*, ed. K. Bojar and N. Naples, 9–21. New York: Routledge.

———. 2002b. Teaching community action in the introductory Women's Studies classroom. In *Teaching feminist activism: Strategies from the field*, ed. K. Bojar and N. Naples, 71–94. New York: Routledge.

Parpart, J.L., and M. Zalewski, eds. 2008. *Rethinking the man question: Sex, gender and violence in international relations.* London: Zed Books.

Patai, D., and N. Koertge. 2003. *Professing feminism: Education and indoctrination in Women's Studies.* Lanham, MD: Lexington Books.

Philips, D., and E. Westland. 1992. Men in Women's Studies classrooms. In *Working out: New directions for Women's Studies,* ed. H. Hinds, A. Phoenix and J. Stacy, 36–47. London: Falmer.

Prendergast, P., and H. Grace. 2006. Bringing the male voice to the gender agenda: The task of male organisations in the Caribbean. *Caribbean Quarterly* 52 (2–3): 14–21.

Rexroat, J. 2002. Bridging feminist theory and feminist practice in a senior seminar. In *Teaching feminist activism: Strategies from the field,* ed. K. Bojar and N. Naples, 95–107. New York: Routledge.

Rinehart, J. 2002. Collaborative learning, subversive teaching, and activism. In *Teaching feminist activism: Strategies from the field,* ed. K. Bojar and N. Naples, 22–35. New York: Routledge.

Rose, Ellen. 2002. Activism and the Women's Studies curriculum. In *Teaching feminist activism: Strategies from the field,* ed. K. Bojar and N. Naples, 108–20. New York: Routledge.

Ruth, S., ed. 1990. *Issues in feminism: An introduction to Women's Studies.* Mountainview, CA: Mayfield.

Soares, J. 2006. Addressing the tensions: Reflections on feminism in the Caribbean. *Caribbean Quarterly* 52 (2–3): 187–97.

Tang Nain, G., and B. Bailey, eds. 2003. *Gender equality in the Caribbean: Reality or illusion?* Kingston: Ian Randle.

Vassell, L. 2004. Feminisms, gender studies, activism. In *Gender in the 21st century: Caribbean perspectives, visions and possibilities,* ed. B. Bailey and E. Leo-Rhynie, 687–706. Kingston: Ian Randle.

14

Passionate Realities

Students' Perceptions of Sexuality at the University of the West Indies, Mona

ANNECKA MARSHALL

To name ourselves rather than be named we must first see ourselves. For some of us this will not be easy. So long unmirrored, we may have forgotten how we look. Nevertheless, we can't theorize in a void; we must have evidence.

– Lorraine O'Grady, "Olympia's Maid: Reclaiming Black Female Subjectivity"

Introduction

This chapter addresses female undergraduate students' beliefs about the regulation of sexuality in Jamaican society. I argue that silence and prejudice about multiple sexual identities and same-sex relationships restrict the potential of the classroom as a space to offer new debates about sexual liberation. The general argument that sexual diversity is abnormal, pathological, evil and a racial treachery limits students' willingness to appreciate choices of sexual lifestyles. My pedagogical approach broadens students' awareness of alternative sensuality in order to reduce the dangerous repression and victimization of people who are stigmatized as being sexually deviant. Increased dialogue about sexual variation can resocialize students to celebrate creative erotic autonomy. Research on understanding safer sex practices and the joy of different sexual desires has the capacity to work towards transforming local communities to redefine and embrace love instead of violence.

In lectures and tutorials I have asked students to query the limits of sexual acceptability and gender-crossing. My primary motivation in doing so is to counteract not only the primacy which is usually given to heterosexuality but also secrecy about divergent erotic encounters, in order to encourage students to recognize the restrictions which they themselves, and others, have placed on their sexualities. Knowledge about defying sexual stereotypes contributes to a healthier and more fulfilling eroticism that enhances students' sense of well-being and self-worth. My classes teach students that sexuality refers to erotic identities, feelings and pleasures that are culturally constructed and reinforced by gender, class, racist and ethnic power inequalities (Mohammed 1994; Vance 1984). Students learn to appreciate both that the term "all-sexual" refers to people who are "bisexual", "same-gender loving", "transgender" or "transsexual", and that their own experiences are significant (http://www.jflag.org).

This chapter examines the relevance of the relatively underresearched area of multiple sexual variants and sexual paraphilias. Sexual variants are practices that people engage in for variety, not as their preferred means of becoming sexually aroused. Sexual paraphilias describe the situation whereby an individual's only or preferred source of sexual gratification depends exclusively on being preoccupied with or satisfying persistent, compulsive and intense sexual urges that are typically considered unusual (King 2001). In pairs and in group-work, feminist dialogue about sexual variants and paraphilias is instrumental to developing an understanding of divergent ideas and sensual emancipation.

The chapter delves into the emotional and physical spectrum of erotic desires in Jamaica to demonstrate the importance of the social manipulation of sexuality in university courses and in wider society. It questions stigmatized sexual attitudes in an attempt to understand why some activities are ignored or regarded as being perverted as opposed to others. A questionnaire about sexual beliefs and behaviour was distributed to 160 female undergraduate students at the Mona campus. In particular, questions about what students considered to be appropriate sexual conduct, sexual variants and sexual paraphilias were asked. Students discuss the way in which power relationships dictate opinions about dynamic sexual identities, attraction and conduct. Caribbean women's sexualities are generally depicted in terms of cultural expectations regarding passivity, chastity, faithfulness, demureness, serial monogamy, procreation and financial obligations (Douglas, Reid and Reddock 2008). Despite cultural and religious opposition to various sexual antics, my analysis indicates that allegedly atypical behaviours are more wide-spread than we are aware of. The responses to the questionnaire, as well as conversations in lectures and tutorials, show divergences between students' cultural and religious notions about sexuality and their actual experiences.

Methodology

I initiated my research after being a guest on a local interactive radio pro-gramme entitled *Sex Fetish and Kinky Sex*. During this exciting debate, I identified core themes that I wanted to revise and pose as questions in a survey of female undergraduate students. During the four-hour radio show on RJR, forty male and five female callers discussed provocative and controversial sex-ual realities. The audience probed the necessity for increased sex education to know, accept and experiment with sexual behaviours that are perceived as being out of the ordinary without moral judgements about what is wrong and perverse. We addressed the correlation between pleasure, pain, danger and shame. Callers explained how they define and set their own personal param-eters about what is risky and liberating. They considered how sexual fetishism is typically regarded as an unnatural attachment to an inanimate object or body part in order to achieve sexual arousal. The callers confirmed Bruce M. King's assertion that male fantasies have more explicit and visual imagery than female fantasies, because of men's sexual lifestyles (King 2001). King claims that 90 per cent of women have romantic fantasies that frequently help arousal during sex (ibid.).

We addressed the degree to which a person's sexual fetishism also incorpo-rates concern about the feelings of partners. Callers questioned whether their own upbringing triggered the association between sexual behaviour, power, order, authority and taking control. They asserted that typically lonely and shy men who are unable to express themselves in intimate relationships con-centrate on sex in terms of kinky sensations (King 2001). Kinky sex describes sexual contact that mainstream society considers to be unhealthy, irregular and bizarre, such as sadomasochistic relations of pain, humiliation, domi-nance, discipline, bondage and submission (http://en.wikipedia.org/wiki /Kink_(sexual). Callers generally assumed that women are more emotionally

connected than men to sex, which women associate with loving feelings, spir-
ituality, safety and trust. (Appendix 14.1 provides details of the questions that
callers answered.)

The discussion during the radio programme helped me to revise my central
research questions about heterosexuality, homosexuality, lesbianism, bisexuality, sadomasochism, transgender relationships, bestiality and necrophilia. I
distributed questionnaire surveys to 160 female undergraduate students at the
Mona campus in Jamaica in order to investigate the extent to which a better
understanding of complicated sexual realities contributes to feminist analyses
of gender justice. The students are between eighteen and forty-six years old.
Of the respondents, 157 state that their racial identity is black, while 2 students
are Indian and 1 is white. Out of a total of 160 women, 157 explain that they
are heterosexual. Only 1 woman defines herself as a lesbian, and 2 women are
bisexual. Responses to the questionnaire suggest that tensions surround the
enjoyment of equal sexual partnerships. They also elucidate different connotations of sexual complexity beyond preconceived, dichotomous thinking, and
interrogate the "either/or" mentality (male/female, gay/straight, healthy/
unhealthy, safe/dangerous and liberating/repressive).

Students' Views about Heterosexuality

Studies on the historical and cultural construction of sexuality unveil the social
control of diverse erotic feelings and pleasures. Based on scholarship about the
association between social interventions, different sexual meanings, and knowledge and power relations, I assess the surveillance of sexual relations in Jamaica
(Foucault 1976; Weeks 1995; Mohammed 1994). Respondents maintain that,
since enslavement, stereotypes of black women as immoral, lascivious and diseased have been used to legitimate subordination. During slavery, the sexual
violation of black women by white men symbolized a wider system of white,
male domination. Sexual exploitation was an institutionalized method of terrorism that aimed to demoralize and dehumanize slave women as well as slave
men (Davis 1982). The historical depiction of black women as sexually denigrated, animalistic and licentious continues to be used to justify sex tourism
(Kempadoo 2003). Many students are concerned that debates about sexual variants and sexual paraphilias reinforce the historical depictions of sexually
aggressive black women which are still influential in Caribbean societies.

Participants are concerned about perpetuating the belief that black women are promiscuous, hypersexual and licentious. Most respondents argue that these myths are utilized to justify black female oppression by black men and whites.

According to cultural prescriptions in the Caribbean, women's sexuality is usually defined in terms of fidelity to men, procreation and financial resources (Kempadoo 2003). Patricia Mohammed argues that Caribbean female sexuality is socially dominated by men's desires, but it is also autonomous and fluid. Mohammed criticizes the rigid ordering in Caribbean societies that prioritizes male pleasure and control. Religion, popular culture, peer pressure and language restrict women's sexual beliefs and experiences in order to satisfy men. Women, however, are negotiating their needs within cultural ideals about passivity, purity and chastity that attempt to subvert the historical stereotype of promiscuity (Mohammed 1994).

The responses to the questionnaire largely reflect Carole Vance's analysis of female sexuality within the historical and social context of racialized, gendered and class-based inequalities. Vance argues that female sexual orientation is an ambiguous and contradictory site of personal and social dominance (Vance 1984). Women experience restriction, repression and danger, but they also encounter pleasure, agency, exploration and safety. Vance maintains that women internalize conventional cultural norms of acceptable sexual attitudes and behaviours. Women who do not conform to coercive expectations of heterosexuality, marriage and motherhood are deemed "bad" women. This negative labelling legitimates stigma, violation and punishment by the state, religion, medicine and public opinion (ibid.).

Many respondents expressed concern that black women's involvement in sexual variants and sexual paraphilias perpetuates denigration. Most students expressed the popular notion that "normal" sexual orientation is characterized by heterosexuality, preferably within marriage. They spoke disapprovingly of lesbians and bisexual women because Jamaican society defines these sexual lifestyles as taboo. Their knowledge of the shifting boundaries of eroticism enabled them to make informed choices whereby they could articulate their heterosexual options. Despite their awareness of the broad range of passionate relations, their responses demonstrated that there is still an imbalance of power between the ways in which men and women perceive and approach sex, evident in women's greater vulnerability to involvement in risky sexual practices (Douglas, Reid, and Reddock 2008).

Respondents believed that double standards about the expression of sexuality place restrictions and penalties on women that are not placed on men. They stated that women are expected to be obedient, submissive and dutiful sexual partners. The icon of the devoted, pure and chaste woman circumscribed their sexual activities, to a large extent. In addition, they felt that historical and biblical myths about evil temptresses and seductresses who were responsible for the "fall" of men have caused women to be viewed as outcasts. Students' testimonies revealed that imagery of male sexual prowess and female fidelity serves to justify male control and female subordination (Collins 1990). Kamala Kempadoo maintains that more theorizing about evolving sexual proclivities is necessary to counteract the tendency for research to portray sexuality in the Caribbean mainly in terms of male heterosexual privilege and promiscuity, female sexual fidelity and homophobia (Kempadoo 2003).

Participants identified that, despite institutionalized beliefs and practices that dictate which forms of attraction are natural and normal, sexual identities may shift over the course of an individual's lifespan, and cross-culturally over time. Common ideas about what constitutes improper, incorrect, unusual and unnatural sexual behaviour are historically and culturally specific (King 2001). Lesbophobia and homophobia, for example, involve a fear and hatred of same-sex attraction, and therefore reinforces patriarchy. Women who have sex with women (WSW) and men who have sex with men (MSM) are castigated as socially unacceptable, indiscernible, corrupt, diseased and destructive, and this negative branding leads to hostile prejudice, discrimination and violence (Lorde 1984). "Irregular" or "abnormal" sexual choices are regarded as consensual sexual acts in which the majority of people do not engage. The following quote provides an example of an undergraduate student's perception of abnormal sexuality: "I believe that any sexual behaviour extremely outside the norm of normal sex, such as an adult engaging into [sic] sexual activities with a child, is perverted. Why? Because it goes far beyond the limit of what is sexually acceptable." Like this student, most other participants in the survey stated that they adhere to strict and conventional religious beliefs about heterosexuality and procreation. Their accounts reflect Adrienne Rich's findings that religious ideals about heterosexuality, marriage and the nuclear family describe appropriate sexual conduct (Rich 1980). Other types of sexual encounters that deviate from these ideals are, by and large, seen as filthy and threatening to traditional social mores and Christian ideology. Lesbianism and homosexuality, in particular, are viewed pejoratively and are perceived, as Valerie Mason-John and Ann Khambatta assert, as unnatural sins derived from Western society – as a kind of "white man's disease" that is alien and detrimental to black culture (Mason-John and Khambatta 1993)

Adrienne Rich argues that cultural ideas and institutionalized preferences confer higher status, power and privileges on those who are presumed to be heterosexual, since heterosexuality is generally perceived as the only natural and normal expression of sexual identity (Rich 1980). Rich asserts that, although women are primarily attached to each other, they are socialized to be heterosexual: immense social pressures manipulate women into being heterosexual, instead of allowing them to make their own, individual decisions about sexual preference. Rich also examines the ways in which the historical and social construction of heterosexuality limits freedom of sensual expression. She explains that the invisibility of enforced heterosexist ideologies and strategies prevents recognition of women's lack of options. The socio-economic and political surveillance of heterosexuality denies women the opportunity to define adequately and meet the needs of their own, independent lust. Rich challenges the binary descriptions of being either heterosexual or homosexual and the prioritization of male supremacist heterosexuality over other sexual preferences. According to Rich, "the absence of choice remains the great unacknowledged reality, and in the absence of choice, women will remain dependent upon the chance or luck of particular relationships and will have no collective power to determine the meaning and place of sexuality in their lives" (ibid., 135).

Students' Objections to Sexual Variation

Participants' views reflect embedded cultural expectations about required heterosexual perceptions and conduct in Jamaica. (Appendix 14.2 provides the questions that students answered.) There is fierce denunciation of those who presumably deviate from prescribed heterosexual roles. For instance, respondents firmly believed that homosexuals, lesbians and bisexuals are abnormal and should be chastized in Jamaican culture. They vehemently argued that homosexuality, lesbianism and bisexuality are unsettling and immoral types of deviance that require psychological and spiritual support. Statements such as the following highlight the general sense of the responses: "Bisexuals are confused people who can't figure their sexual identity and just want to have fun"; "They are confused about their sexuality. They need to choose one sexual orientation, not two."

Research conducted by Janet Brown and Barry Chevannes explains that violent hatred of homosexuality is a central aspect of Caribbean male sexualities in particular. Boys are encouraged to be sexually active and to have several female sexual partners to prove that they are heterosexual (Brown and Chevannes 1998). Gregory M. Herek (2000) argues that anti-gay prejudice and hate crimes are linked to authoritarianism. He maintains that homophobic stigmas and practices are most intense among men who strongly believe in heteropatriarchy and religious fundamentalism and have limited education. Men's overt attacks on MSM are attempts to repress their own attraction to other men and to prove their manhood (Herek 2000). In a similar vein, Kamala Kempadoo asserts that brutal anti-gay sentiments reinforce aggressive male heterosexuality (Kempadoo 2004).

Michael Kimmel (1993) states that homophobia represents men being afraid of other men perceiving them as failing to meet the criteria of hegemonic masculinity and suspecting that they are gay. Homophobia is an informally imposed social mechanism that monitors the beliefs and conduct of boys and men. The institutionalization of deep hatred of homosexuality is a form of surveillance that sanctions against open displays of same-sex attraction (ibid.). Homophobia reinforces a hierarchy of hegemonic male power and social status whereby men dominate and gain the respect of each other. This kind of policing disciplines men to adhere to conventional definitions of appropriate heteronormative masculine traits to demonstrate that they are not gay. Men are terrified that their same-sex orientation may be discovered, and repress homoerotic expression in order to confirm that they are heterosexual (ibid.).

It would be interesting to investigate the extent to which Kimmel's analysis applies to social constraints on female sexuality. Patricia Mohammed asserts that rigid taboos about homosexuality limit the flexible expression of sexual preferences in the Caribbean region. Mohammed encourages people to interrogate how sex allows them to transcend isolation. She explains that heterosexuals who are satisfied with their sexual experiences are not threatened by homosexuality, and suggests that future studies should investigate the causes of homophobia (Mohammed 1994).

Joceline Clemencia (1996) argues that derogatory name-calling and brutal rejection of WSW are dangerous aspects of patriarchal domination. Female same-sex relations are segregated as sick and immoral offences to religion and Caribbean societies. Michele Cave and Joan French (1996) explain that legislation and cultural regimes restrict woman-woman relationships in Caribbean societies. These liaisons are denigrated and discriminated against because of the fear that women's sexual autonomy threatens and undermines patriarchy. Dominant ideas in society contribute to harassment, criminalization and violation which restrain female sexuality as well as institutionalize shocked silence and terror about same-sex intimacy (ibid.). M. Jacqui Alexander (2007) maintains that fragile nation states police and discipline the female body, sex workers, bisexuals, lesbians and gay men for disrupting the prevalent values of heterosexuality and the nuclear family. Patriarchy, hegemonic masculinity and heterosexuality are naturalized as central to maintaining the stability of Caribbean societies. Legislation perpetuates oppressive sanctions against same-sex partnerships, which are castigated as perverse, corrupt, diseased, destructive, unnatural and deviant.

Ruth C. White and Robert Carr (2005) state that the stigma of and discrimination against HIV/AIDS lead to low levels of HIV/AIDS testing, treatment and care services. HIV-positive people feel hesitant and vulnerable about informing their partners about their serostatus. White and Carr argue that Christian fundamentalist norms are used to justify family rejection, community violations and police attacks (ibid.). The article "Hated to Death" (2004) documents severe levels of violence, hate crimes and abuse of gay men, lesbians and bisexuals in Jamaica. This type of discriminatory behaviour perpetuates social exclusion, poverty and inadequate health care and employment opportunities. The institutionalization of homophobic and lesbophobic power and privilege within the government and police force, and among state officials and health workers, is a harsh form of criminalization and punishment. Moral and social policing contribute to the HIV/AIDS crisis because health workers often sabotage interventions to prevent and treat the epidemic. Official indifference to victimization by police and HIV/AIDS workers contributes to hostile coercion ("Hated to Death", 2004). The students surveyed, however, tended either to ignore these types of violations of human rights or to proclaim that they are exaggerated.

Sadomasochism as Feminist Revenge?

Students were aware that sadism entails inflicting pain on others to achieve sexual arousal. A minority of female students expressed the belief that reversing gender roles, so that women are sexually aggressive and men are sexually submissive, is an important goal. They argued that female sexual dominance over submissive men would compensate for patriarchal domination in Jamaican society. The women who gave these responses realized that masochism involves suffering, harm and humiliation. They asserted that this gives women control over men as a means of obtaining male obedience. In their opinions, women would feel more authoritative if they obtained sexual pleasure from causing men pain and humiliation. It is important to note, however, that these respondents adhered to an exploitative form of sexual enslavement in theory but not in practice. Most students expressed their opinions about sexual decency by stating that sadomasochistic (S/M) relationships involving one person dominating a submissive partner are wrong, weird and dangerous. Participants reported feeling disturbed by sadism and masochism, which they regarded as satanic, filthy and unhealthy. Nevertheless, several students stated that they enjoy watching pornographic films which portray the subjective meanings and imagery by which they claim to be offended.

The students' descriptions of their disapproval of alleged sexual perversion suggest that there is an unclear distinction between fantasies and behaviours that are generally regarded as unconventional, yet are followed in their personal relationships. Many students were ambivalent about the extent to which sadomasochism, even with a partner's consent, is characterized by gross humiliation and submission. They questioned whether sadomasochistic relations of superiority and inferiority have evolved as a consequence of the painful control, suffering and degradation forced upon blacks during slavery (Beckles 1989). A few respondents did think that sadomasochism is a legacy of the harsh punishment administered by slave masters, and expressed the belief that these historical instances of brutality can explain contemporary experiences of socio-sexual power and powerlessness. One student criticized sadomasochism because, she proclaims, "I believe that persons engaging in such relationships have some mental or emotional imbalance and should seek psychological aid."

Religious Criticisms of Transgendered People

Valerie Mason-John and Ann Khambatta (1993) refute the notion that black communities are more homophobic than other societies. They suggest that cultures with strong religious convictions are prone to homophobia. Since religion is central to many black cultures, they argue, black people may seem to be more narrow-minded, bigoted and homophobic than whites. Respondents to the survey discussed transgender roles in which a person's inner gender identity is opposite to his or her physical, bodily characteristics at birth. Most participants expressed a belief that transgender individuals should sanctify God's creation of masculinity and femininity rather than claiming that they belong to a sex different from that indicated by their genitalia. Students stated that, instead of feeling as if they are "trapped in the body of the wrong gender", transgender people should accept the gender identity that nature has assigned them. The majority of respondents made arguments such as the following:

> God created persons the way [i.e., gender] they ought to be. It is their perverted mind that is playing tricks on them.

> I believe that God made you a particular sex for a reason and that is how you should be. There is no such thing as being "trapped in the wrong body".

> We are all made in the likeness of God. And a person should just accept who she or he is.

> The Bible says the Lord made us beautifully and wonderfully. He makes no mistakes. If you are born female you are to be female and not male. Learn to have confidence in yourself and accept yourself, as you are faithfully and wonderfully made in the eyes of the Lord.

> They were blessed with the gender God gave them. Feeling as if he made a mistake is insulting and thus I would not encourage such feelings.

Responses such as these ignore the rights of transgendered individuals to have gender reassignment and to adapt their civil statuses to live out their perceived gender identities. The questionnaire data reveal that several students used religion as a yardstick to measure sexual mores and condemn others, but their own sex lives frequently did not reflect that understanding. Some students argued that any sexual activity that is not heterosexually oriented is eccentric and should not be tolerated. Students' responses demonstrate that religious traditions, beliefs and organized institutions clearly distinguish concepts of appropriate male and female sexual conduct that religious adherents do not always obey. Participants explained, for example, that traditional religious notions about female virtue that have strongly influenced sexual values, decisions, roles and responsibilities in the past are now changing (Mohammed 1994).

Students addressed the manner in which ethical and medical arguments affect seduction, dominance, subordination and surrender. Further research is necessary to establish how strongly religion influences opinions about orgasmic fulfilment. Many students quoted biblical teachings to explain that they reject transgender people because they regard them as sinful. Traditional ideas about heterosexuality are seen as the norm, and other sexual preferences are considered immoral, unnatural and dangerous. Most students claimed that they are disgusted by unconventional means of sexual pleasure, which they view as outrageous violations of general values of acceptable romantic conduct. Given the students' responses, it is evident that increasing the dialogue about respecting the fluidity of an individual's sense of sexual identification is necessary. An open dialogue would allow students the opportunity to acknowledge the fact that dynamic and transformational sexualities do not discredit religious values. Participants in the survey maintained that they refute divergent erotic behaviour because they believe it is strange, bad and unhygienic. They expressed revulsion at forms of sexual satisfaction that mainstream society typically perceives as indicative of mental illness. Respondents claimed that sexual variance increases the likelihood of unprotected sex and the spread of the HIV and AIDS pandemic. Exposing students to more debates about sexuality might make them reconsider their original opinions.

Taming the Beast?

The students surveyed were both repelled by and fascinated with sexual variants and paraphilias. They asserted that sexual paraphilias are unethical and usually caused by men's need to control women. Few students believed that women also willingly engage in these activities, although they do. I will concentrate here on participants' objections to bestiality and necrophilia because the students were more disgusted by these practices and so discussed them in greater detail. All respondents vehemently condemned people who have sexual contact with animals. Bestiality and zoophilia are often transitory phases among adolescents, and adults who practice bestiality are generally men who are socially isolated and who have poor interpersonal skills. To eradicate bestiality, experts recommend a holistic system of therapy that resocializes men (King 2001).

Respondents claimed that bestiality is a forbidden abuse of animals that destroys ethical and sexual values. Students maintained that bestiality is motivated by a yearning for non-human, quiet and passive objects when consenting female partners are not available. Participants were appalled by bestiality because, in their view, it is morally deplorable, horrible and nasty. Students expressed belief that individuals who participate in bestiality require imprisonment, or psychiatric or spiritual help. The following descriptions of aversion to bestiality highlight respondents' common sentiments:

> This person is absolutely crazy and has some sexual disorder, one which is rooted in the mind!

> I would be shocked, disgusted and angry. The violation of an animal is the violation of its right of being. Rather it's disgusting, sick and the person should go to a mental institution.

> I would feel violated myself. I am strongly against the ill treatment of animals and I would report this person and hope to see them incarcerated.

Grave Taboos

There are relatively few reported instances of necrophilic fantasies and acts. Respondents consistently argued that necrophilia is a psychological problem that necessitates professional healing. They think that individuals who are sexually attracted to human corpses are extremely strange and disgusting. Students' testimonies confirm the results of general studies of necrophilia, which indicate that men's sexual excitement, obsession and activities with dead people largely result from their inability to find enthusiastic female companions (King 2001). Necrophiles also fear rejection by women (ibid.). Participants in the survey claimed that necrophilic men desire non-responsive female "partners" because they fail to create romantic attachments with women. They argued that such men desperately attempt to remedy their feelings of alienation by dominating women who are incapable of resisting them (ibid.).

Expressing power over dead bodies enables the necrophile to deal with low self-esteem and feeling unloved. Bruce M. King explains that 90 per cent of necrophiles are men, most being heterosexuals between the ages of twenty and fifty. Necrophiles have a tendency to be lonely and depressed men who have lacked affection in their childhood. Controlling a limp and lifeless body arouses them. Necrophiles often choose careers, such as morgue attendants or grave diggers, that enable them to have close contact with dead people (ibid.). In the survey, respondents asserted that men's desire to engage in sexual acts with deceased females is a horrendous expression of their perverted need to subjugate women, as the following comments indicate:

> Men like to be in control, they feel powerful being dominating.
>
> I think that it is usually men who have sex with dead bodies because by patriarchal society's rules, men should dominate. Perhaps those men find it hard to dominate women in the way they would [dominate] a dead body, which will offer no objections.
>
> They are desperate, they have a psychological problem, or they have developed a fetish where they only get aroused by dead bodies and the control they can have over the dead body.

On the whole, the students considered bestiality and necrophilia to be terrible and illegal forms of male superiority, aggression, self-loathing and control. The students' ability to discuss their attitudes towards sexual variants and paraphilias without inhibitions highlights the wider boundaries of sexualized power relations. Further research is required to interrogate the way in which non-linear and conflicting sexual conduct challenge the prevalent, dichotomous view of sex as being either "freaky" or "regular". This kind of work will help us to understand the vital influence of institutionalized practices, such as religious rituals, that shape ideas about correct versus atypical sexual lifestyles. It will also allow us to provide treatments for conditions such as sexual anorexia, which involves anxiety and aversion to emotional relationships (see http://en.wikipedia.org/wiki/Sexual_anorexia).

The Ways Forward

Most participants in the survey supported bell hooks's assertion that black women must embrace independent self-perceptions and sexual agency that are based on equality, mutual respect and lustful fulfilment, three qualities that can transform their lives. The necessity of research on the spectrum of sexual persuasions is evident in hooks's analysis (2003) of journeys towards sexual self-discovery, self-acceptance, love and liberation. Audre Lorde (1984) explains the transformation of erotic energy needed to re-create the power to enhance deep conscious and unconscious desires. Lorde maintains that women's powerful assertion of creative energy, sensuality and knowledge offers new ways of living that enrich all areas of our existence.

The re-creation of erotic power in both personal and political preferences is crucial to well-being. Intimate relationships and feminist activism need to encompass inspirational subjectivities (ibid.). Lorde's analysis encourages us to consider the ways in which we should tackle heterosexist, racist, patriarchal, elitist, religious and moralistic constructions of sexuality. We must reject male-dominated, homophobic, ageist and anti-disabled prescriptions of female erotic power in the Caribbean region. This process entails confronting censorship, anxieties, ambivalence and tensions that repress erotic urges (ibid.).

It is essential both to query fears that reflect pervasive Western, bourgeois and patriarchal values, and to enjoy the elasticity of sexual tastes and creativity. Audre Lorde states that sensuality has personal, socio-economic and political power (ibid.). She asserts that women must understand and reclaim new expressions of eroticism. It is important that women transcend suppressive portrayals of femininity to resist alienation in an "anti-erotic society" in order to achieve social change. According to Roger Horrocks, "the solution may lie in the direction of a model of 'diverse sexualities', that is, a spectrum of sexual orientations, feelings and acts, without the privileging of any particular one over the other" (Horrocks 1997, 141).

Interrogating moral judgements about what is deemed sexually ab/normal and un/natural is intricately linked to M. Jacqui Alexander's analysis of "erotic autonomy" (Alexander 2005). Alexander explains the demand for de-colonization from brutal, heteropatriarchal state power. Radical self-definitions and self-determination that affirm individual and collective sexual agency challenge the narrow construction of a nuclear family (ibid.). Freedom of sexual pleasure is addressed by bell hooks: "We need an erotics of being that is founded on the principle that we have a right to express sexual desire as the spirit moves us and to find in sexual pleasure a life-affirming ethos. Erotic connection calls us away from isolation and alienation into community. In a world where positive expressions of sexual longing connect us we will all be free to choose those sexual practices which affirm and nurture our growth" (hooks 2003, 92).

Conclusion

This chapter explores the importance of the continuum of diverse sensual experiences to women's sexual liberation. The responses of callers to a local radio programme increased my realization that there is a void in the analysis of sexual variation that needs to be filled. For most of the callers, the Radio RJR show on sexual issues was their main arena to address their feelings. There is a dire need for more media and academic forums to debate sexual diversity. Paying attention to callers' concerns, I designed a questionnaire about sexual differences and distributed it to 160 female undergraduate students on the Mona campus of the University of the West Indies. The students' opinions demonstrate the impact of cultural and religious dogma on sexual attitudes and behaviours. Like the RJR show, students' responses emphasize the necessity of increasing our awareness, negotiation and validation of multiple sexual encounters. I approve of sexual diversity, variants and paraphilias among consenting adults. Therefore, like my students, I oppose paedophilia, bestiality and necrophilia. I find, however, that some of the students' religious objections to sexual behaviour were often hypocritical, such as criticizing sex before marriage, when classroom debates suggested that students were more sexually adventurous than the questionnaire responses imply.

The questionnaires probe the way in which our autonomous senses of our own sexual personas and rights rebel against societal taboos and repression. Students highlighted concerns about the extent to which we are challenging (or merely reproducing) moralistic, religious fundamentalist, elitist and conventional attitudes about acceptable forms of sexual expression. They raised the issue of how we can meet the need to appreciate and explore our erotic agency in a sensitive, non-prescriptive and non-exploitative manner. Students identified how the encouragement of alternative sexual realities premised on mutual and self-respect may contradict social and religious dictates. It is my goal here to raise queries that need to be addressed by families, the educational system, mass media, religious organizations, legislation and social policies, in order to move beyond opposition to and distortion of the concerns of sexual "minorities". Replacing ignorance with effective recommendations for open dialogue is critical to the implementation of interventions for loving, safe and free relationships. It is beneficial to everyone to sensitize and train groups such as counsellors, priests, teachers, police and social service providers to resolve the segregation, ambivalence and insecurity that currently surround sexual politics in the Caribbean region.

Appendices

Appendix 14.1

RJR radio, 12 September 2005: A summary of the questions that Sandra Joy Alcott, Chandis Alcott and Annecka Marshall asked people who called in to the radio programme.

1   What turns you on?
2   What are your sexual needs?
3   What do you enjoy sexually?
4   What does your partner (do your partners) want sexually?
5   How do you keep the passion going?
6   How do you keep sex hot?
7   How do you keep it loving and sexy?
8   What is natural?
9   What is unnatural?
10 What is conventional?
11 What is unconventional?
12 What is usual?
13 What is unusual?
14 What is normal?
15 What is abnormal?
16 What is healthy?

17   What is unhealthy?
18   What is clean sex?
19   What is dirty or nasty sex?
20   How seductive are your dreams, fantasies and imagination?
21   What would you call a sexual fetish?
22   Is a sexual fetish a psychological disorder?
23   Do you have a sexual fetish?
24   What is your fetish?
25   Why do people use a fetish to satisfy their desires?
26   What do you consider to be kinky sex?
27   What is kinky for you?
28   What makes sex naughty, strange and extreme?
29   Is there something kinky in your sex life?
30   What is sexually bizarre?
31   What is a step beyond kinky sex?
32   Why do some people want to feel pain?
33   What is the difference between kinky and freaky?
34   How freaky is Jamaica?
35   What are your own sexual limits?
36   What is sexual liberation?
37   Do you have the freedom to do what you want?

Appendix 14.2

Sexual Diversity Questionnaire, completed by 160 female undergraduate students at the Mona campus, Jamaica.

1   How old are you?
2   What is your racial / ethnic identity?
3   What is your sexual identity?
4   Do you feel great about the quality of your sex life? Why or why not?
5   Do you believe that consenting adults should engage in any sexual activities they want in private? Why or why not?
6   Describe a sexual relationship that you consider to be sexually normal.
7   What do you think is perverted sexual behaviour? Why?

8 Which sexual experiences do you disapprove of? Why?

9 What is the general view of lesbians in Jamaica? Why?

10 How would you feel if a member of your family told you that she is a lesbian? Why?

11 What are your opinions about bisexuals?

12 What do you think about sexual relationships that involve painful control and humiliating submission?

13 Do you believe that if your best friend feels that s/he is "trapped in the body of the wrong gender" s/he should be encouraged to "become the opposite sex"? Why or why not?

14 How would you react if you heard that someone in your neighbourhood has sexual contact with animals? Why?

15 Why do you think that it is usually men who have sex with dead bodies?

16 Do you believe that women need to be in more control of their sexual relationships? Why or why not?

17 Would you like to add any other comments?

References

Alexander, M.J. 2005. *Pedagogies of crossing: Meditations on feminism, sexual politics, memory, and the sacred.* Durham, NC: Duke University Press.

———. 2007. Danger and desire: Crossings are never undertaken all at once or once and for all. *Small Axe: A Caribbean Journal of Criticism* 24 (October): 154–66.

Beckles, H.McD. 1989. *Natural rebels: a social history of enslaved black women in Barbados.* London: Zed Books.

Brown, J., and B. Chevannes. 1998. *Why man stay so: An examination of gender socialization in the Caribbean.* Kingston: University of the West Indies Press.

Cave, D.M., and J. French. 1996. Sexual choice as a human right issue. *Lolapress* 5. http://www.lolapress.org/artenglish/cavee5.htm (accessed 6 October 2008).

Clemencia, J. 1996. Women who love women in Curacao: From cachapera to open throats: A commentary in collage. *Feminist Studies* 22 (1): 81–88.

Collins, P. Hill. 1990/1991. *Black feminist thought: Knowledge, consciousness, and the politics of empowerment.* New York: Routledge.

Davis, A. 1982. *Women, race and class.* London: Women's Press.

Douglas, D., S. Reid and R. Reddock. 2008. Gender and sexuality: Behaviour, attitudes and taboos among UWI students on the St Augustine campus. In *Sex, power and taboo:*

Gender and HIV in the Caribbean and beyond, ed. D. Roberts, R. Reddock, D. Douglas and S. Reid, 216–38. Kingston: Ian Randle.

Foucault, M. 1976. *The history of sexuality: An introduction.* Vol. 1. New York: Pantheon.

Herek, G.M. 2000. The psychology of sexual prejudice. *Current Directions in Psychological Science* 9 (1): 19–22.

hooks, b. 2003. *Communion: The female search for love.* London: Women's Press.

Horrocks, R. 1977. *An introduction to the study of sexuality.* New York: St Martin's.

Hated to death: Homophobia, violence and Jamaica's HIV/AIDS epidemic. 2004. *Human Rights Watch* 16 (6): 1–81.

Kempadoo, K. 2003. Sexuality in the Caribbean: Theory and research (with an emphasis on the anglophone Caribbean). *Social and Economic Studies* 52 (3): 59–88.

———. 2004. *Sexing the Caribbean: Gender, race and sexual labour.* London: Routledge.

Kimmel, M. 1993. Masculinity as homophobia: Fear, shame, and silence in the construction of gender identity. In *Cracking the armour: Power, pain and the lives of men,* ed. M. Kaufman, 213–19. Toronto: Viking Canada.

King, B.M. 2001. *Human sexuality today.* Upper Saddle River, NJ: Prentice Hall.

Lorde, A. 1984. *Sister outsider: Essays and speeches.* Freedom, CA: Crossing Press.

Mason-John, V., and A. Khambatta. 1993. *Lesbians talk making waves.* London: Scarlet Press.

Mohammed, P. 1994. Ruminations on sexuality. *CAFRA News: Newsletter of the Caribbean Association for Feminist Research and Action* 8 (1–2): 5–6.

O'Grady, L. 1992. Olympia's maid: Reclaiming black female subjectivity. *Afterimage* (Summer): 14–23.

Rich, A. 1980. Compulsory heterosexuality and lesbian existence. *Signs: Journal of Women in Culture and Society* 5 (4): 631–60.

Vance, C.S., ed. 1984. *Pleasure and danger: Exploring female sexuality.* London: Routledge and Kegan Paul.

Weeks, J. 1995. *Sexuality.* London: Routledge.

White, R.C., and R. Carr. 2005. Homosexuality and HIV/AIDS stigma in Jamaica. *Culture, Health and Sexuality* 7: 1–13.

PART 6

Looking Back to the Future of Gender

15

Locating Gender in the History of Science, Technology and Medicine in the Caribbean

TARA INNISS

THE PLANTER AND PHYSICIAN David Collins published his *Practical Rules for the Management and Medical Treatment of Negro Slaves in the Sugar Colonies* in 1803. He described the selection of appropriate midwives for the safe delivery of enslaved newborns at a time when planters and managers were seeking to increase the plantation labour force by natural means prior to the anticipated abolition of the transatlantic slave trade. Collins wrote that any experienced, sensible woman could perform the function of a midwife as long as she was sufficiently trained by "any gentlemen of the faculty [i.e., a physician] or other midwives"; however, if a difficult case presented itself, only "men of science must be early resorted to" (Collins 1803/1971, 159). Medical provision and scientific practice occupied a contested space in the early nineteenth century, a space where women and men competed for jurisdiction over medical and scientific knowledge and authority in the region. From Collins's perspective, it was acknowledged that enslaved women had intimate knowledge of the female body, but it was male medical practitioners and slave masters who allowed them the space to perform their skills; moreover, it was "men of science" who defined the contours of scientific knowledge and practice.

Collins could order reproduction on the plantation because he defined his knowledge as dominant and subordinated the knowledge of midwives and the women in their care. He arranged the information in a publication that could be disseminated widely among other planters and managers. The need for order and control in the management of the enslaved, however, did little to respond to the needs or wishes of enslaved women, who often opted for the familiar supervision of midwives over the haphazard attendance of male physicians who likely had a very limited knowledge of the female body (Mott 2003, 40; Loudon 1992, 192–93).

Even this brief extract implores historians to consider the following questions: Is the pursuit of "science" a masculine enterprise that can only be understood and reproduced by some men and not others? And what about the authorities who are silenced? What about the female as practitioner and the female as patient? Where do they fit into historical narratives? This chapter will begin to map some of the theoretical and methodological issues surrounding the exploration of gender in the history of science, technology and medicine (HSTM) in the Caribbean, and will suggest some new areas for inquiry among the scholarship.

Gender in the History of Science, Technology and Medicine in the Caribbean

Feminist readings of the development of science, technology and medicine demonstrate how gender has played a key role in defining how the natural world is viewed and explained. Gendered constructions of scientific knowledge have also determined who is "(cap)able" of doing the explaining and what subjects are explored. The HSTM has developed as a field of inquiry for other regions, namely in the United Kingdom, Europe and North America. Increasingly, historians are turning their attention to the HSTM in regions such as those in the Global South to begin to articulate how social constructions of science, technology and medicine (STM) have intersected with ideas of race, gender, colonization and the development of empire. This is no less true for the Caribbean, which has a rich history in the production of scientific knowledge and practitioners of science.

In the Caribbean, historians can look at the ways in which gender operates *as* science – where "women"/ "female" and "men"/ "male" are the subjects of scientific and medical inquiry – creating meanings and constructions of sexual difference which dominate human understanding of the natural world. Race also plays an important role in gendered constructions of the body. Racialized notions of the capacities and capabilities of non-white men and women were used to justify their subjugation, and these notions were grounded in the scientific discourse of the day.

Caribbean historians can also examine how gender has determined men's and women's participation in science. Throughout the region's history, the practice of science and medicine has remained a contested space among all women and men. Gender, race and ethnicity play significant roles in both the creation of opportunities and the denial of participation by women and men in practising science and medicine in the region.

Men and women in the Caribbean have engaged with scientific principles and explained the natural world from the beginning of their settlement in the region. They have created explanations for heavenly bodies, fashioned tools to make life easier and used the natural environment around them to heal the body and community within their own systems of belief. It was the process of colonization, however, that brought these philosophies into contact with other ways of knowing, which were also developing in Africa and Europe (Pickstone 2001). Since contact and colonization, the Caribbean has witnessed the large-scale in-and-out migration of several ethnic groups which brought their own understandings of STM with them. Knowledge and practice in the region developed alongside the more widely known (and recognized) development of Western STM. Knowledge exchange, adaptation and transformation have been the products of contact and competition between ethnicities and traditions. Caribbean women and men have played integral roles in the development of Caribbean STM and have influenced the development of STM traditions elsewhere, as both subjects and practitioners.

It is critical that the Caribbean region also plays its part in the development of its own HSTM to ensure that the experiences and contributions of Caribbean people are recognized. As the discipline matures, gender analysis (particularly feminist analysis) of STM has come to transform understandings of the development of STM and the role these ideas play in human societies and cultures. The HSTM has helped us to acknowledge STM as a range of social constructions. Although some may argue that STM enterprises seek to be rational and objective, they are not. They are products of human society, and are therefore subject to the inequalities, incongruities and deviations that define human culture. STM *is*, quite simply, gendered.

The HSTM, Gender and Caribbean Scholarship

Little work has been done in the field of HSTM for the region, and there have been even fewer contributions to the understanding of how gender has operated in the regional development of STM. Scholars have developed a demographic and health history of the Caribbean to a limited extent, particularly in the area of colonization and the enslaved experience (Sheridan 1985; Kiple 1984; Kiple and Kiple 1981; Higman 1984). These contributions are useful, but they do not situate demography or health history within belief systems or social constructions of healing that are relevant to the entire Caribbean experience (not just as a peripheral discussion of European-dominated medical science in the eighteenth and nineteenth centuries). And although these histories often include information on gender in a descriptive sense, gender analysis is rarely used to explain mortality rates, the social construction of disease, or power relations among medical practitioners and their patrons. Moreover, law has explored "bodies" in representations through crime and punishment, but it has not treated these bodies as biological subjects that can be inscribed with racialized and gendered ideas based on scientific and medical meanings (Paton 2001; Paton 1996).

Histories of public health have been published recently, but again, gender remains on the periphery of investigation, with women and men as biological subjects and with little discussion of the operation of Caribbean masculinities and femininities as central to the discussion of the development of public health policy (De Barros 2003). The HSTM in the post-emancipation period and in the twentieth century has been limited. Regionally, gender as a mode of analysis in these disciplines has also been limited. The subject area is vast, with immense opportunities for development in all time periods, and can begin to answer questions about the silenced contributions of Caribbean women and men to the development of STM – for instance, in the origins of cosmological and epistemological Caribbean scientific traditions and the place of women and men in them; in the knowledge, use and acceptance of technologies in the region by different groups; and in how notions of health and healing are engendered and gendered in the region.

Beginning to answer these questions is essential to creating a discourse with STM in Caribbean society, and to determining its place in shaping Caribbean identity (or identities) and forging relationships with an increasingly globalized world in which knowledge and technology are frequently downloaded to the region without debate or analysis, and often even without a basic understanding of the region's role in developing modern STM. It is incumbent on the historian to play a role in interrogating meanings and representations of STM in order to understand how scientific knowledge is produced, reproduced and transformed. Moreover, the discipline must ensure that Caribbean ways of knowing remain central to these explanations.

Regional development of the discipline will also feed into HSTM's being developed elsewhere, challenging assumptions and beliefs as well as providing a critical discourse on how STM traditions have been propagated through time and space. As a place of empire, the region has had to make space for competing understandings of the natural world. European knowledge systems have existed alongside Amerindian, African, Indian and even Creole knowledge systems, and they have sometimes borrowed from one another, subsuming each other but also often dominating established social and economic hierarchies. The development of the HSTM in the region should also help to close critical knowledge gaps in the development of gender relations by creating representations and analyses that are relevant to Caribbean men and women.

European knowledge systems, therefore, cannot be privileged in the HSTM in the Caribbean without acknowledging the presence, and creation, of other knowledge systems. Men and women have decided which systems hold the answer to their particular problems or curiosities – sometimes choosing one, sometimes choosing all. Any investigation of the HSTM must also consider how ethnicity, race and class operate in the region. Scientific constructions of race inform constructions of gender in the Caribbean.

The Quest for Sources

The quest for sources is a key concern for any emerging topic for historical investigation. The documentary evidence for STM, particularly for the history of medicine, is quite vast for most time periods during the colonial period. A number of visitors to the region recorded and collected specimens from the natural environment, and published their findings widely throughout Europe (Sloane 1725; Chamberlaine 1792; Ligon 1657/1998). During slavery, physicians were equally proficient in publishing treatises and manuals for the successful management of plantations, including the health and welfare of enslaved persons. Archival sources, such as plantation journals and correspondence, are also very useful for mapping the health concerns of colonialists. Moreover, birth and death registers also give some insight into mortality rates, especially among free white communities. Military records can also be used to investigate the health concerns of soldiers and colonial officers in the region. In addition, as public health and sanitation became increasingly important to the government and ordering of the colonies, colonial office correspondence lends significant insight into the motivations of the colonial government in its bid to control disease and public health.

Historians of STM in the region, however, will almost immediately recognize the silences in these early records, particularly because these predominantly written sources privilege European-derived scientific and medical knowledge, to which only some "learned" men had access. Accounts of the role of women as practitioners and subjects, described in their own voices, are virtually non-existent, with the valued exception of practitioner Mary Seacole and the handful of colonial white women who wrote of their experiences as subjects and patients (Seacole 1857/1988). It is far more common to read about the medical diagnoses and treatment of enslaved or free men, women and children in the journals and reminiscences of visiting male physicians and practitioners of science. Although they are filtered through the viewpoints of elite male practitioners of medicine or science, it is possible to get a glimpse of the experiences of Caribbean people who not only sought the assistance of established European medical authorities, but also solicited a wide variety of other sources of medical knowledge.

The history of technology is somewhat more tangible, because some of the artefacts of technological history remain intact (although left abandoned and disintegrating) on the region's plantations, in urban centres and government laboratories. There is, as yet, no culture of preservation or interpretation of this part of the region's material culture. Moreover, the gendering of technologies or tools created or used widely in the region has not received satisfactory attention.

Oral sources can prove to be very useful for the historian of STM, especially in investigations of twentieth-century medical or scientific practice. They are promising sources for evaluating the experiences of Caribbean men and women as practitioners and subjects of science; as users and consumers of technology; and as patients or beneficiaries of healing systems. For insight into women's health in particular, the collection and analysis of oral sources is likely to shed light on perceptions of medical diagnoses and the medical establishment in general. Moreover, deep silences exist between and among Caribbean women and men about several sexual and reproductive disorders that often result in social isolation and poor survival rates. The collection and analysis of oral histories is critical to unearthing these silences and providing science and medicine with some knowledge of the social understandings of disease, health and healing among the region's people.

Male and Female *as* Science in the Caribbean

In Western scientific traditions, the sexual differences between men and women have long been a subject with which natural philosophers, modern scientists and medical professionals have concerned themselves. The anatomical differences between the male and the female in animal species have puzzled scientific thinkers for ages. As a result, human physiology and biology have been influenced by the different opinions that have dominated over time. The female reproductive system and genitalia have frequently been compared to those of the male. Some of the first thinkers to differentiate between the two saw the female reproductive system as being similar in structure, except for being located within the body. Aristotle, for example, believed that female genitalia were lesser forms of male genitalia. In fact, he posited that male testes have analogous structures in what he called female testes. In his worldview, everything in the universe had the potential to become male. Other thinkers, like Galen, simply turned the male organs inwards to reveal the female reproductive system (Laqueur 1992).

It begins to become apparent that, within Western knowledge traditions, biological representations and understandings of the body and sexual differences influenced the ways in which men and women were viewed and how they viewed themselves (Laqueur 1992). For much of its history, the dominant view in Western thought was that male physiology was normal, perfect in structure and causing little or few health concerns or biological abnormalities.

Female physiology was, by contrast, abnormal and imperfect in structure. Medicine linked female health complaints and behaviour inextricably to the presence of the uterus (Digby 1989). Because of the peculiar structure and function of the female reproductive organs, women's health was thought to revolve around one system. Women's health complaints were ascribed to their being female.

Arguably, such views have dominated the development of Western STM, which has traditionally found perfection and normality in the male specimen, while either ignoring the female or studying her only when sexual reproduction or abnormality was under investigation. Men as producers of technologies have been designated as the creators of tools to adapt and control the natural environment, while women have merely been designated as the consumers of these technologies, with little appreciation of women's roles in producing and using them (Berg and Lie 1995, 336). Medical traditions evolved to privilege the health complaints of the male patient (as treated by men), while women's health complaints were relegated to the peripheries of formal medical investigation (often treated by women). Even diseases were viewed as gendered. Physiological and psychological illnesses in women were often ascribed to menstruation and to being *female*, and received little or no treatment, while diseases in men were rationalized – diagnosed, treated and prevented.

Just as Western scientific knowledge and practice were being formalized into what is known as "modern" science and medicine, the Caribbean became a locus for the development of modern scientific inquiry. The natural environment of the region became a living laboratory where specimens could be described, collected and classified. They were taken to Europe to be organized and catalogued (Sloane 1725; Chamberlaine 1792). Captive indigenous, European and African men and women were also specimens who could be organized and catalogued in this living laboratory. Caribbean men and women were gendered and racialized subjects of observation and experimentation on the plantations, and as possessions of their European masters (Sloane 1725; Chamberlaine 1792; Lascelles et al. 1786; Collins 1803/1971; Hillary 1766; Dancer 1801). As a means of production and reproduction, procreation became a singular fascination of the planter class, which exchanged knowledge of observations that assisted in the successful reproduction of the enslaved, who were often the unknowing or unwilling subjects of experiments to find new treatments for diseases or improve existing practices to preserve human life.

As a counterpoint to the perceived dominance of Western traditions, indigenous African and Indian traditions had their own perceptions of sexual difference which also influenced perceptions of the human body and its relationship to the community. Much more research must be done in this area to begin to chart how other knowledge systems viewed and gendered the body and the natural world. It is in a similar way that human gender perceptions can influence our biological understanding of other organisms. It would be worthwhile to investigate to what extent gender perceptions have shaped and continue to influence how the Caribbean natural environment is explored and explained.

Women and Men in Science

Women and men were as much actors in 'modern' science as they were subjects. The participation of men and women in the sciences is indeed gendered, with the contributions of some women and men being silenced, while those of others are glorified. Appreciation of STM is often confused with the "cult of achievement" that surrounds it – the elevation of persons who cultivate progress in human thought and enterprise – but this perception is in itself gendered, since the work of science is often carried out by persons who receive no credit at all.

The historian of STM rarely acknowledges the men and women who were clerks in laboratories or on exploratory expeditions, or who did experiments, recorded observations or refined calculations (Rossiter 1995). This lack of acknowledgment is fruitful ground, however, for anyone seeking an explanation of the power dynamics in the pursuit of scientific knowledge. Moreover, the contributions of men and women who are often designated as "non-scientific" practitioners are often ignored because of power dynamics based on gender, race and ethnicity. Their work is rarely recorded, and is often handed down through memory and practice. In addition, power dynamics have often dictated who receives credit for the work of science. Enslaved doctors and doctresses were often not acknowledged for showing planter-physicians treatments for afflictions which endangered the lives of either the enslaved or the enslavers. The remedy was subsumed under the name of the planter-physician who was the property owner who "sanctioned" medical knowledge for dissemination to other members of the planter class (Chamberlaine 1792; Long 1774, 828).

The work of Caribbean women in science and medicine, in particular, has not been acknowledged. Women have been at the forefront of popular health-care as healers, midwives, sick nurses and doctresses on slave plantations. As women, they were often seen on the peripheries of Caribbean medical practice, especially because they dealt with the health of black people. They provided an invaluable service at a time when European medical practitioners were largely unavailable or inaccessible to many people (Sheridan 1985, 89). Moreover, European medicine and practitioners may not have been trusted on account of their own shortcomings in healing practices (ibid., 90). In the case of midwifery, for example, it is reported that many enslaved women, during childbirth, preferred being in the company of relatives and other women from their communities to that of plantation physicians (Higman 1984, 352; Long 1774, 436).

During the nineteenth and twentieth centuries, Caribbean medical practice became more closely aligned with the development of European medicine. As in Europe, women's roles in medicine required more formal training and practice, particularly within the nursing profession. As one of the few options for women seeking careers, nursing became popular among many socially mobile women; so much so, in fact, that Caribbean nurses continue to be sought as immigrants to countries with nursing shortages. From the 1950s to 1970s, nurses trained in the English-speaking Caribbean, as well as those seeking training, left as part of the massive out-migration of people seeking opportunities in the United Kingdom, Canada and the United States (Beckles 2001). Their role in the development of nursing abroad is often overlooked, but it has been crucial to their ability to provide for families in the Caribbean. Unfortunately, their out-migration signalled the onslaught of the "brain-drain", or human capital loss, in Caribbean nursing. Some nurses opted to stay in the countries where they received their qualifications and training, and their knowledge was not transferred back to the Caribbean. Some of these women, however, went on to pioneer teaching and public health initiatives, or even to enter medical or other therapeutic professions.

In spite of the presence of women in scientific professions, there have been limitations on the full access and participation of women in the sciences. Inequalities in science education are one area in which gender has operated to undermine the participation of women. Even when women were permitted access to the necessary educational resources, the availability of that education was gendered. Victorian middle-class education for women did teach some scientific principles, but only as part of an effort to ensure that women had a rudimentary understanding of science so that they could teach their children, especially their sons (Dyhouse 1977). But many more barriers were established. For instance, women were refused entry to universities and medical schools, because medical perceptions about "women's educability" in the Victorian period limited the extent of women's participation in higher education. At the time, women were perceived to be unfit for the task of pursuing higher education because of their reproductive function, their "excitability" and the supposed ill effects of overwork on the female body. Moreover, women's pursuit of higher education was considered to be contrary to their maternal destiny (Digby 1989).

Throughout the colonial world, education (especially science education) was segregated and serviced the interests of empire. In Barbados, secondary schools such as Harrison College and Queen's College, for boys and girls, respectively, developed as top-tier schools in the education system. They offered bright students an opportunity to pursue a secondary education, but rarely did these students move beyond their status as colonial subjects. These schools were largely reserved for members of the middle and upper classes, who were intended to hold a particular station above the labourers who benefitted from the elementary system (Mayers 1995, 259). Students who could not earn money to pay fees by winning highly competitive scholarships had only limited access to the secondary system (ibid., 261). Race and class were critical determinants for access to education, but girls also experienced the limitations of a gender-based education system and curriculum (ibid.).

From the inception of Queen's College in 1883, girls were taught more "feminine" and "practical" subjects, such as reading, writing and domestic science. In the early twentieth century, this kind of education prepared girls to become good wives and mothers, or to enter female-oriented careers such as secretarial work (ibid., 264–66). When Elsie Payne (*née* Pilgrim), a student from Queen's College, became the first woman to win the prestigious Barbados Scholarship in 1946, it was a milestone for Barbadian women and their access to higher education. Although a stellar achievement, Pilgrim's academic choices were limited to pursuing an arts-based education at the tertiary level. By the 1950s, girls who wanted to pursue science-related courses had to, for a time, use the laboratories at the all-male Harrison College – posing a severe limitation on their ability to contribute equally to Caribbean science. Harrison College, by contrast, offered a wider variety of courses, including science, to prepare largely middle-class and elite young men to be loyal citizens of the empire, with many of those interested in science being encouraged to pursue agricultural science to continue to develop the region's sugar and other agricultural industries.

The fall-out over gendered ideas about science and scientific ability has resulted in women shunning the sciences in favour of the arts and social sciences. The legacy of imperial and colonial notions of race and gender has left many postcolonial societies dealing with skewed gender participation in the sciences. In spite of the increased access to tertiary-level education, women still largely enter non-scientific disciplines. This is a worldwide problem facing many societies striving to achieve gender equality.[1] Women continue to be underrepresented in science-related fields. Women comprise more than 60 per cent of the overall undergraduate enrolment at the Cave Hill campus of the University of the West Indies (UWI Cave Hill 2007/8, 4). Although women have achieved parity with men in enrolment in the scientific disciplines (women comprise 46 per cent of the overall enrolment in the medical sciences and pure and applied sciences), this trend is not reflective of overall enrolment patterns, where one would expect to see women outnumbering men, as in non-science disciplines (UWI Cave Hill 2007/8). Although these trends are widely acknowledged, there has been little investigation into why these notions have become so entrenched in Caribbean society, and there is little historical data or analysis by which to gauge whether this is changing at any level in the education system.

Conclusion

This chapter establishes some positionings for gender and the HSTM, and poses some theoretical and methodological considerations for the historian of STM. But, more importantly, it establishes the need for a HSTM for the region, placing gender squarely at the centre of the discipline. The disciplines of STM are becoming important actors in the region's development, as policymakers are increasingly looking at modern STM to promote and safeguard continued economic and social development. But without an understanding of the historical evolution of STM in the lives of Caribbean men and women (past and present), there can be little success if external knowledge systems are merely transferred, and in some cases adapted. There are wider implications for gender and STM, particularly because health policies and reproductive technologies are often imported with little regard to the ways in which Caribbean men and women interpret their health status or perceive reproductive challenges. There must be a dialogue between these social understandings of scientific knowledge and authority, and STM. Historians of STM can bridge this divide if they are sensitive to the roles gender, race, ethnicity and class play in the construction of Caribbean STM.

Note

1.   In some countries, women's participation in the sciences, or at least in certain disciplines, does not reflect this trend. In India, the number of women studying higher mathematics almost exceeds the number of men. The experience of women scientists and doctors in post-Communist countries, where women and men have been expected to participate fully in society, is also very different. See Hays 2005, 119–33.

References

Beckles, H. McD. 2001. Nursing colonial wounds: Nita Barrow and public health reform after the 1930s workers' revolution. In *Stronger, surer, bolder: Ruth Nita Barrow: Social change and international development,* ed. E. Barriteau and A. Cobley, 26–48. Kingston: University of the West Indies Press.

Berg, A.-J., and M. Lie. 1995. Feminism and constructivism: Do artifacts have gender? *Science, Technology and Human Values* 20 (3): 332–51.

Chamberlaine, W. 1792. *A practical treatise on the efficacy of stizolobium: Or, cowhage (the dolichos pruriens of Linnaeus) internally administered, in diseases occasioned by worms. To which are added observations on other anthelmintics of the West-Indies.* 5th ed. London: n.p.

Collins, D. 1803/1971. *Practical rules for the management and medical treatment of Negro slaves in the sugar colonies.* London: Vernor, Hood and Sharp.

Dancer, T. 1801. *The medical assistant; Or, Jamaica practice of physic: Designed chiefly for the use of families and plantations.* Kingston: Aikman.

De Barros, J. 2003. Sanitation and civilization in Georgetown, British Guiana. *Caribbean Quarterly* 49 (4): 65–86.

Digby, A. 1989. Women's biological straitjacket. In *Sexuality and subordination: Interdisciplinary studies of gender in the nineteenth century*, ed. S. Mendus and J. Rendall, 192–220. London: Routledge.

Dyhouse, C. 1977. Good wives and little mothers: Social anxieties and the schoolgirl's curriculum, 1890–1920. *Oxford Review of Education* 3 (1): 21–35.

Hays, J.N. 2005. *Epidemics and pandemics: Their impacts on human history*. Santa Barbara: ABC-CLIO.

Higman, B. 1984. *Slave populations of the Caribbean, 1807–1834*. Bridgetown: University of the West Indies Press.

Hillary, W. 1766. *Observations of the changes of the air and the concomitant epidemical diseases in the island of Barbadoes and other West India islands*. London: Hawes, Clarke and Collins.

Kiple, K. 1984. *The Caribbean slave: A biological history*. Cambridge: Cambridge University Press.

Kiple, K., and V. Kiple. 1981. *Another dimension to the black diaspora: Diet, disease, and racism*. Cambridge: Cambridge University Press.

Laqueur, T. 1992. *Making sex: Body and gender from the Greeks to Freud*. Cambridge: Harvard University Press.

Lascelles, E., et al. 1786. *Instructions for the management of a plantation in Barbadoes and for the treatment of Negroes*. London: n.p.

Ligon, R. 1657/ 1998. *A true and exact history of the island of Barbadoes*. London: Frank Cass.

Long, E. 1774. *History of Jamaica*. Vol. 2. London: Lowndes.

Loudon, I. 1992. *Death in childbirth: An international study of maternal care and maternal mortality, 1800–1950*. Oxford: Clarendon Press.

Mayers, J. 1995. Access to secondary education for girls in Barbados, 1907–43: A preliminary analysis. In *Engendering history: Caribbean women in historical perspective*, ed. V. Shepherd, B. Brereton and B. Bailey, 258–78. Kingston: Ian Randle.

Mott, M.L. 2003. Midwifery and the construction of an image in nineteenth-century Brazil. *Nursing History Review* 11: 31–49.

Paton, D. 1996. Decency, dependence and the lash: Gender and the British debate over slave emancipation, 1830–34. *Slavery and Abolition* 17 (3): 163–84.

———. 2001. Punishment, crime, and the bodies of slaves in eighteenth-century Jamaica. *Journal of Social History* 34 (4): 923–54.

Pickstone, J. 2001. *Ways of knowing: A new history of science, technology and medicine*. Chicago: Chicago University Press.

Rossiter, M. 1995. *Women scientists in America: Before affirmative action*. Baltimore, MD: Johns Hopkins University Press.

Seacole, M. 1857/ 1988. *Wonderful adventures of Mrs Seacole in many lands.* Oxford: Oxford University Press.

Sheridan, R. 1985. *Doctors and slaves: A medical and demographic history of slavery in the British West Indies, 1680–1834.* Cambridge: Cambridge University Press.

Sloane, H. 1707–1725. *A voyage to the islands Madera, Barbados, Nieves, St. Christopher and Jamaica: With the natural history . . . of the last of those islands. To which is prefix'd an introduction, wherein is an account of the inhabitants, air, waters, diseases, trade, etc.* 3 vols. London: British Museum.

University of the West Indies, Cave Hill. 2007/8. *Annual Statistics, 2007/8.* Bridgetown: University of the West Indies.

16

Contemporary Gender Relations among Afro-Costa Ricans

CARMEN HUTCHINSON MILLER

Introduction

Scholarly work that focuses on the Afro-Costa Rican population is scarce. The contribution of Meléndez and Duncan (1989), considered a classic not only for academia but also for the Afro-Costa Rican population, was the first publication in the country that had as its subject the Afro-Costa Rican population, whom it did not depict in a stereotypical manner. Meléndez and Duncan's work is considered an important historical documentation of the life of Afro-Caribbean migrant workers and eventually Afro-Costa Rican citizens. Their research mentions two distinct waves of African presence in Costa Rica: the first wave, which began during the period of colonization, and a second wave, which occurred during the late nineteenth century with the immigration of Caribbean labourers for the construction of the railroad. The people of the present Afro-Costa Rican population are direct descendants of this second wave of Africans.

While Meléndez and Duncan's work continues to be an important publication, especially for the younger Afro-Costa Rican generation, it does not focus on relations of gender. Recent research by Senior (2007) places the Afro-Costa Rican community of the twentieth century at the centre of analysis.

Like Meléndez and Duncan, however, Senior does not deal with the issue of relations of gender. Putnam's (2002) publication, while it deals with the issue of relations of gender among those who migrated for the construction of the railroad, does not focus specifically on the Afro-Caribbean and Afro-Costa Rican populations of the late nineteenth century to the mid-twentieth centuries, but also includes other ethnic groups, such as mestizos.

In this analysis, I focus on contemporary Afro-Costa Ricans specifically from the port of Limón, and enquire into the ways in which the social relation of gender plays out among them. Since there is a lack of statistical data on the various ethnic groups within the country, I gathered the information used for this analysis from interviews with sixteen respondents in Costa Rica during 2006. The interviewees were all Afro-Costa Ricans whose ages ranged between twenty-three and eighty-seven years old, with a sex composition of ten females and six males.

Acknowledging and Fighting to Eradicate Gender Inequalities

Most women and men who have internalized power relations and practise the established and unquestioned gender roles that have been perpetuated through existing patriarchal institutions are unaware that these roles are ideologies constructed by classical political thinkers. Scholars such as Agonito (1977) and Bell (1973) present a comprehensive analysis of these philosophers, theologians and educators, and their thoughts about women.

The resilience of misogynistic ideas and practices over the centuries could suggest that these ideas, which are still present, have remained uncontested. Fortunately, this is not the case. The history of humanity has demonstrated that human beings have always fought against injustice, and women of every race and class are no exception.

Over the centuries, feminist scholars have challenged misogynistic ideas in their efforts to promote equality for women. Following in their footsteps, contemporary scholars continue to challenge the persistent misogynistic and androcentric ideas that are still manifest, in overt and covert ways, throughout different societies. Scholars such as Groag (1973), Agonito (1977), Schüssler (1992), hooks (1984), Lerner (1986), Scott (1986), Gunew (1990), Loades (1990), Hill Collins (1990), Yuval-Davis (1997), Leitinger (1997) and Barriteau (2001) have dealt with the various and distinct aspects of women's inequality, oppression, subordination and exploitation. They have identified androcentric biases, critiquing them, suggesting alternatives and taking the actions necessary to bring about changes at the social, political and economic levels.

Costa Rica, like other former colonized countries, did not escape Western misogynist influences. Research by Chavarria (1993) gives an insight into twentieth-century Costa Rican women's battles to be recognized as full citizens. On the question of Costa Rican women's right to vote, an article published in *La Tribuna* in 1923 shows how Costa Rican politicians would consider women's suffrage an important point on their agenda when they wanted to gain sympathy. The article also records the continuous lobbying of La Liga Femenina (The Feminine League) with petitions for women's suffrage, which the different congresses discussed from 1923 up to 1943 without any positive results for the advocates (see Leitinger 1997).

Fortunately, the Liga Femenina was not alone in its struggle for women's equality. While it did not get the results it desired in the early 1920s and 1940s, Costa Rican women would soon enjoy the right to vote by the early 1950s, along with women in many other countries. Tables 16.1 and 16.2 provide a list of countries that gave women the right to vote in the Americas and the Caribbean in the twentieth century.

Table 16.1. Women's Suffrage in the Americas

Country	Year	Country	Year
Canada	1917	Mexico	1947
United States	1920	Argentina	1947
Ecuador	1929	Costa Rica	1949
Uruguay	1932	Chile	1949
Brazil	1934	Mexico	1953
Bolivia	1938	Colombia	1954
El Salvador	1939	Honduras	1955
Guatemala	1946	Nicaragua	1955
Panama	1946	Peru	1955
Venezuela	1946	Paraguay	1961

Source: Compilation from the Human Development Report 2005.

Table 16.2. Women's Suffrage in the Caribbean

Country	Year	Country	Year
Cuba	1934	Dominica	1951
Dominican Republic	1942	Grenada	1951
Jamaica	1944	St Lucia	1951
Trinidad and Tobago	1946	St Kitts and Nevis	1951
Suriname	1948	St Vincent and	
Barbados	1950	the Grenadines	1951
Haiti	1950	Guyana	1953
Antigua and Barbuda	1951	Belize	1954
		Bahamas	1964

Source: Compilation from the Human Development Report 2005.

Gaining the right to vote did not guarantee better conditions for women. During the twentieth century, after gaining suffrage, women did not enjoy the formal equality they anticipated. Faced with this reality, women continued their quest for this elusive equality through local, national, regional and international organizing.

In the twentieth century, women's collective efforts have resulted in the organization of four World Conferences on Women[1] and the enactment of the Convention on the Elimination of All Forms of Discrimination Against Women (CEDAW).[2] A list of Hispanic countries signatory to CEDAW is shown in table 16.3, and other conventions for the protection of women and children are shown in table 16.4.

Table 16.3. Hispanic American States That Are Parties to CEDAW

State	Date of Signature
Argentina	17 July 1980
Bolivia	30 May 1980
Brazil	31 March 1981

Table continues

422

Table 16.3. Hispanic American States That Are Parties to CEDAW (*cont'd*)

State	Date of Signature
Chile	17 July 1980
Colombia	17 July 1980
Costa Rica	17 July 1980
Ecuador	17 July 1980
El Salvador	14 November 1980
Guatemala	8 June 1981
Honduras	11 June 1980
Mexico	17 July 1980
Nicaragua	17 July 1980
Panama	26 June 1980
Peru	23 July 1981
Uruguay	30 March 1981
Venezuela	17 July 1980

Source: Compilation from CEDAW states parties, http://www.un.org/womenwatch/daw/cedaw/states.htm.

Table 16.4. Other United Nations Conventions and Declarations on Women

Conventions	Declarations	Year
Protocol to prevent, suppress and punish trafficking in persons, especially women and children, supplementing the United Nations Convention against Transnational Organized Crime		2003
Convention on consent to marriage, minimum age for marriage and registration of marriages		1962
Convention against discrimination in education		1960

Table continues

Table 16.4. Other United Nations Conventions and Declarations on Women (*cont'd*)

Conventions	Declarations	Year
Convention on discrimination (employment and occupation)		1958
Convention on the nationality of married women		1957
Convention on the political rights of women		1952
Convention on equal remuneration		1951
Convention for the suppression of the traffic in persons and of the exploitation of the prostitution of others		1949
	Declaration on the elimination of violence against women	1994
	Declaration on the protection of women and children in emergencies and armed conflicts	1974

Source: UNIFEM 2004, 56.

Social Relations of Gender

Costa Rica, like other former colonies of Europe, inherited European sexist ideology. Nineteenth-century political leader Dr José María Castro Madriz, influenced by the liberal ideas of the period, thought that he was being progressive when he passed a decree to establish a school for women called the *escuela normal para mujeres* (normal school for women) in 1847. The fact that a decree had to be passed to make education available to women is just another indication of the inequality of women within Costa Rican society.

Zeledón (1997, 260) quotes part of Dr Castro Madriz's speech, delivered in 1847. Castro Madriz states that one of the most important objectives of public morality and social benefit is the education of the beautiful sex, from which springs the loving daughter who flatters and sweetens her parents in old age, the faithful wife who makes the happiness of the domestic home, and the tender mother destined by nature to form, like the first teacher, the heart of man. Madriz was voicing the ideological sentiments of an androcentric society, and while he was considered very progressive at the time, his statement confirms the gender inequality within the society. Costa Rican women were not being educated for personal empowerment; they were being educated within the public sphere to be better daughters, wives and mothers. Madriz was only echoing Jean-Jacques Rousseau's position on women in the eighteenth century when, according to Hamilton (1999), Rousseau stated that "the whole education of women ought to be relative to men. To please them, to be useful to them, to make themselves loved and honoured by them, to educate them when young, to care for them when grown, to counsel them, to console them and to make life sweet and agreeable to them – these are the duties of women at all times, and should be thought of from infancy" (Hamilton 1999, 4). Presently there is the false perception that the situation of Costa Rican women is optimal, since Costa Rica is signatory to the CEDAW convention and Costa Rican women legally enjoy the privileges and responsibilities that come with being citizens. There is a need to be cautious with these gender equality illusions, especially when embedded androcentric ideologies continue to be maintained.

Some of these inequalities are evident today in legal documents that appear to seek equality, as in the case of Costa Rica's Family Code. In article 16.2, concerning marriage prohibition, the code states that a woman wanting to remarry after a divorce should wait three hundred days from the dissolution or annulment of a previous marriage before marrying again, unless she gives birth before the prescribed term is complete, or proves that she is not pregnant through examination by two official medical doctors (Family Code 1974, 16.2). The inequality in this piece of legislation is that the prohibition does not apply to divorced Costa Rican men. This inequality stands in stark contrast to Costa Rican women's continuous contribution to the development of their country, with their active participation in almost every field within the public sphere.

The *Human Development Report* (2007/8) ranks Costa Rica relatively highly, in the forty-eighth position among countries. On the gender-related Development Index, Costa Rica ranks forty-seventh, with women's literacy at 95.1 per cent. On the Gender Empowerment Measure, Costa Rica ranks twenty-fourth, with 38.6 per cent of the seats in parliament held by women, and 44.9 per cent of women age fifteen and over are involved in economic activity (*Human Development Report* 2007/8, 326, 330, 338).

Despite these rankings, Costa Rican women still suffer inequalities within their society. Their active participation in the public sphere, as reflected by the figures in the *Human Development Report* (2007/8), would suggest that, in the private sphere where they are safe and protected, their spouses, boyfriends, and partners support their involvement in public matters. Regrettably, this is untrue in many cases.

Tangible evidence of the inequalities suffered by Costa Rican women appears in their earning capacity. The Human Development Report states that the estimated earned income for Costa Rican women is US$6,983, while the earnings of Costa Rican men is 53 per cent more, US$13,271 (*Human Development Report* 2007/8, 326). This is not surprising since efforts made in changing the conditions of Costa Rican women have focused on political and educational participation and less so on economic empowerment.

Another worrisome manifestation of gender inequality within Costa Rican society is that of violence, which is more evident within the private sphere. Here, the CEDAW convention and the Ley de Promoción de la Igualdad Social de la Mujer (Law to Promote Women's Equal Social Rights, law 7142),[3] along with the Ley Contra la Violencia Doméstica (Law Against Domestic Violence, law 7586) and Costa Rica's ratification of the BELEM DO PARA convention in 1995,[4] are unable to guarantee the protection that Costa Rican women need from abusive partner relationships in the privacy and "sanctuary" of their homes.

According to *Al Día*, the Costa Rican newspaper (12 April 2007), statistics on the increase in domestic violence in Costa Rica reveal that, in 2006 alone, 5,327 women attended La Delegación de la Mujer, and 35 women were murdered by their spouses. As is well known in cases related to domestic violence, these estimates are conservative. Table 16.5, compiled from information that appeared in *Al Día* between 2003 and 2007, illustrates selected reports of some of the violent acts and the types of violence perpetrated against women by men.

As a result of this alarming situation, beginning in 2000, under the leadership of then-president Miguel Angel Rodriguez, some ministers and feminist

Table 16.5. Some Headlines on Domestic Violence: *Al Día* Newspaper, 2003–2007

Date	Headline	Brief Summary of Report
9 October 2003	Domestic violence is worrisome	"Sarapiquí . . . The office in charge of minor contravention has processed 315 reports for domestic violence in the first nine months of the year . . ."
28 January 2004	Violence without a truce	"They did know how to protect themselves from those who supposedly loved them . . . in at least seven cases, the women had the protective measures and their aggressors had antecedents . . ."
16 March 2004	Domestic violence out of control	"Nicaraguan Marlene Vargas Morera is the ninth victim for the year of domestic violence . . . Vargas, 50 years of age, died last night of a stab [wound] in her thorax, allegedly by her partner, surnamed Moya . . ."
8 March 2005	Domestic violence does not cease	"In Ciudad Quesada. Today on International Women's Day the worrying numbers of reports and consultations on domestic violence blurs the message of respect and equality for them . . ."
13 December 2006	67 thousand reports for domestic aggression	"On the afternoon of February 21st Carolina Duarte, age 26, received a shot in the head, allegedly after a discussion with her partner, who shot himself in the head afterward in the house where both were living in Limón . . ."
3 October 2007	Housewife saved from being buried alive	"In Pococí of Limón a man with the surname Mendoza tried to bury her alive after putting a 22-calibre rifle to her chest and hitting her unconscious . . ."

Source: Compilation from *Al Día* newspapers, 2003 to 2007. The articles have been translated from Spanish.

groups concerned with the conditions of women made an effort to turn the project "La Ley para la Penalización de la Violencia contra las Mujeres" (Law to Penalize Violence Against Women) into a law. For seven years they faced resistance, since many thought that some of the punishments that appear in the law were too harsh for the perpetrators. An *Al Día* report of 1 March 2004 described some of the punishments that would be included in the proposed law: twenty to thirty-five years' imprisonment for femicide; twelve to eighteen years for sexually abusing a woman; two to ten years for restricting or prohibiting women's freedom (with one to twelve years applied to the aggressor, as well as an inhibition to practise in the post or profession in the ambit where the crime was committed); three to six years for forcing a woman into painful and humiliating acts during sexual intercourse; two to five years for forcing a woman to have sexual intercourse with third parties for economic gain; and six months to two years' imprisonment for physically abusing a woman or stopping her from expressing her right to self-determination.

Those against the project argue that it would be discriminatory if it were to become law, since it punishes only abuse and aggression against women. Others dispute that it would be unconstitutional. Among those who disputed the law was parliamentarian Carlos Ricardo Benavides, who stated that, because of the law's ambiguity, if it is not clear that a relationship a man has with a woman is that of confidence, it is impossible for him to know if his behaviour can result in imprisonment (*Al Día,* 25 February 2005).

Despite opposition from members of parliament and the general public, the reality is that women are abused, to the point of death in many cases. It is the inherited misogynistic views embedded in our societies that allow for systematic and continuous injustices against women. As long as women continue to be perceived as men's property within marriage as well as in common-law and visiting unions, the suffering they endure in their homes will continue to be seen as non-political. Therefore, concerned individuals and institutions are in for a long, hard battle.

The expressions of parliamentarian Luis Antonio Barrantes echo the perception of domestic violence as a private matter. On 24 May 2007, *Al Día* quoted him as saying that the proposed Law to Penalize Violence Against Women not only goes against the Political Constitution and individual rights, but also encroaches on the private sphere, and involves penalties that are too open and indeterminate. Notwithstanding implicit concerns about sentiments such as "a man's house is his castle", voiced by Barrantes and many like him, the seven-year legal stale mate over the law ended in May 2007, with the sanctioning of the law by then-president Oscar Arias Sanchez. According to *Al Día* (24 May 2007), the law was approved in its first debate in December 2004, and ratified in the second debate in April 2005 after many discussions and constitutional consultations. The same report listed some of the punishments that would be applied to those found guilty. Two of the penalties discussed in the *Al Día* report three years prior (24 May 2004) remained: thirty-five years' imprisonment for killing a woman, and eighteen years' imprisonment for sexually abusing a woman. This report also included two new punishments that were not mentioned before, a maximum imprisonment of six years for anyone insulting and shaming a woman, publicly or privately, and six years' imprisonment for any man who forces his woman to maintain him. The article reports that the former of these punishments is still questionable, because alleged victims can abuse it.

The sanctioning of the law, while celebrated by those in favour of it, is far from ending endemic domestic violence. I argue that the law will actually cause more violence against women, since many men continue to believe that women are their property. Instituting laws that will deprive them of the right to do as they like with "their" property will only serve to infuriate them further, thus threatening more women's lives. Costa Rica is a patriarchal society and patriarchy is going to fight back. Despite this gloomy forecast, the executive president of the Instituto Nacional de la Mujer (National Institute for Women) was in a celebratory mood when she stated to *Al Día* (24 May 2007) that Costa Rica is at the forefront in the protection of women's rights, since Spain is the only other country that has a similar law. As it relates to the condition of women and the struggle for a violence-free life of equality, what does this scenario say about gender relations among the Afro-Costa Rican population?

Gender Relations among Afro-Costa Ricans

Within the Costa Rican context, data on domestic disputes are not disaggregated according to ethnic groups. As a matter of fact, there are no data of any type that are disaggregated by groups. If one were to be guided by the newspapers and radio reports which feature mainly mestizos (the leading ethnic group) in demographic pieces, one might get the wrong impression that Afro-Costa Ricans, as well as other ethnic groups such as the Chinese and the Amerindians, do not suffer from this societal ill. This is just an indication of racial neglect, and of an area of research that needs to be explored.

Contemporary Afro-Costa Ricans do have difficulties in their relationships. They might not report them, however, because of cultural differences in handling these kinds of situations. I suspect that Afro-Costa Ricans, living within a racist society such as this one, are cognizant of the fact that they would get too much media attention, which would not only help perpetuate the stereotype that this group is aggressive but would also deflect attention from the issue at hand: unequal gender relations.

Historical evidence taken from newspapers attests to the fact that, even if articles do not clearly state that the subjects involved are Afro-Costa Ricans, people were certainly engaged in romance, divorce and violent relationships in the province of Limón. It is important to note that Port Limón is the area where the largest number of Afro-Costa Ricans lives. This has been so since the construction of the railroad in the late nineteenth century, when the area was peopled by a large number of Afro-Caribbean migrant workers.

One newspaper of the late 1920s reports a woman being charged for the murder of her husband. It is not clear if she was of African descent because the report highlights the race of the man who helped her in the crime, not the woman's own race. One could speculate that, based on her name, Roslin Dunkley, she could have been a black woman, because in those days it was more likely that people of Afro-Caribbean descent would have English names.

The *Search Light* reported in 1930: "Mrs Roslin Dunkley, the wife of Luther Stanford Dunkley, is now held in the Limón jail along with one William Ford, a black Jamaican farmer, charged with the murder of her husband which occurred between the 26th and the 28th of June 1929 at 18 miles near the village of Estrada." According to the records of the proceedings, Mrs Dunkley conspired with William Ford to kill her husband because of some dispute in connection with a banana farm owned and managed by the woman accused, and because the deceased had made known his disapproval of Ford's pretentions to be the husband of his eldest daughter, Josephine.

In 1946 the *Atlantic Voice* reported on the proceedings for a divorce and highlighted some of the intimate difficulties that individuals, and certainly Afro-Limonenses,[5] faced in that period: "The Civil Court of Limón has

granted divorce to Mr John Rogers Wright and cancels the marriage union
with his former wife, Mrs Rowena Da Costa Biene. The divorce is obtained
by Mr Rogers free of any claim of pension or any financial obligation in favour
of the wife, the trial judge having found her liable in the act." The historical
evidence continues to demonstrate other types of violent acts perpetrated
against spouses. In 1940 the newspaper *La Prensa Libre* reported a case in
which a wife caused her husband serious burns by pouring hot water on him.

As in the brief historical evidence above, contemporary Afro-Costa Ricans
do not feature in the mass media as perpetrators or victims of domestic violence, but they certainly have relationship difficulties with which they deal on
a daily basis.

Inherited Caribbean Gender Relations

When Afro-Caribbean migrants arrived on the Costa Rican coast in the late
nineteenth century to work on the construction of the railroad, they did so
with their particular and distinct cultural differences, including social relations
of gender. The social relations of gender which Caribbean migrants brought
with them to Costa Rican shores were similar to those of Costa Rican society.
Ideologically, Caribbean migrants, when they settled, expected women to be
submissive and subservient, even when social and economic conditions created
different expressions of gender relations.

Caribbean scholars in academic fields such as the social sciences, history
and gender studies have dealt with the issues of female–male socialization and
the social relations of gender. Some of these include Wilson (2001), Massiah
(1982; 1986), Mohammed and Shepherd (1988), Barrow (1998), Mohammed
and Perkins (1999), Chevannes and Brown (1998), Shepherd, Brereton and
Bailey (1995), Reddock (2004a), Barriteau (2002), and Tang Nain and Bailey
(2003).The history of Caribbean slavery and, later, the push and pull factors
that motivated massive migration construed an interesting but tension-riddled
relationship between what is expected from both sexes and what was practised
in Costa Rica.

When dealing with migrants, gender and work, Putnam (2002) speaks of
what men would have liked to happen, but what reality forced them to do in
terms of the daily domestic organization within the private sphere:

In migrants' societies of origin, as in most places and times, the labor that ensured daily social reproduction was usually performed by women rather than men and provided under the structure of kinship obligations rather than market exchange. In Limón this was not the case. Here most men found themselves far from aunts or mothers, sweethearts or wives. Of course in theory men could perform maintenance chores for themselves, and sometimes they did.

A knife-and-pistol duel in 1901 began when Jamaican Simon Clark, a "contractor who weeds banana farms . . . went with my crew. . . down to the river to wash our clothes, as we do every Sunday", and James Taylor, also Jamaican, came by and with "vulgar words" ordered the men away from their accustomed spot. (Putnam 2002, 51–52)

This quotation highlights the daily domestic situation of Afro-Caribbean migrant workers. It also reveals the fact that these men knew how to do chores generally perceived as belonging to women. It also suggests, however, that they would have expected the women to do these chores if they had migrated with female counterparts.

This is not surprising. Based on Barriteau's (2001) work on the unequal relations of gender which the Caribbean inherited from European colonizers, this type of sexual division of labour is expected. Peter Wilson's research (2001) demonstrates unequal relations of gender and the double standards imposed on women (while not identifying it in those terms) in the Caribbean of the 1960s. These unequal relations of gender are still prevalent because of the importance given to reputation in the case of men, and respectability in the case of women. Pursuit of the latter concept restricts women to the private sphere, where they are sheltered and controlled.

Within contemporary Caribbean and Costa Rican societies these perceptions are still expected, even if many are not practised. The collective hysteria among many Caribbean men and women about "Caribbean men in crisis", and the male marginalization thesis, provide evidence of men's loss of total control over women. These reactions represent another way in which the relentless ideology of male superiority wants to ignore the advances that Caribbean women have made over the past thirty years.

During the late nineteenth and into the twentieth century, Caribbean labour migrants in Costa Rica recreated their relations of gender through prevailing gender ideologies. Putnam (2002) demonstrates how the range of values and characteristics relating to reputation and respectability played out among the Afro-Caribbean community of the nineteenth century. Anecdotes from older Afro-Costa Ricans reveal defined gender roles in relation to discipline that were ascribed to both the mother and father: when a child misbehaved, the mother would wait until the end of the day when the father returned home before punishing the unruly child.

Another aspect of the relations of gender evident among Afro-Costa Ricans – and another inheritance from Afro-Caribbean migrants – is the social and economic value of marriage. In a 2001 research paper I reported on the importance of marriage, especially to older Afro-Limonense women. One sixty-three-year-old Afro-Limonense female affirmed: "In my days I always ask the Lord to help not to go and live with anybody because if I am good enough to live with you, I am good enough to marry you. If [I] even marry and divorce" (Hutchinson Miller 2002). What we can note from this account is the practice of common-law relationships in the Afro-Costa Rican community, notwithstanding the popular belief that marriage is the respectable and desirable thing to do. There is respectability in marriage, especially for women, even if they divorce later.

Another social relation Afro-Costa Rican women inherited from their Caribbean grandmothers is the issue of wage work. In my 2002 research paper I highlighted some of the informal economic activities in which many Afro-Jamaican women and Afro-Costa Ricans were involved, in order to take care of themselves and their families. Afro-Costa Ricans, specifically Afro-Limonenses who are over forty years of age and who would have grown up during the period when baskets were heavily used by vendors, have memories of women with their baskets on their heads or around their hips, waiting at every train station to hop on a train or reach through the train windows to sell what they had prepared. Their goods included foods like yucca roll (fried cassava with meat filling), grater cake, pan bon, patty, gizzada, cut cake, plantain tart, fried fish and many other goodies made from cassava, coconut, flour, plantain or any other edible product that was plentiful. A lot of these products are still sold today at the bus stops in the city of Limón, but the vendors are not only women, but also mestizos and Afro-Costa Rican men. Men's return to historical and informal ways of making money, such as selling food, is an indication of the labour conditions of the provinces.

While Putnam's research does not focus directly on Afro-Caribbean women and work, it substantiates the type of economic activities in which women were involved during the period of the construction of the railroad. 'The word "higgler" was never widely used in Limón, but that was the exact role of women like Sarah Simon, who rode the train back from San José to Zent in 1899 with a market basket filled with eighty eggs and three pounds of coffee, or Ella Kelly, who left her home in Matina centre at four o'clock as usual one morning in 1906 to "see to her obligation, that of picking up the milk at Mile 23 and carrying it to sell at Zent Junction"' (Putnam 2002, 53). According to Putnam's research, other types of economic activities among women included managing stores; for example, "In 1898 Jamaican Ada Gale owned a storefront in Cimarrones with a room behind, where she lived with her four teenage sons and daughters and her consensual partner" (Putnam 2002, 53). One of my respondents testifies to another type of economic activity in which Afro-Limonense women were involved. The respondent mentions that his mother was an "adventurer" (i.e., higgler) from Limón who had a cook shop in Cartago, one of Costa Rica's seven provinces. In sharing where his parents came from, he commented that his father was from Jamaica but had never returned to his homeland after migrating to Costa Rica in 1903. This respondent also gave other evidence of Afro-Caribbean women's economic involvement. He commented that his maternal grandmother was born in Jamaica. During her lifetime she travelled to Cuba, and lived in Panama. He thinks she also went to India. He notes she was very adventurous, and finally died in the United States. It is not clear in his conversation if the purpose of his grandmother's travels was for business or pleasure. One can surmise that his grandmother's travels would have had an impact on his mother, who was an Afro-Costa Rican involved in commercial activities, including setting up a cook shop in Cartago.

Findings on Social Relations of Gender among Contemporary Afro-Costa Ricans

Now I will focus on my own findings from sixteen interviewees, whose responses I will use to illuminate social relations of gender among contemporary Afro-Costa Ricans. I use Barriteau's model of material and ideological relations of gender as my theoretical framework in helping to explain these relationships.

Despite the advances that women have made and continue to make within
the public sphere, within existing patriarchal societies such as Costa Rica there
are still certain social expectations for women at the ideological level. What I
simply call social expectations, Barriteau defines as the ideological dimensions
of gender systems: "I define a gender system as comprising a network of power
relations with two principal dimensions: one ideological and the other material
. . . The material dimension reveals access to and the allocation of power,
status and resources within a given community or society . . . The ideological
dimension involves the construct of masculinity and femininity" (2001, 30).

This definition explains succinctly the reality that plays out in general
within Costa Rican society, of which Afro-Costa Ricans are a part. It alludes
to the influence of patriarchal teachings that are perpetuated through institutions such as the church, school and family. There is no better example of this
perpetuation within the Costa Rican context than the primary-school textbook
Paco y Lola, used for decades within the Costa Rican educational system. In
this text the images leave no doubts about the clearly defined roles for girls,
boys, women and men. They contribute to the construct of femininity and
masculinity in Costa Rica. Girls in this text remain in the home learning to
wash and bake by watching their mothers, while the boy is outside kicking a
ball, and his father is sitting comfortably in the house reading a newspaper.
These images overtly transmit unequal gender roles, which they accept as the
rule of thumb. And what better way to instil ideologies than from an early
age in innocent human beings without much life experience who are going to
accept without question what the images impart?

Despite material changes in gender relations in Costa Rica (evidenced by
the HDR report 2007/8), conservative views about women and men are still
prevalent. These views create tension between those who want unequal conditions for women to change and those who want these conditions to remain,
exacerbating other socio-economic, political, and cultural tensions already
present in the society. The interviewees confirm that material and ideological
relations of gender are present within the Afro-Costa Rican community by
responding to the following questions about their personal relationships: Who
took the initiative in the courting process? At what age did their relationships
(whether common-law union or marriage) start? And who is considered the
head of the house or family?

Women: Initiation of Courtship

All the women interviewed mentioned that men are the ones who take the initiative, although they admitted that this tradition is changing with the younger generation. Nonetheless, the responses confirm that the ideology that the man must be the initiator is still prevalent today. Despite affirming that things are changing and that men of her generation expect women to be aggressive, one twenty-three-year-old year old interviewee stated that it is still a predominant belief that men should initiate relationships, and that women should wait. She admits that she herself once held that belief but that she has realized, along with other women of her generation, that men like women to be aggressive.

While this interviewee's response suggests a slight shift in the expectations of men and women in contemporary Afro-Costa Rican relationships, and probably the entire Costa Rican population, it is certain that, during the era of older respondents, it was clear who did and did not take the initiative. A sixty-two-year-old interviewee stated in her response: "In the relationship the man maybe is who come and say [to start the relationship]. In our generation we were taught that they are to come. We had to wait; we had to wait until them come to you." This convention would have posed a problem for women who either adhered or did not adhere to it. Questions that arise include: What happens if a particular woman likes, or is interested in, someone other than the one who approaches her? What happens to the woman whom no one approaches? Are these women condemned to a life of unhappiness for lack of choice? Patriarchy presents men as the prize/trophy that women should aspire to, and feel lucky and grateful to have.

A fifty-one-year-old respondent raised an interesting point about perception and practice. She stated that, in her time, it was the man who took the initiative, but that this practice has changed slightly; yet she also acknowledged that after the man makes the first move it is the woman who takes control. She suggests that men and women assume one role in the public sphere, and another in private. This idea is understandable within a patriarchal system which has imposed dominant gender roles on men and has left some women to manoeuver their power within the private sphere in order not to make men look as if they are weak or lack control in public.

Men: Initiation of Courtship

While the men were less unanimous than the women in answering the question of who takes the initiative in courtship, their answers confirmed the ideological and material relations of gender that Barriteau (2001) has explained. Three of the men said that men take the initiative, one said that both men and women do, and two others said that women do. One male respondent, between sixty and seventy years of age, clearly demonstrated how power relations play out when he admitted that, in his time, men took the initiative but women were the ones who decided whether or not to accept the advances. His statement indicates that both men and women took the initiative, despite the fact that men were the dominant ones in pursuing.

A sixty-one-year-old Afro-Limonense respondent also showed another dimension to gender relations – that of women being considered suggestive by the way they dress, and the way men interpret this alleged suggestiveness. He agreed with the female respondents, and some of the other men, that men take the initiative, and added that, in some cases, women take the first step through their body language and the way they dress. What he is suggesting is that a man might end up having intercourse with a provocatively dressed woman, since this is the way the patriarchal system understands a woman who is confident and does not conform to established androcentric norms: "In my time it was a male approach. But, for instance, there is a[n] aggressive approach by a woman based on their dress, and style. OK, so you expose so much that it makes it easy for the guys to approach, and sometimes there are no limits."

Women: Proper Age for Courtship

Opinions on the proper age for courtship depend on the upbringing of the young people involved. In many if not all Afro-Costa Rican homes, education takes centre stage in children's development. This attitude is understandable among Afro-Costa Ricans living as an ethnic minority. In previous work, I dealt with the important role that education has played, and continues to play, in the life of Afro-Costa Ricans. In their culture, all young people, whether girls or boys, have to pursue their education before thinking seriously about getting into a relationship.

A fifty-four-year-old Afro-Limonense woman indicated that, in her time, there was not a specific age for starting the courtship process, a practice that she also continued when she became a parent: "*Bueno*, in my time no *edad* [age]. *Edad* was to study, and finish you studies before you could get a boyfriend. And I pass it down to my own [children]. And when my own se [say], 'Ma, but we come out fifth year now', [I say], 'When you finish university . . . !'"A sixty-two-year-old Afro-Limonense woman shared a popular saying from her time on the issue in question: "First come studies, then marriage, then the baby carriage." This statement does not mean in any way that young people did not engage in relationships in the past; many did so without the knowledge of their parents, as the respondent implied. "I say [the best time for relationships is] in you twenties, thirties, because even when you seventeen, eighteen, sometime you wanted to and the parents wouldn't agree", she said. A significant difference can be noted with a younger Afro-Costa Rican respondent, who indicated that young people engage in courting at all ages but do not begin to think seriously about marriage until around age twenty-five. She commented that it is rare for young people to marry at age twenty-two, as one of her friends was about to do.

Men: Proper Age for Courtship

Here again the men's perspectives coincided with those of the women's. They admitted that the age of permission for courting would depend on what kind of family the young person belongs to. They also agreed with the women that the general allowable age is during puberty.

Women: Marriage and Common-Law Unions

An important construct within men's and women's relationships is that of marriage, which women see as something that they should attain. Those who manage to enter into marriage consider themselves, and are considered, to have attained an elevated status within society, and those who do not are frequently questioned and even live with guilt.

All female respondents admitted that both common-law unions and marriage are widespread among Afro-Costa Ricans, but stated that marriage is more prestigious. A young female acknowledged that women of her generation are not preoccupied with getting married, but with getting an education and a good job; women in her generation are more focused on building and taking care of themselves. All respondents agreed that the man is considered the head of the house and/or family but admitted that, in reality, the woman is the one who runs the family.

A seventy-seven-year-old respondent shared what the practice was in her generation when she stated: "Most living together, because as I told you, the parent don't want you to do the thing [i.e., have intercourse], and when you do it them not gwen [i.e., going to] take you. Them run you out . . . If you mada [mother] even try to save you, you bet she going. If you mada try to save you, the fada [father] throw out the two of you outside. Plenty people use to [get] married you know." The suggestion is that many persons decided to live together because they started having intercourse, which parents may have become aware of as a result of a young woman's becoming pregnant. The lack of support offered by some parents creates another difficulty for the youngsters who are thrown out. Unless they are leaving to live with rich partners, being banished from their parents' homes means that they are in for financial hardships, adding to the complexity that is intrinsic to relationships.

A sixty-two-year-old respondent strengthened the point on couples' not being ready for marriage while she also accepted that, in her time there were both marriages and common-law unions: "You had both, you had both. People would try to [get] married because of certain status, but you had a lot of people were living together and they weren't married, or they would go have this relationship, have children inclusive, and when they half way, then they formalize with a marriage." The idea of people's marrying "because of status" (mostly for women), is owed in part to women's financial dependence. Even if its advocates do not want to admit it, marriage is an economic transaction. Many women, because of their economic and emotional dependency, desire marriage in order to gain not only prestige but also financial stability. Of course, many have encountered hardships. According to a forty-two-year-old respondent, there has been a shift in the status which previous generations accorded to marriage: "In these days now, no. In these days you live together [and] if it works well, when twenty years pass you married."

Currently it is easier for many women, because of their financial autonomy, to leave a relationship that is not working out, although there are still many women who will not leave abusive relationships, despite their financial autonomy, because they are emotionally dependent on their partners and find it difficult to leave them. In the process, they expose themselves and their children to constant abuse.

Men: Marriage and Common-Law Unions

Male respondents, along with females, confirmed that the practice of common-law unions is as prevalent as that of marriage within the Afro-Costa Rican community. The men also agreed with the women that marriage is considered respectable. A man between sixty and seventy years of age summed it up well when he admitted that common-law unions were very common during his time, but that children from these unions, when they became adults, would want their parents to marry. He is suggesting that, even when people live in common-law unions, the women in these unions hope or have the desire to reach the altar in their white dresses. Note, based on his input, that it is the women, and not the men, who have this illusion.

Women: Head of the Family

Again, ideological beliefs convince us that men are the leaders in both the public and private spheres. Therefore, it is not surprising that respondents considered men the heads of families, even in cases where the men do not assume leadership and do not comply with the imposed roles of provider and protector of the family. A forty-two-year-old female respondent made a clear distinction between the ideological and the material – what I would call perception versus reality – by noting that "the man is considered the head of the family, even if he is not, even if he is an ornament in the household because of his lack of participation and collaboration within the family, but in reality the woman is the head due to the added role she has to assume".

A forty-five-year-old woman confirms this statement when she shared an anecdote that illustrates the power dynamic between her mother and father in terms of who ultimately makes decisions. When, as a child, she would ask for something that her mother did not want to give her, her mother would send her to ask her father. If his reply was not in agreement with her mother's, she would have to settle with what her mother agreed to, regardless of what her father said. This story demonstrates that the mother would make the final decision. The respondent went on to share, based on accounts she got from her mother, that many women who did not receive financial support from their partners would look for it elsewhere. They would share whatever they received with their male partners who did not contribute because these men were the "heads" of the house. These responses make it clear how ideological and material relations of gender play out. The man is still considered the head of the family even if he is not contributing, and the women is active in both the private and public spheres, making sure that the rest of the family, including the irresponsible men, are provided for.

A fifty-one-year-old respondent presented a different view. She stated that Afro-Costa Rican women are the heads of the home. She affirmed, first, that all men are irresponsible, but then rephrased her statement to say that not all men are irresponsible, but still incapable of running the family. She attributed this deficiency to the strength and persistence of black women. She gave details of men's behaviour through the decades, explaining that the forefathers, including those of the era of her grandfather and father, were men dedicated to their homes, more so than men today. Men today, by contrast, are more into their children, she noted. She shared that Afro-Costa Ricans complain that they have lost a lot of their African heritage, and chuckled while saying that the men have not lost the heritage of engaging in more than one relationship.

Men: Head of the Family

In regard to the question of who is head of the household, one man indicated that the distinction depends on who is bringing in the highest salary. Most of the men agreed that men are perceived as the heads of the family, but that woman are the necks. One man said that the woman is the head. A sixty-one-year-old respondent indicated that women are more reliable since they are typically the ones who finish their studies, despite the sacrifices many of them have to make. He stated women face life by themselves and assume the role of head of the family even when a man is present in their lives, and therefore have to make the decisions with or without a man.

Couples' Expectations

Some societal myths are constructed around marriage and the idea of couples living happily together forever, and give the wrong idea of eternal bliss. This unrealistic perspective can create anxiety, deception and frustration in couples when they are faced with the reality of living with another person (other than a family member) who not only does not share the same family values in terms of relationships, in most instances, but is unconsciously living out the pre-scribed script assigned to each male and female within their societies.

Women

There was a range of responses to questions about couples' expectations and difficulties, opinions about single men and single women, and opinions about people who do not want to have children. On the question of couples' expectations, female respondents described good relationships in which the partners work together as a couple and demonstrate affection and equality. A forty-five-year-old Afro-Limonense woman responded that, presently, there is a consciousness of mutual respect; the traditional idea that the man is the one who rules no longer prevails, which eliminates pressure on the woman. Today, couples are not forced by societal expectations to stay in relationships that do not work. If they think they can be happy elsewhere, they go and search for that happiness. Note the difference between this answer and that of an eighty-six-year-old respondent, who implied that, in her time, having a good life, raising their children properly and enduring a relationship even if it was not working out well, in this case materially, was part of a couple's expectations: "You know, to have a good life, a good future and to have good means of bringing up the children the right way. It wasn't much, but I did what I could. I think I did my best. You expect to get beta (better), but the thing is, you satisfy wid [i.e., with] what you get." A sixty-two-year-old respondent, in high-lighting the differences between contemporary relationships and those of her generation, saw the positive aspect of today's couples trying to make it work:

> I feel like now they are trying to go together, they are trying, they are trying to make things work when they really decide to live together, because,[I] mean, they have this [thing] they call *marinovio* [a visiting relationship] now, and on weekends you sleep over, no formality, but [I] mean, after they decide to be together under the

same roof or whatever, in lots of cases now I notice these young people would try to do things together. For instance, in my days I don't remember [mentions husband's name] visiting me and, ahm, like come in the kitchen and help me make a sandwich, because that was not well seen. You, as the woman, is who had to prepare something and give [it to] him. Now, you would see these couples where both of them would come from university together, or come from a picture [i.e., movie] whatever, and they preparing something to eat because both of them tired, both of them hungry, both of them work . . . One will be doing the dishes, or one will be putting, you know, setting the table, and the other person preparing whatever. When they finish, they both would take up . . . the dishes off the table and wash them, one dry it. You neva [never] use to see that! That was strictly considered a woman's responsibility and that's something that is changing and is good.

These responses demonstrate the shift in the roles which has certainly affected the perceptions of people coming together to form a union within a relationship. Based on this last respondent's contribution, the scenario looks positive.

Other Gender Considerations

Women

The older women's responses suggested that a single woman is a danger to a married woman. If she has multiple relationships, she is considered a whore; if she has children, she is considered an easy sexual opportunity; and some are considered old maids. Younger women tend to see a single woman as someone who is achieving her personal goals if she does not have children; if she has children, it is seen just as another aspect of her life.

As for the single man, the women expressed that they do not consider men single even when they are divorced or out of formal relationships, because men are never without women in their lives. When a man is confirmed to be truly single, meaning that he does not have any type of relationship with a woman, he is viewed as irresponsible, and people suspect that he could be a lazy man or a woman beater. Others perceive single men as happy human beings who either have women catering to their needs, or are gay. On the question of women who have no children, whether by choice or by nature, older female respondents commented that they saw these women as old maids. Younger respondents saw childless women as women who made choices. The men who answered this question commented that they do not face the same scrutiny as women do.

Men

Male respondents expressed that they expect to find women, whether black or not, at their same professional levels, to enter relationships based on equality, or to maintain traditional gender roles. As for the difficulties, they mentioned financial woes, infidelity, lack of black identity, and meeting a woman from a different province.

A sixty-one-year-old male described the division of labour within his relationship and commented that it is equitable because he cooks since his wife is tired of doing it, because he cleans sometimes, and because he is responsible for much of the daily running of the house. His wife is responsible for washing the dishes. He notices that, with this equitable distribution, she is happier and less stressed, and has more time for herself.

Another fifty-one-year-old male respondent gave a different scenario about expectations, and started off by saying that the Afro-Costa Rican male's lack of knowledge about himself works against his aspirations and good relationships. He continues to note that Afro-Costa Rican males seek professional women as partners. If the woman is not a professional, she must at least be a progressive-thinking individual in order not to be an obstacle to men in their quest to build a good family.

A thirty-five-year-old respondent also spoke about the shift in perceptions of people in relationships, and mentioned couples who work together to build their homes. These couples expect fidelity within the context of a still-existing macho society that allows men to have multiple partners. Men's responses did not differ from women's in supporting a shift in gender relations, and in the desire to have good, happy relationships and families.

Males interviewed gave various responses about the issue of single women. Some commented that a woman's status when single depends on the woman herself, since many single women are well respected. Several respondents expressed that being single is a tragedy for women, because a single woman does not have a man to take care of her. Others viewed single women with suspicion, or as old maids, or saw single women as prizes to be obtained.

Concerning single men, male respondents expressed that they have all the freedom; they walk alone but are not alone. Some single men experience a sort of pressure after age forty, they said, and single women sometimes see men as prizes, depending on their financial capabilities and career choices, such as doctors and lawyers.

According to some of the male respondents, women who do not have children are to be pitied; other respondents verbally abused childless women with names such as "old maid". Older interviewees sometimes expressed respect for these women and saw the issue of having children as the woman's choice. They viewed single men similarly to single women – with respect, with pity, or without seeing single status as a problem.

Male and female responses were not that disparate from one another. They all supported the continuous struggle of an archaic, patriarchal ideology, the alternatives to which individuals resort in order to survive, and the determination of many people, whether consciously or unconsciously, to struggle out of ideological webs in order to achieve decent and fruitful lives.

Similarities and Differences among Afro-Costa Rican Couples

Women

Respondents voiced the following initial comments in response to questions about similarities and differences, the definition of family, and women taking over the workplace. They found that both women and men hold more professional occupations now than in the past. The difficulty is that, despite professional preparation, women continue to suffer inequality in the workplace and receive low wages for the same occupations as men.

A sixty-two-year-old female respondent commented on how social relations of gender play out within marriages, when some men are unable to take advice from their spouses: "Our husbands, they don't listen. And there are certain things they were not taught. Them want to handle certain situations but they don't know how to, and they are so proud of being the man that they cannot, like, lower themselves. They feel that [it] is lower[ing] themselves to try to get help from somebody who knows some more." Other problems experienced within Afro-Costa Rican relationships are those of men's inability to express emotion, relationship priorities, infidelity and financial constraints. One respondent, a forty-five-year-old Afro-Limonense woman, summed these problems up succinctly with her reply on the matter of similarities and differences between partners within Afro-Costa Rican couples: "Afro-Costa Rican men, the majority of them don't express their feelings clearly . . . and some of them [are] easy to be influenced by other men, like, 'Don't stay home tonight, come and get a drink. You wife cian [i.e., cannot] do nothing' . . . Having other women outside is part a [i.e., of] that conflict. And another thing, you know, like no money. If no money not there, things cian [i.e., cannot] work because . . . money and love work together, you understand me, money and love and respect work together."

Men

Men's replies in respect to women being on par professionally were very similar to women's. One difference they identified is that women are more educated than men; therefore, some will earn more than their male partners. They considered that women are better administrators of financial resources. Some men may feel jealous of the achievements of their female partners, but Afro-Costa Ricans, as an ethnic group, are proud of the advancement their women are making. A thirty-five-year-old male respondent expressed that he does not feel put out by women's achievements, a feeling that he attributed to the fact that he considers himself a feminist. He thinks that anything an Afro-Costa Rican achieves is an achievement for all Afro-Costa Ricans.

A twenty-three-year-old respondent also expressed that he does not believe women are replacing men. He thinks that women's advancement has to do with their training, implying with this statement that women have the merit because they work for it. The same sentiment is expressed by an older respondent, an Afro-Limonense man between fifty and sixty years old: "I wouldn't say that [women] are replacing the man, but I would say, yes, indeed the woman is, ahm, marching [at] a faster pace than men . . . The woman is marching [at] a quicker pace and that, ahm, is showing more devotion to self-development more than men . . . That is because the women have more opportunity now what they didn't have before and they are taking advantage."

A sixty-one-year-old respondent was not afraid to share his feeling that women are advancing because of men's irresponsibility. Instead of thinking that women are taking over, he is suggesting that they are overworked. Based on the responses of the interviewees, and despite the lack of statistical data disaggregated by ethnic groups, contemporary Afro-Costa Ricans have been influenced not only by the social relations of gender currently practised within their country but also by those gender relations that they have inherited from their grandparents, the Caribbean immigrant workers of the nineteenth century, and continue to practise.

Despite the lack of research on gender relations among the Afro-Costa Rican population, the information afforded through these interviews provides evidence of tension with the old ideology, which expects women to be submissive, obedient and confined to the private sphere. The new ideology, by contrast, speaks about equality between the sexes and allows women the freedom to choose where and to whom they want to belong, or whether they want to or belong to anyone at all. Some of the tensions between the two ideologies are clearly noticeable when respondents' answers are analysed on the framework of ideological and material relations of gender. It is understandable why Afro-Costa Rican women today – partly because of their history as descendants of migrant workers, and especially descendants of those Caribbean women who have worked in the private and public spheres – are expected to take care of themselves and their families within the private sphere, and also find themselves in tension with their male partners when trying to make a better life in the public sphere. The theoretical framework also helps in understanding how difficult this double burden is for them.

A shift in the traditional relations of gender is obvious in some Afro-Costa Rican men's equitable participation in the home. Even so, many Afro-Costa Rican women continue to be heads of households even when a man is present in the home, because Afro-Costa Rican men continue to suffer the ills of un-problematized patriarchal relationships. This kind of relationship allows men to continue to leave all the domestic activities to women, while they continue to practise those activities, such as infidelity and emotional unavailability, that they believe boost macho reputations.

Afro-Costa Rican women continue to advance professionally, with or without the support of their partners. Despite their professional achievements, however, they still suffer all the same difficulties that come with living within a patriarchal society. And although it seems a contradiction, Afro-Costa Rican women are admired by their male counterparts for their constant struggle to better their lives within a society that is racially unequal. At the same time, some individual Afro-Costa Rican men still find it problematic that "their" women are involved in trying to better themselves professionally, and not putting the same energy and effort into the private sphere. In contrast to views in the anglophone Caribbean of women "taking over", this is not an issue within the Afro-Costa Rican population, based on the findings of these interviews.

Notes

1. The first World Conference on Women was in 1975 in Mexico, the second in 1980 in Copenhagen, the third in 1985 in Nairobi, and the fourth in 1995 in Beijing.
2. The CEDAW is an international convention adopted in 1979, with 185 state parties presently. For in-depth information, check United Nations Development Funds publications.
3. For full information on this law, see Investigaciones Jurídicas, *Ley de Promoción de la Igualdad Social de la Mujer* (San José, Costa Rica: Investigaciones Jurídicas, Año XI, no. 7).
4. For full information on this law and the BELEM Convention, see Colección de Leyes, *Ley Contra la Violencia Doméstica* (San José, Costa Rica: Editores, 2003).
5. The term "Afro-Limonense", as used in this paper, refers to individuals of African descent who were born and raised in the province of Limón. "Afro-Costa Rican" designates individuals of African descent who were born in any province other than Limón.

References

Afro-Costa Rican man, sixty to seventy years of age. 2006. Interview by C. Hutchinson Miller. 24 April. San José, Costa Rica.

Afro-Costa Rican man, sixty-one years of age. 2006. Interview by C. Hutchinson Miller. 24 April. San José, Costa Rica.

Afro-Costa Rican man, thirty-five years of age. 2006. Interview by C. Hutchinson Miller. 1 May. San José, Costa Rica.

Afro-Costa Rican woman, forty-two years of age. 2006. Interview by C. Hutchinson Miller. 20 April. San José, Costa Rica.

Afro-Costa Rican woman, sixty-two years of age. 2006. Interview by C. Hutchinson Miller. 20 April. San José, Costa Rica.

Afro-Limonense man, fifty to sixty years of age. 2006. Interview by C. Hutchinson Miller. 20 April. San José, Costa Rica.

Afro-Limonense woman, eighty-six years of age. 2006. Interview by C. Hutchinson Miller. 3 May. Port Limón, Costa Rica.

Afro-Limonense woman, fifty-four years of age. 2006. Interview by C. Hutchinson Miller. 3 May. Port Limón, Costa Rica.

Afro-Limonense woman, fifty-one years of age. 2006. Interview by C. Hutchinson Miller. 3 May. Port Limón, Costa Rica.

Afro-Limonense woman, forty-five years of age. 2006. Interview by C. Hutchinson Miller. 17 April. San José, Costa Rica

Afro-Limonense woman, seventy-seven years of age. 2006. Interview by C. Hutchinson Miller. 17 April. San José, Costa Rica.

Afro-Limonense woman, sixty-three years of age. 2001. Interview by C. Hutchinson Miller. 11 January. Port Limón, Costa Rica.

Afro-Limonense woman, twenty-three years of age. 2006. Interview by C. Hutchinson Miller. 17 April. San José, Costa Rica.

Agonito, R. 1977. *History of ideas on women: A source book.* New York: Putnam.

Barriteau, Eudine. 2001. *The political economy of gender in the twentieth-century Caribbean.* New York: Palgrave.

Barrow, C., ed. 1998. *Caribbean portraits: Essays on gender ideologies and identities.* Kingston: Ian Randle.

Bell, S. Groag, ed. 1973. *Women from the Greeks to the French Revolution.* Palo Alto, CA: Stanford University Press.

Chavarria, C.A. 1993. *Mujer y Democracia.* San José, Costa Rica: Centro Nacional para el Desarrollo de la Mujer y la Familia.

Chevannes, B., and J. Brown. 1998. *Why men stay so: An examination of gender socialization in the Caribbean.* Kingston: University of the West Indies Press.

Collins, P. Hill. 1990/1991. *Black feminist thought: Knowledge, consciousness, and the politics of empowerment.* New York: Routledge.

Gunew, S., ed. 1990. *Feminist knowledge: Critique and construct.* London: Routledge.

Hamilton, M. 1999. *Women and higher education in the Commonwealth Caribbean: UWI — A progressive university for women?* Working paper no. 2. Bridgetown: Centre for Gender and Development Studies, University of the West Indies, Cave Hill.

hooks, b. 1984. *Feminist theory: From margin to centre.* Cambridge: South End.

Hutchinson-Miller, C. 2002. *In memory of my ancestors: Contribution of Afro-Jamaican female migrants in Port Limón, Costa Rica, 1872–1890.* Working paper no. 8. Bridgetown: Centre for Gender and Development Studies, University of the West Indies.

Leitinger, I.A., ed. 1997. *The Costa Rican women's movement: A reader.* Pittsburgh: University of Pittsburgh Press.

Lerner, G. 1986. *The creation of patriarchy.* New York: Oxford University Press.

Loades, A., ed. 1990. *Feminist theology: A reader.* London: Knox.

Massiah, J., ed. 1982. *Women and the family.* Bridgetown: Institute of Social and Economic Research, University of the West Indies.

———, ed. 1986. *Women in the Caribbean.* Bridgetown: Institute of Social and Economic Research, University of the West Indies, Cave Hill.

Meléndez, C., and Q. Duncan. 1989. *El Negro en Costa Rica.* San José: Editorial Costa Rica.

Mohammed, P., and A. Perkins. 1999. *Caribbean women at the crossroads: The paradox of motherhood among women of Barbados, St Lucia and Dominica.* Kingston: Canoe.

Mohammed, P., and C. Shepherd, eds. 1988. *Gender in Caribbean development: Papers presented at the inaugural seminar of the University of the West Indies women and development studies project.* Kingston: University of the West Indies Press.

Putnam, L. 2002. *The company they kept: migrants and the politics of gender in Caribbean Costa Rica, 1870–1960.* Chapel Hill: University of North Carolina Press.

Reddock, R.E., ed. 2004. *Interrogating Caribbean masculinities: Theoretical and empirical analyses.* Kingston: University of the West Indies Press.

Schüssler, F.E. 1992. *A feminist theological reconstruction of Christian origins: In memory of he.* New York: Crossroad.

Scott, J.W. 1986. Gender: A useful category of historical analysis. *American Historical Review* 91 (5): 1053–75.

Senior, A.D. 2007. La incorporación social en Costa Rica de la poblacion Afrocostarricense durante el siglo XX, 1927–1963. Thesis, Ciudad Universitaria Rodrigo Facio, Costa Rica.

Shepherd, V., B. Brereton and B. Bailey, eds. 1995. *Engendering history: Caribbean women in historical perspective.* Kingston: Ian Randle.

Tang Nain, G., and B. Bailey, eds. 2003. *Gender equality in the Caribbean: Reality or illusion?* Kingston: Ian Randle.

United Nations Development Fund for Women (UNIFEM). 2004. *CEDAW made easy: Question and answer booklet.* Bridgetown: UNIFEM.

United Nations Development Programme (UNDP). 2005. *Human development report 2005: International cooperation at a crossroads: Aid, trade and security in an unequal world.* New York: United Nations Development Programme.

———. 2007/2008. *Human development report 2007/2008: Fighting climate change: Human solidarity in a divided world.* Basingstoke, UK: Palgrave Macmillan.

Wilson, J.P. 2001. Reputation and respectability: A suggestion for Caribbean ethnology. In *Caribbean sociology: Introductory readings*, ed. C. Barrow and R. Reddock, 338–49. Kingston: Ian Randle.

Yuval-Davis, N. 1997. *Gender and nation.* London: Sage.

Zeledón, C.E. 1997. *Surcos de lucha.* Heredia, Costa Rica: Instituto de Estudios de la Mujer, Universidad Nacional.

PART 7

The Gaze
Men, Masculinity and Loving

17

Constructing Brotherhood
Fraternal Organizations and Masculinities in
Barbados since 1740

AVISTON DOWNES

Introduction

In his 1995 essay "Sex and Gender in the Historiography of Caribbean
Slavery", Hilary Beckles made the contention that "the advance from
'Women's History' to 'Gender History' is still at the stage of gathering the
troops"(1995, 126). Caribbean feminist history, within its first twenty-five
years, was virtually unwavering in its commitment to a recuperative agenda
to excavate Caribbean women from historical "invisibility". Within the
broader feminist historiography that had developed by the 1980s, however,
there was a growing paradigmatic shift from perceptions of woman as an essentialist category with prescribed sex roles to an emphasis on the historicized,
relativistic, ever-shifting and unstable, pluralistic socio-cultural constructions
of gender identities and gender relations. Joan Scott's influential essay
"Gender: A Useful Category of Historical Analysis" typified this new approach
and the growing influence of post-structuralism, or the so-called linguistic
turn (Scott 1986, 1053–75). These kinds of developments did not go unnoticed
in the region, but the majority of Caribbean feminist historiography kept its
focus on women and the "realities" of female oppression, and thus avoided
the "gender trouble" which erupted within North Atlantic scholarship (Hoff

1994). Beckles observes that "it is here, it seems, that historians of Caribbean slavery have made some headway by refusing to dichotomise the methodologies of women's history and gender history, and by insisting that the two occupy different levels of the same habitat. The implication of this stance is clear; the analysis of 'real experience' and the theorising of 'constructed representation' constitute part of the same intellectual project in the search for meaning and truth" (1995, 137). But embracing gender as a conceptual tool of historical analysis and acknowledging its relational nature has paved the way to interrogating not only the lived human materiality but also the discursive representations of both women and men. It is ironic that, in spite of the authorial dominance of male historians in documenting the region's "his"-story, there is still a relative paucity of substantial historical studies on men and masculinities in the Caribbean.

Of course, one acknowledges the pioneering anthropological and sociological studies of men in the Caribbean from the 1950s with their focus on "lower-class" men within the context of Afro-Caribbean family structures. These studies characterized families as predominantly female-centred or "matrifocal", and projected black males as irresponsible and marginal (Barrow 1998, 339–58). These studies also focused on the fulfilment of sex roles within a Parsonian structural-functionalist framework. Peter Wilson developed a binary schema within which Afro-Caribbean working-class masculinity was shaped by a "reputation" fashioned outside the home in places such as the streets, while black working-class femininity was characterized by a "respectability" nurtured inside the home and church. Although Richard D. Burton has resurrected the schema in order to examine Afro-creole working-class culture, the use of "reputation" to interrogate black Caribbean masculinity has very limited utility (Wilson 1969, 70–84; Burton 1997).

There has been an elaboration of the black male marginality hypothesis, albeit with the focus on education rather than the family. Errol Miller's *Marginalization of the Black Male* (1986) and his subsequent *Men at Risk* (1991) did much to confer intellectual respectability on the male marginalization hypothesis, even though his conclusions have found virtually no support within feminist scholarship in the region (Downes 2003; Barriteau 2003, 324–55). Clearly, then, the foregoing conceptual frameworks for addressing masculinities in the Caribbean have serious limitations. As Christine Barrow contends, "the discourse of multiple and mutable masculinities transcends the limitations of binary theorising inherent in the models of 'marginality' and 'reputation'" (1998, 357–58).

It is obvious, too, that relations of gender are not confined to the so-called opposite sexes but include social struggles among men (and indeed women). I have argued previously for the application of the concept of "hegemonic masculinity" as articulated by R.W. Connell (1998) as a framework for studying the relations among the multiple masculinities in the Caribbean. I defined this predominant masculinity as "a discursively constructed masculinity which gains and maintains its pre-eminence through its ideological linkages with socially dominant men" (Downes 2004, 107). Similarly, Linden Lewis has emphasized that masculinity must be examined in the context of capitalist labour relations, since it is through such relations that one's own material existence is produced and reproduced (Lewis 2003, 8–11). Dominant gender relations are therefore invariably linked to the control of the means of production. Hegemonic masculinity, however, could not be guaranteed on the basis of socio-economic dominance alone. White creole elite men may have exercised extensive power as the "masters" of West Indian slave societies, but hegemonic masculinity assumes some validation and compliance by the "lesser" masculinities and femininities. Though stripped of patriarchal authority, enslaved black men, in some limited contexts, were permitted to dominate some enslaved women and other men. Indeed, Beckles argues that enslaved black men shared with their white masters some common visions of masculinity. He states: "Imported Africans, and their creole progeny, however culturally understood, shared and actively supported the important tenets of the ideology of masculinity as represented by white men within the colonial encounter. Notions of political authority, economic power and domestic dominance as publicly presented by white elite masculinity were culturally sanctioned by enslaved black men" (2004, 229).

Therefore, hegemonic masculinity was not necessarily internally coherent, stable or independent from other masculinities. Preoccupation with the assertion of masculine identity occurs in periods of perceived crises or dramatic social and economic shifts. This was certainly the case at critical moments in the British West Indies and within Britain itself. The rise of industrial capitalism witnessed the birth of a bourgeoisie which was hostile to the mercantilists and slave-owning classes. This confrontation, rooted in shifting capitalist forces, found social expression in discourses on Christian morality and manliness. The allegations of social wantonness levelled at the "fallen" landed English aristocracy were also mobilized against the "fallen" planter class of the British West Indies. The new feminist historiography of abolitionism has done much to reveal the significance of women and gender within abolitionist discourse but tends to fall very short of exploring the "masculinist" dimensions of that discourse (Midgley 1992; Ferguson 1992; Scully and Paton 2005). Melanie Newton (2005a), however, has offered some valuable insights into white colonial masculinity during the abolitionist campaign. Her essay asserts that abolitionism, amelioration and emancipation were implicated in a transatlantic ideological struggle over representations of "moral and civilised masculinities".

But the contestations over masculinity were inextricably linked to contentions over "race", which is as constructed a category as gender. Barbadian whites, on a number of occasions, asserted their status as "Englishmen in the tropics", but metropolitan whites cast suspicions on the whiteness and masculinity of these colonial claimants. The climatic theory linking race, slavery and environment posited that whites were out of their "natural habitat" in the tropics, and that living among enslaved Africans had inevitably resulted in the social and moral decline of these whites. In this milieu, gender relations and identities were often warped, according to the abolitionists. The white men who constituted the West Indian plantocracy were therefore demonized by their metropolitan "cousins" as cruel, unmanly, immoral drunkards (Lambert 2005). Thus, amelioration and emancipation were held out as opportunities for bringing about a genuine new social order.

Fraternities and Masculinity

But what is the relevance of fraternities to Caribbean masculinities in this context? Fraternities are voluntary associations based on a firm belief in the fatherhood of God and the brotherhood of mankind. They are committed to the moral and material uplifting of their membership through a network of charity or mutual self-help, and bound by rituals of mutual recognition (whether secret or not). Although usually philosophically committed to latitudinarian and cosmopolitan inclusiveness, fraternities have historically coalesced around "race", class and gender – the latter being the most consistent base for solidarity (Dumenil 1984). Unfortunately, fraternities have not attracted the historical attention they deserve because of the perception that they are idiosyncratic, esoteric retreats tangential to the major concerns of the communities in which they operate. This, of course, is not the case. Indeed, fraternalism served as the most readily available associational model for collective organization up to the early twentieth century, so that charities, mutual-aid organizations, political parties, trade unions and other mass-based civic movements evolved out of a common fraternal culture.

The recent scholarship of Cecily Jones and Melanie Newton offers some indication of the importance of charitable, temperance and other reform institutions in mediating gender relations. Except for a brief discussion by Newton on friendly societies, however, the many other fraternities remain unexplored (Jones 1998, 2003, 2007; Newton 2005a, 2008). Apart from Jones and Newton's work, there are a number of other studies which have established the linkages between fraternalism and masculinities in the Atlantic world from the eighteenth century (Carnes 1989; Clawson 1989). These studies, however, have tended to focus heavily on white, middle-class elite men in the North Atlantic. This chapter will undertake a more inclusive approach to the fraternal world and will explore a wider context for the interrogation of gender relations and multiple masculine identities in the Caribbean.

There were no parallels in the British Caribbean to the black Catholic confraternities or lay brotherhoods which flourished in Latin America (Mulvey 1982, 39–68; von Germeten 2006). The British fraternities established in the region were secular but invariably promoted faith in God and advocated morality and benevolent brotherhood.

The first British fraternity established in Barbados was the St Michael's Masonic Lodge, founded in 1740. It was followed by a number of other Masonic lodges which catered to a relatively wide cross section of white men of middling to elite status. For the first century of their operations in Barbados, Masonic lodges excluded all enslaved blacks and free persons of colour (Downes 2007). Race and gender were implicated in this exclusion. Women had been securing membership within Freemasonry across Continental Europe from the middle of the eighteenth century, through Lodges of Adoption. British Freemasonry, in all of its permutations – English, Irish, Scottish, Antients and Moderns – all remained stubbornly opposed to the admission of women. Mary Ann Clawson (1989, 182) contends that the United Grand Lodge of England was a project of the mechanical philosophers who

associated rationality and science with masculinity, while they relegated emo-
tionalism, disorder and irrationality as feminine contaminants. Women were
perceived as interlopers and denied initiation except in a few cases where they
witnessed the rituals surreptitiously (Rich 1997; http://www.luckymojo
.com/comasonry.html). Moreover, women were stereotyped as garrulous and
incapable of keeping secrets. There was also a view that women would threaten
fraternal harmony by provoking jealousy or even compromising morality
(Harland-Jacobs 2007, 93). Barbadian Freemasons remained loyal to their
British Orders and kept their local lodges in Barbados as exclusive male
homosocial spaces in which notions of masculinity could be rehearsed and
reinforced.

White Masculinity and the Moral Order

This section of the chapter takes a closer look at the constructions of white
masculinities from the early eighteenth century. Although Barbados lost a significant number of white yeoman small farmers in the wake of the so-called
sugar revolution, the island nevertheless retained a higher percentage of whites
than most of the other West Indian colonies. By 1715, white women slightly
outnumbered white men. Consequently, the island did not have the highly
skewed gender demographic imbalance so characteristic of early colonial
societies.

At the same time, as the enslaved black population and slavery became
firmly entrenched in Barbados, women became the reproducers of enslavement or freedom. Irrespective of the father's identity, enslaved black women's
progeny were born enslaved, while those of all white women were born free.
White womanhood, then, became the means of establishing the boundaries
demarcating freedom from enslavement, civility from degradation. There
were, however, a number of relationships involving black men and white
women up to the early eighteenth century but these soon became taboo
(Beckles 1989, 134). Nevertheless, white elites perceived poor white women as
constituting a potential fracture within white civilization. The problem of economic vulnerability was compounded by a stereotype of poor white females
as lacking in moral and sexual restraint, and likely to cohabit with black men.
While "property-rights in pleasure" characterized white men's access to black
females, sexual contact between black men and any white females soon became

taboo. According to Cicely Jones, poor relief officials of the vestries subjected the sexuality of poor white females to surveillance, insisting on sexual morality as a condition for the receipt of benefits. Ultimately, this kind of surveillance was one of the means employed by white males to police the perceived threatened social boundaries between whites and non-whites (Jones 1998, 9–31; Jones 2003, 219; Jones 2007, 15, 29).

These kinds of phobias were heightened on those few occasions when enslaved black men were arraigned for the rape of white women. For instance, in August 1764, after Sharper, an enslaved black man was found guilty of raping Sarah Sutton, a white woman of Bridgetown, Governor Pinfold authorized "that his privy Members be then cut off and burned before his Face . . . and that the whole execution may be performed with such Solemnity that it may strike the Spectator with the Greatest Awe and Terror" (Welch 2003, 150).

During the 1816 slave rebellion in Barbados, whites were filled with dread over the implications of one of the banners which the blacks took into battle. This unsettling banner depicted a black man and white woman engaged in sexual intercourse. Colonel Codd reported that this "rude drawing served to inflame the passions by representing the union of a black man with a white female"(Watson 2000, 41). Such a deep emotional response was also evident in the case of Robert James, an enslaved black man, who had been convicted of the rape of a poor white widow and mother, Margaret Higginbotham, in St Philip in October 1832. James received a death sentence, but President John Brathwaite Skeete suspended the execution on account of his unease over certain aspects of the trial and referred the case to the Crown for review. White Barbadians were incensed when the British imperial authorities declared the conviction unsound and commuted James's punishment to transportation. Melanie Newton concludes that the case is a reminder that "white masculine authority rested on preventing the kind of 'illegitimate' intercourse between white women and black men" (Newton 2005b, 606–7).

But how were fraternities implicated in the crusade to bolster white masculinities? Charity or discretionary relief was a central tenet within Freemasonry around which masculinity was constructed. Barbadian Freemasons affirmed white masculinity by demonstrating their capacity to take care of poor or widowed white women and to head off any possibility of these women seeking either material or romantic comfort in the arms of black men. Hilary Beckles has suggested that the white governing elite did not perceive the presence of poor whites as ideologically problematic in Barbadian society "unless the integrity of the entire structure was endangered" (1990, 46–50). Cecily Jones and Melanie Newton have noted the absence of any concerted philanthropic effort by white elites to relieve the conditions of poor whites (Newton 2005a, 227; Jones 2007, 18). "Those rare planters who formed charities to improve the condition of poor whites", Newton states, "were motivated by a fear that impoverished Whites contradicted the doctrine of white supremacy" (2005a, 227).

Unfortunately, both Newton and Jones have overlooked the charitable endeavours of the Freemason lodges from 1740. Masonic lodges made critical contributions to the rehabilitation of both poor as well as middle-class whites who fell on hard times. Each lodge contributed to charity funds at home as well as in Britain. In 1808 the Provincial Grand Lodge of Barbados initiated a fund to establish a Charity School (*Barbados Mercury*, 7 May 1808). By 1844, the Albion Lodge had secured the permission of the Education Committee to provide scholarships to two boys and two girls at the Central Schools. With the reorganization of these schools in the late nineteenth century, these scholarships became tenable at Combermere and Queen's College (*Resume of the History of the District Grand Lodge of Barbados*, 1937, 8).

Following the hurricane of September 1898 which killed about 85 people, injured 260 and flattened an estimated 18,000 houses, the Imperial Government granted £40,000, plus an additional £18,000 from the Mansion House fund, to aid the Barbadian victims (Annual Report of Barbados, 1898, 26–27). But, one month later, John Locke, the district grand master of Barbados, made a special appeal to the United Grand Lodge of England on behalf of the poor whites. To justify his request for this kind of discriminatory relief, Locke claimed that the Mansion House Fund had greatly assisted the black victims but that the poor whites suffered in silence because "they cannot mix with negroes" (Locke to Letchworth, 15 October 1898, in *PUGLE* (*Proceedings of the United Grand Lodge of England*) 10 [1898–1900]: 170). This plea for special treatment of whites apart from the imperial public dispensing of aid again underscores the strategy simultaneously to minimize the visibility of white distress and to reinforce the myth of white men's capacity to "take care of their own".

Irrespective of the myth, white resources were limited and other strategies had to be employed to secure the same objective. For instance, while the

Barbados government was always reluctant to fund any assisted migrant schemes for the black working class, it was willing to aid whites in the same circumstances. As early as 1848 the governor proposed a scheme to assist poor whites to emigrate to other West Indian colonies (Roberts 1955, 250). In 1897 the government established the Victoria Emigration Society to assist mainly white women in straightened circumstances to migrate. Of the 229 women who emigrated with the assistance of the society between 1897 and 1900, 179 were white and 50 were coloured (Roberts 1955, 269, 284). By 1913 an enquiry made by Governor Probyn showed that poor whites had benefited significantly from this and other local sponsored mobility and were the recipients of a flow of funds from "crowds" of their relatives who emigrated to North America (CO 28/281, encl. no. 1, A. Percy Haynes to the Colonial Secretary, 29/5/13; encl. no. 2, Richard Haynes to the Colonial Secretary, 7/6/13; and encl. no. 3, W.G. Hutchinson to the Colonial Secretary, 11/6/13; all in Probyn to Harcourt, 17 June 1913). In fact, so successful was this sponsored white mobility that Reverend W.G. Hutchinson, rector of St Joseph Anglican Church, believed that any further special emigration scheme for poor whites would undermine their role as social buffers in Barbados. He noted: "Seeing that the black race has never proved itself capable of self-government or advancement without leading, and how rapidly the white element is disappearing from this Island, I think it regrettable that these 'Red Legs' should be leaving it as they are. There are more openings in the Island for them than ever before" (CO 28/281, encl. no. 3, W.G. Hutchinson to the Colonial Secretary, 11/6/13, in Probyn to Harcourt, 17 June 1913).

But poor whites were not the only beneficiaries of sponsored white elite relief; so too was a class of "genteel poor", invariably middle-class "ladies" who had fallen on hard times. For example, a large number of Freemasons in Barbados petitioned their order in London for funds to assist the wife and family of incarcerated Bridgetown merchant William Bourne for relocation to North America. Owing to questions about the character of Bourne, Grand Lodge in London offered no assistance (UGLE 196, petition enclosed in Wilson to Clerke, 7 February 1887; letter to Clerke, 23 March 1887). But there were other cases which found favour with the United Grand Lodge of England.

The economic depression in the West Indian sugar industry during the latter half of the nineteenth century wrecked a number of small enterprises and brought to light even more of these "genteel poor". For example, the widow of Edward Gascoigne Watts appealed to the St Michael's Lodge and was granted a pension of $5.00 (£1. 10d.) per month from 1900 until her death in September 1906 (St Michael's Lodge Minutes, 21 August 1900, and 21 August 1906). Her husband had been a representative of the parish of St Philip in the House of Assembly from 1886 to 1894. He had also been the receiver of the indebted 75-acre Ivy Plantation in St Michael which was eventually sold off in lots. It was not always within the capacity of local lodges to extend pensions to widows of deceased brethren. The widows of Williams and Poyer were each granted £10 by the United Grand Lodge of England in 1890 and 1892, respectively (Samuel, George, James and Lydia Williams to Letchworth, 9 November 1901, UGLE 196; Clinckett to Assistant Grand Secretary, 3 January 1892, UGLE 196).

Masonic charity was always discreet, and in the Barbadian case, provided a veil to shield any white vulnerability from the public gaze. In spreading a charitable safety net around white females of all classes, white men thereby projected themselves as secure in their masculinity as providers and protectors. Thus, myths of gender reinforced those of race. Fraternal charity was always very deeply gendered and premised on the feminization of economic distress and the masculinization of its relief. For instance, fraternal iconography illustrating certificates, warrants and banners often depicted females and infants as symbols of benevolence.

Lynn Dumenil's research on Freemasonry in the United States demonstrates that although Masonic charity was projected towards widows and orphans, men were also frequent beneficiaries (Dumenil 1984, 106). Similarly, the number of appeals from Barbadian Freemasons for personal assistance, especially during the economic depression of the late nineteenth century, demonstrates the myth of a secure, stable white masculinity. For example, the Board of Benevolence of the Grand Lodge in London granted £30 to the Jewish grocer J.K. Valverde, who claimed that he and his wife were chronically ill and that their son was unemployed (Valverde to Letchworth, 19 July 1902, UGLE 2196). Mr Walton, a Bridgetown merchant, also applied to the Grand Lodge for relief and was granted £40 (Walton to Letchworth, 20 December 1902 and 11 March 1903, UGLE 2196; Walton to Letchworth, 19 November 1904, UGLE 2196; Inniss to Letchworth, 18 November 1904, UGLE 2196). Clearly, though, women were usually seen as more "deserving" and men who persistently sought aid were viewed as unmanly and undeserving. For example, the Master of St Michael's Lodge considered F.B. Mann, a frequent applicant for pecuniary aid, as a "deserving case", but Reverend Clark-Holman was worried that helping Mann "was nothing more nor less than encouraging and upholding pauperism" (St Michael's Lodge Minutes, 18 June 1889).

The mobilization of relief by fraternities and the state to poor whites did not transform fundamentally the status of those impoverished whites but this kind of intervention sufficiently masked white vulnerability, thus enhancing representations of secure masculinity and whiteness. The result was the perpetuation of another misrepresentation: that women, and especially white women, were simply consuming beneficiaries of the slave plantation economy but were themselves uninvolved in that enterprise. In this respect, white women of the plantocracy were discursively projected as "uncontaminated" by the social degradation of the slavery enterprise. It was taken for granted that, inevitably, the white masters would bear that "moral contamination" associated with slave-driven tropical plantations, and that white women held the key to any kind of rehabilitation. As we have already established, Barbados possessed one of the largest white populations among Caribbean slave societies, and by 1715 white women actually outnumbered white men on the island. William Dickson contended that it was this "far greater proportion than elsewhere of ladies, or well-educated women" which mitigated the horrors of Barbadian slave society (Dickson 1814, 440). Of course, the many accounts of the cruelty of white slave mistresses to enslaved black women across the Caribbean raises serious doubts about the Dicksonian hypothesis. In any case, as we will see, the question of morality became part of the ideological arsenal of the English reformers and abolitionists from the late eighteenth century.

Civilizing Masculinities: Abolitionism and the Discourse on White Elite Colonial Masculinity

By the turn of the nineteenth century, metropolitan abolitionists were increasingly reprimanding the predominantly white male plantocracy in the British West Indies for the human degradation of slavery. Abolitionism, however, won no public support in the Caribbean from white women, who were as pro-slavery as their male counterparts. There is, however, some indication of privately expressed criticism and disapproval of the immorality of white men in the private letters and journals of some, mainly expatriate, white women. Maria Nugent, for example, did not support the abolitionist arguments against the slave trade but intimated that if white men were to set a better moral example for their slaves, natural increase would result from slave families, thus obviating any need for a slave trade (Nugent 1966, 86–87).

Nugent vowed to protect her son from the white culture of male indulgence and swore that she would not allow him to be raised "thinking himself a king" and adopting the "petty vices of little tyrants" (ibid., 146). Similarly, Elizabeth Fenwick feared for her grandson in Barbados that he, too, might fall prey to "those vices of Manhood" (Wedd 1927, 169–70). She herself had shattered the stereotype of the dependent housewife when she relocated to Barbados as an independent female entrepreneur following the business failures of her English husband (Beckles 1998, 1–16). Mrs Fenwick also witnessed the failure of her own Barbadian son-in-law to meet the expectations of responsible manhood because he had an "insatiable love of company and late hours" and was in a state of "constant intoxication" (Wedd 1927, 193).

According to a number of keen observers, such as Thomas Verney, Sir Henry Colt and Father Antoine Biet, drunkenness among white men of all classes was ubiquitous in Barbados from the early seventeenth century (Bruce 1853, 194–95; Harlow 1925; Handler 1967). Indeed, white English colonists insisted that drinking was a core expression of their "Englishness" and masculinity. As one Barbadian planter opined in 1710, "upon all the new settlements the Spaniards make, the first thing they do is to build a church, the first thing the Dutch do . . . is to build them a fort, but the first thing the English do . . . is to set up a tavern or drinking house" (*JBMHS* 15 [1947–48]: 35). The Jamaican planter-historian Edward Long sought to implicate enslaved black men in Jamaica in the hedonism frequently levelled against white men. Of black men Long states: "They have no moral sensations; no taste but for women; gormandizing and drinking to excess" (Long 1774, 353). Alcohol consumption among enslaved Africans, however, reflected a wider and more complex socio-cultural repertoire. For instance, libations were important to religious and funerary practices, and were also implicated in slave rebellion (Smith 2000, 212–27).

British abolitionists seem to have been effective by the early nineteenth century in their representation of the moral decay of the West Indian slave societies, "with particular focus on the arbitrary violence, drunkenness, and promiscuity which were the hallmark of wealthy white masculinity"(Newton 2005a, 237). Melanie Newton contends that, during the period of apprenticeship, white Barbadian elite planters and merchants, aided by clergymen, responded to anti-slavery pressure by promoting temperance and other societies to rehabilitate their masculinity. For instance, in 1835 the Barbados Temperance Society was formed to cater, apparently, to white men exclusively (Newton 2008, 169–70; idem 2005a, 237). An examination of a wider range of local "reform" men's organizations, however, would serve to demonstrate a more nuanced and complex perspective. One then needs to question to what extent Barbadian white men were prepared to bow to the ideological and institutional pressures that originated from the English middle class and some local acolytes to determine the parameters of "civilized masculinity". I wish to suggest that British abolitionist campaigns were integral to the processes of asserting the superiority of British morality and manliness (Walvin 1987). Thus, British middle-class men were not simply seeking to spread "civilized masculinity" to the British West Indies; West Indian masculinities were among the colonial "other" so necessary for establishing the hegemony of the metropolitan construct (Sinha 1995).

In Britain, fraternities became targets of temperance campaigns on account of their practice of "wet rents" of lodge rooms in public houses. Temperance propaganda succeeded, to some degree, in associating drinking with unthrifty behaviour, domestic irresponsibility and unmanliness. In Barbados and the wider Caribbean, free women of colour were the principal proprietors of taverns. These operations served as hotels, drinking saloons and brothels, catering to the entertainment needs of the many white male transients found in very busy port cities such as Bridgetown.

By the early nineteenth century, some lodges in the West Indies began to follow the trend in Britain by shifting their operations from rooms in taverns to their own temples. For instance, the Albion Lodge, the first "Antient" Masonic lodge in Barbados, began its operations in the Masons' Arms in Bridgetown in 1790, and moved in 1794 to the Williams' Freemasons' Tavern, where it functioned for a decade before transferring to the "Masonic Temple"(Lane 1895).

In 1816 the Grand Lodge of England ruled that food, alcohol and tobacco were to be excluded from lodge rooms, and in the course of the nineteenth century, saloonkeepers were banned from Masonry in the United States (Hamhill 1986, 81; Dumenil 1984, 76–77). Nonetheless, white men would have found in Freemasonry an avenue to continue convivial drinking in an exclusively male homosocial (and up to the mid-nineteenth century, exclusively white) space. Behind the privacy of the doors of their new temples, Freemasons continued to accord a special place to drinking but with the respectability associated with initiation banquets and the numerous loyal and patriotic toasts to the monarch, governor and other colonial officials. Moreover, although "lodge night" took men away from hearth and home, its convivial activities were balanced by the brotherhood's consideration for charitable duty. In all, each Freemason was to be the model man at the lodge, at home and in the society: "Masons ought to be Moral Men. . . consequently good Husbands, good Parents, good Sons, and good Neighbours, not staying too long from Home and avoiding all Excess" (Harland-Jacobs 2007, 17).

The Flogging of Women and the Discourse about Masculinity

To the colonial catalogue of "unmanly" behaviours such as licentiousness and drunkenness was added the contentious issue of the flogging of enslaved black women by male personnel of the plantations, and the failure of plantocratic legislatures to enact any law to protect women from such measures. It was particularly on this issue that Barbadian planter elites defied the British bourgeoisie constructions of civilized masculinity. North Atlantic visitors to Barbados and the region often expressed their revulsion of the scenes of black drivers mercilessly whipping women with the approval of their white masters. Not surprisingly, the practice became a major focal point for abolitionist propaganda. In 1823, Lord Bathurst, the secretary of state for the colonies, called for a ban on the indiscriminate and unsupervised flogging of enslaved women. As Catherine Hall has argued, English middle-class men by the early 1800s saw true manliness in the support for the weak – women, children, slaves and animals (Hall 2002, 27). White middle-class Englishwomen provided ideological support for this representation of masculinity. They, too, became engaged in redefining themselves as the protectors and spokespersons for their downtrodden "sisters" in the West Indies. But, as Claire Midgley and Moira Ferguson have pointed out, these white middle-class British women virtually negated the persistent rebellion of enslaved black women, misrepresenting them as helpless, virtuous victims (Midgley 1992, 90; Ferguson 1992, 3).

Barbadian planters, however, refused to accept these "new" gender representations of enslaved black women as soft and delicate. The Barbadian plantocracy stuck to their centuries-long entrenched philosophy and practice of refusing to treat black women as any weaker sex. Hamden, a planter-cum-lawyer, eloquently defended the traditional position, contending: "Unfortunately our black ladies have a tendency to the Amazonian cast of character; and believe their husbands would be very sorry to hear that they were placed beyond the reach of chastisement" (Beckles 1989, 40). Barbadian planters remained locked in a test of wills with the Colonial Office on this issue, and although they passed the more reformed Consolidated Slave Laws in 1826, they did not concede on the matter of flogging women. This is yet another case of West Indian elite white men refusing to embrace the dominant representation of masculinity (or lack of it) emanating from Britain. Indeed, as late as 1833, Lord Stanley, secretary of state for the colonies, expressed disappointment that West Indian legislators were still to take "what, in manliness and in humanity should be the first step" to amelioration by abolishing the flogging of women (Paton 1996, 176).

Becoming "True Men" at Last! Fraternities and Black Middle-Class Masculinity

The 1820s also witnessed an acceleration of the quest by free people of colour to secure civil rights. Lovelace Overton, a Barbadian free coloured man who had been initiated into Masonry in England was barred from visiting any of the local lodges, and his efforts to establish a lodge which would accommodate free people of colour was stoutly resisted (Downes 2007, 60–62). To justify their actions, white Barbadian Masons strictly interpreted the Masonic *Constitutions*, which stipulated that "the Persons admitted Members of a *Lodge* must be good and true Men, free-born, and of mature and discreet Age, no Bondmen, no Women, no immoral or scandalous Men, but of good Report" (Anderson 1734, 49). According to local interpretation, persons with any hint of a slave ancestry could not qualify as "true Men". Legally, enslaved persons were property and possessed no property rights and, as Catherine Hall has pointed out, "a man who did not own himself or his property could not be a man" (Hall 1992, 32).

Emancipation coupled with the importunity of coloureds and blacks resulted in a reinterpretation of the *Constitutions* in Britain, and non-whites began to penetrate the membership of Freemasonry from the 1840s. Even so, property holding remained an important consideration, and therefore the black and coloured men approved for admission were invariably substantial property owners and former slave owners (Downes 2007, 63–64).

It was this hurdle which a number of black and coloured men faced in securing initiation into Masonic lodges, which led to the introduction of the second wave of secret fraternities in the island: the affiliated friendly society orders, often referred to as "poor men's freemasonry". Many of them originated in the industrializing heartland of Britain, where they attracted the better-paid skilled workers or the "aristocracy of labour". In Barbados their core membership was urban and drawn primarily from the black artisan class and some sections of white-collar workers, such as clerks and elementary school teachers. The largest of these, the Independent Order of Oddfellows (Manchester Unity) and the Ancient Order of Foresters were launched in Barbados in 1842 and 1846, respectively. These new societies may have broadened the access to quasi "masonic" fraternalism, but they initially insisted on the exclusion of women, as British Freemasonry had done.

There were apparently a few of these affiliated societies in early nineteenth-century Britain which were organized by women, but the male fraternities forbade their members from associating with these kinds of lodges. For example, one Order of Oddfellows in 1832 expelled a member for acting as secretary to a lodge of Odd Women, and cited the following resolution: "That should any Brother or Brothers belonging to the Grand Order, persist in, or become in any way connected with Odd Women, or any other similar Female Secret Societies whatsoever; he or they so offending, we do most earnestly request (upon due proof) that Grand Lodge will expel them *from the Grand United Order for ever*" (Smith 1932, 10).

The Oddfellows in the United States formulated the honorary Degree of Rebekah in 1851 for their spouses and widows. Women in Rebekah Lodges remained under the tutelage of the men. This type of lodge required a minimum of ten members – five of each sex. The initiation of a woman normally required the sanction and presence of her husband and "involve[d] no indelicacy" (*Complete Manual of Oddfellowship* 1879, 253). Her duties were said not to be of "a light character, merely ornamental and pleasing to vanity", but rather given to the visitation and relief of the sick, burying the dead and the education of orphans (ibid., 254). It was not until 1893, however, that the Oddfellows in Britain, at their Oxford Annual Moveable Committee, approved a new general rule to admit women to exclusive female lodges (Moffrey 1905, 66; Moffrey 1910, 115, 130). In 1887, after just over fifty years of opposition to female membership, the Ancient Order of Foresters mandated its executive to draw up tables of contributions for women, but it was not until 1892 that the order agreed to admit women as members, albeit within separate female courts (Stead, Stead and Stead 1914, 77–78). In Barbados, neither the Ancient Order of Foresters nor the Independent Order of Oddfellows (Manchester Unity) admitted women until the twentieth century.

A few smaller fraternities did admit women in Barbados from the 1880s. One such lodge was the Empress Victoria, established under the Improved Independent Order of Oddfellows, London Unity, in 1886. This female lodge met separately from the gatherings of its male counterparts of the George and Victor Lodge. According to the *Blue Book* for 1888, the Empress Victoria had sixty-five members and just over £66, compared to twenty-four men in the Loyal George and Victor, which had a balance of just over £4. In 1902 the Loyal Order of Ancient Shepherds (Ashton Unity) established Palm Tree Lodge 2568 for women in Bridgetown (*Loyal Order of Ancient Shepherds [Ashton Unity] Guide and Directory for the Year 1922–23*, 63). Up to the 1920s its membership did not surpass twenty-five.

As already indicated, the social classes from which these organizations drew their membership reinforced the masculinist bias of "secret" fraternities. In expressing his support of the petition to grant the Myrtle Flower Lodge of the British Order of Ancient Free Gardeners its own act of incorporation, Mr Walter Reece informed his parliamentary colleagues that this lodge had a restricted membership which "consisted of forty or fifty of the better class of labouring men – people of the class of stevedores, ship carpenters, Master carpenters and men of that class" (House of Assembly Debates, 28 January 1908). One of the features of the labour force of Barbados throughout slavery and afterward was men's domination of highly rewarded, skilled positions. Consequently, women, who had a narrower range of employment possibilities, were overrepresented in agricultural field labour.

Not surprisingly, the aristocracy of labour which dominated these new, urban-based fraternities distanced themselves from those employed in agricultural labour. Nevertheless, their fates, too, were determined by the island's plantation economy. By the late nineteenth century, poor economic conditions caused by depression in the sugar industry threatened the male labour aristocracy. The ranks of the skilled and semiskilled workers had expanded more rapidly than the market could accommodate. As early as the 1870s, the Poor Relief Commission observed that carpenters, coopers, masons, tailors and shoemakers had experienced reduced wages because those trades "were so overcrowded that continuous occupation cannot be obtained by those who follow them" (Report of the Poor Law Commission, Barbados, 1878). Two decades later, in the midst of the deepened economic crisis, conditions were no better. Charles Alleyne, a shopkeeper-speculator, remembered that crowds of men, including coopers, carpenters and masons, begged him for work – "any kind of employment, no matter how menial or arduous" (WIRC 1898, appendix C, part 3, paragraph 927).

The lack of labour opportunities struck a severe blow to upper-working-/lower-middle-class masculinity. These middling fraternities reinforced the ideal that economic independence and mutual self-help were important foundations of masculinity. To be charitable was desirable but to be the object of charity was unmanly. The Oddfellows' Order taught its members "to respect one another, and help themselves, without the degradation of receiving charity" (Spry 1867, 179). During an initiation into this order, the master of the lodge would charge: "The man who would willingly exist upon the charity of others rather than labour for his daily bread, by that very act forfeits his claim to our brotherly consideration. Neither the relief granted by the Society in sickness, nor the money paid upon the death of a member or his wife, is to be regarded in the light of a charitable donation, but as the payment of a just claim, the honestly earned reward of the member's prudence and forethought" (*Complete Manual of Oddfellowship*, 92).

Significantly, these ideals were not applicable to women. The Oddfellows, for example, converted their Charity Fund to a permanent widows and orphans fund in the 1890s. Masculinity, then, was predicated on economic independence and prudent provision for dependent women and children. Reverend Caldecott, former principal of Codrington College, was one of a number of European observers who conceded that it was nigh impossible to designate masculinity among Afro-West Indians through female dependence and compliance. He noted: "There is in the Negro race a nearer approach to equality than is found in European races. The woman is almost as capable a the man; at any rate she can, in early and middle life, easily earn enough to keep a house for herself and two or three children; and not infrequently it is the woman whose affection cools or changes, and from whom arises the abandonment of the connection and the choice of another mate" (Caldecott 1898/1970, 195).

In some sectors of colonial employment, there were efforts to enhance middle-class masculinity by ensuring that men received a so-called family wage. For instance, in 1898, the Board of Education in Barbados introduced regulations to debar married women from teaching and to reduce the salaries of the remaining single female teachers to 25 per cent of that of a man doing the same work. Rule 1c declared: "Masters will in the majority of cases marry and have families to support. Mistresses must remain single if they continue in the service: they therefore cannot have the same claims on the salaries that a man with a wife and children would have" (*Official Gazette*, 14 July 1898, 2311). Notwithstanding this regulatory change, a number of masters and male teachers buckled under the burden of masculinity defined as principal or sole breadwinner. A cursory examination of the Board of Education minutes in the first decade of the twentieth century reveals that there were a number of embarrassing cases of the colonial secretary referring educators for discipline on account of their indebtedness. All were men.[1] Interestingly, fees earned from providing management services to working-class fraternities may have saved this sector of the lower middle-class from further embarrassment.

Black middle-class fraternalists also became targets of temperance campaigners, although they did not have the same reputation as the white planters, who were known as inveterate boozers. In the tradition of the Masons, affiliated friendly society orders often convened in taverns. For instance, in the late 1860s Court Western Star 2066 of the Ancient Order of Foresters convened at the Defy Rascality Inn on Nelson Street, Bridgetown, every first and last Monday of the month (*Ancient Order of Foresters Directory and Almanack* 1868–69, 239). At its Annual Movable Conference at Oxford in 1898, the Independent Order of Oddfellows (Manchester Unity) passed a resolution requiring its lodges to cease the practice of "wet rents" or face expulsion from the Order (*Independent Order of Oddfellows [MU] Quarterly Report*, October 1898, 258).

In Britain, some of the temperance societies organized themselves along the lines of fraternities. The Independent Order of Rechabites, for example, was perhaps the most popular of these, but there is no evidence of any of its tents (lodges) operating in Barbados. The Independent Order of Good Templars (IOGT) did establish a foothold on the island from 1877. This society did not pay the usual benefits associated with a friendly society but managed to attract enthusiastic support from local Moravian clergyman James Young Edghill, who worked tirelessly in promoting this society's temperance campaign. The Excelsior and Lodge No. 2 were the main Good Templars lodges operating in Bridgetown. The movement extended its influence into rural Barbados with the establishment of the St Joseph Faithful Lodge in the parish of St Joseph. By 1880, Barbados was constituted as a district with seventeen Good Templar lodges under its jurisdiction.

The launch of the Good Templars in 1877 also attracted the interest of the Anglican bishop of Barbados. He observed that the vice of drunkenness was in no way as deleterious as it was in England, but noted that poor whites and young Bridgetown clerks seemed vulnerable to it (Bishop's Court Church Council and Diocesan Synod Minute Book 1877–1891, 26 September 1877). In June 1880, the British Foreign Bible Society launched the Young Men's Christian Association in Bridgetown as a strategy to dissuade young men in the city from frequenting the drinking saloons (*Herald*, 21 June 1880; *Herald*, 23 October 1882; *Times*, 13 May 1893). The vast majority of young urban males refused to join, and by 1883 only sixty persons had enrolled. One correspondent to a local newspaper perhaps spoke for the majority of the island's young men when he derisively dismissed the mission of the Young Men's Christian Association as a "Salvation Army" (*Herald*, 4 June 1883).

British evangelicals, in concert with amelioration advocates and abolitionists, may have succeeded, as Newton suggests, in stimulating moral outrage at the decadent masculinity of the slave owners. But it is evident that in Barbados, up to the apprenticeship and well beyond it, both white elite and black middle-class men rejected much of the agenda to reform or reconstruct their masculinity. Temples may have replaced taverns as acceptable sites for fraternal activity, but in these new locations men could, and did, redefine the ritual of drinking from a symbol of dissolute manhood to one of patriotism.

Civic Processions and the Symbolic Construction of Masculinity

Street processions or parades have a long association with fraternities, trade unions, political parties and other civic movements. Originally, these displays were more inclusive, but by the early nineteenth century, working-class street displays had attracted the disapproval of the social elites. These elites also engaged in severe self-restriction in their own parades in order to accentuate the processions' ritual value and differentiate them from the "vulgar spectacles" of the working class. One noted feature of the recognizably elite parade by the nineteenth century was its masculine character. Participation symbolized one's citizenship and right to occupy the street. Property holding was a fundamental qualification for citizenship, and the legal framework for property ownership was highly discriminatory against women. The civic procession, therefore, became an important, relatively rare but very public, visible tableau of social and political patriarchal power at both the local and imperial levels. The colonial state organized these kinds of processions to mark coronations, royal jubilees, the monarch's birthday and other highly auspicious occasions. The public and political import of these displays invariably stamped them as exclusively masculinist. All of the major participants were themselves institutions of patriarchy: the governor, members of parliament, military and paramilitary organizations, the church and other institutions such as fraternities, which could add colour, pomp, éclat and commitment to the status quo. Nevertheless, the organizers were careful not to miss an opportunity for crafting hegemonic displays by ensuring participation from a cross-class alliance of men ranging from the "respectable" black artisans to the white colonial elites. It was important to attract the barefoot working classes and women, but to restrict them to a position of awestruck spectatorship.

Civic street processions, with their unmistakable military tone symbolized the imposition of order on the streets and colonial spaces of Barbados. Urban areas in particular were projected as physically and morally dangerous sites, especially for unchaperoned members of the "fairer sex" and for "respectable" citizens in general. A partial solution to this problem was a succession of Vagrancy Acts, which criminalized congregating on public streets (Vagrancy Acts 1840–41 and 1897 cap. 14; Bridgetown, Speightstown and Hole Town Act 1891 cap. 41; Police Act 1890 cap. 19).

As I have indicated, fraternities have had their own, long history of street processions. Freemasons, for example, engaged in regular processions in the early years of their history, but on account of the unflattering mimicry of street "roughs" such as the "Scald Miserable Masons", the Grand Lodge forbade Masonic processions from 1747, except by its grant of a special "dispensation". Lodges of Oddfellows were similarly forbidden from appearing publicly in regalia without prior consent of their Grand Lodge (Hamhill 1986, 77–78; *Complete Manual of Oddfellowship*, 341). The rarity of these public appearances by fraternities served to deepen their impression on spectators.

Fraternities, then, shared a common culture of imperial masculinity underscored by militarism. Military and quasi-military displays spread like a cultural epidemic in Britain and her empire in the latter half of the nineteenth century. Victorian reformers contended that the injection of paramilitarism fostered manliness and would stimulate the interest of young men in areas in which their participation was low. Consequently, organizations such as the Boys' Brigade, Boy Scouts, Church Lads Brigade, and Cadet Corps were promoted to stimulate manly interest in school and church. Simon Cordery has pointed to the martial nature of fraternal processions: the brotherhoods often carried ensigns, staves and even battle-axes (2003, 39–40). For instance, the procession through Bridgetown to mark the celebration of Queen Victoria's Golden Jubilee in June 1887 involved a Masonic contingent of Royal Arch and Knights Templars headed by the Tyler with a drawn sword (*Times*, 25 June 1887). This Masonic display was entirely consistent with that of the Oddfellows, whose *Manual* stipulated that each procession was to be headed by the OG (Outer Guard) with his drawn sword (*Complete Manual of Oddfellowship*, 342). Colour was also essential to the creation of an attractive and bedazzling display.

The significance attached to civic pomp and pageantry should not be underestimated. For instance, Governor Hay, himself a Freemason, seemed to have forgotten that fact when he arrived in "an ordinary tweed suit instead of the regular official Windsor uniform" to inspect the trooping of the colours on the occasion of Queen Victoria's seventy-fourth birthday. According to the editor of the *Times*, it was "calculated to inspire into the minds of 'ordinary mortals,' a spirit of disloyalty" (*Times*, 27 May 1893).

On the occasion of its fifteenth anniversary, the Livesey Comet Lodge of the Grand United Order of Oddfellows was reported to have drawn crowds to witness its procession to St Ambrose Church for divine service. They followed some of the principal thoroughfares of Bridgetown to the church and back, in an "orderly and respectable" manner (*Weekly Recorder*, 5 August 1905). The procession of members of the Independent Order of Mechanics was reported to draw no fewer than a thousand spectators, besides those in the hills and gaps who gathered to watch as members of the fraternity marched from their lodge room at St Silas School to the chapel, accompanied by a band of music. The *Times* observed that, "notwithstanding this monster gathering, the strictest decorum was observed" (27 August 1892).

Consistently, then, processions were tableaux intended to inspire loyalty to empire, order and control. There was at least one occasion on which a procession constituted a clash of patriarchies. In 1902 the governor of Barbados faced the censure of the House of Assembly, following the official coronation procession on 26 June of that year. On that occasion, the governor deviated from the Colonial Office Order of Precedence by placing all officers of the army and navy (including junior ranks) ahead of the members of the House of Assembly in the procession, "in order that the effect of the general scene might be heightened". But Mr Yearwood, who tabled the motion of censure, contended, "The massing of colour might impress savages and ignorant people, but it will not impress the educated people of Barbados. Good, strong rule, and adherence to principle – not massing of colour – will impress the people of Barbados" (House of Assembly Debates, Barbados, 29 July 1902, 113–15). A certain degree of caution, then, must qualify any analysis of the impact of these civic rituals and to what extent they significantly achieved what Lindsay calls the "symbolic manipulation" of the colonized (Lindsay 1981).

Participation in all of these processions was generally restricted to men. The procession through Bridgetown to the Garrison on the occasion of the island's tercentenary celebration in 1905, however, included a solitary woman, Sister S. Antoinette Esterbrook, among the Ancient Order of Foresters, the Grand United Order of Oddfellows, the Improved Order of Oddfellows, the Loyal Order of Ancient Shepherds, the Free Gardeners and the Independent Order of Mechanics (*Weekly Recorder*, 2 December, 1905). Esterbrook enjoyed this exceptional honour because she participated as head of a small Christian denomination on the island known as the Anchor Mission.

On 21 June 1911, the fraternities in Barbados staged a massive procession to celebrate the coronation of George V (*Barbados Standard*, 2 May 1911). Estimated to be nearly half a mile long, it consisted of about four hundred members. All except the Ancient Free Gardeners were fully attired in regalia, preceded by the police band and three decorated wagons illustrating aspects of the British influence. The march left Trafalgar Square and made its way to Government House, attracting massive crowds along the route. After having read and delivered their address to be submitted to the king and queen, the governor inspected and addressed the procession. He noted that "an expression of loyalty from the Secret Societies of Barbados was of special value, because it was of importance that members of these Societies should realise very fully the obligation of citizenship, and it was by fulfilling the obligations and duties of citizens that the Empire was made strong" (*Coronation Handbook* 1911, 10–11). The governor's sentiments were consistent with the prevailing narrow, masculinist view of citizenship and patriotism.

Boys to Men?

A number of scholars have endeavoured to explain the construction of middle-class masculinity by "retreat from domesticity" hypotheses. Mark Carnes has contended, for instance, that the emergence and growth of fraternities such as Freemasonry reflected some attempt by men to escape the overweening presence of women in the domestic sphere. Carnes postulates that fraternal orders provided "solace and psychological guidance" through the difficult transition to middle-class manhood in the Victorian United States (Carnes 1989, 12–14; idem 1990, 48–52). Paul Rich, too, has identified Freemasonry as a rite of passage for boys in many English Public Schools (1988). These hypotheses are fascinating but remain speculative on account of the absence of empirical evidence.

The qualifying age for membership in Freemasonry was twenty-one years. There was, however, special provision for the initiation of a "Lewis", usually the eldest son of a Master Mason who had not attained the qualifying age. "Lewises", however, were rare in Barbadian lodges, and only four are identified in the records of the Masonic lodges of Barbados between 1880 and 1914. One such Lewis was Evan Walter Roberts, an eighteen-year-old Harrison College student who was initiated on the evening of 15 June 1907 into the Thistle No. 14 (Scottish) Lodge, of which his father, Fitzgerald Clairmonte Roberts, headmaster of Roebuck Boys' School, was co-founder and master (Grand Lodge of Scotland Registration Book 18, fol. 849). An analysis of initiation ages between 1880 and 1914 indicates that the average initiation age for the Albion Lodge was thirty-two, for Victoria it was thirty-six, and for both St Michael and Scotia it was thirty-three. There is a clear indication, then, that the men who joined Masonry in Barbados did so as mature men and not as some rite of passage from boyhood to manhood.

The Ancient Order of Foresters was one of the better-documented societies, and published for actuarial purposes the size and average age of the membership of each lodge around the world. The lowest average age recorded for any Barbadian Ancient Order of Foresters Lodge was twenty-nine, for the Western Star 2066 in 1920. The average age for both Western Star 2066 and St Michael's Diamond 2203 between 1890 and 1930, however, ranged between the thirties and age fifty. More generally, the average hovered around the early to mid-forties. It was, however, customary for some fraternities to make provision for the maintenance of juvenile sections. The Alpha Lodge of the Loyal Order of Ancient Shepherds inaugurated at the St Mary's Boys' School in September 1890 a juvenile lodge called the Hopeful Friendly, with a membership of forty boys (*Times*, 27 September 1890). There is, however, no indication of juvenile lodges in Barbados among the annual data from the major lodges.

So while the arguments in support of "psychological guidance" for young men remains interesting, the secret fraternities in Barbados catered overwhelmingly to mature men and seemed not to have played the kind of role I have identified for cricket and paramilitary youth movements. Fraternities in Barbados were indeed bastions of male homosociality but no evidence exists to suggest that they provided solace or even rites of passage for Barbadian boys. Fraternities did, however, facilitate the construction of masculinity in other ways.

Working-Class Friendly Societies and Black Masculinity

Abolitionism, as we have seen, served to catalyse new discourses and representations of elite and middle-class masculinities. Amelioration and emancipation, then, were presented as "civilizing" processes which held at their core the correction and reordering of gender relations warped by centuries of slavery. The Colonial Office approved the role of the church as a major civilizing agent, especially in promoting education, values and morality.

In 1823 Lord Bathurst, the secretary of state for the colonies, advocated a number of measures aimed at the amelioration of slavery. One of the conundrums of slavery was the aggressive participation and significant control by enslaved men and women of the internal marketing system. This economic activity was a significant area of resistance by enslaved persons legally rendered as property themselves. Although amelioration efforts in some colonies involved attempts to curb Sunday markets, Lord Bathurst supported the establishment of friendly societies and savings banks to encourage enslaved persons to be thrifty, industrious and moral. No action was taken on these proposals in Barbados until William Hart Coleridge was appointed the first bishop of Barbados and the Leeward Islands. He encouraged the Anglican clergy to set up these kinds of societies, and the first was established in the rural parish of St John in July 1832 (*Barbadian*, 18 May 1833). Although this very first society may have been poor white or free coloured, the movement was soon dominated by non-whites (*Barbadian*, 7 January 1835).

Unlike their "secret" middle-class counterparts, these working-class friendly societies admitted women from the inception. Certainly black women were consistently critical to the labour force on the estates during slavery and continued to be independent wage earners thereafter. Nevertheless, the church supported as an ideal the evolving separate spheres ideology. In 1834 the local Anglican church adopted a policy of separating the sexes within the friendly society movement. For example, in that year two societies – one male and one female – with membership drawn from among the free coloured population of the city were established at St Mary's Anglican Church in Bridgetown (*Barbadian*, 7 January 1835; Goodridge 1977, 31). The female branch of St Mary's, the St Michael's Female Friendly Society, had a membership of 75 in 1834, and by their second anniversary in 1836 the male and female societies together had a membership of 430 (*Barbadian*, 25 May 1836).

The separation of the sexes also reflected a preoccupation with bridling the allegedly "loose" sexual morality which had characterized slavery but now needed to be reversed to foster familial stability. As the *Barbadian* newspaper observed, the societies "are made instrumental to the encouragement of a moral and religious life. The members are bound to a strict observance of their practical duties as christians [*sic*]" (*Barbadian*, 7 January 1835). Reverend Thomas Watt, chaplain to the estates of the Society for the Propagation of the Gospel in St John, observed, "The formation of Friendly Societies in all the Parishes [was] so eminently calculated, as experience has proved, to diffuse habits of industry, frugality, order, and generally a religious and moral feeling among the labouring classes" (*Barbadian*, 18 May 1833).

The Methodists and Moravians also promoted friendly societies as civilizing institutions on the island. The United Bridgetown Friendly Society, established in 1844 at the Bethel Methodist Church in Bridgetown, excluded all those found guilty of adultery, fornication, drunkenness, gambling, swearing and violating the Sabbath, among other sins (Rules of the United Bridgetown Friendly Society 1846).

But black men in these church-based fraternities were especially targeted as if they possessed some proclivity for immorality. For instance, in 1835 at least twenty-nine men were expelled from their society at St Mary's Church because "they persisted in their choice to live in concubinage rather than in the honourable state of marriage" (*Barbadian*, 25 May 1836). While expressing satisfaction in 1836 that none of the 270 members of St Mary's Female Friendly Society had been expelled over the previous year, Bishop Coleridge was "evidently disappointed to find [the men] very much behind the Sisters" (*Barbadian*, 17 May 1837). When American abolitionists Sturge and Harvey visited the island in 1837, they claimed that the St Mary's friendly societies had limited their membership to married persons (Sturge and Harvey 1838/1968, 142).

Abolitionists and missionary reformers expected black women to serve as moral catalysts to civilize black men, as white women had ostensibly done for white males. William Knibb, the famous Baptist missionary to Jamaica, contended that, "until the female character is raised, we shall never far advance in civilisation and virtue". Similarly, the Anglican bishop of Barbados charged that "things will not be much better until the coloured woman has learnt to value her honour as much as her white sister" (Hall 1992, 323; National Library Service BS33B, BS34, Bishop's Court Church Council and Diocesan Synod Minute Book 1891–1909: Annual Session of the Diocesan Synod, 3 March 1909). The austere standards of moral conduct demanded by the church friendly societies were unrealistic, and a number of members withdrew, as one police magistrate observed (*Parliamentary Papers* 29 [1842]: 83).

Nevertheless, the early nineteenth-century missionary reformers shared with the abolitionists a vision for the restoration of the black man to his "rightful place" as absolute head of his household, a role which was negated by their white masters during slavery. As John Scoble, secretary of the Anti-Slavery Society, announced at Emancipation, "To the number of many thousands, [who] were held the property of other men; today, they were their own property – husbands could embrace their wives as their own property, and slavery, with all its gloomy and revolting features, was at an end, he trusted, forever" (Hall 1992, 33).

Here, one observes the marriage of the gendered anti-slavery discourse and the emerging Victorian ideology. Part of the recovery of black masculinity involved the construction of weak, dependent black women. Black women, who had emerged as the very backbone of production on the plantations, were being re-presented as physically weak and to be restricted to light, preferably domestic work. For instance, John Scoble of the Anti-Slavery Society is quoted as saying, "We hope and trust that, whatever the consequences for the crops, the negro labourers throughout the colonies will, ere long, insist on their wives and daughters keeping out of the field, except in reaping time to assist in the lighter works of harvest" (*Liberal*, 30 March 1839). Bridget Brereton has explored the dynamics of the "flight from the estates" by women at emancipation. While not negating the influence of abolitionist and Christian missionary discourse on the apparent decision by black women to keep some distance between themselves and the plantation fields, Brereton argues persuasively that responses by black women were more driven by pragmatic "family strategies" rather than by some unreflective genuflection to Euro-Victorian Christian notions about gender relations (Brereton 1999, 77–107).

Black women, therefore, were rarely dependent housewives, as was reflected in their active membership and sometimes leadership of friendly societies when the movement became secularized from the 1880s. For example, the Empress of India was registered in 1888 with 411 members (*Barbados Blue Book* 1888), and was the largest female society registered between 1880 and 1914. It operated for eighteen years and still had about sixty members when it ceased operations after its treasurer, Mary Bonnett, allegedly absconded with $61 (£12. 14s), more than half of its total funds (Minutes of Legislative Council and House of Assembly 1905–6, document 102, "Report of the Registrar of Friendly Society for the Half-Year July–Dec. 1905", 2–3). There were a number of other societies organized by women, such as the Ladies' United Provident (1889), the Ladies' Excelsior (1891) and the Culloden Sisterhood (1895). Other evidence indicates clearly that women were numerically dominant in late-nineteenth-

century societies, and were among the most consistent contributors. The St
George's Friendly Society, for example, had a membership ratio of over three
women to each man. Between 1895 and 1900, the number of men averaged
twenty-seven, compared to an average of ninety-nine women (*Monthly
Subscription Book of the St George's Friendly Society* in the Barbados
Department of Archives). Women were also the very life of the St Ambrose
Friendly Society between 1884 and 1925 (*St Ambrose Friendly Society Book,
1884–1925* in the Barbados Department of Archives). Women's participation
in these societies clearly underscores the extent of the economic autonomy of
many black working-class women. One woman's autonomy is poignantly
illustrated by a letter from her husband, who belatedly discovered his wife's
friendly society affairs:

> Sir I am riteng to you with a Heart of love as a christian Brother sir my wife Careline
> Layne she has ben Dead November gone 1911 and I now Have the Privalege of riteing
> to you: coming cross the card I understand she was in saint ambrose society and I
> want you sir to see into This matter for me to Help me if there is anything for me I
> will be glad for it from the debt she leave me in awaiteing me down. (*St Ambrose
> Friendly Society Book* in Barbados Department of Archives, Joseph Layne, Campion
> Land, Martindale's Rd, 7 October 1912,unbound letter between fols. 208–9)

Unlike middle- and upper-class fraternities, working-class friendly societies
were not unequivocally committed to the separate spheres of the Victorian
mould within which hegemonic masculinity had been cast. By participating
in mutual-aid fraternities, women provided some prospects for tempering their
vulnerability in a male-dominated society. In the 1890s a woman's daily wage
as an agricultural labourer was about four to eight pence, compared to eight
to ten pence for men. When task work became universal around 1894, some
women took an entire week to earn ten pence by "farming" weeds
(*Parliamentary Papers* 50 [1898], c. 8657; WIRC 1898, appendix C, vol. 2, part
3, memorandum 239 of George Gay Daniel, p. 219). One reason why the large
affiliated friendly societies in England had objected to female membership
was based on a perception of women as medical liabilities. One benefit exclusive to women was the accouchement, the "lying-in" or maternity payment.
Stillbirths and the death of mothers during childbirth were ever-present possibilities in this period. It was not uncommon for the funeral benefit to follow
on the heels of the accouchement payment. Take the case of Rose Prescod,

who in February 1894 received a childbirth payment of 8s. 4d., and exactly nine months later the same amount was paid to her for the burial of the child. In February 1896 she received 8s. 6d. for another birth and an equal amount *the very same day* to bury the baby. She was more fortunate with her two subsequent births, in December 1896 and December 1908 (ANG 28/4/14, *St Ambrose Friendly Society Book*, 172). It was the stark reality of these experiences, felt so intimately by women, that prompted them to become full, independent members of society organizations rather than remaining content with the unrealistic expectation that they would benefit adequately as dependent partners.

Conclusion

In this chapter I have attempted the ambitious project of exploring the shifting and unstable boundaries of masculinities between Britain and Barbados against the background of abolitionism, amelioration, emancipation and post-slavery "reconstruction". England's industrial capitalist bourgeoisie, buoyed by neo-Puritanism, sought to have their colonial "cousins" become "civilized men" who would abandon their drunkenness, sexual immorality and cruelty to women. While supporting certain gender ideals, hegemonic masculinity constructed on an edifice of a Euro-Victorian ideology of separate spheres and notions of the woman as the weaker sex, to be protected and provided for, proved elusive. Clearly, material resources were critical to the making of hegemonic masculinity but were not enough to sustain it. Fraternities were critical institutions for the mobilization of economic resources, as well as the ideology and ritual practices so central to the construction of masculinities. West Indian men were conscious of the unflattering perspective on their masculinity their metropolitan cousins had, but at every level Barbadian men rejected many of the fundamental elements of Victorian, Euro-Christian prescriptions of "civilized masculinity".

Note

1.   See BDA: ED 1/10 Minutes of the Proceedings of the Education Board, 9 January 1902–16, January 1911. Meeting of 22 September 1902, 34 (re: R.M. Cummins, Hincks' Infant School); meeting of 18 May 1903, 71 (re: St C. Blackman, Master of St Mary's Boys' School); meeting of 24 January 1910, 381–82 (re: Mr Gale of Holy Trinity).

References

Ancient Order of Foresters directory and almanack 1868–69.

Anderson, J. 1734. *The constitutions of the Free-Masons.* Ed. B. Franklin. Philadelphia: Benjamin Franklin.

Barriteau, E. 2003. Requiem for the male marginalization thesis in the Caribbean: Death of a non-theory. In *Confronting power, theorizing gender: Interdisciplinary perspectives in the Caribbean*, ed. E. Barriteau, 324–55. Kingston: University of the West Indies Press.

Barrow, C. 1998. Caribbean masculinity and family: Revisiting marginality and reputation. In *Caribbean portraits: Essays on gender ideologies and identities*, ed. C. Barrow, 339–58. Kingston: Ian Randle.

Beckles, H. McD. 1989. *Natural rebels: A social history of enslaved black women in Barbados.* London: Zed Books.

———. 1990. *A history of Barbados: From Amerindian settlement to nation-state.* Cambridge: Cambridge University Press.

———. 1995. Sex and gender in the historiography of Caribbean slavery. In *Engendering history: Caribbean women in historical perspective*, ed. V. Shepherd, B. Brereton and B. Bailey, 125–40. Kingston: Ian Randle.

———. 1998. White women and a West India fortune: Gender and wealth during slavery. In *The white minority in the Caribbean*, ed. H. Johnson and K. Watson, 1–16. Kingston: Ian Randle.

———. 2004. Black masculinity in Caribbean slavery. In *Interrogating Caribbean masculinities: Theoretical and empirical analyses*, ed. Rhoda Reddock, 225–43. Kingston: University of the West Indies Press.

Brereton, B. 1999. Family strategies: Gender and the shift to wage labour in the British Caribbean. In *The colonial Caribbean in transition: Essays on post-emancipation social and cultural history*, ed. B. Brereton and K.A. Yelvington, 77–107. Kingston: University of the West Indies Press.

Bruce, J. 1853. *Letters and papers of the Verney family down to the end of the year 1639.* London: Camden Society.

Burton, R.D.E. 1997. *Afro-Creole: Power, opposition, and play in the Caribbean*. Ithaca: Cornell University Press.

Caldecott, A. 1898/1970. *The church in the West Indies*. London: Frank Cass.

Carnes, M.C. 1989. *Secret ritual and manhood in Victorian America*. New Haven, CT: Yale University Press.

———. 1990. Middle-class men and the solace of fraternal ritual. In *Meanings for manhood: Constructions of masculinity in Victorian America*, ed. M.C. Carnes and C. Griffen, 37–52. Chicago: University of Chicago Press.

Clawson, M.A. 1989. *Constructing brotherhood: Class, gender, and fraternalism*. Princeton, NJ: Princeton University Press.

Complete manual of Oddfellowship. 1879. London: privately printed.

Connell, R.W. 1998. *Masculinities*. Cambridge: Polity.

Cordery, S. 2003. *British friendly societies, 1750–1914*. Basingstoke, UK: Palgrave Macmillan.

Coronation handbook. 1911.

Dickson, W. 1814. *Mitigation of slavery*. Westport, CT: Negro Universities Press.

Downes, A. 2003. Gender and the elementary teaching service in Barbados, 1880–1960: A re-examination of the feminization and marginalization of the black male theses. In *Confronting power, theorizing gender: Interdisciplinary perspectives in the Caribbean*, ed. E. Barriteau, 303–23. Kingston: University of the West Indies Press.

———. 2004. Boys of the empire: Elite education and the socio-cultural construction of hegemonic masculinity in Barbados, 1875–1920. In *Interrogating Caribbean masculinities: Theoretical and empirical analyses*, ed. R. Reddock, 105–36. Kingston: University of the West Indies Press.

———. 2007. Freemasonry in Barbados, 1740–1900: Issues of ethnicity and class in a colonial polity. *Journal of the Barbados Museum and Historical Society* 53:50–76.

Dumenil, L. 1984. *Freemasonry and American culture, 1880–1930*. Princeton, NJ: Princeton University Press.

Ferguson, M. 1992. *Subject to others: British women writers and colonial slavery, 1670–1834*. New York: Routledge.

Goodridge, S.S. 1977. *St Mary's Barbados, 1827–1977*. Bridgetown: n. p.

Grand Lodge of Scotland Registration Book, volume 18 (January 1907–December 1908). In Grand Lodge of Scotland, Freemasons' Hall, Edinburgh.

Hall, C. 1992. *White, male and middle class: Explorations in feminism and history*. London: Polity.

———. 2002. *Civilising subjects: Metropole and colony in the English imagination, 1830–1867*. Chicago: University of Chicago Press.

Hamhill, J. 1986. *The craft: A history of English Freemasonry*. London: Crucible.

Handler, J.S. , ed. 1967. Father Antoine Biet's visit to Barbados in 1654. *Journal of the Barbados Museum and Historical Society* 32:56–76.

Harland-Jacobs, J. 2007. *Builders of empire: Freemasonry and British imperialism, 1717–1927*. Chapel Hill: University of North Carolina Press.

Harlow, V.T., ed. 1925. *Colonising expeditions to the West Indies and Guiana, 1623–1667*. London: Hakluyt Society.

Hoff, J. 1994. Gender as a postmodern category of paralysis. *Women's History Review* 3 (2): 149–68.

House of Assembly Debates (Barbados): 29 July 1902; 28 Jan. 1908.

Independent Order of Oddfellows (MU) Quarterly Report, October 1898.

Journal of the Barbados Museum and Historical Society (JBMHS) 15 (1947–48).

Jones, C. Forde. 1998. Mapping racial boundaries: Gender, race, and poor relief in Barbadian plantation society. *Journal of Women's History* 10 (3): 9–31.

———. 2003. Contesting the boundaries of gender, race and sexuality in Barbadian plantation society. *Women's History Review* 12 (2): 195–232.

———. 2007. *Engendering whiteness: White women and colonialism in Barbados and North Carolina, 1627–1865*. Manchester, UK: Manchester University Press.

Lambert, D. 2005. *White creole culture, politics and identity during the age of abolition*. Cambridge: Cambridge University Press.

Lane, J. 1895. *Masonic records, 1717–1894*. London: Letchworth.

Lewis, L. 2003. Exploring the intersections of gender, sexuality, and culture in the Caribbean: An introduction. In *The culture of gender and sexuality in the Caribbean*, ed. L. Lewis, 1–21. Gainesville: University Press of Florida.

Lindsay, L. 1981. *The myth of a civilizing mission: British colonialism and the politics of symbolic manipulation*. Institute of Social and Economic Research working paper, no. 31. Kingston: Institute of Social and Economic Research.

Long, E. 1774. *History of Jamaica*. Vol. 2. London: Lowndes.

Loyal Order of Ancient Shepherds, Ashton Unity. 1922–23. *Guide and Directory for the Year 1922–23*. Edinburgh: Loyal Order of Ancient Shepherds.

Midgley, C. 1992. *Women against slavery: The British campaigns, 1780–1870*. London: Routledge.

Miller, E. 1986. *Marginalization of the black male: Insights from the development of the teaching profession*. Kingston: Institute of Social and Economic Research, University of the West Indies.

———. 1991. *Men at risk*. Kingston: Jamaica Publishing House.

Moffrey, R.W. 1905. *The rise and progress of the Manchester Unity of the Independent Order of Oddfellows, 1810–1904*. Manchester, UK: Independent Order of Oddfellows, Manchester Unity.

———. 1910. *A century of Oddfellowship*. Manchester, UK: Independent Order of Oddfellows, Manchester Unity.

Mulvey, P.A. 1982. Slave confraternities in Brazil: Their role in colonial society. *Americas* 39 (1): 39–68.

Newton, M. 2005a. Philanthropy, gender, and the production of public life in Barbados, ca. 1790–ca. 1850. In *Gender and slave emancipation in the Atlantic world*, ed. P. Scully and D. Paton, 225–46. Durham, NC: Duke University Press.

———. 2005b. The king v. Robert James, a slave, for rape: Inequality, gender, and British slave amelioration, 1823–1834. *Comparative Studies in Society and History* 47 (3): 583–610.

———. 2008. *The children of Africa in the colonies: Free people of color in Barbados in the age of emancipation*. Baton Rouge: Louisiana State University Press.

Nugent, M. 1966. *Lady Nugent's journal of her residence in Jamaica from 1801 to 1805*. Ed. P. Wright. Kingston: Institute of Jamaica.

Paton, D. 1996. Decency, dependence and the lash: Gender and the British debate over slave emancipation, 1830–34. *Slavery and Abolition* 17 (3): 163–84.

Proceedings of the United Grand Lodge of England (PUGLE) 10 (1898–1900).

Resume of the history of the District Grand Lodge of Barbados, 1740–1936. 1937. Bridgetown: n.p.

Rich, P.J. 1988. Public-School Freemasonry in the empire: "Mafia of the mediocre"? In *"Benefits bestowed"? Education and British imperialism*, ed. J.A. Mangan, 174–92. Manchester: Manchester University Press.

———. 1997. Female Freemasons: Gender, democracy and fraternalism. *Journal of American Culture* 20 (1): 105–10.

Roberts, G. 1955. Emigration from the island of Barbados. *Social and Economic Studies* 4 (3): 245–88.

Rules of the United Bridgetown Friendly Society. 1846. Bethel Methodist Church Friendly Society Accounts, 1844–53. In Barbados National Library Service.

Scott, J.W. 1986. Gender: A useful category of historical analysis. *American Historical Review* 91 (5): 1053–75.

Scully, P., and D. Paton, eds. 2005. *Gender and slave emancipation in the Atlantic world*. Durham, NC: Duke University Press.

Sinha, M. 1995. *Colonial masculinity: The "manly Englishman" and the "effeminate Bengali" in the late nineteenth century*. Manchester, UK: Manchester University Press.

Smith, C. 1932. *Centenary history of the Ancient Noble Order of United Oddfellows, Bolton Unity, 1832–1932*. Manchester, UK: Executive of the Ancient Noble Order of United Oddfellows, Bolton Unity.

Smith, F.H. 2000. Alcohol, slavery and African cultural continuity in the British Caribbean. In *Drinking: Anthropological approaches*, ed. I. de Garine and V. de Garine, 212–27. Oxford: Berghahn Books.

Spry, J. 1867. *The history of Odd-Fellowship*. London: Fred Pitman.

Minutes of the St Michael's Lodge 2253 (1880–1914). 1900. (In possession of the District Grand Secretariat of Barbados.) Held by the District Grand Secretary of Barbados.

Stead, T.B., J.L. Stead and W. Stead. 1914. Female Foresters. In *The Foresters' directory* 17:77–78.

Sturge, J. , and T. Harvey. 1838/1968. *The West Indies in 1837*. Reprint. London: Dawsons of Pall Mall.

United Grand Lodge of England (UGLE) Papers. Annual Returns and Correspondence. Freemasons' Hall, London.

Von Germeten, N. 2006. *Black blood brothers: Confraternities and social mobility for Afro-Mexicans*. Gainesville: University Press of Florida.

Walvin, J. 1987. Symbols of moral superiority: Slavery, sport and the changing world order. In *Manliness and morality: Middle-class masculinity in Britain and America, 1800–1940*, ed. J.A. Mangan and J. Walvin, 242–60. Manchester: Manchester University Press.

Watson, K. 2000. The iconography of the 1816 revolt. *Journal of the Barbados Museum and Historical Society* 46 (December): 40–46.

Wedd, A.F., ed. 1927. *The fate of the Fenwicks: Letters to Mary Hays, 1798–1828*. London: Methuen.

Welch, P. 2003. *Slave society in the city: Bridgetown, Barbados, 1680–1834*. Kingston: Ian Randle.

Wilson, P. 1969. Reputation and respectability: A suggestion for Caribbean ethnology. *Man* 4 (1): 70–84.

West Indies Royal Commission (WIRC) (1897). 1898. *Parliamentary Papers* 50, c. 8657.

18

The Harder They Fall
Masculinity and the Cinematic Gaze

PATRICIA MOHAMMED

Casting Emotions in Dramatic Conflict

There are several scenes in director Ang Lee's *Brokeback Mountain* that pull the viewer helplessly into an emotional vortex. Some of this is achieved by forcing the viewer to empathize with the dilemma of the main protagonists. This is not an easy task in a film that handles the taboo subject of a homosexual affair between two men which combines the elements of both eros and agape.[1] Among other films, perhaps only *La Cage aux folles* (*The Birdcage*)[2] has attempted to create a similar degree of empathy with a homosexual couple; even so, *La Cage aux folles* has done so through comedic humour and within the genre of the "gay" film. Soliciting viewer empathy is even more difficult to accomplish if the subject matter of the film challenges a sacrosanct symbol that underscores the dominant hetero-machismo of a nation; in the case of *Brokeback Mountain*, the homosexual relationship between the film's two leading men destabilizes the character of the quintessential US western cowboy. Yet, almost effortlessly, the film draws you in. When the director wrests from you a huge gulp of emotion – not a slight teardrop successfully held back in a darkened cinema, but the gut-wrenching kind that leaves you unsettled for the duration of the film and afterwards – he has already caught you by the seat of your pants.

The first scene in which Lee fully captures his viewers' emotions is when Ennis Del Mar (Heath Ledger) and Jack Twist (Jake Gyllenhaal) separate after their initial encounter as sheep herders at Brokeback Mountain, a landscape portrayed as a harsh yet penetrable beauty. They return to the dusty trailer shed and flat terrain where they first met. The parting is a laconic one, in the non-verbal style and temperament befitting that of the cowboy characters that have been inscribed in film grammar for nearly a century now – a monosyllabic silence. Jack drives off in his beaten-down van. He looks at Ennis's lonely, receding figure, a visual reference to the earlier scene in which he spied on Ennis through his wing mirror while they were both waiting to be considered for the job. and it becomes clear that Jack's previous glance at Ennis acts as a powerful foreshadowing of the intimacies of this later gaze. Ennis walks up the deserted street; he slips into an abandoned doorway, doubles over and explodes in a torrent of grief. The pain of separation is so great that he literally throws up the feeling that has welled up inside him, a taciturn character whose emotions have emerged thus far in playful and not-so-playful violence rather than in words. He punches the walls as if to shift the internal torment, which he cannot placate, into physical pain. He transforms his emotional agony into a pain he can feel, see and touch, in bruises and dried blood. A chance male passes by just at this time, again providing another masculine moment for diffusing deep emotion. Ennis curses him violently ("What the fuck are you looking at?"), immediately conveying the intemperate language and mood to the viewer. After all, men don't cry, much less cowboys. At the end of the movie we see that Ennis's constrained exterior is a thin skin over his passionate desperation and fear of public retribution should he choose a redefined manhood. In conveying these ideas, Ang Lee sets the tone for a film which is profoundly destabilizing, whether you like it or not, and which recasts the boundaries of masculinity in a field that film (unlike written fiction) has not been able to render with sufficient emotional depth or breadth thus far.

In *The Harder They Come* another play of masculinity unfolds, with multiple roles and stereotypes, culturally borrowed and redefined gender schemas, a brutal landscape of Caribbean gender relations, and the classic portrayal of men's continuing inhumanity to one another in a battle for survival of the most cunning and exploitative. In this pioneering film, released three decades before *Brokeback Mountain*, director Perry Henzell also situates culturally for this region another construction of masculinity, described by Julianne Burton as the main character, Ivanhoe Martin's, "attempt to live out the American dream on that colonized Caribbean island" of Jamaica (Burton 1975, 5). In the film grammar of the region, *The Harder They Come* establishes one archetype of masculinity, in much the same way, perhaps, that Charlie Chaplin created the character of the lovable tramp: Ivan (played by Jamaican reggae singer Jimmy Cliff) has a family resemblance to other characters in the region's fiction, like Fisheye without the deathwish from Earl Lovelace's *The Dragon Can't Dance* (1979/1986), or Hat from V.S. Naipaul's *Miguel Street* (1959/1982).

The Harder They Come and Brokeback Mountain continue to position manhood as an unfinished project – the pathos of the failure of Ivanhoe Martin's dream of succeeding in the face of all odds and Jack Twist's dream of farming the land with his male partner. Both directors present the raw underbelly of a masculine emotional range that is rarely dissected and held up for close scrutiny. The same way in which *Brokeback Mountain* ushers in the shuffling, inarticulate Ennis who invites immediate sympathy, so also *The Harder They Come* draws the viewer, from the beginning, into the boyish naïveté of country lad Ivanhoe Martin, who is at first too easily deceived. When the rickety bus and a more modern flatbed truck encounter each other in a face-off on Flatbridge between country and town (symbolic of all the encounters that will take place between Ivanhoe and the more sophisticated urban men in Kingston), Ivan pulls a mango out of one of his bags. Another passenger asks him for it but he says he is taking it to his mother. Ivan's answer is respected as a sentiment to be honored "in country". The mango continues to recur in the film as a metaphor, the Caribbean fruit of temptation, like the apple in the book of Genesis, the site of temptation of one sort or another. As soon as Ivan lands in Kingston, two conmen easily relieve him of all the worldly goods he brings with him, hoping to make a new life for himself. When he goes to see his mother, she asks if he has brought her anything, even just a mango, from the country. He lies. Better the lie than the truth that will hurt and worry her – it was not a good mango season this year. Outside her one-room barrack flat, he runs into the two other conmen playing dominoes, and the man Jose, who will contribute to his fall from paradise.

Like Dick Whittington heading for London, Ivanhoe goes to Kingston to seek his fortune, and if the streets are not paved with gold, at least there is the possibility of adventure or earning a living. He is guileless, trusting, innocent, and still a gawky, outmoded country boy with liquid dark eyes, already a swagger in his walk. He gazes at the world in wonder, greets it openly and expects that it will return his greeting similarly, just as he expects when he looks out from the back of the country bus and waves to the occupants of a small, sporty convertible, as if he does not differentiate between the modes of transportation or the disparate social conditions of the people in the car, as compared to himself. This naïveté, coupled with shrewdness and innate intelligence, perhaps the hallmarks by which the colonized small-islander survives, best describes the mixture found in Ivan's character. Like many colonized subjects before him, he has an unwillingness to remain in the box that others have designed for men of his race and class. The dramatic tension between the two streams of his personality, trusting and optimistic yet skeptical and wily, will be Ivan's downfall but also his redemption as a tragic hero in defense of Caribbean masculinity.

This chapter explores the theme of masculinity in these two films, *The Harder They Come* (1972), written and directed by Jamaican filmmaker Perry Henzell, and *Brokeback Mountain* (2005), directed by Ang Lee.[3] Over three decades separate the release of the two films. In the intervening years between their making, cinematic styles, film technology and discourses on gender have undergone tremendous change. Yet these films speak to universal and timeless questions of gender and sexual identity, to how one finds a place in the world and makes meaning of existence, in the context of cultural norms or conditions of birth which set the primary boundaries and possibilities of a life. The heroism of both films is found in the complete candour and honesty that the main protagonists demonstrate. As actor Heath Ledger observed in regard to the making of *Brokeback Mountain*, he liked to give a little of himself in a film; it was therapeutic. This quality has, in fact, become a hallmark of his acting and, perhaps, of his personality – already recognizable in the making of a new screen icon who was unfortunately prematurely taken away in his prime.

Jimmy Cliff's rendition of Ivan is an unselfconscious one, the overconfident young upstart, poor and almost undernourished in his slim appearance but with hope and a readiness to dream. He represents a kind of purity with which all men and women possibly start out in life, before they have to acquire the arts of deception of one sort or another. This faculty to give of oneself unselfconsciously on camera, the capacity of directors, screenwriters and cinematographers to elicit this kind of performance from an actor and from the raw material of the script that is cobbled together in no logical sequence, to be made sense of and converted into a seamlessly finished product by editorial and sound skills, is itself the magic of the screen, and some of it is untranslatable into words as each viewer brings to it a personal history and experience. Thus there are as many Ivanhoes and Ennises as there are viewers who have seen and interpreted these characters. Nonetheless, it is possible to read some recurrent metaphors and codes in each of these films.

This analysis concentrates on some of the metaphors that reveal, whether explicitly or implicitly, a gender narrative – that is, the filmic codes that the directors employ to unwrap or reveal gender schemas or behaviours. In the chapter, I examine how devices such as *mise en scène*, plot, symbol, camera work and carefully constructed cinematic effects convey these themes and ideas to viewers. I argue that cinema and the visual gaze, in its emergence in the twentieth century, are powerful forces for transforming how we look at and think about many issues that we were unable to interrogate sufficiently in the past.

The most obvious reason for the exploration and comparison of these two films is that they are both linked by the idea of the "cowboy", a figure that generations have defined as the prototype of masculinity in the American west. In *The Harder They Come*, the displaced country boy Ivanhoe becomes an outlaw in the rough terrain of music and drug-trading in an unvarnished snapshot of urban life in Jamaica in the 1970s. He is killed in a shootout on a beach that takes its cues from the spaghetti westerns of that era, films well patronized by cinema-going audiences in the Caribbean. In the 2005 film *Brokeback Mountain*, the real-life cowboy occupation of herding sheep in the mountains of Wyoming in 1963 is converted into the space where compulsory homo-sociality transforms gradually and naturally into a site for a homosexual relationship between two men, Ennis Del Mar and Jack Twist. Prior to this film, only 1969's *Midnight Cowboy* (dir. John Schlesinger), the story of naive male prostitute Joe Buck's (Jon Voight) struggle to survive on the streets of New York City, together with his sickly friend Ratso (Dustin Hoffman), came close to portraying not only the homosexual encounters that Buck agreed to for money, but also the fact that the relationship between Buck and Ratso might be, if not homosexual, certainly founded on a sincere act of caring between two men. The recasting of the "Marlboro" country image of man-hood in *Brokeback Mountain* is doubly haunting, as homosexuality – "the Love that dare not speak its name"[4] – is indeed named, and by a director who is not American born, but of Chinese origin and descent.[5] The troubled, passionate and secretive relationship that Ennis and Jack continue for nineteen years, and which ends only after Jack's tragic death, has parallels, in some ways, with the death of Ivan in Henzell's Jamaican film: both represent another desire unfulfilled, as if constructs of masculinity must be maintained, even at the cost of self-destruction. And here, perhaps there is an echo of another subtext of the song which gave the film and this paper its title: *the harder they come, the harder they fall.*

Feminist Apertures on Gender and Sexuality

Men must wear multiple masks in their quest for living out predefined notions of masculinity. Feminism and, recently, masculinity studies have emerged as two distinctive yet interrelated discourses. One of these is the multiple masks that men must wear in their quest for living out predefined notions of masculinity. There is no happy marriage between the two, as some writers place them in opposition.[6] Even so, it was inevitable that the centring and reclaiming of a space for a female voice and position, consistently, over three decades in a world that presented itself to women as phallocentric, would evoke a male response. At the same time, the male response has developed alongside and in partnership with advances in feminist thought in the work of postmodern theorists, particularly that of Roland Barthes (1972) (differentiation of the signifier and the signified in the image), Jacques Derrida (1978) (deconstruction of the binary), Jacques Lacan (1979) (desire and the signification of the phallus) Judith Butler (1990) (gender and performativity) and Luce Irigaray (2001) (*écriture féminine* and the challenge to phallogocentrism).

These theorists have allowed for greater fluidity in thinking through the sameness yet difference between masculinity and femininity, and have provided a far more productive way in which we can now both understand and critique archetypes. In *real* life, stereotypes do not exist, even if *reel* life needs to use shortcuts to position and flesh out characters in accelerated time. While film depends on rapidly establishing for an audience the basic markers good and evil, ugly and pretty, ethical and unethical, and so on, and the symbols which hold these markers in place, the medium also allows for refraction of these symbolic representations, just as plays have done on the stage for centuries. For example, one can argue that deconstruction of the western began long before it was recognized as disassembly – think of the character Kitty Russell, the kind yet spirited saloon keeper in the long-running series *Gunsmoke*, which aired on television from 1955 to 1975. *Gunsmoke* to date holds the "distinction of not only being the longest-running TV western series, but also the longest-running dramatic series in network television history . . . [and] can be aptly described as TV's first 'adult' western, featuring three-dimensional characters with all-too-human flaws and weaknesses, and stark, austere, realistic storylines".[7]

Queer theory has also challenged the essentialist notion that sexuality is biologically determined, or that it is a product of social construction, proposing that our gender and sexual identities are continuously being defined, forever undergoing change, mercilessly dependent on our minds as well as bodies. Queer theory has upended the cart of theories that could safely position people on one or the other side of the assumed binary, allowing for the multiplicity of human emotions, interactions, decisions and behaviours, contradictions and varied expressions of sexual desire.[8] Next to Neil Jordan's 1992 film *The Crying Game*,[9] Ang Lee's *Brokeback Mountain* represents one of the finest examples of this nuancing of gender and sexual characterization as raised in ideas expounded in queer theory.

Gender and the cinematic gaze is a fascinating field of enquiry and, in my view, one of the areas that is propelling radical thought in progressive and, some might argue, transgressive directions. It acknowledges the importance of developing our visual intelligence in technologically driven environments where visuality has taken prominence over the text. An early essay by Laura Mulvey, "Visual Pleasure and Narrative Cinema" (1975), unwraps the filmmaking process vis-à-vis a gender lens. Drawing on a psychoanalytical viewpoint, Mulvey argues that Hollywood films have depended largely on the "male gaze" and that cinema provides visual pleasure through the systemic framing of "the look" as the primary semiotic representation of women in cinema as the sexual objects of men, primarily for the pleasure of men. This dominant feature of cinematic representation across cultures cannot be dismissed or underestimated. At the same time we might also critique the radical feminist stance of Mulvey's comments, written over three decades ago, and point out that directors and filmmakers also cater to male audiences that look to films for gender roles of all kinds, including men who desire male bodies (or women who desire female bodies). In the scopophilic pleasure afforded by cinema,[10] we have to imagine that the filmmaker consciously plays all audiences like a violin,[11] touching the strings here and there so that each viewer picks up the resonances differently, based on, among other elements, personal experience, psychological predisposition and temperament, and sexual orientation.

Visual Tropes of Masculinity in *The Harder They Come* and *Brokeback Mountain*

Not only are both films differentiated by time, space and cultural distance, but they are vastly different in *mise en scène*, camera movement, editing techniques, lighting and sound. *The Harder They Come* is set primarily in an urban landscape, a profusion of noise, mechanical objects, voices, lyrics, grotty inner-city yards and zinc fences, seascapes that still hold the city in proximity. When Ivan arrives in Kingston the camera moves rapidly, highlighting the congested nature of the city. Even when the camera focuses on natural vegetation, emphasis still lies on the seamy underbelly of city life. In one scene, a plane lands in a green field, but the central object in view soon becomes a huge bag of ganja, thrust out toward the pilot to be transported away. The white plane, like a small bird, lands and takes off gracefully, but the underlying echo of the violence of the drug trade dominates the organic feel of green and grass.

Brokeback Mountain, by contrast, tells of huge spaces, wide mountain views balanced by the domestic turf and streams that the two young protagonists have made their safe haven, sheltered from the gaze of others by the mountain that surrounds them. The music is soft and meandering, like the stream, lulling the viewer into the love song Jack and Ennis have created for themselves. *The Harder They Come* represents a contrast, the antithesis almost, to *Brokeback Mountain*. The musical score of Caribbean sounds cannot be ignored in *The Harder They Come*; the transistors are always on, the radio announcers are on the air, the horns screech, the city dominates, raw poverty and cramped, overcrowded spaces imprison the viewer as they do Ivan, who has come from the country and is more used to unfettered oxygen and space. Yet, in this setting the hero refuses to comply and lives out his dream. Like

Jack Twist, his passions lead him to a dramatic death rather than a safe, regretful life that is only partially fulfilled.

Island-Style Cowboy

Cultural codes may be subject or regionally specific and lost from one film to another. For example, some of the "cowboy" image that Ivan adopts in *The Harder They Come* – like the clothes he acquires even before he has money to buy food, or after he has made his first record – is symbolic of a type of masculinity that is identified with the figure of the "dandy" (the "rude bwoy" in 1950s Jamaica, the "saga boy" in Trinidad). He is dressed sharply, if flashily, with matching hat, shirt, waistcoat and pants, not unlike the cowboy of the western films, except no holster is slung across his hip. In Jamaica Ivan has to emulate this style of dress to perform and represent the role of the cowboy. In *Brokeback Mountain* it is the natural garb of the mountaineering shepherd, not out of sync with the western dress of the early film cowboy.

When he enters the film, Ivan's narrow-brimmed pork pie hat is the first sign of his difference and the stylishness he will continue to adopt. It is also the hat of the respectable man from the country. He next wears a serviceable, saffron-coloured corduroy beret, which he exchanges soon enough for a showy, shiny, white leather beret once his song has been released. White is the colour typically associated with a film's "good guy", but it is equally associated with the rich man who can afford the luxury of frequent laundering. Ivan's wardrobe will take on the palette of white more and more as he acquires wealth. But by the last scene, when Ivan is shot on the beach, he is hatless. Why is this an important, or unimportant, symbol of masculinity?

The cowboy in western fiction is almost always associated with a hat (its type can vary according to its wearer's occupation, status or fashion, although variations on the Stetson, a hat with a wide brim to keep the sun out of the cattleman's or outback rider's eyes, are the most dominant). Wearing hats sets Ivan apart immediately from the other men he encounters on the streets of Kingston, some of whom also wear caps and tams of varying sorts. Yet he wears his hat consciously, sporting it always at a jaunty angle that is consistent with the spring in his step and the confident air he has to present to Elsa, his woman, and to the largely low-life characters he becomes embroiled with. He is constantly adjusting the hat, tipping it this way and that depending on the situation, almost in the way that men in the Caribbean hold onto their crotches as a crutch in situations of unease or tension, or perhaps to remind themselves of their manhood constantly. When Ivan is on an upbeat, or in an optimistic space, he is hatted; when he is not, the hat is not evident.

Ivan is the quintessential heterosexual, Jamaican male. *The Harder They Come* does not admit to any other dimensions of sexuality than the heterosexual. This is consistent with the general outlook of Jamaican society, where the idea of male homosexuality is not only taboo but attracts violent reactions. While the man–woman gender dynamic appears secondary to the main plot of this film, the allusion to a deep-seated Christianity that provides the blueprint for gender roles in Jamaica is replayed in several indexical forms. Ivan meets his love interest, Elsa, at the same time that he receives help from Preacher. Elsa is a member of Preacher's flock as well as his ward, but she eventually shifts her loyalty from Preacher to Ivan, who seduces Elsa with his youthfulness, his sweet talk and high-flying visions of what he wants to become, and perhaps his bravery in confronting Preacher who uses religion to exert close control of those around him. Ivan, therefore, like the serpent in the Garden of Eden, gives Elsa the opportunity to break with the cloying and dubious protection of Preacher, who, the other girls say, has his eye on Elsa. But it is eventually to Preacher that Elsa returns, when she betrays Ivan's whereabouts to him, and he, in turn, informs the police.

By the time she betrays Ivan, Elsa feels forced to end the fantasy of a possible life with him. It is the action she must take to save the child she has adopted and is caring for. She never enters the cinematic world of make-believe in which Ivan lives. Elsa is not merely a soulmate in this film; she is Ivan's saviour and conscience, a replacement for his grandmother and mother, not a joyful sexual partner who will go to the club to celebrate with him the night his first record is released. The play between seduction and betrayal, between religious and secular, between competing male lust and ultimate female betrayal clearly involves metaphoric references to Christianity. Male characters comment on women's sexuality and sexual maturity, such as the discussion, in the masculine sphere of the shed in Preacher's yard, of who has the right "to pick the ripe fruit". The apple of the story in Genesis is here replaced by the mango: on the bus, Ivan refuses to give up the mango that he is bringing to his mother; then it is stolen from him when he arrives in Kingston; the fruit that he does pick (i.e., Elsa) is from Preacher himself; and it is this same fruit that later betrays Ivan to Preacher, albeit for an honourable reason. Jose, the man he meets playing dominoes after his first visit to his mother, and who has drawn him into the web of criminal life, goes to inform on him to the policeman, A call from Preacher comes in to complete the triangular betrayal of Ivan. This scene takes place with the policeman sitting in a hammock under the mango tree, and the camera lingers on the three or four mangos hanging over his head,[12] inverting fruit and serpent in the biblical text. The mango that Ivan never brought to his mother recurs as a symbol of the forbidden fruit. Only those like the policeman and the studio manager Hilton, who both exploit Ivan mercilessly, can savour the taste of this sweetness, won through the fruits of corruption of one sort or another.

Ivan is not a rough character, although he is capable of extreme and menacing violence; for example, he repeatedly slashes the face of the man who works for Preacher when the man attempts to relieve him of his bicycle. In his first encounter with his mother Ivan is soft and well spoken. He is a jovial character, not a cruel one. He never becomes a rude, rough speaker like Jose, nor does he have the sleazy, dishonest tone of Hilton, the record studio magnate who rips him and many others off and who monopolizes the record industry. Nor does he have the middle-class accent of the policeman, whose colour, lifestyle and connections to all levels of society are important for his work. There is a hierarchy of power in the drug trade, the police force and the record industry. All the players presented in the various hierarchies are male, and the drug trade is a masculine domain. Women in the film are represented as whores and as objects relegated to the private sphere and the "collaborative and regressive agency of the church" (Burton 1975, 7). The plot revolves around Ivan's quest to raise his status in his respective hierarchy, but he must prove his manhood in a system that does not offer promotion easily, if at all.

Ivan maintains a spectatorial attitude towards the events that shape his life, as if he is outside of these inconvenient realities; for instance, he takes Elsa's last twenty dollars to go out with, because he believes his record will instantly make him rich and famous. As the plot evolves we see him change into another, still naïve but shrewder, operator. Like Adam in the book of Genesis, he has lost his innocence after tasting the fruit. In the scenes in which he becomes involved in trading and smoking ganja, the lighting is clever: Ivan's underhanded dealings with the underworld, with its smoke and darkness, contrast with his previous naïve openness. The darkness feeds his growth into unreality, not unlike the viewer's experience in the space of the darkened cinema, where one can escape pleasurably into the character of the leading role. Ironically, Ivan fools neither himself nor others, despite the apparent fantasy world in which he functions. His astuteness is obvious; he figures out very quickly that Hilton, the record magnate, will exploit him, and tries to create his own market. When he is used as a middleman who carries out the most dangerous part of the trade, he knows that he is being paid a pittance – "spit", as he describes it, with graphic eloquence. But his initial lack of aggression, as well as his innocence and willingness to earn his keep and make his fortune through talent and wit, or by hiring himself out for manual labour, has brought him nothing but deeper poverty and further disillusionment. He walks off the street into a garden whose front gate has been left open, and asks the lady of the house for something to do to earn money; he is prepared to wash her car. She drives him off unceremoniously, inferring that he is unemployed and hungry because he is a lazy good-for-nothing. The colonial legacies of Jamaica are still tightly embedded in the class relationships between the haves and have-nots, as Ivan soon learns. Poor and unemployed young black men are on the lowest rung of the ladder, for if they are not viewed as criminals or intent on crime, their crime is perceived to be that of laziness.

When Ivan's attempt to earn a decent living within legal bounds does not work, he turns back to the sphere which men in urban ghettos or inner-city areas are drawn into, without volition. He has already met Jose, who has an almost predatory feel, as if he is always looking for raw talent to recruit for the forces of the unsavoury. The ringleader of the criminal underworld, Jose is also a two-faced character who works as a spy for the police and as we noted above turns Ivan in after he becomes a wanted man. At Ivan and Jose's first meeting, it is Jose who treats Ivan to his first outing to the Rialto cinema, a place he had only read about before. The film that Ivan sees at the Rialto is a spaghetti western starring Franco Nero in which the hero kills off the posse that is after him with a blazing machine gun. The posse approaches head on, walking into the trap bravely, without flinching, their faces covered by red bandanas. The red bandanas the cowboys wear in the film might be read symbolically as the blood and bloodletting that is to come in Ivan's life. Jose berates a heckler in the cinema audience, "You shut your mouth; yuh think hero can dead till the last reel." This seeming throwaway line sounds ominous.

Ivan gradually begins to recede from a state of reality as the film's plot unfolds. But this recession is logical. The film starts off with the optimism of a country boy who believes that "you can get it if you really want it", that if *you try, try and try, you'll succeed at last.* The title song "The Harder They Come", however, already portends the film's denouement:

> Well, they tell me of a pie up in the sky,
> waiting for me when I die,
> but between the day you born and when you die,
> they never seem to hear even your cry
> So, as sure as the sun will shine,
> I am going to get my share now of what's mine.
> Then the harder they come, the harder they'll fall, one and all.

Ivan prefers notoriety and an earthly fortune rather than any imaginary reward in an imaginary heaven. In one scene, as a policeman on a motorcycle is chasing him, Ivan's mind flashes back to the ignominy of being whipped in jail after his first offence, for assaulting someone. Rather than endure this shame again, he chooses to retaliate and takes out his gun and shoots the policeman. When Ivan becomes a "wanted man", although no "wanted" posters are actually plastered on the walls of the city, as in westerns, the writing is still on the wall, like a challenge – I am everywhere, and I disappear – and graffiti is scrawled on the concrete. He has already disappeared into himself in one sense; he was always elusive and unwilling to play by the rules. He has written his own script and the rules by which he lives his life. Perhaps unconsciously, Ivan perceives himself to be the cowboy hero meant to save the people from those who hold power over the masses.

When Ivan is on the run, dressed in a leopardskin waistcoat, white trousers, white shirt and white beret, he goes to a photographer to have his likeness taken to send to the press. He re-enacts a western scene in front of the camera, emulating the gun-slinging posture of the cowboy, guns drawn from their holsters. On the streets he is the good guy; the crowd is behind him. Not unlike the comic-book Spiderman, who sends pictures to the newspaper to prove that he is on the side of good, not evil, Ivan chooses to be his own spin doctor, creating his own mythology of what he represents. It is a foolhardy and dangerous courage, but courage all the same, and one of the characteristics of human nature that provides the plots of many films. In *The Harder They*

Come, the men and women of Jamaica know that Ivan has challenged the men in power, who have also ripped them off; his rise from poverty is a story of success, not failure. He has outsmarted those who would outsmart him. He is the sung hero of this too-consistent tale of power and greed between those who control and earn on the backs of others and by emasculating other men. Hilton the entrepreneur is completely unscrupulous and unfair; the policeman will use every informer to get his man; Jose befriends Ivan for his own ends but is essentially a police informer. Even the Preacher, the man of God, shows little understanding of the young man whose masculinity threatens his control over the women of his flock.

Ivan meets his death hardened by reality but by also disappearing from reality, entering the dreamlike state of being himself in a film in which the bullets are not real and, after the final scene is shot, the hero literally gets up and dusts himself off. He walks unflinchingly towards the group of lawmen who have been stalking him; he comes out like the "good guy" in the western, toting his two guns and asking for a fair fight. In fact, the sounds that surround Ivan in his first outing to the Rialto cinema become the soundtrack to the final shootout between Ivan and the lawmen. His mind has escaped into the cinema, where that first pleasure of the city embraced him, and into the notion that the good guy wins over the bad. "We are going to do a frontal assault", the police shout. Ivan has by then lost all hold on the gravity and reality of his situation and replies: "All right, hold on . . . Don't worry with the armour business, one man just come out, who is the bad man who can draw." The film's soundtrack plays over and over again in Ivan's head; in his mind, he is not on a beach facing death but has been transported to the darkened cinema in Rialto where Jose's words ring in his ears – "You tink hero can dead till the last reel." The symbol on Ivan's dark T-shirt is a big star, worn like a bullseye on his chest. It represents not only the easy target he is for the lawmen, but also the other quintessential hero of the western, the sheriff, the good guy who outshoots the baddies, and who also sports the tin star prominently displayed on his shirt front. Jose is prescient – the hero does not die until the last reel. The final denouement is a fitting end. Ivan has fallen hard, but is still standing on his own two feet, and this is the way we would have it. We want him to die like a hero, not be captured by the police, dragged through the ignominy of a trial and end up hanged. His death is honourable and one that he has, in a sense, chosen.

While Shepherds Watch Their Flocks by Night

Ang Lee, director of the film *Brokeback Mountain*, comments on the unspoken aspects of gender that he has attempted to tap into. From the first moment Jack lays eyes on Ennis, scuffing his shoe, head down, face partially obscured by his Stetson, he smiles secretly to himself. Then he peeks at Ennis in his rear view mirror while he is shaving. Ennis is the shy partner. The die is cast, and the idea of sexual attraction is hinted at, if not established. A short time later, after they have begun to work on the mountain, Jack looks through the valley from the cold and lonely, moonlit perch from which he oversees the sheep at night and sees the single light that comes from the campsite where Ennis stays. The camera focuses on a close-up of Jack's face, turned completely towards the audience; then it follows the direction of his gaze, by briefly moving into a long shot of the glowing light of the distant campsite, before moving back to Jack's face. The look has become one of longing for companionship and comfort.

While the trailer for the film posits Jack and Ennis's relationship as a friendship that has to be kept secret, already branding the film as a specific genre of gay film, *Brokeback Mountain* contains both heterosexual and homosexual sexual relationships. There are heterosexual marital and parental relationships, and dynamics between parents and children, all of which affect the decisions that Jack and Ennis make (or do not make) about the choice of their sexual lives. We see the development of the relationship between the two main protagonists change – there are times when it is not primarily a physical relationship but simply a friendship. In an essay on "policing manhood", David Plummer discusses the term "compulsory homosociality", commenting that, "during primary school, peer culture expresses a strong expectation that boys should socialize only with other boys" (Plummer 2001). *Brokeback Mountain*'s protagonists are employed in the male-dominated occupation of sheep herding and are out in the wilderness with other men, but there is a line that cannot be crossed. Yet, one might ask, when does homosociality turn into homosexuality?

The basic rules of the herding job, as established by the foreman (Randy Quaid), already set up the paradigm of a typical marital household division of labour between the two men hired to work for months at a time on the forsaken mountain. One tends the camp, staying by it and creating a basis of domesticity – doing the home chores, cooking the meals – while the other, the herder, goes out all day with the sheep and even sleeps with the animals at night to guard them from predators. A thought occurs to me: Is this a delib-erate rule to ensure separation between the two men during the night? In any event, the arrangement reproduces the domesticity of two heterosexual part-ners so closely that certain scenes function as a parody, however slight, of the minutiae of a domestic marital scene. For instance, Jack's parting shot to Ennis one morning is simply, "No more beans." The next time Ennis orders supplies, he orders soup, and the deliveryman reminds him that he once said he did not like soup. When Jack later returns to the campsite and finds that his meal has not been prepared, he drunkenly berates Ennis when he comes in late: "Where the hell have you been? I been up with the sheep all day and when I get down here all I find is beans."

As the routine of inside and outside, home and world, sets in, Jack com-plains that the division of labour, in which he is up half the night with the sheep, is not fair. A role reversal occurs. Jack now becomes the domestic part-ner, taking on the "feminine" role, one could say, in the campsite as well as in his relationship with Ennis, until the end of his life. He continues to pursue Ennis, to desire him and go out of his way to please him, to set up meetings that cannot be kept, to dream about a domesticity with Ennis that he can never realize. Jack and Ennis's role-changing has a parallel in the method in which the film's director diffuses binary constructions of the characters. The choices of framing and editing in the film direct viewers towards a combina-tion of perspectives. There are times in the film when the camera's gaze is Jack's and other times when it is Ennis's – we are allowed to see the world from their different points of view. Through this technique, the director also disrupts the division that typically exists between characters as active partici-pants in the story and the film's viewers; he invites them/us to judge the film's events, even if with a different set of values.

Jack and Ennis slowly get to know each other at the campsite by sharing their family histories. In particular, they talk about their relationships with their fathers. There is a period of bonding and sharing of confidences over alcohol. Ennis does not go back to watch the sheep one night after a prolonged bout of drinking whisky. Preserving masculine distance, he attempts to sleep near the campfire but wakes up shivering. Jack calls him into the tent to sleep and get warm. Their closeness and body heat lead to the first, fairly rough sexual encounter between them, sounds of belt buckles opening, the men heaving and grunting, with very little tenderness and few emotional connections established. Ennis rises early and sets off to the mountaintop without a word to Jack. The ensuing camera shots and angles take on an interesting sexual connotation in the daylight. He rides up the hill and across the undulating ridge of the mountain, the ascendancy and grandeur of the landscape drawing viewers into the sense of peace that Ennis possibly feels, but as he looks down over the mountainous terrain he sees in the distance that a coyote has killed and eviscerated one of the sheep during the night. He rides down to the body, splayed open on the hillside, representing in shape and symbol the open and raw, bloodied vagina or the insides of a body ripped apart. First blood has been drawn.

The evidence of blood as sign of deflowering of a virgin, referring in this case to Ennis's first encounter with a homosexual experience, recurs again later. When he learns that he and Jack are being recalled from the job, because the weather has turned nasty and the sheep are being moved, in the only way he knows how to express emotional pain, Ennis begins a fight with Jack. Blood is spilt on both their shirts. Like the symbol of the mango in *The Harder They Come*, blood and violent retribution for sexual transgression are recurrent themes in *Brokeback Mountain*. As the plot continues to unfold, Jack is possibly beaten to death, his body left bloodied, to be discovered. The full significance of the bloody shirt is only evident after Jack's death. Ennis visits Jack's parents' house to pay his respects after his friend's death. Jack's mother allows him to look at Jack's room, which she has kept exactly as it was since Jack was a boy. Ennis finds the two shirts, dried blood still on the cuffs, one shirt placed inside the other on the same hanger in the small cupboard in Jack's room. Only then, we the viewers realize that Jack deliberately squirrelled away the shirt Ennis thought he had forgotten at the campsite, and kept it as a memento for sentimental reasons. This moment of realization – about the significance of their love and their brotherhood/friendship, and the extent to which the relationship completely consumed Jack – comes to Ennis in an epiphany of comprehension, with an unbearable sadness and regret. It comes too late. Ironically, this is the real moment in which Ennis loses his virginity to Jack and to the value of such a relationship – he has denied the possibilities between them for nearly twenty years.

Heterosexual Performances of Gender Relations

As Jack and Ennis leave the homosocial world of their jobs in the wilderness and return to society, they now engage in what Adrienne Rich calls "compulsory heterosexuality". They obey the heteronormative rules of society and get married and have children. Perhaps this, too, is just another of the many masks that men must wear in their quest for masculinity. Perhaps it is a necessary one, and the act of fathering or giving birth to a child is a human need, despite one's sexual orientation. Although *Brokeback Mountain* does not attempt to privilege the viewpoint or perspective of either of the main protagonists, Ennis nevertheless keeps his bisexuality intact; the film shows that he actually wants to maintain a sexual relationship with his wife, Alma, while Jack's sex life with his wife is never depicted. Alma is aware of Ennis's proclivities from the first time Jack visits their marital home, four years after their first encounter on Brokeback Mountain. She looks out of the window and catches them kissing at the side of the house. Her silence then, and for years afterward, whenever Ennis left to go on one of the fishing trips in which no fish were ever caught, is more painful to swallow than the angry confrontation which comes much later. She never reveals or talks about Ennis's relationship with Jack until after they are divorced, at a Thanksgiving dinner with her new husband and her two daughters. Lureen, Jack's wife, wonders why her husband always goes to meet Ennis but Jack never invites Ennis down to fish in Texas, but she does not seem to be the pondering kind. The friendship between the two men, as long as it involves fishing or hunting or camping in the mountains, is partially understood and accepted as normal, as it were, because the heterosexual performance of gender is maintained on both sides. In *The Harder They Come*, Ivan also lives out other expectations of heterosexual masculinity. After he becomes a drug runner, he sleeps with Jose's girlfriend, who, consistent with the tenor of the film's portrayal of femininity, is set up to betray him.

Marlboro Country

The most dominant element of *Brokeback Mountain* is the landscape – the raw beauty of craggy mountains and sparkling streams, green hills and lowlands, blue skies decorated by just enough clouds to temper the visual monotony of blueness, and the brutality of seasons that shift into cold, wintry chills and monochromatic colours. All of these elements come to reflect the changing moods and situations of the characters in the film. Unlike *The Harder They Come*, it is not an urban movie, despite moments of semi-urban life, but one set in the expanse of the countryside. This notion of space allows the characters the possibility of escape – of running and hiding, of moving from one state to another. For Jack Twist it suggests the possibility of his and Ennis's living out their lives together on a farm as partners and lovers. Yet the other elements of the landscape – the large mass of sheep moving like maggots on the hillside, juxtaposed with the recurrent flatness hemmed in by well-ordered roads and fields, or the grey urban poverty in which Ennis and Alma live – all add up to constrain the character of Ennis, who reciprocates desire but must be guarded about his choices. Throughout the film the camera gives us sweeping vistas of the western frontier. And although this frontier is supposed to be a savage place, the opposite of the civilized world of manmade towns, in this film it is, ironically, the space where Jack and Ennis have the freedom to be together. Even within this vast expanse of land in which they have their freedom, there is still a need for secrecy. When the foreman comes to the mountain one day to give Jack a message that his uncle is ill, he sees them horsing around half naked near the campsite, and he immediately draws his own conclusion, a correct one, to be sure. This episode returns us to a consideration of what allowed masculinity is, and where it can exist – the football or rugby field legitimizes manly horseplay and bodily contact, not the western outback. Marlboro men are always seen riding their horses, bedding down camp-style around a fire for the night, not safely tucked away together in tents.

If Jack represents the intensity of Brokeback Mountain (his last wish is to have his ashes scattered over the mountain), Ennis's character represents the flatness of the terrain which they both inhabit in daily life, the flatness of emotions kept under control, and his life kept away from prying eyes or, yet worse, weapons that wound. Whenever he lashes out, however, there is violence of another sort: he interrupts the structured immobility of his features and expressions; he must hurt himself or another to express anger and frustration. For instance, after Alma discloses that she has been aware of his affair with Jack, and reduces it to something "nasty", he crosses a road indiscriminately and deliberately picks a fight with a driver who almost runs him over, through no fault of his own. Ennis had learned the tragedy of homosexual love very early in life. When Jack tries to encourage the idea of both of them working a farm together as a couple, Ennis recounts the story of two men who farmed together in the village where he lived. One was viciously killed, his body left on the mountainside for all to see – again bloodied prey is left to be discovered. Ennis was nine years old when his father took him to see this sight as a warning, and he observes that it might very well have been his father who killed the man.

This anecdote fixes the tragedy of the film and pathos of its plot. The memory of the violently dismembered man whom his father took him to see serves to restrain Ennis from committing to Jack as anything other than as secondary partner in their love affair. Jack is the more obviously "gay" homosexual character. He has pursued Ennis, whereas Ennis is positioned as the heterosexual male who falls in love with Jack against his will but maintains his heterosexual position and status at all costs. Jack crosses both physical and mental borders and goes to Mexico to satisfy his sexual desires. Ennis maintains the semblance of a heterosexual existence; he is a father to his daughters and has a supportive and loving relationship with them. The circumstances of Jack's death are never clearly spelled out, and we are left to imagine one of two scenarios – either that he is killed, just as Ennis feared, by other men who brutally attack and kill homosexuals, or, as Jack's wife tells Ennis over the phone, that he has met with an unfortunate accident while fixing his car. Either way, he meets with an early death. Like Ivanhoe Martin and Jim Stark (the character James Dean plays in *Rebel without a Cause*), Jack Twist is an outsider, daring to live beyond defined codes of safety. The penalty is excommunication and death. Desire and imagination are two elements of the human condition that cannot be tolerated if they do not fall within the boundaries of what is socially permitted.

Conclusion: Confronting Masculine Tropes of Gender and Sexuality

The two films, separated by over three decades (1972 and 2005), present different constructions of masculinity and, in the case of *Brokeback Mountain*, a movement away from the pure binary construction of gender relationships that once predominated. This is not unexpected. During the decades that intervened between the two films, film production technologies have undergone a revolution, as has sexuality itself,[13] the latter perhaps signified by an increasing acceptance of homosexuality as a normative expression of human sexuality, at least in the matter of human rights. It is not unexpected (culturally) that *The Harder They Come* would be completely silent on this theme, maintaining heterosexuality as a complicit norm. In any event, this was not the key focus of that film. *Brokeback Mountain*, on the other hand, is well situated in time to tackle these kinds of issues head on. It does so intelligently. It is not a film merely about homosexuality but about the many sexual worlds that people inhabit, the contradictions and problems that come with each, and the problems which real life presents to ordinary individuals. Jack is driven by homosexual desire but lives out a part of his life as bisexual. Ennis does love his wife and children, and part of him is both happy and committed to a heterosexual frame of reference, but he falls in love with Jack. This is the essence: Jack draws him out of a non-responsive exterior ("Hell, this is more words than I have spoken for a year", he admits to Jack). How sexual desire is learned, as well as how we are products of both biological and psychoanalytic drives over which we have little control, underscores the nature of the dilemma which the film presents for analysis. Just as it raises the issue of silences between men and women in marital relationships, it presents power plays between men – the increasingly unfriendly behaviour of Jack's father-in-law towards Jack, and the persistently disapproving eyes of the foreman, for example – as "society's" watchful presence over those who do not quite subscribe to the unwritten cardinal rules of human sexuality. A parallel might still be drawn to Ivan's transgressive nature, as he challenges another set of cardinal rules – those established by the capitalist owner of the music studio, the legal authorities and the assumed code of honour established among thieves. In this sense, both films deal with the pleasures and dangers of living out one's desires on terms set by oneself rather than others.[14]

Both films also present different planets for scopophilic pleasure. Ivan's struggle against exploitation is not set within the conventional narrative of the western – the good guys against the bad guys. He enters a life of crime to survive as well as to resist the condition of being the underdog in society. We identify with this character as a heroic one – he is the proletarian hero in Marx's *Das Kapital*; he is the new, unemasculated male in postcolonial Jamaica; he is the working-class, underprivileged country boy come to town. But there is a constant bounce and swagger to his walk, and scenes shift from tropical exteriors suffused with natural light, to motorcycle chases and stolen car rides to tropical interiors, and dark, smoky rooms alive with the pungency of ganja spliffs. There is some success to the film's forays into sexuality. Burton comments that "in the close-ups of mouth and tongue and hard-to-identify skin surfaces (Ivan's making love to one of Jose's women), we see an incorporation of techniques confined not too long ago to underground cinema" (Burton 1975). More convincing as a culturally Caribbean method of conveying sexual excitement on the screen are the episodes of emotional tension or playfulness between characters; the orgasmic gyrations of the choir and congregation in their songs of praise; the preacher's dawning suspicion of the attraction between Elsa and Ivan, and his invasion of her room and violent accusations against her; Elsa's sexual fantasies; and the bicycle ride taken by Ivan and Elsa on his handcrafted machine. The still-innocent courting of two young people is convincingly real and hauntingly complex, composed of multiple horizontal planes, including two silver bands of water, glinting like a thousand pieces of broken glass in sunlight. When the camera draws away in a long shot, we see that the scene is another dump full of debris, but the cinematic aphorism is nonetheless apposite – the lotus can grow on a dung heap.

The treatment of sexuality in *The Harder They Come* brings to mind a question that has occupied me in the business of how Caribbean audiences deal with film. There is always audience interaction, especially in emotive moments, as observed by Keith Warner (2000), Richard Fung (2002) and Bruce Paddington (2005) . The audience becomes part of the film's narrative, entering the dialogue at places either to question the filmmaker's veracity or to diffuse a particularly stressful or disturbing moment. The enaction of the sexual act onscreen is one such moment – if it is acceptable behaviour for "foreigners" onscreen, by 1972 it would have been at least daring in a film based and made in the Caribbean. Displays of emotion, kissing in public and too affectionate behaviour between couples have never really been acceptable in the region, although raunchy and sexually expressive dances fill this vacuum completely. Even the filmmaker diffuses the frank sexual forays – for instance, when Ivan jumps out from the landing after making love to Jose's girlfriend and, finding out that he has been set up, makes his escape wearing only his underwear. Then a comic scene plays out in which he steals clothes from an unfortunate man who is returning home late at night. The filmmaker has anticipated and produces the relief that the Caribbean cinema audience requires to recover from the embarrassment of this scene, even if they are hidden in dark cinemas.

Jack and Ennis of *Brokeback Mountain*, like Ivan, are of humble, working-class origins. Ennis spends his life struggling to make ends meet – the under-belly of middle American poverty is evident both in his fulmination against the loss of one month's wages when the job on Brokeback Mountain closes down early because of bad weather, and in the balancing act of domestic tasks and work that he shares with Alma in the colourless houses that he moves into one after the other. Visually, the camera draws viewers into the monotones of Ennis's existence outside of his escapes with Jack. On Brokeback Mountain they constantly recapture the zest of a full-bodied life; away from prying eyes, they revel in the clear-running streams, in horseback riding on trails, in naked plunges into lakes, combined with the deep angst of separation at each parting. They are two beautiful-looking men, pleasing to the eye. Gyllenhaal's lips and eyelashes are seductively presented to the camera, time and again, keeping Ledger's more structured features hard edged and masculine – the ying and yang of it.

There is no gratuitous sex in this film; each sexual act, either between Jack and Ennis or Jack and Alma, is carefully crafted to achieve a mood, carry forward the narrative and elicit a feeling from the audience. The first time Jack and Ennis copulate, it is cold and grey inside the tent. The second time, they make love; their relationship is now one of volition, and the light in the tent changes from grey to gentle browns and hues of candlelit yellows. Their light brown bodies merge together at rest. Like the mountains and plains, their beauty is equally compelling. Is this the view of all audiences? When the film was first screened by myself in a course I taught on gender and cinema, it elicited very different responses, with one or two students actually being repelled by the enactments of passion between two men. Do men view the film differently from women? What gaze is being compelled here? I return to my critique of Mulvey's seminal article – that the cinematic gaze has refracted the lens with which we must now view gender – to propose that the "subject" and "object" positions are slowly merging or becoming interchangeable, just as Jack and Ennis exchange their domestic and herding jobs. As Teresa de Lauretis proposes, the re-presentation of gender is itself its deconstruction (de Lauretis 1987).

The two films present different soundscapes as backdrops for cowboy films. One is set against the faster, rhythmic tones of Caribbean music, with widely varied lyrical scores that are themselves part of the narrative sequencing. The other unfolds against a repetitive theme, a slowly drawn out, epic western sound haunting its way back to the peaceful, mountainous presence that has quieted the storm of passion and the friendship between the two leading men.

Ivan's conception of himself as the cowboy is partially built on the real-life story of an outlaw in Jamaica, and partially invented from the myth of cinema. His psychological escape into the celluloid fantasy that leads to his death is a product of both cinema and the social constraints that present such escapism as more palatable than reality. Jack and Ennis, by contrast, are modern-day cowboys, with all the appurtenances in dress, occupation, skills and props – horses, camping gear and vittles, baked beans in tins notwithstanding.

Ultimately, the two films destabilize the basis of another fiction that is itself an invention of the cinema. The west never existed in the way in which both directors conceive of it, yet both build on this cinematic trope as if it originated in some truth or memory that might be preserved. The appeal of the cowboy, which influences both films, is a hard-edged, strong, resilient and resourceful masculinity. These traits, too, are the invention of fiction and film – throughout the ages, human beings have come in every shape and size, with some being indoor scholars and others being better suited to outdoor pursuits or skilled labour. What is the appeal of the cowboy, that it has persisted with such vigour, and why is *Brokeback Mountain* invested in undermining this trope of masculinity in cinematic history? In *The Harder They Come* the western movie itself is revealed as a thing of falsity which can be harmful to those who cannot suspend disbelief outside of the cinema. In bringing together gender and sexuality to undermine the cowboy character, Ang Lee proposes that if the virtual world of cinema can serve to destabilize these myths that have underpinned society and kept many imprisoned for life, then we can in time destabilize some of the widely held myths about gender and sexuality that are guilty of other kinds of imprisonment.

Notes

1. If eros is used as erotic love and desire, then agape is used here not as Christian brotherhood but as an unconditional, self-sacrificing, active, volitional and thoughtful love.

2. *La Cage aux folles*, directed by Edouard Molinaro, was first released in French in 1979. It is essentially the story of two gay men living in St Tropez who have their

lives turned upside down when the son of one of the men announces he is getting married. An English-language production was released as *The Birdcage* in 1996, directed by Mike Nichols and starring Robin Williams, Nathan Lane and Gene Hackman.

3. My thanks to research assistant Laura Battersby, who carried out some preliminary research for me on both films and shared her insights from the perspective of gender and cinema.

4. Testimony of Oscar Wilde, under examination by Sir Edward Clarke, 1895. See http://www.law.umkc.edu/faculty/projects/FTRIALS/wilde/Crimwilde. html.

5. This could be interpreted as the undermining of the icon by an "outsider". So far I have not come across such a critique of director Ang Lee.

6. See Clatterbaugh 1997 for a description of the different streams of masculinity studies and positions that have emerged.

7. See http://movies.msn.com/movies/movie-synopsis/gunsmoke-tv-series (accessed 17 January 2009).

8. Queer theory took its cue from the fields of gay and lesbian studies as well as feminist studies, and was heavily influenced by the work of Michel Foucault, particularly his *History of Sexuality, Volume One* (1978). Foucault's remarkable insight that sexuality is itself a product of social construction – what he refers to as the "technology of sex" – presents a major challenge to the ideas of what might itself be taken as natural or normal – heteronormativity, for instance.

9. In Jordan's *Crying Game* (1992), a British soldier kidnapped by IRA terrorists befriends one of his captors, ultimately drawing him into his world.

10. "Scopophilia" refers to the pleasure derived from the act of looking itself. In *Three Essays on the Theory of Sexuality* (1905/1962), Freud defines scopophilia as a component instinct of sexuality that is independent of stimulation of the erotogenic zones – in other words, it is desire, whether sexual or other, stimulated by visuality.

11. See, for example, films by Isaac Julien, especially his *Looking for Langston* (1989), 40 minutes, 16mm, black and white.

12. Franklyn St Juste, cinematographer on the film *The Harder They Come*, admits that the fruit hanging over the policeman's head in this scene was purely coincidental. Nonetheless, visually it works to continue the analogy.

13. Michel Foucault's *Histoire de la sexualité* was published in France in 1976, and translated into English in 1977. The last three decades of the twentieth century began the revolutions of gender and sexuality that shifted ideas and the concept of rights to, if not attitudes towards, homosexuality.

14. There are different possibilities for men and women in this regard: Do female characters have fewer options? Are they more hemmed in? What boundaries are established for lesbianism that are less blurred? This is a useful comparative point to pursue in films.

References

Barthes, R. 1972. *Mythologies.* Ed. and trans. A. Lavers. New York: Hill and Wang.

Burton, J. 1977. The harder they come: Cultural colonialism and the American dream. *Jump Cut: A Review of Contemporary Media* 6: 5–7. http://www.ejumpcut.org/archive /onlinessays/JC06folder/HarderThey Come.html.

Butler, J. 1990. *Gender trouble: Feminism and the subversion of identity.* New York:

Clatterbaugh, K. 1997. *Contemporary perspectives on masculinity: Men, women and politics in modern society.* Boulder: Westview.

de Lauretis, T. 1987. *Technologies of gender: Essays on theory, film, and fiction.* Theories of Representation and Difference. Bloomington: Indiana University Press

Derrida, J. 1978. *Writing and difference.* Trans. A. Bass. Chicago: University of Chicago.

Foucault, M. 1978. *The history of sexuality: An introduction.* Trans. R. Hurley. Vol. 1. New York: Pantheon Books.

Freud, S. 1905/1962. *Three essays on the theory of sexuality.* Trans. James Strachey. New York: Basic Books.

Fung, R., dir., prod. 2002. *Islands.* An experimental video that deconstructs a film by John Huston to comment on the Caribbean' relationship to the cinematic image.

Irigaray, L. 2001. *Democracy begins between two.* Trans. K. Anderson. New York: Routledge.

Lacan, J. 1979. *The Four fundamental concepts of psycho-analysis.* Ed. J-A. Miller; trans. A. Sheridan. Middlesex: Penguin Books.

Lovelace, E. 1979/1986. *The dragon can't dance* London: Longman.

Mulvey, L. 1975. "Visual pleasure and narrative cinema". *Screen* 16 (Autumn): 6–18.

Naipaul, V.S. 1959/1982. *Miguel Street.* London: Heinemann.

Paddington, B. 2005. Caribbean cinema: Cultural articulations, historical formation, and film practices. PhD diss., University of the West Indies, St Augustine.

Plummer, D. 2001. *Policing manhood: New theories about the social significance of homo-phobia.* http://www.xyonline.net/downloads/policingmanhood.pdf.

Warner, K. 2000. *On location: Cinema and film in the anglophone Caribbean.* Warwick and London: Warwick University Caribbean Studies and Macmillan.

Contributors

V. Eudine Barriteau is Professor of Gender and Public Policy, Institute for Gender and Development Studies: Nita Barrow Unit, and Deputy Principal, University of the West Indies, Cave Hill, Barbados. Her edited publications include *Confronting Power, Theorizing Gender: Interdisciplinary Perspectives in the Caribbean*, and, with Alan Cobley, *Enjoying Power: Eugenia Charles and Political Leadership in the Commonwealth Caribbean* and *Stronger, Surer, Bolder: Ruth Nita Barrow Social Change and International Development*.

April Bernard is Lecturer in Sociology and Deputy Dean (Distance and Outreach), Faculty of Social Sciences, University of the West Indies, Cave Hill, Barbados.

Roxanne Burton is Lecturer in the Department of History and Philosophy, University of the West Indies, Cave Hill, Barbados. She is co-editor, with F. Ochieng-Odhiambo and Ed Brandon, of *Conversations in Philosophy: Crossing the Boundaries*.

Jessica Byron is Senior Lecturer in International Relations and Head of the Department of Government, University of the West Indies, Mona, Jamaica.

Charmaine Crawford is Lecturer in the Institute for Gender and Development Studies: Nita Barrow Unit, University of the West Indies, Cave Hill, Barbados.

Halimah A.F. DeShong is Lecturer in the Institute for Gender and Development Studies: Nita Barrow Unit, University of the West Indies, Cave Hill, Barbados

Aviston Downes is Senior Lecturer, Department of History and Philosophy, University of the West Indies, Cave Hill, Barbados.

Wendy C. Grenade is Lecturer in Political Science, University of the West Indies, Cave Hill, Barbados.

Tonya Haynes has her PhD in Gender and Development Studies, Institute for Gender and Development Studies: Nita Barrow Unit, University of the West Indies, Cave Hill, Barbados.

Kristina Hinds Harrison is Lecturer in Political Science and Coordinator of the MSc Integration Studies Programme, University of the West Indies, Cave Hill, Barbados.

Gabrielle J. Hosein is Lecturer in the Institute for Gender and Development Studies, University of the West Indies, St Augustine, Trinidad and Tobago.

Carmen Hutchinson Miller is a historian and research assistant, Institute for Gender and Development Studies: Nita Barrow Unit, University of the West Indies, Cave Hill, Barbados.

Tara Inniss is Lecturer in the Department of History and Philosophy, University of the West Indies, Cave Hill, Barbados.

Jonathan Lashley is a Fellow at Sir Arthur Lewis Institute of Social and Economic Studies, University of the West Indies, Cave Hill, Barbados.

Annecka Marshall is Lecturer in the Institute for Gender and Development Studies, University of the West Indies, Mona, Jamaica.

Don D. Marshall is Senior Research Fellow, Sir Arthur Lewis Institute of Social and Economic Studies, University of the West Indies, Mona, Jamaica.

Patricia Mohammed is Professor of Gender and Cultural Studies, Institute for Gender and Development Studies, University of the West Indies, St Augustine, Trinidad and Tobago.

www.ingramcontent.com/pod-product-compliance
Lightning Source LLC
Chambersburg PA
CBHW022344280326
41935CB00007B/69

9 7 8 9 7 6 6 4 0 2 6 5 5